MW01000335

Polish

A Comprehensive Grammar

Polish: A Comprehensive Grammar is a complete reference guide to the Polish grammar system for intermediate to advanced learners. It presents an accessible and systematic description of the language, focusing on real patterns of use in contemporary Polish.

The *Grammar* is a comprehensive work and an invaluable resource for students and anyone interested in linguistics and the way modern Polish works.

Features include:

- coverage of all parts of speech
- full cross referencing
- clear and illuminating examples.

The book is organized in such a way to promote a thorough understanding of Polish at all levels of structure: the sound system through to the formation of words and phrases, and sentence construction. It offers a stimulating analysis of the complexities of the language, providing clear explanations and examples for each point.

Polish: A Comprehensive Grammar is the essential reference work on Polish grammar for all learners and users of the language.

Iwona Sadowska teaches Polish and Russian language, literature, and film studies at Georgetown University, USA.

Routledge Comprehensive Grammars

Comprehensive Grammars are available for the following languages:

Bengali
Cantonese
Catalan
Chinese
Danish
Dutch
Greek
Indonesian
Japanese
Modern Welsh
Modern Written Arabic
Polish
Slovene
Swedish
Turkish
Ukrainian

Polish

A Comprehensive Grammar

 **Iwona Sadowska**

 Routledge
Taylor & Francis Group

LONDON AND NEW YORK

First published 2012
by Routledge
2 Park Square, Milton Park, Abingdon, Oxon OX14 4RN

Simultaneously published in the USA and Canada
by Routledge
711 Third Avenue, New York, NY 10017

Routledge is an imprint of the Taylor & Francis Group, an informa business

British Library Cataloguing in Publication Data
A catalogue record for this book is available from the British Library

Library of Congress Cataloging in Publication Data
Sadowska, Iwona.
  Polish : a comprehensive grammar / Iwona Sadowska.
    p. cm.
  Text in English and Polish.
  1. Polish language—Grammar. 2. Polish language—Textbooks for
foreign speakers—English. I. Title.
  PG6112.S23 2011
  491.8'582421–dc22
                                    2011016344

ISBN: 978-0-415-47540-2 (hbk)
ISBN: 978-0-415-47541-9 (pbk)
ISBN: 978-0-203-61073-2 (ebk)

Typeset in Sabon and Gill Sans
by Graphicraft Limited, Hong Kong

Contents

List of tables

List of abbreviations

(!)	example of an incorrect form
ACC	accusative
ADJ	adjective
ADV	adverb
coll.	colloquial
COMP	comparative
CONJ	conjunction
DAT	dative
DIM	diminutive
FEM	feminine
GEN	genitive
IMPER	imperative
IMPFV	imperfective
INF	infinitive
INS	instrumental
lit.	literally
LOC	locative
MHPL	male human plural form
MSC	masculine
NT	neuter
NO-MHPL	no male human plural form
NOM	nominative
PFV	perfective
PR	person
1 PR	first person
2 PR	second person
3 PR	third person
PL	plural
PRON	pronoun
SG	singular
VOC	vocative
Ø	zero ending, null ending

Chapter 1

Pronunciation and spelling

1.1 Alphabet

The Polish alphabet is based on the Latin alphabet.

Aa Ąą Bb Cc Ćć Dd Ee Ęę Ff Gg Hh Ii Jj Kk Ll Łł Mm Nn Ńń Oo Óó Pp Qq Rr Ss Śś Tt Uu Vv Ww Xx Yy Zz Źź Żż

The letters **q**, **v**, and **x** appear in words of foreign origin and are sometimes not listed as part of the Polish alphabet. For alphabetization, each letter is ordered separately; **troska** precedes **trójca** in the dictionary (unlike French where **élixir** precedes **elle**).

In Polish, the letter **x** is called "**iks**," **y** is called "**igrek**," and **z** is called "**zet**."

There are 12 letter combinations that can be pronounced as a single sound:

ch, ci, cz, dz, dź, dż, ni, rz, si, sz, zi, and **dzi**.

Table 1.1 Polish alphabet

Letter	International Phonetic Alphabet	English approximation	English example	Polish example
Aa	a	a	as in f<u>a</u>ther	**fala** 'wave'
Ąą	ɔ̃ʷ	on	(nasalized vowel) as in the French word b<u>on</u>	**są** 'they are'
Bb	b	b	as in <u>b</u>oy	**banan** 'banana'
Cc	t͡s	ts	as in ba<u>ts</u> or as in no<u>te</u>s	**noc** 'night'
Ćć	t͡ɕ	ch	soft/palatalized, as in <u>ch</u>eer	**robić** 'to do'
Dd	d	d	as in <u>d</u>og	**dobry** 'good'
Ee	ɛ	e	as in m<u>e</u>t	**tekst** 'text'

1

Table 1.1 (*cont'd*)

Letter	International Phonetic Alphabet	English approximation	English example	Polish example
Ęę	$\varepsilon^{\tilde{w}}$	en	(nasalized vowel) as in the French word _fin_; when "ę" is the final letter of a word it tends to be pronounced like "e"	**język** 'language'
Ff	f	f	as in fun	**fajka** 'pipe'
Gg	g	g	as in good	**góra** 'mountain'
Hh	x	kh	as in yahoo (same pronunciation as "ch")	**handel** 'commerce'
Ii	i	ee	as in beet	**lis** 'fox'
Jj	j	y	as in yes	**jutro** 'tomorrow'
Kk	k	k	as in kite	**królik** 'rabbit'
Ll	l	l	as in last	**lampa** 'lamp'
Łł	w	w	pronounced like the English letter "w"	**mały** 'small'
Mm	m	m	as in may	**mapa** 'map'
Nn	n	n	as in no	**noc** 'night'
Ńń	ɲ	ni	as in onion	**koń** 'horse'
Oo	ɔ	o	as in no (U.S.) as in law (England)	**noga** 'leg'
Óó	u	oo	as in through (same pronunciation as "u")	**ósmy** 'eighth'
Pp	p	p	as in pan	**praca** 'work'
Qq	k	q	only in foreign words, as in status quo	*Quo vadis?* (a novel by Henryk Sienkiewicz)
Rr	r	r	as in room	**rano** 'morning'
Ss	s	s	as in sit	**sobota** 'Saturday'
Śś	ɕ	sh	soft/palatalized, as in sheet	**środa** 'Wednesday'
Tt	t	t	as in tap	**tam** 'there'
Uu	u	oo	as in through (same pronunciation as "ó")	**ulica** 'street'
Vv	v	v	only in foreign words, as in via	via, vice versa
Ww	v	v	as in van	**wino** 'wine'
Xx	k͡s	x	only in foreign words, as in Pax Romana	Pax Romana
Yy	ɨ	i	as in whim	**syn** 'son'
Zz	z	z	as in zoo	**zupa** 'soup'
Źź	ʑ	zh	soft/palatalized, as in Indonesia	**późno** 'late'
Żż	ʐ	zh	hard/unpalatalized, as in measure	**życie** 'life'

Table 1.2 Letter combinations

Letters	International Phonetic Alphabet	American English approximation	English example	Polish example
ch	x	kh	as in Bach (same pronunciation as "h")	**chleb** 'bread'
ci	t͡ɕ or t͡ɕi	ch	soft/palatalized, as in <u>ch</u>eer	**ciało** 'body' **nici** 'thread'
cz	t͡ʂ	ch	hard/unpalatalized, as in <u>ch</u>air	**czas** 'time'
dz	d͡z	dz	as in pa<u>ds</u>	**dzwon** 'bell'
dzi	d͡ʑ or d͡ʑi	j	soft/palatalized, as in <u>j</u>eans	**dziecko** 'child' **budzik** 'alarm clock'
dź	d͡ʑ	j	soft/palatalized, as in <u>j</u>eans	**dźwięk** 'sound'
dż	d͡ʐ	j	hard/unpalatalized, as in <u>j</u>am (mainly found in words of foreign origin)	**dżem** 'jam'
ni	ɲ or ɲi	ni	as in o<u>ni</u>on	**tani** 'cheap' **nic** 'nothing'
rz	ʐ	zh	hard/unpalatalized, as in mea<u>s</u>ure (same pronunciation as "ż"); note: on rare occasions the "r" and "z" are pronounced separately (**marznąć**— 'to freeze')	**morze** 'sea'
si	ɕ or ɕi	sh	soft/palatalized, as in <u>sh</u>eet	**siła** 'strength' **siedem** 'seven'
sz	ʂ	sh	hard/unpalatalized, as in <u>sh</u>ow	**szynka** 'ham'
zi	ʑ or ʑi	zh	soft/palatalized, as in Indone<u>si</u>a	**zima** 'winter' **zielony** 'green'

1.2 **Vowels**

1.2.1 *Oral*

Polish has seven letters that represent oral vowels: **a, e, i, o, ó, u,** and **y.**
Two of these letters represent the exact same sound and are pronounced
identically: **ó** and **u.**

The primary pronunciations of the oral vowels are as follows (based on a
comparison with general American English pronunciation and Received
Pronunciation in England). In general, Polish vowels are shorter in duration than English vowels.

a   as in f<u>a</u>ther   **fala** 'wave' [fala]

A is pronounced in Polish with the tongue in the front of the mouth, rather
than in the back as in English.

e   as in m<u>e</u>t   **tekst** 'text' [tɛkst]
i   as in b<u>ee</u>t   **lis** 'fox' [lis]

I in Polish is pronounced like the vowel sound in the English word "b<u>ee</u>t,"
but the Polish **i** is shorter in duration.

o   as in n<u>o</u>   **noga** 'leg' [nɔga]

An approximation of the Polish **o** in general American English pronunciation is the first part of the "o" sound in the word "n<u>o</u>." However, the
American English "o" is a diphthong, consisting of two sounds together.
To approximate the Polish **o,** start to say "n<u>o</u>" but stop short before
completing the word. Additionally, the Polish **o** is pronounced with the
tongue further toward the bottom of the mouth than in American
English.

The Polish **o** is pronounced like the vowel sound in the word "law" in
English Received Pronunciation, except that the Polish vowel **o** is shorter
in duration.

ó   as in thr<u>ou</u>gh   **ósmy** 'eighth' [usmɨ]
u   as in thr<u>ou</u>gh   **ulica** 'street' [ulitsa]

In Polish, **ó** and **u** are pronounced exactly the same; both letters are pronounced like the vowel sound in the English word "through," except that
the Polish vowel sound is somewhat shorter in duration.

y   as in wh<u>i</u>m   **syn** 'son' [sɨn]

The Polish y is pronounced with the tongue higher—up at the roof of the mouth—and with the tongue in the center of the mouth, rather than in the near-front of the mouth as in English.

1.2.2 | Nasal

Polish has two letters that represent nasal vowels: ą and ę.

The primary pronunciation of the nasal vowels are:

ą approximated in the French word b<u>on</u>   **są** 'they are' [sɔ̃]
ę approximated in the French word f<u>in</u>   **język** 'language' [jɛ̃zɨk]

While there is no equivalent in English, ą can very roughly be approximated by "on" in English (pronounced like the English word "own"), and ę can be approximated by "en" in English – except stop short just before you are about to pronounce the "n" in "on" ("own") or "en".

In word final position ę can be either pronounced with slight nasality (more careful pronunciation) or pronounced without nasality, e.g., "idę" or "ide"; "kredę" or "krede."

Ą before ł is pronounced as "o."

wziął 'took' is pronounced as "**wzioł**" [vʑɔw] <3 PR PAST, SG, MSC>

Ę before l and ł is pronounced as "e."

wzięła 'took' as "wzieła" [vʑɛwa] <3 PR PAST, SG, FEM>
wzięli 'took' as "wzieli" [vʑɛli] <3 PR PAST, PL, MALE HUMAN>

Before p and b, ą is pronounced as "om" and "ę" is pronounced as "em."

ząb 'tooth' as "zomp" [zɔmp]
kąpiel 'a bath' as "kompiel" [kɔmpjɛl]
zęby 'teeth' as "zemby" [zɛmbɨ]
pępek 'belly button' as "pempek" [pɛmpɛk]

Before t, d, c, dz, and cz, ą is pronounced as "on," and ę as "en."

ręcznik 'towel' as "rencznik" [rɛntʂɲik]
rząd 'government' as "rzont" [ʐɔnt]

Before ć and dź, ą is pronounced as "oń," and ę is pronounced as "eń."

zdjęcie 'picture' as "zdjeńcie" [zdjɛɲtɕɛ]
zdjąć 'to take sth off' as "zdjońć" [zdjɔɲtɕ]
bądź 'be' <IMPER> as "bońdź" [bɔɲtɕ]

Before **k** and **g**, **ą** is pronounced as "**eŋ**," and **ę** as "**oŋ**." (The sound "ŋ" is the same as the pronunciation of the letter "n" in the English word "ba<u>n</u>k.")

dziękować "to thank" as "dzieŋkować" [dʑɛŋkɔvatɕ]
pociąg 'train' as "pocioŋk" [pɔtɕɔŋk]

Note: In spoken Polish, words with the ending -ą, such as nouns in the instrumental case, are sometimes pronounced as [-om] (**kanapka z szynką** as "szynkom" ('ham sandwich')). However, this is not considered standard pronunciation.

1.2.3 | *Vowel combinations*

Two vowels next to each other are usually pronounced one at a time. For example, **nauka** is pronounced in three syllables as **na-u-ka**. Zoopark is pronounced in three syllables as **zo-o-park**.

In some words of foreign origin, two vowels next to each other are pronounced as diphthongs. **Autor** is pronounced as **au-tor** [aw.tɔr] and not as **a-u-tor**. Euro is pronounced as eu-ro [ɛw.rɔ].

1.2.4 | *The letter i*

The letter i has a special role in Polish where it can soften the preceding consonant (see 1.3 Consonants below). Where the combinations **ci, si, zi,** and **dzi** precede a vowel, the letter i is not pronounced; the role of the letter i in these cases is solely to soften the preceding consonant or consonant cluster. There is no i sound in the word **siew** 'planting'; **siew** is pronounced as "śef" [ɕɛf].

Where the combinations **ci, si, zi,** and **dzi** do not precede a vowel, the i in those combinations is pronounced (e.g., **siła** 'strength' [ɕi.wa]; **nici** 'threads' [ɲi.tɕi]).

In other cases (besides **ci, si, zi,** and **dzi**) where i precedes another vowel, the letter i is generally pronounced similar to the letter "y" in English. **Pies** 'dog' is pronounced as "pyes" in English ([pjɛs] or [pʲɛs]) (not as **pi-es**). Exceptions to this can occur in words of foreign origin, such as **via**, usually pronounced as in English vi-ya [vija] and less commonly as vya [vja].

1.3 Consonants

1.3.1 Single letter

The Polish consonants b, d, f, g, h, k, l, m, n, p, q, r, s, t, v, x, and z are generally pronounced similarly to their English versions.

The following Polish consonants are pronounced differently than in English. The list below provides the Polish consonant(s) followed by their closest approximation in English.

c "ts"	as in ba<u>ts</u>	noc 'night' [nɔts]
ć "ch"	as in <u>ch</u>eer, soft/palatalized (tongue against roof of mouth)	robić 'to do' [rɔbitɕ]
j "y"	as in <u>y</u>es	jutro 'tomorrow' [jutrɔ]
ł "w"	pronounced like the English letter 'w'	mały 'small' [mawɨ]
ń "ny"	as in o<u>ni</u>on	koń 'horse' [kɔɲ]
ś "sh"	as in sheet, soft/palatalized	środa 'Wednesday' [ɕrɔda]
w "v"	as in <u>v</u>an	wino 'wine' [winɔ]
ź "zh"	as in 'Indone<u>si</u>a,' soft/palatalized	późno 'late' [puʑnɔ]
ż "zh"	hard/unpalatalized, as in mea<u>s</u>ure	życie 'life' [ʑɨtɕɛ]

1.3.2 Combinations of letters

The following letter combinations are generally pronounced as a single sound.

ch "kh"	as in Johann Sebastian Ba<u>ch</u> (same pronunciation as h)	chleb 'bread' [xlɛp]
ci "ch"	soft/palatalized, as in <u>ch</u>eer (same pronunciation as ć)	ciało 'body' [tɕawɔ]
cz "ch"	hard/unpalatalized, as in <u>ch</u>air	czas 'time' [tʂas]
dz "dz"	as in pa<u>ds</u>	dzwon 'bell' [dzvɔn]
dzi "j"	soft/palatalized, as in <u>j</u>eans (same pronunciation as dź)	dziecko 'child' [dʑɛtskɔ]
dź "j"	soft/palatalized, as in <u>j</u>eans (same pronunciation as dzi)	dźwięk 'sound' [dʑvɛŋk]

dż "j"	hard/unpalatalized, as in jam (mainly found in words of foreign origin)	**dżem** 'jam' [dʒɛm]
ni "ni"	as in o<u>ni</u>on (same pronunciation as **ń**)	**niebo** 'sky' [ɲɛbɔ]
rz "zh"	hard/unpalatalized, as in measure (same pronunciation as **ż**). (Note: On rare occasions the "**r**" and "**z**" are pronounced separately; e.g., **mar-znąć** 'to freeze' [marznɔɲtɕ].)	**morze** 'sea' [mɔʐɛ]
si "sh"	soft/palatalized, as in <u>sh</u>eet (same pronunciation as **ś**)	**siedem** 'seven' [ɕɛdɛm]
sz "sh"	hard/unpalatalized, as in <u>sh</u>ow	**szynka** 'ham' [ʂɨŋka]
zi "zh"	soft/palatalized, as in Indone<u>si</u>a (same pronunciation as **ź**)	**zielony** 'green' [ʑɛlɔna]

1.3.3 | Types of consonants

Consonants can be divided into:

1. Hard consonants (including velar consonants k, g, ch/h)
2. Soft and palatalized consonants.
3. "Historically" soft consonants, consonants which were soft in Old Polish. (See Table 1.3)

Note: Today, the "historically" soft consonants often cause problems not only for learners of Polish, but also for Poles, for example in the genitive plural forms.

> **gra<u>cz</u>** 'player' <NOM MSC SG> **graczy** <GEN MSC PL> rarely **gra<u>czów</u>**
> **me<u>cz</u>** 'game' <NOM MSC SG> **me<u>czów</u>** (not meczy) <GEN MSC PL>
> **spina<u>cz</u>** 'paper clip' <NOM MSC SG> **spina<u>czy</u>** (not spinaczów) <GEN MSC PL>

1.3.3.1 | Hard consonants

Both **i** and **y** can be written after the hard consonants:

b, p, w, f, d, t, z, s, m, n, r, h/ch

<u>mi</u>ły 'nice' <ADJ MSC SG>	my<u>ł</u>y 'wash' <PAST 3 PR PL NO-MHPL>
by<u>ć</u> 'to be'	b<u>i</u>ć 'to beat'
nowy<u>y</u> 'new'	now<u>i</u> <ADJ NOM MHPL>

It is important to realize that depending on the softness or hardness of the consonants, the words may acquire a different meaning.

mała 'small' <FEM>   **miała** 'she had'
pasek 'belt'   **piasek** 'sand'
burka 'burka'   **biurka** 'desks'

Only i (not y) can be written after **k**, **g**, and **l** (with a few exceptions such as **kynolog** 'cytologist' and in modified Polish last names, as in Kowalsky) (1.3.5.1).

Egipt 'Egypt'
polski 'Polish' (pertaining to Poland)
gimnazjum 'gymnasium'

Write **y** (not **i**) after **cz**, **sz**, **rz**, **ż** (except for a few foreign words such as **reżim** 'regime').

Waszyngton 'Washington, DC'
maszyna 'machine'
życie 'life'

Hard consonants before -i or -'e become palatalized.

kasa 'cashier' vs. **Kasia** [kaśa] (female first name)

Some hard consonants before -i or -'e shift as a result of palatalization, such as **r** shifts to **rz**, **t** shifts to **ci**, etc. (1.3.4)

kobieta 'woman'   **kobiecie** <DAT/LOC FEM SG>
teatr 'theatre'   **teatrze** <LOC MSC SG>

| 1.3.3.2 | *Soft consonants* **dź, ć, ź, ś, ń** *before vowels* |

Soft consonants dź, ć, ź, ś, ń (diacritical mark above the letters indicates the softness of the consonants) are written **dzi, ci, zi, si, ni** (-i after the letters indicates the softness of the consonants) *before vowels* (except for -y).

koń 'horse' <NOM SG>
konia <GEN SG>
koniowi <DAT SG>
koniu <LOC SG>
konie 'horses' <NOM PL>

The sounds **ć, ś, ń, ź**, and **dź** do not occur with the vowel **y**. Therefore, the letter combinations **ciy, siy, niy, ziy**, and **dziy**, are not possible. The letters **i** and **y** are mutually exclusive counterparts, with **i** relating to a soft role and **y** relating to a hard role. The letters **ć, ś, ń, ź,** and **dź** are soft consonants and are incompatible with **y**.

Note for heritage speakers: Softness is indicated either by the diacritical mark above the letter (´) or by an "**i**" after the letter, but *not both*—"**śi**" does not exist in Polish.

Soft consonants **dź/dzi, ć/ci, ź/zi, ś/si, ń/ni** are written before other consonants.

ślub 'wedding'	**silny** 'strong'
cho<u>dzi</u>my 'we are walking'	**cho<u>dź</u>my** 'let's go'

Soft consonants **dź/dzi, ć/ci, ź/zi, ś/si, ń/ni** are written at the end of the words.

koń 'horse'	**koni** 'horses' <GEN PL>
gałąź 'branch'	**gałęzi** <GEN SG/PL>

When **dzi, ci, zi, si, ni** are at the end of the words, **-i** is pronounced.

When **dzi, ci, zi, si, ni** are in the middle of the words, **-i** only softens the consonants and is not pronounced separately.

koni (**i** pronounced)
konie (**i** not pronounced separately)

See 1.2.4.

Note for heritage speakers: Every syllable in Polish must have a vowel. In order to decide whether to write **ś** or **si, ń** or **ni**, etc., before consonants or at the end of the words, divide the word into syllables. When **i** serves as a syllable, it will be written **dzi, ci, zi, si, ni**. Otherwise there must be another vowel in the syllable.

sil-ny vs. **śli-mak**　　　**ga-łąź** vs. **ga-łę-zi**

| 1.3.3.2.1 | **ć** or **ci, ś** or **si, ń** or **ni, ź** or **zi, dź** or **dzi**? |

It is impossible for the letters **ć, ś, ń, ź,** and **dź** to be written before any vowel. These letters must be written as **ci, si, ni, zi,** and **dzi** before a vowel. For example, before the vowel "**a**," the sound **ś** is written as **si**, as in **siano** 'hay.' Likewise, the sound **ś** is written as **si** before **ą** in **siąknąć** 'to sniffle'; as **si** before **e** in **sieć** 'net'; as **si** before **ę** in **sięgnąć** 'to reach'; as **si** before **o** in **siostra** 'sister'; as **si** before **ó** in **siódmy** 'seventh'; as **si** before **u** in **siusiu** 'pee.'

Before the vowel sound **i**, **ś** is written as **si** as in **siwy** 'grey.' In this case, the letter **i** in **siwy** serves two purposes: it denotes that **si** is pronounced as **ś** and it serves as the vowel sound **i**. The letter combinations **cii, sii, nii, zii,** and **dzii** are not used (effectively, the two letters **i** are combined into one letter). An exception to this rule can occur in words of foreign origin: Japonia, Japonii 'Japan' <GEN>.

The letters **ć, ś, ń, ź,** and **dź** do not occur with the vowel **y**. Therefore, the letter combinations **ciy, siy, niy, ziy,** and **dziy** are not possible. The letters **i** and **y** are mutually exclusive counterparts, with **i** relating to a soft role and **y** relating to a hard role. The letters **ć, ś, ń, ź,** and **dź** are soft consonants and are incompatible with **y**.

Words that pronounce **i** after **z** and **s** are: **sinus** [s-i-nus], **cosinus** [cos-i-nus], **Zanz-i-bar,** s-i-dol, calc-i-pirina, **peps-i.**

1.3.3.3 | Soft p^j, b^j, m^j, w^j

Nouns with hard **p, b, m, w, f** and soft p^j, b^j, m^j, w^j, f^j look identical in the nominative singular. Consonants p^j, b^j, m^j, w^j in **Oświęcim** 'Auschwitz,' **Wrocław** (city in Poland), **Radom** (city in Poland), **jedwab** 'silk,' **gołąb** 'dove,' and in a few other masculine nouns are soft and have -**u** in the locative singular after **w** 'in' and **o** 'about': **Oświęcimi-u, we Wrocławi-u, w Radomi-u, o jedwabiu, o gołębiu.** Also, as a consequence, the nouns have the ending -**iem** (instead of -**em**) in the instrumental singular: **Oświęcim<u>iem</u>, Wrocław<u>iem</u>, Radom<u>iem</u>, jedwab<u>iem</u>, gołęb<u>iem</u>.**

The letter **i** is generally pronounced similarly to the letter "y" in English where **i** precedes another vowel, e.g., **w Oświęcimiu** is pronounced [w Oświęcimyu]. (1.2.4)

1.3.3.3.1 | Soft w^j in feminine nouns

A few feminine nouns have a soft w^j, e.g., **krew** 'blood,' **marchew** 'carrot,' **brew** 'eyebrow.' The softness is seen in certain cases which end in -**i** instead of -**y**: **krw<u>i</u>, marchw<u>i</u>, brw<u>i</u>, krwi<u>ą</u>, marchwi<u>ą</u>, brwi<u>ą</u>** (to compare: **kawa** 'coffee'—**kaw<u>y</u>, kaw<u>ą</u>**). Additionally, the fleeting **e** is observed in all oblique cases (any case other than the nominative): **kr<u>e</u>w** <NOM> **krwią** <INS>.

sok z marchwi 'carrot juice'

1.3.4 Consonant shifts

The Polish alphabet has 32 letters. There are also 12 combinations of letters (digraphs) representing single sounds.

Predictable consonant shifts occur in the final consonant(s) of the stem in many nouns, adjectives, adverbs, numerals, pronouns, and verbs before **i, y, 'e**. These shifts are very systematic and allow learners to trace constant changes in both directions; for example, whenever -**r**- shifts, it will always change to -**rz**-, and whenever -**rz**- shifts, it will always change to -**r**-, e.g., **bar** 'bar'—**w barze** 'in a bar,' **Węgier** 'Hungarian'—**Węgrzy** 'Hungarians.'

Table 1.3 Possible consonant shifts

Hard consonants	Soft and palatalized consonants	"Historically" soft consonants
b	bi	
p	pi	
w	wi	
f	fi	
d	dź/dzi	
t	ć/ci	c
z	ź/zi	ż
s	ś/si	sz
m	mi	
n	ń/ni	
r		rz
ł	l	
g	gi	ż, dz
k	ki	c, cz
h/ch	ś/si	sz
zg		żdż

teatr 'theatre' <NOM MSC SG>: **w teatrze** 'in a theatre' <LOC MSC SG>
marzec 'March' <NOM MSC SG>: **w marcu** 'in March' <LOC MSC SG>

In English the process can be compared to the changes within the words:

confuse   confusion
duke   duchess
fallacy   fallacious

Predictable consonant shifts in the final consonant of the stem mostly occur:

1. in the locative singular forms before endings -'e and -i
2. in the dative singular feminine forms before endings -'e and -i
3. in the nominative male human plural forms before endings -y/-i
4. in comparative forms of adjectives and adverbs
5. in the formation of adverbs from adjectives
6. when non-past endings are added to the infinitives, before verb endings -ę and -ą (See 6.6.1.5)
7. in the formation of female professions from the male ones before -ka
8. in the formation of diminutives before endings -yk/-ik and -ek

Table 1.4 Consonant and vowel shifts in nominative male human plural forms before endings **-y** and **-i**

	Nominative singular	Nominative male human plural
a:e	**sąsiad** 'neighbor'	**sąsiedz**-i
ch:si	**Czech** 'Czech'	**Czes**-i
d:dzi	**Szwed** 'Swede'	**Szwedz**-i
g:dz	**kardiolog** 'cardiologist'	**kardiolodz**-y
k:c	**Polak** 'Pole'	**Polac**-y
ł:l, o:e	**anioł** 'angel'	**aniel**-i
n:ni	**Litwin** 'Lithuanian'	**Litwin**-i
p:pi	**chłop** 'peasant'	**chłop**-i
r:rz	**premier** 'prime minister'	**premierz**-y
s:si	**prezes** 'chairman'	**prezes**-i
t:ci	**student** 'student'	**studenc**-i
z:zi	**Francuz** 'Frenchman'	**Francuz**-i

Examples of predictable consonant shifts in nominal and verbal forms:

r↔rz

teatr 'theatre' <NOM MSC SG>:   **teatrzyk** <DIM>

siostra 'sister':   **siostrze** 'to (my) sister' <DAT FEM SG>

aktor 'actor' <NOM MSC SG>:   **aktorzy** 'actors' <NOM MHPL>

dobry 'good' <NOM MSC SG>:   **dobrzy** 'good' <ADJ NOM MHPL>

dobry 'good' <ADJ>:   **dobrze** 'well' <ADV>

gorszy 'worse' <ADJ>:   **gorzej** 'worse' <ADV>

dworzec 'station':   **na dworcu** 'at the station'

dziennikarz 'journalist' <NOM MSC SG>:   **dziennikarka** <NOM FEM SG>

ch↔si

Wło**ch** 'Italian' <NOM MSC SG>:   Wło**si** 'Italians' <NOM MHPL>

ch↔sz

bla**ch**a 'baking sheet' <NOM FEM SG>:   na bla**sz**e <LOC FEM SG>

brzu**ch** 'stomach' <NOM MSC SG>:   brzu**sz**ek <NOM MSC SG DIM>

Sta**ch** (male name):   Sta**sz**ek <DIM>

d↔dzi

Mag**d**a <NOM FEM SG>:   Mag**dzi**e <DAT FEM SG>

wo**d**a 'water' <NOM FEM SG>:   w wo**dzi**e <LOC FEM SG>

Szwe**d** 'Swede' <NOM MSC SG>:   Szwe**dzi** <NOM MHPL>

ty**dzi**eń 'week' <NOM MSC SG>:   w tygo**dni**u <LOC MSC SG>

ló**d** 'ice' <NOM MSC SG>:   po lo**dzi**e <LOC MSC SG>

samochó**d** <NOM MSC SG>:   samocho**dzi**k <NOM MSC SG DIM>

mło**d**y 'young' <NOM MSC SG>:   mło**dzi** <ADJ NOM MHPL>

mło**d**o 'young' <ADV>:   mło**dzi**ej <ADV, COMP>

when non-past endings are added to infinitives, before verb endings **-ę** and **-ą**

dzi↔dz

cho**dzi**ć 'to walk':   cho**dz**ę <1 PR SG>

    cho**dz**ą <3 PR PL>

g↔dz

dro**g**a 'road' <NOM FEM SG>:   na dro**dz**e <LOC FEM SG>

Kin**g**a (female name) <NOM>:   Kin**dz**e <DAT FEM SG>

dru**g**i 'second' <NOM MSC SG>:   dru**dz**y <ADJ NOM MHPL>

pedago**g** 'teacher' <NOM MSC SG>:   pedago**dz**y <NOM MHPL>

kole**g**a 'friend':   kole**dz**y <NOM MHPL>

na**g**i 'naked' <NOM MSC SG>:   na**dz**y <ADJ NOM MHPL>

g↔ż

mo**g**ę 'I can' <1 PR SG>:   mo**ż**esz 'you can' <2 PR SG>

in comparative forms of adjectives and adverbs

dro**g**i 'expensive':   dro**ż**szy 'more expensive'

dro**g**o 'expensively':   dro**ż**ej 'more expensively'

k↔c

mat**k**a 'mother' <NOM FEM SG>:   mat**c**e <DAT FEM SG>

Pols**k**a 'Poland' <NOM FEM SG>:   w Pols**c**e 'in Poland' <LOC FEM SG>

Pola**k** 'Pole' <NOM MSC SG>:   Pola**c**y <NOM MHPL>

when non-past endings are added to infinitives that end in **c**, before verb endings **-ę** and **-ą**

piec 'to bake' <INF IMPFV>: **piekę** <I PR SG>
pieką <I PR PL>

k↔cz
urzędnik 'clerk': **urzędniczka** 'female clerk'
rok 'year': **roczek** <DIM>

when non-past endings are added to infinitives, before verb endings **-e(sz)**

piekę 'I bake' <I PR SG>: **pieczesz** <2 PR SG>
pieczemy <2 PR PL>

ł↔l
szkoła 'school' <NOM FEM SG>: **w szkole** <LOC FEM SG>
stół 'table' <NOM MSC SG>: **na stole** <LOC MSC SG>
stół 'table': **stolik** 'coffee table' <DIM>
miły 'nice': **milszy** 'nicer'
stały 'permanent' <ADJ>: **stale** 'permanently' <ADV>

s↔ż in comparative forms of adjectives and adverbs

niski 'short': **niższy** 'shorter'
nisko 'low': **niżej** 'lower'

sł↔śl
Wisła '(the) Vistula' <NOM FEM SG>: **w Wiśle** <LOC FEM SG>
dorosły 'adult' <NOM MSC SG>: **dorośli** <NOM MHPL>

sn↔śni
wiosna 'spring' <NOM FEM SG>: **o wiośnie** <LOC FEM SG>
wczesny 'early' <ADJ>: **wcześnie** <ADV>
jasno 'brightly' <ADV>: **jaśniej** <ADV COMP>
jasny 'bright' <ADJ>: **jaśniejszy** <ADJ COMP>

st↔ści
czysto 'clean' <ADV>: **czyściej** <ADV COMP>
artysta 'artist' <NOM MSC SG>: **artyści** 'artists' <NOM MHPL>
miasto 'city' <NOM NT SG>: **w mieście** <LOC NT SG>
most 'bridge' <NOM MSC SG>: **na moście** <LOC MSC SG>
dwieście 'two hundred' <NOM>: **w dwustu** <LOC>

sz↔si
nasz 'our(s)' <NOM MSC SG>: **nasi** <NOM MHPL>
wasz 'your(s)' <NOM MSC SG>: **wasi** <NOM MHPL>
starszy 'older' <NOM MSC SG>: **starsi** <NOM MHPL>
prosić 'to request' <INF IMPFV>: **proszę** <I PR SG>
proszą <3 PR PL>

t↔ci

student 'student' <NOM MSC SG>:   **studenci** <NOM MHPL>

tata 'dad' <NOM MSC SG>:   **tacie** <DAT/LOC MSC SG>

kobieta 'woman' <NOM FEM SG>:   **kobiecie** <DAT/LOC FEM SG>

brat 'brother' <NOM MSC SG>:   **bracia** <NOM MHPL>

tort 'tort' <NOM MSC SG>:   **torcik** <DIM>

kwiecień 'April' <NOM MSC SG>:   **w kwietniu** <LOC MSC SG>

ż↔zi

duży 'big' <ADJ NOM MSC SG>:   **duzi** <ADJ NOM MHPL>

when non-past endings are added to infinitives, before verb endings
-ę and **-ą**

wozić 'to transport' <INF IMPFV>:   **wożę** <I PR SG>

                                           wożą <3 PR PL>

zd↔ździ

wyjazd: 'exit' <NOM MSC SG>:   **przy wyjeździe** <LOC MSC SG>

gwiazda 'star' <NOM FEM SG>:   **o gwieździe** <LOC FEM SG>

when non-past endings are added to infinitives, before verb endings
-ę and **-ą**

ździ↔żdż

jeździć 'to drive' <INF IMPFV>:   **jeżdżę** <I PR SG>

                                           jeżdżą <3 PR PL>

j↔i

mój 'my' <ADJ NOM MSC SG>:   **moi** <ADJ NOM MHPL>

czyj 'whose' <NOM MSC SG>:   **czyi** <NOM MHPL>

Maja (female name) <NOM FEM SG>:   **Mai** <DAT/LOC FEM SG>

soja 'soy' <NOM FEM SG>:   **soi** <DAT/LOC FEM SG>

when non-past endings are added to infinitives, before verb endings
-ę and **-ą**

kleić 'to glue' <INF IMPFV>:   **kleję** <I PR SG>

kroić 'to cut' <INF IMPFV>:   **kroją** <3 PR PL>

1.3.5 *Palatalization*

Palatalization is a process of modification (softening) of the hard consonants
before -**i** and -'**e**. It is important to distinguish hard consonants from palatalized

ones in the written form as well as in pronunciation. The meaning of the word often depends on whether the consonant is palatalized (soft) or not.

Hard consonants	Palatalized consonants
my 'we'	**mi** 'to me'
był 'he was'	**bił** 'he was hitting something'

Additionally, consonants and vowels shift as a result of palatalization (Table 1.3) e.g., **listopad** 'November': **w listopadzie** <LOC MSC SG> (1.3.3)

See 3.10 for examples of locative case consonants and vowel changes within the singular locative case for masculine, feminine and neuter nouns to illustrate the process of softening—also called palatalization.

The locative singular illustrates the process of palatalization. When the ending -e is attached to the final consonant of the stem, the hard consonant undergoes softening (-i follows the consonant, or the consonant shifts). Softening of consonants often results in consonant shifts. The list of possible consonant shifts allows tracing of the changes.

mama 'mom': **mamie**	**m** <hard m>: **mie** <palatalized m>	
kobieta 'woman': **kobiecie**	**t** <hard t>: **cie** <palatalized t→consonant shift>	

(see Table 1.3)

Below note the formation of the dative singular and locative singular cases for feminine nouns to illustrate the process of palatalization. Only hard and velar-stem (-k, -g, -h/-ch) consonants are affected.

	Nominative case (basic form)	Dative/locative singular
b:bi	**choroba** 'disease'	**chorobie**
ch:sz	**blacha** 'baking sheet'	**blasze**
d:dzi	**ambasada** 'embassy'	**ambasadzie**
f:fi	**szafa** 'wardrobe'	**szafie**
g:dz	**droga** 'road'	**drodze**
h:sz	**Doha** 'Doha'	**Dosze**
k:c	**książka** 'book'	**książce**
ł:l	**szkoła** 'school'	**szkole**
m:mi	**mama** 'mom'	**mamie**
n:ni	**żona** 'wife'	**żonie**
p:pi	**kanapa** 'sofa'	**kanapie**
r:rz	**góra** 'mountain'	**górze**
s:si	**klasa** 'classroom'	**klasie**
t:ci	**kobieta** 'woman'	**kobiecie**
w:wi	**Warszawa** 'Warsaw'	**Warszawie**
z:zi	**teza** 'thesis'	**tezie**

1.3.5.1 | Softening **k** and **g**

-k and -g before -e are palatalized. When -k and -g are the final consonants of the stem in feminine nouns, -k shifts to -c and -g shifts to -dz before -e in locative singular and dative singular.

Ameryka 'America':	**w Ameryce** 'in America'
Praga 'Prague':	**w Pradze** 'in Prague'
Kinga (female name):	**Kindze** 'to Kinga'

When -k and -g are the final consonants of the stem in masculine and neuter nouns, -k softens to -ki and -g softens to -gi before -e in instrumental singular.

When -k and -g are the final consonants of the stem in male human nominative plural nouns, -k shifts to -c and -g shifts to -dz before the ending -y.

kolega 'friend'	**koledzy** 'friends'
Anglik 'Englishman'	**Anglicy** 'English people'

Write i before e, after k and g with the exception of a few foreign words such as **kelner** 'waiter,' **kemping, ketchup, poker, wegetarianin** 'vegetarian,' **agent**.

pisać ołówkiem 'to write with a pencil'
jestem Anglikiem 'I am an Englishman'
wysokie 'tall' <NO-MHPL>
kiedy 'when'
żakiet 'jacket'

The instrumental singular case illustrates the process of softening (palatalization) of **k** and **g**.

Nominative case (basic form)	Instrumental case
Belg 'Belgian'	**Belgiem**
embargo 'embargo'	**embargiem**
kurczak 'chicken'	**kurczakiem**
mleko 'milk'	**mlekiem**
nowojorczyk 'New Yorker'	**nowojorczykiem**
ołówek 'pencil'	**ołówkiem**
Polak 'Pole'	**Polakiem**
sok 'juice'	**sokiem**
szpieg 'spy'	**szpiegiem**

It also explains why in the singular neuter and no male human plural forms of adjectives that end in -k and -g in the masculine singular, -i is present before the ending -e (and not before the feminine ending -a).

wysoki <MSC SG>	**wysoka** <FEM SG>	**wysokie** <NT SG/NO-MHPL>
drogi	**droga**	**drogie**

1.3.6 | Voiced and voiceless pairs

> Note for heritage speakers: You write **chleb**, you hear 'chlep'. There is final devoicing [xlɛp].

Poles do not pronounce voiced consonants in the final position (at the end of the phrase). Therefore, you hear 'chlep' but you write **chleb** 'bread.' The process of final devoicing explains the way Polish words are spelled. Note the voiced and voiceless pairs below. These shifts are very systematic and allow learners to predict changes in both directions; for example, whenever -**f**- in the final position is heard, you will always hear -**w**- before a vowel, unless -**f**- is the final consonant in the word.

Consonants **m, n, r, l, ł, j** are always voiced (in the final position you will still hear **m, n, r, l, ł**). Pronunciation of clusters in the final position can be reduced, such as -**gł** in **mógł** 'he could' to [muk] ‖ [mukw][1] (1.3.8).

1. **Mam alergię na pyłki <u>traw</u>** 'I'm allergic to pollen,' you hear [traf], because the final sound of the word is the voiceless [f], not the voiced [v] that is written. Once you modify the sentence, so that the final consonant is followed by a vowel, you will hear [v]. It means that in the word you write **w** even though you hear [f].

   Mam alergię na tra<u>w</u>y. 'I'm allergic to grass.'

2. **Co za traf!** What luck! You hear [traf]
   When you modify the sentence, so that the final consonant is followed by a vowel, and you still hear [f] it means that **f** is written at the end of the word.

   Szczęśliwym tra<u>f</u>em, udało mi się was znaleźć.
   'As luck would have it, I managed to find you.'

Table 1.5 Voiced and voiceless pairs

Voiced	Voiceless	Example	Translation	Pronounced as
b	p	chle<u>b</u>	bread	'chlep'
d	t	samochó<u>d</u>	car	'samochót'
dz	c	je<u>dz</u>!	eat!	'jets'
g	k	śnie<u>g</u>	snow	'śniek'
rz	sz	ku<u>rz</u>	dust	'kusz'
w	f	kre<u>w</u>	blood	'kref'
z	s	tera<u>z</u>	now	'teras'
ź	ś	we<u>ź</u>!	take it!	'weś'
ż	sz	ju<u>ż</u>	already	'jusz'
dź	ć	cho<u>dź</u>!	come!	'choć'

tusz 'ink' or **tuż** <particle to emphasize that something or someone is close> are pronounced identically.

Święta tuż, tuż.
'The holidays are just around the corner.'

Kup tusz!
'Buy ink!'

It is useful in adding a vowel to a final consonant that is not voiced in pronunciation to check whether the word is spelled with a voiced or a voiceless consonant.

chle<u>b</u>	chle<u>ba</u> (the [b] sound is clear)
samochó<u>d</u>	samocho<u>du</u> (the [d] sound is clear)
śnie<u>g</u>	śnie<u>gu</u> (the [g] sound is clear)
cho<u>dź</u>	cho<u>dzi</u> (the [dzi] sound is clear)
tu<u>sz</u>	(nie ma) tu<u>szu</u> (the [sz] sound is clear)

1.3.7 | Assimilation

This is a process in which sounds change. Just as Poles do not pronounce voiced consonants at the end of the phrase but instead pronounce a voiceless counterpart (1.3.6), they assimilate sounds that are next to each other. This process—called assimilation—explains the way that Polish words are spelled. In the process of assimilation, which can be progressive and regressive, the second consonant usually influences the first.

przepraszam [pṣɛpraṣam]/[reads pszepraszam] 'I'm sorry'/
  'excuse me'
łóżko [wuṣkɔ]/[reads wuszko] 'bed': ż before voiceless **k** is
  pronounced [sz]
także [tagʑɛ]/[reads tagże] 'as well': **k** before voiced ż is
  pronounced [g]
prośba [prɔʑba]/[reads proźba] 'request': ś in front of voiced **b**
  is pronounced [ź] [proźba]
buźka 'cheers'(GB coll.) or 'mouth': ż before voiceless **k** is
  pronounced [ś] [reads buśka]

The process in English can be compared to the pronunciation of 's' after voiced 'd,' or voiceless 't.'

kid<u>s</u> [kid<u>z</u>]
kit<u>s</u> [kit<u>s</u>]

| 1.3.7.1 | *Prepositions*

Prepositions are pronounced with the following word, as if glued together. For example, the preposition **w** 'in(side)' before voiceless consonants is pronounced [f], and before voiced consonants and vowels is pronounced [v].

w domu [vdomu] 'at home'
w Ameryce [vameryce] 'in America'
w pokoju [fpokoju] 'in a room'
w Polsce [fpolsce] 'in Poland'

If a preposition ends in the same letter as the following word the sound of the preposition is longer.

w Waszyngtonie [w·aszyngtonie] 'in Washington, DC'
w Warszawie [w·arszawie] 'in Warsaw'

Note: Potential difficulties in pronunciation of compound adjectives:

podziemny   reads **pod-ziemny**, not podziemny 'underground'
tysiączłotowy   reads **tysiąc-złotowy**, not tysiączłotowy
                      'thousand-zloty' <ADJ>
tysiąchektarowy reads **tysiąc-hektarowy**, not tysiąchektarowy
                      'thousand-hectare' <ADJ>

| 1.3.8 | **Consonant clusters**

Consonant cluster is a sequence of two or more consonants. Consonant clusters often occur in Polish. There can be up to six consonants in a sequence.

Chrząszcz brzmi w trzcinie w Szczebrzeszynie
(łamaniec językoway 'tongue twister')
    bezwstydny 'shameless'
    bezwzględność 'ruthlessness'
    chrzczony 'baptized'
    jabłko 'apple'
    językoznawstwo 'linguistics'
    społeczeństwo 'society'
    Wrocław (city in Poland)
    wtorek 'Tuesday'

When a cluster is at the beginning of the word, an extra vowel may be required on the preposition—also called the buffer e—as in **we wtorek** 'on Tuesday.'

When a cluster is in positions in the word other than at the beginning, the process of assimilation often occurs, as in **sześćset** 'sześset' [ʂɛɕt͡set] or 'szejset' [ʂɛjset] 'six hundred' (1.3.7).

Extra **-e**

This buffer vowel is attached to the single-consonant prepositions (**w** and **z**) before consonant clusters to ease the pronunciation of the phrase.

The use of the extra -e may be or may not be triggered by the cluster—it "depends on the phonological structure of the potential cluster at the juncture of preposition and word."[2]

Two forms are used in modern Polish: **w młynie** and **we młynie**, with the former being used more often. Here, the consonant cluster is **mł-**.

Ze sobą 'with each other' is not a consonant cluster, however extra **e** occurs to ease the pronunciation of the phonologically close sounds **z** and **s**.

> **Gdzieżeś ty bywał, czarny baranie? We młynie, we młynie, mój mości panie.** (children's song)
> 'Where were you black ram? In a mill, in a mill, my petty nobleman.'

we occurs before clusters beginning with **w** and **f**.

we wtorek 'on Tuesday'	consonant cluster **wt-**
we Włoszech 'in Italy'	consonant cluster **wł-**
we Francji 'in France'	consonant cluster **fr-**
we Wrocławiu 'in Wrocław'	consonant cluster **wr-**
we wszystkim 'in everything'	consonant cluster **wsz-**

"The ligature is likely to occur before roots that lack a vowel (in oblique cases)."[3]

> **we krwi** 'in blood' (**-i** is the genitive singular ending)
> **we łzach** 'in tears' (**-ach** is the locative plural ending)
> **we łbie** 'in head' (**-ie** is the locative singular ending)

W środę [fśrode] 'on Wednesday,' even though it has a cluster -śr-, does not require an extra -e because the cluster does not start with either **w** or **f**. The same occurs in the phrases **w czwartek** [fczfartek] 'on Thursday,' **w Szczecinie** 'in Szczecin' (a city in Poland), and **w Pszczynie** 'in Pszczyna' (city in Poland).

Z**e** occurs before clusters of which the first consonant is: **z, s, ź, ś, sz** and before **wz-, ws-, łz-**:

> **ze łzami w oczach** 'with tears in eyes'
> **ze Stanów Zjednoczonych** 'from the United States'
> **ze Szwecji** 'from Sweden'
> **ze wszystkimi** 'with everyone'
> **ze złością** 'with anger'
> **ze zmęczenia** 'from fatigue'
> **ze szczęścia** 'from happiness'
> **ze Szczecina** 'from Szczecin' (city in Poland)
> **ze źródła** 'from the source'

Clusters **chl, chrz, chł, chw, brz,** and combinations of letters (**rz, dz, dź, dż**) do not trigger the extra -e after **z**.

> **z chlebem** 'with bread' **w chlebie** 'in bread'
> **z chrzanem** 'with horseradish' **w chrzanie** 'in horseradish'
> **w chłodnym pokoju** 'in a cold room'
> **z chłodnego pokoju** 'from a cold room'
> **w chwili rozpoczęcia filmu** 'at the very beginning of the film'
> **z rzeki** 'from a river'
> **z Rzymu** 'from Rome'

The extra -e is also attached to monosyllabic prepositions that end with a consonant (**bez, od, pod, przed, nad, spod**).

bez**e** 'without' appears before the personal pronoun **mnie**

> **beze mnie** 'without me'

od**e** 'from' appears before the personal pronoun **mnie**

> **czego ode mnie chcesz?** 'what do you want from me?'
> **pozdrów go ode mnie** 'say hello from me to him'

before a set phrase: **ode złego** (as in the Lord's Prayer), otherwise

> **od złego** 'from evil'

pod**e** 'under, by' appears before the personal pronouns **mnie** and **mną**

> **pode mną** 'below me'

and also in books: in Prus's *Lalka* Żeromski's *Popioły*, Reymont's *Chłopi* we can encounter the forms **pode drzwiami** 'by the door,' **pode płotem** 'under the fence'

prze<u>de</u> 'in front of' appears before the personal pronouns **mnie** and **mną**

> **przede mną** 'in front of me'

and in the set phrase **przede wszystkim** 'first of all' (but: **przed wszystkimi** 'in front of everyone')

na<u>de</u> 'above' appears before the personal pronouns **mnie** and **mną**

> **nade mną** 'above me'

and in the set phrase **nade wszystko** 'above all' (bookish), (but: **czuwać nad wszystkim** 'to keep watch on everything')

spo<u>de</u> 'from' appears before the personal pronoun **mnie**

> **spode mnie** 'from under me' and in the set phrase **patrzeć spode łba** 'to scowl'

The clusters **chl, chrz, chł, chw, brz,** and combinations of letters (**rz, dz, dź, dż,**) do not trigger the extra -e after **bez, od, pod, przed, nad, spod**.

> **bez <u>chrząszcza</u>** 'without a beetle'
> **przed <u>chrzczonym</u>** 'in front of the baptized'
> **spod <u>krzyża</u>** 'from under the cross'

The clusters **-dł, -zł, -gł, -rł** in the final position tend to be reduced to a single voiceless consonant [t], [s], [k] or to [r].

> **zmarł** [zmar] ‖ [zmarw̦]
> **znalazł** [znalas] ‖ [znalasw̦]
> **szedł** [ʂɛt] ‖ [ʂɛtw̦]
> **mógł** [muk] ‖ [mukw̦]

1.4 Stress

1.4.1 Regular word stress

In Polish, generally the stress falls on the penultimate syllable (next to the last).

tel<u>e</u>fon 'phone'	muz<u>e</u>um 'museum'
telef<u>o</u>ny 'phones'	lic<u>e</u>um 'high school'
na<u>u</u>ka 'science'	bibliot<u>e</u>ka 'library'
<u>i</u>gloo	

1.4.2 | Irregular word stress

Standard references for Polish prescribe rules for some irregular word stress, but some Poles apply word stress on the penultimate syllable instead.

Stress falls on the final syllable of a phrase when a monosyllabic word is preceded by other words: **eks** 'former,' **wice** 'deputy,' **pół** 'half'

eksmąż ex-husband   **pół Fin** half Finnish

In words borrowed from French:

attaché, exposé, esemes 'SMS'

Some abbreviations have stress on the last syllable.

PKP PeKaPe   Polish Railway Service
PKS PeKaeS   Polish Bus Service
UJ [ujot]

skończyć UJ 'to graduate from Jagiellonian University in Cracow'

Words with the endings -yka/-ika, usually denoting disciplines, and a few other words have stress on the third syllable from the last.

fizyka 'physics'
matematyka 'maths'
uniwersytet 'university'

With the hundred numerals ending in -set, -sta, -stu, the hundred suffix is not counted in determining word stress. This means that if there are three syllables or more, the stress falls on the third syllable from the end.

czterysta 'four hundred'
siedemset 'seven hundred'
osiemset 'eight hundred'
dziewięćset 'nine hundred' **dziewięciuset** <GEN PL>

The stress falls on the next to last syllable of the verb, with the exception that parts of the verb that can be moved are not counted. For example, in **robiłby**, the suffix -by can be moved to attach to another part of the sentence, such as żeby robił. Stress never falls on the markers of the conditional mood -by, -byśmy, -byście.

ro-bił 'he was doing'
ro-bi-ła 'she was doing'
ro-bi-li 'they were doing'<MHPL>
ro-bi-li-śmy 'we were doing'   żebyśmy ro-bi-li

ro-_bi_-li-ście 'you were doing' <MHPL>
_ro_-bił-by 'he would be doing'
ro-_bi_-ła-by 'she would be doing'   **żeby ro-_bi_-ła**
ro-_bi_-li-byśmy 'we would be doing' <MHPL>
rob_i_-libyście 'you would be doing' <MHPL>
rob_i_-liby 'they would be doing' <MHPL>
rob_i_-łyby 'they would be doing' <NO-MHPL>

| 1.4.3 | **Sentence stress** |

Sentence stress is placed on a whole word or words to emphasize the importance of it or them within the sentence.

Ogród jest _niesamowity_!
'Garder is _unbelievable!_'

Czekamy, _jak zwykle_, na ciebie.
'We are waiting, _as usual_, for you.'

Czego się spodziewałeś?
'_What_ were you expecting?'

| 1.4.4 | **With prepositions and particles** |

| 1.4.4.1 | *Prepositions* |

| 1.4.4.1.1 | Monosyllabic prepositions with monosyllabic pronouns |

Primary prepositions, e.g., **z** 'from,' **do** 'to,' **dla** 'for,' are normally unstressed, however before a monosyllabic pronoun, e.g., **mną** 'me,' **was** 'you, PL,' **nas** 'us' *the stress shifts to the preposition.*

pisz _do_ mnie często 'write _to_ me often'
co masz _dla_ mnie? 'what do you have _for_ me?
trzymamy _za_ was kciuki 'we keep our fingers crossed _for_ you'

| 1.4.4.1.2 | Monosyllabic prepositions with monosyllabic nouns |

With monosyllabic prepositions, e.g., **na** 'on,' **do** 'to,' **za** 'behind' before a monosyllabic noun e.g., **głos** 'voice,' or a monosyllabic possessive pronoun **mój** 'my,' or a monosyllabic numeral e.g., **trzy** 'three,' **dwóch** 'two,' the stress falls on the noun, possessive pronoun or numeral, respectively.

pracować za <u>dwóch</u> 'to do the work *of two men*'
liczymy na <u>głos</u> senatorów w tej sprawie 'we count on the
   senators' vote in this matter'
ćwiczenia na <u>krzyż</u> 'exercises for back [pain]'

An exception from that rule is observed for set phrases. Then the stress
falls on the prepositions.

wyszła <u>za</u> mąż 'she got married'
miał kilka włosów <u>na</u> krzyż 'he was practically bald'
liczyć <u>na</u> głos 'to count out loud'
wyprowadzić się <u>na</u> wieś 'to move to the country'
pochodzę <u>ze</u> wsi 'I come from a village'

| 1.4.4.1.3 | Change of meaning as a result of stress shift |

The meaning of the phrase can differ depending on the stress.

z dnia <u>na</u> dzień or **dzień po <u>dniu</u>** 'day by day'
żyć z dnia <u>na</u> dzień 'to live day by day'
z dnia na <u>dzień</u> 'suddenly, within 24 hours'
z dnia na <u>dzień</u> straciliśmy wszystko 'we lost everything within
   24 hours'

| 1.4.4.1.4 | Stress with the negated particle **nie** 'no' |

Nie is joined directly to the verb to express negation: *nie* śpię 'I'm not
sleeping' and receives the stress when the verb is monosyllabic.

<u>nie</u> śpię 'I am *not* sleeping'
<u>nie</u> chcę 'I *don't* want'
<u>nie</u> ma 'there isn't/there aren't'

| 1.4.4.2 | *Particles* |

Stress does not fall on the particles **-bym, -byś, -by, -byśmy, -byście**. The
stress falls on the penultimate syllable in the word after the elimination of
the particles (1.4.2. Irregular word stress).

r<u>o</u>bił-by
rob<u>i</u>ła-by
rob<u>i</u>li-byśmy

27

1.5 Intonation

Intonation is the rise and fall of speech.

In Polish, like in English, falling intonation is typical for statements.

Rising intonation and a rapid change in pitch would suggest a question or emphasis.

> **To wszystko.** 'That's it.'
> **To wszystko?** 'That's it?'
> **Naprawdę.** 'Really.'
> **Naprawdę?** 'Really?'

The focal phrase is pronounced higher than the rest of the sentence.

> **Jak często chodzisz do kina?**
> 'How often do you go to the movies?'

1.6 Spelling rules

Some common spelling rules:

sz, rz, ż, cz never take -i, and **k, g, l** never take -y, e.g.,

książka 'book'	**książki** <GEN SG>
noga 'leg'	**nogi** 'legs' <GEN SG>
sól 'salt'	**soli** 'salts' <GEN SG>
kasza 'kasha'	**kaszy** <GEN SG>
burza 'storm'	**burzy** <GEN SG>
tęcza 'rainbow'	**tęczy** <GEN SG>

except in a few words, e.g., **kynolog** 'cynologist,' **a kysz!** 'be gone!', **lycra** 'Lycra fabric'

> **Egipt** 'Egypt'
> **gips** 'gypsum, plaster'

(1.3.3, 1.3.5)

This is especially important for the nominative plural no male human forms (except for neuter plural) and genitive singular feminine forms. In both, endings are spelled -i when the final consonant of the word (after dropping any vowel endings) is **k** or **g**.

> **książka** 'book': **książki** <NOM PL/GEN SG FEM>
> **bank** 'bank': **banki** <NOM NO-MHPL>

The nominative male plural ending is spelled -y when the final consonant of the word (after dropping any vowels) is **k** or **g**, because both **k** and **g** shift; **k** shifts to **c**, and **g** to **dz**.

kolega 'male friend': **koledzy** <NOM MHPL>
Polak 'Pole': **Polacy** <NOM MHPL>.

1.6.1 | ó and u

Both **ó** and **u** are pronounced identically.

ulica 'street' [uliṱsa]   **ósmy** 'eighth' [usmɨ]

U is written at the beginning of a word (except for **ósmy** 'eighth,' **ów** 'that' (bookish), **ówczesny** 'contemporary,' **ówdzie** 'elsewhere' (bookish))

ulica 'street'   **umrzeć** 'to die'
urodzić się 'to be born'   **uśmiechnij się** 'smile'

Ó is never written at the end of a word.

In the middle of a word both **ó** and **u** occur.

sól 'salt'   **susza** 'drought'

The letter **ó** can shift to **o, e, a**.

stół 'table'   **stoły** 'tables'
ósmy 'eighth'   **osiem** 'eight'
kościół 'church'   **w kościele** 'in the church'
siódmy 'seventh'   **siedem** 'seven'
skrócić 'to shorten' <PFV>   **skracać** 'to shorten' <IMPFV>
wymówić 'to pronounce' <PFV>   **wymawiać** 'to pronounce' <IMPFV>

The exception to the rule is all conjugated forms of verbs with **-ować**: **pracuj** is spelled **-u**, even though the infinitive is **pracować**.

1.6.1.1 | ó ↔ o shifts

Ó in the final syllable shifts to **o** when a new syllable occurs.

mój 'my'   **moja** 'my'
samochód 'car'   **samochodem** 'by car'
stół 'table'   **stoły** 'tables'
stój! 'halt'   **stoję** 'I am standing'

Ó in the final syllable before ż does not shift to o before vowels.

stróż 'guard'   **stróża** <GEN SG>
podróż 'trip'   **podróże** <NOM PL>

O in the final syllable (after dropping vowel endings) shifts to ó in genitive plural feminine and neuter nouns.

morze 'sea'   **mórz** <NT GEN PL>
woda 'water'   **wód** <FEM GEN PL>

The genitive plural of masculine nouns is spelled -ów [uf].

zabrakło lodów 'there is no more ice cream'
pięć domów 'five houses'
dużo rowerów 'many bikes'

Suffixes -ówna, -ów, -ówka are spelled with ó.

krówka (name for Polish fudge)
starówka 'the Old Town'
Barbara Radziwiłłówna (name of the Polish Queen)
Kraków 'Cracow' (city in Poland)

Note: Kraków in its name has the genitive plural ending -ów; 'a city of Krak.'

| 1.6.1.2 | **u** |

U is written in augmentative and diminutive forms, with the suffixes **-uch**, **-utki**, **-uszek**, **-uś**.

starucha 'old woman' (coll.)   **dziadziuś** 'grandpa'
brzuszek 'tummy'   **malutki** 'tiny'

| 1.6.2 | *rz and ż* |

Both **rz** and **ż** are pronounced identically.

Może nad morze? 'How about [going to] the sea?'

może '(s)he can' [mɔʒɛ]
morze 'sea' [mɔʒɛ]
nie każ się prosić 'don't make me beg you'
nie karz go 'don't punish him'
powietrze 'air'

rz can shift to **r**.

mo<u>rz</u>e 'sea'	**mo<u>r</u>ski** 'pertaining to sea'
nie ka<u>rz</u> 'do not punish'	**ka<u>ra</u>ć** 'to punish'
powiet<u>rze</u> 'air'	**wiat<u>r</u>** 'wind'

ż can shift to **g, ź, z, s**.

mo<u>ż</u>e '(s)he can'	**mo<u>g</u>ę** 'I can'
nie ka<u>ż</u> się prosić	**ka<u>za</u>ć** 'to order'
ksią<u>ż</u>ka 'book'	**ksi<u>ęg</u>arnia** 'bookstore'
kole<u>ż</u>eński 'friendly'	**kole<u>g</u>a** 'friend'
du<u>ż</u>y 'big'	**du<u>z</u>i** 'big' <ADJ MHPL>

It is especially useful in the formation of the comparative forms of adjectives and adverbs.

ni<u>ż</u>ej 'lower'	**ni<u>s</u>ko** 'low'
dro<u>ż</u>szy 'more expensive'	**dro<u>g</u>i** 'expensive'

The traces of **rz** and **ż** in Polish words can also be found in their foreign equivalents with **r** and **g**, respectively.

in<u>ż</u>ynier 'engineer'	**baga<u>ż</u>** 'baggage'
And<u>rz</u>ej 'And<u>rew</u>'	**gara<u>ż</u>** 'garage'
cmenta<u>rz</u> 'cemete<u>ry</u>'	**ma<u>rz</u>ec** 'Ma<u>rch</u>'
k<u>rz</u>yż 'c<u>r</u>oss'	**presti<u>ż</u>** 'prestige'

Note: **żona** 'wife' is spelled with ż because of the root *gen-* in Latin *genus* and then in Greek *gynē* 'wife.'

Consequently, all related words such as **małżonek** 'spouse,' **małżeństwo** 'marriage,' **ożenić się** 'to get married' (for a man) are spelled with ż.

There is also a correlation between Polish words spelled with **rz** and Russian words spelled with 'r.'

<u>rz</u>eka 'river' <u>р</u>ека

For **r** ↔ **rz** shifts see 1.3.4.

Suffixes that denote an actor: **-arz, -erz, -mistrz**, are spelled with **-rz**. Note that many of these forms correspond to "-er" in English.

pis<u>arz</u> 'writ<u>er</u>'
zegarmistrz 'watchmak<u>er</u>'
żołni<u>erz</u> 'soldi<u>er</u>'

After initial **p** write **rz**.

przedwojenny 'prewar' ("pre-" in English)
przedhistoryczny 'prehistoric'
przyjaciel 'friend'
przespać się 'to take a nap'
przemoc 'violence'

(except for **pszenica** 'wheat,' **pszczoła** 'bee' and nouns related to the two)

Many particles with -eż and -uż, -óż, -iż, -że, -żeby at the end are spelled with ż (not rz).

a nuż 'maybe'
cóż 'oh well'
jakże 'how'
już 'already'
niż 'than'

| 1.6.3 | *ch and h* |

There are pronounced identically

hełm [xɛwm] 'helmet'
Chełm [xɛwm] (city in Poland)

For words of foreign origin, the Polish spelling of **ch** or **h** will generally reflect the foreign spelling.

Chiny 'China'
chemia 'chemistry'
charakter 'character'
charytatywny 'charity'
alkohol 'alcohol'
pracoholik 'workaholic'
hermetyczny 'hermetic'
historia 'history'

Write **ch** in the locative case endings -ach, -ych, -óch, -ech.

w tych dwóch lub trzech nowych domach
'in these two or three new houses'

ch can shift to sz, si.

ucho 'ear'	**uszy** 'ears'
mucha 'fly'	**muszka** 'small fly' or 'bow tie'
Włoch 'Italian'	**Włosi** 'Italians'
brzuch 'stomach'	**brzuszek** 'tummy'
dach 'roof'	**zadaszenie** 'canopy'

Write **ch** at the end of words (except for **druh** 'scout').

1.6.4 | s, z, ś, wz, *and* ws

> Note for heritage speakers: The perfective form of verbs can begin with z, s, and ś.

Write **s** before voiceless consonants.

spytać 'to inquire' <PFV>
skontaktować się 'to get in touch' <PFV>
spieszyć się 'to hurry' (or **śpieszyć się**)

Write **z** before voiced consonants and s, sz, ś, ć even though you hear [s] [si].

zszyć [sʂɨt͡ɕ] 'to sew something up' <PFV>
zsumować [s·umɔvat͡ɕ] 'to add up' <PFV>
zsiąść z roweru 'to get off the bike' <PFV>

Write **ś** before **ci**.

ściszyć 'to turn [radio] down'	**ściskać** 'to hug'
ścigać 'to chase'	**ściemnia się** 'it is getting dark'

Perfective forms of verbs can begin with **wz-, ws-, wes-**.

Write **wz-** before voiced consonants:

wzbogacić się 'to become rich'

Write **ws-** before voiceless consonants:

wspominać 'to recall'
wspierać 'to support' <IMPFV>
wskoczyć 'to jump on'

Write **wes-** before verbs with consonant clusters (voiceless).

wesprzeć 'to support' <PFV>

(See 6.4.14.13)

1.7 Capitalization

Days of the week, months, adjectives of nationalities, languages, natives of cities, religions, and the personal pronoun 'I' are not capitalized except as the first word of the sentence.

Dzisiaj jest sobota. 'Today is Saturday.'
w maju 'in May'
(język) polski 'Polish (language)'
szwajcarski zegarek 'Swiss watch'
warszawianin 'native of Warsaw'   **warszawianie** <PL>
krakowianin 'native of Cracow'   **krakowianie** <PL>
lublinianin 'native of Lublin'   **lublinianie** <PL>
nowojorczyk 'native of New York'   **nowojorczycy** <PL>
waszyngtończyk 'native of Washington, DC'   **waszyngtończycy** <PL>
buddyzm 'Buddhism'
islam 'Islam'
katolicyzm 'Catholicism'

Personal pronouns and polite forms when addressing one person or a group of people: **Pan** 'Sir,' **Pani** 'Madam,' **Państwo** 'Mr and Mrs,' can be capitalized as a sign of respect in written correspondence.

Szanowni Państwo 'Dear Sir or Madam'
Dziękuję Ci za list. 'Thank you for the letter.'

1.7.1 Proper nouns

Proper nouns that relate to a designated entity are written with a capital letter, e.g.,

W którym roku była *bitwa* **pod Grunwaldem?**
'In which year was the *battle* of Grunwald?'
W którym roku została namalowana *Bitwa* **pod Grunwaldem?** 'In which year was *The Battle* of Grunwald (a painting by Matejko) painted?'
Jaka jest odległość między *Słońcem* **a** <u>*Ziemią*</u>**?**
'What is the distance between the Sun and *the Earth*?'
Nie siadaj na *ziemi.*
'Don't sit on the *ground.*'
W sobotę *słońce* **zajdzie o 20.10.**
'*Sunset* will be at 8:10 p.m. on Saturday.'

1.8   Letter alternations

Table 1.6 Consonant alternations

t	ć/ci	c
student	o studencie	studencki
bogaty	bogaci	bogactwo
uniwersytet	na uniwersytecie	uniwersytecki
miasto	w mieście	miejsce
demokrata	o demokracie	demokracja

k	c	cz	-kiem
rok		roczny	rokiem Wołu
piekę	piec	piecze	wypiekiem
smak		smaczny	ze smakiem
mleko		mleczny	z mlekiem
ręka	w ręce	ręczny	

d	dź/dzi
jadę	jedziesz
ambasada	w ambasadzie

g	dz	ż	gi
noga	na nodze	piłka nożna	nogi
kolega	koledze	koleżeński	kolegi
droga	po drodze	dorożka	drogi

ch	s	sz	si
Włoch	włoski	we Włoszech	Włosi
Czech	czeski	w Czechach	Czesi

z	ź
zły	źle

35

Table 1.7 Vowel alternations

soft consonant + **a** or + **o**	**e** + soft consonant
obiad	po obiedzie
sąsiad	o sąsiedzie
gwiazda	o gwieździe
wiatr	na wietrze
gniazda	w gnieździe
miara	w dużej mierze
wiara	w wierze
siadać	siedzieć
niosę	niesiesz
wiozę	wieziesz
biorę	bierzesz
piorę	pierzesz

Verbs that end with -eć, e.g., **mieć** 'to have,' **widzieć** 'to see' write **a** before
ł and **e** before **l** (plural masculine forms) in the past tense.

on miał   oni   mieli
ona miała   one   miały

A remains in the penultimate position when it is not preceded by a soft
consonant.

sad   w sadzie
osada   w osadzie
warta   na warcie

Ó in the final syllable shifts to **o** before another vowel.

ó   o
pokój   pokoje
nóż   noże
samochód   samochodem

Ó changes to **e** when ó follows a soft consonant.

ó   e
kościół   w kościele
ziół   ziele
pióro   pierze
but
miód   w miodzie

Ą generally changes to ę.

When the first person of the verb ends with -ę, the third person plural **oni, one** has -ą

chcę	**chcą**	**chcieć** 'to want'
pracuję	**pracują**	**pracować** 'to work'
mówię	**mówią**	**mówić** 'to speak'
tańczę	**tańczą**	**tańczyć** 'to dance'
zacznę	**zaczną**	**zacząć** 'to begin'

Ą before **ż, dz, c** in the final syllable shifts to ę before another vowel.

mąż	**męża**
pieniądz	**nie mam pieniędzy**
miesiąc	**pięć miesięcy**
ksiądz	**z księdzem** (NOM PL **księża**)

Ą → ę in front of labial and dental consonants: **dąb** 'oak' **dęby, urząd** 'office' **urzędy** but nasal consonant **ą** does not change to ę in all oblique cases before consonant **s: wąs, wąsy** 'moustache,' **pląs, pląsy** 'lively dance.'

Ą in verbs with the ending -ąć, e.g., **zacząć** 'to begin,' remains ą in masculine singular forms of the past tense; in all other forms of the past tense ą changes to ę.

(**ja**, MSC) **zacząłem**	(**ja**, FEM) **zaczęłam**
	oni zaczęli
	one zaczęły

For the pronunciation of ą and ę before ł and l see 1.2.2.

For the full conjugation paradigm of the past tense of **zacząć**, see Table 6.8.

1.9 Fleeting vowel

The fleeting vowel is a vowel that is found in some forms of the nouns, but not in others.

dziadek 'grandfather'	**dziadka** <ACC/GEN SG>
książka 'book'	**książek** <GEN PL>
Niemiec 'German'	**Niemcy** <NOM PL>
okno 'window'	**okien** <GEN PL>

For the fleeting vowel with prepositions before clusters, such as **we wtorek**, see 1.3.8.

In Polish the fleeting vowel is mostly -e and in rare examples -o such as in osioł 'donkey' osła <GEN SG>. The fleeting vowel often occurs before the consonants -(i)ec, -ek, -eł, -el, and in a few words that end with -(i)er and -en, plus pies 'dog', psy 'dogs'.

Fleeting vowel -e also occurs in a few monosyllabic feminine nouns that end with a consonant.

wieś 'village'	**wsie** <NOM PL>
krew 'blood'	**krwi** <GEN SG>
brew 'eyebrow'	**brwi** <NOM PL>

The fleeting vowel disappears in all forms of the nouns except for the nominative singular case.

-(i)ec

chłopiec 'boy'	**Niemiec** 'German'
cudzoziemiec 'foreigner'	**ojciec** 'father'
goniec 'messenger'	**strzelec** 'rifleman'
krawiec 'tailor'	**wdowiec** 'widower'
kupiec 'buyer'	**widelec** 'fork'
mędrzec 'wise man'	

bez <+GEN> **ojca** 'without a father'
zostałem <+INS> **ojcem** 'I became a father'
nasi <+NOM PL> **ojcowie** 'our fathers'

-ek

budynek 'building'	**stryjek** 'uncle'
dziadek 'grandfather'	**wujek** 'uncle'
marszałek 'speaker of Sejm'	

w **budynku** 'in the building'
z **dziadkiem** i **wujkiem** 'with grandpa and uncle'

-el/-eł/-oł

Nobel	**poseł** 'Member of Parliament'
orzeł 'eagle'	**wróbel** 'sparrow'

zostać ministrem 'to become a minister'
być posłem 'to be an MP'
wróble 'sparrows'
Nagroda Nobla 'Nobel Prize'

-en

len 'linen'	lnu <GEN SG>
sen 'dream'	snu <GEN SG>

-er

The fleeting vowel -e before -r disappears after soft -ki as well as in a few foreign-influenced words in all noun forms, except for the nominative singular case. In most words with the final -er, -e stays in all forms of the words.

Fleeting -e

cukier 'sugar'	**cukru** <GEN SG>
lukier 'icing'	**lukrem** <INS SG>
minister 'minister'	**ministrem** <INS SG>
sweter 'sweater'	**swetra** <GEN SG>

No fleeting -e

folder	**foldery** <NOM PL>
kasjer 'cashier'	**kasjera** <GEN SG>
komputer 'computer'	**komputera** <GEN SG>
mikser 'blender'	**miksera** <GEN SG>
rower 'bicycle'	**roweru** <GEN SG>
toster 'toaster'	**tostera** <GEN SG>

Chapter 2

Case usage

2.1 Case names and order

Polish is a highly inflected language, with words taking many different endings (suffixes) to show their many meanings. Case endings are added to words to indicate their function in a sentence. These case endings vary for different classes (also referred to as genders, see 3.2.1) and numbers. In other words, Polish is a case language.

What is a case?

Case is a grammatical concept that through a set of different endings attached to the nominal forms (noun, adjective, pronoun, numeral, and/or participle) explains *who does what to whom* without heavily relying on word order.

> **Ludzie** _{<who NOM>} **ludzi*om*** _{<to whom DAT>} **zgotowali** _{<VERB>} **ten los** _{<what ACC>} 'People _{<who NOM>} created _{<VERB>} this fate _{<what ACC>} for [other] people _{<to whom DAT>}'
>
> Zofia Nałkowska, *Medallions*

The Polish case marking system

The parts of speech that can be declined with different case endings are: *nominal forms*, generally nouns, adjectives, pronouns, numerals, and adjectival participles (which decline like adjectives). The parts of speech that are generally not declined with different case endings—*verbal forms*—are adverbs, prepositions, conjunctions, interjections, verbs, and adverbial participles (which are formed from verbs). Verbs are conjugated with different endings to show mood, tense, class (also referred to as gender, see 3.2.1), number, and person but they are not declined by case, with the exception of most participles.

In Polish there are seven kinds of distinctive relationships, overtly marked on nominal forms. The seven distinctive relationships correspond to the seven cases in Polish.

Table 2.1 Cases in Polish

English name	Polish name	General case questions		Abbreviation
		Person	Thing	
nominative	**mianownik**	**kto?**	**co?**	NOM
accusative	**biernik**	**kogo?**	**co?**	ACC
genitive	**dopełniacz**	**kogo?**	**czego?**	GEN
dative	**celownik**	**komu?**	**czemu?**	DAT
locative	**miejscownik**	**(o) kim?**	**(o) czym?**	LOC
instrumental	**narzędnik**	**kim?**	**czym?**	INS
vocative	**wołacz**	—	—	VOC

Polish has seven cases for each number—singular and plural—thus a total of 14 forms for each fully developed nominal form. Some words have only singular forms (also called *singularia tantum*) or only plural forms (*pluralia tantum*). A few words in Polish retain the dual number, e.g., **uszy** 'ears,' **oczy** 'eyes,' **plecy** 'back.'

2.2   Cases and the process of communication

Different endings on nominal forms can denote which nominal form is the subject in a sentence, which is the object in a sentence, and which words function in other roles. Each word has a range of functions it can fulfill within a sentence or a clause which is marked by case. Each case has a set of endings that are added to a word to indicate this function. In practice, the process of inflection can be compared to putting a puzzle together— once all the elements are accurately assigned we can see and express the whole picture to others.

Each case provides a set of endings that are added to the stem of the noun, as if to give a new birth to the word. It is not a *tabula rasa* any more; the word is assigned to perform certain functions amidst other players on the scene—amidst other words in the sentence, a clause or within a larger context such as a paragraph. Rather than in separate words or individual clauses, people communicate in longer chunks of text that usually consist of a few sentences or clauses.

2.3 Polish and English

2.3.1 Word order

English relies heavily on word order (subject—verb—object) to indicate what function certain words play in a sentence or a clause. In Polish, the word order is more fluid as case endings have a primary role in determining relationships between words. However, word order is still important, and particularly it can be used to put emphasis on certain words.

Subject before object is a natural word order in Polish. When object stands before subject, the sentence is slightly emotionally charged.

Kupiłem dom. 'I bought a house.'
Dom kupiłem [a nie mieszkanie]. 'I bought a house [and not an apartment].'
Anna <NOM> **lubi *Ewę*** <ACC>. 'Anna likes *Ewa*.'
Annę <ACC> **lubi Ewa** <NOM>**, a nie Basia.** 'Ewa, and not Basia, likes *Anna*.'

2.3.2 Case usage

It is useful to recognize that case usage occurs in English too, although only to a very limited extent. When "she" is a direct object, the word changes to "her"; the same happens in Polish, where **on** 'he' changes to **go** 'him,' for example:

On lubi Ewę. Ewa go lubi. 'He likes Ewa. Ewa likes *him*.'

Another example of case usage in English is the possessive case, which is marked by an apostrophe "s" in the singular or by an apostrophe in the plural.

samochód siostry 'sister's car'
samochód sióstr 'sisters' car'

Case usage in Polish is similar to this but is *much more extensive than in English*. Polish has seven cases, and each case has a set of endings based on class (also referred to as gender, see 3.2.1) and number. The cases are: nominative, accusative, genitive, dative, locative, instrumental, and vocative. (This order of cases is used to more readily show overlap of similar endings between cases, especially when depicted in tables of case endings.) An overview of their functions is found in Table 2.2; for simplicity, the table provides only some main uses of each case. A more detailed description of the uses of each case follows.

Table 2.2 Case usage

Case	Main use(s)	Example(s)
Nominative	Subject	**Anna jest silna.** *'Anna* is strong.'
Accusative	Direct object	**Lubię Annę.** 'I like *Anna.'*
	Object of directed motion or directed movements after the prepositions **między, na, nad, po, pod, poza, przed, przez, w, za** after motion verbs	**Anna jedzie w góry.** 'Anna is going to *the mountains.'* **Nie chodź pod stół.** 'Don't go under *the table.'*
Genitive 'of'	Absence	**Nie ma Anny.** *'Anna* is not [here].' **Brakuje wody.** 'There is no *water.'*
	Negation of an accusative object	**Nie lubię Anny.** 'I do not like *Anna.'*
	Possession, 'of' something, quantity	**dom Anny** *'Anna's* house' **pełna energii** 'full *of energy'* **prezes firmy** 'president *of the firm'* **butelka wody** 'a bottle *of water'*
Dative 'to'	Indirect object	**Dałem go Annie.** 'I gave it *to Anna.'*
	Impersonal constructions	**Zimno mi.** 'I'm cold.' (Literally: [It is] cold *to me.)*
Locative (Prepositional) Must be used with a preposition.	Location, object of the prepositions **na, przy, w, po**	**na stole** 'on *the table'* **przy Annie** 'near *Anna'* **w domu** 'at *home'* **po Azji** 'all over *Asia'*
	'After'	**po pracy** 'after *work'*
	'About'	**o Annie** 'about *Anna'*
	Telling time	**o piątej** 'at *five o'clock'*
Instrumental 'with'	Tool, means to an end, means of transportation	**Piszę ołówkiem.** 'I'm writing *with a pencil.'* **jechać autobusem** 'to go *by bus'*
	Accompaniment	**Idę z Anną.** 'I'm going [together] *with Anna.'*
	'Being' or 'becoming'	**Anna jest prezydentem.** 'Anna is *the president.'*
Vocative	Direct address	**Dzień dobry Anno!** 'Hello *Anna!'*

2.4   Nominative

"Nominative" is derived from *nomen*, which in Latin means "name." Words in the nominative case serve as the subjects of a sentence. Names such as nouns, pronouns, numerals and adjectives in their *entry* or *basic form* are in the nominative case. This is the form you can find in a dictionary.

The entry form in a dictionary for nouns (including verbal nouns) and pronouns is the nominative case, e.g., **dom** 'house,' **zmęczenie** 'tiredness,' **my** 'we.' The entry form for adjectives is the nominative case in the masculine singular, e.g., **dobry** 'good.' Other forms of adjectives are usually not listed, unless they are irregular. The entry form for numerals is the standard nominative case form, e.g., *trzy* (**psy**) 'three (dogs)'; however, the nominative male human form is not usually listed, e.g., *trzech* (**chłopców**) or *trzej* (**chłopcy**) 'three (boys).' The entry word for verbs is the infinitive, e.g., **zmęczyć** 'to tire.' Participles that are used extensively (and thought of as common adjectives) are listed in the nominative masculine singular form, e.g., **zmęczony** 'tired.' Less commonly used participles are not listed independently, but may be found under the entry for the infinitive, e.g., **przeczytany** 'read' found under **przeczytać** 'to read.'

2.4.1 │ *Importance of nominative noun endings*

The endings a nominal form (a noun, adjective, pronoun, numeral, and/or participle) will have in different cases depend on the ending the nominal has in nominative singular.

In Polish, a noun is the most important nominal in a phrase, a clause or a sentence, because it imposes the form that other modifying nominals will have. Nouns are classified *masculine*, *feminine*, or *neuter* based on the ending of the noun in the nominative singular case. For people, nouns classes are based on the biological gender/gender identity of the noun.

Ten mężczyzna jest przystojny. 'This man is handsome.'
Profesor Nowak jest miły <MSC>. 'Professor Nowak is nice.'
  (Professor Nowak is male.)
Profesor Nowak jest miła <FEM>. 'Professor Nowak is nice.'
  (Professor Nowak is female.)

The most typical endings for nouns in the nominative singular are:

For masculine nouns: a consonant (**-Ø**) (**pies** 'dog') (less commonly:
  -a (**poeta** 'poet'), **-o** (**dziadzio** 'grandpa <DIM>'))

For feminine nouns: **-a** (**siatka** 'net') (less commonly: a consonant (**-Ø**) (**podróż** 'trip'), **-i** (pani, 'Mrs./Ms./you <FORMAL>'))
For neuter nouns: **-o, e, -ę** (**dziecko** 'child,' **mieszkanie** 'apartment,' **imię** 'first name') (less commonly: **-um** (**muzeum** 'museum'))

The most typical endings for plural nouns in the nominative are -y and -i.

Nouns ending in a soft consonant (ones with a diacritical mark (accent) above the consonant) and "historically" soft consonants (ż, rz, sz, dz, dż, cz) make up a separate group and may be either masculine or feminine, e.g., **ten koc** <MSC> 'this blanket,' **ta noc** <FEM> 'this night.'

For simplicity this is just an overview of most typical endings in the nominative case. A more detailed description of the endings for each class follows. (See 3.3)

2.4.2 | Generic questions

The nominative case has a set of interrogatives:

kto? 'who?'; **co?** 'what?'; **który?** 'which one?'; **jaki?** 'what kind?'

In the nominative case a noun or noun phrase denotes the subject of a sentence and answers the questions: kto/co? 'who/what?'

Two generic questions that call for the use of the nominative case are:

Kto to jest? 'Who is that?' **Kto** 'who' *refers to people.*
Co to jest? 'What is that?' **Co** 'what' *refers to objects.*

The answers to the nominative questions kto/co? 'who/what?' will also be in the nominative case.

Kto **kupił ten obraz?** Who bought the painting?
Matka. 'Mother' [bought the painting].

Kto **ci się podoba?** 'Who do you like? (Who appeals to you?)'
Ewa **bardzo mi się podoba.** 'I like Ewa a lot.'

Co **ci się podoba?** 'What do you like (what appeals to you)?'
Ten obraz **mi się podoba.** 'This painting appeals to me.'

Jaki **jest dzisiaj dzień?** 'What's the day today?'
Dzisiaj jest *sobota* <NOM>. 'Today is Saturday.'

Jaki **był wczoraj dzień?** 'What day was it yesterday?'
Wczoraj był *piątek* <NOM>. 'Yesterday was *Friday*.'

Który **dzień jest dzisiaj?** 'What's the date today?'
Dzisiaj jest *trzeci* <NOM> **maja.** 'Today is the third of May.'

Który **(dzień) był wczoraj?** 'What was the date yesterday?'
Wczoraj był *drugi* <NOM> **maja.** 'Yesterday was the second of May.'

The days of the week and months in Polish are not capitalized (See 1.7.).

In exclamations beginning with **jaki** 'such, what a...' or **co za** 'what a...,' the nominative case is used. **Jaki** agrees with the noun or noun phrase in class (also referred to as gender, see 3.2.1) and number.

Jaka piękna torebka! 'What a beautiful purse!'
Jaki piękny dom! 'What a beautiful house!'
Co za piękny dom! 'What a beautiful house!'

2.4.3 Generic responses

These frequent patterns of response all take the nominative <+NOM> case:

To (nie) jest ... 'This is (not) ...' <+NOM>
To (nie) ... 'This is (not) ...' <+NOM>
To (nie) są ... 'These are (not) ...' <+NOM>
To (nie) ... 'These are (not) ...' <+NOM>
Oto ... 'Here is/are ...' <+NOM>
Oto nasze dzieci. 'Here are our children.'
Oto mój mąż. 'Here is my husband.'

Nie jestem tutaj na urlopie, ale w pracy.
'I am not here on vacation, but for work.' (2.4.9)

2.4.4 Omission of "to be" in present tense after to 'this'

The forms of the verb **być** 'to be' can be omitted in the present tense when used in Polish with the unchanging pronoun **to** 'this' for introduction: **to jest/to są** 'this is, that is/these are, those are,' and naming (in definitions): **jest to/są to** 'it is.' The forms of the verb **być** 'to be' cannot be omitted in the past and future tenses.

Kto to jest? 'Who is that/this?'   **Kto to?** 'Who [is] that/this?'
To jest Ewa. 'This is Ewa.'   **To Ewa.** 'This [is] Ewa.'
To są psy. 'These are dogs.'   **To psy.** 'These [are] dogs.'

chory (jest) to osoba, która źle się czuje
'sick it is a person who does not feel well'

skrzypce (jest) to instrument muzyczny, który ma cztery struny
'violin it is a musical instrument that has four strings'

2.4.5 | Kto, ktoś, nikt, co, coś

The subject **kto** 'who,' **ktoś** 'somebody,' and **nikt** 'nobody' of a verb is in the nominative case. **Kto** 'who,' **ktoś** 'somebody,' and **nikt** 'nobody' are used with a masculine form of an adjective and with a verb in the third person singular. With the past-tense form, **kto, ktoś,** and **nikt** take the masculine form—even if it is known that **kto, ktoś,** or **nikt** refer to a female subject. The subject **nikt** 'nobody' takes a negated verb and negated complements.

Kto śpiewa? 'Who is singing?'
Ktoś śpiewa. 'Somebody is singing.'
Kto dołączył do grupy? 'Who joined the group?'
Ktoś nowy dołączył do grupy. 'Someone new joined the group.'
Nikt nikogo nie znał. 'Nobody knew anyone.'

(The female form, **ktoś nowa dołączyła,** is not used even if it is known that the subject is female.)

On the contrary, the object **co** 'what,' **coś** 'something,' and **nic** 'nothing' combine with the neuter form of the adjective in the genitive singular (2.6). **Nic** takes a negated verb and negated complements.

Co kupiłaś nowego? 'What new thing did you buy?'
Zobaczyłam coś błyszczącego. 'I saw something shiny.'
Nikomu nie stało się nic złego. 'Nothing bad happened to anyone.'

2.4.6 | *Noun phrases*

Noun phrases can occur in all cases. The main function of the nominative case is to denote the subject of a sentence. Noun phrases that can serve as the subject of a sentence can be formed from a number of parts of speech: adjectival nouns (**krewny** 'relative,' **przełożony** 'superior'—a group of words that are nouns in meaning, but are declined like adjectives), numerals (**jeden** 'one,' **szóstka** 'six'), pronouns (**ja** 'I'), infinitives (*Słuchać* **go nie będzie przyjemnie.** '*Listening* to him will not be pleasant.'), verbal nouns—also called *gerunds* (*mycie* okien jest nudne 'washing windows is boring') adjectival participles (kobieta pracująca 'working woman') and set phrases (Nowy Rok 'New Year,' Wielki Tydzień 'Holy Week').

A noun phrase as the subject imposes the forms on other nominals in the clause or a sentence.

Mój przełożony kupił dom.
'My superior <MSC> bought a house.'

Moja przełożona kupiła dom.
'My superior <FEM> bought a house.'

2.4.7 | Infinitives and verbal nouns as subjects

A gerund, also called a verbal noun (in English this is the noun with the marker "-ing" e.g., "walking," "listening") is often used as the *non-personal subject* of a sentence.

Częste *picie* <NOM> skraca życie.
'Frequent *drinking* shortens [one's] life.' (coll. saying)

A gerund as the subject of a sentence is in the neuter form (ending -e). The object attached to the gerund is in the genitive case unless there is a preposition, and then the preposition imposes the case on the noun.

Częste picie alkoholu <GEN> skraca życie.
'Frequent drinking of alcohol shortens [one's] life.'

Picie bez umiaru skraca życie.
'Drinking without moderation shortens [one's] life.'

Mycie <NOM, NT SG> okien <GEN> jest nudne <ADJ, NT SG>.
'Washing [of] windows is boring.'

Te ciągłe narzekania <NOM, NT PL> muszą się skończyć.
'This constant complaining has to stop.'

Chodzenie <NOM, NT SG> po <+LOC> górach <LOC>
jest zdrowe <ADJ, NT SG>.
'Hiking in the mountains is healthy.'

An infinitive can also be used instead of the gerund as the subject of a non-personal sentence. The object attached to the infinitive is in the nominative case, unless there is a preposition, and then the preposition imposes the case on the noun.

Pić <INF, SUBJECT> **alkohol** <NOM> **nie jest zdrowo** <ADV>.
'To drink alcohol is not healthy.'

Myć <INF, SUBJECT> **okna** <NOM> **jest nudno** <ADV>.
'To wash windows is boring.'

Chodzić <INF, SUBJECT> **po** <+LOC> **górach** <+LOC> **jest zdrowo** <ADV>.
'To hike in the mountains is healthy.'

The infinitive of a verb must be modified by an adverb (**nudno** 'boringly,' **zdrowo** 'healthily'); in English, this is often translated as an adjective ("boring," "healthy"), as in the examples above.

Nouns in cases other than the nominative case can be used in the position of the subject of the sentence (2.4.10.1).

Wielu ludzi szuka pracy. '*Many people* look for a job.'
Jedzenia <GEN> **było pod dostatkiem.** 'Food was in plenty.'
(2.6.12.1)

| 2.4.8 | *Sentence structure: the subject* |

In Polish, the subject may be at the beginning of a sentence or at the end of a sentence, or somewhere in between.

Boli mnie *głowa*. 'I have a headache.' [[*my*] *head* hurts]
Dzisiaj jest *wtorek*. 'Today is *Tuesday*.'
W kawiarni mogą pracować tylko *studenci piątego roku*.
  'Only *seniors* [students of the last year] can work at the café.'
W naszej szkole uczą się sami *obcokrajowcy*.
  'Only *foreigners* study in our school.'

The most important information tends to be towards the end or at the end of the sentence, and if the subject is the most important (new and unknown) information, in Polish it is placed towards the end of the sentence.

Some set phrases with inanimate subjects often have the verb placed before the subject.

wieje *wiatr* 'the wind is blowing'
pada *deszcz* 'it is raining'
świeci *słońce* 'the sun is shining'
nadciągają *chmury* 'the clouds are approaching'
nadciąga *jesień* 'fall is approaching'

| 2.4.9 | *Constructions of absence* |

When **być** is negated and used to denote location in time or space—the whereabouts—and the emphasis is on the valid location, the subject remains in the nominative case. The verb agrees in person and number with the subject.

Profesor <NOM> **nie jest w domu, *tylko* w szpitalu.**
'The professor is not at home, *but* in hospital.'

Dzieci <NOM> **nie są na obozie, *tylko* u babci.**
'The kids are not at camp, *but* with grandma.'

Nie jestem[ja] <NOM> **w pracy, *ale* na urlopie.**
'I am not at work, but on vacation.'

Kiedy nie jestem <NOM> **w pracy, jestem w domu z dzieckiem.**
'When I am not at work, I am at home with [my] baby.'

Gdańsk nie jest na południu, *lecz* na północy Polski.
'Gdańsk is not in the south *but* in the north of Poland.'

Dzisiaj nie jest piątek, tylko poniedziałek.
'Today is not Friday, but Monday.'

Compare with constructions of absence using genitive case: 2.6.4.

| 2.4.10 | *Usage* |

The nominative case is used in a sentence or a clause:

1. To designate the grammatical *subject of the verb*—somebody or something that performs the action of the verb.

   Ojciec pomalował dom.
   '*Father* painted the house.'

   Dorośli nie rozumieją dzieci.
   '*The adults* don't understand the children.'

   Znajomy zaprosił mnie na drinka.
   '*Friend* <noun, declines like ADJ> invited me for a drink.'

   Ktoś podniósł słuchawkę.
   '*Somebody* picked up the receiver.'

The subject can be a person, thing, animal, plant, phenomenon (**burza** 'storm,' **pogoda** 'weather') or abstract concept (**życie** 'life,' **dobroć** 'good').

Życie płata nam figle. '*Life* plays tricks on us.'
Idzie zima. '*Winter* is coming.'
Wieje wiatr. '*The wind* is blowing.'

The implied subject, on the other hand, is usually expressed in genitive or dative cases.

Zimno mi. 'I am cold.'→Subject expressed in dative (2.7)
Wielu studentów jest chorych. 'Many students are sick.'
   →Subject expressed in genitive: (2.4.10.1, 2.4.11)

The subject can be one word or a group of words.

Gdzie są *dziadkowie, rodzice i dzieci*?
'Where are the *grandparents, parents, and children*?'

Iwona, księżniczka Burgunda to dramat Witolda Gombrowicza.
'*Yvonne, Princess of Burgundy* is a drama by Witold Gombrowicz.'

Kubuś Puchatek należy do moich ulubionych książek.
'*Winnie-the-Pooh* is among my favorite books.'

2. To mark the subject of a sentence or a clause with the interrogatives **jaki?** 'what kind?'; **który?** 'which?'; and **czyj?** 'whose?' The interrogatives agree in number and class (also referred to as gender, see 3.2.1) with the subject.

Jaki *on* jest? What is *he* like?
Jaka *ona* jest? 'What is *she* like?'
Jaka jutro będzie *pogoda*? 'What will *the weather* be like tomorrow?'
Który *dom* jest wasz? 'Which *house* is yours?'
Które to było *miejsce*? 'Which *place* was it?'
Czyj to plecak? 'Whose *backpack* is it?'

Note that while the subject of a sentence with the interrogative **czyj?** will be in the nominative, the answer will be in the genitive case (except for the possessive pronouns).

Czyj to plecak <NOM>?
To mój <NOM> plecak <NOM>. 'This is my backpack.'
or **Mój <NOM>.** 'Mine.'
To plecak <NOM> Adama <GEN>. 'This is Adam's backpack.'
or **Adama <GEN>.** 'Adam's.'

3. After the construction **to jest** 'this/that is' and **to są** 'these/those are' (2.4.4).

> ***To jest* Jan.** 'This is Jan.'
> ***To jest* moja rodzina.** '*This is* my family.'
> ***To są* moje dzieci.** '*These are* my children.'
> ***To był* mój dom.** '*It was* my house.'
> ***To były* dziwne czasy.** '*These were* strange times.'

4. With verbs indicating *being* or *becoming*. These have special uses of case. If the object of the verbs indicating being or becoming is an adjective, the adjective is in the nominative case.

> **Jan** <NOUN NOM> **jest ambitny** <ADJ NOM>.
> 'John is ambitious.'
> **Jan** <NOUN NOM> **stał się nerwowy** <ADJ NOM>.
> 'John became nervous.'
> **Berlin** <NOUN NOM> **jest wielokulturowy** <ADJ NOM>.
> 'Berlin is multicultural.'
> **Ten spektakl** <NOUN PHRASE NOM> **był ciekawy** <ADJ NOM>.
> 'That play was interesting.'

The subject imposes the form of the adjective(s) so that the adjective(s) agree in number and class (also referred to as gender, see 3.2.1) with the subject.

If the object of the verb indicating *being* or *becoming* is a noun or a noun phrase, the noun or the noun phrase is in the instrumental case.

> **Jan** <NOM> **jest studentem** <INS>.
> 'John is a student.'
>
> **Jan** <NOM> **jest ambitnym** <INS> **studentem** <INS>.
> 'John is an ambitious student.'
>
> **Jan** <NOM> **stał się nerwowym** <INS> **człowiekiem** <INS>.
> 'John became a nervous individual.'
>
> **Berlin** <NOM> **jest miastem** <INS>.
> 'Berlin is a city.'
>
> **Berlin** <NOM> **jest wielokulturowym** <INS> **miastem** <INS>.
> 'Berlin is a multicultural city.'
>
> **Ten spektakl** <NOUN PHRASE NOM> **był ciekawym** <ADJ INS>
>   **wydarzeniem** <NOUN INS> **kulturowym** <ADJ INS>.
> 'That play was an interesting cultural event.'

(See also 2.9.)

In spoken Polish it is possible to use the nominative when a noun or a noun phrase is the object of the verb indicating being or becoming.

Janek jest student na medal. 'Janek is a first-class student.'
Jej mąż jest Polak. 'Her husband is a Pole.'

5. For the object of the preposition **jako** 'as.'

Objects of the preposition **jako** 'as,' may also be used in cases other than the nominative case. With the preposition **jako** 'as,' both sides of the construction are in the same case.

Przed wojną *dziadek* <NOM> **pracował jako** *notariusz* <NOM>.
  'Before the war, *grandfather* worked as *a notary*.'
Znali *go* <ACC> **jako** *notariusza* <ACC>.
  'They knew *him* as *a notary*.'

When using **jako** 'as,' one subject is in the same case as the other implied subject. In the sentences below, **profesor** 'a professor' does not disclose the gender identity of the subject; **miała** informs us about the gender identity and number of the subject. Because two clauses share the same subject, the subject is she, not he, or they.

Jako *profesor* <NOM>, **miała** <NOM> **prawo do urlopu macierzyńskiego.**
  'As *a professor*, [*she*] was entitled to maternity leave.'

Dobiegnie do mety jako *pierwsza* <NOM FEM SG>.
  '[*She*] will finish [as] *first*.'

The object in comparative constructions with **jak** 'like, as' remains in the nominative regardless of other changes in the sentence.

Piotr jest głodny <NOM> **jak wilk** <NOM>.
  'Piotr is very hungry.' [lit. as hungry as a wolf]

Wyglądasz na głodnego <ACC/GEN> **jak wilk** <NOM>.
  'You look very hungry.'

6. For definitions. A dash is often used to separate two words that would be connected by the unchanging pronoun **to**.

Tatry <NOM>—**najwyższe** <NOM> **góry** <NOM> **w Polsce.**
  'Tatras: the highest mountains in Poland.'
or **Tatry** <NOM> **są to najwyższe** <NOM> **góry** <NOM> **w Polsce.**

Nauczyciel <NOM>—**osoba** <NOM>, **która pracuje w szkole.**
Nauczyciel <NOM> **jest to osoba, która pracuje w szkole.**
  Teacher <NOM> it is a person who works at school.

7. To address somebody or something (instead of the vocative case).

Cześć *Krzysiek*! 'Hi *Krzysiek!*'

Piotrek, oddaj aparat! '*Piotrek*, pass the camera!'

Kaśka, czego ty ode mnie oczekujesz?

'*Kaśka*, what do you expect from me?'

Witaj *Olka*! 'Hi *Olka!*'

Vocative forms are used more often in the written form. In spoken Polish, the vocative forms are sometimes displaced by nominative forms. There is a tendency to use diminutive forms of names without an emotional tinge, like **Krzysiek, Piotrek, Kaśka,** in the nominative case more often than in the vocative. (See also 2.10.2) Compare:

Cześć Krzysiek <NOM>! (**Krzysiek** is neutral and used in nominative case)

Cześć Krzysiu <VOC>! (**Krzyś** is friendly and put in vocative case)

Cześć Krzysztofie <VOC>! (**Krzysztof** is respectful and put in vocative case)

Piotrek <NOM>, **oddaj aparat!** (neutral)

Piotrusiu <VOC>, **oddaj aparat!** (friendly)

Piotrze <VOC>, **oddaj aparat!** (respectful)

Kaśka <NOM>, **dokąd idziesz?** (neutral)

Kasiu <VOC>, **dokąd idziesz?** (friendly)

Katarzyno <VOC>, **dokąd idziesz?** (respectful)

Cześć Magda <NOM>! (neutral)

Cześć Madziu <VOC>! (friendly)

Cześć Magdaleno <VOC>! (respectful)

8. After introductions with the verb **nazywać się** 'to be named' (literally: 'to call oneself').

Nazywam się Maria Kowalska.

'My name is Maria Kowalska.'

Ta miejscowość nazywa się Ełk.

'This city is called Ełk.'

Note: The verb **nazywać** 'to name, to call' can be used to call one thing (in the accusative case) another thing (in the instrumental case).

Nazywała go <ACC> **wujkiem** <INS>.

'She was calling him [her] uncle.'

Żona nazywała męża <ACC> **skarbem** <INS>.

'The wife was calling her husband sweetheart.'

9. With compound numbers: in compound numbers, the last two digits
   are declined and other parts remain in the nominative case.

> **W 1989 (tysiąc** <NOM> **dziewięćset** <NOM> **osiemdziesiątym** <LOC>
> **dziewiątym** <LOC>**) roku.**
> 'In the year 1989.'
>
> **W 2011 (w dwa** <NOM> **tysiące** <NOM> **jedenastym** <LOC>**) roku.**
> 'In 2011.'
>
> **Do dwa** <NOM> **tysiące** <NOM> **dziesiątego** <GEN> **roku**
> **mieszkaliśmy w Londynie.**
> 'We were living in London until 2010.'
>
> **Do dwutysięcznego** <GEN> **roku mieszkaliśmy w Londynie.**
> 'We were living in London until 2000.'
>
> **Do tysiąc** <NOM> **setnego** <GEN> **roku** <GEN>**.**
> 'Until the year 1100.'

| 2.4.10.1 | Subject expressed in the genitive case

The subject is expressed in genitive case with numerals five and up (except
for compound numerals that end in **dwa/dwie**, **trzy**, **cztery**), all collective
numerals **dwoje** 'two,' **troje** 'three,' nouns referring to male human beings
with the numerals **dwóch** 'two,' **trzech** 'three,' **czterech** 'four,' and with
quantitative adverbs (words that relate to numerals and have a nominal
nature, e.g., **dużo** 'a lot,' **wiele** and **wielu** (the latter is used with nouns
referring to male humans) 'many,' **dwukrotnie** 'twofold,' **wielokrotnie**
'manyfold'). The verb is in the third person singular form, with the past
tense of the verb taking the singular neuter form (-**ło**).

> **Dwoje dzieci** <GEN> **było w parku.**
> 'Two children were in the park.'
> **Wielu mężczyzn pracuje/pracowało w tym banku.**
> 'Many men work/worked in this bank.'
> **Wiele kobiet pracuje/pracowało w tym banku.**
> 'Many women work/worked in this bank.'
> **Dwóch chłopców** <GEN> **bawiło się w parku.**
> 'Two boys were playing in the park.'
> **Jedzenia** <GEN> **było pod dostatkiem.**
> 'Food was in plenty.'
> **Pacjentów** <GEN> **było dwuktornie więcej niż lekarzy.**
> 'There were twice as many patients as doctors.'

Sentences with nouns referring to male human beings can have alternative nominative forms, e.g.

> **Dwóch chłopców** <GEN> **bawiło się w parku.**
> 'Two boys were playing in the park.' (2.4.11.2)

or

> **Dwaj chłopcy** <NOM> **bawili** <VERB PL> **się w parku.**
> 'Two boys were playing in the park.' (2.4.11.1)

2.4.11 | Numeral governance and nominative case

2.4.11.1 | Male human forms in the subject position with numerals
dwaj 'two,' **trzej** 'three,' **czeterej** 'four'

This is the case for nouns referring to male human beings used with numerals ending in the words **dwaj, trzej,** and **czterej.** (For five and up see 2.4.11.2)

Numerals **dwaj, trzej, czterej** can only be used with nouns referring to a male human being in the subject position. When numerals **dwaj, trzej, czterej** are used in the subject position, verb and other nominals have plural forms—plural numerals **dwaj, trzej, czterej** in the nominative impose plural forms on verbal and nominal forms.

> **Dwaj** <NOM PL> **mali** <NOM PL> **chłopcy** <NOM PL> **grają** <PL>
> **w piłkę.**
> 'Two boys are playing soccer.'

> **Dwaj** <NOM PL> **mali** <NOM PL> **chłopcy** <NOM PL> **grali** <PL>
> **w piłkę.**
> 'Two boys were playing soccer.'

> **Trzej** <NOM PL> **wysocy panowie** <NOM PL> **grają** <PL> **w piłkę.**
> 'Three tall men are playing soccer.'

> **Trzej** <NOM PL> **wysocy panowie grali** <PL> **w piłkę.**
> 'Three tall men were playing soccer.'

> **Czterej** <NOM PL> **studenci** <NOM PL> **są** <PL> **chorzy** <NOM PL>.
> 'Four students (male) are sick.'

> **Czterej** <NOM PL> **studenci** <NOM PL> **byli** <PL> **chorzy** <NOM PL>.
> 'Four students (male) were sick.'

Adjectival nouns with the numerals **dwaj, trzej, czterej** in the subject position also have the plural male human form, the verb in the plural and other nominals in the plural.

Ci <NOM PL> **dwaj** <NOM PL> **twoi** <NOM PL> **znajomi** <NOM PL> **są** <PL>
bardzo mili <NOM PL>.
'These two your friends are very nice.'

Nasi <NOM PL> **dwaj** <NOM PL> **znajomi** <NOM PL> **kupili** <PL> **dom.**
'Our two friends bought a house.'

| 2.4.11.2 | *Male human forms in the subject position with numerals* **dwóch, trzech, czterech, pięciu** and up |

The numerals **dwóch, trzech, czterech, pięciu** and up in the subject position can only be used with nouns referring to male human beings. When the numerals **dwóch, trzech, czterech, pięciu** and up are used in the subject position, the verb is in the singular (in the past-tense form with the marker -ło), and other nominals take genitive plural forms—plural numerals **dwóch, trzech, czterech, pięciu** and up in the subject position impose the genitive plural on nominal forms and singular on verbs. To remember that constructions like **dwóch chłopców** 'two boys' require use of the genitive, the construction can be thought of as meaning 'two of the boys'—as 'of' in English often corresponds to using genitive in Polish. (See 8.1.1.9)

Dwóch <GEN PL> **małych** <GEN PL> **chłopców** <GEN PL> **gra** <SG>
w piłkę.
'Two [of the] small boys are playing soccer.'

Dwóch <GEN PL> **małych** <GEN PL> **chłopców** <GEN PL> **grało** <SG>
w piłkę.
'Two [of the] small boys are playing soccer.'

Trzech <GEN PL> **wysokich** <GEN PL> **panów** <GEN PL> **gra** <SG>
w piłkę.
'Three tall men are playing soccer.'

Trzech <GEN PL> **wysokich panów gra** <SG> **w piłkę.**
'Three tall men were playing soccer.'

Czterech <GEN PL> **studentów** <GEN PL> **jest** <SG> **chorych** <GEN PL>.
'Four students (male) are sick.'

Czterech <GEN PL> **studentów** <GEN PL> **było** <SG> **chorych** <GEN PL>.
'Four students (male) were sick.'

Adjectival nouns with the numerals **dwóch, trzeh, czterech, pięciu** and up in the subject position also take the genitive plural male human form and the verb in the singular.

> **Tych** <GEN PL> **dwóch** <GEN PL> **twoich** <GEN PL> **znajomych** <GEN PL>
> **jest** <SG> **bardzo miłych** <GEN PL>.
> 'These two friends of yours are very nice.'

> **Naszych** <GEN PL> **dwóch** <GEN PL> **znajomych** <GEN PL> **kupiło** <SG>
> **dom.**
> 'Our two friends bought a house.' or 'Two of our friends bought a house.'

2.4.12 Translation difficulties

When translating between Polish and English, each language can have a different subject in certain constructions, even though both languages are saying the same thing. The subject in Polish in the nominative case may be the object in the English version. The subject in the English version may be rendered as an object (often in the dative and genitive cases) in the Polish version.

> **Podoba mi** <DAT> **się Wawel** <NOM>. (**Wawel** is the subject.)
> 'I like Wawel.' (Literally: 'Wawel appeals to me.')

> **Potrzebny mu** <DAT> **spokój** <NOM>. (**Spokój** 'rest' is the subject.)
> 'He needs some rest.' (Literally: 'Rest is needed by him.')

> **Boli mnie** <ACC> **głowa** <NOM>. (**Głowa** 'head' is the subject.)
> 'I have a headache.' (Literally: '[My] head hurts me.')

> **Bolą mnie** <ACC> **plecy** <NOM>. (The word **plecy** is the subject.)
> 'I have a backache.' (Literally: '[My] back hurts me.')

> **Smakuje ci** <DAT> **obiad** <NOM>? (**Obiad** is the subject.)
> 'Do you like dinner?' (Literally: 'The dinner is tasty to you?')

> **Jest mi** <DAT> **smutno.** (The subject is an implied 'it.')
> 'I'm sad.' (Literally: '[It] is sad to me.')

2.5 Accusative

Miej serce <ACC> i patrzaj w serce <ACC>.
'Have a heart and look into [your] heart.'

Adam Mickiewicz

2.5.1 | Of an object

In the quote above **serce** 'heart' is used in the accusative case—the case for the direct object. In the first clause **serce** 'heart' is the object of the verb **mieć** 'to have.' In the second clause **serce** is the object of the preposition **w** 'into' and the verb of directed action **patrzeć** 'to look.'

The phrases **Miej . . . patrzaj w . . .** are incomplete. Therefore, they require an object to be completed.

Have (what?) a heart   Look into (what?) a heart

In both clauses **serce** is used in the accusative case.

The Polish name for the accusative case is **biernik**, which comes from the word **bierny** 'passive.' The accusative is the direct object and can generally be thought of as passively undergoing the action of the verb.

Note the sentence: **Pies gryzie kość.** 'A dog is biting a bone.' **Kość** 'bone' is in the accusative case. **Pies** 'a dog' is the active subject that **gryzie** 'is biting' **kość** 'a bone,' the passive object.

In the sentences below, the nouns or noun phrases such as **obraz, książkę, Piotra, małego kota** undergo the direct action of the verb. They are in the accusative case.

Ewa maluje *obraz*. 'Ewa is painting *a picture*.'
Piotr czyta *książkę*. 'Piotr is reading *a book*.'
Ewa lubi *Piotra*. 'Ewa likes *Piotr*.'
Dzieci głaszczą *małego kota*. 'The children pet *a small cat*.'

2.5.2 | As direct object

Noun phrases in Polish that are in the accusative case generally correspond to the *direct object* in English.

Anna zbudowała dom <ACC>. 'Anna built a house <ACC>.'
Ktoś zepsuł telewizor <ACC>. 'Someone broke a TV <ACC>.'
Kto wbił gwóźdź <ACC> **w ścianę** <ACC>? 'Who hammered a nail <ACC> into the wall <ACC>?'
Anna pisze list <ACC>. 'Anna is writing a letter <ACC>.'
Grzegorz uwielbia szarlotkę <ACC>. 'Grzegorz loves apple pie <ACC>.'
Rodzice kupili nam dom <ACC>. '[Our] parents bought us a house <ACC>.'

The accusative can be an object of certain prepositions and verbs. (See also 2.5.7, 2.5.8, 2.5.12.)

2.5.3 *Generic questions*

In the accusative case, the following question words are used.

Kogo? Co? 'Who? What?'

In formal English, **kogo?** overlaps with 'whom?' **Kogo rysujesz?** 'Whom are you drawing?'

Kogo 'who' refers to people; **co** 'what' refers to things. The answer to the accusative case questions **kogo/co** must also be in the accusative case.

Co <ACC> **chcesz na kolację?** 'What do you want for dinner?'

(**Kogo** <ACC> **chcesz na kolację?** would necessarily mean cannibalism; it does not mean 'Who do you want to come for dinner?')

Co <ACC> **rysujesz?** 'What are you drawing?'
Kota <ACC> **i dom** <ACC>. 'A cat and a house.'

Kogo <ACC> **rysujesz?** 'Who are you drawing?'
Dziadka <ACC>. 'Grandfather.'

2.5.4 *Without a preposition (transitive verbs)*

When there is no preposition in the accusative, a transitive verb (a verb that can be made passive) is used and the direct object rendered by the accusative case has the ability to become the subject of a corresponding construction using the passive voice. The accusative is the case in statements and questions but *not* in negatives. In negatives the genitive is used instead of the accusative (2.5.5).

Kobiety czytają tę <ACC> **gazetę** <ACC>.
'Women read *this paper*.' (active voice)
(**tę gazetę** 'this paper' is the direct object and is in the accusative case)

Ta gazeta **jest czytana przez kobiety.** (passive voice)
'*This paper* is read by women.'
(**ta gazeta** 'this paper' is the subject and is in the nominative case)

The direct object in English is often rendered in Polish by using the accusative case, but it can also be rendered in Polish by using the genitive and instrumental cases.

2.5.5 Accusative versus genitive as object of negation

The genitive is used when the *accusative direct object of transitive verbs is negated*.

Kobiety *nie* czytają *tej* <GEN> gazety <GEN>.
'Women do not read *this paper.*' (active voice)

Anna nie pisze *listu* <GEN>.
'Anna is not writing *a letter* <GEN>.'

Accusative vs. Genitive as object

1. The genitive can be used instead of the accusative case in the meaning of *some*—also called partitive genitive.

   Chcesz herbaty <GEN>? 'Do you want *some* tea?'
   Nalej mi piwa <GEN>. 'Pour me *some* beer.'
   Mogę pożyczyć cukru <GEN>? 'Can I borrow *some* sugar?'
   Dodaj wody <GEN> do sosu. 'Add *some* water to the gravy.'

   The sentences can be modified so that the verbs are followed by the accusative case.

   Chcesz filiżankę <ACC> herbaty <GEN>? 'Do you want a cup of tea?'
   Nalej mi kufel <ACC> piwa <GEN>. 'Pour me a mug of beer.'

2. In the accusative case, the direct object of the verb is obtained or impacted *wholly and completely* (eternally), as opposed to the genitive case where the object is obtained partially or incompletely (temporarily).

   Sąsiad dostał zawału <GEN>. 'A neighbor had a heart attack.'
   Sąsiad dostał spadek <ACC>. 'A neighbor came into an inheritance.'
   Studiuję polonistykę <ACC>. 'I study Polish.' (as my major)
   Uczę się polskiego <GEN>. 'I learn/study Polish' (as an elective)

   The examples below will also illustrate that the direct object is rendered in Polish by using the genitive case because the object is being obtained temporarily (for a limited time) and not eternally.

   Syn znowu dostał wysypki <GEN>.
   '[My] son again has had an allergic reaction.'

   Mogę pożyczyć roweru <GEN>?
   'Can I borrow [your] bike?'

3. The genitive case is used instead of the accusative case for the objects of certain verbs, but there is no easily identifiable pattern for this.

Słucham muzyki <GEN>.
'I am listening to the music.'

Oczekuję dziecka <GEN>.
'I am expecting a child.'

Szukam mieszkania <GEN>.
'I am looking for an apartment.'

2.5.6 **Accusative versus instrumental as object**

The instrumental case is used instead of the accusative case for the objects of certain verbs, also with no easily identifiable pattern.

Zarządzam przerwę <ACC>.
'I call a break.'

Piotr sprawnie zarządza przedsiębiorstwem <INS>.
'Piotr efficiently manages the company.'

Kadaffi od ponad 40 lat rządził Libią <INS>.
'Gaddafi governed Libya for over 40 years.'

Policjant kieruje ruchem ulicznym <INS>.
'A policeman directs traffic.'

Some verbs can govern the accusative or instrumental.

Ktoś ruszał moje rzeczy <ACC>.
'Somebody moved my stuff.'

Pacjent bez przerwy rusza głową <INS>.
'The patient can't stop moving [his/her] head.'

Anna rzuciła pracę <ACC>.
'Anna left [her] job.'

Anna rzuciła książką <INS> **o podłogę** <ACC>.
'Anna threw a book on the floor.'

| 2.5.7 | *As object of directed motion* |

The accusative is used as the object of directed motion and directed action after the prepositions **w, na, przez, za, pod, między, pomiędzy, nad, przed, poza, po**. The accusative is the case in statements, questions, and in negatives.

w	indicates that the motion is directed *in, inside*
na	indicates that the motion is directed *on, onto*
przez	indicates that the motion is directed *across, through* from one side of the object to the other
za	indicates that the motion is directed *behind*
pod	indicates that the motion is directed either under the object or not far from the object
między	indicates that the motion is directed between objects
pomiędzy	indicates that motion is directed *in amongst* objects
nad	indicates that motion is directed *above or over* something
przed	indicates that the motion is directed *in front* of something
poza	indicates motion *beyond* something
po	indicates that the motion is directed in order to fetch or get something or someone

Biegnij za <ACC> **bramę** <ACC>. 'Run behind <ACC> the gate <ACC>.'
Jadę w <ACC> **góry** <ACC>. 'I am going to the mountains.'
Przeprowadźmy się pod Warszawę. 'Let's move not far from Warsaw.'
Wskocz na <ACC> **stół** <ACC>. 'Jump on <ACC> the table <ACC>.'
Nie lubię chodzić pod <ACC> **górę** <ACC>. 'I don't like walking uphill.'
Wepchnij to za <ACC> **szafę** <ACC>. 'Stuff it behind the dresser.'
Biec na <ACC> **łeb** <ACC>**, na szyję** <ACC>. 'To run fast [carelessly].' (idiom)
Kot uciekł pod łóżko <ACC>. 'The cat ran under the bed.'
Biegnę na <ACC> **pocztę** <ACC>. 'I'm running to the post office.'
Przejdźmy przez ulicę <ACC>. 'Let's cross the street.'
Chodźmy przez park <ACC>. 'Let's walk through the park.'
Leć po pielęgniarkę <ACC>. 'Rush to get a nurse.'

Note: The locative is used as object of location after the prepositions **w**, **na**, and **po** (when describing the whereabouts of someone or something).

Jestem w <LOC> **górach** <LOC>. 'I am in the mountains.' (location)
Masz coś na <LOC> **szyi** <LOC>. 'You have something on [your] neck.'
Jestem na <LOC> **poczcie** <LOC>. 'I'm at the post office.'

The instrumental is used as object of location after the prepositions między, pomiędzy, nad, pod, poza, przed, za.

> **Mieszkamy pod Warszawą.** 'We live not far from Warsaw.'
> **Kot leżał pod** <INS> **łóżkiem** <INS>. 'The cat was lying under the bed.'
> **Lampa wisi nad** <INS> **biurkiem** <INS>. 'A lamp is hanging above the desk.'

Both accusative and instrumental can be objects of the preposition **nad** 'above'.

> **Powieś to nad łóżkiem/nad łóżko.** 'Hang it above the bed.'

2.5.8 | *Sports and games*

The accusative is the object of directed motion and directed movement. As such it is also the object of the preposition **w** in constructions denoting playing sports and games.

> **Lubię grać w piłkę** <ACC>. 'I like to play soccer.'
> **Często gram w gry** <ACC> **komputerowe** <ACC>. 'I often play computer games.'
> **Dziewczynki bawią się w matkę** <ACC> **i dziecko** <ACC>. 'Girls play mom and child.'
> **Dzieci bawią się w dom** <ACC>. 'Children play house.'

Note: Many games and sports have genitive case endings rather than the accusative case.

> **grać w pokera** <ACC> 'to play poker'
> **grać w tenisa** <ACC> 'to play tennis'
> **grać w golfa** <ACC> 'to play golf'
> **grać w chowanego** <ACC> 'to play hide-and-seek'

This paradigm is characteristic of masculine animate nouns and noun phrases, as in **mam psa** <ACC> 'I have a dog,' **znam dobrego** <ACC> **fryzjera** <ACC> 'I know a good hairdresser.'

2.5.9 | *In passive construction*

When an active construction is changed into the passive, the direct object rendered by the accusative case becomes the subject of a corresponding construction using the passive voice. The preposition **przez** '[done] by' is used when the agent of the action is mentioned. Only transitive verbs can be made passive (verbs with **się**—called *reflexive verbs*—are not transitive).

Kobiety <NOM> **czytają tę** <ACC> **gazetę** <ACC>.
'Women read this paper.' (active voice)
(**tę gazetę** 'this paper' is the direct object and is in the accusative case)

Ta gazeta <NOM> **jest czytana przez kobiety.** (passive voice)
'This paper is read by <ACC> women.'
(**ta gazeta** 'this paper' is the subject and is in the nominative case)

Maria <NOM> **Skłodowska** <NOM>**-Curie** <NOM> **odkryła Polon** <ACC>.
'Marie Skłodowska-Curie discovered Polonium.'

Polon <NOM> **został odkryty przez Marię** <ACC>
  Skłodowską <ACC> **-Curie** <ACC>.
'Polonium was discovered by Marie Skłodowska-Curie.'

(See passive voice at 6.12)

2.5.10   O *and* na *with verbs of aimed movement*

The accusative is the case in statements, questions, and in negatives.

Czekam *na Annę* <ACC>. 'I am waiting for *Anna.*'
(**na Annę** 'for Anna' is the direct object and is in the accusative case)
Nie czekam na Annę <ACC>. 'I am not waiting for Anna.'

Martwię się *o Annę* <ACC>. 'I worry about *Anna.*'
(**o Annę** 'about Anna' is the direct object and is in the accusative case)
Nie martwię się *o Annę* <ACC>. 'I do not worry about *Anna.*'

błagać o przebaczenie <ACC> 'to beg for forgiveness'
czekać *na* **matkę** <ACC> 'to wait for mother'
patrzeć na tablicę <ACC> 'to look at the blackboard'
wpływać na decyzję <ACC> 'to influence the decision'
spojrzeć na matkę <ACC> 'to have a look at mother'
Dbam o chorą siostrę <ACC>. 'I take care of a sick sister.'
Martwię się o brata <ACC>. 'I worry about [my] brother.'
Poprosiłam go <ACC> **o przerwę** <ACC>. 'I asked him for a recess.'
Proszę o pomoc <ACC>. 'I'm asking for help.'
Troszczę się o rodziców <ACC>. 'I take care of [my] parents.'
zaprosić na kawę <ACC> 'to invite for coffee'

The accusative is the object of verbs that indicate *requesting*: **prosić** 'to ask'; **błagać** 'to beg'; **zapraszać** 'to invite.' **Prosić** and **błagać** are used to ask someone for something by putting the someone in the accusative and using the preposition **o** 'for' + something, also in the accusative.

Poproszę matkę <ACC> **o pomoc** <ACC>. 'I will ask mother for help.'
Proszę cię <ACC>. 'I beg you.'

Prosić can be used with or without the preposition **o** 'for' with concrete noun phrases, while **prosić** is generally used with the preposition **o** 'for' with abstract noun phrases.

Proszę kawę <ACC>. 'Coffee please.'
  (**kawa** is concrete, so **o** is optional)
Proszę o ciszę <ACC>. 'Silence please.'
  (**cisza** is abstract, so **o** is used)

Also, in the constructions with a clearly stated person we request from, the preposition **o** must be used to link the requested object with the person/object we request from.

Czasami proszę siostrę <ACC> **o pieniądze** <ACC>.
'I ask my sister for money from time to time.'

| 2.5.11 | *Przez with verbs of overt agent*

Przez with the accusative is used to indicate the agent *'because of'* whom something happened.

Przez ciebie spóźniłam się do pracy <ACC>.
'I was late for work because of you.'

Nie lubią nas przez polityków.
'They do not like us because of the politicians.'

Przez <+ACC> in the meaning 'because of' suggests a negative circumstance. In contrast, **dzięki** <+DAT> means 'thanks to' and has a positive connotation.

Dzięki mikrofalówce możesz odgrzać obiad w pięć minut.
'Thanks to the microwave you can reheat lunch in five minutes.'

Dzięki kredytowi kupiliśmy dom.
'Thanks to the credit we bought the house.'

Dzięki tobie dostałam tę pracę.
'Thanks to you I got the job.'

The accusative is the object of many time expressions (See 2.5.14.).

The accusative is used following the particle **co** 'every' when indicating frequency.

co chwilę <ACC> **patrzysz na zegarek** 'you are looking at the clock every now and then'

co godzinę <ACC> 'every hour'

co tydzień <ACC> 'every week'

co rok <ACC> 'every year' (**co roku** is also used)

2.5.12 Governed accusative

Verbs that require their objects to be in the accusative case are numerous. To compile an exhaustive list of all the verbs that require the accusative case is beyond the capacity of this book. *Praktyczny słownik łączliwości składniowej czasowników polskich*. (A practical dictionary of Polish verbal collocations) by Stanisław Mędak offers an exhaustive list of verbs that can take certain cases.[1]

Conceptually, verbs that require the accusative case can be thought of as usually embracing, seizing, comprehending, or otherwise impacting the direct object *wholly and completely*. (See 2.5.5)

The examples below only apply to statements and questions, not to negatives. (In negatives they would require the genitive case.)

The accusative is used:

1. With verbs indicating a sense of *possession*, including the following verbs and other similar verbs: **mieć** 'to have'; **posiadać** 'to own'; **obejmować** 'to include, to take'; **zawierać** 'to contain'; and **osiągać** 'to achieve.'

   Mam siostrę <ACC> **i brata** <ACC>.
   'I have a sister and a brother.'

   Produkt posiada atest <ACC> **Ministerstwa Zdrowia.**
   'The product has the seal of approval of the Ministry of Health.'

   Teren obejmuje las <ACC> **i rzekę** <ACC>.
   'The area includes the forest and the river.'

   Obejmij mnie <ACC>. 'Embrace me.'

   Kawa zawiera kofeinę <ACC>. 'Coffee contains caffeine.'

   Osiągnąć cel <ACC>. 'To achieve the goal.'

2. With verbs indicating a sense of *consuming*: jeść 'to eat'; pić 'to drink'; **konsumować** 'to consume'; **spożywać** 'to consume'; **pochłaniać** 'to devour.'

> **Jem kanapkę** <ACC>.
> 'I'm eating a sandwich.'
>
> **jeść pączka** <ACC>.
> 'to eat a donut' (See 3.3.5.4)

3. With verbs indicating *sensing*: widzieć 'to see'; oglądać 'to watch'; obserwować 'to observe'; dotykać 'to touch (figuratively)'; czuć 'to feel'; stwierdzać 'to certify.'

> **Czuję ból** <ACC> **i zmęczenie** <ACC>.
> 'I feel pain and fatigue.'
>
> **Czuliśmy nadchodzącą** <ACC> **wiosnę** <ACC>.
> 'We felt the approaching spring.'
>
> **Notariusz stwierdził autentyczność** <ACC> **podpisu.**
> 'The notary certified the authenticity of the signature.'

Czuć in the meaning of 'to feel' takes the accusative case, but in the meaning of 'to smell' **czuć** takes the instrumental case: **czuć farbą** <INS>, **czosnkiem** <INS>, **kapustą** <INS> 'to smell like paint, garlic, cabbage.'

Dotykać means 'to touch.' When **dotykać** is used in a figurative sense, 'to touch, to affect,' it is used with the accusative case.

> **Kryzys dotknął także naszą** <ACC> **rodzinę** <ACC>.
> 'The crisis touched/affected our family too.'

When **dotykać** is used to mean 'to touch' in a literal/physical sense, it takes the genitive.

> **dotknąć ust** <GEN>, **sufitu** <GEN>, **lampy** <GEN>
> 'to touch her lips, the ceiling, a lamp'

4. With verbs indicating *causality*: **powodować** 'to cause'; **robić** 'to do'

> **Brak witamin powoduje anemię** <ACC>.
> 'Lack of vitamins causes anemia.'
>
> **robić awanturę** <ACC>
> 'to make a scene'

5. With verbs indicating *stating something*: **mówić** 'to say'; **opowiadać** 'to tell'; **opisywać** 'to describe'; **oznajmać** 'to announce.' Note that the addressee of the action of these verbs is in dative case.

> **Mówię prawdę** <ACC>.
> 'I am telling the truth.'

> **Opowiedz mi** <DAT> **bajkę** <ACC>.
> 'Tell me a fairy tale.'

> **opisać wypadek** <ACC>
> 'to describe an accident'

> **przekazać informację** <ACC>
> 'to transmit information'

6. With verbs connected with *being a student*: **studiować** 'to study'; **czytać** 'to read'; **analizować** 'to analyze'; **powtarzać** 'to repeat, review'; **pisać** 'to write' (**co** 'something,' **do kogo** 'to somebody') *czym* '*with something*'; **prowadzić** 'to conduct'; **rozumieć** 'to understand.'

> **studiować historię** <ACC> 'to study history (as a major)'
> **powtarzać gramatykę** <ACC> 'to review grammar'
> **czytać książkę** <ACC> 'to read a book'
> **odrabiać pracę** <ACC> **domową** <ACC> 'to do homework'
> **prowadzić badania** <ACC>, **doświadczenie** <ACC> 'to conduct research, an experiment'
> **zrozumieć tekst** <ACC> 'to understand the text'

Note: **Studiować** 'to study' has the sense of studying and learning something in depth or completely; with the sense of completeness, the object is in the accusative case. **Uczyć** 'to teach' and **uczyć się** 'to study, learn' (literally 'to teach oneself') have less of a degree of completeness. **Uczyć** is therefore used with the genitive case. **Uczyć się**, as a reflexive verb, is not used with the accusative, but uses the genitive like **uczyć**. The object of the verb **uczyć** that undergoes the process is in the accusative case.

> **Studiuję polski** <ACC>.
> 'I study Polish (as a major).'

> **Uczę dziecko** <ACC> **angielskiego** <GEN>.
> 'I'm teaching the child English.'

> **Uczę się arabskiego** <GEN>.
> 'I am learning Arabic.'

7. With verbs connected to *performing errands*: **sprzątać** 'to clean, tidy up'; **gotować** 'to cook'; **przygotowywać** 'to prepare'; **prasować** 'to iron'; **załatwiać** 'to take care of, fix.'

> **posprzątać pokój** <ACC> 'to clean the room'
> **ugotować obiad** <ACC> 'to prepare dinner'
> **przygotować raport** <ACC> 'to prepare a file'
> **wyprasować koszulę** <ACC> 'to iron a shirt'
> **załatwić formalności** <ACC> 'to take care of formalities'

8. With verbs indicating *loss*: **gubić** 'to lose, misplace,' **tracić** 'to lose (irretrievably)'; **przegrywać** 'to lose (in a contest).'

> **zgubić paszport** <ACC>, **klucze** <ACC>
>   'to lose a passport, keys'
> **stracić kontrakt** <ACC>, **kontakt** <ACC>, **kontrolę** <ACC>
>   'to lose a contract, contact, control'
> **przegrać samochód** <ACC> **w pokera**
>   'to lose a car in poker'
> **przegrać mecz** <ACC> 'to lose a game'

Increasingly, there is a tendency in everyday Polish to apply the genitive ending -a in the accusative to masculine inanimate objects of foreign origin, e.g., **podłączyć laptopa** <ACC> 'to connect the laptop' and **podłączyć prąd** <ACC> 'to connect the electricity.'

> **grać w Xboxa** <ACC> 'to play Xbox'
> **podłączyć laptopa** <ACC> 'to connect the laptop'
> **kupić iPhone'a** <ACC> 'to buy an iPhone'
> **wysłać SMS-a** <ACC> or **SMS** <ACC> 'to send an SMS'
> **wysłać e-maila** <ACC> or **e-mail** <ACC> 'to send an email'

(See 3.3.5.4)

2.5.13 | *Other meanings without prepositions*

1. The accusative without a preposition can be used to indicate a certain period of time.

> **Byłem tam *tydzień*** <ACC>.
> 'I was there for *one week*.'
>
> ***Całą*** <ACC> ***wiosnę*** <ACC> **przygotowywał się do podróży.**
> 'He was preparing for the trip *the entire spring*.'
>
> ***Całą*** <ACC> ***noc*** <ACC> **pisałam wypracowanie.**
> 'I was writing [my] paper *all night*.'

The adjective **cały** 'whole, entire' agrees with the noun in class (also referred to as gender, see 3.2.1) and number.

Chwileczkę <ACC> **proszę.** 'Just a minute.'

Godzinę <ACC> **czekałam na lekarza.**
'I was waiting for a doctor *for an hour.*'

2. The accusative is often used to express the cost or weight of something.

Czy krowa może ważyć tonę <ACC>**?**
'Can a cow weigh a ton (about 2000 pounds)?'

Co dzisiaj kosztuję złotówkę <ACC>**?**
'What costs one złoty today?'

Ważysz chyba tonę <ACC>**.**
'You must weigh a ton.'

3. The accusative is also used to express distance traveled.

Przebiegłam *milę* <ACC>**.** 'I ran *for a mile.*'

| 2.5.14 | *Time* |

The accusative is also used to indicate time, recurring events with the preposition **co** 'every,' duration (from beginning to end) with prepositions **na** 'for' and **przez** 'through,' and **w** 'on' with days of the week.

w środę 'on Wednesday' (See Table 9.5)

Wróce *za godzinę* <ACC>**.**
'I'll be back *in an hour.*'

W sobotę <ACC> **idziemy do kina.**
'*On Saturday* we are going to the movies.'

Jadę *na tydzień* <ACC>**.**
I am going *for a week.*

Przez chwilę <ACC> **nie mogłam oddychać.**
'I could not breathe *for a moment.*'

Babcia oszczędzała *przez całe* <ACC> *życie* <ACC>**.**
'Grandmother was saving *for [her] whole life.*'

2.5.15 Ponad

The accusative is used as the object of the preposition **ponad** 'more than, over.'

> **Rozmawiasz *ponad godzinę*** <ACC>. 'You have been talking *for over an hour.*'
>
> **Żyjecie *ponad stan*** <ACC>. 'You live beyond *your means.*'

2.5.16 *Accusative and nominative with identical case markings*

Inanimate masculine nouns and noun phrases in the accusative case have the same case markings as in the nominative case in both the singular and plural.

> **Gdzie jest nasz** <NOM> **samochód** <NOM>? 'Where is our car?'
> **Czy widzisz nasz** <ACC> **samochód** <ACC>? 'Do you see our car?'
>
> **Gdzie są kwiaty** <NOM>? 'Where are the flowers?'
> **Kupiłeś kwiaty** <ACC>? 'Did you buy the flowers?'

No male human plural nouns and noun phrases have the same case endings in the accusative plural as they have in the nominative plural.

Male human plural class covers male humans or any group with at least one male human. No male human plural class covers all other plural subjects (e.g., women, **dzieci** <N PL> 'children,' animals, things).

> **Gdzie są kobiety** <NOM> **i dzieci** <NOM>? 'Where are the women and children?'
> **Czy widzisz kobiety** <ACC> **i dzieci** <ACC>? 'Do you see women and children?'
> **Gdzie są psy** <NOM>? 'Where are the dogs?'
> **Czy widzisz psy** <ACC>? 'Do you see the dogs?'

Feminine nouns that end in a consonant in the singular have identical case markings in the singular and plural for both the accusative and nominative cases.

> **Gdzie jest maść** <NOM>? 'Where is the ointment?'
> **Kupiłam maść** <ACC>. 'I bought the ointment.'
> **Gdzie jest straż** <NOM> **miejska** <NOM>? 'Where is the city police?'
> **Czy widziałeś straż** <ACC> **miejską** <ACC>? 'Have you seen the city police?'

For accusative with food, drink, vehicles, currencies, dances, tobacco and technology, see 3.3.5.4.

2.6 Genitive

Bez pracy <GEN> **nie ma kołaczy** <GEN>.
'Without work there is no pay.' (saying)

The genitive case can perform a number of functions. It can be attached to verbs and noun phrases with prepositions and without prepositions. The Polish name for the genitive case is **dopełniacz**. The verb **dopełnić** 'to fill up, complete' suggests to replenish, to complete, and to complement where there is a lack of something. The genitive case is often used to indicate this lack of something, as illustrated in the saying above, and in the examples below.

brak wody <GEN> 'water shortage'
Brakuje Anny <GEN>. 'Anna is missing.'
Jestem bez <+GEN> **pracy** <GEN>. 'I am without a job.'
Dokroję chleba <GEN>. 'I'll cut some more bread.'
dołóż drewna <GEN> **do kominka** 'put some more wood to [in] the fire place'

The word **dopełniacz** 'genitive' is composed of a combination of the preposition **do** 'to, up to, until' and the adjective **pełny** 'full.' This underscores that the preposition **do** 'to, up to, until' is *always used* with the genitive case (e.g., **dolej wody** <GEN> **do sosu** <GEN> 'pour some more water into the sauce' <IMPER>). Additionally, the adjective **pełny** 'full' is also used with the genitive case (e.g., **pełny** <NOM> **wody** <GEN> 'full of water').

The genitive case can perform a number of functions. (For the subject expressed in genitive, see 2.4.10.1, 2.4.11.1, 2.4.11.2.)

2.6.1 Generic questions

The genitive answers the questions **kogo?** 'who?'; **czego?** 'what?'; **czyj?** 'whose?'

Kogo 'who' refers to people; czego 'what' refers to everything else.

Kogo <GEN> **szukasz?** *'Who are you looking for?'*
Dziadka <GEN>. *'Grandpa.'*

Czego <GEN> **szukasz?** *'What are you looking for?'*
Okularów <GEN>. *'[My] glasses.'*

Czyj to dom? 'Whose house is it?'
Adama <GEN>. 'Adam's.'

The genitive (also possessive) is a distinctive case form typically marking a relative, close, or exclusive relationship and to express ownership. This is the most frequent use of the genitive.[2] Whereas in English "of" or "'s" would be used, in Polish such a relationship is expressed in the genitive case. Please note that the word with an apostrophe in English will be in the genitive case and placed after the subject in Polish. Otherwise the emphasis is shifted to the possessor, instead of the possessed object.

prawo <NOM> **jazdy** <GEN> 'driver's license'
data <NOM> **urodzenia** <GEN> 'date of birth'
poezja <NOM> **Szymborskiej** <GEN> 'Szymborska's poetry'
źródło <NOM> **wody** <GEN> 'a source of water'
adres rodziny <GEN> **Simpsonów** <GEN> 'the Simpsons' home address'
    (Literally: 'address of the family of Simpsons')
Pałac Kultury i Nauki 'Palace of Culture and Science'
numer telefonu <GEN> 'phone number' [number of the phone]
lęk wysokości 'fear of heights'
koniec lekcji 'end of the lecture'
początek pięknej jesieni 'beginning of a beautiful fall'
dom <NOM> **matki** <GEN> 'mother's house'
matki <GEN> **dom** <NOM>**, a nie ojca** 'house of [my] mother, and not of [my] father'

With a gerund (with a marker "-ing") the phrase can be ambiguous. Compare these phrases. Also, after the gerund the noun is in the genitive.

przesłuchanie sędziego
'judge's hearing' or 'interrogation of the judge'
    (judge is interrogated or judge is interrogating)

jedzenie psa
'dog food' or 'eating a dog'

małpowanie/przedrzeźnianie syna doprowadza mnie do szału
'[my] son's mimicking/mocking drives me crazy' (it drives me crazy when my son is mocking)
'mimicking my son/mocking my son drives me crazy' (it drives me crazy when [someone] is mimicking/mocking my son)

Constructions with the possessive genitive can be long and complex. It is easier to locate the subject first to establish the relationship between the subject and its objects.

miejsce <NOM> **urodzenia** <GEN> **narzeczonego** <GEN> **mojej** <GEN> **przyrodniej** <GEN> **siostry** <GEN>
'my stepsister's fiancé's place of birth'

Ministerstwo <NOM> **Spraw** <GEN> **Zagranicznych** <GEN> **Rzeczypospolitej** <GEN> **Polskiej** <GEN>
'Ministry of Foreign Affairs of the Republic of Poland'

| 2.6.3 | *Negation of a direct object in accusative* |

When a sentence with a direct object in the accusative case is negated, the direct object is changed to the genitive case. The genitive plays the role of depicting absence or unfulfillment of the action (2.5.5).

Czytam książkę <ACC>. 'I am reading a book.'
Nie czytam **książki** <GEN>. 'I am not reading a book.'
Ewa *nie kocha* **Piotra** <GEN>. 'Ewa does not love *Piotr*.'
Nie znam **tego mężczyzny** <GEN>. 'I don't know *this man*.'
Nie wolno **jej** <GEN> **ograniczać**. 'You must not limit *her*.'
Nie chcę **czytać tego artykułu** <GEN>. 'I don't want to read *the article*.'

Be careful when negating a sentence with a direct object and an intensifier, e.g., **bardzo** 'very,' or with adverbs of frequency, e.g., **często** 'often,' **zawsze** 'always.' Negation **nie** placed in front of **bardzo** or adverbs of frequency will result in a change of intensity; **nie** placed in front of the verb will result in the genitive case.

Nie bardzo lubię kawę <ACC>.
'I don't like coffee much.'

Bardzo nie lubię kawy <GEN>.
'I really don't like coffee.'

Nie często oglądam telewizję <ACC>.
Literally: 'Not often I watch television.'

Nie oglądam często telewizji <GEN>.
'I don't watch television often.'

2.6.4 | Constructions of absence

The genitive is used to denote the nonexistence, lack, or absence of something or someone. To denote absence, three constructions are used with all noun and noun phrases (SG and PL, MSC, FEM, and NT):

nie ma <+GEN> in the present tense
nie było <+GEN> in the past tense
nie będzie <+GEN> in the future tense

The noun or noun phrase to which the absence refers is in the genitive case.

The neuter form of the verb **nie było** is used in the past tense. This is because of the lack of an overt subject in the sentences. **Nie ma, nie było, nie będzie** is used regardless of the class (also referred to as gender, see 3.2.1) and number of nouns or noun phrases. In such constructions in English the subject is clear. In Polish the subject is implied (it is not in the nominative case).

Profesora <GEN SG> **nie ma w pokoju.**
'The professor is not in the room.'

Profesora <GEN SG> **nie było w pokoju.**
'The professor was not in the room.'

Profesora <GEN SG> **nie będzie jutro w pracy.**
'The professor won't be at work tomorrow.'

(See also 2.4.9.)

Rodziców <GEN PL> **nie ma/nie było/nie będzie w domu.**
  '[My] parents are not/were not/will not be at home.'
Nie ma sprawiedliwości <GEN>. 'There is no justice.'
Nie ma mnie <GEN> **jutro w biurze.** '*I am not* in the office
  tomorrow.'
Nie będzie go <GEN> **jutro w pracy.** 'He won't be at work
  tomorrow.'
Nikogo <GEN> **nie było w domu.** 'No one was at home.'
Kogo <GEN> **nie ma?** 'Who is not here?'
Kogo <GEN> **nie było?** 'Who was not in?'
Nie ma sprawy <GEN>. 'No problem.'
W hotelu jest sauna <NOM>. 'There is a sauna in the hotel.'
W hotelu nie ma sauny <GEN>. '*There is not* a sauna in the hotel.'

W hotelu nie było sauny <GEN>. 'There wasn't a sauna in the hotel.'

W hotelu nie będzie sauny <GEN>. 'There won't be a sauna in the hotel.'

Dzisiaj nie ma lekcji <GEN>. '*There are no* classes today.'

Wczoraj nie było lekcji <GEN>. 'There weren't any classes yesterday.'

Jutro też nie będzie lekcji <GEN>. 'Tomorrow there won't be any classes either.'

Nie ma prądu <GEN MSC SG>, **wody** <GEN FEM SG> **i ogrzewania** <GEN NT SG>. 'There is no electricity, water, and heating.'

Nie ma dodatkowych kosztów <GEN PL>. 'There are no additional costs.'

| 2.6.5 | *Partitive genitive "some"*

With a direct object, a distinction can be made by putting the object in the accusative to denote the whole object or a specific object or putting the object in the genitive (the partitive genitive **dopełniacz cząstkowy**) to denote part of the object. This is often used with food or drink, but can be used with other objects that can be treated as the whole object or a specific object or to denote part of the object. The use of the partitive genitive is optional; the accusative form can be used with either meaning, with the meaning understood from the context (e.g., you can say **daj mi wino** <ACC> with the meaning of either 'give me some wine' or 'give me the wine'). The partitive genitive form, however, is not used with the accusative meaning (e.g., **daj mi wina** <GEN> is not said with the meaning of 'give me the wine' but only 'give me some wine').

Chcesz kawy <GEN>?
'Do you want some coffee?'

Podaj mi wino <ACC>.
'Give me the wine.' (e.g., a specific bottle of wine)

Nalej mi wina <GEN>.
'Pour me some wine.' (some of any wine)

Poproszę sera <GEN>.
'Some cheese please.'

Poproszę ser <ACC> **tylżycki** <ACC>.
'Tylżycki cheese please.' (a specific kind of cheese)

Verbs that can impact the whole object or a specific object or only part of the object can be used to denote a partitive meaning:

> **dostarczyć** 'to provide (some)' <+GEN> **dostarczyć wody** <GEN>
> 'to provide some water'
> **dostarczyć walizkę** <ACC> 'to deliver a suitcase'
> **podać sól** <ACC>/**soli** <GEN> 'to pass the salt/some salt'
> **podać długopis** <ACC> 'to pass a pen'
> **nabyć doświadczenia** <GEN> 'to gain some experience'
> **nabyć mieszkanie** <ACC> 'to purchase an apartment'

but only **dobudować garaż** <ACC> 'to build on a garage' [add on a garage]. Garage is a specific object.

Such verbs often have the prefix **do-**, **po-**, **na-**.

| 2.6.6 | *Governed genitive* |

Praktyczny słownik łączliwości składniowej czasowników polskich. (*A Practical Dictionary of Polish Verbal Collocations*) by Stanisław Mędak offers an exhaustive list of verbs that can take certain cases.[3]

The verbs that the genitive case is used with include:

> **bać się** 'to be afraid of'
> **doczekać się** 'to wait until'
> **domagać się** 'to demand'
> **dopełnić formalności** 'to go through the formalities'
> **dotrzymać słowa** 'to keep [your] word'
> **nadużywać** 'to abuse'
> **oczekiwać gości** 'to expect guests'
> **potrzebować** 'to need (to have need of)'
> **pozbawić prawa głosu** 'to deprive of the right to vote'
> **pozbywać się** 'to get rid of'
> **pożądać** 'to crave' (genitive shows a lack of the thing you crave)
> **pragnąć** 'to desire' (genitive shows a lack of the thing you desire)
> **przestrzegać** 'to obey'
> **słuchać** 'to listen to'
> **strzec się złodziei** 'beware of thieves'
> **szukać** 'to look for'
> **unikać słońca** 'to avoid the sun'
> **używać** 'to use (to make use of)'
> **życzyć** 'to wish (for)'

Adam nadużywa alkoholu. 'Adam abuses alcohol.'

Boję się ciemności i pająków.

'I am afraid of the dark and spiders.'

doczekał się odpowiedzi 'he waited until he got a response'

domagać się zwrotu pożyczki

'to demand repayment of a loan'

gratuluję mu <DAT> **nagrody** <GEN>

'to congratulate him on [his] award'

Potrzebuję odpoczynku. 'I need a break.'

Słucham opery. 'I am listening to the opera.'

Szukam mieszkania/pracy.

'I am looking for an apartment/a job.'

Używam komputera i telefonu.

'I'm using the computer and the phone.'

Życzę ci <DAT> **szybkiego** <GEN> **powrotu** <GEN> **do zdrowia** <GEN>.

'I wish you <DAT> a speedy recovery <GEN>.'

2.6.7 | As object of certain prepositions

The genitive must always be used for noun phrases that are the objects of
the following prepositions: **do** 'to'; **od** 'from, made of'; **u** 'at someone's
place, business'; **bez** 'without'; **dla** 'for'; **koło** 'by, next to'; **zamiast** 'instead
of'; **oprócz** 'except'; **mimo** 'despite'; **obok** 'next to'; **naprzeciw** 'across
from.'

The genitive is used with the preposition z in the meaning of 'from' (**Jestem
z Polski.** 'I'm from Poland.'); z can also be used with the instrumental in
the meaning of 'together with' (**z nami** 'with us') and with the accusative
in the meaning of 'about, around' (**Czekam już z godzinę.** 'I've been waiting for about an hour.')

2.6.7.1 | With prepositional phrases

The genitive is used after these common prepositional phrases:

w ciągu **tygodnia** 'during the week' (mostly with time phrases)
w czasie **wojny** 'during the war'
w trakcie **rozmowy** 'in the course of the conversation'
z okazji **urodzin** 'on the occasion of [your] birthday'
z powodu **choroby** 'because of the illness'

$\boxed{2.6.7.2}$ As *object of* **do** 'until,' **od** 'since,' **podczas** 'during,'
sprzed 'before,' **za** 'during,' **w czasie** 'during'

za komuny 'during Communism'
Mieszkamy w Kanadzie od lat osiemdziesiątych.
  'We have been living in Canada since the '80s.'
Od roku szukam mieszkania. 'I have been looking for
  an apartment for a year now.'
od poniedziałku do piątku 'from Monday to Friday'
od maja aż do grudnia 'from May until December'
od wczoraj 'since yesterday'

$\boxed{2.6.7.3}$ As *object in expressing time without prepositions*

The genitive is used in the constructions "every day," "every summer,"
etc. (See also 4.21.2.3 and 7.10.1)

każdego dnia 'every day'
każdego roku 'every year'
każdego lata 'every summer'

$\boxed{2.6.7.4}$ As *object of* **do** 'to,' 'for'

The preposition **do** 'to,' 'for' <+GEN> can have the meaning 'for the purpose
of': **coś do czytania** 'something to read'; **coś do jedzenia i picia** 'something
to eat and drink.' (See 9.7.2)

Where one noun modifies another noun in English, the genitive is often
used in the equivalent in Polish; the preposition **do** 'to,' 'for' <+GEN>
expresses the sense of 'for the purpose of.'

widelczyk do ciasta 'dessert fork'
pasta do zębów 'toothpaste'

It is also used after verbs with the preposition **do** 'to,' such as **pisać do** 'to
write to' somebody, **dzwonić do** 'to call' somebody (make a phone call to
somebody).

Zadzwoń do Piotra <GEN>. 'Call Piotr.'
Piszę e-mail do profesora <GEN>. 'I am writing an email to
  the professor.'

2.6.7.5 | As *object of* **bez** 'without' *and* **dla** 'for (the benefit of)'

człowiek bez charakteru
'a man without character'

kawa bez cukru
'coffee without sugar'

dom dla syna
'a house for the son' (See 9.7.2)

2.6.8 | *Full dates*

The genitive is marked on the last two numerals in a full date (a date that consists of a day, month and year, or a day and month) denoting when something occurs/occurred or will occur. (See 9.2.6)

Mój brat urodził się pierwszego maja, dwa tysiące drugiego roku.
'My brother was born on the first of May, two thousand two.'

Wracamy piątego stycznia.
'We will be back on the fifth of January.'

2.6.9 | *As object of lack, loss, deficiency, and reduction*

To follow the general idea of the genitive to express replenishment, the genitive case is also used to denote lack, loss, absence, excess, deficiency, and reduction.

After certain verbs and nouns the genitive is used:

brak/deficyt/niedostatek/niedobór 'a lack of something'
brakować 'to be lacking something' (used only in third person)
  (See 6.6.1.3, point 9)

  brak czasu i pieniędzy 'lack of time and money'
  nadmiar wapnia 'excess of calcium'
  niedostatek wiedzy 'lack of education'
  niedobór witamin 'a vitamin deficiency'
  redukcja etatów 'job cuts'
  strata czasu 'waste of time'

2.6.10 Regrets and dislikes

The genitive is used after certain verbs and nouns that denote regret or disgust:

żałować 'to regret' **nie cierpieć** 'to be unable to stand'
żal 'a pity' **nienawidzić** 'to hate'
szkoda 'a waste, pity' **nie znosić** 'to be unable to bear'

Żałuję wielu rzeczy. 'I regret many things.'
Szkoda słów. 'Waste of breath.' (coll.)

2.6.11 Quantifiers

The genitive case is used with words that denote containers, e.g., **pudełko** 'box,' **butelka** 'bottle.'

butelka wody <GEN> 'a bottle of water'
talerz zupy <GEN> 'a plate of soup'
kawałek pizzy <GEN> 'a piece of pizza'

To denote measurement: **kilogram cukru** 'a kilo of sugar'; **galon mleka** 'a gallon of milk'; **szklanka mąki** 'a cup of flour.'

After nouns to express 'a group of':

tłum ludzi 'a crowd of people'
gromada dzieci 'a bunch of children'
banda złodziei 'a band of thieves'
grupa naukowców 'a group of scholars'

2.6.12 Adverbs of quantity

Quantitative adverbs, words that relate to numerals and have nominal nature, e.g., **dużo** 'a lot,' **wiele** and **wielu** 'many,' **dwukrotnie** 'twice,' 'twofold,' **dużo** 'a lot'; **mało** 'not much, (a) little, few'; **trochę** 'a little bit'; **kilka** and **kilku** 'a few'; **ile** and **ilu** 'how much, how many'; **niewiele** and **niewielu** 'a little, few'; **tyle** and **tylu** 'so much, many' take the genitive. (See 8.1.5.)

Profesor ma dużo ciekawych książek <GEN>.
'[The] professor has many books.'

Rodzice mają mało czasu <GEN>.
'[My] parents do not have much time.'

Adam ma wielu przyjaciół <GEN>.
'Adam has many friends.'

Piję dużo kawy.
'I drink a lot of coffee.'

Mamy kilka świetnych filmów na DVD.
'We have a few great films on DVD.'

| 2.6.12.1 | *Quantitative adverbs in the subject position (genitive in the subject position)* |

When quantitative adverbs are used in the subject position, the genitive is used and the verb is in the third person singular form (in the past the neuter form (marker -ło)).

Dużo ciekawych książek <GEN> **było/jest** <SG 3 PR> **w pokoju profesora.**
'Many interesting books were/are in [the] professor's room.'

Wielu studentów <GEN> **zachorowało.**
'Many students <mixed group> got sick.'

Wiele studentek <GEN> **zachorowało**.
'Many students <only women> got sick.'

Pacjentów <GEN> **było dwuktornie więcej niż lekarzy.**
'There were twice as many patients as doctors.' (2.4.10.1)

| 2.6.13 | **Numeral case governance and genitive** |

To indicate "one and a half," the numeral **półtora** is used for masculine and neuter subjects and **półtorej** is used for feminine subjects. The genitive is used after both **półtora** and **półtorej**.

półtora roku 'a year and a half'
półtorej godziny 'an hour and a half'

The genitive plural is used with numbers five and up, except compound numbers ending in the words **dwa/dwie** 'two,' **trzy** 'three,' or **cztery** 'four.'

> **trzydzieści pięć książek** <GEN PL> '35 books'
> **dwadzieścia jeden godzin** <GEN PL> '21 hours'
> **osiemnaście lat** <GEN PL> '18 years'
> **jedenaście godzin** <GEN PL> '11 hours'
> **dwanaście książek** <GEN PL> '12 books'
> But: **trzydzieści trzy książki** <NOM PL> '33 books'

When numbers five and up, except compound numbers ending in the words **dwa/dwie** 'two,' **trzy** 'three,' or **cztery** 'four,' are used in the position of the subject, the verb is in the third person singular (in the past tense the neuter form with the marker -ło), and the adjective or other modifying noun word is in the genitive plural.

> **35 starych** <GEN PL> **książek** <GEN PL> **jest/było** <VERB SG> **na półce.**
> '35 old books are/were on the shelf.'

→Subject expressed in the genitive case (2.4.10.1, 2.4.11)

2.6.14 As object of certain adjectives

The genitive is used as the object of certain adjectives: **bliski** 'close (to),' **ciekawy** 'curious (of, about),' **niepewny** 'unsure (of),' **nieświadomy** 'unaware (of),' **pewien** 'sure (of),' **spragniony** 'yearning (for),' **świadomy** 'aware (of),' **winny** 'guilty (of),' **pełny** 'full (of),' **wart** '(to be) worth.' In Polish, the genitive is often used in place of the words 'of something' in English.

> **pełny zapału** 'full of enthusiasm'
> **bliski płaczu** 'close to tears'
> **On jest tego ciekawy.** 'He is curious about that.'
> **kościół pełen ludzi** 'church full of people'
> **to jest warte zachodu** 'it's worth the trouble'
> **film wart obejrzenia** 'film worth watching'

2.6.15 Co, coś, cokolwiek, co bądź

> **co** 'what'   **coś** 'something'
> **cokolwiek** 'anything'   **co bądź** 'whatever'

> **Co nowego?** 'What's new?'
> **cokolwiek białego** 'anything white' (See 2.4.5)

2.6.16 Ani . . . , ani . . .

The objects after the connectors **ani . . . , ani . . .** 'neither . . . , nor . . .' are put in the genitive case. The verb in such a sentence must be negated.

Ewa nie ma ani ojca <GEN>**, ani matki** <GEN>**.**
'Ewa has neither a father nor a mother.'

2.7 Dative

The dative case of nouns is the least used.[4] However, the personal pronouns in the dative are used frequently as logical subjects (the most important argument), and with impersonal forms of the verbs.

Zimno mi <DAT>**.** 'I am cold.'
Jak ci <DAT> **się podoba w Polsce?** 'How do you like Poland?'
Dobrze im <DAT> **się wiedzie.** 'They are well off.'
Chce mi <DAT> **się spać.** 'I want to sleep.'
Ukradli mi <DAT> **dokumenty** <ACC/NOM>**.** 'I had my documents stolen.'
Zabrali mi <DAT> **walizkę** <ACC>**.** 'I had my suitcase taken away.'
Jak ci <DAT> **się spało?** 'How did you sleep?'

The dative case in Polish is called **celownik**—**cel** 'an aim,' 'goal' (person or object) the action is directed to (towards).

The dative case is typically used to mark the indirect object of a verb; to denote the person or thing the direct object is directed to. In English "to" or "for" is often used to indicate the addressee, experiencer, or receiver of the verb.

While the indirect object in English can be expressed with the preposition "for" or "to," in Polish the dative is expressed without prepositions. Remember that a direct or indirect object in Polish can go at the beginning of a sentence, as required by context.

Człowiek <NOM> **człowiekowi** <DAT> **wilkiem** <INS>**.**
'Homo homini lupus (est).' ['A man is a wolf *to his fellow man*.']

Matka czyta bajkę dziecku <DAT>**.**
'A mother is reading a story to a child.'

Kupiłam mamie <DAT> **perfumy.**
'I bought a perfume for [my] mom.'

Często pomagam siostrze <DAT>**.**
'I often [extend] help [to] my sister.'

Generic questions

Komu się sprzeciwiasz? 'Who do you oppose?'
Rodzicom [się sprzeciwiam]. '[I oppose] [my] parents.'

Czemu się sprzeciwiasz? 'What do you oppose?'
Wojnom [się sprzeciwiam]. '[I oppose] wars.'

After certain verbs

The dative case is often used to denote the receiver or the beneficiary of an action. This often corresponds to the indirect object in English, marked by "to." **Dałem *mu*** <DAT> **książkę.** 'I gave a book *to him*.' (See 5.2.9)

The dative case is used with many verbs with meanings related to "giving," "conveying," "transferring" or the lack thereof. An item given is often in the accusative case and the addressee/receiver is in the dative case.

dać 'to give'	**pokazać** 'to show'
darować 'to give'	**przebaczyć** 'to forgive'
doręczyć 'to deliver'	**przekazać** 'to hand over'
dziękować 'to thank'	**przydać się** 'to be useful'
dziwić się 'to be surprised at somebody'	**przynosić** 'to bring'
	sprezentować 'to present'
odmawiać 'to refuse'	**szkodzić** 'to harm'
ofiarować 'to donate'	**towarzyszyć** 'to accompany'
podać 'to pass'	**zawdzięczać** 'to owe'
podobać się 'to be attracted to'	**zazdrościć** 'to envy'
pomagać 'to help'	

The dative case is used with several verbs with meanings related to "looking," "listening closely."

przyglądać się 'to observe'	**przedstawić** 'to introduce'
przypatrywać się 'to look carefully'	**zwierzyć się** 'to confide'
przysłuchiwać się 'to listen'	

The dative case is used with several verbs with meanings related to "power and control."

dokuczać 'to tease'	**ulegać** 'to give in'
podporządkować się 'to yield'	**zabraniać** 'to prohibit'
pozwolić 'to allow'	**zakazać** 'to forbid'
przeszkadzać 'to interrupt'	**zapobiegać** 'to prevent'
sprzeciwiać się 'to oppose'	

The dative case is used with verbs with meanings related to "believing and trusting."

ufać 'to trust'   **zaprzeczać** 'to deny'
wierzyć 'to believe'

The dative case is used with verbs with meanings related to "passing information" to a listener.

mówić 'to tell'   **powiedzieć** 'to say'
opowiedzieć 'to tell'

Praktyczny słownik łączliwości składniowej czasowników polskich. (A practical dictionary of Polish verbal collocations) by Stanisław Mędak offers an exhaustive list of verbs that can take certain cases.[5]

2.7.3 | As object of certain prepositions and prepositional phrases

dzięki 'thanks to'
przeciw(ko) 'against'
ku 'towards'
wbrew 'against'
na przekór 'out of spite'

Dzięki niej spłaciłam kredyt.
'Thanks to her I paid off [my] credit.'

Note: **Jej** as a possessive pronoun does not change to **niej**. Compare the two sentences. (See 5.2.6)

Dzięki jej pomocy spłaciłam kredyt.
'Thanks to *her help* I paid off [my] credit.'

Dzięki niej spłaciłam kredyt.
'Thanks to her I paid off [my] credit.'

2.7.4 | In impersonal constructions

chce *mi* **się jeść** '*I* want to eat'
jest *mi* **zimno** '*I* am cold'
nie wolno *ci* **się poddawać** '*you* can't give up'

wdzięczny 'grateful'
potrzebny 'needed'
Jestem wdzięczna rodzicom <DAT> **za pomoc.**
  'I am grateful to [my] parents for help.'

2.7.5.1 *Potrzebny 'is needed/to need'*

In order to express the need for something, use the adjective **potrzebny** with the object that is needed in the nominative case, preceded by the person who is in need in the dative case (or by a personal pronoun). **Potrzebny** agrees in class (also referred to as gender, see 3.2.1) and number with the object needed. The construction is used with nouns, not with verbs: '*I need* to rest.' *Muszę* odpocząć.

Potrzebny mi **nowy sweter.** '*I need* a new sweater.'
Potrzebna mi **nowa koszula.** '*I need* a new shirt.'
Potrzebne mi **nowe okulary.** '*I need* new glasses.'
Potrzebni nam **wykwalifikowani sprzedawcy.**
  'We *need* professional salesmen.'

2.8 Locative

The Polish name for the locative case is **miejscownik**. This case is used to show the location (**miejsce**) of a person, animal or thing. In English, this case is also sometimes called the prepositional case. The two names in English capture the two main attributes of the case: (1) it denotes location— where and wherein; and (2) this case must be used with a preposition. This is the only case where a preposition is mandatory. However, it is important to note that following a preposition many different cases can be used.

Martwię się o <+ACC> **siostrę.** (See 2.5.10)
  'I worry about [my] sister.'

Myślę o <+LOC> **siostrze.**
  'I am thinking about [my] sister.'

Praktyczny słownik łączliwości składniowej czasowników polskich. (A practical dictionary of Polish verbal collocations) by Stanisław Mędak offers an exhaustive list of verbs that can take certain cases.[6]

It is easy to know when to use the locative case, but it is not easy to form it, because of the many consonant and vowel shifts.

See 3.10 for examples of locative case consonants and vowel changes within the singular locative case for masculine, feminine and neuter nouns to illustrate the process of palatalization.

2.8.1 | Generic questions

O kim? 'about whom?'; o czym? 'about what?'; gdzie? 'where' (with certain prepositions)

O kim rozmawiacie? 'Who are you talking about?
O tobie. 'About you.'

O czym rozmawiacie? 'What are you talking about?'
O polityce. 'About politics.'

Gdzie mieszkasz? 'Where do you live?'
W Gdańsku. 'In Gdańsk.'

2.8.2 | Usage

It is used with certain prepositions **na, w, po, przy** to express *locality*: gdzie? 'where?'

1. To denote objects of the prepositions **na** 'on,' 'on top' and **w** 'in,' 'inside' to show location

   Od tygodnia jesteśmy w górach.
   'We have been in the mountains for a week now.'

2. With the object of the preposition **po** 'along,' 'movement over a surface or an area'

   podróżować po Europie 'to travel around Europe'
   spacerować po parku 'to walk along the park'
   chodzić po ulicach 'to walk around the streets'
   bić po rękach 'to slap the hands'
   poszło jak po maśle 'it went swimmingly [like clockwork]'
      (saying)

3. With the object of the preposition **przy** 'by', 'in front of'/'in the presence of'

> **siedzimy przy stole** 'we are sitting at the table'
> **zaparkowałem przy sklepie** 'I parked by the store'
> **Nie kłóćmy się przy wszystkich.** 'Let's not argue in front of everybody.'

4. With the object of speech or thought; object of the preposition **o** 'about'

> **artykuł o bezrobociu** 'an article about unemployment'
> **film o dzieciach** 'a film about children'
> **książka o Lechu Wałęsie** 'a book about Lech Wałęsa'

The locative as object of speech or thought is mostly used with verbs indicating speaking, talking or thinking.

> **Myślę o tobie.** 'I am thinking about you.'
> **Marzę o wakacjach.** 'I dream about [the] vacation.'
> **Dyskutujemy o polityce.** 'We are discussing [about] politics.'
> **Rozmawiam o koncercie.** 'I am talking about the concert.'
> **Pisać o muzyce Chopina.** 'To write about Chopin's music.'
> **Zapomnieć o urodzinach brata.** 'To forget about brother's birthday.'
> **Śpiewać o wolności.** 'To sing about freedom.'
> *But:* **Pytać o cenę** <ACC>. 'To ask about the price.'
> **Czytać o korupcji.** 'To read about corruption.'

| 2.8.3 | *Temporal prepositions po, w, o* |

po 'after'
w 'in' with months and years (see Table 9.6)
o 'at what time'
po wakacjach 'after [the] vacation'
po obiedzie 'after lunch'
w maju 'in May'
o godzinie piątej 'at five o'clock'

A week, month, year, and a century that is the object of the preposition **w**, denoting time and answering the question **kiedy?** 'when?' is used in the locative case.

> **w tym/zeszłym/przyszłym/następnym tygodniu/miesiącu/roku/ stuleciu**
> 'this/last/next/following week/month/year/century'

(9.2.6)

2.8.4 | As object with instruments and equipment

The object of the verbs **grać na** 'to play an instrument', and **pracować na** 'work on' takes the locative, after the preposition **na**.

Gram na fortepianie i na gitarze. 'I play piano and guitar.'
pracować na komputerze 'to work on the computer'

With certain sport equipment after prepositions **na** and **w**

jeździć na nartach 'to ski'
jeździć na rolkach 'to rollerblade'
jeździć na koniu 'to ride a horse'

Note: Note that nouns are used in the instrumental case in Polish to indicate means of transportation: **jeździć samochodem/pociągiem** 'to go by car/by train'; **latać samolotem** 'to fly by plane.' Some of the nouns have two equal forms: **jeździć rowerem/jeździć na rowerze** 'to ride by bike/on a bike'; **jeździć na koniu/jeździć konno** 'to ride a horse.' (See 9.2.1 for prepositions **w** and **na**).

2.8.5 | To mark the object of verbs

Praktyczny słownik łączliwości składniowej czasowników polskich. (A practical dictionary of Polish verbal collocations) by Stanisław Mędak offers an exhaustive list of verbs that can take certain cases.[7]

After verbs indicating *thinking about somebody or something*:

myśleć o 'to think about'
marzyć o 'to dream about'
pamiętać o 'to remember about'
zapominać o 'to forget' (a fact)

After verbs indicating *talking about somebody or something*:

mówić o 'to talk about'
rozmawiać o 'to converse about'
dyskutować o 'to discuss something'
wspominać o 'to mention about'
gadać o 'to chat about (coll.)'
opowiadać o 'to tell stories about'

After verbs of indicating *to know a lot about something, participate in something*.

> **znać się na czymś** 'to know a lot about something'
> **brać udział w czymś** 'to participate in something'
>
> **Ewa zna się na sztuce.** 'Ewa knows a lot about art.'

2.9 Instrumental

In Polish, the instrumental case is called **narzędnik. Narząd** means 'instrument,' and the instrumental case is used to denote a tool or a means through or by which an action is taken. Instrumental is the case of the objects that fulfill the action of the verb. In English, the means or instrument is often expressed with the help of the prepositions "with," "by," and "in." In Polish, such constructions usually have no preposition.

> **Proszę nie pisać *ołówkiem*** <INS>.
> 'Please do not write *in pencil*.'
>
> **Sushi je się *pałeczkami*** <INS>, **nie *widelcem*** <INS>.
> 'Sushi is eaten *with chopsticks*, not *with a fork*.'
>
> ***Ogniem*** <INS> **i *mieczem*** <INS>
> *With Fire* and *Sword* (a novel by Henryk Sienkiewicz)

It is important to note that Polish makes a distinction between a noun phrase that denotes an instrument used to fulfill an action and a noun phrase that denotes another actor that joins in the performance of an action. Both are in the instrumental case, but only an actor joining in the performance of an action is denoted with the preposition **z** '(together) with.' In English both meanings can be translated using the preposition "with" which can lead to mistakes in Polish.

Czyszczę szczotką. 'I'm cleaning with a broom.' I'm using the **szczotka** 'broom' as an instrument to do something, so the preposition **z** 'with' is not used.

Incorrect: **Czyszczę ze szczotką.** 'I'm cleaning with a broom.' With the preposition **z** 'with' in this sentence, the sentence means that the **szczotka** 'broom' is joining in the performance of the action; the broom and I are both doing the cleaning. This would only be possible in a situation like a fairy tale, such as a Harry Potter movie, where a magical broom is helping a character to clean a room. It is important to note this to avoid a common mistake that creates an absurd sentence.

Another example for clarification can be made with the word **pilot**, which can mean 'remote control' or 'pilot' in Polish.

Steruję pilotem. 'I'm steering with a remote control.' (I'm using the **pilot** 'remote control' as an instrument to do something, so the preposition **z** 'with' is not used.)

Steruję z pilotem. 'I'm steering with the pilot.' (The **pilot** 'pilot' is joining in the performance of the action; the pilot and I are both steering, so the preposition **z** 'with' is used.)

> **Podróżować *rowerem*.** 'To travel *by bike*.' (riding on a bike)
> **Podróżować *z rowerem*.** 'To travel *with a bike*.' (such as having a bike in the trunk of your car as you travel)

> **kroić coś** <ACC> ***nożem*** <NOM> 'to cut something *with a knife*'
> ***z nożem*** <NOM> **w ręce** <LOC> '*with a knife* in a hand'
> **Ewa bawi się *lalką*.** 'Ewa is playing *with the doll*.' (Ewa is using the doll as an instrument so the preposition **z** 'with' is not used.)
> **Ewa bawi się *z dzieckiem*.** 'Ewa is playing *with the child*.' (The child and Ewa are both playing so the preposition **z** 'with' is used.)

(See 4.11.3)

2.9.1 | *Generic questions*

Kim? or **z kim?** generally mean 'with whom?' and **czym?** or **z czym?** generally mean 'with what?' These questions are used with the instrumental case.

In English, when asking "who with?" or "what with?" the word "who" or "what" can often begin the sentence with the preposition "with" coming at the end of the question. This is not possible in Polish; the question must be asked as **z kim . . . ?** 'with whom' or **z czym . . . ?** 'with what?'

> **Z kim** <INS> **idziesz do kina** <GEN>**?** 'Who are you going to the movies with?'
> **Z żoną.** 'With [my] wife.'

> **Z czym** <INS> **chcesz pizzę** <ACC>**?** 'What do you want the pizza with?'
> **Z bazylią.** 'With basil.'

> **Czym** <INS> **je się sushi?** 'With what does one eat sushi?'
> **Pałeczkami** <INS>**, nie widelcem** <INS>**.** 'With chopsticks, not with a fork.'

Kto <NOM> *kim* <INS> **zarządza?** 'Who manages *whom?*'
Prezes zarządza *pracownikami*. 'A president manages *the employees*.'

Kto <NOM> *czym* <INS> **zarządza?** 'Who manages *what?*'
Prezes zarządza *bankiem*. 'A president manages *the bank*.'

| 2.9.2 | *Usage* |

The instrumental is used as the object of instruments with which or by means of which something is being done (without the use of any preposition). Note that the object of the verb is mostly in the accusative, and the tools used by the object in the accusative are in the instrumental.

Leczyć pacjenta <ACC> **antybiotykami** <INS>.
'To cure a patient with antibiotics.'

Pisać list <ACC> **zielonym** <INS> **długopisem** <INS>.
'To write a letter with green ink.'

Myć zęby <ACC> **pastą** <INS>.
'To brush [the] teeth with toothpaste.'

Czesać dziecko <ACC> **szczotką** <INS>.
'To brush a child's hair with a brush.'

Kroić chleb <ACC> **nożem** <INS>.
'To cut bread with a knife.'

1. To express mode of travel

   While in English a preposition is usually used to describe a mode of travel, in Polish this is done without any preposition.

   jeździć *samochodem, autobusem, pociągiem* 'to go *by car,*
   by bus, by train'
   latać *samolotem, helikopterem* 'to fly *by plane, by helicopter*'
   pływać *kajakiem, żaglówką* 'to sail *by kayak, by sailboat*'

2. Noun complement of verbs indicating "being" or "becoming": **być** 'to be,' **zostać** 'to become,' **stać się** 'to become,' **okazać się** 'to turn out to be,' **jawić się** 'to appear,' **wydawać się** 'to seem.'

   Chcę zostać *politykiem*. 'I want to become *a politician*.'
   Piotr został *policjantem*. 'Piotr became *a police officer*.'
   Po wojnie stał się *innym* <INS> *człowiekiem* <INS>. 'After the war he became *a new person*.'

However, predicate adjectives that are not used in a noun phrase are put in the nominative case.

Chcę być *miły* <NOM>.
'I want to be kind.'

Chcę być *miłym* <INS> *człowiekiem* <INS>.
'I want to be a kind person.'

Predicate adjectives after the infinitive of the verb "to be" are in the instrumental case when used in an impersonal construction.

Warto być *miłym* <INS>. 'It is worth it to be *kind*.'

3. Complement of certain verbs (without the use of any preposition).

bawić się 'to play with'
czuć 'to smell'
gardzić 'to despise'
handlować 'to trade'
interesować się 'to be interested in'
kierować 'to manage'
machać 'to wave'
martwić się 'to worry about'
myć się 'to wash oneself with'
okazać się 'to turn out, end up being'
opiekować się 'to take care of'
poruszać 'to move' (a body part)
przejmować się 'to be worried by'
rozczarować się 'to be disappointed with'
rządzić 'to rule'
zachwycać się 'to admire'
zajmować się 'to be occupied with'
zarazić się 'to infect with'
zarządzać 'to manage'

Czuć *papierosami.*
'It smells *of cigarettes.*'

Interesuję się *historią.*
'I am interested *in history.*'

Zaraził się *malarią.*
'He got infected *with malaria.*'

Proszę nie poruszać *głową.*
'Please do not move *[your] head.*'

95

2.9.3 | Z

2.9.3.1 | *Complement of adjectival phrases with* **z** *'with'*

identyczny z 'identical with'   **zbieżny z** 'coincidental with'
sprzeczny z 'contrary to'   **zgodny z** 'in accordance with'
zaręczony z 'engaged to'   **związany z** 'bound together with'

Anna jest zaręczona z Ewą. 'Anna is engaged *to Ewa.*'
akt zgodny z *prawem* 'an act in accordance *with the law*'

2.9.3.2 | *Complement of verbs with* **z** *'with'*

dzielić się z 'to share with'
kłócić się z 'to argue with'
kontaktować się z 'to get in touch with'
pogodzić się z 'to make up with'
pożegnać się z 'to say good-bye to'
przywitać się z 'to say hello to'
radzić sobie z 'to manage, make do with'
rozmawiać z 'to talk with'
spotykać się z 'to meet up with'
umówić się z 'to arrange to meet with'
współpracować z 'to cooperate with'

Chodź przywitamy się z *babcią*.
'Let's go say hello *to grandma.*'

Współpracujemy z *wieloma firmami*.
'We cooperate *with many firms.*'

Często spotykam się ze *znajomymi*.
'I often meet up with *my friends.*'

2.9.3.3 | *Object of* **z** *'together with' to express group subject*

My z żoną mieszkamy od lat z teściową.
'My wife and I live [have been living] with mother-in-law for many years.'

My z bratem się nigdy nie kłócimy.
'My brother and I never argue.'

| 2.9.3.4 | *Complement of a noun with* **z** *'together with'* |

kawa z mlekiem 'coffee *with milk*'
herbata z cytryną i cukrem 'tea *with lemon* and *sugar*'
kurczak z frytkami 'chicken *with fries*'
pierogi z mięsem 'dumplings *with meat*'
bułka z masłem 'a roll with butter,' also a saying meaning "a piece of cake" (something that is very easy)

| 2.9.4 | **Classifying a person, animal, object or abstract** |

The instrumental case is used when classifying a person, animal, object or abstract idea as belonging to a particular category.

Kim jest Piotr? 'Who is Piotr?'
Piotr jest mężem Ewy. 'Piotr is Ewa's husband.'

Kim on jest? 'Who is he?'
On jest naszym sąsiadem. 'He is our neighbor.'

Czym jest pistolet? 'What is a pistol?'
Pistolet jest bronią. 'A pistol is a weapon.'

In comparison, asking the name of a person or an object would require the nominative case, e.g., **Kto to jest?** 'Who is it?', **Co to jest?** 'What is it?'

The verb **nazywać** 'to name,' 'to call' can be used to call one thing (in the accusative case) another thing (in the instrumental case).

Nazywała go <ACC> **wujkiem** <INS>. 'She was calling him uncle.'
Żona nazywała męża <ACC> **skarbem** <INS>. 'The wife was calling her husband sweetheart.'

(See also 2.4.10, points 3–4)

| 2.9.4.1 | *With* **być** *when the subject is given a noun label or category (except when used in a* **jest to** *'this is' construction)* |

Warszawa jest dużym <INS> **miastem** <INS>. 'Warsaw is *a large city*.' (noun)
On jest *lekarzem*. 'He is *a doctor*.'
Ewa jest *Polką*. 'Ewa is *a Pole*.'
***Romeo i Julia* jest dramatem Szekspira.** '*Romeo and Juliet* is *a play by Shakespeare*.'

When only an adjective and no noun is used with **być** 'to be,' the adjective is in the nominative case.

> **Warszawa jest *duża*** <NOM>. 'Warsaw is *large*.' (no noun)

Constructions with the verb **być** 'to be' along with the demonstrative pronoun **to** (e.g., **jest to . . .** 'this is . . .') are followed by the nominative case. A noun can be used with **to** plus nominative without any verb.

> **Pan Nowak to sąsiad** <NOM> **Basi.**
> 'Mr. Nowak is a neighbor of Basia.'
>
> **Pan Nowak jest sąsiadem** <INS> **Basi.**
> 'Mr. Nowak is a neighbor of Basia.'
>
> **Warszawa to stolica** <NOM> **Polski.**
> 'Warsaw is the capital city of Poland.'
>
> **Warszawa jest stolicą** <INS> **Polski.**
> 'Warsaw is the capital city of Poland.'

2.9.5 | As object of certain prepositions

2.9.5.1 | *Object of prepositions to show location:* **za** 'behind,' **przed** 'in front of,' **pod** 'under,' **nad** 'above,' **między** 'between,' **pomiędzy** 'among,' **poza** 'beyond'

> **Siedzimy za *stołem*.**
> 'We are sitting behind *the table*.'
>
> **Samochód stoi przed *domem*.**
> 'The car is parked in front of *the house*.'
>
> **Piotr mieszka piętro nad *nami*.**
> 'Piotr lives one floor above *us*.'
>
> **Lampa stoi między krzesłami.**
> 'A lamp stands between the chairs.'

2.9.5.2 | *Object of the prepositions* **nad** 'at' *and* **przed** 'before' *indicating time.* 'When?' **Kiedy?**

> **nad ranem** 'at dawn'
> **przed nocą** 'before nightfall'
> **przed południem** 'before the afternoon'

2.9.5.3 | "In a season," "in the evening," "at night"

While a preposition is used in English, no preposition is used in Polish in these constructions.

wieczorem 'in the evening'
wiosną 'in the spring'
latem 'in the summer'
nocą 'at night'
jesienią 'in the fall'
zimą 'in the winter'

2.9.5.4 | *Object of preposition* **nad** *to indicate location* 'by'
an expanse of water

wakacje nad morzem 'vacation by the sea'
piknik nad Wisłą 'a picnic by [the] river Vistula'

(See 9.2.5)

2.9.6 | *In adverbial expressions*

2.9.6.1 | *Instrumental as object of adverb indicating a manner in*
which something has been done

biec truchtem 'to jog'
pływać kraulem 'to swim the crawl'
pisać maczkiem 'to write in a tiny hand'
iść nierównym krokiem 'to walk at an uneven pace'
mówić szeptem 'to speak in a whisper'

2.9.6.2 | *Adverbial expressions of motion*

After verbs meaning "to go" the instrumental is used to denote the manner in which the movement was performed.

iść ulicą/ścieżką
'to go on the street/on the path'

jechać drogą/ulicą/autostradą
'to drive on the road/on the street/on the highway'

2.10 Vocative

The vocative case is called **wołacz** in Polish, from the verb **wołać** 'to call.'

2.10.1 Written Polish

The vocative case is generally used to indicate written forms of address in letters, documents and applications.

Szanowny Panie 'Dear Sir'
Szanowna Pani Profesor [no last name] Dear Professor <female>
Szanowny Pani Profesorze [no last name] Dear Professor <male>

2.10.2 Spoken Polish

In the spoken form there is a tendency to use the nominative case instead of the vocative: **Zosia!, Tadeusz!, Henryk!, Joanna!**

In refined Polish, including written Polish, it is advisable to use the traditional form of the vocative: **Zosiu!, Tadeuszu!, Henryku!, Joanno!** When the noun is preceded by an adjective (or **pan/pani** etc.) the forms of the vocative are used to address people.

Drogi Tadeuszu! (not: Drogi Tadeusz!) 'Dear Tadeusz!'
Pani Joanno! (not: Pani Joanna) 'Mrs. Joanna'

2.10.3 Exclamations

O Boże! O my God!
Ty ośle! You donkey!

The vocative forms are marked with a comma: **Witaj, Agnieszko!**

After the vocative form we can put an exclamation.

Litwo! Ojczyzno moja! Ty jesteś jak zdrowie.
'O Lithuania! My fatherland! You are like good health.'

Adam Mickiewicz

Chapter 3

Nouns

3.1 Overview

Nouns, also called *substantives*, are traditionally considered one of the nine classes of words next to pronouns, verbs, adverbs, adjectives, conjunctions, prepositions, interjections, and particles.

"Noun" in Polish is **rzeczownik**, from **rzecz** 'thing.' Traditionally, nouns denote things and individual physical entities, like **stół** 'table,' **kot** 'cat,' **syn** 'son,' **wierzba** 'willow,' **Kościuszko** (last name).

Nouns are inflected (changed) for case (e.g., **okno** 'window,' **na oknie** 'on the window') and number (e.g., **okna** 'windows'), and classified for class (also referred to as 'gender'). Nouns can represent abstract ideas and concepts, e.g., **piękno** 'beauty,' **wymowa** 'pronunciation' or actions, e.g., **pisanie** 'writing,' **kronikarstwo** 'writing a chronicle.' Each fully developed noun has 14 ending forms (seven each in singular and plural).

New nouns are constantly being added to the Polish vocabulary—they are either invented, like **podomka** 'housecoat' (**po** 'along,' **dom** 'house') or borrowed from other languages such as **lobbysta** 'lobbyist.'

Nouns represent a very rich group. They can be simple, e.g., **kraj** 'country' or compound, as **obcokrajowiec** 'foreigner' (**obcy** 'foreign,' **kraj** 'country').

3.1.1 Types of nouns

Nouns are divided into:

common: **dom** 'house'
proper (written in capital letters): **Biały Dom** 'White House'

animate (referring to living beings and divided further into male human and no male human classes)

male human (referring to a male human being): **chłopiec** 'boy'

no male human: **pies** 'dog,' **kobieta** 'woman,' **stół** 'table'

inanimate (referring to lifeless objects and concepts): **dom** 'house,' **piękno** 'beauty'

concrete: **książka** 'book'

abstract (referring to concepts): **wstręt** 'disgust'

countable (referring to nouns that can be counted so have singular and plural forms): **długopis** 'pen'

non-countable (refer to non-count, mass nouns, that can be quantified in units of measure and counted, but the noun itself cannot be counted): **mięso** 'meat'

individual: **członek** 'member'

collective: **członkostwo** 'membership'

3.1.2 | Main functions of nouns: case usage

A primary function of nouns is to denote the subject of the sentence or the object in oblique cases (cases other than the nominative case; for case usage see Chapter 2).

Some examples of the noun as the object include:

- direct object in accusative case: **Czytam** <+ACC> <u>książkę</u>. 'I'm reading <u>a book</u>.'
- indirect object in dative case: **Czytam** <+DAT> <u>dziecku</u> książkę. 'I'm reading a book <u>to a child</u>.'
- noun as a predicate (after the form of the verbs indicating *being* and *becoming* in the instrumental case—to classify the role or function of the subject: **Jan jest** <+INS> <u>studentem</u>. 'Jan is <u>a student</u>.' (instrumental case)
- object of belonging and relation, used to link two nouns: **Biblioteka** <+GEN> <u>Kongresu</u> 'Library <u>of Congress</u>'
- prepositional phrase—a phrase consisting of a preposition and a noun phrase serving as its object: **w** <+LOC> **domu** 'at home'
- noun used as a form of address: **Szanowny Panie** <VOC> 'Dear Sir'

Nouns can describe the time of the day: **wieczorem** 'in the evening,' time of the year (season): **wiosną** 'in the spring,' on a specific day: **pierwszego stycznia** 'on the first of January,' place: **w pociągu** 'on a train,' manner (way of traveling): **pociągiem** 'by train,' purpose: **rodzinie** 'for a family.'

Endings on nouns change when the noun is used in a phrase or a sentence, to show its function within the phrase, sentence, or clause. In Polish there are seven kinds of distinctive relationships, overtly marked on nominal forms. The seven distinctive relationships correspond to the seven cases in Polish (2.1).

3.1.3 Nouns with verbal forms and other nominals

Verbs and prepositions, some adjectives and adverbs can impose a form on a noun (its case), e.g.,

napić się <+GEN> **kawy** 'to drink some coffee'   [verb]
Nie umiem żyć bez <+GEN> **kawy.** 'I can't live   [preposition]
  without coffee.'
bliski <+GEN> **płaczu** 'on the verge of tears' (masc.)   [adjective]
blisko <+GEN> **domu** 'closely to home'   [adverb]

(See 3.4)

A noun is "the chief" among other nominal forms in a phrase or a sentence.

Two nouns can be connected with or without a preposition. If two nouns in a phrase or a sentence are connected without a preposition, one of the nouns is "the chief" and the other noun accommodates the former, e.g.,

ból <GEN> **głowy** 'headache'
jazda pociągiem <INS> 'a ride on a trian'
kwiaty mamie <DAT> 'flowers for mom'

In the sentences below notice how the nouns **wieczór** <MSC>, **zabawa** <FEM>, and **spotkanie** <NT> impose endings on other nominals and the past tense.

Ten pierwszy letni *wieczór* **był cudowny.** 'This first summer
  evening was wonderful.'
Ta pierwsza letnia *zabawa* **była cudowna.** 'This first summer
  party was wonderful.'
To pierwsze letnie *spotkanie* **było cudowne.** 'This first summer
  meeting was wonderful.'

3.1.4 Noun structure

A noun consists of a stem (**temat**) and an ending (**końcówka**).

The stem is the *base* of the noun to which endings are added, e.g.,

in the noun **ulic|a** 'street', the base is **ulic** and the ending is **-a**
in the noun **miejsc|e** 'place', the base is **miejsc** and the ending is **-e**.

Based on the stem-final, nouns attach certain endings, e.g., stem-final **sz**, **rz**, **ż**, **cz** never take **i**, and stem-final **k**, **g**, **l** never take **y** (1.6).

stem-ending

książk-a 'book'	**książk-i** <GEN SG>
nog-a 'leg'	**nog-i** <GEN SG>
kasz-a 'kasha'	**kasz-y** <GEN SG>
burz-a 'storm'	**burz-y** <GEN SG>
tęcz-a 'rainbow'	**tęcz-y** <GEN SG>

3.1.4.1 | Shared endings

Some endings can be identical in more than one case. For example, the ending -a can indicate different things for different words. It can be nominative feminine singular, as in **gdzie jest poczta?** 'where is the post office?'; nominative masculine animate singular, as in **mam kota** 'I have a cat'; genitive neuter singular, as in **szukam dziecka** 'I'm looking for the baby'; nominative neuter plural, as in **dwa okna** 'two windows'; exceptionally, it can be a nominative plural no male human noun: **akta sprawy** 'case records,' **cuda techniki** 'marvels of modern technology'; and it can even be accusative masculine inanimate singular: **jem pączka** 'I'm eating a donut.'

Within a case, different classes and/or numbers can share the same case endings. An example of this is -om, which is the dative plural ending for nouns of all classes: **Dają prezenty ciociom, wujkom, i rodzicom.** 'They are giving presents to aunts, uncles, and parents.'

Animacy/Inanimacy Shared Endings: In the masculine singular accusative case, masculine animate nouns have the same endings as in genitive singular, and masculine inanimate nouns have the same endings as in nominative singular. (See 3.3.5.2)

3.1.4.2 | Unique endings

Some endings, on the other hand, are used with only one combination of case, class (also referred to as gender, see 3.2.1), number, and part of speech. For example, the ending -owi, as in **profesorowi** 'to the professor,' is used exclusively for the dative masculine singular of nouns.

1. Studentka <NOM> przedstawiła dziadka <ACC> *profesorowi* <DAT>.
   'The student introduced her grandfather *to the professor*.'

2. Studentka <NOM> przedstawiła profesora <ACC> *dziadk<u>owi</u>* <DAT>.
'The student introduced the professor *to her grandfather.*'

Endings that are added to nouns or noun phrases in Polish are used to show the function that certain nouns or noun phrases play in a sentence or a clause. In the two examples above, the subject of the sentences in the nominative case in 1 and 2 is **studentka**; the direct object in the accusative case in 1 is **dziadka** and in 2 it is **profesora**; and the indirect object in the dative case in 1 is **profesorowi** 'to the professor,' and in 2 it is **dziadkowi** 'to her grandfather.'

| 3.1.4.3 | *Translation difficulties* |

Dziecko wychowuje rodzeństwo.
'A child raises sibling(s)' Or: 'Sibling(s) raise(s) a child.'

Some forms of nominal words in Polish can be identical, e.g., **dziecko** 'child' and **rodzeństwo** 'siblings' have identical forms in the nominative and accusative singular/plural cases. It means that both **dziecko** and **rodzeństwo** have identical forms in the subject case (nominative) and in the object case (accusative). Because forms are identical, it is better to use the sentence in the passive.

> **Dziecko jest wychowywane przez rodzeństwo.** 'A child is raised by (his/her) sibling(s).'
> **Rodzeństwo jest wychowywane przez dziecko.** 'Sibling(s) is/are raised by a child.'

| 3.1.4.4 | *Consonant shifts with inflection* |

Predictable consonant shifts occur in the final consonant(s) of the stem in many nouns (and adjectives, adverbs, numerals, pronouns, and verbs) during the process of inflection before [i], [y], ['e] (see 1.3.4). (The ending ['e] denotes that the preceding consonant(s) become palatalized.) These shifts are very systematic and allow learners to trace constant changes in both directions; for example, whenever -**r**- shifts, it will always change to -**rz**-, and whenever -**rz**- shifts, it will always change to -**r**-, e.g.,

> **dwo<u>rz</u>ec** 'railway station' **na dwo<u>rc</u>u** 'at the station'
> **ba<u>r</u>** 'bar' **w ba<u>rz</u>e** 'in the bar.'

> **Młoda pa<u>ra</u>** <NOM FEM> **dziękuje orkiest<u>rz</u>e** <DAT FEM>.
> 'The newlyweds thank the music band.'

> **Orkiest<u>ra</u>** <NOM FEM> **dziękuje młodej pa<u>rz</u>e** <DAT FEM>.
> 'The music band thanks the newlyweds.'

The soft consonants ć, ń, ś, ź, dź before a vowel ending become ci, ni, si, zi, dzi, e.g., styczeń 'January' w styczniu 'in January' (1.3.3.2).

Fleeting -e with inflection

The fleeting vowel is a vowel that is found in some forms of the nouns, but not in others. The fleeting vowel -e/-'e is removed in inflected forms of a noun, often occurring before the consonants -(i)ec, -ek, -eł, -el, and in a few words that end with -er and -en, as well as in the word pies 'dog' (see 1.9).

stycz<u>e</u>ń <NOM> 'January' **w styczniu** <LOC> 'in January'

Ojc<u>ie</u>c <NOM> **martwi się o dziadka** <ACC>.
'Father worries about grandfather.'

Dziad<u>e</u>k <NOM> **martwi się o ojca** <ACC>.
'Grandfather worries about father.'

3.2 Class

3.2.1 Why "class" and not "gender"?

Class is often traditionally referred to as "gender," but calling class "gender" seems to be imprecise and can be confusing. There is nothing masculine about the noun słoik 'jar' which is considered to be of masculine grammatical gender in Polish, and nothing feminine about the word książka 'book' which is of feminine gender. If kobieta 'woman' is of feminine gender, why is poeta 'poet' of masculine gender even though it ends in -a like kobieta?

"Class" can better highlight the fact that the <u>classification</u> of objects into masculine, feminine, and neuter can be arbitrary and not actually based on gender. "Class" also brings to light that certain words can be grammatically of one gender but semantically of another gender, as well as how the assignment of certain "genders" to words may be due to the fact that certain roles were traditionally held by men—rather than due to anything inherently related to gender.

Dyplomata 'diplomat' has the feminine ending marker -a but is a masculine word in Polish taking masculine complements.

Polish "gender" is further complicated by "subgenders" of masculine animate and masculine inanimate. Referring to these classes as genders is confusing as animacy has nothing to do with gender. The Polish plural paradigm is focused on whether there is a male human as part of the subject—incorporating a focus on gender (male) plus personhood (human), where personhood has nothing to do with gender. "Class" will be used throughout this book to refer to all these divisions and subdivisions that cover imprecise gender divisions and issues beyond gender.

3.2.2 | What is "class"?

Each nominal (a noun, adjective, pronoun, numeral, and/or participle) in its basic form shows class—a division that will classify it as *masculine*, *feminine* or *neuter* (neuter being neither masculine nor feminine). Class can show the corresponding biological gender or gender identity of the words referring to human beings, as well as whether the word references a human being, an animal, or an object. Each noun in Polish belongs to the *masculine*, *feminine* or *neuter* class. The noun is the most important nominal in a phrase, a clause or a sentence, because it imposes the form other modifying nominals will have. (See 3.1.3)

3.2.3 | How is class assigned?

Nouns are classified *masculine*, *feminine* or *neuter* based on two conditions:

the ending in the nominative case (basic form)
the biological gender/gender identity of the noun (applies to nouns referring to human beings only)

The class of loan words that do not refer to human beings can be based on the noun the loan word refers to, e.g., **Pepsi** is feminine, as is **Cola**, however **grizzly** [grizli] is masculine as it refers to the masculine noun **niedźwiedź**, and **sushi** is neuter as it refers to the neuter noun **danie** 'dish' (3.2.9.8).

3.2.4 | The most typical endings in the nominative case

The most typical ending for masculine nouns is: a consonant
The most typical ending for feminine nouns is: -**a**
The most typical endings for neuter nouns are: -**o**, -**e**, and -**ę**
The most typical endings for plural nouns are: -**y** and -**i**

(See 2.4.1)

Here are the examples for each class, based on the specification of the noun's endings:

> masculine: **ten obraz** 'this painting,' **ten stół** 'this table'—all nouns end in a consonant
>
> feminine: **ta książka** 'this book,' **ta fotografia** 'this photograph'—all nouns end in -**a**
>
> neuter: **to łóżko** 'this bed,' **to zdjęcie** 'this picture,' **to imię** 'this first name'—all nouns end in -**o**, -**e**, or -**ę**.

For simplicity this is just an overview of most typical endings in the nominative case (basic case). A more detailed description of the endings for each class follows.

Note that some nouns can have endings other than the typical ones, e.g., both masculine and feminine nouns can end in a soft or "historically" soft consonant.

> **ta kość** 'this bone'
> feminine noun that ends in a soft consonant
>
> **ten gość** 'this guest'
> masculine noun that ends in a soft consonant

A more detailed description of the endings for each class follows (3.2.5).

| 3.2.5 | *Masculine and feminine nouns ending in a consonant* |

The most typical feminine ending is -a, however there is a large group of nouns with soft and "historically" soft final consonants that can be either feminine or masculine. Below please note numerous examples of *feminine and masculine nouns* that end in a consonant.

Masculine

owoc 'fruit'	**grzebień** 'comb'
gość 'guest'	**kosz** 'basket'
paznokieć 'nail'	**paź** 'page'
bicz 'whip'	**ktoś** 'somebody'
nóż 'knife'	**małż** 'a clam'
kurz 'dust'	**ból** 'pain'
pokój 'room'	**bal** 'ball'

baśń 'fairy tale'
brew 'eyebrow'
chorągiew 'banner'
ciecz 'liquid, fluid'
dobroć 'kindness'
gałąź 'branch'
goleń 'shin'
grabież 'plunder'
grań 'ridge'
jabłoń 'apple tree'
kąpiel 'bath'
maść 'ointment'
maź 'gunk'
młodzież 'young people'
mysz 'mouse'
noc 'night'
odzież 'clothes'
oś 'axis'
ość 'fish bone'
otchłań 'abyss'
pamięć 'memory'
paproć 'fern'
pieczęć 'seal'
pieśń 'song'
podróż 'journey'
pomoc 'help'
pościel 'bed linen'

kibić 'waist'
kieszeń 'pocket'
kiść 'bunch, cluster'
klacz 'mare'
kolej 'railway'
kość 'bone'
krawędź 'edge'
krew 'blood'
łódź 'boat'
macierz 'motherland, matrix'
marchew 'carrot'
powieść 'novel'
przyjaźń 'friendship'
rtęć 'mercury'
rzecz 'thing'
sień 'entrance hall'
skroń 'temple'
śmierć 'death'
sól 'salt'
spowiedź 'confession'
stal 'steel'
straż 'guard'
szadź 'hoar frost'
treść 'content'
twarz 'face'
wieś 'countryside'

3.2.6 | Nouns ending in a soft or "historically" soft consonant

One of the ways to help learners to determine whether a noun with a soft or "historically" soft consonant is masculine or feminine is to create a diminutive (emotive form), as emotive forms usually show the class of the original noun.

kieszonka <FEM> <kieszeń <FEM> 'pocket'
grzebyk <MASC> <grzebień <MASC> 'comb'
kostka <FEM> <kość <FEM> 'bone'

| 3.2.7 | **Soft bʲ, pʲ, wʲ, mʲ**

These nouns occur in both the masculine and feminine class. Nouns with hard
p, b, m, w, and soft pʲ, bʲ, mʲ, wʲ, look identical in the nominative singular,
however in all cases other than the nominative singular the soft versions
show *systematic change*, and are declined following *soft-stem* nouns, e.g.,

	Final-stem hard consonants	Final-stem soft consonants
NOM	**kaw-a** 'coffee'	**marchew** 'carrot'
GEN	**kaw-y**	**marchw-i**
INS	**kaw-ą**	**marchw-ią**

In feminine nouns that end in -eś, -ew, the fleeting vowel disappears in all
forms other than the nominative singular (see 1.9).

Uwielbiam sok z marchwi! 'I love carrot juice!'

Table 3.1 Systematic change of feminine nouns with soft consonants

NOM/ACC SG with soft stem	GEN/DAT/LOC/VOC SG with soft stem	NOM: GEN SG with hard stem
chorągiew <FEM>	**chorągwi**	**kawa: kawy**
krew <FEM>	**krwi**	**krowa: krowy**
marchew <FEM>	**marchwi**	**Warszawa: Warszawy**

See the full declension at Table 3.30 (Section 3.3.6.15).

Table 3.2 Systematic change of masculine nouns with soft consonants in
nominative and locative

NOM SG with soft stem	LOC SG with soft stem	NOM: LOC SG with hard stem
ołów <MSC> 'lead'	**ołowiu**	**zlew: zlewie** 'sink'
gołąb <MSC> 'dove'	**gołębiu**	**klub: klubie** 'club'
jedwab <MSC> 'silk'	**jedwabiu**	**chleb: chlebie** 'bread'
drób <MSC> 'poultry'	**drobiu**	**grób: grobie** 'grave'
karp <MSC> 'carp'	**karpiu**	**etap: etapie** 'stage'
Oświęcim <MSC> (city)	**Oświęcimiu**	**album: albumie**
Radom <MSC> (city)	**Radomiu**	**islam: islamie**
Bytom <MSC> (city)	**Bytomiu**	**reżim: reżimie**
Wrocław <MSC> (city)	**we Wrocławiu**	**Kraków: Krakowie**

For full declension see Table 3.10 (Section 3.3.5.10).

Note ó shifts to o with a new syllable, **ołów-ołowiu** and ą shifts to ę: **gołąb-gołębiu** (1.6).

3.2.8 | *Biology wins!*

For nouns referring to human beings *biological gender wins* and the noun is classified as either masculine or feminine even though the noun has an atypical ending for its class.

Here are the examples for nouns having an atypical ending for their class. Because all of the nouns refer to human beings, their class is based on the biological gender—biology wins!

ten mężczyzna 'this man'	masculine noun
ten książę 'this prince'	masculine noun
ten macho 'this macho' (coll.)	masculine noun
ten tata 'this dad'	masculine noun
ta pani 'this woman'	feminine noun

The ending -i in the nominative is common for nouns that refer to a female human being, e.g., **gospodyni** 'host,' **zwyciężczyni turnieju** 'championship's winner.'

Note: The ending -i in nominative singular nouns that do not refer to a female human being is common for neuter nouns that are indeclinable (have one form in all cases), e.g., **to sushi** 'this sushi,' **to spaghetti** 'this spaghetti.' (See 3.8)

3.2.9 | *Class of various nouns*

3.2.9.1 | *Status and titles*

Status and titles of nouns referring to human beings are masculine when referring to a male human being, and feminine when referring to a female human being.

Ten/ta świadek 'this witness [in court]' is classified masculine when referring to a male human being, and feminine when referring to a female human being.

Ten/ta kaleka 'this handicap' is classified masculine when referring to a male human being, and feminine when referring to a female human being.

Ten/ta prezydent 'this president' is classified masculine when referring to a male human being, and feminine when referring to a female human being.

Senator Clinton jest ambitna <FEM>.
'Senator Clinton is ambitious.'

Prezydent Clinton jest ambitny <MSC>.
'President Clinton is ambitious.'

Nouns in this class become indeclinable if they have an ending other than -a when referring to a woman.

Profesor Nowak jest miły <MSC>.
'Professor Nowak is nice.' (Prof. Nowak is a man.)

Profesor Nowak jest miła <FEM>.
'Professor Nowak is nice.' (Prof. Nowak is a woman.)

Rozmawiam z profesorem Nowakiem <MSC>.
'I'm speaking with Profesor Nowak.' (Prof. Nowak is a man.)

Rozmawiam z profesor Nowak <FEM>.
'I'm speaking with Profesor Nowak.' (Prof. Nowak is a woman.)

3.2.9.2 | *First and last names*

First and last names are classified masculine or feminine based on the biological gender or gender identity of the subject the nouns refer to. This can apply to a range of subjects including people, pets, and dolls.

Alex jest mądra.   noun referring to a female
 'Alex is smart.'

Alex jest mądry.   noun referring to a male
 'Alex is smart.'

Frodo jest lojalny.   noun referring to a male
 'Frodo is loyal.'

Margo jest lojalna.   noun referring to a female
 'Margo is loyal.'

Nowak jest chory.   noun referring to a male
 'Nowak is sick.'

Nowak jest chora.   noun referring to a female
 'Nowak is sick.'

Obama jest życzliwa.   noun referring to a female
 'Obama is kind.'

Obama jest życzliwy.   noun referring to a male
 'Obama is kind.'

Nouns in this group become indeclinable when they refer to a female and end in anything other than -a.

Rozmawiam z Alexem   noun referring to a male
  'I'm speaking with Alex.'
Rozmawiam z Alex.   noun referring to a female
  'I'm speaking with Alex.'

Last names of females that have an ending other than -a can be preceded by a title (e.g., **pani** 'Mrs./Ms.,' **profesor** 'professor,' **prezydent** 'president') to indicate the subject is female.

Rozmawiam z panią Nowak. 'I'm speaking with Ms. Nowak.'
Rozmawiam z Nowakiem. 'I'm speaking with [Mr.] Nowak.'

| 3.2.9.3 | *Pejorative and augmentative nouns* |

Pejorative and augmentative (indicating larger size) forms are classified masculine, feminine or neuter based on their ending in the nominative singular case (basic form).

ten babsztyl 'this old hag'   masculine noun **okropny babsztyl**
                              'horrible old hag'
to chłopisko 'this chap'   neuter noun **silne chłopisko**
                              'strong chap'

A pejorative form of male human plural nouns can be formed by adding the ending -y instead of the standard -i or -owie. This form is described as pejorative as it gives the male human group a no male human plural ending. In other words, the male group in the pejorative form has the same plural ending marker as a group of females, animals, or objects. This identifies a perceived difference in status between male human plural and no male human plural, with the former being of higher status. (It is not possible to reverse this formation to create a pejorative plural by adding the male human plural ending to a noun denoting females.)

dobrzy generałowie 'good generals'
beznadziejne generały 'hopeless generals'

pracowici urzędnicy 'hard-working officials'
skorumpowane urzędniki 'corrupt officials'

(See also 3.3.5.9)

| 3.2.9.4 | Diminutive nouns |

Diminutive nouns are classified masculine, feminine or neuter based on the biological gender/gender identity of an individual when referring to human beings.

ten dziadzio 'this grandpa' noun referring to a male human being
ten Zbyszko 'this Zbyszko' noun referring to a male human being
ten wujcio 'this uncle' noun referring to a male human being
but **to miłe dziewczę** neuter noun referring to a female
  'this nice girl' human being

Diminutive nouns are classified masculine, feminine or neuter based on the ending in the basic noun (before being modified) when referring to things and animals.

to zwierzątko 'little animal' **<zwierzę 'animal'** <NT>
ten brzusio 'tummy' **<brzuch 'stomach'** <MSC>

| 3.2.9.5 | Fairy tale characters |

Names of fairy tale characters are classified masculine, feminine or neuter based on the noun ending in the nominative case.

Czerwony Kapturek był w lesie. 'Little Red Riding Hood was in a forest.'
Ten kapturek 'this hood' is a masculine noun.
Kopciuszek był sierotą. 'Cinderella was an orphan' is a masculine noun.

| 3.2.9.6 | Abbreviations and acronyms |

Abbreviations and acronyms are classified masculine, feminine or neuter mostly based on the ending in the nominative case (basic form) of the main noun that was abbreviated.

SLD był *Sojusz* **Lewicy Demokratycznej**
PO była *Platforma* **Obywatelska**
UJ był *Uniwersytet* **Jagielloński**
SGH była *Szkoła* **Główna Handlowa**

3.2.9.7 | Foreign abbreviations and acronyms

Abbreviations and acronyms of foreign words can be classified masculine, feminine or neuter based on the ending of the Polish equivalent of the main noun that was abbreviated in the nominative case, or based on the ending the abbreviation or acronym has.

NATO była feminine form because of the feminine noun
   organizacja, *Organizacja* **Paktu Północnego Atlantyku**
   'North Atlantic Treaty *Organization*'
NATO było (as in **dziecko było,** neuter form)
ONZ był masculine form (rarely feminine **była**) **Organizacja**
   Narodów Zjednoczonych 'UN'

3.2.9.8 | Loan nouns

Loan nouns are invariable (have one form in all cases) when the noun has an atypical ending for its class. Compare: **piję zimną colę** 'I'm drinking a cold cola' (as in **piję zimną wodę** 'I'm drinking cold water') vs. **piję zimną Pepsi** 'I'm drinking a cold Pepsi.' (Pepsi is feminine just like the noun it refers to: **cola** 'cola').

Loan nouns are masculine, feminine or neuter mostly based on the meaning they refer to in Polish.

ten grizzly 'this grizzly'	masculine noun just like the noun it refers to: **niedźwiedź** 'a bear'
ta pepsi 'this pepsi'	feminine noun just like the noun it refers to: **cola** 'cola'
ta brandy 'this brandy'	feminine noun just like the noun it refers to: **wódka** 'vodka'
ta Barbi 'this Barbie'	feminine noun just like the noun it refers to: **lalka** 'doll'

For the class of adjectives as nouns, see 3.6.4.

3.2.10 Social preference

Sometimes there is a disparity between the class the noun is supposed to be in and the way in which the nouns are actually used. It is social preference that decides whether the abbreviation, acronym or a loan word is masculine, feminine or neuter.

WAT by<u>ł</u> masculine	**Wojskowa Akademi<u>a</u> Techniczna**
	'Military and Technical *Academy*'
ASP by<u>ła</u> or **było**	**Akademi<u>a</u> Sztuk Pięknych**
feminine or neuter	'*Academy* of Fine Art'

Miłość type feminine nouns

-ość

Nouns that are derived from adjectives with the ending -ość denote an abstract meaning. They are feminine.

jakość 'quality' <**jaki** 'what's like'
kobiecość 'femininity' <**kobiecy** 'feminine'
liczebność 'number' <**liczebny** 'numerical'
litość 'mercy' <**luty** 'merciful'
męskość 'maleness' <**męski** 'masculine young'
miłość 'love' <**miły** 'dear'
młodość 'youth' <ADJ **młody** 'young'
nowość 'newness' <**nowy** 'new'
radość 'joy' <**rad** 'pleased'
spontaniczność 'spontaneity' <**spontaniczny** 'spontaneous'
starość 'old age' <**stary** 'old'
szybkość 'speed, velocity' <**szybki** 'fast'
wielkość 'size, greatness' <**wielki** 'great'
złość 'anger' <**zły** 'evil'

For the declension pattern of nouns ending in -ość see Table 3.29.

Feminine suffixes -ini/-yni

The suffixes -ini/-yni belong to the suffixes that have the ability to change certain masculine nouns (which have stems ending in a velar (-k, -g, -ch/-h) or "historically soft" consonant) into feminine (compare with the suffixes -ka: aktorka 'actress,' -owa: cesarzowa 'empress'). (See 12.2)

bóg—bogini 'goddess'	**znawca—znawczyni** 'expert'
mistrz—mistrzyni 'champion'	**sprzedawca—sprzedawczyni**
	'salesman'

3.2.13 Indeclinable feminine nouns

A few indeclinable nouns are feminine, e.g., **kakadu** (a type of parrot, **papuga**, which in Polish is of feminine class, based on the semantic (meaning) **kakadu**). (For indeclinable nouns, see 3.2.9.1, 3.2.9.2, 3.2.9.8, 3.3.7.6)

3.2.14 Class variation

Some nouns have an unfixed class or may belong to one class or another depending on their meaning. Class variation presents a rich repertory in Polish. It often has its base in lexical (grammatical), semantic (meaning) or syntactic (how the words fit together in a sentence or a phrase with other words) differences among nouns. While most nouns in Polish have a fixed grammatical class, there is a group that presents a problem not only to learners of Polish, but to Poles as well. Such a situation often results from an influx of new vocabulary in political, economic, and social life.

> **grać w nowego Xboxa** <MSC ANIMATE> 'to play on a new Xbox'
> **grać w nowy Xbox** <MSC INANIMATE> 'to play on a new Xbox'
> **ten piszczel, ta piszczel** 'shinbone'
>
> **Mam złamaną** <ACC> **piszczel** <FEM>. 'I have a broken shinbone.'
> **Mam złamany** <ACC=NOM> **piszczel** <MSC>. 'I have a broken shinbone.'

1. There is a group of identical nouns which have different classes depending on their meaning:

   > **ten boa** <MSC> 'this boa (snake),' **to boa** <NT> 'this boa (shawl)'
   > **ten dorosły kiwi** <MSC> 'this grown kiwi (bird),' **to dojrzałe
   > kiwi** <NT> 'this ripe kiwi (fruit)'
   > **ten żołądź** <MSC> 'acorn,' **ta żołądź** <FEM> 'gland'

2. Augmentative forms (to express a notion of large size) with the affix -isko/-ysko are *neuter* or *masculine*: **chłopisko** 'bloke' <MSC/NT>, **psisko** 'huge dog' <NT>, **kocisko** 'big, fat cat' <NT>, **to paskudne dziewczynisko** 'this nasty girl' (<**dziewczyna** 'girl') <NT>; **wstrętne muszysko** 'disgusting huge fly' (<**mucha** 'fly') <NT>

3. Proper and common nouns referring to male human beings are masculine regardless of the ending, e.g., **Zbyszko** and **Mieszko** (such as in the first ruler of Poland, Mieszko I 'Mieszko the first'), **Fredro** (as in the Polish writer Aleksander Fredro), and **Moniuszko** (as in the composer Stanisław Moniuszko), **Czesio** (<**Czesław** as in Czesław Miłosz), **wujcio** (<**wujek** 'uncle'), **dziadzio** or **dziadunio** 'grandpa' (<**dziadek** 'grandfather'),

papcio, tatunio 'daddy,' **wnusio** 'grandson.' Forms with the affix -**ajło**
are masculine: **rębajło** 'swashbuckler,' **wykidajło** 'bouncer,' **zapiewajło**
'leading singer.'

4. Diminutive forms with -**ątko** added to the animate nouns, which usually
   denote offspring, e.g., **dziewczątko** 'girlie' (<dziewczyna 'girl' <FEM>),
   słoniątko (<słoń 'elephant') <MSC> are *neuter*;
5. Nouns that denote offspring or minors take on the *masculine* class in
   a colloquial form: **cielak** 'calf,' **źrebak** 'foal,' **szczeniak** 'puppy.' The
   suffix -**ak** belongs to the most common suffixes. The change from **cielę**
   'calf' <NT> to **cielak** <MSC> seems to be a natural way for Poles to avoid
   complications with collective numbers, e.g.:

NOM **pięcioro cieląt**   **pięć cielaków** (coll.)
GEN **pięciorga cieląt**   **pięciu cielaków** (coll.)

Cielę declines like **zwierzę** 'animal' (see Table 3.39).

6. Some nouns have alternative forms of class for the semantically
   identical words **ten rodzynek** <MSC> or **ta rodzynka** <FEM> 'rising,'
   ten podkoszulek <MSC>, **ta podkoszulka** <FEM> (coll.) 'undershirt', **ten
   piszczel, ta piszczel** 'shinbone.'
7. Both masculine and feminine class are typical for many nouns that
   denote names of certain professions, ranks, titles and posts, such as
   ambasador 'ambassador,' **mecenas, obrońca** 'defense attorney,' **profesor**
   'professor,' **dziekan** 'dean,' **doktor** 'doctor,' **redaktor** 'editor,' **specjalista**
   'specialist,' **krytyk** 'critic,' **psycholog** 'psychologist,' **komisarz** 'commissar,' **kierowca** 'driver.' Titles, ranks, and professions are not declined
   if they have an ending other than -**a** and are used together with a female
   name.

Rozmawiam z doktor <NOT DECLINED> **Kowalską** <INS>.
  'I'm speaking with Dr. Kowalska.' (a woman)
Rozmawiam z doktorem <INS> **Kowalskim** <INS>. 'I'm speaking
  with Dr. Kowalski.' (a man)

Dzień dobry Pani <VOC> **Profesor!** <NOT DECLINED>
  'Hello Professor!' (addressing a woman)
Dzień dobry Panie <VOC> **Profesorze!** <VOC> 'Hello Professor!'
  (addressing a man)

3.2.15 Class divisions

The table below shows a breakdown of the classes of nouns.

Table 3.3 Class divisions

Singular	Plural
1 Masculine animate (SG only) • Accusative = Genitive	5 Male human (PL only) • Accusative = Genitive • Plural nouns and adjectives have **-i/-y** ending plus <u>consonant shift</u> • Plural verbal ending **-li**
ten student 'this student' **widzę <u>tego studenta</u>** <ACC=GEN> 'I see this student'	**ci studen<u>ci</u> przyszli** 'these students came' **widzę <u>tych studentów</u>** <ACC=GEN> 'I see these students'
	NO MALE HUMAN (PL only) • Accusative = Nominative • adjectives end in **-e** in NOM PL without consonant shift • Plural verbal ending **-ły**
	6 No male human plural – MSC
ten kogut 'this rooster' **widzę <u>tego koguta</u>** <ACC=GEN> 'I see this rooster'	**te koguty przyszły** 'these roosters came' **widzę <u>te koguty</u>** <ACC=NOM> 'I see these roosters'
2 Masculine inanimate (SG only) • Accusativie = Nominative **ten portret** 'this portret' **widzę <u>ten portret</u>** <ACC=NOM> 'I see this portrait'	**te portrety tam były** 'these portraits were there' **widzę <u>te portrety</u>** <ACC=NOM> 'I see these portraits'
3 Feminine singular **ta matka** 'this mother' **widzę tę matkę** 'I see this mother'	7 No male human plural – FEM **te matki przyszły** 'these mothers came' **widzę <u>te matki</u>** <ACC=NOM> 'I see these mothers'
ta krowa 'this cow' **widzę tę krowę** 'I see this cow'	**te krowy przyszły** 'these cows came' **widzę <u>te krowy</u>** <ACC=NOM> 'I see these cows'
4 Neuter singular **to dziecko** 'this child' **widzę to dziecko** 'I see this child'	8 No male human plural – NT **te dzieci przyszły** 'these children came' **widzę <u>te dzieci</u>** <ACC=NOM> 'I see these children'

Feminine and neuter nouns are not affected by the distinction between animate and inanimate nouns.

3.2.16 Male human and no male human plural

While the category of animacy among masculine nouns is the determining factor for the accusative endings in the singular (see 3.3.5.2), in the plural it is the category of "male human." One scholar of Polish has referred to this classification as: "men—rest of the universe" ("mężczyźni—reszta uniwersum").[1] Plural nouns that refer to groups of at least one male human, e.g. **ojcowie** 'fathers,' **bracia** 'brothers,' **chłopcy** 'boys,' **mężczyźni** 'men,' **poeci** 'poets,' **ludzie** 'people,' have *accusative* endings that are the same as in *genitive*.

All other plural nouns that do not refer to male human beings, or that do not have at least one male human in the group—the "no male human" class (masculine no human, feminine, neuter)—have an ending in the *accusative plural* that is the same as that in the *nominative plural*. Put simply, male human plural has ACC=GEN and no male human plural has ACC=NOM.

The table below shows how masculine, feminine, and neuter nouns are affected by the distinction between nouns that do and do not refer to male humans, or to a group with at least one male human being. Note that **dzieci** 'children' and **osoby** 'persons' both take no male human plural forms. (See 5.2.4.1 and 6.5.2.2)

Table 3.4 Male human and no male human plural nouns

Masculine		
NOM PL	ACC PL	GEN PL
ci **ludzie** 'these people'	tych **ludzi**	tych **ludzi**
ci **ojcowie** 'these fathers'	tych **ojców**	tych **ojców**
ci **mężczyźni** 'these men'	tych **mężczyzn**	tych **mężczyzn**
te **koguty** 'these roosters'	te **koguty**	tych **kogutów**
te **notesy** 'these notebooks'	te **notesy**	tych **notesów**

Feminine		
NOM PL	ACC PL	GEN PL
te **osoby** 'these persons'	te **osoby**	tych **osób**
te **mapy** 'these maps'	te **mapy**	tych **map**
te **matki** 'these mothers'	te **matki**	tych **matek**
te **gospodynie** 'these hostesses'	te **gospodynie**	tych **gospodyń**
te **kury** 'these hens'	te **kury**	tych **kur**
te **myszy** 'these mice'	te **myszy**	tych **myszy**

Neuter		
NOM PL	ACC PL	GEN PL
te **dzieci** 'these children'	te **dzieci**	tych **dzieci**
te **szczenięta** 'these puppies'	te **szczeniąt**	tych **szczeniąt**
te **biura** 'these offices'	te **biura**	tych **biur**
te **muzea** 'these museums'	te **muzea**	tych **muzeów**

3.2.17 | Modifiers with male human and no male human plural

Male human plural noun phrases as subjects take the plural verbal ending -li.

mężczyźni byli 'men were'

No male human plural phrases as subjects take the plural verbal ending -ły.

kobiety i dzieci były 'women and children were'

Nominals that modify male human plural nouns (adjectives, pronouns, ordinal numbers) in the nominative and vocative cases have the ending -i/-y **plus consonant shift**. Nominals that modify no male human plural nouns in the nominative and vocative cases have ending the ending -e (with no corresponding consonant shift).

Ci pracowici mężczyźni byli pierwsi na wiecu.
'These hard-working men were the first at the rally.'

Te pracowite kobiety i dzieci były pierwsze na wiecu.
'These hard-working women and children were the first at the rally.'

The predictable consonant shifts that occur with male human plural forms are described at 1.3.4.

For male human plural adjectives see 4.6.

For male human pronouns see 5.4.7.2 and 5.5.

See also 5.2.4.1 for use of the words **osoby** 'persons,' **ludzie** 'people,' and **dzieci** 'children.'

Exceptionally, when a female human and a masculine animal are the subjects of a sentence, the whole phrase takes a male human plural form.

Dziewczynka i pies bawili się w parku. 'A girl and a dog were playing in the park.'
Dziewczynki i psy bawili się w parku. 'The girls and dogs were playing in the park.'

Krasnoludki 'dwarfs,' **smerfy** 'smurfs,' **skrzaty** 'goblins,' **elfy** 'elves,' **chochliki** 'imps' and other fictional characters are treated as "no male human": **krasnoludki były** (not **byli**) along with emotive nouns denoting children (not fully developed male human beings) like **urwis(y)**, **łobuz(y) był(y)** (not **byli**) 'rascal(s), hooligan(s) were.'

993 <u>kobiety</u> <no male human form> **<u>były</u>** <no male human form>
na wiecu wyborczym.

'993 <u>women</u> <u>were</u> at an election rally.'

993 <u>kobiety</u> <no male human form> **i jeden mężczyzna** <male human form>
<u>byli</u> <male human form> **na wiecu wyborczym.**

'993 <u>women</u> and <u>one man</u> <u>were</u> at an election rally.'

3.3 Declension patterns

In the singular, the main declension patterns for nouns are: masculine animate, masculine inanimate, feminine, and neuter. In the plural the main declension patterns for nouns are: male human plural and no male human plural (with no male human plural patterns subdivided into masculine, feminine, and neuter).

3.3.1 Nouns following masculine pattern

The following nouns are declined according to the masculine pattern:

- singular common masculine nouns that end in a consonant in the nominative singular: **dom** 'home,' **stół** 'table';
- singular common nouns that refer to a male human being, e.g., **dziadek** 'grandfather,' **książę** 'prince';
- proper nouns that refer to a male human being that end in a consonant, e.g., **Jan** 'John' or the vowel -o, e.g., **Zbyszk<u>o</u>** (first name), **Carl<u>o</u>** (first name), **Canalett<u>o</u>** (last name), **Pacino** (last name) (except for last names that end in -ko, e.g., **Matejko**, and -a, e.g., **Obama**),
- singular diminutive nouns created from masculine nouns, e.g., **dom<u>ek</u>** 'little house,' **stol<u>ik</u>** 'coffee table,' **dziadzi<u>o</u>** 'grandpa,' **piesi<u>o</u>** <pies 'doggy,' **brzusi<u>o</u>** <brzuch 'tummy.'

Note: Singular common and proper nouns referring to male human beings with the ending -a in the nominative singular, e.g., **mężczyzna** 'man,' **poeta** 'poet,' **Obama** are declined in the singular according to the feminine singular pattern and in the plural according to the male human plural pattern.

Common adjectival masculine nouns, e.g., **narzeczony** 'fiancé' are declined according to the masculine adjectival pattern, and proper adjectival nouns (first and last names) referring to a male human being, e.g., **Zachary**, **Hillary** (e.g., Edmund Hillary), are declined according to the masculine adjectival pattern (3.6.4).

Plural masculine nouns, e.g., **domy** 'houses,' that do not refer to a male human being share significant overlap with all other nouns that do not refer to a male human being—the so-called *no male human* plural pattern. Additionally, these no male human plural nouns all take the same modifiers (the same adjectival plural declensions and the plural verbal ending **-ly**) regardless of whether they are masculine, feminine, or neuter.

For a description of the no male human plural pattern, see section 3.3.9. For charts with examples of the full declension of nouns following the masculine patterns, see Tables 3.8 to 3.19.

Plural masculine nouns referring to a male human being in the plural have a distinct pattern—the so-called *male human* plural pattern. Plural masculine nouns referring to male human beings with the ending -a, e.g., **mężczyzna** 'man,' **poeta** 'poet,' **kierowca** 'driver,' and proper nouns (first and last names) that refer to male human beings with the endings -a and -ko, e.g., **Kucia, Wałęsa, Matejko** are declined according to the male human plural pattern.

3.3.2 *Nouns following feminine pattern*

The following nouns are declined according to the feminine pattern:

- singular common feminine nouns with the ending -a: **mama** 'mom,' **książka** 'book.'
- singular common feminine nouns with soft and "historically" soft consonants: **rzecz** 'thing,' **miłość** 'love'
- singular common nouns referring to a female human being: **pani** 'Mrs./ Ms./you <SG>' (respectful form of address), **gospodyni** 'hostess'
- singular masculine nouns referring to male human beings with ending -a e.g., **mężczyzna** 'man,' **poeta** 'poet,' **kierowca** 'driver,' and proper nouns (first and last names) that refer to male human beings with the endings -a (case for both first and last names) and -ko (case for last names), e.g., **Alosza** (first name), **Obama** (last name), **Matejko** (last name). First names ending with -(k)o, e.g., **Janko, Pedro,** are declined according to the masculine pattern.

Plural feminine nouns share the pattern with all nouns that do not refer to a male human being—the so-called no male human plural pattern. For the no male human plural pattern, see section 3.3.9.

Plural masculine nouns referring to male human beings with the nominative singular ending -a, e.g., **mężczyzna** 'man,' **poeta** 'poet,' **kierowca** 'driver,' and proper nouns (first and last names) that refer to male human beings with the endings -a and -ko in nominative singular, e.g., **Kucia, Wałęsa, Matejko** are declined in the plural according to the male human plural pattern.

For charts with examples of the full declension of nouns following the feminine pattern, refer to Tables 3.20 to 3.32.

3.3.3 | Nouns following neuter pattern

The following nouns are declined according to the neuter pattern

• neuter nouns with the nominative singular endings -o, -ę, -e and -um

Note: Loan words with the ending -um, e.g., **muzeum, akwarium, stypendium** have the nominative form in all cases in the singular. In the plural however neuter nouns with the ending -um have different endings in all cases. Nouns ending with -um in nominative singular can be neuter or masculine. The small group of masculine nouns with -um includes: **szum** 'noise,' **tłum** 'crowd,' **album** 'album,' **kostium** 'suit,' **rozum** 'mind, reason.' Masculine nouns with the ending -um decline similarly to **bursztyn** 'amber' (see Table 3.11a).

3.3.4 | Plural

Plural nouns are declined according to two patterns:

> male human plural pattern
> no male human plural pattern

All plural nouns that refer to a male human being are declined according to the male human plural pattern.

This also means that nouns like **mężczyzna** 'man,' **poeta** 'poet,' **kierowca** 'driver' which are declined in the singular according to the feminine pattern, are declined in the plural according to the male human plural pattern. Adjectival nouns referring to male human beings, e.g., **narzeczeni** 'engaged couple' are declined according to the male human plural pattern.

All plural nouns other than those referring to a male human being are declined according to the no male human plural pattern.

3.3.4.1 | *Pattern for male human plural and no male human plural forms*

The charts below show the differences in treating nouns in the plural—the male human plural pattern and the no male human plural pattern. Note the systematic changes in the accusative and genitive cases, and the distribution of the demonstrative pronouns **ci** vs. **te** in the nominative plural. (See 3.2.16)

Table 3.5 Nouns that refer to male human beings

NOM SG	NOM PL	ACC PL =	GEN PL
ten chłopiec 'the boy'	<u>ci</u> **chłopcy**	**tych chłopców**	**tych chłopców**
ten narrator 'narrator'	<u>ci</u> **narratorzy**	**tych narratorów**	**tych narratorów**
ten mężczyzna 'the man'	<u>ci</u> **mężczyźni**	**tych mężczyzn**	**tych mężczyzn**
ten brat 'the brother'	<u>ci</u> **bracia**	**tych braci**	**tych braci**
ten ojciec 'the father'	<u>ci</u> **ojcowie**	**tych ojców**	**tych ojców**
ten człowiek 'the man'	<u>ci</u> **ludzie**	**tych ludzi**	**tych ludzi**

Table 3.6 Nouns that do not refer to male human beings

NOM SG	NOM PL	ACC PL =	GEN PL
ten dzieciak 'the kid' (coll.)	<u>te</u> **dzieciaki**	**te dzieciaki**	**tych dzieciaków**
ten pies 'the dog'	<u>te</u> **psy**	**te psy**	**tych psów**
ten dom 'the house'	<u>te</u> **domy**	**te domy**	**tych domów**
ta kobieta 'the woman'	<u>te</u> **kobiety**	**te kobiety**	**tych kobiet**
ta mapa 'the map'	<u>te</u> **mapy**	**te mapy**	**tych map**
ta osoba 'the person'	<u>te</u> **osoby**	**te osoby**	**tych osób**
to dziecko 'the child'	<u>te</u> **dzieci**	**te dzieci**	**tych dzieci**
to biuro 'the office'	<u>te</u> **biura**	**te biura**	**tych biur**

Table 3.7 Consonant shifts in male human plural

NOM SG	NOM MHPL	NOM SG	NOM no-MHPL
ten Wło<u>ch</u> 'this Italian'	**ci Wło<u>si</u>** 'Italians'	**ten da<u>ch</u>** 'this roof'	**te dach<u>y</u>** 'roofs'
ten Pola<u>k</u> 'this Pole'	**ci Pola<u>cy</u>** 'Poles'	**ten pta<u>k</u>** 'this bird'	**te ptak<u>i</u>** 'birds'

Masculine singular

Masculine declension pattern—animacy and humans

Masculine declension patterns are based on what the noun phrase refers to (a male human being, a male animal or an object that ends in a consonant), and on the stem-final consonant in the nominative case. (See 3.1.4.1)

Nouns classed as masculine based on what they refer to are:

animate (referring to living beings and divided further into human and non-human)

- male human (referring to a male human being): **dziadek** 'grandpa'
- non-human (referring to an animal): **kot** 'cat'

inanimate (referring to an object): **telefon** 'phone'

Type of the final-stem consonant in the nominative case:

1. **k, g, ch/h**—also called *velar*
2. **c, dz, sz, ż, rz, cz, dż**—also called *"historically" soft*
3. **ś, ć, ź, dź, ń, l, bi, pi, mi, wi, j**—also called *soft*
4. all other consonants (**b, p, f, w, m, ł, t, d, s, z, n, r**)—also called *hard*

For the declension patterns in the plural, see the male human plural overview at 3.3.8 and the no male human plural overview at 3.3.9.

Masculine singular pattern overview

NOM *consonant* (rarely **-o**)
ACC animate nouns: = GEN **-a**
 inanimate nouns: = NOM (see 3.3.5.3.1)
GEN animate nouns: **-a** (except for **woł-u** 'ox,' **bawoł-u** 'buffalo')
 inanimate nouns: **-u/-a** (see 3.3.5.3.2 and 3.3.5.5 to 3.3.5.7)
DAT **-owi/-u** (see 3.3.5.3.3 and 3.3.5.8)
LOC **-'e/-u** (see 3.3.5.3.4, 3.3.5.3.5)
INS **-em/-iem** (see 3.3.5.3.6, 3.3.5.3.7)
VOC **-e/-u** (see 3.3.5.3.8)

Note: The LOC ending **'e** denotes that the preceding consonant(s) become palatalized (see 1.3.4, 1.3.5).

For charts with examples of the full declension of masculine nouns, refer to Tables 3.8 to 3.19.

3.3.5.3 | Masculine pattern endings

3.3.5.3.1 | Masculine accusative inanimate singular -a

-a is the ending in accusative masculine inanimate singular nouns not determined by the final consonant but rather by other factors: -a is the ending with many grammatically masculine food, drink, vehicles, currencies, dances, tobacco and technology products, e.g., **jem pączka** <ACC=GEN> 'I eat a donut' but **jem obiad** <ACC=NOM> 'I am eating lunch,' **przerwa na papierosa** <ACC=GEN> 'smoke break,' **przerwa na obiad** <ACC=NOM> 'lunch break' (3.3.5.4).

3.3.5.3.2 | Masculine genitive inanimate singular -u

-u/-a endings in the genitive case for inanimate masculine nouns are not determined by the final consonant but rather by other factors: **nie ma parasola** 'there is no umbrella' but **nie mam spadochronu** 'I don't have a parachute.' (see 3.3.5.5)

3.3.5.3.3 | Masculine dative singular -owi/-u

-owi is the predominant ending (3.3.5.8).

-u is the ending in the dative singular for some masculine nouns, e.g., **pan-u** 'you' (formal way of address), **brat-u** 'brother,' **ojc-u** 'father,' **chłop-u** 'peasant,' **chłopc-u** 'boy,' **ps-u** 'dog,' **kot-u** 'cat,' **diabł-u** 'devil' but **męż-owi** 'husband.' Note that for the same nouns the genitive/accusative ending is -a, e.g., **ojciec** <NOM>, **ojca** <ACC/GEN>, **ojcu** <DAT> (by contrast **ząb, dom** have dative **zębowi, domowi,** with accusative identical to nominative).

3.3.5.3.4 | Masculine locative singular -u

-e/-u endings in the locative case are determined by the stem-final consonant.

-u in the locative is the ending after velar, soft and "historically" soft-stem nouns (ć, ś, ń, ź, dź before a vowel shift to ci, si, ni, ź, dzi (1.3.3.2).

3.3.5.3.5 | Masculine locative singular -'e

-'e in the locative is the ending after hard-stem nouns. Systematic stem changes occur, and the hard consonant undergoes softening: -i follows the consonant, or the consonant shifts, e.g., **klub-klubie, bar-barze** (1.3.5, 1.3.4) (exceptions: **w domu** 'at home', **o panu** 'about you' (respectful form of address), **o synu** 'about [my] son.'

See 3.10 for examples of locative case consonant and vowel changes within the singular locative case for masculine, feminine and neuter nouns to illustrate the process of *palatalization*.

3.3.5.3.6 | Masculine instrumental singular -iem

-iem in the instrumental is the ending after **k, g** and soft stems (except for **l, j**)

pisać ołówkiem (1.3.5.1)

Note the systematic changes where the soft stem ć, ś, ń, ź, dź shifts to ci, si, ni, zi, dzi before a vowel (1.3.3.2), e.g., **koń-koniem**.

3.3.5.3.7 | Masculine instrumental singular -em

-em in the instrumental is the ending after **ch/h, l, j**, "historically" soft, and hard stems.

3.3.5.3.8 | Masculine vocative singular -u

-e/-u endings in the vocative are as in the locative (except for a few nouns that end in -iec, as in **ojciec**: *ojcze*, **chłopiec**: *chłopcze*, **skąpiec**: *skąpcze* or *skąpcu*).

-u is the ending in the vocative after velar, soft and "historically" soft stems: **dziadku, dziadziu, dziaduniu** 'grandpa' <diminutives>. A fleeting vowel occurs in many nouns, e.g., **dziadek-dziadku** (1.9).

3.3.5.4 | Accusative and genitive with food, drink, vehicles, currencies, dances, tobacco and technology

The accusative case of masculine inanimate singular objects normally has the same ending as the nominative. However, there are many semantically inanimate nouns in the masculine singular, particularly, drink, vehicles, currencies, dances, tobacco and technology products, that follow the pattern of masculine animate singular nouns (such as 'dog': **pies** <NOM>, **psa** <ACC>, **psa** <GEN>) taking the genitive ending for the accusative singular -a.

The reason for this is the nouns are perceived as being impacted partially, in the meaning of "some," and temporarily (not eternally), which is a general characteristic of using the genitive endings in the accusative case, e.g., **sąsiad dostał list** <ACC> '[my] neighbor got a letter' and **sąsiad dostał zawału** <ACC> '[my] neighbor had a heart attack.' "This is a growing category; any masculine count noun with genitive singular in *a* is a potential member." (Comrie and Corbett, 2002)

Mam pysznego <ACC> **pączka** <ACC>. 'I have a tasty donut.'
Jem gofra <ACC>. 'I'm eating a waffle.'
pić szampana <ACC>. 'to drink champagne'
Pali papierosa <ACC> **za papierosem** <INS>. 'He smokes one cigarette after another.'
Jem pomidora <ACC>. 'I am eating a tomato.'
Zapłaciłam jednego dolara <ACC>. 'I paid one dollar.'
Lubię tańczyć walca <ACC>. 'I like to dance a waltz.'
Kupiłem mercedesa <ACC>. 'I bought a Mercedes.'

| 3.3.5.5 | Endings **-u**/**-a** *in genitive singular masculine inanimate nouns* |

| 3.3.5.5.1 | Ending **-u** |

Masculine inanimate nouns mostly take the ending -u when they denote:

concepts (connected with human perception)

czasu 'time,' **bólu** 'pain,' **smutku** 'sorrow,' **spokoju** 'peace,' **strajku** 'strike,' **widoku** 'view,' **zapachu** 'smell,' **smaku** 'taste,' **szacunku** 'respect,' **hałasu** 'noise,' **wiatru** 'wind,' **śniegu** 'snow,' **deszczu** 'rain,' **wschodu** 'east';

loan words

handlu 'trade,' **Holokaustu** 'Holocaust,' **stresu** 'stress,' **gotyku** 'gothic,' **filmu** 'film,' **terroryzmu** 'terrorism,' **komunizmu** 'communism';

(temporal) illness

kaszlu 'cough,' **kataru** 'runny nose,' **okresu** 'period';

non-countable nouns (mass nouns, that can be quantified in units of measurment and counted, but the noun itself cannot be counted);

materials and liquids

> **kleju** 'glue,' **oleju** 'oil,' **papieru** 'paper,' **gipsu** 'plaster,' **materiału** 'fabric,' **jedwabiu** 'silk,' **cukru** 'sugar,' **piasku** 'sand,' **gazu** 'gas,' **prądu** 'electricity,' **soku** 'juice,' **tlenu** 'oxygen,' **tuszu** 'ink,' **długopisu** 'pen,' **budyniu** 'pudding,' **bigosu** 'Polish dish with cabbage and meat,' **ryżu** 'rice,' **sosu** 'sauce' and their diminutive forms;

spices

> **pieprzu** 'pepper,' **cynamonu** 'cinnamon,' **imbiru** 'ginger,' **kopru** 'dill';

days of the week

> **piątku** 'Friday,' **wtorku** 'Tuesday,' **czwartku** 'Thursday';

means of transportation

> **pociągu** 'train,' **autobusu** 'bus,' **samolotu** 'plane,' **samochodu** 'car,' **tramwaju** 'street car,' **statku** 'ship,' **roweru** 'bike,' **motoru** 'motorcycle';

buildings

> **budynku** 'building,' **gmachu** 'edifice,' **sejmu, bloku, schronu** 'bunker,' **przystanku** 'bus stop,' **basenu** 'pool,' **hotelu** 'hotel' but **wieżowca** 'skyscraper,' **biurowca** 'office block';

cities other than Polish ones

> **Waszyngtonu, Londynu, Madrytu** but **Paryża, Berlina, Wiednia**;

nouns with the ending -**unek**

> **gatunku** 'type,' **rysunku** 'drawing,' **rachunku** 'check';

nouns transmitting information or sounds

> **faksu** 'fax,' **aparatu** 'apparatus, camera,' **telefonu** 'telephone,' **domofonu** 'intercom,' **automatu** 'payphone, vending machine,' **instrumentu** 'instrument,' **kontrabasu** 'double bass,' **fortepianu** 'piano,' **klawesynu** 'harpsichord.'

3.3.5.5.2 | Ending -**a**

Masculine inanimate nouns mostly take the ending -*a* when they denote:

some/a piece of food

> **chleba** 'bread,' **sera** 'cheese,' **arbuza** 'watermelon' (but **tortu** 'cake') and their diminutives **serka** 'cheese <DIM>';

concrete countable objects and gestures

> **języka** 'tongue,' **koca** 'blanket,' **telewizora** 'TV,' **stolika** 'coffee table,' **całusa** 'kiss,' **buziaka** 'kiss,' and their diminutives;

tools

> **kija** 'stick,' **pędzla** 'brush,' **słupa** 'pole,' **komputera** 'computer,' **słownika** 'dictionary';

months

> **maja** 'May,' **grudnia** 'December,' etc. except for **luty:lutego** (declines like adjective);

measurement units

> **centa, funta, kilograma, metra, hektara, dolara**;

most parts of the body

> **palca** 'finger,' **paznokcia** 'nail,' **zęba** 'tooth,' **nosa** 'nose,' **kciuka** 'thumb,' **brzucha** 'stomach,' but **bark-u** 'shoulder,' **kark-u** 'nape';

cities with a suffix -urg, -uk

> **Hamburga** (analogous to **chirurga** <GEN MSC SG> 'surgeon'), **Petersburga, Insbruka, Edynburga, Strasburga**;

nouns with an ending -nik

> **czajnika** 'kettle,' **chodnika** 'rug';

nouns that end with -iec

> **tańca** (analogous to **chłopca** <GEN MSC SG> 'a guy') 'dance,' **sińca** 'bruise,' **końca** 'end.'

| 3.3.5.5.3 | Endings **-u/-a** |

A few masculine inanimate nouns have two endings, which signalize a change in the meaning of the noun: **-u** (for a conceptual meaning) and **-a** (for a figurative meaning):

> **wieczor-u** 'soiree' and **wieczor-a** 'evening, part of the day'
> **od rana do wieczora** 'from morning till night,' and **miłego wieczoru** 'Have a nice evening.'
> **przypadk-a** 'case,' as in **mianownik-a, przypadk-u** 'chance': **od przypadku do przypadku** 'now and then'
> **światu** and **świata**
> **ulica Nowego Światu** (street name in Warsaw) and **Nowego świata nie będzie** 'There won't be a new world.'
> **tłok-u** 'crowd' **tłok-a** 'piston'
> **zamku** 'castle' **zamka** 'lock, zipper'

3.3.5.6 | Conclusion on the distribution of -a and -u, in the inanimate genitive case in singular

This conclusion draws on the one presented in the book: *A Study in Polish Morphology: The Genitive Singular Masculine* by Stanisław Westfal, 1956.

3.3.5.6.1 | Ending -a

-a is used when the noun in form/shape/size relates to a human size (able to cover it but "must not exceed the size of man/animal"). Nouns with an ending -a have four points of resemblance to humans:

1. form/shape
2. size, "must not exceed the size of man/animal" and "there is no lower limit"
3. "essentially definite character of form/shape: whatever deserves -a, must be of a definite form/shape"
4. "whatever moves, is likely to take (the mobility) -a, even though the size exceeds the upper limit."[2]

Examples:

> **szlafrok** 'robe'—**szlafroka** "the essential form/shape is that which the dressing gown acquires whenever worn by man, *with* the man wrapped up with it."[3]
>
> **fotel** 'armchair'—**fotela** but **tron** 'throne' **tronu** (exceeds the size of man/animal)
>
> **chodnik** 'rug'—**chodnika** but **dywan** 'carpet'—**dywanu** (exceeds the size of man/animal)
>
> **parasol** 'umbrella'—**parasola** but **spadochron** 'parachute'—**spadochronu** (exceeds the size of man/animal)

3.3.5.7 | Social preference of -a/-u

Usage of the ending -a or -u for genitive singular masculine inanimate nouns is often dictated by social preference. In many nouns it is not either -a or -u; it is both, e.g., **tapczanu** 'futon' or **tapczana**, **krawatu** 'tie' or **krawata**.

In agreement with Westfal's conclusions "whatever moves, is likely to take (the mobility) -a," loan words have the ending -a, e.g., **nie mam laptopa, Xboxa, premiera iPoda w Polsce, operator iPhone'a w Polsce** but **wydarzenia empiku**, like **budynku** (exceeds the size of man/animal).

| 3.3.5.8 | When the underdog wins: ending **-owi** in dative masculine singular |

Because the ending -**u** can be the ending in the locative, e.g., **o mężu** 'about a husband,' **o wilku** 'about a wolf,' and in the genitive, e.g., **miodu** 'honey,' the more distinctive ending -**owi** expanded and became the predominant ending in the masculine dative singular instead of -**u**, e.g., **mężowi** 'husband,' **wilkowi** 'wolf.' In Proto-Slavic the forms of **mąż** and **wilk** had the ending -**u**.[4]

-U is the ending in the dative singular for a few masculine nouns, e.g., **pan-u** 'you' (formal way of address), **brat-u** 'brother,' **ojc-u** 'father,' **chłop-u** 'peasant,' **chłopc-u** 'boy,' **ps-u** 'dog,' **kot-u** 'cat,' **diabł-u** 'devil,' **ksiądz-u** 'priest,' but **męż-owi** 'husband.' Note that for the same nouns the genitive/ accusative ending is -**a**, e.g., **ojciec** <NOM>, **ojca** <ACC/GEN>, **ojcu** <DAT>.

Social preference means that for some nouns both endings are used, e.g., **orł-u/orł-owi** 'eagle.'

| 3.3.5.9 | Male human plural emotive nouns |

Some male human plural emotive nouns (with an emotional tinge) show inflectional behavior similar to no male human plural nouns, e.g., *te* **domy** 'these houses'—*te* **łobuzy** 'these rascals' instead of **ci łobuzi** like **ci mężczyźni**. The process is to show depreciation of the noun, and makes the noun colloquial in meaning. When the nouns are used in non-emotive language, e.g., **ci łobuzi**, they are declined like male human plural nouns (see 3.2.9.3).

Compare:

> **Ach te chłopy!** (coll.) or **Ach ci chłopi!** 'O! Those guys!'
> **Zdrowe chłopaki wróciły z treningu** (coll.) or **Zdrowi chłopcy wrócili z treningu.** 'The healthy boys are coming back from [their] training.'

Sometimes the change brings new stylistically charged language, like in *Wesele* "Wedding" by Wyspiański, a conversation between a master, **pan**, and a peasant. The regular form for Chinese is **Chińczycy**, but the author decided to use **Chińczyki** to undermine the language of the peasant:

> **Cóż tam, panie, w polityce?** 'Well, sir, what's new in politics?'
> **Chińczyki trzymają się mocno!?** '[The] Chinese hold on tight!?'
> Stanisław Wyspiański, *Wesele*

Other examples of masculine emotionally charged nouns:

te dzikusy or **ci dzikusi** 'these loners'
te dziwaki or **ci dziwacy** 'these weirdoes'
te huligany or **ci huliganie** 'these hooligans'
te lenie or **ci lenie** 'these lazybones' GEN **tych leniów** (only about men) or **leni**
te lesery or **ci leserzy** 'these goof-offs'
te łobuzy or **ci łobuzi** 'these rascals'
te wałkonie or **ci wałkonie** (either a female or a male) 'these loafers'
te wariaty or **ci wariaci** 'these madmen'

With some, the no male human plural form is the (almost) only possible one: **te grubasy** 'these fat people (coll.).'

| 3.3.5.10 | *Masculine noun tables*

In Tables 3.8 to 3.19 note that singular animate masculine nouns that end in a consonant have the same ending in the accusative case as in the genitive while singular inanimate masculine nouns have the same ending in the accusative as that in the nominative.

ACC = NOM for singular masculine inanimate nouns
ACC = GEN for singular masculine animate nouns
LOC = VOC for singular masculine nouns ending in a consonant

Exceptions to that rule are explained in detail in 3.3.5, e.g.,

jem pączka <ACC> 'I'm eating a doughnut' (3.3.5.4)
Nie ma kija <GEN> 'I don't have a stick' and **nie ma kleju** <GEN> 'I don't have any glue' (3.3.5.5)

The tables below show masculine pattern and male human plural pattern nouns with a stem-final consonant in the nominative singular, where the stem-final consonant is:

1. k, g, ch/h—also called *velar* (see Tables 3.8 to 3.8e)
2. c, dz, sz, ż, rz, cz, dż—also called "*historically*" *soft* (see Tables 3.9 to 3.9d)
3. ś, ć, ź, dź, ń, l, bʲ, mʲ, wʲ, pʲ, j—also called *soft* (see Tables 3.10 to 3.10f)
4. all other consonants (b, p, f, w, m, ł, t, d, s, z, n, r)—also called *hard*

They also show:

5. the ending -*anin*: **Amerykanin** 'American,' **Rosjanin** 'Russian'
6. *the fleeting vowel*: **ojciec** 'father,' **poseł** 'MP,' **pies** 'dog,' **dzień** 'day,' **tydzień** 'week,' **budynek** 'building,' **widelec** 'fork'
7. the nasal vowel -ą in the penultimate position: **mąż** 'husband,' **wąż** 'snake,' **błąd** 'mistake,' **ząb** 'tooth'
8. irregular forms: **człowiek** 'human, man,' **ludzie** 'human beings, people,' **brat** 'brother' and **bracia** 'brothers'
9. the irregular declension **książę** 'duke,' **ksiądz** 'priest'
10. the ending -o in the nominative singular in emotive nouns: **dziadzio** 'grandpa,' **Henio** (first male name diminutive), **piesio** 'doggy,' **brzusio** 'tummy'
11. proper nouns with the ending -o (except for last names in -**ko**), e.g., **Pedro** (first name), **Canaletto** (last name)
12. the ending -**izm**

1. Velar stem

In the instrumental singular, final-stem velar nouns with **k**, **g** have the ending -**iem** (not just -**em**).

In the locative final-stem velar nouns take -**u**.

Predictable consonant shifts occur in nominative plural nouns referring to a male human being: **k:cy, g:dzy, ch:si.**

Table 3.8 Masculine nouns with velar stem

Case	Singular	Plural	Singular	Plural
NOM	**Polak** 'Pole'	**Polac-y**	**biolog** 'biologist'	**biolodz-y** or **biolog-owie**
ACC	**Polak-a**	**Polak-ów**	**biolog-a**	**biolog-ów**
GEN	**Polak-a**	**Polak-ów**	**biolog-a**	**biolog-ów**
DAT	**Polak-owi**	**Polak-om**	**biolog-owi**	**biolog-om**
LOC	**Polak-u**	**Polak-ach**	**biolog-u**	**biolog-ach**
INS	**Polak-iem**	**Polak-ami**	**biolog-iem**	**biolog-ami**
VOC	**Polak-u**	**Polac-y**	**biolog-u**	**biolodz-y**

Note: Many nouns that denote professions end with -(lo)g and decline like **biolog**:

filolog 'philologist' **pedagog** 'teacher'
ginekolog 'gynecologist' **psycholog** 'psychologist'
kardiolog 'cardiologist' **teolog** 'theologian'

Many nouns that denote professions end with -ik/-yk. **Anglik** 'Englishman' and **Tadżyk** 'Tadzhik' decline like **Polak**:

mechanik 'mechanic'   **pułkownik** 'colonel'
pracownik 'employee'   **muzyk** 'musician'
informatyk 'IT specialist'   **urzędnik** 'clerk'
kierownik 'manager'   **rolnik** 'farmer'

Table 3.8a

Case	Singular	Plural	Singular	Plural
NOM	**kurczak** 'chicken'	**kurczak-i**	**pstrąg** 'trout'	**pstrąg-i**
ACC	**kurczak-a**	**kurczak-i**	**pstrąg-a**	**pstrąg-i**
GEN	**kurczak-a**	**kurczak-ów**	**pstrąg-a**	**pstrąg-ów**
DAT	**kurczak-owi**	**kurczak-om**	**pstrąg-owi**	**pstrąg-om**
LOC	**kurczak-u**	**kurczak-ach**	**pstrąg-u**	**pstrąg-ach**
INS	**kurczak-iem**	**kurczak-ami**	**pstrąg-iem**	**pstrąg-ami**
VOC	**kurczak-u**	**kurczak-i**	**pstrąg-u**	**pstrąg-i**

Note there are discrepancies in the distribution of the endings -a vs. -u in genitive singular inanimate masculine nouns: **parku** vs. **szlafroka** and **dialogu** vs. **pługa**. For explanation see 3.3.5.5.

Table 3.8b

Case	Singular	Plural	Singular	Plural
NOM	**park** 'park'	**park-i** 'parks'	**szlafrok** 'robe'	**szlafrok-i** 'robes'
ACC	**park**	**park-i**	**szlafrok**	**szlafrok-i**
GEN	**park-u**	**park-ów**	**szlafrok-a**	**szlafrok-ów**
DAT	**park-owi**	**park-om**	**szlafrok-owi**	**szlafrok-om**
LOC	**park-u**	**park-ach**	**szlafrok-u**	**szlafrok-ach**
INS	**park-i-em**	**park-ami**	**szlafrok-i-em**	**szlafrok-ami**
VOC	**park-u**	**park-i**	**szlafrok-u**	**szlafrok-i**

Table 3.8c

Case	Singular	Plural	Singular	Plural
NOM	**dialog** 'dialogue'	**dialog-i**	**pług** 'plough'	**pług-i**
ACC	**dialog**	**dialog-i**	**pług**	**pług-i**
GEN	**dialog-u**	**dialog-ów**	**pług-a**	**pług-ów**
DAT	**dialog-owi**	**dialog-om**	**pług-owi**	**pług-om**
LOC	**dialog-u**	**dialog-ach**	**pług-u**	**pług-ach**
INS	**dialog-i-em**	**dialog-ami**	**pług-iem**	**pług-ami**
VOC	**dialog-u**	**dialog-i**	**pług-u**	**pług-i**

Note the nominative plural endings for masculine nouns referring to male human beings. (See 3.3.8.3)

Table 3.8d

Case	Singular	Plural	Singular	Plural
NOM	Czech	Czes-i [ch:si]	Kazach 'Kazakh'	Kazach-owie
ACC	Czech-a	Czech-ów	Kazach-a	Kazach-ów
GEN	Czech-a	Czech-ów	Kazach-a	Kazach-ów
DAT	Czech-owi	Czech-om	Kazach-owi	Kazach-om
LOC	Czech-u	Czech-ach	Kazach-u	Kazach-ach
INS	Czech-em	Czech-ami	Kazach-em	Kazach-ami
VOC	Czech-u	Czes-i	Kazach-u	Kazach-owie

Table 3.8e

Case	Singular	Plural	Singular	Plural
NOM	duch 'ghost'	duch-y 'ghosts'	dach 'roof'	dach-y
ACC	duch-a	duch-y	dach	dach-y
GEN	duch-a	duch-ów	dach-u	dach-ów
DAT	duch-owi	duch-om	dach-owi	dach-om
LOC	duch-u	duch-ach	dach-u	dach-ach
INS	duch-em	duch-ami	dach-em	dach-ami
VOC	duch-u	duch-y	dach-u	dach-y

2. "Historically" soft stem

In this group genitive plural endings can be: ów/y (see 3.3.8.12 to 3.3.8.15 and Table 3.52).

c, dz in the genitive plural take -ów with a few exceptions: owoc-ów 'fruits,' koc-ów 'blankets' but miesięc-y 'months.'

rz, ż, dż in the genitive plural take -y: lekarz-y, komentarz-y, kalendarz-y, noż-y (a few can take both -y and -ów: wąż 'snake'-węż-y/węż-ów, małż 'clam' małży/małżów).

sz, cz referring to male human beings take -y and rarely -ów: działacz-y 'activists,' gracz-y 'players,' palacz-y 'smokers.'

sz, cz referring to objects take -ów and rarely -y: kosz-ów 'baskets,' mecz-ów 'games,' płaszcz-ów 'coats' but klucz-y 'keys.'

All "historically" soft-stem masculine nouns take -u in the locative and vocative singular.

Many nouns have a fleeting vowel, e.g., **chłop***iec* 'boy'—**chłopca** (1.9).

-mi is an older ending in the instrumental plural, preserved in a few nouns including **pieniędzmi** 'monies <INS PL>' (see Table 3.9a).

Table 3.9 Masculine nouns with "historically" soft stem

Case	Singular	Plural	Singular	Plural
NOM	**tasiemiec** 'tapeworm'	**tasiemc-e**	**związkowiec** 'union member'	**związkowcy**
ACC	**tasiemc-a**	**tasiemc-e**	**związkowc-a**	**związkowc-ów**
GEN	**tasiemc-a**	**tasiemc-ów**	**związkowc-a**	**związkowc-ów**
DAT	**tasiemc-owi**	**tasiemc-om**	**związkowc-owi**	**związkowc-om**
LOC	**tasiemc-u**	**tasiemc-ach**	**związkowc-u**	**związkowc-ach**
INS	**tasiemc-em**	**tasiemc-ami**	**związkowc-em**	**związkowc-ami**
VOC	**tasiemc-u**	**tasiemc-e**	**związkowc-u**	**związkowc-y**

The suffix -iec as in **związkow***iec* belongs to the productive suffixes for doers. Other popular nouns that decline like **związkow***iec* include:

akowiec AK-owiec 'Home Army soldier'
chłopiec 'boy'
krawiec 'tailor'
Niemiec 'German'
skąpiec 'miser'
wdowiec 'widower'

Note the fleeting vowel -e (1.9).

A few examples below are exceptional and take -y in the genitive plural after c and dz. Note that also the nasal -ą shifts to -ę in the penultimate position in the genitive plural, and in **pieniądze** in the instrumental plural as well.

'Money' is mostly used in the plural.

Piotr ma dużo pieniędzy. 'Piotr has a lot of money.'
Jego żona wie, co robić z pieniędzmi. 'His wife knows what to do with the money.'
Pieniądz robi pieniądz. 'Money makes money.'
Rok ma dwanaście miesięcy. '[A] year has twelve months.'

Table 3.9a

Case	Singular	Plural	Singular	Plural
NOM	miesiąc 'month'	miesiące	pieniądz 'money'	pieniądze
ACC	miesiąc	miesiące	pieniądz	pieniądze
GEN	miesiąca	miesięcy	pieniądza	pieniędzy
DAT	miesiącowi	miesiącom	pieniądzowi	pieniądzom
LOC	miesiącu	miesiącach	pieniądzu	pieniądzach
INS	miesiącem	miesiącami	pieniądzem	pieniędzmi
VOC	miesiącu	miesiące	pieniądzu	pieniądze

Table 3.9b

Case	Singular	Plural	Singular	Plural
NOM	zając 'hare'	zając-e	koc 'blanket'	koc-e
ACC	zając-a	zając-e	koc	koc-e
GEN	zając-a	zajęc-y	koc-a	koc-ów
DAT	zając-owi	zając-om	koc-owi	koc-om
LOC	zając-u	zając-ach	koc-u	koc-ach
INS	zając-em	zając-ami	koc-em	koc-ami
VOC	zając-u	zając-e	koc-u	koc-e

Note that nouns with "historically" soft-stem -rz and -cz take -y in the genitive plural, with a few exceptions, e.g., mistrz and compound nouns with mistrz, e.g., burmistrz 'mayor.'

A few nouns have the alternative ending -ów, e.g., słuchacz 'listener,' mecz 'game, match' (see 3.3.8.11).

Table 3.9c

Case	Singular	Plural	Singular	Plural
NOM	lekarz 'doctor'	lekarz-e	słuchacz 'auditor'	słuchacz-e
ACC	lekarz-a	lekarz-y	słuchacz-a	słuchacz-y/ słuchacz-ów
GEN	lekarz-a	lekarz-y	słuchacz-a	słuchacz-y/ słuchacz-ów
DAT	lekarz-owi	lekarz-om	słuchacz-owi	słuchacz-om
LOC	lekarz-u	lekarz-ach	słuchacz-u	słuchacz-ach
INS	lekarz-em	lekarz-ami	słuchacz-em	słuchacz-ami
VOC	lekarz-u	lekarz-e	słuchacz-u	słuchacz-e

The suffix -*arz* as in lek*arz* belongs to the productive suffixes for doers. Other popular nouns that decline like **lekarz** include:

cesarz 'emperor'	**piekarz** 'baker'
dziennikarz 'journalist'	**piłkarz** 'football player'
kucharz 'cook'	**piosenkarz** 'singer'
malarz 'painter'	**pisarz** 'writer'

Other nouns that decline like **słuchacz** include:

działacz 'activist'	**siłacz** 'strong man'
gracz 'player', 'gambler'	**palacz** 'smoker'
tułacz 'wanderer' (bookish)	

Table 3.9d

Case	Singular	Plural	Singular	Plural
NOM	**kalendarz** 'calendar'	**kalendarz-e**	**mecz** 'game'	**mecz**
ACC	**kalendarz**	**kalendarz-e**	**mecz**	**mecz-e**
GEN	**kalendarz-a**	**kalendarz-y**	**mecz-u**	**mecz-ów**
DAT	**kalendarz-owi**	**kalendarz-om**	**mecz-owi**	**mecz-om**
LOC	**kalendarz-u**	**kalendarz-ach**	**mecz-u**	**mecz-ach**
INS	**kalendarz-em**	**kalendarz-ami**	**mecz-em**	**mecz-ami**
VOC	**kalendarz-u**	**kalendarz-e**	**mecz-u**	**mecz-e**

Other nouns include: **komentarz** 'commentary,' **talerz** 'plate,' **spinacz** 'paper clip,' **klucz** 'key,' **nóż** 'knife'; genitive plural forms: **komentarz-y, talerz-y, spinacz-y, klucz-y, noż-y**, respectively.

3. Soft-stem masculine nouns

-**u** is the ending in the locative and vocative singular.

-**e** is the ending in the nominative plural (with the exception of male humans **królowie** 'kings').

-soft-stem **ć, ś, ń, ź, dź** show *systematic changes* to **ci, si, ni, zi, dzi** before vowels (except for -**y**) (1.3.3.2)

-**i** is the ending in the genitive plural, e.g., **dużo szpitali, dużo nauczycieli**. Hotel exceptionally has two alternative endings: **hoteli** and **hotelów** (see 3.3.8.15).

Note there are discrepancies in the distribution of endings -**a** vs. -**u** in genitive singular inanimate masculine nouns **pokoj̲u** vs. **kij̲a**. For explanation see 3.3.5.5.

-**mi** is an older ending in the instrumental plural, preserved in a few nouns, including: **końmi, gośćmi** (see Tables 3.10a, 3.10c).

Table 3.10 Masculine nouns with soft stem

Case	Singular	Plural	Singular	Plural
NOM	pokój 'room'	pokoj-e 'rooms'	kij 'stick, bat'	kij-e 'sticks, bats'
ACC	pokój	pokoj-e	kij	kij-e
GEN	pokoj-u	pokoj-ów (or pokoi)	kij-a	kij-ów
DAT	pokoj-owi	pokoj-om	kij-owi	kij-om
LOC	pokoj-u	pokoj-ach	kij-u	kij-ach
INS	pokoj-em	pokoj-ami	kij-em	kij-ami
VOC	pokoj-u	pokoj-e	kij-u	kij-e

Table 3.10a

Case	Singular	Plural	Singular	Plural
NOM	koń 'horse'	koni-e	kamień 'rock'	kamieni-e
ACC	koni-a	koni-e	kamień	kamieni-e
GEN	koni-a	koni	kamieni-a	kamien-i
DAT	koni-owi	koni-om	kamieni-owi	kamieni-om
LOC	koni-u	koni-ach	kamieni-u	kamieni-ach
INS	koni-em	koń-mi	kamieni-em	kamieni-ami
VOC	koniu	koni-e	kamieni-u	kamieni-e

Table 3.10b

Case	Singular	Plural	Singular	Plural
NOM	uczeń 'schoolboy'	uczni-owie	zięć 'son-in-law'	zięci-owie
ACC	uczni-a	uczni-ów	zięci-a	zięci-ów
GEN	uczni-a	uczni-ów	zięci-a	zięci-ów
DAT	uczni-owi	uczni-om	zięci-owi	zięci-om
LOC	uczni-u	uczni-ach	zięci-u	zięci-ach
INS	uczni-em	uczni-ami	zięci-em	zięci-ami
VOC	uczni-u	uczni-owie	zięci-u	zięci-owie

Table 3.10c

Case	Singular	Plural	Singular	Plural
NOM	gość 'guest'	gości-e	nauczyciel 'teacher'	nauczyciel-e
ACC	gości-a	gośc-i	nauczyciel-a	nauczyciel-i
GEN	gości-a	gośc-i	nauczyciel-a	nauczyciel-i
DAT	gości-owi	gości-om	nauczyciel-owi	nauczyciel-om
LOC	gości-u	gości-ach	nauczyciel-u	nauczyciel-ach
INS	gości-em	gość-mi	nauczyciel-em	nauczyciel-ami
VOC	gości-u	gości-e	nauczyciel-u	nauczyciel-e

Some occupations in Polish, similarly to Russian, end with -el: **nauczyciel** (учитель) 'teacher.' Other nouns that decline like **nauczyciel** include:

głosiciel 'proponent'   **właściciel** 'owner'
kapral 'corporal'   **zbawiciel** 'savior'
marzyciel 'dreamer'

Note the older INS PL **-mi** (like **gość-mi** 'guests,' **koń-mi** 'horses').

The frequently used noun **przyjaciel** 'friend' has a specific set of endings in the plural, e.g., **zero ending** (-Ø) in the accusative and genitive, as well as the older instrumental plural form **-mi**. Please note there are changes within the stem in the plural, **el:ół:oł. Nieprzyjaciel** 'enemy' is declined like **przyjaciel**.

Table 3.10d

Case	Singular	Plural
NOM	**przyjaciel** 'friend'	**przyjaciel-e** 'friends'
ACC	**przyjaciel-a**	**przyjaciół**
GEN	**przyjaciel-a**	**przyjaciół**
DAT	**przyjaciel-owi**	**przyjacioł-om**
LOC	**(o) przyjaciel-u**	**(o) przyjacioł-ach**
INS	**przyjaciel-em**	**przyjaciół-mi**
VOC	**przyjaciel-u**	**przyjaciel-e**

Table 3.10e

Case	Singular	Plural	Singular	Plural
NOM	**krasnal** 'dwarf'	**krasnal-e**	**hotel** 'inn'	**hotel-e** 'inns'
ACC	**krasnal-a**	**krasnal-e**	**hotel**	**hotel-e**
GEN	**krasnal-a**	**krasnal-i**	**hotel-u**	**hotel-i/hotel-ów**
DAT	**krasnal-owi**	**krasnal-om**	**hotel-owi**	**hotel-om**
LOC	**krasnal-u**	**krasnal-ach**	**hotel-u**	**hotel-ach**
INS	**krasnal-em**	**krasnal-ami**	**hotel-em**	**hotel-ami**
VOC	**krasnal-u**	**krasnal-e**	**hotel-u**	**hotel-e**

Nouns with a hard **p, b, m, w** and soft **p^j, b^j, m^j, w^j** look identical (and are both pronounced as hard) in the nominative singular.

In all other cases the nouns follow a soft-stem pattern, similar to that in **kamień** 'rock.'

Soft **b^j, p^j, w^j, m^j** show *systematic change* in all forms other than the nominative singular. The nouns follow the pattern of soft-stem nouns even though in the nominative singular they end in a hard stem. e.g., **we Wrocławiu, w Radomiu, w Oświęcimiu, karpiu, gołębiu**. (See 3.2.7)

Table 3.10f

Case	Singular	Plural	Singular	Plural
NOM	karp 'carp'	karpi-e	gołąb 'dove'	gołębi-e
ACC	karpi-a	karpi-e	gołębi-a	gołębi-e
GEN	karpi-a	karpi	gołębi-a	gołębi
DAT	karpi-owi	karpi-om	gołębi-owi	gołębi-om
LOC	karpi-u	karpi-ach	gołębi-u	gołębi-ach
INS	karpi-em	karpi-ami	gołębi-em	gołębi-ami
VOC	karpi-u	karpi-e	gołębi-u	gołębi-e

Note that in **gołąb** nasal **ą** shifts to **ę** in all forms other than the nominative singular.

4. Hard-stem masculine nouns

-'e is the ending in the locative singular. The ending -'e denotes that the preceding consonant(s) become palatalized (see Table 3.64 and section 1.3.5). Systematic stem changes occur, and the hard consonant undergoes softening: -i follows the consonant, or the consonant shifts, e.g., **bursztyn-bursztynie** 'amber,' **rower-rowerze** 'bicycle' (1.3.5).

-y is the ending in nominative plural nouns that refer to animals and objects: **bar-bary**.

-y is the ending in nominative plural nouns that refer to male human beings and end in -r in the nominative singular: **aktor-aktorzy**.

-owie/-y are used in the nominative plural. The ending -owie is added to hard-stem titles and positions as an alternative ceremonious ending except for titles and positions in -(a)t, -tor, -(m)an.

Table 3.11 Masculine nouns with hard stem

Case	Singular	Plural	Singular	Plural
NOM	aktor 'actor'	aktorz-y	rower 'bicycle	rower-y
ACC	aktor-a	aktor-ów	rower	rower-y
GEN	aktor-a	aktor-ów	rower-u	rower-ów
DAT	aktor-owi	aktor-om	rower-owi	rower-om
LOC	aktorz-e	aktor-ach	rowerz-e	rower-ach
INS	aktor-em	aktor-ami	rower-em	rower-ami
VOC	aktorz-e	aktorz-y	rowerz-e	rower-y

Note: Many occupations in Polish, similarly to English, end with -or, -er: reżyse̱r 'direc<u>tor</u>,' keln<u>er</u> 'wait<u>er</u>.' Other nouns that decline like **aktor** include:

ambasador 'ambassador'	**premier** 'prime minister'
dyrektor 'manager'	**profesor** 'professor'
inżynier 'engineer'	**prokurator** 'prosecutor'
lektor 'lecturer'	**redaktor** 'editor'

Table 3.11a

Case	Singular	Plural	Singular	Plural
NOM	**bursztyn** 'amber'	**bursztyn-y** 'ambers'	**stół** 'table'	**stoł-y** 'tables'
ACC	**bursztyn**	**bursztyn-y**	**stół**	**stoł-y**
GEN	**bursztyn-u**	**bursztyn-ów**	**stoł-u**	**stoł-ów**
DAT	**bursztyn-owi**	**bursztyn-om**	**stoł-owi**	**stoł-om**
LOC	**bursztyni-e**	**bursztyn-ach**	**stol-e**	**stoł-ach**
INS	**bursztyn-em**	**bursztyn-ami**	**stoł-em**	**stoł-ami**
VOC	**bursztyni-e**	**bursztyn-y**	**stol-e**	**stoł-y**

Table 3.11b

Case	Singular	Plural
NOM	**profesor** 'professor'	**profesorz-y/profesorowie**
ACC	**profesor-a**	**profesor-ów**
GEN	**profesor-a**	**profesor-ów**
DAT	**profesor-owi**	**profesor-om**
LOC	**profesorz-e**	**profesor-ach**
INS	**profesor-em**	**profesor-ami**
VOC	**profesorz-e**	**profesorz-y/profesorowie**

5. Hard-stem masculine nouns ending -**anin**

The extended stem is reduced in plural forms. **Jesteśmy Amerykanami** (not: Amerykaninami). Note the distribution of -**ów** vs. the **zero ending** (-Ø) in the genitive plural (see 3.3.8.12 and 3.3.8.16).

Table 3.12 Masculine nouns with hard stem ending -**anin**

Case	Singular	Plural
NOM	**Amerykanin** 'American'	**Amerykani-e** 'Americans'
ACC	**Amerykanin-a**	**Amerykan-ów**
GEN	**Amerykanin-a**	**Amerykan-ów**
DAT	**Amerykanin-owi**	**Amerykan-om**
LOC	**Amerykanini-e**	**Amerykan-ach**
INS	**Amerykanin-em**	**Amerykan-ami**
VOC	**Amerykanini-e**	**Amerykani-e**

Table 3.12a

Case	Singular	Plural
NOM	**Rosjanin** 'Russian'	**Rosjani-e** 'Russians'
ACC	**Rosjanin-a**	**Rosjan** (zero ending)
GEN	**Rosjanin-a**	**Rosjan** (zero ending)
DAT	**Rosjanin-owi**	**Rosjan-om**
LOC	**Rosjanini-e**	**Rosjan-ach**
INS	**Rosjanin-em**	**Rosjan-ami**
VOC	**Rosjanini-e**	**Rosjani-e**

6. Fleeting vowel

This is a vowel that is found in some forms of nouns, but not in others. In Polish it is often the vowel -e. The fleeting vowel often occurs in the penultimate syllable before the consonant -ec, -ek, -eł, -el, -er and **pies** 'dog,' **dzień** 'day,' **ogień** 'fire' (see 1.9).

Table 3.13 Masculine nouns with fleeting vowel

Case	Singular	Plural	Singular	Plural
NOM	**ojciec** 'father'	**ojc-owie** 'fathers'	**poseł** 'MP'	**posł-owie** 'MPs'
ACC	**ojc-a**	**ojc-ów**	**posł-a**	**posł-ów**
GEN	**ojc-a**	**ojc-ów**	**posł-a**	**posł-ów**
DAT	**ojc-u**	**ojc-om**	**posł-owi**	**posł-om**
LOC	**ojc-u**	**ojc-ach**	**pośl-e**	**posł-ach**
INS	**ojc-em**	**ojc-ami**	**posł-em**	**posł-ami**
VOC	**ojcz-e**	**ojc-owie**	**pośl-e**	**posł-owie**

Note the older vocative form **ojcze**, (as also in **chłopcze** <VOC> 'boy,' **kupcze** <VOC> 'merchant').

Table 3.13a

Case	Singular	Plural	Singular	Plural
NOM	**dzień** 'day'	**dni** 'days' (not dnie)	**tydzień** 'week'	**tygodnie** 'weeks'
ACC	**dzień**	**dni**	**tydzień**	**tygodnie**
GEN	**dnia**	**dni**	**tygodnia**	**tygodni**
DAT	**dniowi**	**dniom**	**tygodniowi**	**tygodniom**
LOC	**dniu**	**dniach**	**tygodniu**	**tygodniach**
INS	**dniem**	**dniami**	**tygodniem**	**tygodniami**
VOC	**dniu**	**dni**	**tygodniu**	**tygodnie**

Note there are discrepancies in the distribution of the endings -**u** and -**owi** in the dative singular, **ojcu** <DAT SG> 'father' vs. **posłowi** <DAT SG> 'envoy, member of parliament.' For an explanation, see 3.3.5.8.

Note: **Dnie** is an old form, as illustrated in the title of the four-volume novel *Noce i dnie* 'Days and nights' by Maria Dąbrowska, published in 1931–34.

Table 3.13b

Case	Singular	Plural	Singular	Plural
NOM	budynek 'building'	budynk-i	widelec 'fork'	widelc-e 'forks'
ACC	budynek	budynk-i	widelec	widelc-e
GEN	budynk-u	budynk-ów	widelc-a	widelc-ów
DAT	budynk-owi	budynk-om	widelc-owi	widelc-om
LOC	budynk-u	budynk-ach	widelc-u	widelc-ach
INS	budynki-em	budynk-ami	widelc-em	widelc-ami
VOC	budynk-u	budynk-i	widelc-u	widelc-e

7. Nouns with a nasal vowel in the penultimate position.

The nasal vowel **ą** is changed to **ę** in all oblique cases (except ACC for male inanimate nouns where ACC=NOM) in front of labial and dental consonants: **dąb** 'oak' **dęby**, **urząd** 'office' **urzędy**.

The nasal vowel **ą** does not change to **ę** in all oblique cases before the consonant **s**: **wąs**, **wąsy** 'moustache', **pląs**, **pląsy** 'lively dance' (1.6).

Table 3.14 Masculine nouns with nasal vowel -**ą**

Case	Singular	Plural	Singular	Plural
NOM	mąż 'husbands'	męż-owie	wąż 'snake'	węż-e 'snakes'
ACC	męż-a	męż-ów	węż-a	węż-e
GEN	męż-a	męż-ów	węż-a	węż-y/węż-ów
DAT	męż-owi	męż-om	węż-owi	węż-om
LOC	męż-u	męż-ach	węż-u	węż-ach
INS	męż-em	męż-ami	węż-em	węż-ami
VOC	męż-u	męż-owie	węż-u	węż-e

The genitive plural has two alternative endings: -y/-ów, e.g., **węży/węzów**, **małży/małżów**, **małż** 'clam'. (See sections 3.3.8.12 to 3.3.8.15 and Table 3.52)

The nasal vowel **ą** is changed to **ę** in the genitive plural only in a few nouns.

Table 3.14a

Case	Singular	Plural	Singular	Plural
NOM	błąd 'mistake'	błęd-y 'mistakes'	ząb 'tooth'	zęb-y 'teeth'
ACC	błąd	błęd-y	ząb	zęb-y
GEN	błęd-u	błęd-ów	zęb-a	zęb-ów
DAT	błęd-owi	błęd-om	zęb-owi	zęb-om
LOC	błędzi-e	błęd-ach	zębi-e	zęb-ach
INS	błęd-em	błęd-ami	zęb-em	zęb-ami
VOC	błędzi-e	błęd-y	zębi-e	zęb-y

Note **ząb** is pronounced like "zomp" [zɔmp] and **zęby** like "zemby" [zɛmbɨ] (see 1.2.2).

8. **Człowiek** and its irregular form **ludzie, brat** and its old form **bracia**.

Note the old shorter ending -**mi** in the instrumental singular.

Table 3.15 Irregular masculine forms

Case	Singular	Plural	Singular	Plural
NOM	człowiek 'person'	ludzi-e 'people'	brat 'brother'	braci-a 'brothers'
ACC	człowiek-a	ludzi	brat-a	brac-i
GEN	człowiek-a	ludzi	brat-a	brac-i (not: bratów)
DAT	człowiek-owi	ludzi-om	brat-u	braci-om
LOC	człowiek-u	ludzi-ach	braci-e	braci-ach
INS	człowieki-em	ludź-mi	brat-em	brać-mi
VOC	człowiek-u	ludzi-e	braci-e	braci-a

Note the irregular dative singular -**u**, also in **panu, ojcu** (see 3.3.5.8).

Note the older instrumental plural -**mi**.

9. Irregular declension of **książę** and **ksiądz**

Table 3.16 Książę and **ksiądz**

Case	Singular	Plural
NOM	książę 'prince'	książęt-a 'princes'
ACC	księci-a	książąt
GEN	księci-a	książąt
DAT	księci-u	książęt-om
LOC	księci-u	książęt-ach
INS	księci-em	książęt-ami
VOC	książę	książęt-a

Table 3.16a

Case	Singular	Plural
NOM	ksiądz 'priest'	księż-a 'priests'
ACC	ksiedz-a	księż-y
GEN	ksiedz-a	księż-y
DAT	ksiedz-u	księż-om
LOC	ksiedz-u	księż-ach
INS	ksiedz-em	księż-mi
VOC	księże	księż-a

Książę is classified as a masculine noun because it refers to a male human being, but declined according to the neuter pattern, similiarly to zwierzę 'animal'—zwierzęcia. Today the noun is declined in two ways: modern and archaic. The modern, more popular declension is shorter.

Ksiądz has two different stems for singular and plural declensions.

10. Nouns referring to a male human being with the ending -o

These carry an emotive meaning and usually denote a male family member. Other examples include: wujcio 'uncle,' dziadunio or dziadzio 'grandpa,' papcio 'daddy.' In the nominative plural they have the ending -owie. Some male first names have the ending -o to carry an emotive meaning as well: Zbysio (<Zbyszek), Czesio (<Czesław), Henio (<Henryk).

Table 3.17 Masculine nouns ending **-o**

Case	Singular	Plural	Singular	Plural
NOM	dziadzi-o 'grandpa'	dziadzi-owie	brzusi-o 'tummy'	brzusi-e
ACC	dziadzi-a	dziadzi-ów	brzusi-o	brzusi-e
GEN	dziadzi-a	dziadzi-ów	brzusi-a	brzusi-ów
DAT	dziadzi-owi	dziadzi-om	brzusi-owi	brzusi-om
LOC	dziadzi-u	dziadzi-ach	brzusi-u	brzusi-ach
INS	dziadzi-em	dziadzi-ami	brzusi-em	brzusi-ami
VOC	dziadzi-u	dziadzi-owie	brzusi-u	brzusi-e

11. Proper nouns ending in -o

Table 3.18 Masculine proper nouns ending **-o**

Case	Singular	Plural	Singular	Plural
NOM	**Pedro**	**Pedrowie**	**Canaletto**	**Canalettowie**
ACC	**Pedra**	**Pedrów**	**Canaletta**	**Canalettów**
GEN	**Pedra**	**Pedrów**	**Canaletta**	**Canalettów**
DAT	**Pedrowi**	**Pedrom**	**Canalettowi**	**Canalettom**
LOC	**Pedrze**	**Pedrach**	**Canaletcie**	**Canalettach**
INS	**Pedrem**	**Pedrami**	**Canalettem**	**Canalettami**
VOC	**Pedro**	**Pedrowie**	**Canaletto**	**Canalettowie**

12. Nouns ending in **-izm**. Note the pronunciation in the locative and vocative singular.

Table 3.19 Masculine nouns ending **-izm**

Case	Singular
NOM	**komunizm** 'communism'
ACC	**komunizm**
GEN	**komunizm-u**
DAT	**komunizm-owi**
LOC	**komuni<u>zm</u>i-e** [reads komuni<u>źm</u>ie]
INS	**komunizm-em**
VOC	**komuni<u>zm</u>i-e** [reads komuni<u>źm</u>ie]

3.3.6 | Feminine singular

3.3.6.1 | Feminine singular declension pattern

The feminine singular declension pattern is based on the type of final letter—whether it is a vowel (**a, i** or **o**), or a consonant, and on the final-stem consonant.

Types of final-stem consonants in the nominative case:

1. **k, g, ch/h**—also called *velar*
2. **c, dz, sz, ż, rz, cz, dż**—also called *"historically" soft*
3. **ś, ć, ź, dź, ń, l, bʲ, pʲ, mʲ, wʲ, j**—also called *soft*
4. all other consonants (**b, p, f, w, m, ł, t, d, s, z, n, r**)—also called *hard*

For the declension patterns in the plural, see the no male human pattern overview at 3.3.9.

3.3.6.2 *Feminine singular pattern overview*

Less common endings are listed in parentheses.

NOM **-a** (**-i**, **-o**, -soft and "historically" soft consonants)
ACC nouns ending in a vowel take **-ę** (exception **panią**)
    (nouns ending in a consonant: as in nominative)
GEN **-y/-i** (**-ii**)
DAT as in locative
LOC **-'e**, **-y/-i** (**-ii**)
INS **-ą** (**-ią**)
VOC nouns ending in **-a**: **-o/-u**
    (nouns ending in **-i**: as in nominative)
    (nouns ending in a soft consonant: **-i**)
    (nouns ending in a "historically" soft consonant: **-y**)

The locative singular ending -'e denotes that the preceding consonant(s) become palatalized (see Table 3.64 and section 1.3.5).

For charts with examples of the full declension of feminine nouns, refer to Tables 3.20 to 3.32.

3.3.6.3 *Feminine singular final-vowel **-a** nouns DAT = LOC*
                *Feminine singular final-consonant and final-vowel **-i** nouns have*
                identical endings in genitive, dative, locative, and vocative singular

GEN = DAT = LOC = VOC
noc <NOM FEM SG> 'night': **nocy** <GEN>, **nocy** <DAT>, **nocy** <LOC>, **nocy** <VOC>
miłość <NOM FEM SG> 'love': **miłości, miłości, miłości, miłości**
pani <NOM FEM SG> 'Mrs./Ms./you [formal]': **pani, pani, pani, pani**

Feminine nouns that end in a consonant, e.g., **rzecz** 'thing,' **powieść** 'novel,' **miłość** 'love,' have three forms in singular: nominative—accusative, genitive—dative—locative—vocative, and instrumental.

Nouns referring to a female human being with the ending -i (except for **pani**) have three forms in singular: (1.) nominative—genitive—dative—locative—vocative, e.g., **mistrzyni** 'champion,' (2.) accusative **mistrzynię**, and (3.) instrumental **mistrzynią**. Pani ('Mrs./Ms./you,' formal way of addressing a woman) has an irregular declension pattern. In the singular, **pani** is the form for all cases except for the accusative and instrumental, where the form is **panią** (Table 3.27).

3.3.6.4 | Feminine genitive singular -y

The feminine genitive singular ending is -y for nouns ending in -a with hard and "historically" soft stem consonants, as well as with the ch/h stem (e.g., praca 'work' pracy, noc 'night' nocy, rzecz 'thing' rzeczy, burza 'storm' burzy, mama 'mom' mamy, poeta 'poet' poety, kierowca 'driver' kierowcy, mężczyzna 'man' mężczyzny, blacha 'cookie sheet' blachy).

3.3.6.5 | Feminine genitive singular -i

-i in the genitive singular is the ending for feminine nouns ending in -a with the k and g-stem, and with a soft stem consonant (książka 'book' książki, kolacja 'dinner' kolacji, miłość 'love' miłości, ziemia 'ground' ziemi, kawiarnia 'cafe' kawiarni). Soft-stem ć, ś, ń, ź, dź shift to ci, si, ni, zi, dzi (1.3.3.2).

3.3.6.6 | Feminine genitive singular -ii

-ii in the genitive singular is the ending for loan nouns with the -i-stem (usually denoting scientific and academic words, e.g., chemia 'chemistry' chemii, historia 'history' historii, foreign countries Belgia-Belgii, Holandia-Holandii, Anglia-Anglii). The nouns have identical forms in the genitive singular, genitive plural, dative and locative singular. The pronunciation in all the forms is with a final [-yee], [historyee].

3.3.6.7 | -i, -ji, and -ii endings in the genitive, dative and locative singular of feminine nouns which end in -a in the nominative singular

3.3.6.7a | -i

pani, gospodyni and other nouns referring to female humans ending in -i in the nominative singular have an identical form in the genitive, dative and locative singular.

Oto pani <NOM SG> **Ewa.** 'Here is Ms. Ewa.'
Nie ma pani <GEN SG> **Ewy.** 'Ms. Ewa is not here.'
Podaj to pani <DAT SG> **Ewie.** 'Pass it to Ms. Ewa.'
Myślę o pani <LOC SG> **Ewie.** 'I'm thinking about Ms. Ewa.'

Feminine nouns that end in nominative singular in vowel + -ja, e.g., **aleja** 'avenue' have the ending -i in the genitive, dative, and locative singular.

aleja—alei [read: aleji, not ale-i]   **Maja** (female name) **Mai**
szyja 'neck' **szyi**   **nadzieja** 'hope' **nadziei**

3.3.6.7b -ji

Feminine nouns that end in nominative singular in a consonant + -ja have the ending -ji in the genitive, dative, and locative singular.

restauracja 'restaurant'—**restauracji**, **Rosja** 'Russia'—**Rosji**,
Azja 'Asia'—**Azji**, **Szkocja** 'Scotland'—**Szkocji**.

Other nouns with the endings -zja, -cja, -sja include:

agresja 'aggression'   **Francja** 'France'
amnezja 'amnesia'   **Galicja** 'Galicia'
awersja 'dislike'   **inwazja** 'invasion'
dymisja 'resignation'   **kolacja** 'dinner'
Eurazja 'Eurasia'

3.3.6.7c -i/-ii

Feminine common and proper nouns that end in nominative singular in consonant + ia have the endings -i or -ii.

Loan common nouns (e.g., scientific words) and loan proper nouns (geographical places) that end in nominative singular with -ia have the ending -ii in genitive singular, genitive plural, dative singular, and locative singular, e.g.,

chemia 'chemistry' **chemii**   **Japonia** 'Japan' **Japonii**
armia 'army' **armii**   **Austria** 'Austria' **Austrii**
Daria (first name) **Darii**   **historia** 'history' **historii**

Words of Slavic origin that end in nominative singular with -ia have the ending -i (just drop the ending -a) in the genitive, dative, and locative singular, e.g.,

Ania—Ani (first name)   **kawiarnia—kawiarni** 'café'
babcia—babci 'grandma'   **Sonia—Soni** (first name)
ciocia—cioci 'aunt'   **ziemia—ziemi** 'soil'

Speakers of other Slavic languages, especially Russian, might see that in the words история, Дарья, химия, Япония the final consonant is softened by 'i' and the sound я 'ja' is separate, while in земля (ziemia), Соня (Sonia), Аня (Ania) the final consonant is softened by the sound я 'ja' and there is nothing left.

<hr>

3.3.6.8 | Feminine locative/dative singular -'e

-'e in the locative and dative singular is the ending after a hard stem and a velar stem (k, g, ch/h). Systematic stem changes occur, and the hard consonant undergoes softening (-i follows the consonant, or the consonant shifts, e.g., mama-mamie, Ameryka-Ameryce) (see section 1.3.3 and Table 3.64).

The locative singular ending -'e denotes that the preceding consonant(s) become palatalized. For the process of palatalization, see 1.3.5.

3.3.6.9 | Feminine locative and dative singular -y

-y in the locative and dative singular is the ending after "historically" soft-stem (praca-pracy 'work,' noc-nocy 'night,' rzecz-rzeczy 'thing,' burza-burzy 'storm').

3.3.6.10 | Feminine locative and dative singular -i

-i in the locative and dative singular is the ending after soft stems (kolacja-kolacji 'dinner,' ziemia-ziemi 'ground,' kawiarnia-kawiarni 'café').

3.3.6.11 | Feminine locative and dative singular -ii

-ii in the locative and dative singular is the ending for loan nouns ending in -ia (usually denoting scientific and academic words, e.g., chemia-chemii 'chemistry,' historia-historii 'history,' and foreign countries Belgia-Belgii 'Belgium,' Holandia-Holandii 'Holland,' Anglia-Anglii 'England'). The nouns have identical forms in the genitive singular, genitive plural, dative and locative singular. The pronunciation in all the forms is with a final [-yee] [historyee].

3.3.6.12 Feminine instrumental singular -ią

-ią in the instrumental singular is the ending for all feminine nouns with soft stems (except for l, j), e.g., miłość-miłością 'love,' krew-krwią 'blood' (1.3.3.3).

3.3.6.13 Feminine vocative singular -o

-o in the vocative singular is the ending for feminine nouns ending -a with velar and hard stems (matka-matko 'mother', aktorka-aktorko 'actress', mama-mamo 'mom', and diminutives with -ka, e.g., dziewczynka-dziewczynko 'little girl').

3.3.6.14 Feminine vocative singular -u

-u in the vocative singular is the ending in diminutive nouns (except for those with -ka), e.g., Kasia-Kasiu 'Kasia <DIM> [female name],' babunia-babuniu 'grandma <DIM>'.

3.3.6.15 Feminine noun tables

For pattern specificities and ending distribution in the singular see 3.3.6.1. For pattern specificities and ending distribution in the plural see 3.3.9.

Note that locative = dative singular for all feminine nouns.

Examples follow for feminine nouns that end in the vowel -a:

1. with a velar stem: książka 'book,' droga 'road,' cecha 'characteristic'
2. with a "historically" soft stem: praca 'job,' burza 'storm'
3. with a soft stem: armia 'army,' ziemia 'land,' kawiarnia 'cafe,' Japonia 'Japan,' restauracja 'restaurant,' aleja 'avenue,' sala 'room, hall,' willa 'villa,' Ekscelencja 'Excellency'
4. with a hard stem: kobieta 'woman,' mama 'mom,' szkoła 'school,' opera 'opera'
5. with a vowel stem: idea 'idea,' and the irregular noun statua 'statue'
6. *mixed pattern*: Nouns referring to a male human being (e.g., mężczyzna 'man,' poeta 'poet,' kolega 'male colleague,' specjalista 'specialist,' obrońca 'defender') are declined according to the feminine pattern in

the singular only. In the plural the nouns are declined according to the male human plural pattern. (See 3.3.8)

7. *mixed pattern*: Proper nouns (first and last names) that refer to male human beings with the endings -a and -ko, e.g., **Wałęsa, Kucia, Kościuszko**

There are also examples of:

8. feminine nouns that end in the vowel -i: **pani** (respectful form of address), **gospodyni** 'hostess'
9. feminine nouns with a "historically" soft stem: **podróż** 'trip,' 'journey,' **rzecz** 'thing'
10. feminine nouns with a soft stem: **miłość** 'love,' **przyjaźń** 'friendship'
11. feminine nouns with a fleeting vowel: **wieś** 'village,' 'countryside,' **krew** 'blood'
12. the irregular declension **ręka** 'hand' (older dual form)
13. *mixed pattern*: **sędzia** 'judge'

Type of stem-consonant:

k, g, ch/h—also called *velar*

c, dz, sz, ż, rz, cz, dż—also called *"historically" soft*

ś, ć, ź, dź, ń, l, bʲ, pʲ, mʲ, wʲ, j—also called *soft*

all other consonants (**b, p, f, w, m, ł, t, d, s, z, n, r**)—also called *hard*

1. feminine nouns ending -a with a velar stem

nominative plural=genitive singular; **k, g** takes **-i**, **ch** takes **-y**

locative and dative singular **-'e**; predictable shifts occur: **k:ce, g:dze, ch:sze** (see 3.3.6.8)

vocative singular **-o**

Table 3.20 Feminine nouns ending **-a** with velar stem

Case	Singular	Plural	Singular	Plural
NOM	książk-a 'book'	książk-i	drog-a 'road'	drog-i
ACC	książk-ę	książk-i	drog-ę	drog-i
GEN	książk-i	książek	drog-i	dróg
DAT	książc-e	książk-om	drodz-e	drog-om
LOC	książc-e	książk-ach	drodz-e	drog-ach
INS	książk-ą	książk-ami	drog-ą	drog-ami
VOC	książk-o	książk-i	drog-o	drog-i

Table 3.20a

Case	Singular	Plural
NOM	cech-a 'characteristic'	cech-y
ACC	cech-ę	cech-y
GEN	cech-y	cech
DAT	cesz-e	cech-om
LOC	cesz-e	cech-ach
INS	cech-ą	cech-ami
VOC	cech-o	cech-y

2. "historically" soft stem -a

Feminine nouns ending in -a with a "historically" soft stem have the same ending -y in genitive, locative, and dative singular.

Note the **zero ending** (-Ø) (no ending added) in the genitive plural (see 3.3.9.10 to 3.3.9.12).

vocative -o

nominative plural -e

Table 3.21 Feminine nouns ending **-a** with "historically" soft stem

Case	Singular	Plural	Singular	Plural
NOM	prac-a 'work'	prac-e	burz-a 'storm'	burz-e
ACC	prac-ę	prac-e	burz-ę	burz-e
GEN	prac-y	prac	burz-y	burz
DAT	prac-y	prac-om	burz-y	burz-om
LOC	prac-y	prac-ach	burz-y	burz-ach
INS	prac-ą	prac-ami	burz-ą	burz-ami
VOC	prac-o	prac-e	burz-o	burz-e

3. soft stem -a

nominative plural -e

locative = dative = genitive singular

-ii is the ending in genitive loan words with the ending -ia, e.g., arm**ia**
<GEN SG=GEN PL=LOC SG=DAT SG>

-i in the genitive for places in -nia, diminutives, e.g., **Ania-Ani**, and -cja, -zja, -sja-stem, e.g., **Rosja-Rosji** 'Russia,' **Azja-Azji** 'Asia,' **kolacja-kolacji** 'dinner'

-i in the genitive with a vowel before a soft stem, e.g., **szyja-szyi** 'neck,' **nadzieja-nadziei** 'hope,' **aleja-alei** 'avenue'

See Table 3.22b.

Table 3.22 Feminine nouns ending **-a** with soft stem

Case	Singular	Plural	Singular	Plural
NOM	armia 'army'	armie 'armies'	ziemia 'land'	ziemie
ACC	armię	armie	ziemię	ziemie
GEN	arm*ii*	arm*ii*	ziemi	ziem
DAT	arm*ii*	armiom	ziemi	ziemiom
LOC	arm*ii*	armiach	ziemi	ziemiach
INS	armią	armiami	ziemią	ziemiami
VOC	armio	armie	ziemi	ziemie

Table 3.22a Feminine nouns ending **-a** with soft stem

Case	Singular	Singular	Plural
NOM	Japonia 'Japan'	kawiarni-a 'café'	kawiarni-e
ACC	Japonię	kawiarni-ę	kawiarni-e
GEN	Japon*ii*	kawiarn*i*	kawiarn*i*
DAT	Japon*ii*	kawiarn*i*	kawiarni-om
LOC	Japon*ii*	kawiarn*i*	kawiarni-ach
INS	Japonią	kawiarni-ą	kawiarni-ami
VOC	Japonio	kawiarni-o	kawiarni-e

Many nouns that denote a place end with -nia:

ciemnia 'dark room'
cukiernia 'pastry shop'
Gdynia (city name)
księgarnia 'bookstore'
kuchnia 'kitchen'
kwiaciarnia 'florist'

masarnia 'meat processing plant'
piekarnia 'bakery'
pralnia 'laundry room'
przymierzalnia 'fitting room'
stajnia 'stable'
szatnia 'coatroom'

W Krakowie jest dużo <u>kawiarni</u>. 'There are many <u>cafés</u> in Kraków.'

Narnia and other nouns of foreign origin that end in -ia have the ending -ii in GEN, DAT, LOC SG and GEN PL: Nar*nia*—Narn*ii*.

Austria 'Austria'—**Austr<u>ii</u>**
Dania 'Denmark'—**Dan<u>ii</u>**
Hiszpania 'Spain'—**Hiszpan<u>ii</u>**

Japonia 'Japan'—**Japon<u>ii</u>**
Rumunia 'Romania'—**Rumun<u>ii</u>**
Kolumbia 'Colombia'—**Kolumb<u>ii</u>**

Table 3.22b Feminine nouns ending **-a** with soft stem

Case	Singular	Plural	Singular	Plural
NOM	**restauracj-a** 'restaurant'	**restauracj-e**	**alej-a** 'avenue'	**alej-e**
ACC	**restauracj-ę**	**restauracj-e**	**alej-ę**	**alej-e**
GEN	**restauracj-i**	**restauracj-i**	**alei**	**alej/alei**
DAT	**restauracj-i**	**restauracj-om**	**alei**	**alej-om**
LOC	**restauracj-i**	**restauracj-ach**	**alei**	**alej-ach**
INS	**restauracj-ą**	**restauracj-ami**	**alej-ą**	**alej-ami**
VOC	**restauracj-o**	**restauracj-e**	**alej-o**	**alej-e**

Mieszkam przy alei Wolności w Rosji. 'I live at Wolności Avenue in Russia.'

Table 3.22c Feminine nouns ending **-a** with soft stem

Case	Singular	Plural
NOM	**Ekscelencj-a** 'Excellency'	**Ekscelencje**
ACC	**Ekscelencję**	**Ekscelencje**
GEN	**Ekscelencji**	**Ekscelencji**
DAT	**Ekscelencji**	**Ekscelencjom**
LOC	**Ekscelencji**	**Ekscelencjach**
INS	**Ekscelencją**	**Ekscelencjami**
VOC	**Ekscelencjo**	**Ekscelencje**

Often used in phrases:

Jego Ekscelencja ambasador Polski 'His Excellency [the] ambassador of Poland'
Wasza Ekscelencjo 'Your Excellency'
Wasza Eminencjo 'Your Eminence' declines like **Ekscelencja**.

Table 3.22d Feminine nouns ending **-a** with soft stem

Case	Singular	Plural	Singular	Plural
NOM	**sal-a** 'room'	**sal-e**	**will-a** 'villa'	**will-e**
ACC	**sal-ę**	**sal-e**	**will-ę**	**will-e**
GEN	**sal-i**	**sal**	**will-i**	**will-i/will**
DAT	**sal-i**	**sal-om**	**will-i**	**will-om**
LOC	**sal-i**	**sal-ach**	**will-i**	**will-ach**
INS	**sal-ą**	**sal-ami**	**will-ą**	**will-ami**
VOC	**sal-o**	**sal-e**	**will-o**	**will-e**

Most feminine nouns with the stem ending -l have a zero ending in the genitive plural: sal*a*—sal, hal*a* 'hall'—hal, a few have *–i*: aul*a* 'auditorium' aul*i*, aureol*a*—aureol*i*. Will*a* 'villa' has two endings: will*i* and will.

4. hard stem -a

-'e is the ending in the locative singular. Systematic stem changes occur, and the hard consonant undergoes softening: -i follows the consonant, or the consonant shifts, c.g., ma<u>m</u>a-ma<u>mi</u>e, kobie<u>t</u>a-kobie<u>ci</u>e, ope<u>r</u>a-ope<u>rz</u>e (see 1.3.5 and Table 3.64).

-y is the ending in the nominative plural

Note the **zero ending** (-Ø) in the genitive plural (see 3.3.9.10). For an explanation of the **zero ending** with the vowel shift o to ó, as in szkoła-szkół 'school,' see 3.3.9.11.

Table 3.23 Feminine nouns ending **-a** with hard stem

Case	Singular	Plural	Singular	Plural
NOM	kobiet-a 'woman'	kobiet-y 'women'	mam-a 'mom'	mam-y 'moms'
ACC	kobiet-ę	kobiet-y	mam-ę	mam-y
GEN	kobiet-y	kobiet	mam-y	mam
DAT	kobieci-e	kobiet-om	mami-e	mam-om
LOC	kobieci-e	kobiet-ach	mami-e	mam-ach
INS	kobiet-ą	kobiet-ami	mam-ą	mam-ami
VOC	kobiet-o	kobiet-y	mam-o	mam-y

Table 3.23a Feminine nouns ending **-a** with hard stem

Case	Singular	Plural	Singular	Plural
NOM	szkoła 'school'	szkoł-y	oper-a 'opera'	oper-y
ACC	szkoł-ę	szkoł-y	oper-ę	oper-y
GEN	szkoł-y	szkół	oper-y	oper
DAT	szkol-e	szkoł-om	operz-e	oper-om
LOC	szkol-e	szkoł-ach	operz-e	oper-ach
INS	szkoł-ą	szkoł-ami	oper-ą	oper-ami
VOC	szkoł-o	szkoł-y	oper-o	oper-y

5. locative -i

Table 3.24 Feminine nouns ending -a with vowel stem

Case	Singular	Plural	Singular	Plural
NOM	**idea** 'idea'	**idee** 'ideas' [idɛɛ]	**statua** 'statue'	**statuy** 'statues'
ACC	**ideę**	**idee**	**statuę**	**statuy**
GEN	**idei**	**idei**	**statui**	**statui**
	[idɛji ‖ idɛi]			**[statuji ‖ statui]**
DAT	**idei**	**ideom**	**statui**	**statuom**
LOC	**idei**	**ideach**	**statui**	**statuach**
INS	**ideą**	**ideami**	**statuą**	**statuami**
VOC	**ideo**	**idee**	**statuo**	**statuy**

Artysta otrzymał pięć statui. 'An artist received five statues.'
Widziałem Statuę Wolności. 'I saw the Statue of Liberty.'

IKEA is an acronym and is indeclinable: **zakupy w IKEA,** however it is often declined in the media and in everyday speech: **zakupy w ikei** 'shopping in IKEA,' following the pattern of feminine nouns that have a vowel stem.

6. **Mixed pattern:** There are many nouns referring to a male human being with the ending -a in Polish. They have a mixed declension pattern. In the singular the nouns are declined according to the feminine pattern (typical feminine ending -a in the nominative singular, as in **kobieta** 'woman'), but in the plural the nouns are declined according to the male human pattern, since they refer to a male human being. (See 3.3.2 and 3.3.8)

The genitive plural of the nouns is -ów except for **mężczyzna**, which has the zero ending **mężczyzn.**

Nominative plural forms refer to mixed groups. To address a group of females see 12.1.

Table 3.25 Mixed pattern with ending -a

Case	Singular	Male human plural
NOM	**kolega** 'male colleague'	**koledzy** 'colleagues, friends'
ACC	**kolegę**	**kolegów**
GEN	**kolegi**	**kolegów**
DAT	**koledze**	**kolegom**
LOC	**koledze**	**kolegach**
INS	**kolegą**	**kolegami**
VOC	**kolego**	**koledzy**

Table 3.25a Mixed pattern noun with ending **-a**

Case	Singular	Plural	Singular	Plural
NOM	poet-a 'male poet'	poeci 'poets'	mężczyzn-a 'man'	mężczyźni 'men'
ACC	poetę	poetów	mężczyznę	mężczyzn
GEN	poety	poetów	mężczyzny	mężczyzn
DAT	poecie	poetom	mężczyźnie	mężczyznom
LOC	poecie	poetach	mężczyźnie	mężczyznach
INS	poetą	poetami	mężczyzną	mężczyznami
VOC	poeto	poeci	mężczyzno	mężczyźni

The noun **mężczyzna** used to be a collective noun like **szlachta** 'nobility' or **starszyzna** 'elders': **ta mężczyzna, ta starszyzna**, until the seventeenth century. After that **mężczyzna** became a masculine singular noun to denote **ten mężczyzna** 'this man,' but the remnants are seen in certain cases of its declension pattern, which is according to the feminine declension: **widzę mężczyznę** 'I see a man' as in **widzę kobietę** 'I see a woman' and **widzę szlachtę** 'I see nobility' in the singular, and in the plural it has a typical zero ending in the genitive plural.

Other male human nouns with the ending -a include many professions:

atleta 'athlete'
dozorca 'janitor'
dyplomata 'diplomat'
katecheta 'catechist'
kierowca 'driver'
obrońca 'defender'

patriarcha 'patriarch'
patriota 'patriot'
pracodawca 'employer'
zdrajca 'tailor'
znawca 'connoisseur'

Table 3.25b Mixed pattern nouns with ending **-a**

Case	Singular	Plural
NOM	specjalist-a 'expert'	specjaliści 'experts'
ACC	specjalistę	specjalistów
GEN	specjalisty	specjalistów
DAT	specjaliście	specjalistom
LOC	specjaliście	specjalistach
INS	specjalistą	specjalistami
VOC	specjalisto	specjaliści

161

Male human nouns that end with the productive suffix -sta include many professions:

anglista 'English scholar'
lobbysta 'lobbyist'
humanista 'specialist in humanities'
maszynista 'train driver'
polonista 'specialist in Polish studies'
stażysta 'intern'

Table 3.25c Mixed pattern nouns with ending **-a**

Case	Singular	Plural
NOM	**obrońc-a** 'defender'	**obrońcy** 'defenders'
ACC	**obrońcę**	**obrońców**
GEN	**obrońcy**	**obrońców**
DAT	**obrońcy**	**obrońcom**
LOC	**obrońcy**	**obrońcach**
INS	**obrońcą**	**obrońcami**
VOC	**obrońco**	**obrońcy**

7. Mixed pattern. Proper names ending in -a have a mixed declension similar to that of **poeta**. **Wałęsa** in the singular is declined like the hard-stem **kobieta**, and **Kucia** with a soft stem is declined like **kawiarnia**.

Table 3.26 Mixed pattern proper nouns with ending **-a**

Case	Singular	Plural	Singular	Plural
NOM	**Wałęsa**	**Wałęsowie**	**Kucia**	**Kuciowie**
ACC	**Wałęsę**	**Wałęsów**	**Kucię**	**Kuciów**
GEN	**Wałęsy**	**Wałęsów**	**Kuci**	**Kuciów**
DAT	**Wałęsie**	**Wałęsom**	**Kuci**	**Kuciom**
LOC	**Wałęsie**	**Wałęsach**	**Kuci**	**Kuciach**
INS	**Wałęsą**	**Wałęsami**	**Kucią**	**Kuciami**
VOC	**Wałęso**	**Wałęsowie**	**Kucio**	**Kuciowie**

Last names with the ending -ko are declined like **książka** in the singular and follow the male human pattern in the plural. They are declined when referring to a male human being and a mixed group. When referring to a female human being, last names with -ko are indeclinable.

Znam Tadeusza Kościuszkę! 'I know Tadeusz Kościuszko!'
Widzę Ewę Kościuszko. I see Ewa Kościuszko.'

(See Chapter 12)

Only proper names with the ending -**a** are declined when referring to a female human being.

Table 3.26a Mixed pattern proper nouns with ending **-ko**

Case	Singular	Plural
NOM	Kościuszk-o	Kościuszk-owie
ACC	Kościuszk-ę	Kościuszk-ów
GEN	Kościuszk-i	Kościuszk-ów
DAT	Kościuszc-e	Kościuszk-om
LOC	Kościuszc-e	Kościuszk-ach
INS	Kościuszk-ą	Kościuszk-ami
VOC	Kościuszk-o	Kościuszk-owie

Książka o Tadeuszu Kościuszce.
'A book about Tadeusz Kościuszko.'

8. Nouns referring to a female human being often end in -**i**. **Pani** (respectful form of address) and other nouns that refer to a female human being share all the endings, except for the accusative singular ending, where **pani** alone takes -**ą**, while all the other nouns take -**ę**.

Table 3.27 Feminine nouns ending **-i**

Case	Singular	Plural	Singular	Plural
NOM	gospodyni 'hostess'	gospodynie	pani	panie
ACC	gospodynię	gospodynie	panią	panie
GEN	gospodyni	gospodyń	pani	pań
DAT	gospodyni	gospodyniom	pani	paniom
LOC	gospodyni	gospodyniach	pani	paniach
INS	gospodynią	gospodyniami	panią	paniami
VOC	gospodyni	gospodynie	pani	panie

For an explanation of the zero ending (-Ø) in genitive plural, see 3.3.9.10.

Other similar nouns include:

bogini 'goddess'   **sprzedawczyni** 'saleswoman'
członkini 'member'   **świadkini** 'witness'
dawczyni 'female donor'   **znawczyni** 'female expert'
mistrzyni 'female champion' **zwyciężczyni** 'female winner'
monarchini 'queen'

9. There are three forms for "historically" soft-stem feminine nouns in the singular: NOM=ACC, GEN=DAT=LOC=VOC, and INS. These nouns take -e in the nominative plural. **Podróż** keeps **ó** in all cases. **Rzecz** exceptionally takes -y in the nominative plural.

Table 3.28 Feminine nouns ending in final-stem "historically" soft consonant

Case	Singular	Plural	Singular	Plural
NOM	**podróż** 'trip'	**podróże** 'trips'	**rzecz** 'thing'	**rzeczy**
ACC	**podróż**	**podróże**	**rzecz**	**rzeczy**
GEN	**podróży**	**podróży**	**rzeczy**	**rzeczy**
DAT	**podróży**	**podróżom**	**rzeczy**	**rzeczom**
LOC	**podróży**	**podróżach**	**rzeczy**	**rzeczach**
INS	**podróżą**	**podróżami**	**rzeczą**	**rzeczami**
VOC	**podróży**	**podróże**	**rzeczy**	**rzeczy**

10. Final-stem soft consonant

Table 3.29 Feminine nouns ending in final-stem soft consonant

Case	Singular	Plural	Singular	Plural
NOM	**miłość** 'love'	**miłości** 'loves'	**przyjaźń** 'friendship'	**przyjaźnie** 'friendships'
ACC	**miłość**	**miłości**	**przyjaźń**	**przyjaźnie**
GEN	**miłości**	**miłości**	**przyjaźni**	**przyjaźni**
DAT	**miłości**	**miłościom**	**przyjaźni**	**przyjaźniom**
LOC	**miłości**	**miłościach**	**przyjaźni**	**przyjaźniach**
INS	**miłością**	**miłościami**	**przyjaźnią**	**przyjaźniami**
VOC	**miłości**	**miłości**	**przyjaźni**	**przyjaźnie**

Feminine nouns ending in a final-stem soft consonant have three forms in the singular: (1.) nominative is the same as accusative (NOM=ACC); (2.) genitive, dative, locative, and vocative have the same form ending in -i (GEN=DAT=LOC=VOC); and (3.) the instrumental ending -ią.

Other nouns with -ość/-źń endings include:

bojaźń 'fear' (bookish)   **niezależność** 'independence'
ciekawość 'curiosity'   **radość** 'joy'
głębokość 'depth'   **samodzielność** 'self-reliance'
młodość 'youth'   **samotność** 'loneliness'
nienawiść 'hate'   **spontaniczność** 'spontaneity'
niewierność 'infidelity'   **starość** 'old age'

uprzejmość 'courtesy'   **złość** 'anger'
wrażliwość 'sensitivity'

Nouns with a hard **p**, **b**, **m**, **w** and soft **pʲ**, **bʲ**, **mʲ**, **wʲ** are spelled and pronounced the same in the nominative singular.

In all other cases the nouns follow a soft-stem pattern, similar to that of **wieś**.

Soft **bʲ**, **pʲ**, **wʲ**, **mʲ** show *systematic change* in all forms other than the nominative singular. These nouns occur in both the masculine and feminine gender, e.g., jedwab 'silk'—jedwabiu, Wrocław—we Wrocławiu, Radom—w Radomiu, Oświęcim—w Oświęcimiu, karp—karpiu, gołąb—gołębiu and krew—krwi, brew—brwi, chorągiew—chorągwi, marchew—marchwi. In all monosyllabic feminine nouns the fleeting vowel disappears in all forms other than the nominative.

11. Fleeting vowel

Table 3.30 Feminine nouns with fleeting vowel

Case	Singular	Plural	Singular
NOM	wieś 'village'	wsie 'villages'	krew 'blood'
ACC	wieś	wsie	krew
GEN	wsi	wsi	krwi
DAT	wsi	wsiom	krwi
LOC	wsi	wsiach	krwi
INS	wsią	wsiami	krwią
VOC	wsi	wsie	krwi

12. **ręka** has an older dual form in the plural and locative singular.

Table 3.31 Ręka

Case	Singular	Plural
NOM	ręka 'hand'	ręce
ACC	rękę	ręce
GEN	ręki	rąk
DAT	ręce	rękom
LOC	ręce *or* ręku	rękach (not ręcach)
INS	ręką	rękami *or* rękoma
VOC	ręko	ręce

13. **sędzia** 'judge' has a mixed pattern, where in the accusative, genitive and dative singular it takes adjectival endings.

Table 3.32 Sędzia

Case	Singular	Plural	Singular
NOM	**sędzia** 'judge'	**sędziowie** 'judges'/ **sędzie** 'female judges'	**sędzia** 'female judge'
ACC	**sędziego**	**sędziów/sędzie**	**sędzię**
GEN	**sędziego**	**sędziów/sędzi**	**sędzi**
DAT	**sędziemu**	**sędziom**	**sędzi**
LOC	**sędzi**	**sędziach**	**sędzi**
INS	**sędzią**	**sędziami**	**sędzią**
VOC	**sędzio**	**sędziowie**	**sędzio**

Piotra powołano na now_ego_ sędz_iego_. 'Piotr was appointed to be a new judge.'

Ewę powołano na nową sędzię. 'Ewa was appointed to be a new judge.'

3.3.7 | Neuter singular

3.3.7.1 | Neuter declension singular pattern

These are based on the type of final letter and what the nouns refer to (an animal, **zwierzę** 'animal' or an object, **imię** 'first name').

Neuter nouns based on what they refer to are:

animate (referring to an animal): **zwierzę** 'animal'
inanimate (referring to an object): **okno** 'window'
human (referring to human offspring): **dziewczę** 'girl' (bookish),
    dziecię 'child' (bookish)

Neuter nouns with the ending **-um**, e.g., **muze_um_** 'museum' *are indeclinable in the singular*—all case forms are identical to that of the nominative case. Note that some nouns ending in **-um** are masculine (e.g., **kostium** 'suit,' **album** 'album'). (See 3.3.3)

Type of stem consonant in the nominative case:

1. **k, g, ch/h**—also called *velar*
2. **c, dz, sz, ż, rz, cz, dż**—also called *"historically" soft*
3. **ś, ć, ź, dź, ń, l, bⁱ, pⁱ, mⁱ, wⁱ, j**—also called *soft*
4. all other consonants (**b, p, f, w, m, ł, t, d, s, z, n, r**)—also called *hard*

For the declension patterns in the plural, see the no male human pattern overview at 3.3.9.

Declension patterns

| 3.3.7.2 | Neuter singular pattern overview |

NOM **-o, -e, -ę (-um)**
ACC as in nominative
GEN **-a** (systematic stem changes occur for all neuter nouns with ending **-ę**), **-um**
DAT **-u** (systematic stem changes occur for all neuter nouns with ending **-ę**), **-um**
LOC **-e/-u** (systematic stem changes occur for all neuter nouns with ending **-ę**), **-um**
INS **-em/-iem** (systematic stem changes occur for all neuter nouns with ending **-ę**), **-um**
VOC as in nominative

For charts with examples of the full declension of neuter nouns, refer to Tables 3.33 to 3.43.

| 3.3.7.3 | Specificities of neuter pattern endings |

For all neuter nouns the nominative singular is identical to the accusative and vocative singular.

For all neuter nouns the nominative plural is identical to the accusative and vocative plural. For the declension pattern in plural, see no male human pattern in section 3.3.9.

NOM = ACC = VOC

Table 3.33 Neuter pattern endings

NOM SG	ACC SG	NOM PL	ACC PL
to nowe okno 'this new window'	**to nowe okno**	**te nowe okna**	**te nowe okna**
to miłe dziecko 'this nice child'	**to miłe dziecko**	**te miłe dzieci**	**te miłe dzieci**
to duże zwierzę 'this big animal'	**to duże zwierzę**	**te duże zwierzęta**	**te duże zwierzęta**

Table 3.33a

NOM PL	ACC PL	(for contrast: GEN PL)
tych dwoje dzieci 'these two children'	**tych dwoje dzieci**	**tych dwojga dzieci**
tych dwoje szczeniąt 'these two puppies'	**tych dwoje szczeniąt**	**tych dwojga szczeniąt**

The noun **państwo** 'a country' and 'a couple' is declined differently, depending on its meaning (see Table 3.43).

In the genitive, dative, locative and instrumental singular *systematic stem changes* occur for all neuter nouns with the ending -ę.

Table 3.33b

NOM SG	GEN SG	DAT = LOC SG	INS SG
to zwierzę 'this animal'	**tego zwierzęcia**	**zwierzęciu**	**tym zwierzęciem**
to imię 'this first name'	**tego imienia**	**imieniu**	**tym imieniem**

Neuter nouns with the ending -ę referring to human offspring and animals have their stem extended in all singular forms except for nominative and accusative by -ci and then the endings are added: **zwierzę—zwierzęcia, zwierzęciu, zwierzęciem**, and **dziecię—dziecięcia, dziecięciu, dziecięciem**.

Neuter nouns with the ending -ę referring to the object lose the ending -ę, have their stem extended in all singular forms except for nominative and accusative by -eni and then the endings are added: **imię—imienia, imieniu, imieniem**.

3.3.7.3.1 | Neuter locative singular -'e

-'e in the locative singular is the ending after a hard stem. Systematic stem changes occur, and the hard consonant undergoes softening (-i follows the consonant, or the consonant shifts, e.g., **biuro** 'office' **w biurze** 'in the office,' **słowo** 'word'—**słowie**). Predictable consonant and vowel shifts occur: **lato-lecie, miasto-mieście**) (see 1.3.5 and Table 3.64).

3.3.7.3.2 | Neuter locative singular -u

-u in the locative is the ending after velar, soft and "historically" soft stems: **pole—polu** 'field,' **mieszkanie—mieszkaniu** 'apartment,' **morze—morzu** 'sea,' **serce**—**sercu** 'heart,' **zwierzę**—**zwierzęciu** 'animal,' **imię**—**imieniu** 'first name.'

Neuter instrumental singular **-em**

-em in the instrumental singular is the ending after hard stems plus **ch/h**, **l**, **j**, e.g., **echo-echem**.

3.3.7.3.4 Neuter Instrumental singular **-iem**

-iem in the instrumental is the ending after velar and soft-stem (except for **ch/h**, **l**, **j**), e.g., **jajko** 'egg'—**jajkiem**, **zwierzę** 'animal'—**zwierzęciem**, **imię** 'first name'—**imieniem**.

3.3.7.4 Neuter noun tables

For all neuter nouns:

NOM SG = ACC SG = VOC SG   NOM PL = ACC PL = VOC PL

The tables below show neuter pattern nouns in the singular and no male human pattern nouns in the plural with a final-stem consonant in the nominative singular, where the final-stem consonant is:

1. **k, g, ch/h**—also called *velar*: **jajko** 'egg,' **wojsko** 'army'
2. **c, dz, sz, ż, rz, cz, dż**—also called *"historically" soft*: **morze** 'sea,' **łącze** 'link, connection'
3. **ś, ć, ź, dź, ń, l, b^j, p^j, m^j, w^j, j**—also called *soft*: **pole** 'field,' **molo** 'pier,' **zdjęcie** 'photo,' **pytanie** 'question'
4. all other consonants (**b, p, f, w, m, ł, t, d, s, z, n, r**)—also called *hard*: **słowo** 'word,' **jezioro** 'lake,' **miasto** 'city'

They also show:

5. mixed pattern: emotive (augmentative) nouns that can be both masculine and neuter with **-isko/-ysko**: **chłopisko** 'bloke,' **psisko** 'big dog'
6. the ending **-ę** denoting an animal, **zwierzę**, and human offspring, or, for example, **imię** 'first name'
7. the *mixed pattern* with the ending *-um*: **muzeum** 'museum,' **centrum** 'center' and with other consonant endings: **opus**
8. irregular forms: **dziecko** 'child,' **dzieci** 'children'
9. the irregular declension of **oko** 'eye' and **ucho** 'ear'
10. the *mixed pattern* of **państwo** 'country,' and **państwo** 'couple' vs. **rodzeństwo** 'siblings'

1. Neuter nouns with velar stem (**k**, **g**, **ch/h**) have:

-u in locative singular
-iem in instrumental (except for **ch/h**)
zero ending (-Ø) in genitive plural (see 3.3.9.10)
-a in nominative plural (see 3.3.9.6)

If the stem ends with a consonant cluster with **k** or **g** (a combination of two or three hard consonants, except for the **-sk** combination), a fleeting/ buffer **e** is inserted in genitive plural between the consonants to ease the pronunciation and to compensate for the dropped vowel ending, e.g., **jajko** <NOM SG> 'egg,' **jajek** <GEN PL> (see 3.3.9.12).

Table 3.34 Neuter nouns with velar stem

Case	Singular	Plural	Singular	Plural
NOM	**jajk-o** 'egg'	**jajk-a** 'eggs'	**wojsk-o** 'army'	**wojsk-a** 'armies'
ACC	**jajk-o**	**jajk-a**	**wojsk-o**	**wojsk-a**
GEN	**jajk-a**	**jajek**	**wojsk-a**	**wojsk**
DAT	**jajk-u**	**jajk-om**	**wojsk-u**	**wojsk-om**
LOC	**jajk-u**	**jajk-ach**	**wojsk-u**	**wojsk-ach**
INS	**jajki-em**	**jajk-ami**	**wojski-em**	**wojsk-ami**
VOC	**jajk-o**	**jajk-a**	**wojsk-o**	**wojsk-a**

Note the **zero ending** (-Ø) in genitive plural (see 3.3.9.10).

2. Neuters nouns with a "historically" soft stem have:

-u in locative singular
zero ending (-Ø) in genitive plural (see 3.3.9.10)
-a in nominative plural (see 3.3.9.6)

The vowel **o** in the penultimate position in neuter nouns shifts to **ó** in the genitive plural **zero ending** (-Ø), except with **cz**-stems, e.g.:

koło 'wheel'—**kół**
morze 'sea'—**mórz**
pole 'field'—**pól** (except for **molo** 'pier'—**mol**)
słowo 'word'—**słów**
zboże 'grain'—**zbóż**

cz-stem neuter nouns and a few **ż**-stem nouns take **-y** in the genitive plural

Table 3.35 Neuter nouns with "historically" soft stem

Case	Singular	Plural	Singular	Plural
NOM	morz-e 'sea'	morz-a	łącz-e 'link'	łącz-a
ACC	morz-e	morz-a	łącz-e	łącz-a
GEN	morz-a	mórz	łącz-a	łącz-y
DAT	morz-u	morz-om	łącz-u	łącz-om
LOC	morz-u	morz-ach	łącz-u	łącz-ach
INS	morz-em	morz-ami	łącz-em	łącz-ami
VOC	morz-e	morz-a	łącz-e	łącz-a

Neuter nouns with a stem ending with the "historically" soft consonant -cz, -ż, -rz have the ending -y in the genitive plural (see 3.3.9.8):

obrzeż-y (<obrzeż-e) 'edge'
podnóż-y (<podnóż-e) 'base'
półrocz-y (<półrocze) 'half-year'
ubocz-y (<ubocze) 'out-of-the-way place'
wybrzeż-y (<wybrzeże) 'coast'
zbocz-y (<zbocze) 'hillside'
złącz-y (<złącze) 'connector'

The genitive plural -y also applies to the feminine noun **poręcz-y** (<**poręcz**) 'railing.'

3. Neuter nouns with soft stems have:

-u in the locative singular
zero ending (-Ø) in genitive plural (see 3.3.9.10)
-a in nominative plural (see 3.3.9.6)

The vowel o in the penultimate position in neuter nouns shifts to ó in the genitive plural **zero ending** (-Ø), except with **cz**-stems, e.g.: **pole** 'field'-**pól**, **koło** 'wheel'-**kół** (except for **molo** 'pier'—**mol**).

The **zero ending** (-Ø) is the ending in genitive plural neuter and feminine nouns (except for feminine nouns ending in a consonant). Systematic stem changes occur in nouns with the soft stem **ci, si, ni, zi, dzi**. Before **zero ending** (-Ø), softness of the soft stem is expressed with a diacritical mark, e.g., **zdjęcie** 'photo'-**zdjęć, pytanie** 'question'-**pytań**.

Table 3.36 Neuter nouns with soft stem

Case	Singular	Plural	Singular	Plural
NOM	pol-e 'field'	pol-a 'fields'	mol-o 'pier'	mol-a 'piers'
ACC	pol-e	pol-a	mol-o	mol-a
GEN	pol-a	pól	mol-a	mol
DAT	pol-u	pol-om	mol-u	mol-om
LOC	pol-u	pol-ach	mol-u	mol-ach
INS	pol-em	pol-ami	mol-em	mol-ami
VOC	pol-e	pol-a	mol-o	mol-a

Molo can also be indeclinable:

spacer po molo/po molu 'a walk along the pier'
Jesteśmy na sopockim molu. 'We are on Sopot's pier.'
Spacer sopockim molem 'A walk along Sopot's pier.'
Kino letnie na sopockim molu 'Summer movies on Sopot's pier.'

Table 3.36a Neuter nouns with soft stem

Case	Singular	Plural	Singular	Plural
NOM	zdjęcie 'photo'	zdjęcia 'photos'	pytanie 'question'	pytania
ACC	zdjęcie	zdjęcia	pytanie	pytania
GEN	zdjęcia	zdjęć	pytania	pytań
DAT	zdjęciu	zdjęciom	pytaniu	pytaniom
LOC	zdjęciu	zdjęciach	pytaniu	pytaniach
INS	zdjęciem	zdjęciami	pytaniem	pytaniami
VOC	zdjęcie	zdjęcia	pytanie	pytania

4. Neuter nouns with a hard stem have:

Neuter nouns with hard stems have the ending -'e in the locative singular. The ending -'e denotes that the preceding consonant(s) become palatalized. Systematic stem changes occur, and the hard consonant undergoes softening: -i follows the consonant, or the consonant shifts, e.g., słowo 'word'—słowie, lato 'summer'—lecie, miasto 'city'—mieście, biuro 'office,' w biurze 'in the office' (For the process of palatalization or softening, see 1.3.5. For examples of the process, see Table 3.64 in section 3.10.). Predictable consonant and vowel shifts occur, e.g., -a in the penultimate position shifts to -e: lato-lecie, wiatr 'wind'—wietrze, miasto-mieście (except for wiadro-wiadrze, which in old Polish had a form vedře).

Alternative forms:

czoło 'forehead'—**na czole**
czoło 'in the first rows, at the head of something'—**na czele**

Zero ending (-Ø) in the genitive plural (see 3.3.9.10).

-a in nominative plural (see 3.3.9.6).

Table 3.37 Neuter nouns with hard stem

Case	Singular	Plural	Singular	Plural
NOM	miast-o 'city'	miast-a 'cities'	jezior-o 'lake'	jezior-a 'lakes'
ACC	miast-o	miast-a	jezior-o	jezior-a
GEN	miast-a	miast	jezior-a	jezior
DAT	miast-u	miast-om	jezior-u	jezior-om
LOC	mieśc-ie	miast-ach	jeziorz-e	jezior-ach
INS	miast-em	miast-ami	jezior-em	jezior-ami
VOC	miast-o	miast-a	jezior-o	jezior-a

Table 3.37a Neuter nouns with hard stem

Case	Singular	Plural
NOM	słow-o 'word'	słow-a 'words'
ACC	słow-o	słow-a
GEN	słow-a	słów
DAT	słow-u	słow-om
LOC	słowi-e	słow-ach
INS	słow-em	słow-ami
VOC	słow-o	słow-a

otworzyć/zamknąć cudzysłów
    'to open/close quotation marks'
w cudzysłowie 'in quotation marks'

5. Neuter nouns with a mixed pattern. Emotive nouns with the ending -o in the nominative singular referring to a male human being have the male human pattern ending -ów in the genitive plural, instead of the zero ending (-Ø), e.g., **psisk** <GEN PL> 'big dogs' (from **psisko** <NOM SG>). The accusative singular is identical to the nominative singular, and the accusative plural is the same as the nominative plural. Animacy and personhood are irrelevant.

Table 3.38 Mixed pattern emotive nouns ending in **-sko**

Case	Singular	Plural	Singular	Plural
NOM	**chłopisko**	**chłopiska**	**psisko**	**psiska**
	'bloke'	'blokes'	'big dog'	
ACC	**chłopisko**	**chłopiska**	**psisko**	**psiska**
GEN	**chłopiska**	**chłopisków**	**psiska**	**psisk** or **psisków**
DAT	**chłopisku**	**chłopiskom**	**psisku**	**psiskom**
LOC	**chłopisku**	**chłopiskach**	**psisku**	**psiskach**
INS	**chłopisk**iem	**chłopiskami**	**psisk**iem	**psiskami**
VOC	**chłopisko**	**chłopiska**	**psisko**	**psiska**

6. Neuter nouns with ending -ę

Singular neuter nouns with the ending -ę referring to human offspring and animals have their stem extended by -ci in the singular and then the endings are added: zwierzę—zwierzęcia, zwierzęciu, zwierzęciem.

Plural neuter nouns with the ending -ę referring to human offspring and animals have their stem extended by -ęt and then the endings are added. Additionally, ę shifts to ą in the genitive plural: zwierzę 'animal'—zwierząt <GEN PL>, zwierzętom <DAT PL>.

Singular neuter nouns with the ending -ę referring to objects lose the ending -ę in the singular, have their stem extended by -eni and then the endings are added: imię—imienia, imieniu, imieniem.

Neuter nouns with the ending -ę in nominative singular referring to objects lose the ending -ę in plural, have their stem extended by -on and then the endings are added: imię 'name'—imiona, imion, imionom.

Note the extended stem in all the cases except for the nominative and accusative singular.

Example:

    cielę 'calf' **szczenię** 'puppy'
    dziewczę 'lass' **prosię** 'piglet'

There are a few neuter inanimate nouns with the ending -ę:

    imię 'first name' **strzemię** 'stirrup'
    plemię 'tribe' **wymię** 'udder'
    ramię 'shoulder' **znamię** 'birthmark'

    Ewa to ładne *imię*. 'Ewa is a pretty *name*.'
    Nie pamiętam jej *imienia*. 'I don't remember her *name*.'

Na liście brakowało kilku *imion.*
'A few *names* were missing in the list.'
Żubr to duże *zwierzę.* 'A bison is a big *animal.*'
Nie mogę trzymać w domu żadnego *zwierzęcia.*
'I can't keep an *animal* at home.'
W zoo jest dużo *zwierząt.*
'There are many *animals* in the zoo.'

Table 3.39 Neuter nouns ending -ę

Case	Singular	Plural	Singular	Plural
NOM	imię	imi-ona	zwierzę	zwierzę-ta
	'first name'	'first names'	'animal'	'animals'
ACC	imi-ę	imion-a	zwierz-ę	zwierzęt-a
GEN	imieni-a	imion	zwierzęci-a	zwierząt
DAT	imieni-u	imion-om	zwierzęci-u	zwierzęt-om
LOC	imieni-u	imion-ach	zwierzęci-u	zwierzęt-ach
INS	imieni-em	imion-ami	zwierzęci-em	zwierzęt-ami
VOC	imi-ę	imion-a	zwierz-ę	zwierzęt-a

3.3.7.5 | *Neuter animate nouns ending with* **-ę**

Neuter animate nouns ending in -ę (referring to human offspring and baby animals) take collective numerals. When used in the subject position with collective numerals, neuter animate plural nouns ending in -ę take a singular verb (in the past tense formation they take the neuter singular marker -ło) and they take nouns and adjectives in the genitive plural (see 8.1.2 and 2.4.10.1).

In colloquial usage, nouns that denote offspring or minors can have the masculine suffix -ak added: *ten* cielak 'calf' (from cielę), źrebak 'foal' (from źrebię), szczeniak 'puppy' (from szczenię).

Dwoje <PL> **szczeniąt** <GEN PL> **było** <VERB SG> **głodnych** <ADJ PL>.
'Two puppies were hungry.'

Pięcioro <PL> **wysportowanych** <ADJ PL> **dziewcząt** <GEN PL> **gra**
<VERB SG> **w drużynie.**
'Five athletic girls play in the team.'

7. Mixed pattern **-um** ending. Neuter nouns with the ending **-um** are indeclinable in the singular. In the plural they are declined.

Table 3.40 Mixed pattern neuter nouns with the ending **-um**

Case	Singular	Plural	Singular	Plural
NOM	muzeum	muzea	centrum	centra
	'museum'	'museums'	'center'	'centers'
ACC	muzeum	muzea	centrum	centra
GEN	muzeum	muzeów	centrum	centrów
DAT	muzeum	muzeom	centrum	centrom
LOC	muzeum	muzeach	centrum	centrach
INS	muzeum	muzeami	centrum	centrami
VOC	muzeum	muzea	centrum	centra

Other nouns that decline like **muze*um*** include:

forum
honorarium 'remuneration'
sanatorium 'sanitarium'
stypendium 'scholarship, grant'

Nouns that follow the **muzeum** type are loan words, e.g., **liceum** 'high school,' **stypendium**. A small group of nouns ending in **-um** are masculine (e.g., **album** 'album,' **kostium** 'suit,' **rozum** 'reason, mind,' **szum** 'noise,' **tłum** 'crowd').

Table 3.40a Other consonant endings (e.g., **opus**)

Case	Singular	Plural
NOM	opus 'opus'	opusy 'opuses'
ACC	opus	opusy
GEN	opusu	opusów
DAT	opusowi	opusom
LOC	opusie	opusach
INS	opusem	opusami
VOC	opusie	opusy

Opus dziwiąte (not dziewiąty) 'opus nine'

8. **Dziecko** has an irregular pattern in the plural. Note the old instrumental ending **-mi**.

Dziećmi <INS PL> has an old form as in **ludźmi** 'people,' **końmi** 'horses,' **gośćmi** 'guests.'

Table 3.41 Dziecko

Case	Singular	Plural
NOM	dziecko 'child'	dzieci 'children'
ACC	dziecko	dzieci
GEN	dziecka	dzieci
DAT	dziecku	dzieciom
LOC	dziecku	dzieciach
INS	dzieckiem	dzie*ćmi*
VOC	dziecko	dzieci

When **dzieci** 'children' is used in the subject position with numerals, the collective numeral must be used; additionally, the verb in this construction is in the singular (with the past tense marker -ło) and all modifiers and the word **dzieci** are in the genitive plural (see 2.4.10 and 8.1.2), e.g.:

Dwoje <COLLECTIVE NUMERAL> **miłych** <GEN PL> **dzieci** <GEN PL> **czytało** <3 PR NT SG> **książkę.**
'Two nice children were reading a book.'

9. The irregular patterns of **oko** 'eye' and **ucho** 'ear' result from the fact that the nouns used to have singular, plural and dual forms (3.5.1.3).

Table 3.42 Oko and ucho

Case	Singular	Plural	Singular	Plural
NOM	ok-o	ocz-y	uch-o	usz-y
	'eye'	(oka 'drops')	'ear'	(ucha 'handles')
ACC	ok-o	ocz-y	uch-o	usz-y
GEN	ok-a	ocz-u	uch-a	usz-u
DAT	ok-u	ocz-om	uch-u	usz-om
LOC	ok-u	ocz-ach	uch-u	usz-ach
INS	oki-em	ocz-ami (oczyma)	uch-em	usz-ami
VOC	ok-o	ocz-y	uch-o	usz-y

na obojgu oczach 'on both eyes'
specjalista chorób oczu 'eye infections specialist'

10. *Państwo* and *rodzeństwo*

Państwo, meaning 'country,' is a collective noun and as such *takes singular verbs* as does **rodzeństwo** 'siblings,' and have ending -'e in locative singular, e.g.:

Moje *rodzeństwo* **zostało**: <3 PR NT SG> **w domu.** 'My *siblings* stayed at home.'

państwo <collective noun> *ufundowało* <3 PR NT SG> **wakacje dzieciom** '*state funded* vacation for children'

Mieszkam w tym państwie <LOC SG>. 'I live in this country.'

Państwo meaning 'couple' or 'a group of people' uses *plural verbs and adjectives.*

Locative singular ending is -**u**.

Państwo Nowakowie *kupili* <3 PR MHPL> **nowy dom.**
'Mr. and Mrs. Nowak *bought* a new house.'

Rozmawiam o państwu <LOC SG> **Kwaśniewskich.**
'We are talking about the Kwaśniewski couple.'

Gratulować państwu <LOC SG> **młodym.**
'To congratulate the newly weds.'

Rodzeństwo takes collective numerals: **Mam** *dwoje* **rodzeństwa.** 'I have *two* siblings' (see 8.1.2).

Table 3.43 Państwo

Case	Singular	Plural	Male Human Plural
NOM	**to państwo** 'this country'	**te państw-a**	**ci państwo** 'this couple'
ACC	**państw-o**	**państw-a**	**państwa**
GEN	**państw-a**	**państw**	**państwa**
DAT	**państw-u**	**państw-om**	**państw-u**
LOC	**państw-*ie***	**państw-ach**	**państw-*u***
INS	**państw-em**	**państw-ami**	**państwem**
VOC	**państw-o**	**państw-a**	**państwo**

Rodzeństwo 'siblings' is declined like the singular form of **państwo** (e.g., **Rozmawiamy o moim rodzeństwie** <LOC SG>. 'We are talking about my siblings.').

| 3.3.7.6 | *Indeclinable neuter nouns* |

Many indeclinable nouns are neuter, and they can have a range of endings.

sushi (3.2.9.8)	dementi 'denial'	kombi
etui '(eyeglasses)case'	euro	'station wagon'
graffiti	fatum 'fate'	argot
spaghetti	wotum 'vote'	dossier
harakiri 'hara-kiri'	lokum 'accommodation'	hobby
alibi	kukuryku 'tuft of hair	
kakao 'cocoa'	sticking up'	

Notes:

1. A few nouns with the ending -**um** are masculine: **rozum** 'mind,' 'intellect,' **kostium** 'costume,' 'suit,' **album**. They are declined in both the singular and plural like a masculine noun that ends with **m** such as **krem** 'cream': GEN SG **kremu, albumu,** NOM PL **kremy, albumy.**
2. The plural form of the noun **forum** is **fora,** however for a very long time it was referred to as a noun without a plural form until it was necessary to look at the noun closer due to a better understanding that someone was chatting on several forums or fora. This example illustrates how the Polish language is still developing.
3. **Metro** 'metro,' **studio** 'studio', **radio** 'radio,' are declinable in Polish (e.g., **Często jeżdżę metrem.** 'I often travel by metro.').
4. Neuter nouns with the ending -**um**, e.g., **muzeum** 'museum' are indeclinable in the singular (do not inflect for case, have one form—nominative form), however they are declinable (inflect for case) in the plural, e.g., **muzea** 'museums' except for nouns that have only a singular form, such as the proper nouns **Monachium** 'Munich,' **Bizancjum** 'Byzantium.'
5. **Książę** 'prince, duke' is of masculine class: *Mały Książę The Little Prince* by Antoine de Saint-Exupèry.

3.3.8 | Male human plural

3.3.8.1 | Male human plural declension pattern

The male human plural declension pattern is based on the stem in the nominative singular.

Type of stem consonant in the nominative case:

1. **k, g, ch/h**—also called *velar*
2. **c, dz, sz, ż, rz, cz, dż**—also called *"historically" soft*
3. **ś, ć, ź, dź, ń, l, bʲ, pʲ, mʲ, wʲ, j**—also called *soft*
4. all other consonants (**b, p, f, w, m, ł, t, d, s, z, n, r**)—also called *hard*

| 3.3.8.2 | Male human plural pattern overview |

NOM **-y/-i/-owie/-e/-anie**
ACC **-ów/-y/-i/zero ending** (-Ø)
GEN as in accusative
DAT **-om**
LOC **-ach**
INS **-ami/-iami** (except for a few with the old ending **-mi**: **gość<u>mi</u>**, **ludź<u>mi</u>**, **brać<u>mi</u>**)
VOC as in nominative

For charts with examples of the full declension of masculine nouns, refer to Tables 3.8 to 3.19.

| 3.3.8.3 | Nominative male human plural **-owie** |

-owie is generally the ending for nouns referring to male family members:

dziadkowie 'grandfathers'
mężowie 'husbands'
ojcowie 'fathers'
staruszkowie 'elder men'
synowie 'sons'
wnukowie 'grandsons'
wujkowie 'uncles'
zięciowie 'sons-in-law'

(except for **brat** 'brother,' **braci-a** 'brothers,' a rare display of morphological alternation)

It is generally used with proper (e.g., first and last names, nationalities) non-adjectival nouns referring to human beings (except for **-czy**, **-ży**, e.g., **Ambroży**). (Proper adjectival masculine nouns have the markers **-i/-y**, e.g., **Kowalski**).

[bracia] Coen<u>owie</u>   **Obam<u>owie</u>** 'The Obamas'
  'Coen [brothers]'   **Clinton<u>owie</u>** 'The Clintons'
Bach<u>owie</u> 'The Bachs'   **Wałęs<u>owie</u>** 'The Wałęsas'
Bush<u>owie</u> 'The Bushes'   **Krzyśk<u>owie</u>** 'Christophers'
Chopin<u>owie</u> 'The Chopins'   or 'The Christophers'
Matejk<u>owie</u> 'The Matejkos'   (Christopher and his family)
Mickiewicz<u>owie</u> 'The Mickiewiczs'

Last names with the ending -owie refer to the whole family, e.g., The Clintons. The ending -owe, e.g., **Clintonowe** would refer to female members, and -ówny to the female unmarried members, e.g., **Bushówny** 'Bush's daughters.'

a few nationalities with -owie in the nominative and vocative male human plural:

Arabowie 'Arabs'
Belgowie 'Belgians'
Finowie 'Finns'
Skandynawowie 'Scandinavians'
Kazachowie 'Kazakhs'
Romowie 'Roma'

(but **Włoch-Włosi** 'Italians')

Nationalities with the ending -owie refer to generic names of nationalities. In order to refer to the feminine part of the society only, the noun would need to be modified, e.g., **Arabki, Belgijki, Finki, Skandynawki,** and **Kazaszki,** respectively.

The ending -owie in nominative male human plural is generally used with proper adjectival nouns (e.g., last names) and common adjectival nouns (e.g., professions) referring to human beings in -czy and -ży:

Ambroży-Ambrożowie (last name)
budowniczy 'builder' **budowniczowie**
chorąży 'warrant officer' **chorążowie**
leśniczy 'forester' **leśniczowie**
motorniczy 'tram driver' **motorniczowie**

All cases other than the nominative and vocative have adjectival endings, e.g., **nie ma Ambrożych** 'The Ambrożys are not [here] <ADJ GEN PL>,' **budowniczym** <ADJ DAT PL>.

The ending -owie is used for representing groups referring to male human beings:

królowie 'kings'
ministrowie <**minister** 'ministers'
panowie 'gentlemen'
posłowie <**poseł** 'MPs'
uczniowie <**uczeń** 'pupils'

potomkowie <**potomek** 'descendants'
druhowie <**druh** 'scout leader'
kochankowie 'lovers'
patriarchowie 'patriarch'

Note the fleeting vowel in **poseł, minister, kochanek** and **uczeń** (1.9).

Note: **króle** in NOM PL is used with playing cards, e.g., **dwa króle** 'two kings' and in the phrase **hodować króle** 'to breed rabbits.'

The ending **-owie** is added to hard-stem titles and positions as an alternative ceremonious form except for titles and positions in **-ta, -tor, -(m)an, -(s)ta, -ik, -ich** and soft or "historically" soft consonants, e.g., **artyści** 'artists' <**artysta, stróże** 'watchmen' <**stróż, pułkownicy** 'colonels' <**pułkownik, mnisi** 'monks' <**mnich**, respectively.

Titles that end in **mistrz** can also have the alternative form **mistrzowie** 'masters,' except in the set phrase **mistrz nad mistrze** 'best master.'

ambasadorowie and **ambasadorzy** 'ambassadors'
biologowie and **biolodzy** 'biologists'
bohaterowie 'main characters, heros' and **bohaterzy**
doktorowie and **doktorzy** 'doctors'
filologowie and **filolodzy** 'philologists'
magistrowie and **magistrzy** 'MA'
majstrowie and **majstrzy** 'master'
opiekunowie and **opiekuni** 'minder'
profesorowie and **profesorzy** 'professors'
prezydentowie and **prezydenci** <**prezydent** 'presidents'
burmistrzowie and **burmistrze** 'mayors'
mistrzowie and **mistrze** 'master'

Some nouns referring to male human beings have only one form, e.g.:

generałowie 'generals'
ministrowie 'ministers' <**minister**

generały and **ministry** would have a different meaning (see 3.3.8.5).

| 3.3.8.4 | *Social preference* |

Profesor has two alternative forms: **profesorzy** and **profesorowie** but **profesorowie** is used more often.

Magister has two alternative equally frequent forms: **magistrzy** and **magistrowie**.

Widz, jasnowidz and **wódz** end in the "historically" soft consonant **dz**.

Widz 'spectator' has the plural form **widzowie** 'spectators' while **jasnowidz** has the plural **jasnowidze** and **wódz** 'leader' has the plural **wodzowie**.

3.3.8.5 | Pejorative and disparaging forms

Hard-stem nouns referring to male human beings attach a typical plural ending -y without any consonant shifts to emphasize the pejorative and disparaging character of the nouns, e.g., **pany, ministry, majstry, generały**, as in **darmozjady** 'scroungers,' **nieroby** 'slobs' (see 3.2.9.3).

3.3.8.6 | Colloquial forms and those referring to children

Hard-stem colloquial nouns and nouns referring to children have the ending -y: **śpioch-y** 'sleepyheads,' **łasuch-y** 'gourmands,' **łakomczuch-y** 'big eaters,' **maluch-y** 'toddlers,' **zuch-y** 'scout, brave boy or girl.' **Staruch** 'old man' has two forms in NOM PL: **staruch-y** and **staruch-*owie***.

3.3.8.7 | Nominative male human plural -i

Masculine nouns referring to male human beings ending in a hard stem in the nominative singular (except for -k, -g, -r) take -i to form the nominative male human plural. Nouns ending in -a referring to male human beings with a hard stem (except for -cha) also take -i in nominative plural (e.g., **ten mężczyzna** <NOM SG> 'this man,' **ci mężczyźni** <NOM MHPL> 'these men'). Predictable consonant and vowel shifts occur (k, g, r in plural male human forms shift to c, dz and rz—"historically" soft consonants that do not take -i).

-i is the ending after a hard stem in nominative singular nouns referring to male human beings that end in -a except for -cha. Predictable consonant and vowel shifts occur.

183

Table 3.44 Nominative male human plural ending **-i** with hard stem

NOM SG	NOM PL	Consonant shift
adjunkt 'adjunct'	**adjunkc-***i*	t:ci
adresat 'addressee'	**adresac-***i*	t:ci
adwokat 'lawyer'	**adwokac-***i*	t:ci
anioł 'angel'	**aniel-***i*	ł:l, o:e (or **aniołowie**)
chłop 'peasant'	**chłop-***i*	p:pi
Czech 'Czech'	**Czes-***i*	ch:si
Francuz 'Frenchman'	**Francuz-***i*	z:zi
Litwin 'Lithuanian'	**Litwin-***i*	n:ni
Rumun 'Romanian'	**Rumun-***i*	
pilot 'pilot'	**piloc-***i*	t:ci
prezes 'chairman'	**prezes-***i*	s:si
sąsiad 'neighbor'	**sąsiedz-***i*	d:dzi, a:e
student 'student'	**studenc-***i*	t:ci
Szwed 'Swede'	**Szwedz-***i*	d:dzi
showman	**showman-***i*	
essesman	**essesman-***i*	
jazzman	**jazzman-***i*	
biznesmen 'businessman'	**biznesmen-***i*	
Gruzin 'Georgian'	**Gruzin-***i*	
kinoman 'film buff'	**kinoman-***i*	
lekoman 'pill-popper'	**lekoman-***i*	
meloman 'music lover'	**meloman-***i*	
weteran 'veteran'	**weteran-***i*	
Żyd 'Jewish'	**Żydzi**	d:dzi
but		
brat 'brother'	**braci-a** (old form; mixed pattern)	
Polscy znani jazzmani 'Polish known jazzmen'		

Note: The plural forms **bracia, sąsiedzi** and **anieli** are rare forms of morphological alternations.

Pilot in the meaning of 'remote control' has -y: **piloty** in NOM PL as do other inanimate masculine nouns.

Table 3.45 Nominative male human plural **-i** with hard stem ending **-a**

NOM SG	NOM PL	Consonant shift
anglista 'a specialist in English studies'	**angliśc-i**	st:śc
dyplomata 'diplomat'	**dyplomac-i**	t:ci
katecheta 'catechist'	**katechec-i**	t:ci
lekkoatleta 'athlete'	**lekkoatlec-i**	t:ci
lobbysta 'lobbyist'	**lobbyśc-i**	st:śc
maszynista 'train driver'	**maszyniści**	sta:ści
mężczyzna 'man'	**mężczyźn-i**	n:ni, z:ź
patriota 'patriot'	**patrioc-i**	t:ci
poeta 'poet'	**poeci**	t:ci
stażysta 'intern'	**stażyści**	sta:ści
polonista 'a specialist in Polish studies'	**poloniści**	sta:ści

3.3.8.8 | *Nominative male human plural* **-y**

-y is the ending in the nominative plural after the **k**, **g**, **r**, **-iec** and **-ca** stem in nominative singular nouns referring to male human beings. Predictable consonant shifts occur after **k**, **g**, **r** (1.3.4).

Table 3.46 Nominative male human plural **-y**

NOM SG	NOM PL	Consonant shift
aktor 'actor'	**aktorzy**	r:rz
Anglik 'Englishman'	**Anglicy**	k:c
chłopiec 'boy'	**chłopcy**	
doradca 'advisor'	**doradcy**	
kierowca 'driver'	**kierowcy**	
kolega 'friend'	**koledzy**	g:dz
lektor 'lecturer'	**lektorzy**	r:rz
mechanik 'mechanic'	**mechanicy**	k:c
Norweg 'Norwegian'	**Norwedzy** (or **Norwegowie**)	g:dz
Polak 'Pole'	**Polacy**	k:c
szpieg 'spy'	**szpiedzy**	g:dz
nowojorczyk 'native of New York'	**nowojorczycy**	k:c
waszyngtończyk 'native of Washington, DC'	**waszyngtończycy**	k:c
związkowiec 'union worker'	**związkowcy**	

Note that natives of cities are not capitalized (1.7).

Note the fleeting vowel in **chłopiec-chłopcy** (1.9).

3.3.8.9 | *Nominative male human plural* **-e**

-e is the ending after soft and "historically" soft stems in nominative singular nouns referring to male humans.

Table 3.47 Nominative male human plural **-e**

NOM SG	NOM PL	Consonant shift
cesarz 'emperor'	**cesarze**	
dziennikarz 'journalist'	**dziennikarze**	
geniusz 'genius'	**geniusze**	
gość 'guest'	**goście**	ć:ci before vowel **-e**
kibic 'fan'	**kibice**	
kucharz 'cook'	**kucharze**	
lekarz 'doctor'	**lekarze**	
nauczyciel 'teacher'	**nauczyciele**	
pisarz 'writer'	**pisarze**	
stolarz 'carpenter'	**stolarze**	
słuchacz 'auditor'	**słuchacze**	
działacz 'activist'	**działacze**	
truposz 'stiff' (coll.)	**truposze**	
smakosz [wina] '[wine] connoisseur'	**smakosze**	

3.3.8.10 | *Nominative male human plural* **-anie**

-anie is the ending after the **-anin** and **-an** stem in the nominative singular. The extended stem is reduced in plural forms. **Oni są Amerykanami** (not Amerykaninami) 'They are Americans.'

Table 3.48 Nominative male human plural **-anie**

NOM SG	NOM PL
Afroamerykanin 'African American'	**Afroamerykanie**
Amerykanin 'American'	**Amerykanie**
Hiszpan 'Spaniard'	**Hiszpanie**
Indianin 'Native American'	**Indianie**
krakowianin 'native of Cracow'	**krakowianie**
lublinianin 'native of Lublin'	**lublinianie**
Mołdawianin 'Moldovan'	**Mołdawianie**
poganin 'pagan'	**poganie**
Rosjanin 'Russian'	**Rosjanie**
Rzymianin 'Roman'	**Rzymianie**
Słowianin 'Slav'	**Słowianie**
warszawianin 'native of Warsaw'	**warszawianie**
wegetarianin 'vegetarian'	**wegetarianie**

Note that natives of cities are not capitalized (1.7).

| 3.3.8.11 | Accusative/genitive plural endings in masculine pattern **-y, -ów, -i, zero ending** *(-Ø)* |

| 3.3.8.12 | Genitive and accusative male human plural **-ów** |

-ów is the ending in accusative and genitive plural nouns referring to male human beings after velar, hard, "historically" soft and soft-stem nouns in the nominative singular (except for -rz, -acz, -ć, -l), and in nouns with -kanin and -an in the nominative singular (except for mężczyzna 'man'). Mistrz 'master' and compound nouns with mistrz, e.g., burmistrz 'mayor,' exceptionally take -ów.

Table 3.49 Genitive and accusative male human plural **-ów**

NOM SG	GEN PL
Amerykanin 'American'	**Amerykanów**
Anglik 'Englishman'	**Anglików**
doradca 'advisor'	**doradców**
Hiszpan 'Spaniard'	**Hiszpanów**
kierowca 'driver'	**kierowców**
kolega 'friend'	**kolegów**
królewicz 'prince'	**królewiczów**
leń 'lazy preson'	**leniów**
mąż 'husbands'	**mężów**
poeta 'poet'	**poetów**
Polak 'Pole'	**Polaków**
uczeń 'schoolboy'	**uczniów**
dureń 'fool'	**durniów** (or **durni**)
znawca 'expert'	**znawców**
związkowiec 'union member'	**związkowców**
burmistrz 'mayor'	**burmistrzów**

| 3.3.8.13 | Genitive and accusative male human plural **-y** |

-y is the ending in accusative and genitive plural nouns referring to male human beings after "historically" soft-stem nouns ending -rz, -cz -sz (except forms of mistrz 'master') in the nominative singular.

Table 3.50 Genitive and accusative male human plural **-y**

NOM SG	GEN PL
kucharz 'cook'	**kucharz-y**
lekarz 'doctor'	**lekarz-y**
działacz 'activist'	**działacz-y**
gracz 'player'	**gracz-y**
smakosz [wina] 'wine connoisseur'	**smakosz-y**

A few nouns, referring to male human beings with a **cz** and **sz**-stem, have the alternative ending **-ów** in the genitive plural, for reasons of **social** preference:

słuchacz 'auditor'	**słuchacz-y** (and rarely **słuchaczów**)	
truposz 'stiff' (coll.)	**truposz-y** (and rarely **truposzów**)	
palacz 'smoker'	**palacz-y**	**palacz-ów**
jarosz 'vegetarian'	**jarosz-y**	**jarosz-ów**
Łotysz 'Latvian'	**Łotysz-y**	**Łotysz-ów**
piwosz 'beer drinker'	**piwosz-y**	**piwosz-ów**

3.3.8.14 *Genitive and accusative male human plural* **-i**

-i is the ending in accusative and genitive plural nouns referring to male human beings with soft-stem nouns (except for **ń**, e.g., **uczeń**, **dureń**, which have **-ów**).

Table 3.51 Genitive and accusative male human plural **-i**

NOM SG	GEN PL
gość 'guest'	**gości**
nauczyciel 'teacher'	**nauczycieli**
król 'king'	**króli**
głosiciel 'proponent'	**głosiciel**
marzyciel 'dreamer'	**marzycieli**
właściciel 'owner'	**właścicieli**
zbawiciel 'savior'	**zbawicieli**
and **brat** 'brother' **braci** (old form; mixed pattern)	

Król 'king,' konsul 'consul' have **-ów** in the genitive plural: konsul-ów, król-ów, but note the set phrases Święto Trzech Króli 'Epiphany' and kolory króli 'colors of [cards of] kings.'

3.3.8.15 Social preference: Competitive genitive plural **-ów, -y, -i**

The endings in the genitive plural are still in flux for nouns with **j, cz, sz,** and **l**-stems, e.g.

Table 3.52 Genitive plural **-ów, -y, -i**

NOM SG	GEN PL
pokój 'room'	**pokoj-ów** or **poko-i** [read: pokoyee]
złodziej 'thief'	**złodziej-ów** or **złodzie-i**
hotel 'hotel'	**hotel-ów** or **hotel-i**
słuchacz 'auditor'	**słuchacz-y** or **słuchacz-ów**
truposz 'stiff' (coll.)	**truposz-y** or **truposz-ów**

3.3.8.16 Genitive and accusative male human plural **zero ending (-Ø)**

The **zero ending** (-Ø) (no ending added) is used in the accusative and genitive plural for nouns referring to male human beings ending in -**ianin**, -**janin**. (Additionally, **mężczyzna** 'man' has a zero ending in the accusative and genitive plural (**mężczyzn**).)

Table 3.53 Genitive and accusative male human plural zero ending

NOM SG	GEN PL
Rosjanin 'Russian'	**Rosjan**
Rzymianin 'Roman'	**Rzymian**
Słowianin 'Slav'	**Słowian**
warszawianin 'native of Warsaw'	**warszawian**
mężczyzna 'man'	**mężczyzn**

3.3.8.17 Instrumental male human plural **-iami** and **-mi**

-**iami** is the ending in the instrumental plural after soft-stem nouns (except for **l, j**).

-**mi** is the old ending in some nouns referring to male human beings, e.g., **braćmi** 'brothers,' **ludźmi**, 'people,' **gośćmi** 'guests,' **przyjaciółmi** 'friends.'

Table 3.54 Instrumental male human plural **-iami** and **-mi**

NOM SG	INS PL
uczeń 'school boy'	**uczniami**
dureń 'fool'	**durniami**

3.3.9 No male human plural

3.3.9.1 No male human plural declension pattern

The no male human plural declension pattern is based on the type of the stem consonant in the nominative singular.

Type of stem consonant in the nominative case:

1. **k, g, ch/h**—also called *velar*
2. **c, dz, sz, ż, rz, cz, dż**—also called *"historically" soft*
3. **ś, ć, ź, dź, ń, l, b^j, p^j, m^j, w^j, j**—also called *soft*
4. all other consonants (**b, p, f, w, m, ł, t, d, s, z, n, r**)—also called *hard*

3.3.9.2 No male human plural pattern overview

NOM   **-y/-i, -e**; for neuter plural: **-a**
ACC   as in nominative
GEN   **-ów, -y/-i**; **zero ending** (-Ø) for feminine and neuter
         nominative singular words ending in **-a** or **-o/-e** (exceptionally
         -u after dual **oczu** 'eyes,' **uszu** 'ears')
DAT   **-om**
LOC   **-ach (-ech)**
INS   **-ami/-iami/** (except for a few with the older ending **-mi:**
         nićmi 'threads <INS PL>,' **dziećmi** 'children <INS PL>')
VOC   as in nominative

For charts with examples of the full declension of nouns, refer to the masculine noun charts at Tables 3.8a to 3.19; for feminine see Tables 3.20 to 3.32; and for neuter see Tables 3.33 to 3.43.

3.3.9.3 Nominative no male human plural -y

Masculine nouns not referring to human beings and feminine nouns ending in -a with a hard stem or with a **ch/h** stem take -y in the nominative plural.

It may help to associate the ending **-y** in the plural with personal pronouns referring to a group, as in **my** 'we,' **wy** 'you all.'

Table 3.55 Nominative no male human plural **-y**

NOM SG	Nom PL
ta gazeta <FEM> 'this newspaper'	**te gazety**
ten kot <MSC> 'this cat'	**te koty**
ta góra <FEM> 'this mountain'	**te góry**
ten bar <MSC> 'this bar'	**te bary**
ten dach <MSC> 'this roof'	**te dachy**
ta blacha <FEM> 'this baking sheet'	**te blachy**

3.3.9.4 | Nominative no male human plural **-i**

The no male human plural for masculine nouns ending in **k**, **g** and for feminine nouns ending in **-ka** (except **ręka** 'hand'), **-ga**, **-(ś)ć** take **-i** in the nominative plural.

Table 3.56 Nominative no male human plural **-i**

NOM SG	Nom PL
ta książka <FEM> 'this book'	**te książki**
ten park <MSC> 'this park'	**te parki**
ta noga <FEM> 'this leg'	**te nogi**
ten targ <MSC> 'this market'	**te targi**
ta nić <FEM> 'this thread'	**te nici**

3.3.9.5 | Nominative no male human plural **-e**

-e in the nominative plural is the ending after "historically" soft and soft-stem no male human masculine and feminine nouns, e.g., **noc** <FEM> 'night'—**noce**, **koc** <MSC> 'blanket'—**koce**, **płaszcz** 'coat'—**płaszcze** (except for **brwi** 'brows,' **rzeczy** 'things,' **myszy** 'mice').

3.3.9.6 | Nominative no male human plural **-a**

-a in the nominative plural is the ending for neuter nouns and diminutive no male human masculine nouns ending in **-o**. In all cases *systematic stem changes* occur for all neuter nouns with the ending **-ę**.

191

Neuter nouns with the ending -ę referring to human offspring and animals have their stem extended by -ęt- and then the endings are added. Additionally, ę shifts to ą in the genitive plural: **zwierzę** 'animal'—**zwierząt** <GEN PL>, **zwierzętom** <DAT PL> (see Table 3.39).

Neuter nouns with the ending -ę referring to the object lose the ending -ę, have their stem extended by -on- and then the endings are added: **imię** 'name'—imi**on**a, imi**on**, imi**on**om.

Nouns with the ending -**um** have a mixed declension pattern (indeclinable in the singular, declinable in the plural: **muzeum-muzea**). (See Table 3.40)

3.3.9.7 Genitive no male human plural -**ów**

-ów is the genitive plural ending in no male human masculine nouns after hard and "historically" soft-stem nouns ending in **c, dz, sz, cz** in the nominative singular, e.g., **koców** <GEN PL> 'blankets,' **widelców** 'forks,' **palców** 'fingers,' **koszów** 'baskets,' **afiszów** 'poster,' **meczów** 'games, matches,' **płaszczów** 'coats' (with a few exceptions: **pieniądz** 'money'—**pieniędzy**, **miesiąc** 'month'—**miesięcy**, **zając** 'rabbit'—**zajęcy**, **klucz** 'key'—**kluczy**)

-ów is the ending after soft-stem **j**: **krajów** 'countries <GEN PL>.'

A few nouns with the **sz, ż**-stem can have either the genitive plural ending -ów or the genitive plural ending -ów: **wąż** 'snake' **węż-y/węż-ów**, **małż** 'clam' **małży/małżów**.

-ów is used with nouns ending in -**um**, e.g., **dużo muzeów** 'many museums'.

3.3.9.8 Genitive no male human plural -**y**

-y is the ending in genitive plural masculine no male human nouns with the "historically" soft stem **rz, ż,** and **dż**, e.g., **talerz** 'plate'—**talerzy**, **nóż** 'knife'—**noży**, **komentarz** 'commentary'—**komentarzy**.

-y is the ending in genitive plural feminine and neuter nouns after "historically" soft stems (except for **j, l**), in the nominative singular: **noc** 'night'—**nocy**, **podróż** 'journey'—**podróży**, **wybrzeże** 'coast'—**wybrzeży**, **obroża** 'collar'—**broży**, **łącze** 'connection'—**łączy** (except for **burza** 'storm'—**burz**, **branża** 'trade'—branż, kałuża 'puddle'—kałuż, zboże 'crop'—zbóż, miejsce 'place'—miejsc).

obrzeż-y (<**obrzeż-e** 'edge')
podnóż-y (<**podnóż-e**) 'base'
półrocz-y (<**półrocze** 'half-year')
ubocz-y (<**ubocze** 'out-of-the-way place')
wybrzeż-y (<**wybrzeże** 'coast')
zbocz-y (<**zbocze** 'hillside')
złącz-y (<**złącze** 'connector')
poręcz-y (<**poręcz** 'railing' <FEM>)

3.3.9.9 | Genitive no male human plural **-i**

-i is the ending in genitive plural masculine and feminine nouns after soft stems (except for **j**): **hotel** 'hotel'—**hoteli** <GEN PL>, **szpital** 'hospital'—**szpitali**, **wróbel** 'sparrows'—**wróbli**, **karp** 'carp'—**karpi**, **dzień** 'day'—**dni**, **koń** 'horse'—**koni**, **dłoń** 'palm, hand'—**dłoni**, **pieczęć** 'seal, stamp'—**pieczęci**, **gęś** 'goose'—**gęsi**, **kapsel** 'bottle cap'—**kapsli**, **kolacja** 'supper'—**kolacji**, **pościel** 'bedding'—**pościeli**. Note systematic changes where **ć, ś, ń, ź, dź** shift to **ci, si, ni, zi, dzi** before a vowel (1.3.3.2).

Some nouns can take both the **-i/-y** and **-ów** endings in genitive plural, e.g., **hotel** 'hotel'—**hoteli** or **hotelów**, **pokój** 'room'—**pokoi** or **pokojów**.

-i is the ending in genitive plural neuter nouns after the soft-stem **podziemi** (<**podziemie** 'underground'), **dziesięcioleci** (<**dziesięciolecie** 'decade'), **narzędzi** (<**narzędzie** 'tool').

Dziecko has an irregular declension and **-i** in the genitive plural: **dzieci**.

3.3.9.10 | Genitive no male human plural zero ending

The **zero ending** (-Ø) (no ending added) is the typical ending in genitive plural neuter and feminine nouns (except for nouns ending in a consonant as well certain loan words and nouns that denote a place that end in **-mia/nia** (see Tables 3.22 and 3.22a)). Systematic stem changes occur in nouns with the soft stem **ci, si, ni, zi, dzi**. Before the **zero ending** (-Ø), softness of the soft stem is expressed with a diacritical mark, e.g., **zdjęcie** 'picture'—**zdjęć**, **babcia** 'grandma'—**babć**.

193

Table 3.57 Genitive no male human plural zero ending

Feminine		Neuter	
NOM SG	GEN PL	NOM SG	GEN PL
kobieta 'woman'	kobiet	lato 'summer'	lat
para 'couple'	par	biuro 'office'	biur
burza 'storm'	burz	morze 'sea'	mórz
ulica 'street'	ulic	miejsce 'place'	miejsc
godzina 'hour'	godzin	wino 'wine'	win
sprawa 'matter'	spraw	piwo 'beer'	piw
rzeka 'river'	rzek	wieko 'lid'	wiek
babcia 'grandma'	babć	mieszkanie 'flat'	mieszkań
żona 'wife'	żon	zdjęcie 'photo'	zdjęć
skała 'rock'	skał	kolano 'knee'	kolan
		koło 'wheel'	kół
		zwierzę 'animal'	zwierząt
		imię 'first name'	imion

The **zero ending** (-Ø) is also observed exceptionally in the masculine noun **przyjaciel-przyjaciół** (Table 3.10d), and in *pluralia tantum* (a noun that is invariably plural in form but singular in sense), e.g., **spodnie** 'pants'—**spodni**, **Tatry** 'Tatra Mountains'—**Tatr**, **Alpy** 'Alps'—**Alp**, **Włochy** 'Italy'—**Włoch**, **Czechy** 'Czech Republic'—**Czech**, **Niemcy** 'Germany'—**Niemiec**, respectively.

3.3.9.11 *Zero ending with vowel shift* **o** *into* **ó**

The vowel **o** in the penultimate syllable in the nominative singular of neuter and feminine nouns shifts to **ó** in the genitive plural **zero ending** (-Ø), except with **cz**-stems, e.g.,

morze 'sea'—**mórz**   **słowo** 'word'—**słów**
pole 'field'—**pól**   **pora** 'time'—**pór**
zboże 'grain'—**zbóż**   **noga** 'leg'—**nóg**
koło 'wheel'—**kół**

3.3.9.12 *Zero ending with fleeting* **-e**

If the stem ends with a consonant cluster (a combination of two or three hard consonants including **t**, **d**, **p**, **k**, **g** except for **zd**, **sk** as in gniazdo 'nest,' **gwiazda** 'star,' **wojsko** 'army') a fleeting **e** is inserted between the consonants to ease the pronunciation, to compensate for the dropped vowel ending.

Table 3.58 Zero ending with fleeting **-e**

NOM SG	GEN PL
studentk-a 'female student'	**studentek**
książk-a 'book'	**książek**
jabłk-o 'apple'	**jabłek**
jajk-o 'egg'	**jajek**
cegła 'brick'	**cegieł**
kukła 'puppet'	**kukieł**
druhna 'bridesmaid'	**druhen**
wiadro 'bucket'	**wiader**
listwa 'slat'	**listew**

Note that collective nouns with the suffix -**stwo**, e.g., **społeczeństwo** 'society,' **małżeństwo** 'marriage,' **państwo** 'state,' drop the final -**o** in the genitive plural, without any changes: **państw, małżeństw, społeczeństw.**

| 3.3.9.13 | *Zero ending with fleeting* **-ie-**

-**ie-** is inserted in the genitive plural between two identical consonants and between two different consonants of which one is **k** or **g**.

Table 3.59 Zero ending with fleeting **-ie-**

NOM SG	GEN PL
okno 'window'	*okien*
ścięgno 'tendon'	*ścięgien*
sprzę-gł-o 'clutch'	*sprzęgieł*
i-gł-a 'needle'	*igieł*
gr-a 'game'	*gier*
kr-a 'ice floe'	*kier*
wanna 'bath(tub)'	*wanien*
panna 'miss'	*panien*
(but **mekka** 'Mecca' **mekk**)	

195

Many *pluralia tantum* nouns (nouns with only a plural form) have a zero ending after dropping the final i, y, or e, e.g.,

sanki 'sled'—**sanek, nożyce** 'scissors'—**nożyc, spodnie** 'pants'—**spodni, grabki** 'toy rake'—**grabek, widły** 'pitchfork'—**wideł.**

3.3.9.14 *Genitive no male human plural* **-u** *(dual)*

Exceptionally, **-u** is the ending for the older dual form **oczu** 'eyes', **uszu** 'ears'. (See Table 3.42)

3.4 Class agreement

The class system always requires agreement on some elements other than the nouns themselves:

1. the class of adjectives, also called **noun-adjective agreement**, which means that both noun and its adjectives agree in number, class and case:

dobry <MSC> **mąż** <MSC> 'good husband'
dobry <MSC> **kolega** <MSC> 'good colleague'
dobra <FEM> **żona** <FEM> 'good wife'
dobra <FEM> **powieść** <FEM> 'good novel'
dobre <NT> **dziecko** <NT> 'good child'
dobrzy <MHPL> **ludzie** <MHPL> 'good people'
dobre <NO-MHPL> **psy** <NO-MHPL> 'good dogs'

2. the class of demonstrative pronouns such as *this* and *these*:

ten <MSC> **brat** 'this brother'
ten <MSC> **mężczyzna** 'this man'
ta <FEM> **kobieta** 'this woman'
ta <FEM> **pani** 'this Mrs.'
to <NT> **dziecko** 'this child'
te <NO-MHPL> **znaczki** <NO-MHPL> 'these stamps'
ci <MHPL> **panowie** <MHPL> 'these gentlemen'

3. the class of personal pronouns in the singular:

on 'he' as in *ojciec* śpi '*father* is sleeping,' *on* śpi '*he* (father) is sleeping'

ona 'it' as in *mapa* jest na stole 'a map is on the table,' *ona* jest na stole '*it* is on the table' ono 'it' as in *dziecko* płacze '[the] child is crying,' and *ono* (the child) płacze '*it* is crying'

one 'they' (to replace the noun in the plural which refers to something other than male humans)

psy szczekają '*dogs* bark,' **one szczekają** '*they* (the dogs) are barking'

oni 'they' (to replace the noun or noun phrase in the plural which refers to male humans or to a group that includes any male human noun)

chłopcy grają '*boys* play,' **oni grają** '*they* (boys) play'
rodzice grają '*parents* play,' **oni grają** '*they* (parents) play'

4. the class of first and second person singular and plural possessive pronouns 'my, mine,' **mój, moja, moje, moi**; 'your(s),' **twój, twoja, twoje, twoi**; 'our(s),' **nasz, nasza, nasze, nasi**; 'your(s)' plural, **wasz, wasza, wasze, wasi** agrees with the class of the noun the possessive pronouns modify.

mój ojciec 'my father'

Note: For the third person singular possessive pronouns **jego** and **jej**, *jej* is used with feminine antecedents and *jego* is used with masculine and neuter antecedents. *Matka* **mieszka na drugim piętrze.** *Jej* **syn mieszka piętro wyżej.** '*Mother* lives on the second floor. *Her* son lives a floor above.'

5. the singular past tense form agrees with the class of the noun (see 6.5.2):

żona spała '[the] wife was sleeping'
mąż spał '[the] husband was sleeping'
dziecko spało '[the] child was sleeping'

in the plural a group with at least one human male takes the ending -li:

chłopcy spali '[the] boys were sleeping'

a group with no male humans takes the ending -ły:

psy spały '[the] dogs were sleeping'

With male human forms, "manhood" applies to a fully developed noun, therefore **dzieci** takes the ending -ły;

dzieci spały '[the] children were sleeping'

6. the conditional forms (with forms of -**by** 'would') agree with the class of the noun: **chciałabym** 'I would like <FEM>,' **chciałbym** 'I would like <MSC>,' **dziecko chciałoby** 'the child would like,' **chcieliby** 'they would

like' (groups including one male human), **chciałyby** 'they would like' (groups without one male human).

7. adjectival participles agree with the class of the noun:

śpiąca królewna 'sleeping beauty'   **męczący tydzień** 'tiring week'

3.5   Number

3.5.1 *Singular, plural, dual*

The category of number relates to quantity.

Polish has two numbers: singular **liczba pojedyncza** (**l. poj.** SG **dom** 'house') and plural **liczba mnoga** (**l. mn.** PL **domy** 'houses'). Some nouns have only singular or plural forms—*singularia tantum* (singular form only) such as **wiedza** 'knowledge' and *pluralia tantum* (invariably plural in form but singular in sense), such as **spodnie** 'pants.' A few nouns represent an old dual number, e.g., **uszy** 'ears,' **oczy** 'eyes,' **plecy** 'back,' **dwieście** 'two hundred.'

Old Polish also had dual **liczba podwójna** (dual form), whose remnants are preserved in a few words and phrases, e.g., **Mądrej głowie dość dwie słowie** 'Two words are enough for a smart head,' **dwieście** 'two hundred' (see 3.5.1.3).

3.5.1.1 *Singular*

Singular nouns relate to a single entity which can be distinguished, counted and pluralized:

dzień-dni 'day(s)'
kot(y) 'cat(s)'
dom(y) 'house(s)'

or to and non-count (mass) entity nouns, e.g., **mięso** 'meat' that can be quantified in units of measure.

Those units can be counted, but not the mass entity itself.

kilo mięsa 'a kilo of meat'

Singular nouns relate to abstracts, e.g., **wiedza** 'knowledge,' **wstręt** 'disgust.' The latter by and large do not have plural forms—they are the so-called *singularia tantum* (3.5.2).

| 3.5.1.2 | *Plural* |

Plural nouns relate to two or more entities which can be distinguished and counted:

trzy domy 'three houses'
cztery koty 'four cats'
osiem dni 'eight days'

and to uncountable entities to suggest portions:

dwa piwa 'two bottles, mugs of beer'
dwie kawy 'two cups of coffee'

or relate to entities where the meaning of the original uncountable noun is changed:

wyrazić swoje *uczucia* słowami
'to express one's *feelings* in words'

Uczucia is a plural form from **uczucie** with the meaning of a 'feeling'.

Plural forms in Polish are also often used to refer to the largest possible number of entities: **ludzie** 'people,' '**ssaki**' 'mammals.' Some nouns are plural in form but singular in sense: **spodnie** 'pants'—so called *pluralia tantum* (3.5.3).

Note:

1. In Polish, like English, some nouns can be used to represent a generic group or species in the singular or plural:

   kilogram cebuli <GEN SG> 'a kilo of onions'
   kilogram pomidorów <GEN PL> 'a kilo of tomatoes'
   placek z rabarbarem <INS SG> 'pie with rhubarb'
   placek z truskawkami <INS PL> 'pie with strawberries'

2. When the cardinal number one '**jeden**' accompanies a singular noun, the singular form of the number 'one' agrees in class and case with the noun:

   jeden <MSC> **dom** <MSC> 'one house'
   jedn<u>a</u> <FEM> **kobiet<u>a</u>** <FEM> 'one woman'
   jedn<u>o</u> <NT> **dzieck<u>o</u>** <NT> 'one child'

   The number 'one' has masculine, feminine and neuter forms (see 8.1).

3. When the cardinal number two '**dwa**' accompanies a noun, the plural form agrees in class and case with the noun:

   dwie <FEM> **kobiety** <FEM> 'two women'
   dwa <MSC> **domy** <MSC> 'two houses'
   dwa <NT> **okna** <NT> 'two windows'

dwaj <NOM male human PL> **bracia** <NOM male human PL> 'two brothers'
dwóch <GEN male human PL> **braci** <GEN male human PL> 'of two brothers'

The form **dwie** 'two' is for feminine nouns only, **dwaj** or **dwóch** for male human plural nouns. Numbers three and above are identical for feminine and neuter inanimate nouns: **trzy kobiety** 'three women,' **trzy okna** 'three windows.' Male human plural nouns **dwaj bracia** or **dwóch braci** 'two brothers' and neuter animate nouns with numerals, e.g., **dwoje dzieci** 'two children,' are discussed in Chapter 8.

4. **Półtora** 'one and a half' takes the singular form of nouns in the genitive: **półtora chleba** 'a loaf and a half,' **półtora roku** 'one and a half years.'

3.5.1.3 | Dual

The dual form in Old Polish was used to express duality and everything that naturally comes in pairs, e.g., some organs which are paired such as **oczy** 'eyes,' **uszy** 'ears,' **ręce** 'hands.' The number two was not even necessary. Arabic is one of the languages that has dual forms. In Polish, sentences with dual forms were in use until the sixteenth century.[5]

Today, nouns referring to eyes, ears, hands—natural pairs—have the forms **oczy** 'eyes,' **uszy** 'ears,' **ręce** 'hands' and can also represent more than two objects of **oko** 'eye,' **ucho** 'ear,' **ręka** 'hand.' Next to the old Polish dual forms, the language also has the plural nouns **oka** 'circles on a fabric' or 'fat drops in chicken broth,' and **ucha** 'handles,' whose meaning is different, although refers to the similar shape.

Note the locative forms of **ręka**: **w ręce** 'in one hand' and **w rękach** 'in both hands' (not: w ręcach) <LOC PL>. **W ręku** is the former dual form.

In modern Polish, the dual forms are used less frequently than regular plural forms.

> **ucha dzbana** 'pitcher handles'
> **leżeć z zamkniętymi oczyma** or **oczami** 'to lie with eyes closed'
> **machać rękoma** or **rękami** 'to wave'

3.5.2 | Singular only nouns

Nouns in the singular form only (*singularia tantum*) include **zło** 'evil,' **wstręt** 'disgust,' **uraza** 'resentment.'

There are nouns which are singular in form but not in meaning: **Kiedy państwo przyszli?** 'When did you (Mr. and Mrs.) arrive?

The following are also singular only:

Collective nouns, e.g., **młodzież** 'young people,' **szlachta** 'nobility,' **pierze** 'feathers'

geographical places

concepts with the endings **-izm/-yzm**, e.g., **patriotyzm** 'patriotism,' **komunizm** 'communism.'

| **3.5.3** | *Plural only nouns* |

Plural only nouns (*pluralia tantum*) are nouns that only have a grammatically plural form (they have no singular form). However, they can have a singular meaning:

chrzciny 'christening ceremony'	**nudności** 'nausea'
cymbałki 'chimes'	**ogrodniczki** 'overalls'
drzwi 'door'	**peryferie** 'outskirts'
fusy 'sediment, tea leaves'	**sanie** 'sledge'
grabie 'rake'	**sanki** 'sledge'
grabki 'toy rake'	**skrzypce** 'violin'
imieniny 'name day'	**spodnie** 'pants'
kajdanki 'handcuffs'	**urodziny** 'birthday'
lejce 'reins'	**widły** 'farm fork'
nosze 'stretcher'	**zaręczyny** 'engagement party'
nożyczki 'scissors'	

Konie ciągnęły <u>pięcioro</u> <u>sań</u>. 'Horses were pulling <u>five</u> <u>sleighs</u>.'

> **Dwoje** <collective numeral> **skrzypiec** <GEN PL> **było** <SG verb>
> **opartych** <ADJ GEN PL> **o ścianę.**
> '<u>Two violins were leaning</u> on the door.'

Use collective numbers with *pluralia tantum* (see 8.1.2).

Also geographical places

Alpy 'Alps'	**Katowice** 'city in Poland'
Beskidy 'mountains in Poland'	**Kielce** 'city in Poland'
Bieszczady 'mountains in Poland'	**Malediwy** 'the Maldives'
Chiny 'China'	**Pireneje** 'Pyrenees'
Hawaje 'Hawaii'	**Tatry** 'mountains in Poland'
Himalaje 'Himalayas'	**Wadowice** 'city in Poland'
Indie 'India'	

Plural only nouns in the subject position take no male human plural verbal endings (the past tense formation **były**).

> **Gdzie *są/były* moje spodnie?** 'Where are/were my pants?'

Declension of the *pluralia tantum* follows the no male human pattern

NOM	**długie spodnie** 'long pants'
ACC	**długie spodnie**
GEN	**długich spodni**
DAT	**długim spodniom**
LOC	**długich spodniach**
INS	**długimi spodniami**

For the genitive plural **zero ending** (-Ø), see 3.3.9.10.

3.6   Types of nouns

3.6.1 │ Proper

A proper noun is a noun whose only function is to refer to a designated entity.

> ***Gazeta Wyborcza*** (*Election Gazette*, daily newspaper in Poland)
> **Adam Mickiewicz**
> **Boże Narodzenie** 'Christmas'
> **Dworzec Centralny** (Warsaw main station)
> **Krzyżacy** 'The Order of Teutonic Knights'
> **Lech Wałęsa**
> **Mazury** <PL> 'Masuria'
> **Nowy Rok** 'New Year's Eve'
> **Pałac Kultury i Nauki** 'Palace of Culture and Science'
> **rzeka Wisła** 'River vistula'
> **Tatry** 'Tatra mountains'
> **Warszawa** 'Warsaw'

For the use of capital letters with proper nouns, see 1.7.1.

3.6.2 │ Common

A common noun is a noun which is not a proper noun: **młodość** 'youth,' **gazeta** 'newspaper,' **osoba** 'person.' Nouns can also be *concrete* (their meaning is perceived as a physical entity, e.g., can be felt or seen): **talerz** 'plate,' **mgła** 'fog,' **ściana** 'wall' or *abstract* (their meaning is an abstract concept): **piękno** 'beauty,' **pisownia** 'spelling.' They can be *individual* nouns (denote an individual object or subject): **mieszkaniec** 'resident,' **esej** 'essay' or *collective* nouns (a group of individuals): **społeczeństwo** 'society,' **duchowieństwo** 'clergy,' **szlachta** 'nobility,' **młodzież** 'young people.'

3.6.3 | *Collective*

In English, collective nouns are sometimes used with either a singular or plural verb. In Polish, most collective nouns are used with singular verbs and singular forms of adjectives (e.g., **państwo** in the meaning of 'couple' but not 'state').

> *Społeczeństwo* <collective NT SG noun> **polskie** <NT SG ADJ> *dokonało* <NT SG verb> **wyboru.**
> 'The Polish people have made their decision.'
> *Państwo* <collective NT SG noun> *ufundowało* <NT SG verb> **wakacje dzieciom.**
> 'The state funded vacation for children.'
> *Dziki tłum* <collective MASC SG noun> *rzucił się* <MASC SG verb> **ku drzwiom sklepu.**
> 'A wild crowd rushed to the store's door.'
> *Armia* <FEM SG collective noun> *stała* <FEM SG verb> **już pod miastem.**
> 'The army was standing close to the city.'
> *Igliwie* <NT SG collective noun> *było* <NT SG verb> **pełne olejków eterycznych.**
> 'The pine needles were full of essentials oils.'

Państwo with the meaning of 'couple' *or* 'a group of people' uses a male human plural verb:

> **Państwo Nowakowie <u>kupili</u>** <MALE HUMAN PL verb> **nowy dom.**
> 'Mr. and Mrs. Nowak <u>bought</u> a new house.'
> **Ci państwo stali** <MALE HUMAN PL verb> **za nami.**
> 'These people were behind us.'
> **Czy państwo się znają** <MALE HUMAN PL verb>**?**
> 'Do you know each other?'

Other examples of collective referring to a couple that take male human plural verbs include:

> **wujostwo** 'aunt and uncle'
> **kuzynostwo** 'cousin with his/her wife, husband'
> **hrabiostwo** 'count and countess'

Odwiedzili nas wujostwo z Warszawy. 'Aunt and uncle from Warsaw visited us.'

Kuzynostwo już odjechali. '[Our] Cousin and his wife have already left.'

Adjectival

Pomiędzy ślepcami *jednooki* królem.
'In the country of the blind *the one-eyed* is a king' (Erasmus)

The group of words that are nouns in meaning but are declined like adjectives is called adjectival nouns.

An example in English can be 'superior' referring to a senior officer. Adjectival nouns are masculine or feminine based on the biological gender of the noun they refer to.

znajomy 'friend' referring to a male
znajoma 'friend' referring to a female

Most adjectival nouns refer to human beings. The adjectival nouns that refer to animals or objects are masculine or feminine based on the ending of the adjective in the nominative case.

luty 'February' is masculine just like **dobry** 'good'
czesne 'tuition fee(s)' is no male human plural like **dobre**
Chory **poprosił o wodę.** '[The] *Patient (sick person)* asked for water.'

Adjectival nouns decline like adjectives.

Piotr jest głównym *księgowym*. 'Piotr is the chief *accountant*.'
Zadzwoń do głównego księgowego. 'Call the chief accountant.'
Ania to nasza dobra *znajoma*. 'Ania is our good *friend*.'
Myślę o naszej dobrej znajomej. 'I am thinking about our good *friend*.'
w lutym 'in February'
zasiłek dla bezrobotnych 'benefit *for [the] unemployed*'
Pentagon wymienił *głównodowodzącego* w Afganistanie.
   'The Pentagon changed the *commander-in-chief* in Afghanistan.'
Idę *do krawcowej*. 'I'm going *to the dressmaker*.'
Przejście *dla pieszych*. 'A street crossing [*for pedestrians*].'
średni kurs złotego 'the average *zloty* rate'
córka dobrego *znajomego* 'a daughter of a good *friend*'

Adjectival nouns are mostly used in the masculine and feminine singular forms, and as the male human form in the plural.

bezdomny <MSC>, **bezdomna** <FEM>, 'homeless person',
   bezdomni <male human form> 'the homeless'
narzeczony <MSC>, **narzeczona** <FEM>, 'fiancé',
   narzeczeni <male human form> 'the engaged couple'

(see also 4.12)

| 3.6.4.1 | Usage |

Adjectival nouns (adjectives used as nouns) are common in Polish and decline like adjectives. When adjectives are used alone (without nouns) as predicates with verbs meaning 'to be, to become' they are put in the instrumental case if they have the sense of being a noun that the subject is or is becoming (common with professions), and they are put in the nominative case if they have the sense of being an adjective describing an aspect of the subject.

Piotr jest *wojskowym* <INS>. 'Piotr is *a military man*.'
Piotr jest *uczonym* <INS>. 'Piotr is *a scholar*.'
Piotr jest *chorym* <INS>. 'Piotr is the *patient/sick individual*.'

Piotr jest bezdomny <NOM>. 'Piotr is homeless.'
Piotr jest bezrobotny <NOM>. 'Piotr is unemployed.'
Piotr jest chory <NOM>. 'Piotr is sick.'

Examples of adjectival nouns:

bagażowy 'luggage clerk'
bezdomny 'homeless person'
bezrobotny 'unemployed person'
biegły (sądowy) 'expert witness'
budowniczy 'builder'
chory 'sick'
czesne 'tuition fee(s)'
dyżurny, dyżurna 'duty officer'
głównodowodzący 'commander-in-chief'
krawcowa 'dressmaker'
krewny 'relative'

księgowy 'accountant'
luby, luba 'paramour'
luty 'February'
myśliwy 'hunter'
narzeczony, narzeczona 'fiancé'
niemy 'deaf person'
niewidomy 'blind person'
pieszy 'pedestrian'
podstoli 'master of the pantry'
podwładny, podwładna 'subordinate'
prawoskrzydłowy 'right wing'
przełożony, przełożona 'superior' (NOM PL **przełożeni**)
przewodniczący, przewodnicząca (członek)—'chair (member)'
przyjezdny 'visitor'
radny 'councilor'
ranny 'wounded'
salowy, salowa 'hospital attendant'
uczony 'scholar'
wojskowy 'military man'
woźny 'janitor'
złoty 'zloty' (Polish currency)
znajomy, znajoma (człowiek) 'acquainted (person)'

Many feminine nouns that are declined like adjectives are listed here:

-owa 'a wife of'

baronowa 'baroness'	**królowa** 'queen'
bratowa 'brother's wife, sister-in-law'	**synowa** 'son's wife, daughter-in-law'
cesarzowa 'empress'	**szefowa** 'female boss'
generałowa 'general's wife'	**teściowa** 'mother-in-law'

3.6.4.2 | Declension

Adjectival nouns are generally declined like adjectives—their case marking correlates with the adjective case marking, for example the plural of **znajomy** is **znajomi**, the locative case of **luty** 'February' is **w luty***m* 'in February' (like **w stary***m* from the adjective **stary** 'old').

Table 3.60 Declension of adjectival nouns

Case	MSC SG	FEM SG	NT SG	No male human PL	Male human PL
NOM	znajom-y 'friend'	znajom-a	znajom-e	znajom-e 'friends'	znajom-i
ACC	znajom-ego	znajom-ą	znajom-e	znajom-e	znajom-ych
GEN	znajom-ego	znajom-ej	znajom-ego	znajom-e	znajom-ych
DAT	znajom-emu	znajom-ej	znajom-emu	znajom-ym	znajom-ym
LOC	znajom-ym	znajom-ej	znajom-ym	znajom-ych	znajom-ych
INS	znajom-ym	znajom-ą	znajom-ym	znajom-ymi	znajom-ymi
VOC	znajom-y	znajom-a	znajom-e	znajom-e	znajom-i

Case	MSC SG	MHPL
NOM	chorąż-y 'warrant officer'	chorąż-owie
ACC	chorąż-ego	chorąż-ych
GEN	chorąż-ego	chorąż-ych
DAT	chorąż-emu	chorąż-ym
LOC	chorąż-ym	chorąż-ych
INS	chorąż-ym	chorąż-ymi
VOC	chorąż-y	chorąż-owie

3.6.5 | Mixed pattern

In the mixed pattern (hereclite declension pattern), many proper nouns combine a noun and an adjective, and are declined according to the noun and adjectival patterns, e.g., the town name **Białystok** literally means **biały** 'white' **stok** 'slope.' **Stok** is a masculine inanimate noun.

Table 3.61 Mixed pattern proper nouns

Case	Białystok
NOM	Biał-y-stok
ACC	Biał-y-stok
GEN	Biał-ego-stok-u
DAT	Biał-emu-stok-owi
LOC	Biał-ym-stok-u
INS	Biał-ym-stoki-em
VOC	Biał-y-stok-u

In the phrase **Rzeczpospolita Polska** 'Republic of Poland' (**rzecz** 'thing,' **pospolita** 'common') either only the second, adjectival part of the phrase is declined, as in **obywatel Rzeczpospolitej Polskiej** 'citizen of the Republic of Poland,' or both parts are declined, as in **Prezydent Rzeczypospolitej Polskiej** 'President of the Republic of Poland' (the more formal way).

Table 3.62 Rzeczpospolita Polska

Case	Singular
NOM	**Rzeczpospolit-a Polsk-a** 'Republic of Poland'
ACC	**Rzeczpospolit-ą Polsk-ą**
GEN	**Rzeczpospolit-ej Polski-ej** or **Rzecz-y-pospolit-ej Polski-ej**
DAT	**Rzeczpospolit-ej Polski-ej** or **Rzecz-y-pospolit-ej Polski-ej**
LOC	**Rzeczpospolit-ej Polski-ej** or **Rzecz-y-pospolit-ej Polski-ej**
INS	**Rzeczpospolit-ą Polsk-ą** or **Rzecz-ą-pospolit-ą Polsk-ą**
VOC	**Rzeczypospolit-a Polsk-a**

Krasnystaw (town name, **krasny** 'pretty' from Russian, **staw** 'pond')
Zatrzymał się w Krasnymstawie na obiad. 'He stopped in Krasnystaw for lunch.'
Jadę do Białegostoku. 'I'm going to Białystok.'
Nowy Targ (town name, **nowy** 'new,' **targ** 'market')
Wracamy z Nowego Targu. 'We are coming back from Nowy Targ.'
Królowa Polska (village name, **królowa** 'queen,' **polska** 'Polish')
Babcia mieszka w Królowej Polskiej. 'Grandma lives in Królowa Polska.'

3.6.6 | Homonyms

These are words that have the same form but different meanings—*Homo* means 'the same'—like **pączek** 'donut' or 'bud,' **zamek** 'lock' or 'castle,' **kolejka** 'line' or 'cableway' or 'within city train,' **piec** 'oven' or 'to bake,' **koło** 'wheel' or the preposition 'near,' **bez** 'lilac' or the preposition 'without,' **mam** 'I have' or the genitive form of the noun **mama** 'mother,' **kozak** 'Cossack dance,' 'knee-high boot,' 'birch mushroom' and **Kozak** 'Cossack,' **brać** 'to take' or a 'group of students' as in **brać studencka**, **wieczór** 'evening' or 'soirée.'

Sometimes depending on the meaning of the noun, different endings occur. Compare:

ruiny zamku 'the ruins of a castle'
zasuwa zamka '[the] lock's bolt'
od rana do wieczora 'from morning to evening'
miłego wieczoru 'have a nice evening'

3.6.7 Eponyms

Eponyms or eponymous words are words that are named after the person who inspired or invented them. Capital letters are not used. In Polish there are many words that are related to the people who contribute to Polish vocabulary:

lenonki (John Lennon's style of small round glasses)
amerykanka 'chair-bed': **położyć się na amerykance** 'to lay down on a chair-bed.'
gilotyna 'guillotine' (Joseph Guillotin)
prysznic 'shower' (Vincenz Priessnitz)

3.7 Difference between English and Polish nouns

3.7.1 Definiteness

Polish nouns do not have the indefinite article "a" or "an" or a definite article "the" (for more on definite articles, see 5.5.3.1).

Zjadłem jabłko.
'I ate an/the apple.'

Postaw to na stół.
'Put it on a/the table.'

In Polish, sometimes to signalize the indefinite character of a noun, a form of **jakiś** 'some' or 'any' can be added in front of the noun.

Chcę kupić jakiś prezent dla babci.
'I want to buy a gift for grandmother.'

Jakaś dziewczyna dzwoniła do ciebie godzinę temu.
'A girl called you an hour ago.'

Czy mają państwo jakieś pytania?
Do you have any questions? (formal)

Many Polish nouns that denote professions, ranks or titles do not have a female form, e.g., **dziekan** 'dean,' **premier** 'prime minister,' **pułkownik** 'colonel' (Chapter 12).

Dziekan Jaworska była wybitnym etnografem.
'Dean Jaworska was an outstanding ethnographer.'

3.7.2 | *Structure*

In English two nouns can be linked to each other with "s", the preposition "of" or without any prepositions, e.g., "bank manager" *or* "manager of the bank." In Polish two nouns next to each other are mostly expressed in the genitive case. This is marked on the noun that in English would have "s" or the noun first in the phrase.

> **data** <+GEN> *urodzin* 'date *of birth*'
> **kierownik** <+GEN> *banku* '*bank* manager'
> **dom** <+GEN> *siostry* '*sister's* house'

The partitive genitive is often used in Polish.

> **daj** <+GEN> **wina** 'give some wine'
> **podaj** <+ACC> **wino** 'give a bottle of wine'

Quantitative adverbs (words that relate to numerals and have a nominal nature), e.g., **dużo** 'a lot,' **wiele** and **wielu** 'many,' **dwukrotnie** 'twice, twofold,' **mało** 'not much,' '(a) little,' 'few'; **trochę** 'a little bit'; **kilka** and **kilku** 'a few'; **ile** 'how much, how many'; **niewiele** 'a little,' 'few'; **tyle** 'so much, so many' and numerals denoting more than five (except for numerals ending in the words **dwa, trzy, cztery**) take the genitive plural.

> **W pokoju jest/było** <present/past NT SG> **kilka osób** <GEN PL>.
> 'A few people are/were in the room.'

> **Parę godzin** <GEN PL> **minęło** <past NT SG> **od wypadku.**
> 'A few hours have passed since the accident.'

> **Wiele domów** <GEN PL> **spaliło** <past NT SG> **się do cna.**
> 'Many houses were burnt to the ground.'

> **Siedmiu sędziów** <GEN PL> **było** <past NT SG> **za umorzeniem sprawy.**
> 'Seven judges were in favor that the case was dismissed.'

Also, when quantitative adverbs are used in the subject position, the genitive is used and the verb is in the third person singular form (in the past the neuter form (marker -ło)).

> **Dużo ciekawych książek** <GEN PL> **było/jest w pokoju profesora.**
> 'Many interesting books were/are in the professor's room.'
> **Wielu studentów** <GEN PL> **zachorowało.** 'Many students <mixed group> got sick.'
> **Wiele studentek** <GEN PL> **zachorowało.** 'Many students <all female> got sick.' (See 2.4.10.1)

Polish is an inflected language—it means that it has case markings to signalize the function of the noun in a sentence. **Ewa lubi Piotr-a** 'Ewa likes Piotr,' **Piotr lubi Ew-ę** 'Piotr likes Ewa' (see Chapter 2).

3.7.3 | *Translation difficulties*

Some genitive constructions in Polish could be ambiguous, while in English they are clear:

> **portrety babci** 'grandmother's portraits' or 'portraits of
>   grandmother's'
> **zdjęcia dziadka** 'grandfather's pictures' or 'pictures of grandfather's'

The context in which the sentences are used clarifies the meaning.

3.7.4 | *Number*

Note that a noun in Polish and its equivalent in English can have different numbers.

> **Zdrowe włosy** <PL> **są piękne.** 'Healthy hair <SG> is beautiful.'
> **Drzwi** <PL> **są po prawej stronie.** 'The door <SG> is on the right.'
> **Informacje** <PL> **są potrzebne.** 'Information <SG> is needed.'

Male human plural nouns (groups with at least one male human in them) in Polish take the past tense ending -**li**; no male human plural nouns (groups without any male human in them) take -**ły**.

> panowie **byli** 'men were'   panie **były** 'women were'

In Polish, like English, irregular forms can occur in the plural, where different forms of the word are derived from different stems: **człowiek-ludzie** 'person-people,' **dziecko-dzieci** 'child-children,' **rok-lata** 'year-years.'

3.8   Indeclinable nouns

Many indeclinable nouns are neuter, e.g., **piję kakao** 'I drink cocoa,' **płacę jedno euro** 'I pay one euro,' **gram w gry wideo** 'I play video games,' **słucham stereo** 'I'm listening to the stereo.'

They may have different endings: with -i such as **alibi, sushi, dementi** 'denial,' **kombi** 'station wagon,' **etui** '(eyeglasses) case,' **graffiti, spaghetti, harakiri** 'hara-kiri,' or -o, -u, such as **fatum** 'fate,' **kukuryku** 'tuft of hair sticking up,' **menu, opus, Alleluja, kilo, widzimisię** 'whim (coll.).'

Feminine proper and common loan nouns that end in any letter other than -**a** are indeclinable, e.g.: **Kupiłam lalkę Barbi.** 'I bought a Barbie doll.'

> **Napijesz się pepsi?** 'Would you like some Pepsi?'
> **Zadzwonię do Lee.** 'I'll call Lee.'

Proper nouns referring to a female human being are indeclinable if they do not end in -**a**, e.g.:

> **Rozmawiamy o Hillary.** 'We are talking about Hillary.' (referring to a female)
> **Rozmawiamy o Hillarym.** 'We are talking about Hillary.' (last name, referring to a male)

Neuter proper and common loan nouns that end in -**i** and -**o** are indeclinable (except for nouns that have already become declinable, e.g., **kino** 'cinema,' **radio, metro, Marocco**), e.g.:

> **Jem sushi.** 'I am eating sushi.'
> **Lubię spaghetti.** 'I like spaghetti.'
> **Napij się gorącego kakao przed snem.** 'Have some hot cocoa before going to bed.'
> **Mam alibi.** 'I have an alibi.'
> **Wesołego Alleluja!** 'Happy Easter!'
> **Mam dwa wideo.** 'I have two VCRs.'
> **ty masz swoje, a swoje widzimisię** 'you have your own fussy way and I have my own' (coll.)
> **Nie chcę cappucino.** 'I don't want cappuccino.'
> **Zapłaciłam dwa euro.** 'I paid two euros.'

In colloquial speech it is acceptable to use **dwie łyżki kakaa**.

Many words that in the past were indeclinable in Polish, e.g., **radio, metro, studio** are declinable today. **Ksero** 'photo(copier)', even though officially indeclinable, is declinable in everyday language, e.g.:

> **Nie mamy w biurze ksera.** 'We don't have [a] copier in the office.'
> **Zostawiłeś to na kserze.** 'You left it on the copier.'

It looks like it is just a matter of time when words with already existing patterns will be fully declined in Polish (**ksero** declines like **biuro**).

Serum presents an interesting example. If declined like **muzeum**, it would have the form **sera** in the plural, which overlaps with the genitive form of the noun "cheese," e.g.:

Kupiłam dwa <u>sera</u>.(!) 'I bought two serums.'
Nie ma w domu <u>sera</u>. 'There is no cheese at home.'

Some geographical places are indeclinable: **Monako, Monachium, Notting Hill, Chelsea, Bonn, Buenos Aires, Tibilisi, Tokio, Skopje, Oslo, Kigali, Montevideo, Hanoi, Betlejem, Toronto, Sacramento.** Many U.S. states are indeclinable: **Tennessee, Utah, Kentucky, Delaware, Ohio, Massachusetts, Colorado.**

Mieszkam w Bonn. 'I live in Bonn.'

Many acronyms that end in a vowel sound when pronounced are indeclinable:

PKO [pe-ka-o], **PKP** [pe-ka-pe], **PO** [pe-o], **PZU** [pe-zet-u]
Pracuję w PZU, a mój syn w PKO. 'I work at PZU,
    and my son at PKP.'

In general, acronyms that end in a consonant sound when pronounced are declinable as masculine singular nouns.

Uczę się na UJ-ocie. [from **UJ** 'u-jot,' **Uniwersytet Jagielloński**]
    (Uniwersytet Jagielloński)
'I am studying at Jagiellonian University.'

Titles and professions referring to a female human being with an ending other than **-a** are indeclinable: **doktor** 'doctor,' **psycholog** 'psychologist,' **dziekan** 'dean.'

Mam wizytę u doktor Kowalskiej. 'I have an appointment with
    doctor Kowalska.'
Spotkanie z dziekan Kowalską. 'A meeting with dean Kowalska.'

These nouns used to be indeclinable, now they are not!

Kino, metro, radio, Maroko and **Maryland** are declinable.
wakacje w Maroku 'vacation in Morocco'
podróż do Maroka 'a trip to Morocco'
przyjechać do Marylandu 'to come to Maryland'
Często jeżdżę metrem. 'I often go by metro.'
Idziemy do kina. 'We are going to the movies.'
Nie mam radia. 'I don't have a radio.'

3.9 Declension of first and last names

-ski/-cki are typical adjectival last name endings, e.g., **Kowalski, Jarecki**.

When referring to a female human being, all last names with an ending other than -a are indeclinable.

When referring to a male human being, first and last names ending in a consonant follow masculine animate noun declensions, e.g., **Rozmawiam o Igorze.** 'I'm talking about Igor.'

Nominative male human plural often has the ending -owie.

> **Widzę Adama Kościuszkę.** 'I see Adam Kościuszko.'
> **Widzę Ewę Kościuszko.** 'I see Ewa Kościuszko.'

All first names with an ending other than -a stay indeclinable when referring to a female human being.

> **Widzę Nancy Reagan.** 'I see Nancy Reagan.'
> **Widzę Margaret Thatcher.** 'I see Margaret Thatcher.'
> Compare: **Widzę Ronalda Reagana.** 'I see Ronald Reagan.'

Last names with -ko and -a referring to a male human being are declined according to the feminine pattern (see Tables 3.26, 3.26a).

First and last names with a consonant or -o, e.g., **Nowak, Pacino, Canaletto,** referring to a male human being, are declined according to the masculine pattern (see Table 3.18).

Proper names (first and last names) with the ending -e are declined according to the adjectival pattern, like **urocz-e** 'charming,' **urocz-*ego*,** urocz-*emu*:

> **Nitzsche, Goethe**
> **Czytam Nitzsch*ego*.** 'I'm reading Nitzsche.'
> **Dzięki Nitzsch*emu*.** 'Thanks to Nitzsche.'
> **Rozmawiam o Nitzschem** (like **Zakopanem—**
>   old instrumental ending) 'I talk about Nitzsche'

Osborne is declined similarly to **ogon** 'tail.' Osborne'a, Osborne'owi.

Use the apostrophe when the final letter is a vowel, e.g.,

> **Widzę Billa Clintona.** 'I see Bill Clinton.'
> **Widzę Ozzy'ego Osborne'a.** 'I see Ozzy Osborne.'

Table 3.63 Declension of last names

Case	Singular	MHPL	SG MSC/FEM	MHPL/NO-MHPL
NOM	**Wałęs-a**	**Wałęs-owie**	**Jareck-i/Jareck-a**	**Jarecc-y/Jarecki-e**
ACC	**Wałęs-ę**	**Wałęs-ów**	**Jarecki-ego/Jareck-ą**	**Jareck-ich/Jarecki-e**
GEN	**Wałęs-y**	**Wałęs-ów**	**Jarecki-ego/Jarecki-ej**	**Jareck-ich**
DAT	**Wałęsi-e**	**Wałęs-om**	**Jarecki-emu/Jarecki-ej**	**Jareck-im**
LOC	**Wałęsi-e**	**Wałęs-ach**	**Jareck-im/Jarecki-ej**	**Jareck-ich**
INS	**Wałęs-ą**	**Wałęs-ami**	**Jareck-im/Jareck-ą**	**Jareck-imi**
VOC	**Wałęs-o**	**Wałęs-owie**	**Jareck-i/Jareck-a**	**Jarecc-y/Jarecki-e**
NOM	**Nowak**	**Nowakowie**		
ACC	**Nowaka**	**Nowaków**		
GEN	**Nowaka**	**Nowaków**		
DAT	**Nowakowi**	**Nowakom**		
LOC	**Nowaku**	**Nowakach**		
INS	**Nowakiem**	**Nowakami**		
VOC	**Nowaku**	**Nowakowie**		

3.10 Consonant and vowel changes

Table 3.64 shows examples of consonant and vowel changes within the singular *locative case* for masculine, feminine and neuter nouns to illustrate the process of softening—also called *palatalization*. (See 1.3.5)

Changes within vowels:

> **ó:o** in the penultimate position: **stół:stole, samochód:samochodzie, naród:narodzie, lód:lodzie, powódź:powodzi** but **podróż:podróży**
> **o:ó: noga:nóg, droga:dróg, choroba:chorób, morze:mórz, pole:pól, zboże:zbóż, koło:kół, siostra:sióstr, stopa, stóp, prośba:próśb, podłoga:podłóg**
> **ó:e kościół:kościele, popiół:popiele**
> **e:ó (nie)przyjaciel:(nie)przyjaciół**
> **a:e świat-świecie, obiad-obiedzie, wiatr-wietrze, lato-lecie, sąsiad-sąsiedzie, miasto:mieście, ciasto-cieście, las:lesie** (but **pasi-e**), **wyjazd:wyjeździe, wiara:wierze, miara:mierze** (but **kara:karze**), **gwiazda:gwieździe (gazda:gaździe, mazda:maździe)**
> **ą:ę mąż:mężu, łabądź:łabędziu, gołąb:gołębiu**
> **o:e anioł:aniele, imienia:imion (e:o)**
> **rzec:rc marzec:marcu, dworzec:dworca**
> **ec:c chłopiec:chłopca, kupiec:kupca, ojciec:ojca**
> **ek:k dziadek:dziadka**
> **k:ek matka:matek**

215

Table 3.64 Consonant and vowel changes in locative singular

	Masculine		Neuter		Feminine	
	NOM	LOC	NOM	LOC	NOM	LOC
b:bie	klub 'club'	klub-ie	niebo 'sky'	nieb-ie	szyba 'pane'	szyb-ie
p:pie	sklep 'store'	sklep-ie	tempo 'rate'	temp-ie	zupa 'soup'	zup-ie
m:mie	film	film-ie	pismo 'writing'	piśm-ie	mama	mam-ie
but dom-u, panu, synu, **Radom-iu**, **Bytom-iu**, **Oświęcimiu**!						
n:nie	hymn 'anthem'	hymn-ie	okno 'window'	okn-ie	cena 'price'	cen-ie
but **Bonn**						
w:wie	Kraków	Krakowi-e	piwo 'beer'	piw-ie	Warszawa	Warszaw-ie
but **Wrocław-iu**						
f:fie	szef 'boss'	szef-ie			sofa	sof-ie
s:sie	nos 'nose'	nos-ie	mięso 'meat'	mięs-ie	kasa 'cashier'	kas-ie
z:zie	gaz 'gas'	gaz-ie	żelazo 'iron'	żelaz-ie	wiza 'visa'	wiz-ie
t:cie	brat 'brother'	braci-e	auto 'car'	auci-e	huta 'mill'	huci-e
d:dzie	samochód 'car'	samochodzi-e	rondo 'roundabout'	rondzi-e	woda 'water'	wodzi-e
st:ście	tekst 'text'	tekści-e	miasto 'city'	mieści-e	lista 'list'	liści-e
r:rze	bar	barz-e	biuro 'office'	biurz-e	opera	operz-e
ł:le	stół 'table'	stol-e	mydło 'soap'	mydl-e	szkoła 'school'	szkol-e
k:ce					Ameryka 'America'	Ameryc-e
zd:ździe	wyjazd 'exit'	wyjeździ-e	gniazdo 'nest'	gnieździ-e	gwiazda 'star'	gwieździ-e
sł:śle	umysł 'mind'	umyśl-e	hasło 'password'	haśl-e	Wisła 'Vistula'	Wiśl-e
s(e)n:śnie	sen 'dream'	śni-e	Krosno (city)	Krośni-e	wiosna 'spring'	wiośni-e
g:dze					Praga 'Prague'	Pradz-e
ch/h:sze					Doha 'Doha'	Dosz-e

Note: Velar stem **k**, **g**, **ch/h** changes are observed only in feminine nouns. Both masculine and neuter take the ending **-u** without any alternations.

Alternative forms:

czoło 'forehead' **na czole**
czoło 'in the first rows, at the head of something.' **na czele**

Table 3.65 Noun declensions

	Singular			Plural		
	MSC	NT	FEM	MSC	NT	FEM
NOM	ø (-a, -o)	-o -e -ę	-a (-ø[1] -i)	-i -y -e -owie[2,3]	-a	-i -y -e
ACC	-ø, -a (-ę, -o)		-e[4] (-ø)	= NOM/GEN		
GEN	-a -u[5] (-i/-y)	-a	-i/-y	-ów (-i/-y)	-ø -y[6]	-ø -i -y
DAT	-owi (-u[7], -'e, -i/-y)	-u	-'e -i/-y	-om		
LOC	-'e -u[8] (-i/-y)			-ach		
INS	-(i)em (-ą)		-ą -ią	-ami -mi[9]		
VOC	-'e -u[10] (-o)	= NOM	-o[11] -u[12] -i/-y (-ø)	= NOM		

Notes
[1] Feminine soft consonant endings include: **-ość, kolej, mysz, myśl, noc, pieśń, podróż, rzecz, twarz, wieś.**
[2] **Brat** has the form **bracia.**
[3] **Pan, ojciec, syn, mąż,** and **wuj** have the forms **panowie, ojcowie, synowie, mężowie,** and **wujowie,** respectively.
[4] **Pani** has the accusative singular form **panią.**
[5] The ending **-a** prevails with animate nouns, but inanimate nouns may take **-a** or **-u.**
[6] A small group, mostly three syllables, takes **-y,** e.g., **przymierzy, narzędzi.**
[7] A small group, mostly monosyllabic, takes **-u: Bogu, bratu, chłopu, chłopcu, diabłu, ojcu, panu, lwu, kotu, psu, światu.**
[8] The consonants **-k(o), -g(o),** and **-ch(o)** take the ending **-u,** except **Bóg,** which has the form **Boże.**
[9] **Gość, koń, pieniądz, ludzie** (no SG), **przyjaciel, brat,** and **dziecko** have the forms **gośćmi, końmi, pieniędzmi, ludźmi, przyjaciółmi, braćmi,** and **dziećmi,** respectively.
[10] The ending **-ec** mutates, e.g., **chłopiec** becomes **chłopcze, ojciec** becomes **ojcze, kupiec** becomes **kupcze.**
[11] The ending **-i** remains unchanged.
[12] The endings **-cia, -dzia, -la, -nia, -sia,** and **-zia** take **-u** in first names.

Chapter 4

Adjectives

Wszystkie zwierzęta są równe, ale niektóre są równiejsze od innych.
All animals are equal, but some animals are more equal than others.
George Orwell, *Animal Farm* (Folwark zwierzęcy), 1945

4.1 Overview

An adjective expresses a permanent or temporary attribute or quality of a noun or pronoun. Adjectives have regular and distinct sets of endings. They generally agree with the noun or pronoun they refer to in case, class and number.

Mam <+ACC> **miłego** <+ACC> **sąsiada.** 'I have *a nice neighbor.*'
Rozmawiam z <+INS> **miłym** <+INS> **sąsiadem.** 'I talk *with a nice neighbor.*'

Adjectives are inflected for case, number (singular and plural), and class (masculine, feminine, neuter in singular, and male human and no male human in plural).

4.1.1 Endings in nominative singular

For simplicity this is just an overview of most typical endings in the nominative case (basic case). A more detailed description of the endings for each class follows.

The ending for singular masculine adjectives is **-y** or **-i** (after **k**, **g**, and soft stems).

The ending for singular feminine adjectives is **-a**.

The ending for singular neuter adjectives is -e.

Table 4.1 Adjectival endings in nominative singular, overview

Masculine singular	Feminine singular	Neuter singular
mił-y chłopiec 'nice boy'	**mił-a dziewczyna** 'nice girl'	**mił-e dziecko** 'nice child'
duż-y pies 'big dog'	**duż-a sala** 'big room'	**duż-e zwierzę** 'big animal'
now-y dom 'new home'	**now-a rzecz** 'new thing'	**now-e zdjęcie** 'new picture'
wysok-i mężczyzna 'tall man'	**wysok-a kobieta** 'tall woman'	**wysok-ie drzewo** 'tall tree'
drog-i klub 'expensive club'	**drog-a woda** 'expensive water'	**drog-ie jedzenie** 'expensive food'
tani dom 'cheap house'	**tani-a kawa** 'cheap coffee'	**tani-e mydło** 'cheap soap'

4.1.2 | Endings in nominative plural

For simplicity this is just an overview of most typical endings in the nominative plural. A more detailed description of the endings for each class follows.

Plural adjectives referring to male human beings or to a group with one male human being have either the ending -y or -i—the so-called male human plural form, based on the final-stem consonant.

Plural adjectives that do *not* refer to male human beings (as well as certain feminine and neuter nouns that could include male humans, e.g., **osoby** <FEM> 'persons,' **dzieci** <NT> 'children') have the ending -e—the so-called no male human plural form.

Table 4.2 Adjectival endings in nominative plural

MHPL	NO-MHPL
mil-i chłopy 'nice boys'	**mił-e dziewczyny** 'nice girls'
wysoc-y panowie 'tall gentlemen'	**wysok-ie panie** 'tall women'
mil-i ludzie 'nice people'	**mił-e dzieci** 'nice children'

In Polish, 'adjective' is *przymiotnik*, as one of the main purposes of adjectives is to attribute (qualify) or stand by a noun: *przy imieniu*.

4.1.3 | Adjective–noun position

An adjective can be placed before or after the noun or the noun phrase it refers to. Descriptive adjectives are placed in front of the noun and classifying adjectives are placed after the noun.

Wielkie Jeziora Północnoamerykańskie	'the *Great* Lakes'
Piotr I *Wielki*	'Peter *the Great*'
***odpowiedzialna* osoba**	'*a responsible* person,' 'a person who is reliable'
osoba *odpowiedzialna*	'the person *responsible*,' 'the person who has responsibility'
***najwyższy* sędzia**	'*the tallest* judge'
sędzia *najwyższy*	'*Supreme Court* Judge'

4.1.3.1 | Adjectives in front of a noun

Adjectives that are used in front of a noun have a temporal, incidental or individual character—they can be removed or replaced by other generic adjectives, e.g., **dobry** 'good,' **miły** 'nice,' or **duży** 'big,' and this still would not change the essence of the noun.

> **zimny sok** *cold* juice (juice will still be juice even if it is warm)
> **niejadalne ciasto** *inedible* cake (the cake remains cake even when it is inedible)

'Dzień dobry' and 'dobry wieczór'

For reasons of prosody (rhythm), **dobry** is placed after **dzień** in the very common set phrase **dzień dobry** 'hello/good day.' This maintains a stress on the penultimate syllable of the entire phrase taken as a whole. **Dobry wieczór** 'good evening' already has a stress on the penultimate syllable of the entire phrase without needing to place **dobry** after **wieczór**. **Dobranoc** 'good night' is combined in Polish into a single word to maintain stress on the penultimate syllable of the entire construction taken as a whole.

| 4.1.3.2 | Adjectives after a noun |

An adjective is placed after a noun to classify the noun based on its intrinsic property rather than to describe it, e.g.: **Sędzia** <NOUN> **najwyższy** <ADJ> 'Supreme Court Judge' versus **najwyższy** <ADJ> **sędzia** <NOUN> 'the tallest judge.'

okulary <NOUN> **przeciwsłoneczne**	'sunglasses'
Unia <NOUN> **Europejska**	'European Union'
wybory <NOUN> **parlamentarne**	'parliamentary election'
płaszcz <NOUN> **przeciwdeszczowy**	'raincoat'
sok <NOUN> **jabłkowy** <ADJ>	'apple juice' (the juice that is made of apples)
ciasto <NOUN> **czekoladowe** <ADJ>	'chocolate cake' (the cake that is made of chocolate)

Indeclinable adjectives are used after nouns, e.g., **włosy blond** 'blonde hair.'

Many adjectives modifying food (not its taste or lack of it, temperature or aroma), are used after the noun.

zupa <NOUN> **pomidorowa** <ADJ> 'tomato soup'
lody <NOUN> **czekoladowe** <ADJ> 'chocolate ice cream'

The ingredients used to prepare the food make the food unique. The ingredients classify the food, rather than describe it.

Adjectives that qualify a type of literature or a language are used after the nouns. This is because the adjectives classify what type of literature or language the noun belongs to, rather than describe the noun, e.g.:

literatura <NOUN> **francuska** <ADJ> 'French literature'
język <NOUN> **angielski** <ADJ> 'English language'

| 4.1.3.3 | Difference in meaning of adjectives placed in front of a noun or after it |

Adjective before the noun	Adjective after the noun (quality)
kulturalny attaché	'well-bred attaché'
Attaché *kulturalny*	'Cultural Attaché'
młoda kobieta	'a young woman'
panna *młoda*	'bride, a woman who is getting married'

smaczne **pierogi**	'tasty dumplings'
pierogi *ruskie*	'dumplings with potatoes and cheese'
mały **sklep**	'small store'
sklep *spożywczy*	'grocery store'
zwyczajny **młotek**	'ordinary hammer'
młotek *sędziowski*	'gavel'
polski **król**	'the Polish king'
język *polski*	'Polish language'
zagraniczny **gość**	'foreign guest'
polityka *zagraniczna*	'foreign policy'

4.1.3.4 | Multiple adjectives

Adjectives that normally come before a noun keep their respective positions and are separated by a comma.

> **duża, drewniana łyżka** 'big, wooden spoon'
> **ciekawa, dobra literatura** 'interesting, good literature'

Adjectival modifiers are used with general ones coming before the detailed.

> **To jest mój stary rower.** 'This is my old bike.'

Adjectives that are normally used after a noun keep their respective position.

> **Druga wojna** *światowa* 'Second *World* War'
> **pyszna zupa** *pomidorowa* 'delicious *tomato* soup'
> **trudny egzamin** *końcowy* 'difficult *final* exam'

4.2 Main functions of adjectives

Attribute to a noun, where the attributive adjective *describes* an object in a single phrase and agree with the noun's number, class and case.

> **mocna kawa** 'strong coffee'
> **gotowa pizza** 'pre-cooked pizza'

Predicate to a noun, where the adjective usually *forms a phrase* with the noun after the verb **być** "to be" or **zostać, stać się** "to become" in all tenses.

Sąsiad *jest dobry.* 'The neighbor is good.'
Okna *są duże.* 'The windows are big.'

Note that attributive (descriptive) adjectives can be omitted in the sentence (their role is to add more description), while a predicate adjective (an adjective as a part of the verb) cannot be omitted (their role is essential for understanding the phrase).

Jestem *gotowa.*
'I am ready.' (part of the verb, predicate to a noun)

Nie kupuj *gotowej* **pizzy.**
'Don't buy a pre-cooked pizza.' (descriptive role)

Zrobiła się *czerwona.* 'She got *red.*'

Without the adjective the communicative part *is disrupted.*

Nie kupuj *czerwonych* **butów.**
'Don't buy *red* shoes.'

Without the adjective the communicative part *is not disrupted.*

Jestem *zajęta.* 'I am *busy.*'

Without the adjective the communicative part *is disrupted.*

Zwrot *zajętego* **majątku.**
'Claim of assets in possession of someone else.'

Without the adjective the communicative part *is not disrupted.*

Ewa jest *chora.* 'Ewa is *sick.*'

Without the adjective the communicative part *is disrupted.*

Rozmawiamy *o chorej* **koleżance.**
'We are talking about a sick friend.'

Without the adjective the communicative part *is not disrupted.*

Po prostu jestem *szczery.* 'I am simply *honest.*'

Without the adjective the communicative part is disrupted.

Powiedział ci *szczerą* **prawdę.**
'He told you the *honest* truth.'

Without the adjective the communicative part is not disrupted.

223

Predicate adjectives agree with the nouns they qualify in number and class but are used either in nominative or instrumental cases.

> **On *jest dobry*** <NOM>. (not: **On *jest dobrym*** <INS>.) 'He *is kind*.'
> **Warto *być dobrym*** <INS>. 'It is worthwhile *to be good*.'

Adjectives in the instrumental case are used when the adjectives is accompanied by a noun.

> **On jest dobrym** <INS> **człowiekiem** <INS>. 'He is a good man.'

Adjectives in the *instrumental case* are used in *subjectless* constructions after the infinitive form of **być** "to be."

> **Warto *być dobrym*.** 'It is worthwhile *to be good*.'
> **Lepiej *być mądrym* niż *[być] bogatym*.** 'It's better *to be wise* than *[to be] rich*.'

Adjectives in the *nominative case* are used in a construction with a subject, when the adjective is not accompanied by a noun.

> **On** <subject> **jest** <form of the verb "to be"> **dobry** <ADJ>. 'He is kind.'
> **Lepiej, żebyś** <2 PERSON SG subject marker -ś> **[ty] *był mądry* niż *[był]***
>   ***bogaty*.** (not: żebyś był mądrym)
> 'It'd be better, if *you were wise* than *[you were] rich*.'

For adjectival nouns versus predicate adjectives, see 4.12 (e.g., **Adam jest chorym** 'Adam is the sick one/the patient' versus **Adam jest chory** 'Adam is sick').

4.3 Translation difficulties

Many modal verbs use the infinitive, e.g., **chcę być** 'I want *to be*,' **staram się być** 'I try *to be*.' These constructions have a subject: "I," "you," "they," etc. When the adjective stands alone after such constructions, it is used in the nominative case. When the adjective is accompanied by a noun it is used in the instrumental case.

> **On chce być dobry** <ADJ IN NOM>.
> 'He wants to be kind.'

> **On chce być** <ADJ AND NOUN IN INS> **dobrym człowiekiem.**
> 'He wants to be a kind man.'

The English construction "seem to be," "turned out to be" can be translated:

Ewa wydaje się być szczęśliwą. 'Ewa seems to be happy.'
Ewa wydaje się szczęśliwa. 'Ewa seems happy.' (preferred version)
Wydaje się, że Ewa jest szczęśliwa. 'It seems that Ewa is happy.'
(preferred version)

Okazał się być uczciwym. 'He turned out to be honest.'
(word for word translation)
Okazał się uczciwy. 'He turned out to be honest.' (preferred version)
Okazało się, że on jest uczciwy. 'It turned out that he is honest.'
(preferred version)

4.4 Class

In the singular adjectives are divided into: masculine, feminine or neuter, referring to masculine, feminine or neuter nouns.

ciekawy artykuł <MSC> 'interesting article'
ciekawa książka <FEM> 'interesting book'
ciekawe czasopismo <NT> 'interesting magazine'

Nouns referring to male human beings with the ending -a are modified by masculine adjectives, e.g.,

miły mężczyzna 'nice man'
dobry kierowca 'good driver'
znany artysta 'well-known artist'
straszny oferma 'horrible loser' (coll.)

In the plural adjectives are divided into male human and no male human groups.

Male human adjectives refer to fully developed male human beings and/or a mixed group with at least one male human being. (See 4.6.1)

No male human adjectives refer to everything else. (See 4.6)

Table 4.3 Adjectival endings in male and no male human plural

NOM MHPL	NOM NO-MHPL
now-i sąsiedzi 'new neighbors'	**now-e buty** 'new shoes'
mil-i ludzie 'nice people'	**mił-e dzieci** 'nice children'
mil-i studenci 'nice students'	**mił-e studentki** 'nice students' (referring to female students)

4.4.1 | *Plural of group entities*

The plurals of professions, nationalities, and collective entities will have endings typical for the male human plural (-i/-y), unless the group has no male humans.

A group of either male humans, or mixed males and females:

> *bliscy* **przyjaciele** 'close friends'
> *ambitni* **studenci** 'ambitious students'
> *gościnni* **Polacy** 'hospitable Poles'
> *twórczy* **Amerykanie** 'creative Americans'

A group of females:

> *bliskie* **przyjaciółki** 'close friends'
> *ambitne* **studentki** 'ambitious students'
> *gościnne* **Polki** 'hospitable Poles'
> *twórcze* **Amerykanki** 'creative Americans'

4.4.1.1 | **Ludzie**

Ludzie 'people' takes the male human plural form, while **osoby** 'persons,' takes the no male human plural form, e.g.,

> **mądrzy** <MHPL> **ludzie** 'wise people'
> **mądre** <NO-MHPL> **osoby** 'wise persons'

Ludzie is the plural form of the masculine animate singular noun **człowiek** 'man, human,' while **osoby** is the plural form of the feminine singular noun **osoba** 'person.'

Ludzie and osoby are synonyms. Osoby is used to refer to a group of individuals, and ludzie is used to refer to a larger group as an entity, or an abstract.

> **To ludzie, a nie zwierzęta.** 'These are people, not animals.'

Referring to a small group of people osoby is used, e.g.,

> **parę osób** 'a couple of people'

4.4.1.2 | **Dzieci**

The word **dzieci** 'children' is in the no male human plural class, as it conceptually is a group without a fully developed male human. Therefore, adjectival modifiers of the word **dzieci** 'children' take the no male human plural ending -e, and the word **dzieci** takes the no male human plural past tense verb formation -ły, e.g., **kochane dzieci tam były** 'the darling children were there.'

4.5 Nominative endings

Endings in the nominative singular:

-y or -i (after **k**, **g**, and a soft stem) for adjectives referring to masculine nouns:

dobr-y 'good'   **drog-i** 'expensive'
szybk-i 'fast'   **tan-i** 'cheap'

-a for adjectives referring to feminine nouns:

dobr-a 'good,'

also after a soft stem: **tani-a** 'cheap'

-e; -ie: for adjectives referring to neuter nouns.

dobr-e 'good'

or -ie after **k**, **g** and a soft stem: **tan'-ie** 'cheap'

Table 4.4 Adjectival endings in nominative singular

Masculine	Feminine	Neuter
mił-y	**mił-a**	**mił-e** 'nice'
wysok-i	**wysok-a**	**wysok-ie** 'tall'
tan-i	**tani-a**	**tani-e** 'cheap'

4.5.1 Masculine adjectives in nominative singular

These have the ending -i after velar **k**, **g**, and the soft consonants **p'**, **b'**, **w'**, **ś**, **ń**, **dź**, **ć**;

and the ending -y after all other consonants: **b**, **c**, **d**, **f**, **ch**, **h**, **ł**, **m**, **n**, **p**, **r**, **s**, **t**, **w**, **z**, **sz**, **rz**, **ż**, **dz**, **dż**.

-i examples:

głup'-i 'stupid'   **polsk-i** 'Polish'
tan'-i 'cheap'   **amerykańsk-i** 'American'
gęs'-i adjective from 'gosling'   **drog-i** 'expensive'
angielsk-i 'English'   **ubog-i** 'poor'

227

The ending -i is preserved in all cases in both singular and plural forms, e.g.

Rodzice zatrzymali się *w drogim hotelu*.
'[My] parents are staying *in an expensive hotel.*'
Ta firma buduje *drogie hotele*.
'The company builds *expensive hotels.*'

-y examples:

cich-y 'quiet'	**obc-y** 'foreign'
wspaniał-y 'wonderful'	**duż-y** 'big'
młod-y 'young'	**dżdżyst-y** 'drizzly'

A niechaj narodowie wżdy postronni znają,
 Iż Polacy nie gęsi, iż swój język mają!
And let all the neighboring nations know that Poles have their own
 language, and do not need to use the gosling language.

Mikołaj Rej

4.5.2 | *Feminine adjectives in nominative singular*

These have the ending -a or -ia after a soft stem.

wysok-a 'tall'	**głupi-a** 'stupid'
angielsk-a 'English'	**tani-a** 'cheap'
drog-a 'expensive,' 'dear'	**gęsi-a** 'gosling'
gorąc-a 'hot'	

Softness of consonants is marked by the letter -i before a vowel, hence **tani-a,** (not tańa). (See 1.3.3.2)

In the genitive, dative and locative singular forms and in all cases in the plural, adjectives with a stem ending in k, g have -ki-, -gi-: **wysokiej kobiety** <GEN>, **o wysokiej kobiecie** <LOC>, **o wysokich kobietach** <LOC PL>. (See Table 4.10 and 4.12 in Section 4.7)

In the nominative and the accusative forms, an extra -i is not necessary, e.g., **wysoka kobieta** <NOM>, **wysoką kobietę** <ACC>.

4.5.2.1 | **Wysoka** *but* **wysokie**

The extra -i after k, g results from the neighboring vowel e, and the fact that in Polish k is never followed by -y, but always by -i. The vowel e is a frontal vowel while the consonant k is a back consonant. To ease the pronunciation -i creates 'a bridge' between the two letters.

In the combination -**ka**, the vowel **a** is a back vowel and **k** is a back consonant, so the extra -**i** is not needed:

wysoka but **wysokie** and **wysokich**

-**i** is kept in all cases in singular and plural forms when the adjective is soft-stem, e.g., **tani, tanie, tanich**.

4.5.3 | Neuter adjectives in nominative singular

These have the endings -**e** and -(**i**)**e** after **k**, **g** and a soft stem:

dobr-e wino 'good wine'
ubogi-e państwo 'poor country'
tani-e piwo 'cheap beer'

-**ie** after **k**, **g** and a soft stem is kept in all cases in the singular and plural.

4.6 Plural

Plurals of adjectives are divided into two groups. One group modifies nouns referring to male human beings or to a group with one male human being—so-called *male human* adjectives, and the other group modifies everything else—so-called *no male human* adjectives.

1. male human adjectives have the ending -**y** or -**i**, based on the final-stem consonant in the nominative singular.
2. no male human adjectives have the ending -**e**

Type of the final-stem consonant in the nominative case:

3. **k, g, ch/h**—also called *velar*
4. **c, dz, sz, ż, rz, cz, dż**—also called *"historically" soft*
5. **ś, ć, ź, dź, ń, l, w', b', m', f', w', j**—also called *soft*
6. all other consonants (**b, p, f, w, m, ł, t, d, s, z, n, r**)—also called *hard*

4.6.1 | Male human plural

Plurals of adjectives, referring to a group of male human beings or to a mixed group with one male human being, have either -**i** or -**y** in the nominative plural.

The ending -**i** or -**y** depends on the final-stem consonant in the nominative singular.

-i is the ending in nominative adjectives referring to male human beings or a group with at least one male human being—male human adjectives, after hard and "historically" soft stems plus **ch** (except for **r, c, cz**). Predictable consonant shifts occur (1.3.4).

The ending -y is used in the nominative case for male human plural adjectives with a stem ending in **k, g, r, c, cz** in nominative singular. Predictable consonant shifts occur for: **k:cy, g:dzy, r:rzy**. The endings **c** and **cz** remain unchanged (-**cy**, -**czy**).

> **dob<u>ry</u> człowiek** 'a good man'   **dob<u>rzy</u> ludzie** 'good people'

Adjectives with the ending -**ony** such as **zmęczony** 'tired,' have the shift -**ony**:-**eni** in plural male human forms.

> **Jestem zmęcz*ony*, ale zadowol*ony*.** 'I am tired but happy.' <SG>
> **Jesteśmy zmęcz*eni*, ale zadowol*eni*.** 'We are tired but happy.' <PL>

Table 4.5 Adjectival **-i** ending in male human plural

Masculine singular	Male human form (or a mixed group with a male human)	Predictable changes
sł<u>aby</u> przeciwnik 'weak opponent'	**sł<u>abi</u> przeciwnicy** 'weak opponents'	b:bi
zn<u>any</u> biznesman 'famous businessman'	**zn<u>ani</u> biznesmeni** 'famous businessmen'	n:ni
len<u>iwy</u> student 'lazy student'	**len<u>iwi</u> studenci** 'lazy students'	w:wi
du<u>ży</u> chłopiec 'big boy'	**du<u>zi</u> chłopcy** 'big boys'	ż:zi
mi<u>ły</u> nauczyciel 'nice teacher'	**mi<u>li</u> nauczyciele** 'nice teachers'	ł:li
wes<u>oły</u> staruszek 'jolly older man'	**wes<u>eli</u> staruszkowie** 'jolly older men'	ł:li, o:e
ml<u>ody</u> mężczyzna 'young man'	**ml<u>odzi</u> mężczyźni** 'young men'	d:dzi
pracow<u>ity</u> syn 'hard-working son'	**pracow<u>ici</u> synowie** 'hard-working sons'	t:ci
pro<u>sty</u> człowiek 'simple man'	**pro<u>ści</u> ludzie** 'simple people'	sty:ści
star<u>szy</u> człowiek 'older person'	**star<u>si</u> ludzie** 'older people'	sz:si
zmęcz<u>ony</u> ojciec 'tired father'	**zmęcz<u>eni</u> ojcowie** 'tired fathers'	o:e, n:ni

4.6.1.1 Identical singular and plural forms -i

A small group of masculine adjectives with a soft **p'**, **b'**, **m'**, **n'**-stem have identical forms in the nominative singular and male human plural.

ostatni **zawodnik**	*ostatni* **zawodnicy**
'final contestant'	'final contestants'
olbrzymi **mężczyzna**	*olbrzymi* **mężczyźni**
'giant man'	'giant men'
głupi **człowiek** 'silly man'	*głupi* **ludzie** 'silly people'

4.6.1.2 -y

The ending in nominative male human plural adjectives referring to male human beings that end with **k**, **g** and **r** is -y. Predictable consonant shifts occur: r:rzy, k:cy, g:dzy. Note that -cki changes to -ccy.

Table 4.6 Adjectival **-y** ending in male human plural

Masculine singular	Male human (or a mixed group with male humans)	Predictable changes
dob**ry aktor** 'good actor'	**dobrzy aktorzy** 'good actors'	ry:rzy
wysoki 'tall'	**wysocy**	ki:cy
męski 'masculine'	**męscy**	ki:cy
elegancki 'elegant'	**eleganccy**	ki:cy
lekki 'light'	**lekcy**	ki:cy
ubogi 'poor'	**ubodzy**	gi:dzy
długonogi 'long-legged'	**długonodzy**	gi:dzy

4.6.1.3 Identical singular and plural forms -y

Masculine adjectives with endings -(ą)cy, -czy, -dzy in nominative singular have identical male human plural forms in the nominative case. This group is large, as the ending -ący is also the ending for adjectival participles (in English marking -ing).

Table 4.7 Identical singular and plural adjectival forms

Nominative singular	Nominative plural
pachnący mężczyzna 'nicely smelling man'	**pachnący mężczyźni**
interesujący student 'interesting student'	**intersujący studenci**

Masculine singular/male human (or a mixed group with a male human)

pachnący mężczyzna/mężczyźni 'nicely smelling man/men'
uroczy chłopak/chłopcy 'charming boy/boys'
zaborczy mąż/mężowie 'possessive husband/husbands'

cudzy mąż 'someone else's husband'
cudzy mężowie 'someone else's husbands'

interesujący chłopak 'interesting boy'
interesujący chłopcy 'interesting boys'

płaczący człowiek 'a man who is crying'
płaczący ludzie 'people who are crying'

4.7 Declension

Adjectives have regular declensional patterns. The differences result from velar, soft, "historically" soft and hard stems in the nominative singular.

4.7.1 Shared endings in singular

Masculine adjectives referring to male human beings and animals have an accusative singular identical to the genitive singular. Masculine adjectives referring to objects have an accusative singular identical to the nominative singular.

Table 4.8 Shared endings in singular adjectives

Masculine		
NOM	ACC	GEN
dobry brat 'good brother'	**dobrego brata**	**dobrego brata**
dobry kot 'good cat'	**dobrego kota**	**dobrego kota**
dobry fotel 'good armchair'	**dobry fotel**	**dobrego fotela**

Feminine adjectives have identical adjectival forms in the genitive, dative and locative singular.

Table 4.8a

Feminine			
NOM	GEN	DAT	LOC
dobra kawa 'good coffee'	**dobrej kawy**	**dobrej kawie**	**dobrej kawie**

Neuter adjectives have an accusative singular identical to the nominative singular and an accusative plural identical to the nominative plural.

Table 4.8b

Neuter	
NOM SG/PL	ACC SG/PL
dobre ciastko/dobre ciastka	**dobre ciastko** 'good cookie'

Table 4.9 Adjectives in singular with hard, "historically" soft, and **ch** stem

Case	Masculine	Neuter	Feminine
NOM	**now-y** 'new'	**now-e**	**now-a**
ACC	animate nouns: = GEN inanimate nouns: = NOM (inanimate nouns: **-ego**)	= NOM —	**now-ą** —
GEN	**now-ego**	**now-ego**	**now-ej**
DAT	**now-emu**	**now-emu**	= GEN
LOC	**now-ym** (-**em**)	**now-ym**	= GEN
INS	= LOC	= LOC	**now-ą**
VOC	= NOM	= NOM	= NOM

Note: **-ego**, the accusative singular ending characteristic for an animate masculine noun, is also the ending in the accusative singular for a specific group of inanimate masculine nouns denoting certain sports, dances, food, drink, tobaccos and technologies (3.3.5.4).

> **Jem pyszn<u>ego</u> pączk<u>a</u>.** 'I am eating a delicious donut.'
> **Zapłaciłem jedn<u>ego</u> dolar<u>a</u>.** 'I paid <MSC> one dollar.'
> **Tańczymy walca wiedeński<u>ego</u>.**
> 'We are dancing a Viennese waltz.'
> **Lubię grać w tenisa ziemn<u>ego</u>.** 'I like to play tennis.'

-em instead of **-ym** is the ending in the locative used with geographical names, referring to regions in Poland with the ending **-kie** in the nominative singular, e.g., **Poznańskie**, and with the city **Zakopane**, which is declined like an adjective.

> **w Zakopanem** 'in Zakopane' (city in the south of Poland)
> **w Białostockiem** 'in the Białystok region'
> **w Poznańskiem** 'in the Poznań region'

Table 4.10 Adjectives in singular with **k**, **g**, and soft stem

Case	Masculine	Neuter	Feminine
NOM	**wysok-i** 'tall'	**wysok-ie**	**wysok-a**
ACC	animate nouns: = GEN	= NOM	**wysok-ą**
	inanimate nouns: = NOM	—	—
GEN	**wysoki-ego**	**wysok-iego**	**wysok-iej**
DAT	**wysoki-emu**	**wysok-iemu**	= GEN
LOC	**wysok-im**	**wysok-im**	= GEN
INS	= LOC	= LOC	**wysok-ą**
VOC	= NOM	= NOM	= NOM

Table 4.10a

Case	Masculine	Neuter	Feminine
NOM	**tan-i** 'cheap'	**tani-e**	**tani-a**
ACC	animate nouns: = GEN	= NOM	**tani-ą**
	inanimate nouns: = NOM	—	—
GEN	**tani-ego**	**tani-ego**	**tani-ej**
DAT	**tani-emu**	**tani-emu**	= GEN
LOC	**tan-im**	**tan-im**	= GEN
INS	= LOC	= LOC	**tani-ą**
VOC	= NOM	= NOM	= NOM

4.7.2 | *Shared endings in plural*

Adjectives have *identical endings across the plural forms*, except for the nominative and the accusative cases. Adjectives referring to male human beings or a group with at least one male human being have in the nominative either -y or -i, all other adjectives have -e.

Plural adjectives referring to male human beings or a group with at least one male human being have identical accusative and genitive forms.

4.7.3 | Patriarchy, not animacy, in plural

In Polish, plural forms are classified on the basis of patriarchy. Unlike in Russian, where the division in plural is based on animacy, in Polish it is all about identifying whether there is any male human in the group. If there is a single male human in a group (even a group of one man and 100 women), then the group is classified as male human plural. Otherwise, it is classified as no male human plural. Understanding this concept will aid the production of the correct forms in Polish. (See Table 4.11)

No male human plural

To są _ładne_ kobiety. <NOM PL>.   'These are _pretty_ women.'
Widzę _ładne_ kobiety. <ACC=NOM PL>   'I see _pretty_ women.'
To są _ładne_ dzieci. <NOM PL>   'These are _pretty_ children.'
Widzę _ładne_ dzieci. <ACC=NOM PL>   'I see _pretty_ children.'
To są _ładne_ psy. <NOM PL>   'These are _pretty_ dogs.'
Widzę _ładne_ psy. <ACC=NOM PL>   'I see _pretty_ dogs.'

Male human plural

To są _ładni_ chłopcy. <NOM PL>   'These are _pretty_ boys.'
Widzę _ładnych_ chłopców.   'I see _pretty_ boys.'
    <ACC=GEN PL>

To są _ciekawi_ poeci. <NOM PL>   'These are _interesting_ poets.'
Widzę _ciekawych_ poetów.   'I see _interesting_ poets.'
    <ACC=GEN PL>

Table 4.11 Adjectives in plural with hard, "historically" soft, and **ch** stem

Case	MHPL (referring to male human beings)	NO-MHPL (everything else: no male human MSC/NT/FEM)
NOM	now-i	now-e
ACC	= GEN	= NOM
GEN	now-ych	now-ych
DAT	now-ym	now-ym
LOC	= GEN	= GEN
INS	now-ymi	now-ymi
VOC	= NOM	= NOM

Predictable consonant shifts occur in the nominative case in male human plural. See Tables 4.5 and 4.6.

Table 4.12 Adjectives in plural with **k**, **g** and soft stem

Case	MHPL (referring to male human beings)	NO-MHPL (everything else: no male human MSC/NT/FEM)
NOM	**wysoc-y̲ k:c**	**wysok-i̲e̲**
ACC	= GEN	= NOM
GEN	**wysok-i̲c̲h̲**	**wysok-i̲c̲h̲**
DAT	**wysok-i̲m̲**	**wysok-i̲m̲**
LOC	= GEN	= GEN
INS	**wysok-i̲m̲i̲**	**wysok-i̲m̲i̲**
VOC	= NOM	= NOM

Predictable consonant shifts occur in nominative plural male human adjectives: **k:cy, g:dzy**.

4.8 Agreement

Adjectives agree in number, class and case with the noun they modify.

piękny̲ obraz 'beautiful painting'
piękne̲ obrazy 'beautiful paintings'
na pięknyc̲h̲ obrazach 'on the beautiful paintings'

4.8.1 | Indeclinable adjectives

Indeclinable adjectives such as **bordo** 'claret,' **khaki, blond, frotté, écru, lila** 'lilac color,' **sexy** do not accommodate the nouns they modify, and are used after the nouns.

włosy blond 'blonde hair'
ręcznik frotté 'a terry towel'
buty lila 'lilac color shoes'

4.8.2 | Adjectives with ktoś, nikt, wszystko, wszyscy, coś, nic

Ktoś 'somebody,' **nikt** 'nobody,' **wszystko** 'everything,' **wszyscy** 'everyone,' **coś** 'something,' **nic** 'nothing'

A masculine adjective is used by default with the pronouns **ktoś, nikt**. Male human plural adjectives are used with the pronoun **wszyscy** 'everyone.'

ktoś nowy 'someone new'
nikt znany 'no one famous'
wszyscy nowi 'everyone new'

and in subjectless constructions, after the infinitive **być** 'to be.'

warto być wyrozumiałym
'it is worth it to be understanding' (not: wyrozumiałą)

A neuter adjective is used with the indefinite pronoun **wszystko** 'all,' 'everything.'

wszystko jest gotowe 'everything is ready'

and after the pronoun **to** 'it'

To (jest) interesujące. 'It is interesting.'

Coś 'something,' **cokolwiek** 'anything,' **nic** 'nothing' take an adjective in the genitive masculine singular (with the ending -(i)ego).

coś nowego 'something new'   **nic nowego** 'nothing new'

For agreement with feminine titles and professions, see Chapter 12.

4.9   Adjectives and collective nouns

Modifying adjectives agree in class, number and case with the noun they modify, except for nouns with the ending **-stwo** referring to couples, e.g., **państwo** 'a couple,' **wujostwo** 'aunt and uncle.'

Nouns that denote couples such as **państwo** 'bride and groom' or 'ladies and gentlemen' or 'a couple' take male human form adjectives, and the verb in the plural, e.g.,

Państwo młodzi *kupili* <PL VERB> **nowy dom.** 'The newlyweds *bought* a new house.'
Kosowo to nowe państwo. 'Kosovo is a new country.'
Kowalscy to nowi państwo. 'The Kowalskis are the new couple.'

4.9.1 | Adjective singular with collective nouns

wojsko <NT> **lotnicze** <NT SG> 'the air force'
młodzież <FEM> **uniwersytecka** <FEM SG> 'university students'
państwo <NT> **kapitalistyczne** <NT SG> 'capitalist country'
społeczeństwo <NT> **polskie** <NT SG> 'Polish society'

237

4.9.2 Adjective plural with collective nouns

The noun **państwo** 'a country' and 'a couple' is declined differently, depending on its meaning (see Table 3.43).

szanowni <male human PL> **państwo** <NT> (respectful)
'ladies and gentlemen'

państwo <NT> **Kwaśniewscy** <PL>
'Mr. and Mrs. Kwaśniewski,' 'the Kwaśniewskis'

Kochani <male human PL> **wujostwo** <NT> **napisali do nas.**
'Dear aunt and uncle wrote to us.'

Rozmawiam o państwu Kwaśniewskich z państwem Kowalskimi.
'I talk about Mr. and Mrs. Kwaśniewski with Mr. and Mrs. Kowalski.'

4.10 Short form adjectives

A small group of adjectives have both long and short forms. While long forms inflect for class, number and case with the noun they qualify, short forms, which are considered archaic, occur in the nominative case only (because they are used as predicates). Short form adjectives do not have comparative forms, and are used as a predicate (after the verb "to be"), in comparisons and set phrases.

[jest] zdrów jak ryba '[is] healthy as fish'
[jest] wesół jak szczygieł '[is] as happy as a lark'
jeden [jest] wart drugiego 'one is as bad as another' (saying)
   [lit. one is *worth* the other]

Short adjectives <MSC>	Long adjectives <MSC>
ciekaw	**ciekawy** 'curious'
godzien	**godny** 'worthy'
gotów	**gotowy** 'ready'
pełen	**pełny** 'full'
pewien	**pewny** 'sure'
świadom	**świadomy** 'aware'
wart	**warty** 'worth'
wesół	**wesoły** 'cheerful'
zdrów	**zdrowy** 'healthy'

Adjectives that do not have long forms: **rad** 'glad,' **kontent** 'pleased.'

Masculine forms have a zero-ending and feminine, neuter and plural forms do not differ from regular adjectives, e.g., **wart, warta, warte, warci.**

Jestem pewien <MSC>, **że zadzwonią.**
'I'm sure that they will call.'

Jesteś gotów? <MSC> 'Are you ready?'

4.11 Adjectives imposing a case on nouns

Below are examples of adjectives that dictate the case of the noun.

4.11.1 Genitive

The following adjectives take the genitive case. Generally, the genitive case indicates insatiability, the idea of no fullness, a search to fill a gap.

bliski płaczu 'to be on the verge of tears'
chciwy sławy 'thirsty for fame'
ciekawy świata 'to be curious about the world'
niegodny zaufania 'not trustworthy'
głodny wrażeń 'thrill starving'
niepewny jutra 'unsure of tomorrow'
spragniony wiedzy 'craving for knowledge'
warty obejrzenia 'worth watching'
żądny sensacji 'thirsty for sensations'

4.11.2 Dative

Adjectives that impose the use of the dative case usually bear the idea of transferring benefit or loss to the subject (addressee).

bliski sercu 'close to [my] heart'
(nie)przychylny naszym pomysłom
    '(not) inclined towards our ideas'
(nie)życzliwy rodzinie '(un)kind to the family'
drogi/miły mojemu sercu 'dear to my heart'
obce nam pojęcie 'a concept *foreign* to us'
wierny ideałom 'faithful to the ideas'
znany nam wszystkim 'known to all of us'

4.11.3 Instrumental

The instrumental is used to indicate the agent in a passive construction. Adjectives that impose the use of the instrumental case are often a past participle with the ending -ny, -any, -ty, and are followed in English by the preposition *with* or *by* (which is not used in Polish, as instead, the noun is used in the instrumental case).

> **dotknięty klęską** 'affected by a disaster'
> **[osoba] ogarnięta obsesją** '[a person] with [a] great obsession'
> **zachwycony książką** 'delighted with the book'
> **zajęty pracą** 'occupied with work'
> **zmęczony życiem** 'tired with life'

4.12 Adjectival nouns

The group of words that are nouns in meaning, but are declined like adjectives, is called adjectival nouns. In other words, these are adjectives which are used as nouns—an adjective without the noun, thus acting like a noun itself, e.g., *American* instead of *American man*.

An example in English can also be "superior," referring to a senior officer. Adjectival nouns are masculine or feminine based on the biological gender/gender identity of the noun they refer to.

> **znajomy** 'friend' referring to a male
> **znajoma** 'friend' referring to a female

Most adjectival nouns refer to human beings. The adjectival nouns that refer to animals or objects are masculine or feminine based on the ending of the adjective in the nominative case.

> **luty** 'February' masculine just like **dobry** 'good' (agrees with the masculine noun **miesiąc** 'month')
> **czesne** 'tuition fee(s)' no male human plural like **dobre** (agrees with the plural noun **pieniądze** 'money')

For a list of adjectival nouns, see 3.6.4.

Adjectival nouns can be used by themselves or in noun phrases. Adjectival nouns accompanied by a noun and/or adjective are used in the instrumental case after the verbs 'to be, to become' **być, zostać, stać się.**

Piotr jest znanym <INS> **uczonym** <INS>. 'Piotr is a well-known scholar.'

Piotr jest chorym <INS> **człowiekiem** <INS>. 'Piotr is a sick person.'

Adjectival nouns used by themselves take nominative or instrumental as a predicate.

Piotr jest chory <NOM>. 'Piotr is sick.'

Piotr jest chorym <INS>. 'Piotr is the sick one (the patient).'

Piotr został bezrobotny <NOM>. 'Piotr became jobless.'

Piotr został bezrobotnym <INS>. 'Piotr became an unemployed person.'

Adjectival nouns referring to a profession take the instrumental case after the verbs of being and becoming.

Piotr jest/został wojskowym <INS>.
'Piotr is/became a military man.'

4.12.1 Female titles

Nouns referring to female human beings with the ending -owa are declined like adjectives, e.g.,

Rodowód królowej Bony jest bardzo interesujący.
'Queen Bona's bloodline is very interesting.'

Idę do krawcowej. 'I'm going to the dressmaker.'

Rano mam spotkanie z szefową.
'I have a meeting with my boss in the morning.'

Moja bratowa, Daria, jest piękną kobietą.
'My brother's wife, Daria, is a beautiful woman.'

Many feminine gender nouns have the ending -**owa** to denote titles and positions:

królowa 'queen,' **cesarz**owa 'empress,' **baron**owa 'baroness,' **krawc**owa 'dressmaker,' **szef**owa 'the boss'

Some of the nouns denote 'the wife of': **brat**owa 'brother's wife,' 'sister-in-law,' **syn**owa 'son's wife,' 'daughter-in-law,' **teści**owa 'mother-in-law,' **general**owa 'general's wife.' They decline like adjectives. (See Table 3.60)

(See also Chapter 12)

241

4.13 Compound adjectives

Compound adjectives are typically connected with the letter -o. The adjectival stem is combined with the nominal stem, e.g.,

> **cztery** 'four' + **osobowy** = **czteroosobowy** 'four-person'
> **cały** 'whole, entire' + **dniowy** = **całodniowy** 'daily'
> **woda** 'water' + **odporny** = **wodoodporny** 'waterproof'

> **czterdziestopięcioletni** 'forty-five year old'
> **czterdziestotrzyletni** 'forty-three-year-old'
> **greckokatolicki** 'Greek Catholic'
> **krótkometrażowy** 'a short film'
> **nastoletni** 'teenage'
> **rzymskokatolicki** 'Roman Catholic'
> **sześcioipółroczny** 'six-and-a-half-year-old'

Compound adjectives with **arcy-, eks-, wice- konta-, anty-, ekstra-, pół-, pro-, pseudo-, trans-, ultra-, wszech-** are written as one word (except for a few set phrases written as two words):

> **wiceminister** 'deputy minister'
> **ekschłopak** (also
>   **eks-chłopak**) 'ex-boyfriend'
> **kontrapunkt** 'counterpoint'
> **antypolski** 'anti-Polish'
> **ekstranowoczesny** 'extra-modern'
> **ekstopmodelka** 'former top model'
> **półciepły** 'half warm'
> **półsłodki** 'half sweet'

> **propolski** 'pro-Polish'
> **pseudonaukowy**
>   'pseudo-scientific'
> **transsyberyjski** 'trans-Siberian'
> **ultrakonserwatywny**
>   'ultraconservative'
> **wszechmogący** 'almighty'
> **wszech czasów** 'of all the time'
> **ze wszech miar** 'by all
>   accounts' (bookish)

Two adjectives are used as one compound adjective with colors, when both colors are not separate, but bring a shade to each other.

> **spódnica jasnoniebieska** 'a light blue skirt'
> **kolczyki srebrnopopielate** 'silver gray earrings'

There are potential difficulties in the pronunciation of compound adjectives:

> **podziemny** 'underground' reads [pod-ziemny], not [podziemny]
> **tysiączłotowy** 'thousand-zloty' reads [tysiąc-złotowy], not [tysiączłotowy]
> **tysiąchektarowy** 'thousand-hectare' reads [tysiąc-hektarowy], not
>   [tysiąchektarowy]

4.13.1 Hyphenated adjectives

When two adjectives are used, and both adjectives have the same value, a hyphen is used.

The final adjective agrees with the object qualified, e.g.,

granica polsko-czeska 'Polish-Czech border'
flaga biało-czerwona 'white and red flag'
spódnica niebiesko-biała 'blue and white skirt'
kolczyki złoto-srebrne 'gold and silver earrings'

When three or more adjectives are used, a hyphen is used:

Słownik polsko-angielsko-rosyjski
'Polish–English–Russian dictionary'

Adjectives are hyphenated when used with **quasi-** and **niby-**

quasi-umysłowy 'quasi-intellectual'
niby-romantyczny 'quasi-romantic'

4.13.2 Adverbs with adjectives

Adverbs with adjectives are written separate (except for a few set phrases):

mało znany 'little known'
szybko schnący 'fast drying'
średnio zaawansowany 'intermediate'
świeżo malowany 'wet paint'
szybkoschnący lakier do paznokci 'fast-drying nail polish'

4.14 Negated adjectives

Negated adjectives are written as one word:

czas pracy nienormowany 'irregular working hours'
naczynia nietłukące 'unbreakable dishes'
niebiedny 'not poor or rich'
niemiły 'not kind/unkind'
niepijący 'non-drinking'
niewysoki 'not tall/short'
nieżyjący 'not alive/dead'

However, when a clear contrast or contradiction occurs (usually with the conjunctions **ale**, **lecz**), negated adjectives are written separately:

nie bogaty, lecz biedny 'not rich, but poor'
nie wysoki, ale niski 'not tall, but short'

Negated comparative and superlative forms of adjectives are written separately:

nie lepszy 'not better'
nie najlepszy 'not best'

Many adjectives with the suffix **bez-** have the meaning *not*:

bezdomny 'homeless'
bezrobotny 'unemployed'
bezpłatny 'free of charge'
bezkofeinowy 'caffeineless' (caffeine free)
bezkompromisowy 'uncompromising'

4.15 Intensifiers

Adjectives can be intensified by adverbs, e.g., **bardzo** 'very,' **wyjątkowo** 'exceptionally,' **strasznie** 'awfully.'

wyjątkowo piękny ogród 'exceptionally beautiful garden'
bardzo ładny dom 'very pretty house'
dobrze doprawiona potrawa 'well-spiced dish'
słabo rozwinięty kraj 'underdeveloped country'
strasznie brzydki pies 'awfully ugly dog'

Instead of using the intensifier **bardzo** 'very,' some descriptive adjectives form an adjective with the prefix **prze-** written together with the adjective:

On jest *bardzo miły*. On jest *przemiły*. 'He is *very nice*.'
Ona jest *bardzo piękna*. Ona jest *przepiękna*. 'She is *very pretty*.'
Oni są *bardzo sympatyczni*. Oni są *przesympatyczni*.
   'They are *very friendly*.'

The intensity of the adjectives can also be increased by adding prefixes: **nad-** 'hyper-,' **przy-** '-ish,' **ekstra-**, **super-**, **ultra-**:

Ich syn jest nadpobudliwy. 'Their son is hyperactive.'
Ela jest przewrażliwiona na swoim punkcie. 'Ela is oversensitive
   about herself.'

Jego matka jest zdecydowanie nadopiekuńcza. 'His mother is definitely overprotective.'
Oni są ultrakonserwatywni. 'They are ultraconservative.'
Wujek jest ekstranowoczesny. '[My] uncle is extra-modern.'
Nie rozumiem, dlaczego Amerykanie noszą przykrótkie spodnie. 'I don't understand why Americans wear shortish pants.'

Adjectives used in exclamations are: **jaki, jaka, jakie, jacy. Jaki** agrees with nouns in number, class and case. (See Table 4.21)

Jaka piękna pogoda! Such pretty weather!
Jakie śliczne dziecko! Such a cute child!

4.16 Emotive adjectives

Emotive adjectives have suffixes:

Table 4.13 Emotive adjectives

	mały 'small'	**miły** 'nice'	**słodki** 'sweet'	**młody** 'young'
-utki	malutki 'tiny'	milutki	słodziutki	młodziutki
-eńki	maleńki 'tiny-tiny'	—	słodziuteńki	młodziuteńki
-uśki	maluśki 'tiny'	miluśki	słodziuśki	młodziuśki
-usieńki	malusieńki 'tiny-tiny'	milusieńki	słodziusieńki	młodziusieńki
-uchny	maluchny 'tiny'	miluchny	słodziuchny	młodziuchny

Emotive adjectives are only formed from the positive degree form (e.g., **miły**) of adjectives (not from the comparative or superlative degree forms). When emotive adjectives are formed from negative adjectives the adjectives suggest an ironic, pitiful or pathetic meaning.

słaby 'weak' **słabiutki** 'very weak'
głupi 'stupid' **głupiutki** 'very stupid'

4.17 Comparative

4.17.1 Overview

Adjectives and adverbs have comparative (**stopień wyższy**) and superlative (**stopień najwyższy**) forms.

Comparative and superlative adjectives can be formed in two ways:

1. by adding the suffixes -szy/-ejszy and naj-—so-called *simple comparative*
2. by adding the adverbs **bardziej** 'more' and **najbardziej** 'most' to the positive degree (basic form) of the adjective or adverb—so-called *compound comparative*

Comparative adjectives (in English using the marker "-er," e.g., "smaller") are formed by adding the suffix -szy or -ejszy to the positive degree (basic form).

Superlative adjectives (in English using the marker "-est," e.g., "smallest") are formed by adding the prefix **naj-** to the comparative form.

Table 4.14 Overview of comparative and superlative

Positive degree	Comparative degree	Superlative degree
now-y 'new'	**now-szy** 'newer'	**najnow-szy** 'newest'
młod-y 'young'	**młod-szy** 'younger'	**najmłod-szy** 'youngest'
star-y 'old'	**star-szy** 'older'	**najstar-szy** 'oldest'
mądr-y 'wise'	**mądrz-ejszy** 'wiser'	**najmądrz-ejszy** 'wisest'
ładn-y 'pretty'	**ładn-iejszy** 'prettier'	**najładn-iejszy** 'prettiest'

4.17.2 Lower and lowest degree

Lower and lowest degree is formed by adding the adverbs **mniej** 'less' and **najmniej** 'least' to the positive degree (basic form) of the adjective or adverb, e.g.,

Ten film jest mniej ciekawy od książki.
'The film is less interesting than the book.'

Książka jest mniej zabawna niż film.
'The book is less amusing than the film.'

Ten argument jest mniej poważny.
'This reason is less serious.'

There is one way to express "less" with adjectives and adverbs: **mniej poważny** 'less serious,' **mniej ciekawie** 'less interestingly' while "more" could be expressed in two ways for some adjectives: **bardziej poważny** or **poważniejszy** 'more serious.'

Ten kandydat jest poważniejszy (or **bardziej poważny**).
'This candidate is more serious.

For simplicity this is just an overview of comparative and superlative forms. A more detailed description of the forms follows.

4.17.3 Irregular comparatives

Some adjectives, like in English, have comparative and superlative forms derived from different stems.

dobry 'good'	**lepszy** 'better'	**najlepszy** 'best'
zły 'bad'	**gorszy** 'worse'	**najgorszy** 'worst'
duży 'big'	**większy** 'bigger'	**największy** 'biggest'
mały 'small'	**mniejszy** 'smaller'	**najmniejszy** 'smallest'
lekki 'light'	**lżejszy** 'lighter'	**najlżejszy** 'lightest'

Comparative and superlative adjectives follow the same declension patterns as other adjectives.

Table 4.15 Comparative forms (nominative case)

Masculine	Feminine	Neuter	NO-MHPL	MHPL
nowszy 'newer'	**nowsza**	**nowsze**	**nowsze**	**nowsi**
większy 'bigger'	**większa**	**większe**	**większe**	**więksi**

4.17.4 Adjectives with no comparative or superlative

Relational adjectives have no semantic content other than that of the noun they were formed from. They do not have comparative or superlative forms. However, when used with a metaphorical meaning these adjectives can be intensified or degraded by adding the adverbs **bardziej** 'more' or **mniej** 'less.'

Mam bardziej niebieskie oczy od ciebie.
'My eyes are more blue than yours.'

Za to twoja twarz jest bardziej kwadratowa.
'But your face is squarer.'

Jesteś bardziej tajemniczy niż zwykle.
'You are more secretive than usual.'

dojrzały 'ripe, mature' has two alternative forms:

bardziej dojrzały or **dojrzalszy** 'more mature', e.g.,
  dojrzały mężczyzna 'mature man'

247

bardziej dojrzałe banany 'more ripe bananas'
dojrzalsza Europa 'more mature Europe'
bardziej swojski 'more familiar, more native'

warszawski of or referring to Warsaw and its inhabitants:
    Powstanie Warszawskie 'Warsaw Uprising'
drogowy of or pertaining to road, traffic: **znaki drogowe**
    'traffic, road signs'
studencki pertaining to students: **legitymacja studencka** 'student ID'
dziecięcy pertaining to children, for a child: **dziecięcy wózek**
    'stroller/baby carriage'
bezpłatny 'free of charge' (cannot be more or less free of charge)
pusty 'empty,' 'vacant,' 'blank' (cannot be more or less vacant)
nagi 'naked'
stalowy 'made of steel,' **drewniany** 'made of wood'

Adjectives that end with -ły (adjectives formed from verbs) do not have comparatives:

wyłysiały 'completely bald'
odrętwiały z zimna 'numb with cold'
oniemiały <MSC SG> **oniemiali** <MHPL ADJ> **z zachwytu**
    'speechless with wonder'
zmarły 'dead'
stały 'permanent, solid' as in **prąd stały** 'direct current'

4.17.5 -szy suffix

4.17.5.1 Formation of comparative

When the stem of an adjective ends in a consonant, the suffix -sz is added to it, and it is followed by adjectival endings to make a comparative (rendered in English by "-er," such as "bigger." In male human plural forms the suffix is -si (sz shifts to si).

Table 4.16 Formation of comparative (nominative case)

	Singular			Plural	
	MSC	FEM	NT	NO-MHPL	MHPL
now-y 'new'	**now-szy**	**now-sza**	**now-sze**	**now-sze**	**now-si** 'newer'
star-y 'old'	**star-szy**	**star-sza**	**star-sze**	**star-sze**	**star-si** 'elder'

Predictable consonant and vowel shifts occur:

Adjective	Comparative	Predictable changes
biały	biel-szy 'whiter'	a:e, ł:l
drogi	droż-szy 'more expensive'	g:ż
miły	mil-szy 'nicer'	ł:l
tani	tań-szy 'cheaper'	ni:ń
wesoły	wesel-szy 'more cheerful'	o:e, ł:l

4.17.5.2 Adjectives ending -ki, -oki, -eki

Adjectives with the endings -ki, -oki, -eki, form comparative and superlative forms by dropping the endings, and adding -sz to the stem, followed by adjectival endings. Predictable consonant and vowel shifts occur, e.g., s:ż.

bliski	bliż-szy 'closer'	s:ż
brzydki	brzyd-szy 'uglier'	
ciężki	cięż-szy 'heavier'	
daleki	dal-szy 'further'	
głęboki	głęb-szy 'deeper'	
krótki	krót-szy 'shorter' (length)	
niski	niższy 'shorter' (height)	s:ż
szeroki	szer-szy 'wider'	
wąski	węż-szy 'narrower'	ą:ę, s:ż

4.17.5.3 Consonant clusters plus -ejszy

When a stem ends in a consonant cluster (except for -rdy, -sty), the stem is extended by the suffix -ejsz, and then followed by the adjectival endings. Adjectives with endings -tki, -ski, -dki were discussed in 4.17.5.2.

The consonants before the suffix -ejsz soften.

ciepły	ciepl-ejszy 'warmer'	ł:l
jasny	jaśni-ejszy 'brighter (color)'	sn:śni
ładny	ładni-ejszy 'prettier'	n:ni
łatwy	łatwi-ejszy 'easier'	w:wi
mądry	mądrz-ejszy 'wiser'	r:rz
piękny	piękni-ejszy 'more beautiful'	
szczupły	szczupl-ejszy 'slimmer'	ł:l
trudny	trudni-ejszy 'more difficult'	

wygod<u>n</u>y	**wygod<u>ni</u>-ejszy** 'more comfortable'
zim<u>n</u>y	**zim<u>ni</u>-ejszy** 'colder'

When a stem ends in the consonant cluster -rdy, -sty, a regular suffix -sz is added, and followed by the adjectival endings.

czysty	**czystszy** 'cleaner' (also **czyściejszy**)
gęsty	**gęstszy** 'thicker'
twardy	**tward-szy** 'harder'
prosty	**prost-szy** 'straighter'
częsty	**częst-szy** 'more frequent'
tłusty	**tłust-szy** (also **tłuściejszy** (rarely) or
	bardziej tłusty) 'greasier'

Comparative forms of some adjectives are irregular in the sense that the stem changes, but the comparative degree marker -sz stays.

dobry	**lep-szy** 'better'
zły	**gor-szy** 'worse'
duży	**więk-szy** 'bigger'
mały	**mn-iejszy** 'smaller'
lekki	**lż-ejszy** 'lighter'
miękki	**bardziej miękki** (also **miększy** (rarely)) 'softer'

The suffix -szy is used to make the comparative form of some colors.

biały	**bielszy** 'whiter'	**zielony**	**zieleńszy** 'greener'
czarny	**czarniejszy** 'blacker'	**żółty**	**żółciejszy** 'yellower'
czerwony	**czerwieńszy** 'redder'		

4.17.6 Bardziej/mniej + adjective

4.17.6.1 Comparative and superlative with bardziej/najbardziej

A group of adjectives that end in -ący, -wy, -ty, -sty, -(o)ny (formed from verbs) form comparatives by adding the intensifiers **bardziej** 'more' and **najbardziej** 'most' or diminishers **mniej** 'less' and **najmniej** 'least':

bardziej interesujący	**najbardziej interesujący**
'more interesting'	'most interesting'
mniej interesujący	**najmniej interesujący**
'less interesting'	'least interesting'

bardziej wypoczęty 'more relaxed'
mniej zadowolony 'less satisfied'
bardziej zmęczony 'more tired'

bardziej zajęty 'more busy'
bardziej barczysty 'more broad-shouldered'
bardziej widoczny 'more visible'

Jestem *bardziej zmęczony* **niż wczoraj.**
'I am *more tired* than yesterday.'

Jestem *bardziej zajęty* **niż rok temu.**
'I am *busier* than last year.'

Kiedyś byłam *mniej wyrozumiała.*
'I was *less understanding* in the past.'

Ten album jest *bardziej kolorowy* **niż tamten.**
'This album is *more colorful* than that one.'

Kobieta była *bardziej pijana* **od mężczyzny.**
'The woman was *drunker* than the man.'

bardziej/mniej chory 'more/less sick'	[verb: **chorować**]
bardziej/mniej mokry 'more/less wet'	[verb: **moknąć**]
bardziej/mniej łysy 'more/less bald'	[verb: **łysieć**]
bardziej/mniej siwy 'more/less gray'	[verb: **siwieć**]
bardziej/mniej szczery 'more/less honest'	[verb: **być szczerym**]

Adjectives with the endings **-owy** and **-ski** are mostly used with **bardziej/mniej** in a comparative degree (4.17.4).

Other examples of adjectives with comparative forms using **bardziej/mniej**:

bardziej/mniej wypoczęty 'more/less relaxed'	[verb: **wypoczywać**]
bardziej/mniej typowy 'more/less typical'	[verb: **typować**]
bardziej/mniej wymagający 'more/less demanding'	[verb: **wymagać**]
bardziej/mniej znany 'more/less known'	[verb: **znać**]
bardziej/mniej śliski 'more/less slippery'	[verb: **ślizgać się**]
bardziej/mniej płaski 'more/less flat'	[verb: **płaszczyć się**]
bardziej/mniej łysy 'more/less bald'	[verb: **łysieć**]
bardziej/mniej siwy 'more/less gray'	[verb: **siwieć**]
bardziej/mniej szczery 'more/less honest'	

Some adjectives can form comparatives both ways, based on personal preference, e.g.,

Positive degree	Comparative degree
atrakcyjny 'attractive'	**atrakcyjniejszy** or **bardziej atrakcyjny**
inteligentny 'intelligent'	**inteligentniejszy** or **bardziej inteligentny**

aktywny 'active'	**aktywniejszy** or **bardziej aktywny** (officially)
zabawny 'amusing'	**zabawniejszy** or **bardziej zabawny**
poważny 'serious'	**poważniejszy** or **bardziej poważny**

Note that comparatives with the adverbs **bardziej/najbardziej** are preferred by Poles.[1] This could be the result of a search for more distinct forms.

4.17.6.2 *Bardziej* and *więcej/najbardziej* and *najwięcej*

In English both **bardziej** and **więcej** are translated as 'more,' and **najbardziej** and **najwięcej** are translated as 'most.' **Bardziej** and **najbardziej** are used to intensify the quality of an adjective or adverb. **Więcej** and **najwięcej** are used to indicate a larger quantity of objects, ideas, animals or people.

> **Piotr jest *bardziej nerwowy* niż zwykle.** 'Piotr is *more nervous* than usual.'
> **Piotr ma *więcej pracy*.** 'Piotr has *more work*.'
> **Podróż do Hongkongu była *najbardziej męcząca* i *najwięcej* kosztowała, za to pobyt w Hong Kongu był *najbardziej* relaksujący.**
> 'The trip to Hong Kong was the *most tiring* and it *cost the most*, but [our] stay in Hong Kong was the *most relaxing*.'

4.17.6.3 *Negation with comparative forms*

Negated comparative forms are written separately:

> **Nie gorszy od wczoraj.** 'Not worse than yesterday.'

4.17.7 *Comparative constructions*

Comparison does not require only comparative or superlative forms.

> **nie wysoki, ale niski** 'not tall, but short'
> **wyjątkowo piękny ogród, ale bardzo stary dom**
>   'exceptionally beautiful garden but a very old house'
> **za trudny** 'too difficult'

| 4.17.7.1 | *Comparative of equality* |

To compare two qualities or quantities using the positive degree (basic form) of an adjective, constructions such as **tak . . . , jak** 'as . . . as,' **nie tyle . . . , co** 'so much . . . as,' or just **jak** 'as,' are used.

> **On *(nie)* jest tak wysoki jak jego ojciec.** 'He *is (not) as* tall *as* his father.'
> **Jestem *tak* zajęta *jak* nigdy.** 'I am *as* busy *as* ever.'
> **Był *nie tyle* zmęczony, *co* głodny.** 'He *wasn't so much* tired *as* hungry.'
> **Nasz syn jest zdrowy jak ryba.** 'Our son *is as* healthy *as a* fish.'

| 4.17.7.2 | *Comparison of infinitives* |

> **Wolę *zrobić* to sama, niż kogoś *prosić*.**
> 'I'd rather *do* it myself than *ask* somebody.'

| 4.17.7.3 | *Comparative of superiority* |

To compare two qualities or quantities there are certain constructions, rendered by the English **more . . . than.**

1. Comparative form of the adjective + **niż** 'than' <+NOM>.
2. Comparative form of the adjective + **od** 'than' <+GEN>.
3. **Coraz** + a comparative form of the adjective. Continuous increase/decrease. **Coraz** has the same meaning as the adjective it was used with.
4. **Im . . . tym** 'the more . . . the. . . .'
5. **jest tym bardziej . . . ponieważ** 'all the more . . . as'

> **Herbata jest zdrowsza *niż* kawa.** 'Tea is healthier *than* coffee.'
> **Herbata jest zdrowsza *od* kawy.** 'Tea is healthier *than* coffee.'

> **Pentagon jest większy *od* Białego Domu.** 'The Pentagon is bigger *than* the White House.'
> **Jesteś bardziej zmęczony *niż* ja.** 'You are more tired *than* I am.' (no need to add "I am")
> **Jesteś bardziej zmęczony *ode* mnie.** 'You are more tired *than* I am.'
> **Jestem tym bardziej zaskoczona, ponieważ tego nie oczekiwałam.** 'All the more I am surprised, as I did not expect it.'

> **im droższy, tym lepszy** 'the more expensive, the better'

| 4.17.7.4 | *To show continuous decrease* |

Klimat jest *coraz cieplejszy*. 'The climate is *warmer and warmer*.'

| 4.17.7.5 | **Ode mnie** *'than I'* |

Od in front of the personal pronoun **mnie** changes to **ode** to ease the pronunciation.

Ewa jest dwa lata *starsza ode mnie*.
'Ewa is two years *older than I am*.'

| 4.17.7.6 | *Intensifiers with comparative adjectives and adverbs* |

dużo + comparative form 'much more, much better'
jeszcze + comparative form 'even'

Ojciec jest *wysoki*, a brat *jeszcze wyższy*. '[My] father is *tall* but [my] brother is *even taller*.'
Dziadek jest *dużo starszy* od babci. 'Grandpa is *much older* than grandma.'

4.18 Superlative

The superlative form of an adjective (**stopień najwyższy**) is used to emphasize the highest or lowest level of concentration of a quality among all other subjects or objects.

Pies jest najlepszym przyjacielem człowieka.
'A dog is a man's best friend.'

| 4.18.1 | *naj- prefix* |

The superlative form of adjectives is the same as the comparative form plus the prefix *naj-* added in front of the comparative form.

naj + młodszy 'younger' **najmłodszy** 'youngest'
naj + starszy 'older' **najstarszy** 'oldest'

Irregular forms (see also 4.17.3):

najlep-szy 'best'
najgor-szy 'worst'

najwięk-szy 'biggest'
najmn-iejszy 'smallest'
najbardziej miękki/miększy (rarely) 'softest'
najukochańszy 'the most beloved' (does not have a comparative form)

| 4.18.1.1 | *najbardziej/najmniej + adjective*

Many adjectives, usually longer ones, form the superlative by putting the superlative form of the adverb **bardzo, najbardziej** 'the most' or **najmniej** 'the least,' in front of the adjective. (See 4.17.6)

Adjectives that are formed from verbs (many with the markers **-any, -ony, -ty, -ący**) are used in the superlative form with **najbardziej/najmniej**.

Adjectives with the endings **-owy** and **-ski** are mostly used with **najbardziej/najmniej** in the superlative.

najbardziej/najmniej wypoczęty	[verb: **wypoczywać**]
'the most/least relaxed'	
najbardziej/najmniej typowy	[verb: **typować**]
'the most/least typical'	
najbardziej/najmniej wymagający	[verb: **wymagać**]
'the most/least demanding'	
najbardziej/najmniej znany	[verb: **znać**]
'the most/least known'	

| 4.18.2 | **Superlative constructions**

To compare superlative qualities or quantities certain constructions are used.

1. Superlative form of the adjective + **w** 'in,' **na** 'in, at' plus the locative case
2. Comparative form of the adjective + **z(e)** 'than' plus the genitive plural

(An extra **e** is used before many consonant clusters. See 1.3.8.1.)

Jonathan jest najmądrzejszy z nas wszystkich. 'Jonathan is the smartest among all of us.'
To najwyższy budynek na świecie. 'It is the tallest building in the world.'
Ewa jest najwyższa w grupie. 'Ewa is the tallest in the group.'
To była jedna z moich najpiękniejszych chwil w życiu.
'It was one of my most beautiful moments in my life.'

Negated superlative forms are written separately, e.g.,

Nie najlepszy mecz. 'Not the best game.'

For adjectives without comparative and superlative forms, see 4.17.4.

4.19 Differences between English and Polish adjectives

Polish differs from English in:

- having short and long forms of adjectives
- placement of the adjective before or after the noun (see 4.1.3)
- having more participle types, that can function as adjectival modifiers
- the use of markers, such as **-owy**, **-ski**, and **-ny**, while many English adjectives do not differ from nouns:

      animal farm   farm animal
      a doghouse   a house dog

In English an adjective is used after verbs of perception, e.g.,

She looks *nice* <ADJ>.

In Polish an adverb is used after the verb 'to look,' e.g.,

Ona *ładnie* <ADV> **wygląda.**

(Chapter 7)

4.20 Demonstrative adjectives

Demonstrative adjectives precede and determine the noun with which they agree in number, class and case. In Polish, like in English, **ten, tamten, ta, tamta, to, tamto** 'this/that' **te, tamte, ci, tamci** 'these/those' and **ów** 'that (bookish)' can be used both as adjectives and as pronouns. For the use and declension of **ten/ta/to** and **te/ci**, see 5.5.

As a demonstrative adjective "this" and "that" modify a noun; as a pronoun they replace a noun.

They are declined like adjectives, and like adjectives have masculine, feminine, neuter, singular and plural forms.

i tym podobny 'suchlike'
wszelki 'all' (bookish)

Muszę zapłacić za gaz, prąd i *tym podobne rzeczy.*
'I have to pay for gas, electricity, and *such things.*'

dołożyć *wszelkich starań* 'to make *every effort*'
wszelkimi sposobami 'by all possible means'

Tego dnia było zimno. 'That day, it was cold.' <demonstrative ADJ>
Do kogo należy ten pies? 'Whom does that dog belong to?'
<demonstrative ADJ>
Ten? Nie wiem.
'This one? I don't know.' <demonstrative PRON>

**"W owym czasie [w starożytnym Rzymie] drink nazywał
się aperitivum, co w przekładzie z łaciny brzmi niezbyt
elegancko 'otwieracz', lecz wyjaśnia rolę kieliszka
alkoholu dającego sygnał do rozpoczęcia biesiady."[2]**
'At that time [in ancient Rome] drink was called *aperitivum*, which in
translation from the Latin as "opener" does not sound very elegant,
but explains the role of a glass of alcohol as a signal to open the feast.'

4.20.1 Simple and compound forms

Demonstrative adjectives, as well as demonstrative pronouns, have simple
or compound forms. (see 5.5)

4.20.1.1 Simple

ten, **ta**, **to** correspond to 'this' or 'that'
te, **ci** correspond to 'these' or 'those'
ów, **owa**, **owo** correspond to 'that' (bookish)
owe, **owi** correspond to 'these' or 'those' (bookish)
jedyny 'only, sole'

Jesteś *jedyną osobą,* **która mnie rozumie.**
'You are *the only person* who understands me.'

For an explanation of **ten/ta/to** and **te/ci** and their declensions, see 5.5.

4.20.1.2 Compound

tamten 'that (over there)'/'the other'
i tym podobny or *i temu podobne* '...suchlike...'

Lubię rozmowy z pisarzami <INS PL>, **muzykami i tym
podobnymi** <INS PL> **artystami.**
'I like conversations with writers, musicians and suchlike artists.'

Lubię słuchać pisarzy <GEN PL>**, muzyków i tym podobnych**
<GEN PL> **artystów.**

'I like listening to writers, musicians and suchlike artists.'

Tamten 'that' consists of the pronoun *tam* 'over there,' to convey the idea of distance from the speaker, attached to the simple forms **ten, ta, to** (except ów). The compound form is used to emphasize the opposition.

tam 'over there' + *ten* <MSC> 'that' = *tamten* 'that' ('over there')

tam 'over there' + *ta* <FEM> 'that' = *tamta* 'that' ('over there')

Note that the accusative of **ta** is exceptionally tę:

Proszę spojrzeć w tę stronę, nie w *tamtą***.**

'Please look *this* way, not *the other/that* one.'

Table 4.17 Compound demonstrative adjectives

Case	Singular			Plural	
	'this/that'	'this/that'	'this/that'	'these/those'	'these/those'
	MSC	FEM	NT	NO-MHPL	MHPL
NOM	(tam)ten	(tam)ta	(tam)to	(tam)te	(tam)ci
ACC	= NOM/GEN	tę/tamtą	(tam)to	(tam)te	(tam)tych
GEN	(tam)tego	(tam)tej	(tam)tego	(tam)tych	(tam)tych
DAT	(tam)temu	(tam)tej	(tam)temu	(tam)tym	(tam)tym
LOC	(tam)tym	(tam)tej	(tam)tym	(tam)tych	(tam)tych
INS	(tam)tym	(tam)tą	(tam)tym	(tam)tymi	(tam)tymi

Note that the masculine accusative singular form is identical to that of the genitive for animate nouns (e.g., when referring to a human being or an animal), and to that of the nominative for inanimate nouns.

4.21   Distributive adjectives

Jeszcze się taki nie urodził, co by *każdemu (wszystkim)* **dogodził.**

You cannot please *everyone*. [lit. was not yet born the one who would manage to please each person (everyone)]

Distributive adjectives refer to each, all or some members of a group, such as 'each,' 'every,' **każdy** (modifies a singular entity), 'none,' 'neither' **żaden**, 'some' (in the singular only) **niektóre** or **niektórzy**, 'all' **wszyscy** or **wszystkie** (modifies a plural entity), **wszelki** 'all' (bookish), 'either' (as both **obie, obaj, obydwaj**) 'either' (as one or the other).

In Polish, like in English, "each," "every," "all," "some" and "none" can be used both as adjectives and as pronouns.

As a demonstrative adjective they modify a noun; as a pronoun they replace a noun.

4.21.1 Declension

Distributive adjectives are inflected for class, number and case, like adjectives.

Table 4.18 Distributive adjectives

Case	Singular			Plural	
	'each/every'	'each/every'	'each/every'	'all'	'all'
	MSC	FEM	NT	NO-MHPL	MHPL
NOM	każdy	każda	każde	wszystkie	wszyscy
ACC	= NOM/GEN	każdą	każde	wszystkie	wszystkich
GEN	każdego	każdej	każdego	wszystkich	wszystkich
DAT	każdemu	każdej	każdemu	wszystkim	wszystkim
LOC	każdym	każdej	każdym	wszystkich	wszystkich
INS	każdym	każdą	każdym	wszystkimi	wszystkimi

Note that the masculine accusative singular form is identical to that of the genitive for animate nouns (e.g., when referring to a human being or an animal), and to that of the nominative for inanimate nouns.

4.21.2 Use

Każdy/każda/każde 'each' combines with a noun in the singular to emphasize the distributive sense.

Wszyscy/wszystkie 'all' is used with a noun in the plural to emphasize the collective sense.

Każde dziecko ma prawo do opieki zdrowotnej.
'Each child has a right to health care.'

Wszystkie dzieci mają prawo do opieki zdrowotnej.
'All children have a right to health care.'

Dziadek pożegnał się ze wszystkimi. Każdego z nas przytulił i pocałował.
'Grandfather said goodbye to everyone. He embraced and kissed each of us.'

4.21.2.1 *Consonant cluster*

z(e)—an extra **e** occurs in front of the consonant cluster to ease the pronunciation.

> **ze wszystkimi** 'with everyone'
> **z każdym** 'with each one'

4.21.2.2 **Wszystko** *'the lot of goods,' 'everything' and* **wszyscy** *'all,' 'everyone'*

> **Tęsknię** *za wszystkim.* 'I miss *everything.*'
> **Zadzwoń** *do wszystkich.* 'Call *everyone.*'

4.21.2.3 **Każdy** *with reoccurring time constructions:* *'every day,' 'every year,' etc.*

When used with recurring time, **każdy** has the genitive form. When used with a day of the week, it takes the preposition **w** followed by the accusative case, e.g.,

> *Każdego dnia* **dzwonię do męża.** '*Every day* I call [my] husband.'
> *Każdego roku* **jeździmy nad morze.** '*Every year* we go to the sea.'
> *W każdą sobotę* **jemy obiad u rodziców.** '*Every Saturday* we eat at [my] parents.'

4.22 Niektóre and inny

Niektóre 'so*me*,' '*a few*,' '*certain*' refers to a small number. The noun that niektóre modifies is in the plural. It is often used in comparison with **inne** or **inni** 'others,' e.g.,

> **Niektórzy ludzie nie lubią lodów.** '*Some people* do not like ice cream.'
> **Niektóre osoby mogą jeść lody codziennie.** '*Some persons* can eat ice cream daily.'
> **Niektóre tematy są traktowane jako tabu.** 'Certain topics are regarded as taboo.'

The plural male human or no male human forms are identical except for the nominative and accusative cases.

Table 4.19 Niektóre

Case	NO-MHPL	MHPL
NOM	**niektóre**	**niektórzy**
ACC	**niektóre**	**niektórych**
GEN	**niektórych**	**niektórych**
DAT	**niektórym**	**niektórym**
LOC	**niektórych**	**niektórych**
INS	**niektórymi**	**niektórymi**

Table 4.20 Inny

Case	Singular			Plural	
	MSC	FEM	NT	NO-MHPL	MHPL
NOM	**inny**	**inna**	**inne**	**inne**	**inni**
ACC	**= NOM/GEN**	**inną**	**inne**	**inne**	**innych**
GEN	**innego**	**innej**	**innego**	**innych**	**innych**
DAT	**innemu**	**innej**	**innemu**	**innym**	**innym**
LOC	**innym**	**innej**	**innym**	**innych**	**innych**
INS	**innym**	**inną**	**innym**	**innymi**	**innymi**

Note that the masculine accusative singular form is identical to that of the genitive for animate nouns (e.g., when referring to a human being or an animal), and to that of the nominative for inanimate nouns.

niektórzy 'some' and *inni* 'others' are often used in opposing sentences.

Niektórzy studenci mieszkają w akademiku, *inni* wynajmują mieszkanie.
'*Some students* live in a dormitory, *others* rent an apartment.'

niejeden 'more than one' is used to express 'more than one,' 'many.' The modified noun is singular, as is the verb.

Niejeden student wolałby nie brać kredytu na studia.
'*More than one student would prefer* not to take a student loan.'
Niejeden człowiek chciałby polecieć na Księżyc. (not: niejedni ludzie)
'*More than one person would like* to fly to the moon.'
Niejedno (not: niejedne) **dziecko marzy o podróży w kosmos.**
'*Many children dream* about a trip to the cosmos.'

Z niejednego pieca chleb jeść (saying) 'to have life experience'

4.23 Interrogative adjectives

Which 'który,' what 'jaki,' and whose 'czyj,' modify nouns and are used in questions.

Predictable consonant shifts occur: **k:c, r:rz** (as in **wysoki:wysocy, dobry:dobrzy**).

Jaki changes to **jacy**, and **który** to **którzy, czyj** to **czyi** for male human plural forms.

> *Który rozdział czytasz?* 'Which chapter are you reading?'
> *Jakiego koloru jest pański samochód?* 'What color is your car, sir?'
> *Czyje dziecko krzyczy pod oknem?* 'Whose child screams by the window?'

Jaki is also used in exclamations.

> **Jaki piękny dom!** 'Such a pretty house!'

Table 4.21 Jaki

Case	Singular			Plural	
	MSC	FEM	NT	NO-MHPL	MHPL
NOM	jaki	jaka	jakie	jakie	jacy
ACC	= NOM/GEN	jaką	jakie	jakie	jakich
GEN	jakiego	jakiej	jakiego	jakich	jakich
DAT	jakiemu	jakiej	jakiemu	jakim	jakim
LOC	jakim	jakiej	jakim	jakich	jakich
INS	jakim	jaką	jakim	jakimi	jakimi

Table 4.22 Który

Case	Singular			Plural	
	MSC	FEM	NT	NO-MHPL	MHPL
NOM	który	która	które	które	którzy
ACC	= NOM/GEN	którą	które	które	których
GEN	którego	której	którego	których	których
DAT	któremu	której	któremu	którym	którym
LOC	którym	której	którym	których	których
INS	którym	którą	którym	którymi	którymi

Table 4.23 Czyj

Case	Singular			Plural	
	MSC	FEM	NT	NO-MHPL	MHPL
NOM	czyj	czyja	czyje	czyje	czyi
ACC	= NOM/GEN	czyją	czyje	czyje	czyich
GEN	czyjego	czyjej	czyjego	czyich	czyich
DAT	czyjemu	czyjej	czyjemu	czyim	czyim
LOC	czyim	czyjej	czyim	czyich	czyich
INS	czyim	czyją	czyim	czyimi	czyimi

Note that the masculine accusative singular form is identical to that of the genitive for animate nouns (e.g., when referring to a human being or an animal), and to that of the nominative for inanimate nouns.

4.24 Relative adjectives

Który 'which' or 'that' agrees in number, class and case with the noun it qualifies.

When który is used as a relative pronoun, it replaces the noun it modifies.

Pokaż mi ten dom, który kosztuje milion dolarów.
'Show me the house that costs a million dollars.' <relative PRON>

Który dom kosztuje milion dolarów? <relative ADJ>

Który is declined like a regular adjective (see Table 4.22).

4.24.1 Który in a clause

Który agrees with the class and number of the noun it refers to, but the case of który is determined by the verb in its own clause.

Studentka, z <+INS> którą mieszkam, jest bardzo miła.
'The student I live with is very kind.' [female student]

Student, z <+INS> którym mieszkam, jest bardzo miły.
'The student I live with is very kind.' [male student]

Studenci, z <+INS> którymi mieszkam, są bardzo mili.
'The students I live with are very kind.' [a group of students]

To jest kobieta, której <+DAT> ufam. 'This a woman I trust.'
To jest mężczyzna, któremu <+DAT> ufam. 'This is a man I trust.'
To są ludzie, którym <+DAT> ufam. 'These are the people I trust.'

Table 4.24 Adjective declension

	Singular				Plural	
	MSC		NT	FEM	MHPL[3]	NO-MHPL[4]
	Animate[1]	Inanimate[2]				
NOM	-y/-i		-e	-a	-i/-y	-e
ACC	-ego	-y/-i	-e	-ą	-ych	-e
GEN	-ego		-ej		-ych	
DAT	-emu		-ej		-ym	
LOC	-ym/-im		-ej		-ych	
INS	-ym/-im		-ą		-ymi	
VOC	-y/-i		-e	-a	-i/-y	-e

Table 4.25 To and **te**

	Singular				Plural	
	MSC		NT	FEM	MHPL[3]	NO-MHPL[4]
	Animate[1]	Inanimate[2]				
NOM	ten		to	ta	ci	te
ACC	tego	ten	to	tę[5]	tych	te
GEN	tego		tej		tych	
DAT	temu		tej		tym	
LOC	tym		tej		tych	
INS	tym		tą		tymi	
VOC	ten		to	ta	ci	te

Notes

[1] Animate: masculine animate form, i.e., people and animals.

[2] Inanimate: masculine inanimate form, i.e., things.

[3] MHPL form refers to male human beings.

[4] NO-MHPL form (refers to forms without a man: masculine impersonal (animals and things), neuter and feminine forms).

[5] The form **tę** is irregular (the typical ending for the accusative feminine singular is **-ą**).

Chapter 5

Pronouns

5.1   Overview

"Pronoun" in Polish is **zaimek**. Pronouns are used to point out the identity of the speaker, the addressee or other entities. They can be substituted for nouns and noun phrases.

> **Ojciec mówił do dzieci, ale *one go* nie słuchały.**
> 'Father was talking to the children, but *they* were not listening to *him*.'

> **Studenci studiów zaocznych narzekają, że tylko *oni* płacą za studia. (oni** refers to the whole phrase **Studenci studiów zaocznych,** not only **studenci).**
> 'Part-time students complain that only *they* pay for school.'

> **Dzwoniłam do *tej* firmy kilka razy.**
> 'I called *that* firm several times.'

> **Adam jest strasznym egoistą i myśli tylko *o sobie*.**
> 'Adam is a horrible egoist and thinks only *about himself*.'

Some pronouns, e.g., possessive and demonstrative, decline like adjectives, others have a specific declension, e.g., personal pronouns. The possessive pronouns **jego** 'his,' **jej** 'her,' **ich** 'their' have one form regardless of number, class and case.

5.2   Personal pronouns

Personal pronouns ("I," "you," "she," etc.), regardless of their name, can refer to nouns and noun phrases that denote persons, animals, and objects.

> **Książki leżą *na stole* i pod *nim*.**
> '[The] books are *on the table* and under *it*.' (**nim** refers to the table)

Wszyscy chcieli *psa*, **a teraz ja muszę wyprowadzać** *go* **na spacer.**

'Everyone wanted a dog, but now I have to take *him* for a walk.'

(*him* refers to the dog)

5.2.1 | Declension

Like in English, the declension of personal pronouns in Polish is very specific. The nominative case differs from other cases, e.g., **ja** 'I' and **mnie** 'me'; **my** 'we' and **nas** 'us.'

5.2.1.1 | First and second persons

Ty i ja—teatry to są dwa.

'You and I—to each his own.'

Edward Stachura "Życie to nie teatr" ('Life is not a theater')

The first and second person personal pronouns **ja** 'I,' **ty** 'you' (familiar singular), **my** 'we,' **wy** 'you' (familiar plural) are declined as follows:

Table 5.1 Declension of **ja**, **ty**, **my**, **wy**

NOM	ja 'I'	ty 'you' sing.	my 'we'	wy 'you' pl.
ACC	mn-*ie*/(m-*ię*)	cieb-*ie*/c-*ię*	n-*as*	w-*as*
GEN	= ACC	= ACC	= ACC	= ACC
DAT	mn-*ie*/m-*i*	tob-*ie*/c-*i*	n-*am*	w-*am*
LOC	o mn-*ie*	o tob-*ie*	o n-*as*	o w-*as*
INS	mn-*ą*	tob-*ą*	n-*ami*	w-*ami*
VOC	= NOM	= NOM	= NOM	= NOM

Note: The personal pronouns **ja** and **ty**, and **my** and **wy** share similar endings: **mnie**/**ciebie**, **mną**/**tobą** and **nas**/**was**, **nami**/**wami**.

The accusative form **mię** is very rarely used; mostly in literary works.

Weź mię, ja umrę przy tobie . . .

Take me, I will die beside you . . .

Adam Mickiewicz "**Romantyczność**" ('The Romantic')

5.2.1.1.1 | Notes on first personal pronoun

The first person personal pronoun **ja** is in the nominative case only; all other forms start with the consonant cluster **mn-**. Note that a combination of a consonant cluster and a preposition would require an extra -e sound (see 1.3.8.1).

beze mnie 'without me' but **bez ciebie** 'without you' (familiar form)
przede mną 'in front of me' but **przed tobą** 'in front of you' (familiar form)

5.2.2 | Omission

Generally, personal pronouns, especially the first and second person personal pronouns **ja, ty, my, wy,** are omitted when used as subjects.

Pracuję **w centrum.** '*I work* in the center.'
Znamy się **ze studiów.** 'We know each other from school.'
Nie wiem, **gdzie** *mieszkasz.* '*I don't know* where *you live.*'
Jadę **tak szybko jak** *mogę.* '*I drive* as fast as *I can.*'

The third person personal pronouns are generally omitted when the subject is clear from the context.

Do pokoju weszła kobieta. *Miała* **na sobie płaszcz.** *Usiadła* **i** *zaczęła* **czytać.**
'A woman entered the room. *(She) was wearing* a coat. *(She) sat down* and *started* reading.'

Piotr ma syna. *Ma* **także piękną żonę i duży dom z ogrodem.**
'Piotr has a son. *(He) also has* a wife and a big house with a garden.'

Chciałbyś **kawałek** *ciasta?* **Jest pyszne.**
'*Would you like* a piece of *cake?* [It] *is* delicious.'

However, to emphasize the importance of the subjects (e.g., in opposing sentences), or for clarification, the personal pronouns are used, e.g.,

Tylko *ja* **pracuję w weekendy.** 'Only *I* work on the weekends.'
Czy *my* **się znamy?** 'Do *we* know each other?'
Ja **nie wiem, gdzie** *ty* **mieszkasz, ale** *ty* **wiesz, gdzie** *ja* **mieszkam.**
'*I do not know* where *you* live, but *you* know where *I* live.'

5.2.3 | Third person singular

The third person singular pronouns **on** 'he,' **ona** 'she,' **ono** 'it' are declined as follows:

Table 5.2 Declension of **on, ona, ono**

NOM	**on** 'he'	**ono** 'it'	**ona** 'she'
ACC	**jego/niego/go**	**je/nie**	**ją/nią**
GEN	**jego/niego/go**		**jej/niej**
DAT	**jemu/niemu/mu**		**jej/niej**
LOC	**nim**		**niej**
INS	**nim**		**nią**

Note that **on** 'he' and **ono** 'it' share forms in the genitive, dative, locative and instrumental cases.

The third person pronouns can refer to people, animals and objects. **On** 'he' refers to a masculine noun or noun phrase, and **ona** 'she' refers to a feminine noun or noun phrase, **ono** 'it' refers to a neuter noun or noun phrase, e.g.,

> **Czy *ona (sukienka)* nie jest za krótka?** 'Isn't *it (the dress)* too short?' (she)
>
> **Dlaczego *on (rower)* skrzypi?** 'Why is *it (the bike)* squeaking?' (he)
>
> **Czy *ono (mięso)* jest świeże?** 'Is *it (the meat)* fresh?' (it)
>
> **Pyszne *ciasto*. Sama *je* upiekłaś?** 'A delicious *cake*. Did you bake *it* yourself?' (it)

In the accusative, genitive, and dative, the personal pronouns **on, ono, ona** have more than one form (see 5.2.7).

5.2.4 | *Third person plural*

The third person plural pronoun **oni** 'they' refers to a group of male human beings, or to a mixed group with at least one male human being—the male human form, and **one** 'they' refers to everything else—the no male human form, e.g.,

> <u>**One**</u> **(*psy*) znowu szczekają. Zawołaj *je* (*psy*) do domu.**
> 'They (the dogs) are barking again. Call them (the dogs) home.'
>
> <u>**One**</u> **(*dzieci*) znowu biegają po ulicy. Zawołaj *je* (*dzieci*) do domu.**
> 'They (the children) are running on the street again. Call them (the children) home.'
>
> <u>**Oni**</u> **(*chłopcy*) znowu biegają po ulicy. Zawołaj *ich* (*chłopców*) do domu.**
> 'They (the boys) are running on the street again. Call them (the boys) home.'

5.2.4.1 | **Osoby, ludzie** *and* **dzieci**

Osoby 'persons' and **dzieci** 'children' are referred to by the pronoun **one** 'they', while **ludzie** 'people' are referred to by the pronoun **oni** 'they.'

This is because the singular of **osoby** is **osoba** 'a person'—a feminine noun, while the singular of **ludzie** is **człowiek** 'a man,' a masculine male human noun. **Dzieci** implies a lack of adulthood.

> **Łatwo rozpoznać takie osoby. One noszą kolorowe ubrania.**
> 'It is easy to recognize such *persons*. *They* wear colorful clothes.'
> **Dlaczego oni (ludzie) milczą?** 'Why are *they* (*the people*) silent?'
> **Miłe osoby. Zaprośmy je.** 'Nice *people*. Let's invite *them*.'
> **Mili ludzie. Zaprośmy ich.** 'Nice *people*. Let's invite *them*.'
> **Miłe dzieci. Zaprośmy je.** 'Nice *children*. Let's invite *them*.'

Table 5.3 Declension of *oni* and *one*

NOM	**oni** 'they' <MHPL>	**one** 'they' <NO-MHPL>
ACC	**ich/nich**	**je/nie**
GEN	= ACC	**ich/nich**
DAT	**im/nim**	**im/nim**
LOC	**nich**	**nich**
INS	**nimi**	**nimi**

The third person plural personal pronouns **oni** and **one** share forms in the dative, locative and instrumental cases.

In the accusative, genitive, and dative, the personal pronouns **oni** and **one** have more than one form (see 5.2.7).

5.2.5 | *Identification of the referents* **je** *and* **nie**

Both personal pronouns **je/nie** 'it, them' (**je** and **nie** are the accusative singular of **ono** 'it' and accusative plural of **one** 'they <NO-MHPL>') may refer to a singular neuter noun, e.g., **piwo** 'beer,' **dziecko** 'child,' or to a no male human plural noun, e.g., **dzieci** 'children,' **kobiety** 'women,' **psy** 'dogs' in the accusative case. The context can clarify what **je/nie** refers to. **Nie** is the form of **je** that must be used after a preposition (see 5.2.6).

> **Gdzie jest moje *piwo*? Widziałeś *je*?** 'Where is my *beer*?
> Did you see *it*?'
> **Gdzie są moje *dzieci*? Widziałeś *je*?** 'Where are my *children*?
> Did you see *them*?'

Gdzie jest moje _piwo_? Już dziesięć minut czekam na _nie_.
'Where is my _beer_? I've been waiting ten minutes for _it_.'
Gdzie są moje _walizki_? Już godzinę czekam na _nie_. 'Where are
my _suitcases_? I've been waiting an hour for _them_.'
Ewa urodziła _dziecko_. Widziałeś _je_? 'Ewa gave birth to her _child_.
Did you see _him/her_?'

Note: The pronoun **go** 'him' can be used when referring to a baby boy.

Gdzie jest moje dziecko? Widziałeś _go_? 'Where is my child? Did
you see _him_?'

5.2.5.1 | _"Them" in the context of_ **je** _and_ **ich**

Both personal pronouns **je** (accusative no male human plural) and **ich**
(accusative and genitive male human plural) translate into 'them' in English.

To są moje _koleżanki z pracy_. Chcesz _je_ poznać? 'These are
my (_female_) _colleagues from work_. Do you want to meet _them_?'
To są moi _koledzy z pracy_. Chcesz _ich_ poznać? 'These are my
colleagues from work (a group of female and male colleagues). Do
you want to meet _them_?'

Ich 'them' refers to a group of male human beings or a group with at least
one male human being, e.g., **mężczyźni** 'man,' **sąsiedzi** 'neighbors' and
ludzie 'people.' **Je** 'them' refers to everything else, e.g., **dzieci** 'children,'
kobiety 'women,' **psy** 'dogs' plus **osoby** 'persons.' (See 5.2.4.1)

5.2.6 | _Possessive and personal_

The third person personal pronouns **on, ona, ono, one, oni** in combination
with a preposition have a prepositional form with an **n-** prefix, e.g., **niego,
niemu, (nim) nią, (o) niej, (o) nich, nimi, nim.** (See 5.2.8)

The possessive pronouns **jego** 'his,' **jej** 'her,' **ich** 'their' are indeclinable;
combined with a preposition they do not change. Compare the sentences:

Nie śmiej się _z niego_! 'Don't laugh _at him_!'
Nie śmiej się _z jego fryzury_! 'Don't laugh _at his haircut_!'
Nie pisz _do niego_! 'Don't write _to him_!'
Nie pisz _do jego siostry_! 'Don't write _to his sister_!'
Czekamy _na nich_. 'We are waiting _for them_.'
Czekamy _na ich decyzję_. 'We are waiting _for their decision_.'

5.2.7 | Short and long form

5.2.7.1 | Use and position

Some personal pronouns have more than one form, e.g., 'you' in the accusative and genitive cases can be **cię**—a short (unstressed) form or **ciebie**—a long (stressed) form.

'Him' is represented in Polish by three forms: unstressed (or short) form **go,**

stressed (or long) form **jego,** and **ni-** form **niego.**

Long (stressed) forms are used:

(1) in the initial position when starting a sentence or a clause, and
(2) in opposing constructions, in order to put emphasis on the pronoun.

Ni- forms, characteristic for the third person singular and plural: 'he,' 'she,' 'it,' and 'they,' plus **mnie, tobie, ciebie** are used after prepositions.

Do *not* use short (unstressed) forms in the initial position when starting a sentence or a clause.

This is just an overview of the usage of short, long and **ni-** forms. A detailed explanation follows.

5.2.7.1.1 | Ciebie/cię

Ciebie kocham. 'I love *you.*' (stressed form, initial position)
Kocham cię. 'I love *you.*' (unstressed form)
Nie potrafię żyć bez ciebie. 'I cannot live *without you.*'
(form after preposition)
Ewa kocha Piotra, a nie ciebie. 'Ewa loves Piotr, and not *you.*'
(stressed form, in opposing construction)

5.2.7.1.2 | Jego/niego/go

Jego na pewno nie posłuchają.
'They will not listen to *him* for sure.' (stressed form, initial)

Nigdy go nie słuchają.
'They never listen to *him.*' (unstressed form)

Posłuchali go.
'They listened to *him*.' (unstressed form)

Posłuchali jego, a nie ciebie.
'They listened to *him*, and not to you.' (stressed form, in opposing construction)

Napisali do niego.
'They wrote *to him*.' (form after preposition)

5.2.7.1.3 | Jemu/niemu/mu

Jemu **wszystko się udaje!** '*He* succeeds in everything!' (stressed form, initial)

Podoba *mu* **się projekt?** 'Does *he* like the project?' [Does the project appeal *to him*?]

Ojciec *mu* **wierzy.** 'Father believes *him*.' (unstressed form)

Ojciec tylko *jemu* **wierzy.** 'Father believes only *him*.' (stressed form)

Dzięki niemu **znalazłem pracę.** '*Thanks to him* I found a job.' (form after preposition)

5.2.7.2 | *Unstressed (short) forms*

Unstressed short forms of personal pronouns: **mi, mię** (rarely used), **ci, cię, mu, go** are called "enclitic." These forms are unstressed and pronounced together with the preceding word.

Widzę *cię*. 'I see *you*.'
Podoba *mi* **się ten film.** 'I like the movie.' [The movie appeals *to me*.]
Nie chcę *go* **widzieć.** 'I don't want to see *him*.'
Daj *mi* **to.** 'Give it *to me*.'
Oczekujesz *go*? 'Are you expecting *him*?'

Mię is generally used in literary works.

Kiedy położysz rękę na me dłonie,
'When you put your hand on my palm,'
Luba *mię* jakaś spokojność owionie . . .
'A delightful calmness will envelop *me* . . .'
Adam Mickiewicz, "**Niepewność**" ('Uncertainty')

| 5.2.7.3 | *Stressed (long) forms* |

The long form personal pronouns **mnie, ciebie, tobie, jemu, jego** are stressed personal pronouns.

They are used to emphasize (stress) the persons or the object in comparison with another person or another object. Long forms are used at the beginning of a sentence, with comparisons and in opposing sentences. Long form personal pronouns in a single phrase generally precede the verb.

Zaprosiłam *jego*, a nie *ciebie*. 'I invited *him*, and not *you*.'
(comparison)
Dlaczego akurat *jego* bronisz? 'Why do you defend *him* exactly?'
(emphasis)

Komu ufasz? 'Whom do you trust?' (interrogative)
***Jemu*.** 'Him.' (beginning of the sentence)

Kogo kochasz? 'Whom do you love?'
I *ciebie*, i *jego*. 'You and him.' [Both of you.] (beginning of the sentence, emphasis)

Kocham *cię*. 'I love *you*.'
Ja *ciebie* też. 'I love *you*, too.' (emphasis)

| 5.2.8 | **N-** *prefix* |

A personal pronoun with an extra **n-** prefix is used after the prepositions **niego, niemu, nim, nią, niej, nich, nimi.** These forms are created from the third persons **on, ona, ono, one, oni.**

Jestem z *nią*/z *nim* szczęśliwy. 'I am happy *with her*/*with him*.'
Idę do *niej*. 'I am going *to* [see] *her*.'
***Dzięki nim* znalazłem pracę.** '*Thanks to them* I found a job.'
Dużo o *nich* słyszałem. 'I have heard a lot *about them*.'
Czekasz na *niego*? 'Are you waiting *for him*?'

Be careful when using a preposition in front of a personal pronoun or a possessive pronoun.

While personal pronouns with prepositions take the **n-** prefix, possessive pronouns do not change, e.g.,

Czekam na *niego*. 'I am waiting *for him*.'
Czekam na *jego* siostrę. 'I am waiting *for his sister*.'

(See also 5.2.6)

Instrumental and locative personal pronouns forms

In the instrumental and locative cases only the **n-** prefix forms exist. They are used with or without prepositions, in stressed or unstressed positions: nim, (o) nim, nią, (o) niej, nimi, (o) nich.

> **Kupiłem *rower* i jeżdżę *nim* do pracy.** 'I bought *a bike* and I ride *it* to work.'
>
> **Kupiłem stary *rower* i mam *z nim* same problemy.** 'I bought an old *bike* and I only have problems *with it*.'
>
> **Kocham *Ewę* i jestem *z nią* szczęśliwy.** 'I love *Ewa* and I am happy *with her*.'
>
> **Kocham *Ewę* i chcę się *nią* opiekować.** 'I love *Ewa* and I want to take care of *her*.'

Note the locative of the pronoun **on** 'he' written as one word with the prepositions **w** 'in,' **przez** 'by,' and **dla** 'for.' Even though rarely used in contemporary Polish, such forms are used in literary works.

> weń (= w niego), przezeń (= przez niego), dlań (= dla niego)

> Biegła więc, gdzie stał mały domowy ołtarzyk,
> 'She ran to where a little home-made shrine stood,'
> Wyjęła zeń obrazek i relikwiarzyk . . .
> 'She took out <u>from it</u> a picture and a relic box . . .'
>
> Adam Mickiewicz, **"Pan Tadeusz"**

5.2.9 | *Two pronouns*

Note that personal pronouns that refer to the indirect object come first; personal pronouns that refer to the direct object come second. In English, different word orders are possible (e.g., **Dam <u>ci</u> to.** 'I will give <u>you</u> it.' or 'I will give it <u>to you</u>.').

> ***Pieniądze* na kwiaty? Dam <u>*ci*</u> *je* jutro.**
> '*Money* for flowers? I will give *it* <u>*to you*</u> tomorrow.'

ci 'to you' is the indirect object; je 'it' is the direct object

> **Mam nowy *telefon*. Chcę <u>*ci*</u> *go* pokazać.**
> 'I have a new *phone*. I want to show it <u>*to you*</u>.'

ci 'to you' is the indirect object; go 'it' is the direct object

> **Mam nowy *telefon*. Babcia <u>*mi*</u> *go* dała.**
> 'I have a new *phone*. Grandma gave it <u>*to me*</u>.'

mi 'to me' is the indirect object; go 'it' is the direct object

5.2.10 | Multiple forms of "you"

Note that there is more than one form for saying 'you' in Polish.

The polite forms **pan** 'mister,' **pani** 'madam,' **panie** 'ladies,' **panowie** 'gentlemen,' **państwo** 'ladies and gentlemen' are communicated through the third person singular and plural.

> **Pani Nowak mieszka w domu numer dwa.** '*Miss Nowak* lives in house number two.'
>
> **Czy jest *pan* Nowak?** 'Is *Mr. Nowak* in?'

Ty 'you' (singular) and its respective forms **ciebie, cię, (o) tobie, tobą,** are familiar forms. They are generally used when referring to a person you know or you are familiar with.

Wy 'you' (plural) and its respective forms **(o) was, wam, wami,** are familiar forms. They are generally used when referring to a group of people you know or you are familiar with.

Pani 'you' (singular) and its respective forms **panią, (o) pani** are necessary forms to refer to a woman in a formal setting.

Pan 'you' (singular) and its respective forms **pana, (o) panu, panem** are necessary forms to refer to a man in a formal setting.

Panie 'you' (plural) and its respective forms **panie, (o) paniach, paniom, paniami** are necessary forms to refer to a group of women in a formal setting. (See Table 5.19)

Panowie 'you' (plural) and its respective forms **panowie, (o) panach, panom, panami** are necessary forms to refer to a group of men in a formal setting.

Państwo 'you' (plural) and its respective forms **państwa, (o) państwu, państwem** are necessary forms to refer to a group of men and women in a formal setting. (See Table 5.19)

> **Czy *pani* stoi w kolejce?** 'Do *you* stand in line?'
> **Co *panu* dolega?** 'What does bother *you*?'
> **Gdzie *pani* mieszka?** 'Where *do* you live?'
> **Co *państwo* o tym myślą?** 'What do *you* think about it?'

5.2.10.1 | Capitalization of "you"

Pan, Pani, Panie, Panowie, Państwo can be written with a capital letter in correspondence to show respect.

Szanowni państwo or panie i panowie, 'ladies and gentlemen,' is generally used when referring to a group of people or a couple in a formal setting.

Wy *in singular*

During the Communist period in Poland it was common to address an individual using the second person plural, **wy** 'you':

> **Gdzie** *mieszkacie* <2 PR PL> **obywatelko?** 'Where do *you live* <PL> citizen?'
> **Towarzyszu Grabski, czy** *znacie* **tę osobę?** 'Comrade Grabski, do *you know* <PL> this person?'

Wy *with verbs*

Sometimes, **wy** 'you' (plural) is used with **państwo** 'you' (formal plural) to address a group of people. It is acceptable in spoken Polish. Compare:

> **Gdzie państwo** *mieszkacie* <2 PR PL>**?** 'Where do you <PL> live?' (spoken Polish)
> **Gdzie państwo mieszkają** <3 PR PL>**?** 'Where do you <PL> live?'

5.3   Reflexive pronouns

5.3.1 | Siebie

The reflexive pronoun **siebie** is used when the action reflects back on the subject. Depending on the subject, the reflexive pronoun **siebie** can be translated as 'myself,' 'yourself,' 'herself,' 'himself,' 'itself,' 'ourselves,' 'yourselves' and 'themselves.' **Siebie** cannot serve as the subject; it has no nominative form.

The meaning of the reflexive pronoun **siebie** and its respective forms **się**, **sobie**, **sobą** depends on whom it refers to, e.g.,

> **Spójrz** <2 PR SG> **na siebie!** 'Look at *yourself!*' (SG)
> **Spójrzcie** <2 PR PL> **na siebie!** 'Look at *yourselves!*' (PL)
> **Kupiłem** *sobie* **nowy telefon.** 'I have bought a new phone for *myself.*'
> **Kupiłeś** *sobie* **nowy telefon?** 'Have you bought a new phone for *yourself?*'
> **Mama kupiła** *sobie* **nowy telefon.** 'Mom has bought a new phone for *herself.*'

Ojciec kupił *sobie* **nowy telefon.** 'Father has bought a new phone for *himself*.'

Rodzice kupili *sobie* **nowy telefon.** '[My] parents have bought a new phone for *themselves*.'

Wszyscy kupili *sobie* **nowy telefon.** 'Everybody has bought a new phone for *themselves*.'

Myję *się*. 'I wash *myself*.'

Umyj *się*! 'Wash *yourself*!'

Ona nigdy *się* **nie myje.** 'She never washes *herself*.'

Przyglądam się *sobie* **w lustrze.** 'I am looking at *myself* in the mirror.'

Ona przygląda się *sobie* **w lustrze.** 'She is looking at *herself* in the mirror.'

For the declension of **siebie** see Table 5.4.

| 5.3.1.1 | **Inny** 'other'—*the opposite of* **siebie** 'oneself'

Nie myśl tylko *o sobie*, **pomyśl także** *o innych*!
'Do not think only *about yourself*, think *about others* as well.'

| 5.3.1.2 | *Reciprocal action with* **się**

Się and its respective forms **sobie** and **sobą**, used in constructions with plural verb forms expresses reciprocal (mutual) action. It is generally translated as 'each other,' 'one another,' e.g.,

Znamy się **ze studiów.** '*We know each other* from school.'

Nie mamy *przed sobą* **sekretów.** 'We do not keep secrets *from each other*.'

Oni rozumieją się **bez słów.** '*They understand each other* without words.'

Nie mamy *sobie* **nic do powiedzenia.** 'We have nothing to tell to *each other*.'

Table 5.4 Declension of **siebie**

NOM	—
ACC	**siebie, się**
GEN	= ACC
DAT	**sobie**
LOC	**o sobie**
INS	**sobą**

277

Note: The reflexive pronoun **siebie** declines similarly to the pronoun **ty** 'you.'

> **Mówię o _tobie_/o _sobie_.** 'I am talking *about you/about myself*.'
> **Chcę _być tobą_/_sobą_.** 'I want *to be you/myself*.'

| 5.3.1.3 | **Siebie** *and* **się** *in accusative case* |

In the accusative case there are two forms: shorter, unstressed **się**, and longer, stressed **siebie**.

The stressed form **siebie** is used after a preposition, at the beginning of a sentence, in opposing or contrasting sentences and when we want to emphasize the importance of the subject the reflexive pronoun refers to. Otherwise the unstressed form **się** is used.

> **Spójrz _na siebie_!** 'Look *at yourself*!' (stressed form, after preposition)

> **Komu kupiłaś lody?** 'For whom did you buy ice cream?'
> **Sobie.** '[I bought it for] *Myself*.' (stressed form, beginning of the sentence)

> **_Tylko siebie_ widzę w lustrze.** 'I see *only myself* in the mirror.' (stressed form, *only*)
> **Widzę _siebie_, ale ciebie nie widzę.** 'I see *myself*, but I don't see you.' (stressed form, opposing sentence)

> **_Widzę się_ w lustrze.** '*I see myself* in the mirror.' (unstressed form)
> **Umyj się!** 'Wash *yourself*!' (unstressed form)

Idioms:

> **Czuj(cie) się jak u siebie w domu.** 'Feel (you PL) at home.'
> **Palić za sobą mosty.** 'To burn bridges [behind oneself].'

| 5.3.1.4 | *Reflexive or reciprocal action* |

Sometimes the use of the reflexive pronoun **siebie** can be ambiguous. It has to be seen in its full context to be understood.

> **Myjemy się.** Can be translated as 'We wash *each other*.' or 'We wash *ourselves*.'
> **Koty się liżą.** Can be translated as 'Cats lick *each other*.' or 'Cats lick *themselves*.'

Dzieci *się* ubierają. 'Children dress *each other*.' or 'Children dress *themselves*.'

Nie zróbcie *sobie* krzywdy. 'Don't hurt *one another*.' or 'Don't hurt *yourselves*.'

5.3.1.5 | *Się* as a part of the verb or impersonal form

Się can also be part of a verb that never occurs without się, such as kłócić się 'to argue,' domagać się 'to demand,' part of an impersonal construction such as Ochłodziło się. 'It got cold,' or used with a grammatical subject, as in Jak ci *się* spało? 'How did you sleep?'

5.3.1.6 | Positioning of **się**

Się can be positioned before the verb (but not in the initial position in the clause or sentence), or immediately after the verb. In imperatives, it is generally placed after the verb.

Ubierz *się* ciepło! 'Dress [*yourself*] warmly!'
Poznajcie *się*. 'Meet *each other*.'

5.3.2 | Swój

The reflexive possessive pronoun **swój** means 'my own,' 'your own' (singular and plural), 'his own,' 'her own,' 'our own,' 'their own.'

Swój and its respective forms agree in number, class and case with the noun they refer to.

Masz *swój* paszport? 'Do you have *your own* passport?'
Mam tylko *swój* paszport. 'I only have *my own* passport.'
Kocham *swoją* rodzinę. 'I love *my own* family.'
Jarek kocha *swoją* rodzinę. 'Jarek loves *his own* family.'
Rodzice kochają *swoje* dzieci. 'The parents love *their own* children.'

5.3.2.1 | Use

Mój 'my, mine,' twój 'your, yours <SG>,' jej 'her, hers, its,' jego 'his, its,' nasz 'our, ours,' wasz 'your, yours <PL>,' ich 'their, theirs' and its respective forms can be substituted by **swój** 'one's own' when the possessor, expressed in the *nominative* case, is the subject, in order to differentiate between items that are possessed by someone else and one's own items in sentences with an unclear context.

> **Ewa kocha *swoje* dziecko.**
> 'Ewa loves her (own) child.'

> **Ewa kocha *jej* dziecko.**
> 'Ewa loves her child.' (someone else's)

When the context is clear, possessives are usually omitted in Polish. **Jadę do babci.** 'I am going [to see] my grandma.' It is understood here that I am going to see my (own) grandma. Otherwise, a possessive pronoun would be used to clarify: **Jadę do jego babci.** 'I am going [to see] his grandma.'

5.3.2.2 | **Swój** *and greater specificity*

Swój 'one's own' is also used to point out the specificity of the item possessed.

> **Ewa jeździ do pracy *samochodem*.** 'Ewa drives to work *by car*.'
> (and not by bike)
> **Ewa jeździ do pracy *swoim samochodem*.** 'Ewa drives to work *in her own car*.'
> **Teraz rozumiem *błąd*.** 'Now I understand *the mistake*.'
> **Teraz rozumiem *swój błąd*.** 'Now I understand *my (own) mistake*.'
> **Państwo polskie datuje *swój właściwy początek* w 966 roku.**
> 'Poland dates *its (own) formal beginning* to the year 966.'

> **Weź *swój portfel*.** 'Take *your (own) wallet*.'
> **Wolnoć Tomku *w swoim domku*.** 'A man's house *is his castle*.' (saying)

> **Czcij ojca swego i *matkę swoją*.**
> Honor your father and your mother.

Swój 'one's own' cannot be used:

1. in the nominative case, or to modify a noun in the nominative case, e.g.:

> **To jest *moja matka*.** <NOM> (not swoja) 'This is *my (own) mother*.'
> **Tam jest *jego* dom.** <NOM> (not swój) 'Over there is *his* house.'
> **Nie podoba mi się *mój nos*.** <NOM> 'I don't like *my (own) nose*.'

2. when the possessor is expressed in a case other than the nominative, e.g.:

> **W torebce** *nie było mojego portfela.* 'My (own) wallet wasn't in my purse.' (Logical possessor expressed in GEN.)
> **Brakuje mi** *mojego psa.* (not swojego) 'I miss my (own) dog.' (Logical possessor expressed in DAT.)
> **Syna** *nie było w jego pokoju; był w pokoju swojej siostry.* '[My] son wasn't in his room; he was in his [own] sister's room.'

Idioms:

> **wiek robi swoje** 'age takes its toll'
> **rób swoje** 'take care of your own business'

| 5.3.2.3 | **Swój** *as 'not strange, not foreign'* |

Swój can also be used, in the nominative case, as the opposite of 'strange,' 'foreign'.

> **Nie krępuj się. Możesz mówić o wszystkim.** *Sami swoi* **dookoła.** 'Don't be shy. You can talk about everything. *We are all like family* here.'
> **Nie ma jak** *swoje ciasto.* 'There is nothing better than *the cake you made yourself.'*
> *Sami swoi* 'Our folks' (the title of a popular Polish comedy)

| 5.3.2.4 | *Translation difficulties:* |

> **Podaj mi** *mój* (not swój) *aparat.* 'Pass me *my (own) camera.'*
> **Podaj mi** *swój aparat.* 'Pass me *your (own) camera.'*

| 5.3.2.5 | *Limitation of* **swój** |

Swój 'one's own' refers only to the subject *within its own clause*, e.g.,

> **[Ewa kocha** *swoje* **dziecko** <clause 1>**] i [** *jej* **dziecko to czuje** <clause 2>**.]**
> ['Ewa loves *her own* child] and [*her* child feels it.']

281

| 5.3.2.6 | **Swój** *and its intensifier* **własny**

Własny can be used instead of **swój** to put emphasis on the agency of the possessor.

Wyrzekła się *własnej* (not swojej) **matki.**
'She disowned *her own* mother.'

Jestem na *własnym* (not swoim) **utrzymaniu.**
'I am *self*-supporting.'

Wypisał się ze szpitala na *własną* **prośbę.**
'He discharged [himself] from the hospital at *his own* request.'

Nie wierzę *własnym* **oczom.**
'I don't believe *my own* eyes.'

Ewa jeździ do pracy samochodem.
'Ewa drives to work by car.'

Służbowym?
'A company car?'

Nie *własnym*/**swoim.**
'No, her own.'

Mam dwoje dzieci i każde ma *własny* **[swój] pokój.**
'We have two children and each has *its own* room.'

Idioms:

dbać o *własną* **kieszeń/skórę**
'to take care of one's own interests/oneself'

pracować na *własny* **rachunek**
'to be self-employed'

Na własną rękę
Collateral Damage film [lit. 'on one's own initiative']

| 5.3.2.7 | *Declension*

Swój declines like adjectives and like **mój**. Replace **m-** with **sw-**. Note that the accusative masculine singular form is identical to that of the genitive for animate nouns (e.g., when referring to a human being or an animal), and to that of the nominative for inanimate nouns.

Table 5.5 Declension of **swój**

Case	Singular		
	MSC	NT	FEM
NOM	**swój** 'one's own'	**swoje**	**swoja**
ACC	animate nouns: = GEN	= NOM	**swoj-ą**
	inanimate nouns: = NOM		
GEN	**swoj-ego**	**swoj-ego**	**swoj-ej**
DAT	**swoj-emu**	**swoj-emu**	= LOC
LOC	**swo-im**	**swo-im**	**swoj-ej**
INS	= LOC	= LOC	**swoj-ą**
VOC	= NOM		

Case	Plural	
	Male human PL	No male human PL
NOM	**swoi** 'their own'	**swoje**
ACC	= GEN	= NOM
GEN	**swo-ich**	**swo-ich**
DAT	**swo-im**	**swo-im**
LOC	= GEN	= GEN
INS	**swo-imi**	**swo-imi**
VOC	= NOM	= NOM

5.4 Possessive pronouns

The possessive pronouns are used to express ownership. The form of the possessive pronouns (except for **jego** 'his,' **jej** 'her,' **ich** 'their' which have one form in all cases and numbers) is based on the item(s) possessed and the number of possessors.

> **To jest *mój paszport*, a to *moja wiza*.** 'This is *my passport* and *my visa*.'
> **Gdzie są *moje walizki*?** 'Where are *my suitcases*?'
> **To jest *moje dziecko*.** 'This is *my child*.'
> **To jest *nasze dziecko*.** 'This is *our child*.'
> **Czy to *pani bagaż*?** 'Is this *your luggage*?' (asking a woman)
> **Czy to *pana/pański bagaż*?** 'Is this *your luggage*?' (asking a man)
> **Czy to *państwa bagaż*?** 'Is this *your luggage*?' (asking a couple)

5.4.1 Generic questions

Possessive pronouns answer the question **czyj? czyja? czyje?** or **czyi** 'whose?' (not: kogo?)

The form of the question is based on the item(s) possessed:

> **Czyj to klucz?** 'Whose key is this?
> **Mój.** 'Mine.'

> **Czyje to klucze?** 'Whose keys are these?'
> **Moje.** 'Mine.'

5.4.2 'My' and 'mine'

While in English there are two forms to express possession, such as 'my' and 'mine,' 'your' and 'yours,' etc., in Polish there is just one form, **mój, twój.**

> **Ten samochód jest mój.** 'This car is mine.'
> **To jest mój samochód.** 'It is my car.'

5.4.3 Forms

Table 5.6 Overview of **mój, twój, jego, jej**

	Single item possessed			Many items possessed		
	czyj?	**czyja?**	**czyje?**	**czyje?**	**czyi?**	'whose?'
	MSC	FEM	NT	NO-MHPL	MHPL	
ja 'I'	mój	moja	moje	moje	moi	'my/mine'
ty 'you'	twój	twoja	twoje	twoje	twoi	'your(s)'
on 'he'	jego	jego	jego	jego	jego	'his'
ona 'she'	jej	jej	jej	jej	jej	'her(s)''
ono 'it'	jego	jego	jego	jego	jego	'its'
	jej	jej	jej	jej	jej	

For the declension pattern for **mój,** see Tables 5.10 and 5.11 in section 5.4.7 (**twój** follows the same declension pattern). **Jego** and **jej** have the same form for all cases.

For translating 'its' as either jego or jej, see 5.4.3.2.

Table 5.7 Overview of **pana**, **pani** ('your(s),' 'his,' 'her(s)' used in a formal setting) (for informal 'his,' 'her(s)' see 5.4.3.3)

	Single item possessed			Many items possessed		
	czyj?	**czyja?**	**czyje?**	**czyje?**	**czyi?**	'whose?'
	MSC	FEM	NT	NO-MHPL	MHPL	
pan 'sir'	**pana**	**pana**	**pana**	**pana**	**pana**	'your(s)'
	pański	**pańska**	**pańskie**	**pańskie**	**pańscy**	'your(s)'
pani 'madam'	**pani**	**pani**	**pani**	**pani**	**pani**	'your(s)'

The forms of **pana** and **pani** are not declined as possessive pronouns (e.g., **o pana samochodzie** 'about your <FORMAL SG> car'). The forms of **pański** follow standard adjectival declensions. (See Table 4.24)

Table 5.8 Overview of **nasz**, **wasz**, **ich** ('our(s),' 'your(s) <PL>,' 'their(s)')

	Single item possessed			Many items possessed		
	czyj?	**czyja?**	**czyje?**	**czyje?**	**czyi?**	'whose?'
	MSC	FEM	NT	NO-MHPL	MHPL	
my 'we'	**nasz**	**nasza**	**nasze**	**nasze**	**nasi**	'our(s)'
wy 'you' PL	**wasz**	**wasza**	**wasze**	**wasze**	**wasi**	'your(s)'
oni 'they'	**ich**	**ich**	**ich**	**ich**	**ich**	'their(s)'
one 'they'	**ich**	**ich**	**ich**	**ich**	**ich**	'their(s)'

For the declension pattern for **nasz**, see Table 5.12 in section 5.4.7.2 (**wasz** follows the same declension pattern). **Ich** has the same form for all cases.

Table 5.9 Overview of **pań**, **panów** ('your(s)' and 'their(s)' used in a formal setting)

	Single item possessed			Many items possessed		
	czyj?	**czyja?**	**czyje?**	**czyje?**	**czyi?**	'whose?'
	MSC	FEM	NT	NO-MHPL	MHPL	
panie 'ladies'	**pań**	**pań**	**pań**	**pań**	**pań**	'your(s)'
panowie 'sirs'	**panów**	**panów**	**panów**	**panów**	**panów**	'your(s)'
państwo 'couple'	**państwa**	**państwa**	**państwa**	**państwa**	**państwa**	'your(s)'

Pań, **panów**, and **państwa** have the same form in all cases (e.g., **o państwa dzieciach** 'about your <FORMAL PL> children').

Necessary forms in a formal setting

'Your(s),' 'his,' 'her,' 'their' in formal Polish can be translated into:

pani referring to item(s) that belong to a woman
pana or **pański** referring to item(s) that belong to a woman
pań referring to item(s) that belong to women
panów referring to item(s) that belong to men
państwa referring to item(s) that belong to a couple or a mixed group of people

Czy to *pani* **bilet?** 'Is it *your* ticket?'
Czy to numer telefonu *pani* **Nowak?** 'Is that the phone number of Ms. Nowak?'
Czy to numer pani Nowak? 'Is that *her* number (of Ms. Nowak)?'

While it is common in English to replace the name and title of someone with a possessive pronoun ("his"/"her"/"their") when referring to individuals in a formal setting, in Polish the full name and title are used. Replacing the full name with a possessive pronoun (**jego, jej, ich**) is not considered formal.

'Is that the phone number of Ms. Nowak?' **Czy to numer telefonu pani Nowak?**
'Is that *her* phone number?' **Czy to numer telefonu** *pani* **Nowak?** (formal)
'Is that *her* phone number?' **Czy to** *jej* **numer telefonu?** (informal)

Państwa **dom jest bardzo ładny.** '*Your* house is very pretty.'
Pańskie **zdrowie!** '*To your* health!' (a popular toast)
Czy to *pani* **parasol?** 'Is that *your* umbrella?'
Czy to *pana/pański* **parasol?** 'Is that *your* umbrella?'

Translation of "its"

"Its" is rendered in Polish by **jej** to refer to a feminine noun, **jego** to a masculine noun.

Mam album o Warszawie i *jej* **pomnikach.**
'I have an album about Warsaw and *its monuments*.'
[lit '. . . and her monuments,' because **Warszawa** 'Warsaw' is a feminine noun]

Uwielbiam Kraków i *jego zabytki*. 'I love Cracow and *its monuments*.'
[lit. '…and his monuments,' because **Kraków** 'Cracow' is a
masculine noun]

5.4.3.3 | *Indeclinable possessive pronouns*

Jego 'his'/'its,' jej 'her(s)'/'its' and ich 'their(s)' do not decline. Other
possessives decline like adjectives.

5.4.4 | **Omission**

Possessive pronouns are often omitted when the possessor is clear from
the context.

> **Piszę pracę domową.** 'I am writing [my] homework.'
> (It is understood that I am writing my homework, not somebody
> else's, hence the possessive pronoun is not needed.)
> **Zadzwoniłam do rodziców.** 'I called [my] parents.'
> (It is understood that the caller phoned his or her parents,
> otherwise a possessive pronoun would be used.)
> **Zadzwoniłam do *jego* rodziców.** 'I called *his* parents.'
> **Czego szukasz? Kluczy.** 'What are you looking for? [My] keys.' (If they
> were not mine, I would specify whose keys I am looking for.)

Possessive pronouns are omitted with parts of the body. It is understood
that if one feels pain in one's head, it is one's own head.

> **Boli mnie lewa ręka.** '*My* left hand hurts.' (It is understood that it is
> my hand.)
> **Zamknij oczy.** 'Close [your] eyes.' (You can't really close anyone
> else's eyes.)
> **Skaleczyłam się w palec.** 'I cut [my] finger.'
> **Piotr skaleczył się w palec.** 'Piotr cut [his] finger.'
> **Umyj ręce.** 'Wash [your] hands.'

5.4.5 | **Introducing others**

In introductions possessive pronouns are used, e.g.,

> **To jest Ewa Nowak, *moja koleżanka z pracy*.** 'This is Ewa Nowak,
> *my colleague from work*.'
> **Poznaj, Piotrze, *moją żonę*.** 'Piotr, meet *my wife*.'

Pan pozwoli, że przedstawię *mojego męża.* 'Sir, let me introduce *my husband.'*

5.4.6 | Repetition

Possessive pronouns are generally not repeated when they refer to a noun or a noun phrase of the same class and number.

> **Zapisz mój numer** <MSC> **i adres** <MSC>. 'Write down *my [phone] number* and *address.'*
> **Po co ci moje imię** <NT> **i nazwisko** <NT>? 'Why do you (informal) need *my first and last name?'*

5.4.7 | Declension

First and second person possessive pronouns plus **pański** are declined like adjectives.

mój/twój/nasz/wasz/pański is used in front of a masculine noun or adjective

moja/twoja/nasza/wasza/pańska is used in front of a feminine noun or adjective

moje/twoje/nasz/wasze/pańskie is used in front of a neuter noun or adjective, and in front of a group without a male human being—the so-called no male human group

moi/twoi/nasi/wasi/pańscy is used in front of a group referring to male human beings or a group with at least one male human being—the so-called male human group

5.4.7.1 | Shared possessive pronouns endings in singular—animacy counts!

The possessive pronoun, like adjectives, referring to animate masculine nouns has the accusative ending **-ego**, identical to that in the genitive.

The possessive pronoun referring to inanimate masculine nouns has an accusative ending identical to that in the nominative.

> **Znasz mojego młodszego brata?** 'Do you know *my younger brother?'*
> **Znasz mój nowy adres?** 'Do you know *my new address?'*
> **Widzę naszego psa.** 'I see *our dog.'*
> **Widzę nasz dom.** 'I see *our house.'*

| 5.4.7.2 | *Shared possessive pronouns endings in plural—manhood counts!*

Male human forms—referring to male human beings or a mixed group
with at least one male human being—have an accusative plural identical
to the genitive plural.

No male human forms—referring to a group with no male human beings—
have an accusative plural identical to the nominative plural.

Widzę naszych dobrych sąsiadów. 'I see *our good neighbors*.'
  (either only male or a group of male and female neighbors)
Widzę nasze dobre sąsiadki. 'I see *our good neighbors*.'
  (only female neighbors)
Widzę naszych rodziców. 'I see *our parents*.'
Widzę nasze dzieci. 'I see *our children*.'

Table 5.10 Declension of **mój**, singular

Case	MSC	NT	FEM
NOM	**mój** ('my,' 'mine')	**moje**	**moja**
ACC	animate nouns: = GEN	= NOM	**moj-ą**
	inanimate nouns: = NOM	—	—
GEN	**moj-ego**	**moj-ego**	**moj-ej**
DAT	**moj-emu**	**moj-emu**	= LOC
LOC	**mo-im**	**mo-im**	**moj-ej**
INS	= LOC	= LOC	**moją**
VOC	= NOM		

Table 5.11 Declension of **moi**, plural

Case	Male human PL	No male human PL
NOM	**moi** ('my,' 'mine')	**moje**
ACC	= GEN	= NOM
GEN	**mo-ich**	**mo-ich**
DAT	**mo-im**	**mo-im**
LOC	= GEN	= GEN
INS	**mo-imi**	**mo-imi**
VOC	= NOM	= NOM

The pronouns **twój, twoja, twoje, twoi** 'your,' 'yours' are declined like **mój,
moja, moje, moi** 'my,' mine.'

Table 5.12 Declension of **nasz**, singular

Case	MSC	NT	FEM
NOM	**nasz** ('our,' 'ours')	**nasze**	**nasza**
ACC	personal and animate nouns: **nasz-ego**	= NOM	**nasz-ą**
	inanimate nouns: = NOM	—	—
GEN	**nasz-ego**	**nasz-ego**	**nasz-ej**
DAT	**nasz-emu**	**nasz-emu**	= LOC
LOC	**nasz-ym**	**nasz-ym**	**nasz-ej**
INS	= LOC	= LOC	**nasz-ą**
VOC	= NOM		

Table 5.13 Declension of **nasi**, plural

Case	Male human PL	No male human PL
NOM	**nasi** ('our,' 'ours')	**nasze**
ACC	= GEN	= NOM
GEN	**nasz-ych**	**nasz-ych**
DAT	**nasz-ym**	**nasz-ym**
LOC	= GEN	= GEN
INS	**nasz-ymi**	**nasz-ymi**
VOC	= NOM	

The pronouns nasz, nasza, nasze, nasi are declined like **wasz, wasza, wasze, wasi.**

> **Kto pojedzie *naszym samochodem.*** 'Who will drive *our car?*'
> **Zaprosiłam ich *w twoim imieniu.*** 'I invited them on *your behalf.*'
> **Moim zdaniem, to dobry pomysł.** '*In my opinion*, it is a good idea.'

5.4.8 │ Short forms

The first and second person possessive pronouns have short forms: **ma, me, twa, twe.** Such forms are generally used in stylistically charged texts and in literary works.

They decline like the demonstrative pronouns **ten, ta, to.**

> Dla *twego* zdrowia życia bym nie skąpił,
> 'For *your* health, my life I would not spare,'
> Po *twą* spokojność do piekieł bym zstąpił;
> 'For *your* peacefulness, to hell I would descend;'
>   Adam Mickiewicz, "**Niepewność**" ('Uncertainty')

Table 5.14 Declension of short form possessive pronouns, singular

Case	MSC	NT	FEM
NOM	me/twe ('my/mine,' 'your(s)')	me/twe	ma/twa
ACC	animate nouns: = GEN inanimate nouns: = NOM	= NOM —	mą/twą
GEN	mego/twego	mego/twego	mej/twej
DAT	memu/twemu	memu/twemu	= LOC
LOC	mym/twym	mym/twym	mej/twej
INS	= LOC	= LOC	mą/twą
VOC	= NOM		

5.4.9 -ina

Possessiveness can also be expressed using the suffix -ina with feminine nouns. This is, however, less commonly used in current Polish, and it imparts a sentimental feel.

mamina bransoletka 'mother's bracelet'
mamine okulary 'mother's glasses'
mamina szafa 'mother's wardrobe'

5.5 Demonstrative pronouns

Demonstrative pronouns act and are declined like adjectives. The form of the demonstrative pronoun is based on the noun's number, class and case.

ten and its respective forms refer to singular masculine nouns
ta and its respective forms refer to singular feminine nouns
to and its respective forms refer to singular neuter nouns
te and its respective forms refer to plural no male human nouns (nouns that do not refer to male human beings)
ci and its respective forms refer to plural male human nouns (nouns that refer to male human beings, or a group with at least one male human being)

ten paszport 'this/that passport'
ten mężczyzna 'this/that man'
ta wiza 'this/that visa'
ta pani 'this/that woman'
to zdjęcie 'this/that picture'
te rzeczy 'these/those things'
ci ludzie 'these/those people'

5.5.1 | Simple and compound forms

Demonstrative pronouns have simple or compound forms, e.g., **ten** and **tamten**.

5.5.1.1 | Simple

ten, ta, to correspond to 'this' or 'that'
te, ci correspond to 'these' or 'those'
ów, owa, owo correspond to 'that' (bookish)
owe, owi correspond to 'these' or 'those' (bookish)

5.5.1.2 | Compound

Compound demonstrative pronouns consist of the simple forms **ten, ta, to** (except **ów**) and the word **tam** 'over there,' to convey the idea of distance from the speaker. Compound forms are used to emphasize the object in opposing sentences.

> **tam** 'over there' + **ten** <MSC> 'that' = **tamten** 'that [over there]'
> or 'the other' in opposing sentences

tam<u>ten</u> corresponds to 'that [over there]' or 'the other' in opposing sentences

tam<u>ta</u> corresponds to 'that [over there]' or 'the other' in opposing sentences

tam<u>to</u> corresponds to 'that [over there]' or 'the other' in opposing sentences

tam<u>te</u> corresponds to 'that [over there]' or 'the other' in opposing sentences

tam<u>ci</u> corresponds to 'that [over there]' or 'the other' in opposing sentences

> **Ten paszport jest mój, *a tamten* twój.**
> 'This passport is mine, *and that* [one] is yours.'
> 'This passport is mine, *and the other* [one] is yours.'

> **Ten mężczyzna tu mieszka, a tamten tu pracuje.**
> 'This man lives here, *and that* [one] works here.'
> 'This man lives here, *and the other* [one] works here.'

Ta wiza jest już nieważna, a tamta jest ważna do jutra.
'This visa has already expired *and that* [visa] expires tomorrow.'
'This visa has already expired *and the other* [visa] expires tomorrow.'

Ci ludzie są za, *a tamci* przeciw.
'These people are for, *and those* [people] are against.'
'These people are for, *and the other* [people] are against.'

Demonstrative pronouns

As a demonstrative adjective 'this' and 'that' modifies a noun; as a pronoun it only replaces a noun.

Ten pies jest śliczny. 'This dog is cute.' <demonstrative ADJ>
Ten czy tamten? 'This or that one?' <demonstrative PRON>
Przecież mówię, że ten. 'But I am saying this one.'
  <demonstrative PRON>

In Polish, like in English, ten, tamten 'this'/'that,' **taki** 'such'/'of the kind,' and ów 'that' (bookish), can be used both as adjectives and as pronouns.

5.5.2 Old forms

Even though they are not used in Polish today, **si, sia, sio** used to be demonstrative pronouns as well. They are preserved in a few set phrases:

Do siego roku! 'Happy New Year!'
ni to, ni sio (owo) 'neither this nor that'

5.5.3 Use of simple forms

5.5.3.1 *Ten* as a definite article: **ten, który** 'the ... who/that', **ta, która; to, które; te, które; ci, którzy**

Ten, ta, to, te, ci can be translated as 'the' when combined with **który** 'that'/'who.'

Gdzie jest *ta książka, którą* ci dałam wczoraj? 'Where is *the book that* I gave you yesterday?'
Co zrobiłeś *z tym e-mailem, który* napisałeś? 'What did you do with *the email* you wrote?'

Note: In spoken Polish the combination **ten, co** is acceptable instead of ten, który:

Gdzie jest *ta książka, co* ci dałam wczoraj? 'Where is *the book* I gave you yesterday?'

Ten *in emotionally charged constructions*

Ten, ta, to 'this' in combination with another pronoun becomes emotionally (negatively) charged.

> **Ten jej zięć to niezły oszust.** *'This son-in-law of hers* is quite a swindler.'
> **Nie zależy mi *na tym całym bogactwie.*** 'I don't care *about all that wealth.'*
> **Ten cały szum o nic.** *'All that fuss* about nothing.'

5.5.3.3 **Ten** *in comparative constructions*

Im . . . , tym . . . 'the . . . , the . . .' [+ comparative adjective or adverb]

> **Im starszy, tym lepszy.** 'The older the better.'
> **Im wyżej, tym drożej.** 'The higher, the more expensive.'

5.5.4 *Declension*

Demonstrative pronouns are declined like adjectives, and like adjectives have singular masculine, feminine, and neuter forms, and male human and no male human plural forms.

The form of **ten** 'this' and **tamten** 'that' in the accusative is based on what masculine noun **ten** and **tamten** refer to.

Ten and **tamten** have an accusative identical to the nominative when they refer to an inanimate masculine noun.

Ten and **tamten** have an accusative identical to the genitive when they refer to an animate masculine noun.

> **Widzę ten dom.**
> 'I see *this house.'*
>
> **Widzę *tego psa i tego chłopca i tego mężczyznę.***
> 'I see *this dog,* and *this boy* and *this man.'*

Exceptionally, **ta** 'this, that' has **tę** in the accusative.

Table 5.15 Declension of **ten, tamten**

Case	Singular			Plural	
	MSC	FEM	NT	No male human PL	Male human PL
NOM	**ten** 'this' **tamten** 'that'	**(tam)ta**	**(tam)to**	**(tam)te**	**(tam)ci**
ACC	animate nouns: = GEN inanimate: = NOM	**tę/tamtą**	**(tam)to**	**(tam)te**	**(tam)tych**
GEN	**(tam)tego**	**(tam)tej**	**(tam)tego**	**(tam)tych**	**(tam)tych**
DAT	**(tam)temu**	**(tam)tej**	**(tam)temu**	**(tam)tym**	**(tam)tym**
LOC	**(tam)tym**	**(tam)tej**	**(tam)tym**	**(tam)tych**	**(tam)tych**
INS	**(tam)tym**	**(tam)tą**	**(tam)tym**	**(tam)tymi**	**(tam)tymi**

Ów, owa, owo, owe, owi decline like ten, tamta, to, te, ci.

Idioms:

Muszę kupić to i owo.
'I have to buy *this and that*.'

W owym czasie pisano po łacinie.
'*At that time* they were writing in Latin.'

Ni z tego, ni z owego zaczęła płakać.
'She *suddenly* started crying.'

do tej pory 'up till now,' **do tamtej pory** 'up till then'
od tej pory 'from now on'

Table 5.16 Declension of **taki**

Case	Singular			Plural	
	MSC	FEM	NT	No male human PL	Male human PL
NOM	**taki** 'such'	**taka**	**takie**	**takie**	**tacy**
ACC	animate nouns: = GEN inanimate: = NOM	**taką**	**takie**	**takie**	**takich**
GEN	**takiego**	**takiej**	**takiego**	**takich**	**takich**
DAT	**takiemu**	**takiej**	**takiemu**	**takim**	**takim**
LOC	**takim**	**takiej**	**takim**	**takich**	**takich**
INS	**takim**	**taką**	**takim**	**takimi**	**takimi**

Takich spodni, jakie ona chce, nie kupisz za sto złotych.
'*The kind of pants that she wants*, you won't buy for a hundred zloty.'

W tym roku była *taka zima, jakiej nikt nie pamięta.*
'This year there was *such a winter that nobody remembers*.'
[Nobody can remember a winter like the one we had this year.]

Idioms:

Taki sobie **ten tort.** (coll.) 'The cake is *so-so*.'
Takie buty! (coll.) So that's it!

5.6   Intensifying pronoun sam

Sam, sama, samo, same, sami 'oneself' decline like adjectives.

The pronoun **sam** 'oneself' emphasizes a single-handed performance and it is used to point out that the action was done without anybody's help, personally, on one's own.

Ojciec *sam* **wszystko przygotował.** 'Father prepared everything *by himself*.' (single-handedly, without anybody's help, all on his own)
Dziecko *samo chodzi.* 'The child *walks without anybody's help*.'
Chcę *sam* **tam pójść.** 'I want to go there *by myself*.' (only me and no one else)
Sam **słyszałem.** 'I heard it *personally*.'
Sam **zdecyduj, co chcesz z tym zrobić.** '*Decide yourself*, what you want to do with it.'
Sam **sobie jesteś winien.** 'It is *your* own fault.'
Śmieję się *sam* **z siebie.** 'I laugh at *myself*.' (versus **Śmieję się z ciebie.** 'I laugh at you.')

5.6.1 | Usage

1. Only, nothing but

Na spotkaniu były *same kobiety/sami mężczyźni.* '*Only women/only men* were at the meeting.'
Państwo Klukowscy mają *samych wnuków.* 'The Klukowscys have *only grandsons*.'

Nie samym chlebem **człowiek żyje.** 'Man cannot live *by bread alone*.'

2. To emphasize the specificity of time, action, characteristics

Intensifying
pronoun sam

Od samego rana **pracuję.** 'I work from *the very morning*.'
Mieszkamy *nad samym morzem.* 'We live *right by the sea*.'
Sam **rozumiesz, że inaczej nie mogłem.** 'You *perfectly*
understand that I could do it differently.'
W *samą porę* **przyszliście. Właśnie zaczynamy.** 'You came *just
in time*. We are about to start.'
Garnitur jest *w sam raz* **dla ciebie.** 'The suit is *just right*
for you.'

W samo południe High Noon (western film with Gary Cooper),
[also the title of a famous Polish political poster used in the
1989 election]

3. Alone, by oneself

Po śmierci dziadka, *babcia została sama.*
'After grandpa's death, *grandma stayed alone*.'

Poszłam *sama* **do kina.**
'I went to the movies *by myself*.'

Został *sam jak palec.*
'He is *all alone*.' [lit. 'He stayed alone as a finger,' idiom]

4. To emphasize the importance of the subject

Sam **prezydent przyszedł na spotkanie.**
'*The president himself* came to the meeting.'

Rozmawiałem z *samym reżyserem.*
'I spoke with *the director himself*.'

Sama **chcę się dowiedzieć, co się stało.**
'I want to find out *myself* what happened.'

Sam **jesteś skończonym egoistą.**
'You are a complete egoist *yourself*.'

| 5.6.2 | *Ten sam* and *taki sam* |

'The exact same' is rendered in Polish by **ten sam** <MSC>, **ta sama** <FEM>,
to samo <NT>, **te same** <NO-MHPL>, **ci sami** <MHPL> and **tyle samo** 'the
exact same (amount).' Both parts decline like adjectives. **Tyle samo** is
indeclinable. **Taki sam** means 'the same kind.'

Ten sam *'the exact same'*

Ten sam is used with a masculine noun or noun phrase, **ta sama** with a feminine noun, **to samo** a neuter noun, **te same** a plural non-human noun, and **ci sami** a plural human noun.

> **Jesteśmy *w tym samym wieku*** <LOC SG MSC>. 'We are *the exact same age.*'
> **Córka i syn mieszkają *w tym samym akademiku*** <LOC SG MSC>. My daughter and my son live *in the same dormitory.*
> **Studiują *na tej samej uczelni*** <LOC SG FEM>, **co ich ojciec 20 lat temu.** They study *at the same school* as their father did 20 years ago.

> **Dlaczego używacie *tego samego ręcznika*** <GEN SG MSC>? 'Why are you using *the same towel?*'
> **Nie mogliśmy znaleźć innego.** 'We could not find another.'
> **W tym semestrze mam zajęcia *z tym samym profesorem*** <INS SG MSC>, **z którym miałem zajęcia rok temu.** 'This semester I have classes *with the same professor*, with whom I had classes last year.'
> **To *ci sami ludzie*** <NOM MHPL>, **których spotkaliśmy wczoraj. Chodź, przywitamy się z nimi.** 'These are *the same people* we met yesterday. Let's go and say hello.'

Idiomatic expression:

To samo is often used when ordering the same as our friends at the bar, pub, etc.

> **Proszę frytki i sok.** 'French fries and juice please.'
> **To samo (proszę).** '*The same* (please).' [of course, not the exact same, as I want my own food and drink]

Taki sam

Taki sam means 'the same kind,' and it is used with a noun or noun phrase of masculine class, **taka sama** with feminine class, **takie samo** neuter class, **takie same** no male human plural, **tacy sami** male human plural form. Both parts decline like adjectives.

> **Ładny masz sweter. Mam *taki sam*.** 'You have a pretty sweater. I have *the same kind.*'

Kupię ci *takie same* buty jak ma twoja siostra. Chcesz?
'I'll buy you *the same [kind of]* shoes as your sister has.
Do you want to?'

Moi bracia bez przerwy rywalizują. Jeśli jeden z nich kupi samochód, drugi musi mieć *taki sam*. 'My brothers compete constantly. If one of them buys a car, the other must have *the same* [kind].'

Jesteście *tacy sami* jak wasi rodzice. 'You are *the same* as your parents.'

5.6.3 | Tyle samo

Tyle samo 'the same amount,' 'just as much' is invariable.

Syn *zarabia tyle samo* co dwa lata temu. '[My] son *makes just as much* as two years ago.'

Przygotowałam *tyle samo sałatki* co zwykle, a zabrakło. 'I prepared *the same amount of salad* as usual, but it was not enough.'

5.6.4 | Tak samo

Tak samo 'the same manner' is invariable.

***Jest tak samo* jak było przed wyborami.** '*It is just the same* as it was before the election.'

Dzieci *zachowują się tak samo* jak ich rodzice. 'Children *behave just the same* as their parents.'

5.7   Interrogative, indefinite and negative pronouns

The forms of the interrogative pronouns **kto?** 'who?' and **co?** 'what?' are used to ask questions about subjects or objects.

The forms of the negative pronouns **nikt** 'nobody' and **nic** 'nothing' are used to express the absence of **ktoś** 'somebody,' **coś** 'something.'

Niczyj, niczyja, niczyje, niczyi 'nobody's' is declined like **czyj** 'whose' (see Table 4.23 in section 4.23).

Negative pronouns combine with negated verbs. It is possible to have multiple negations in a sentence.

Nikt nikomu nie wierzy. 'Nobody believes *anybody*.'

Na szczęście, *nikomu nic* **się nie stało.** 'Fortunately, *nothing* happened to *anybody*.' [Nobody was hurt.]

Z *nikim* **o** *niczym* **nie chcemy rozmawiać.** 'We do not want to talk *to anybody about anything*.'

Wyszedł, nie zwracając niczyjej uwagi. 'He left, without catching anyone's attention.'

| 5.7.2 | *Declensions*

Table 5.17 Declension of **kto, ktoś, ktokolwiek, nikt**

Case				
NOM	**kto** 'who'	**ktoś** 'somebody'	**ktokolwiek** 'anyone'	**nikt** 'nobody'
ACC	**kogo**	**kogoś**	**kogokolwiek**	**nikogo**
GEN	**kogo**	**kogoś**	**kogokolwiek**	**nikogo**
DAT	**komu**	**komuś**	**komukolwiek**	**nikomu**
LOC	**kim**	**kimś**	**kimkolwiek**	**nikim**
INS	**kim**	**kimś**	**kimkolwiek**	**nikim**

Table 5.18 Declension of **co, coś, cokolwiek, nic**

Case				
NOM	**co** 'what'	**coś** 'something'	**cokolwiek** 'anything'	**nic** 'nothing'
ACC	**co**	**coś**	**cokolwiek**	**nic**
GEN	**czego**	**czegoś**	**czegokolwiek**	**niczego (nic)**
DAT	**czemu**	**czemuś**	**czemukolwiek**	**niczemu**
LOC	**czym**	**czymś**	**czymkolwiek**	**niczym**
INS	**czym**	**czymś**	**czymkolwiek**	**niczym**

Kto to jest? 'Who is it?'

Co to jest? 'What is it?' (asking about the identity of the object)

Co chcesz na kolację? 'What do you want for dinner?'
   (*Kogo* **chcesz na kolację?** would imply cannibalism)

Czego szukasz? Kluczy. 'What are you looking for? Keys.'

Kogo szukasz? Pana Nowaka. 'Who are you looking for? Mr. Nowak.'

5.7.3 | Kto, ktoś, ktokolwiek, nikt

In the past tense, **kto** 'who,' **ktoś** 'somebody,' **ktokolwiek** 'anyone,' and **nikt** 'nobody' take the third person singular masculine form of the verb (with the marker -ł). They take the masculine form of adjectives, demonstrative pronouns and ordinal numerals, e.g.:

Kto był pierwszy w domu? 'Who was the first home?' (not: kto była pierwsza w domu)

Kto jest głodny? 'Who is hungry?' (not: Kto jest głodna?) **Dzieci.** 'The children.' [are hungry]

Kto pierwszy, ten lepszy. <MSC> 'First come, first served.'

Ktoś pukał? 'Was someone knocking [on the door]?'

Ktokolwiek go widział? 'Has anyone seen him?'

Był taki ktoś. 'There was someone like that.' (not: była taka ktoś)

Nikt nie jest doskonały. <MSC> 'Nobody is perfect.'

Idioms:

Zrobić coś z niczego. 'To make *something from nothing*.'

Wszystko *na nic*. 'All *for nothing*.'

Za nic w świecie nie wsiądę do samolotu! 'I won't get on the plane *for anything in the world*.'

Nie rozumiem *nic a nic*. 'I don't understand *at all*.'

Niby nic, a jednak coś. 'It might look like nothing, but it is something.'

Jakby nigdy nic. 'As if nothing has happened.'

5.7.4 | Nic *and* niczego

Verbs that govern the accusative or genitive cases, such as **mieć** 'to have,' **robić** 'to do,' **znać** 'to know,' **szukać** 'to look for,' **potrzebować** 'to need,' **słuchać** 'to listen to,' etc. combine with **nic** or **niczego** 'nothing' (in the genitive case). Nic is generally used in front of the negated verb; **niczego** after.

Nic **nie mam. Nie mam** *niczego*. 'I have *nothing*.'

Nic **nie szukam. Nie szukam** *niczego*. 'I look for *nothing*.'

Nic **nie potrzebuję. Nie potrzebuję** *niczego*. 'I need *nothing*.'

But only

Niczego **mi nie brakuje.** 'I have everything I need.'

Niczego **nie zapomniałam.** 'I have not forgotten anything.'

| 5.7.5 | Co, coś, cokolwiek, nic |

The form of the interrogative pronoun co 'what,' as well as coś 'something,' cokolwiek 'anything,' and nic 'nothing' combines with adjectives in the genitive masculine ending -ego. The genitive ending -ego could be explained in that while kto establishes the presence of somebody or someone, co relates to absence, just as the genitive case does in Polish.

Co nowego? What's new?
To było coś pięknego. It was something beautiful.
Coś takiego! You don't say! [here used as exclamatory pronouns]

| 5.7.6 | *Other interrogative and indefinite pronouns* |

The interrogative pronouns jaki? 'what like?' który? 'which?' czyj? 'whose?' decline similarly to adjectives. For a full declension and the differences between the use of jaki? and który? see 4.23 and Tables 4.21 and 4.22.

Któż 'whoever,' cóż 'whatever,' jakiż 'what' (bookish) are used in literary works and in stylistically charged texts.

***Jakiż* to ma sens?** 'What is the meaning of it?'
***Któż* to dzwoni o tak późnej porze?** 'Who is calling that late?'
***Cóż* ci lekarz doradził?** 'What did the doctor tell you to do?'

These forms are declined like adjectives, however, the ending -óż (-że after a consonant) is attached.

***Czemu-ż* mi się przyglądasz?** 'Why are you looking at me?'
***Czym-że* zasłużyłem na to?** 'What did I do to deserve it?'

Other indefinite pronouns include: byle kto 'just anybody,' byle co 'just anything,' byle jaki 'any,' kto bądź 'anybody, anyone at all,' co bądź 'anything (at all),' jakiś 'any, some,' któryś 'some, one,' kilka 'several,' wiele 'a lot, many,' byle kto 'anybody.'

Byle in byle kto, byle co, byle jaki is indeclinable.

bądź in kto bądź, co bądź is indeclinable.

Kilka, wiele, wielu declines like numerals. (See Table 8.6)

Nasza dorastająca córka krzyczy z *byle* powodu.
'Our adolescent daughter screams *with no reason at all*.'

Nie jedz *byle czego*—**brzuch będzie cię bolał.**
'Do not eat *just anything*—you will have a stomach ache.'

Bądź co bądź **jesteś dorosły.**
'*After all*, you are an adult.'

5.7.7 | **Exclamatory use**

Jaki 'such,' 'how,' 'what,' taki 'so,' 'this' and co 'what' are used as exclamatory pronouns. Jaki, jaka, jakie, jacy and taki, taka, takie, tacy agree in number, class and case with the noun or noun phrase they refer to.

Jaki [+adjective] **piękny dom!** '*Such/What* a pretty house!'
Jaki [+noun] **ogród!** '*What* a garden!'
Jaka [+personal pronoun] **ona uparta!** '*How* stubborn she is!'
O *jakiej* **podwyżce ty mówisz? Żadnej podwyżki nie będzie.**
   '*What raise* are you talking about? There won't be any raise.'
On jest *taki* **szczęśliwy.** 'He is *so happy.*'
Oni są *tacy* **mili.** 'They are *so nice.*'
Taki malutki. 'This tiny.' (generally, accompanied by a gesture)
Tacy umięśnieni. 'This muscular.'
Co za spotkanie. 'What a meeting.'
Co za miły człowiek. 'What a nice man.'

5.8 **Relative pronouns**

Tyle ..., ile ... 'as many as' or 'as much as'
Ten [+person], **kto ...** 'the ..., who ...'
Ten [+animal or object], **który ...** 'the ... that ...' (5.5.3.1)
Taki ..., który ... 'the one, who ...'
Jaki ..., taki ... 'what ..., that ...'
Kto ..., ten ... 'who ..., that ...'

Kup *tyle* **par butów,** *ile* **chcesz!** 'Buy *as many* pairs of shoes *as* you want.'
Gdzie jest *ten* **notes,** *który* **ci dałem?** 'Where is *the notebook that* I gave you?'
Przeczytałam *ten* **artykuł,** *który* **mi poleciłeś.** 'I have read *the article that* you recommended.'
Myślę o *tym* **artykule,** *który* **mi poleciłeś.** 'I am thinking about *the article that* you recommended.'

Kto szuka, ten znajdzie. 'Who seeks, [*that*] finds.

Jaki tort wybierzesz, taki będzie. 'Whichever tart you choose [*that*] we will have.'

Note: In spoken Polish the combination **ten, co** is acceptable instead of **ten, który**:

Gdzie jest *ta książka,* **co ci dałam wczoraj?** 'Where is *the book* I gave you yesterday?'

Tam sięgaj, *gdzie* wzrok nie sięga
'Reach *the places where* the sight doesn't reach';
Łam, czego rozum nie złamie.
'Break, what the mind cannot break.'

Adam Mickiewicz **"Oda do młodości"** 'Ode to youth'

Table 5.19 Pronoun declensions

	I	You	Mr./You (formal)	Mrs./You (formal)	Miss/You (formal)	He	It	She
NOM	ja	ty	pan	pani	panna	on	ono	ona
ACC	mnie[3]	ciebie, cię[1]	pana	panią	pannę	jego, go[1] (niego[2]) je (nie[2])		ją (nią[2])
GEN	mnie	ciebie, cię[1]	pana	pani	panny	jego, go[1] (niego[2])		jej (niej[2])
DAT	mnie, mi[1]	tobie, ci[1]	panu	pani	pannie	jemu, mu[1] (niemu[2])		jej (niej[2])
LOC	mnie	tobie	panu	pani	pannie		nim	niej
INS	mną	tobą	panem	panią	panną		nim	nią
VOC	ja	ty	panie	pani	panno	on	ono	ona

Table 5.19a

	We	You	Mr. (PL) You (formal)	Mrs. (PL) You (formal)	Misses (formal)	Mr. & Mrs. You (formal)	They (Male human PL)	They (No male human PL)
NOM	my	wy	panowie	panie	panny	państwo	oni	one
ACC	nas	was	panów	panie	panny	państwa	ich (nich[2])	je (nie[2])
GEN	nas	was	panów	pań	panien	państwa	ich (nich[2])	
DAT	nam	wam	panom	paniom	pannom	państwu	im (nim[2])	
LOC	nas	was	panach	paniach	pannach	państwu	nich	
INS	nami	wami	panami	paniami	pannami	państwem	nimi	
VOC	my	wy	panowie	panie	panny	państwo	oni	one

Table 5.19b

	Reflexive	Who	Nobody	Somebody	Anybody	What (Nothing)	Something	Anything
NOM		kto	nikt	ktoś	ktokolwiek	co (nic)	coś	cokolwiek
ACC	siebie, się	kogo	nikogo	kogoś	kogokolwiek	co (nic)	coś	cokolwiek
GEN	siebie, się	kogo	nikogo	kogoś	kogokolwiek	(ni)czego	czegoś	czegokolwiek
DAT	sobie	komu	nikomu	komuś	komukolwiek	(ni)czemu	czemuś	czemukolwiek
LOC	sobie	kim	nikim	kimś	kimkolwiek	(ni)czym	czymś	czymkolwiek
INS	sobą	kim	nikim	kimś	kimkolwek	(ni)czym	czymś	czymkolwiek
VOC		kto	nikt	ktoś	ktokolwiek	co (nic)	coś	cokolwiek

Notes

[1] The short forms (**mi**, **cię**, **ci**, **go** and **mu**) are used after verbs; they cannot be used in the initial position, at the beginning of the clause or a sentence, or after prepositions, or in stressed and emphasized positions (e.g., **Widziałem go**. **Jego widziałem**).

[2] This form is used after prepositions (e.g., **Trudno jest bez niego**.).

[3] The colloquial short form **mię** also exists.

Chapter 6

Verbs

6.1   Overview

Traditionally, verbs express actions, transformations or states: **pada** 'it's raining,' **ściemnia się** 'it's getting dark,' **jestem** 'I am (present).'

In Polish "verb" is **czasownik** (words of **czas** 'time').

It is worth noting that the group of words is open, and new verbs are constantly added to the Polish vocabulary, e.g., **grillować** 'to grill,' **kliknąć ikonę** (w) <+ACC> 'to click on the icon.'

It is interesting how loan verbs referring to different types of action are adapted to become Polish verbs, for example verbs referring to a process usually take the productive suffix **-ować**, while verbs referring to momentary action take the suffix **-ać**, **-ąć**, or **-ić**, e.g.,

> **logować się** 'to log in'
> **studiować** 'to study'
> **parkować** 'to park'
> **grillować** 'to grill'
> **resetować** 'to reset'
> **klikać** and **kliknąć** 'to click'
> **lukać** and **luknąć** (coll.) 'to look, to glance'
> **klaskać** and **klasnąć** 'to clap'
> **certolić** (coll.) 'to make a fuss'

Verbs are *conjugated*. The process is called conjugation, from the Latin *conjugar*, and it indicates the person, number, tense, voice of a verb, and in some forms also the class (also referred to as gender) of the subject of the action, and the aspect of the action. This means that the verb form changes in order to agree with its subject, e.g., **śpię** 'I am sleeping,' śpi*sz* 'you are sleeping,' śpi*my* 'we are sleeping.' Similarly, in English we say "I study" but "she/he studies," adding "-s" to the verb and changing the stem when needed, when the subject is "she," "he" or "it." The personal pronouns "I," "you" (SG and PL), "we" are usually omitted in Polish because each person has a distinct ending by which the subject can be recognized:

Często *pracuję* wieczorami '*I* often *work* in the evenings.'

An exception to these situations occurs when the personal pronoun is required to avoid confusion about whom the verb refers to; for example in the third person singular and plural in the present tense and compound future with the infinitive **będzie spać** 'will be sleeping.' Personal pronouns are also used, when we want to express a contrast or to emphasize the subject:

Tylko *ja pracuję* w weekendy. 'Only *I work* on the weekends.'

Note that the third person singular **ona** 'she,' **on** 'he,' **ono** 'it,' and plural **oni one** 'they' have identical verb forms in the present tense: **on/ona/ono śpi** 'he/she/it sleeps,' **oni/one śpią** 'they sleep.'

Kto 'who' and **nikt** 'nobody' always take a singular verb form, even though the answer is plural, e.g.,

Kto mieszka obok? 'Who lives next door?'
Kowalscy 'The Kowalskis.'

nikt nie przyszedł 'nobody came'

Kto and **nikt** take the masculine verb form in the past tense, and in all verb forms, where the class is recognized (e.g., compound future: **kto będzie pisał?** 'who will be writing?' not: kto będzie pisała; conditional **nikt nie byłby wolny** 'nobody would be free').

Kto kupił <3 PR SG MSC PAST> **tort?** 'Who bought the cake?'
Babcia. Ona zawsze pamięta o moich urodzinach.
'Grandma. She always remembers (about) my birthday.'

Nie is joined directly to the verb to express negation, e.g., **nie śpię** 'I'm not sleeping' and receives the stress when the verb is monosyllabic: *nie* śpię, *nie* chcę 'I don't want,' *nie* ma 'there isn't/there aren't.'

Polish verbs have the following verbal categories:

- number (singular, plural)
- person (1st, 2nd, 3rd)

- class (masculine, feminine, neuter in singular and male human, and no male human in plural)
- tense (present, past, future)
- aspect (perfective, imperfective)
- mood (indicative, conditional, imperative).

Verbs impose certain cases on nouns or certain prepositions: **szukać** <+GEN> **pracy** 'to look for a job,' **dzwonić** *do* <+GEN> **babci** 'making a phone call to grandma.'

6.2 Number and person

Unlike in English, where number is not marked on the verb, except for the third person singular in "-s" suffix the present tense ("*she lives*" but "*I/you/we/they live*"), Polish verbs have a different set of endings for present, past and future tenses and distinguish singular forms from plural forms: **ona mieszka** 'she lives,' but **mieszka***my* 'we live.'

The number in which the verb is used is based on who the verb is referring to: a single or a plural entity. In other words, the subject and verb of a given sentence agree in number, person and class—the process called subject-verb agreement (see 6.5.2). In Polish, there are three persons singular and three persons plural, as shown in the list of person subjects below:

Singular	Plural
1st person **ja** 'I'	**my** 'we'
2nd person **ty** 'you,' 'thou'	**wy** 'you'
3rd person **on/ona/ono** 'he/she/it'	**oni/one** 'they'

Note that there is more than one form for saying 'you' in Polish. Formal ways of address are **pan** 'you,' referring to a man, **pani** 'you,' referring to a woman, **panie** 'you,' referring to women, **panowie** 'you,' referring to men, and **państwo** 'you,' referring to a couple or a mixed group of people.

Pan, pani are communicated through the third person singular, and **panie, panowie, państwo** are communicated through the third person plural.

Gdzie mieszkasz?
'Where *do you* live?' (asking a man or a woman in an informal setting)

Gdzie pani mieszka?
'Where *do you* live?' (asking a woman in a formal setting)

Gdzie mieszkacie?
Where *do you* live?' (asking a couple in an informal setting)

Gdzie państwo mieszkają?
Where *do you* live? (asking a couple in a formal setting)

6.3 Class

Class (also referred to as "gender") is not marked in the present tense by means of suffixes. **Czyta** 'is reading' is ambiguous as it could mean a female or a male is reading, so class is determined by adding a personal pronoun in front of the verb: **on czyta** 'he's reading,' **ona czyta** 'she's reading.'

The same situation occurs in the future tense of imperfective verbs with an infinitive: **będzie czytać** 'will be reading,' **on będzie czytać** 'he will be reading,' **ona będzie czytać** 'she will be reading.' A personal pronoun in front of the verb clarifies the class of the verb.

6.3.1 Singular

Temporal constructions that use the past tense verb forms, e.g., future compound tenses and the conditional mood, have the following endings in singular:

('I') -łem, ('you') -łeś, ('he') -ł when referring to a male human being, a masculine animal or a masculine object

('I') -łam, ('you') -łaś, ('she') -ła when referring to a female human being or a feminine object

-ło when referring to neuter nouns (see 6.6.2.2 for potential forms ('I') -łom, ('you') -łoś)

> **Ojciec** *pisał* **list.** 'Father was writing a letter.'
> **Matka** *pisała* **list.** 'Mother was writing a letter.'
> **Ojciec będzie** *pisał* **list.** 'Father will be writing a letter.'
> **Matka będzie** *pisała* **list.** 'Mother will be writing a letter.'
> **Dziecko** *pisało* **list.** 'A child was writing a letter.'

and in the conditional mood:

> **Gdyby ojciec** *chciał,* **toby coś** *napisał.*
> 'If father felt like writing he *would write* something.'

Discrepancy with the ending -ło

Temporal constructions take a singular verb with the marker -ło with:

1. numerals five and up (except those ending in the words: **dwa/dwie** 'two,' **trzy** 'three,' **cztery** 'four')
2. collective numerals **dwoje** 'two,' **troje** 'three' and upwards (see 8.1.2)
3. nouns referring to male human beings with the numerals **dwóch** 'two,' **trzech** 'three,' **czterech** 'four' and upwards
4. quantitative adverbs (words that relate to numerals and have a nominal nature, e.g., **dużo** 'a lot,' **wiele** and **wielu** (the latter used with nouns referring to a male human) 'many,' **dwukrotnie** 'twofold,' **wielokrotnie** 'manyfold')
5. constructions of absence in the past (see 2.6.4).

> **Dwoje dzieci** <GEN> **było w parku.** 'Two children *were* in the park.'
> **Wielu studentów** <GEN> **zachorowało.** 'Many students (mixed group) got sick.'
> **Mamy *nie było* w domu.** 'Mom *was not* at home.'

6.3.2 | *Plural*

Temporal constructions with past tense verb forms in the plural have the ending -li or -ły.

('we') -liśmy, ('you') -liście, ('they') -li refers to male human beings or a group with at least one male human being—the male human form,

('we') -łyśmy, ('you') -łyście, ('they') -ły refers to a group without a male human being—the no male human form.

> **Byliśmy w domu.** 'We <MHPL> were at home.'
> **Oni (artyści)** *malowali* **obraz.** 'They (artists) *were painting*.'
> **One (artystki)** *malowały* **obraz.** 'They (artists) *were painting*.'

Note that the ending -li is for fully developed male humans, hence **dzieci pisały** 'children were writing,' not pisali.

> **Rodzice** *byli* **w domu.** '[My] parents *were* at home.'
> **Dzieci** *były* **w domu.** '[The] children *were* at home.'

An exception to that rule is a group of one or more female human being(s) and a masculine animal. Such a group takes -li.

> **Córka i pies** *byli* **na balkonie.** '[My] daughter and a dog *were* on the balcony.' (6.1)

6.4 Aspect

Polish has two aspects, **aspekt niedokonany** 'imperfective aspect' (IMPFV) which literally means 'not achieved aspect,' and **aspekt dokonany** 'perfective aspect' (PFV), which literally means achieved aspect.

Aspect is a grammatical concept that allows the speaker to express the status of an action as completed, achieved, terminated, e.g., *namalowałam obraz* 'I *have finished painting* the picture' or as non-completed, to describe a process of happening, e.g., *malowałam* obraz 'I *was painting* a picture.'

In the first example we know that the artist is ready to give the painting to the gallery, because he is finished with the painting, he reached the goal. In the second example we are only informed that the process of painting has occurred, but not that the process has finished. Aspects in Polish allow the speaker to choose what he/she intends to inform us about.

Malowałam obraz. 'I *was painting* a picture.'
Namalowałam obraz. 'I *have finished painting* the picture.'

Technically, linguistic limitations occur as to which aspect of the verb should be used when the sentence is placed within a wider context. For example, to show a sequence of actions, one action must have been completed so that the latter action can occur.

Namalowałam <PFV> **obraz i oddałam go do galerii.** 'I *painted* a picture and gave it to the gallery.'

In other words the process of painting must have been finished (as indicated in the perfective form of the verb) in order for it to have been given to the gallery.

Often, where in English one verb, e.g., "to paint" is used in a series of tenses ('I have painted,' 'I was painting,' 'I used to paint,') to communicate the completion or continuity of ongoing, repeated or habitual action, in Polish an aspectual pair of verbs with fewer tenses is used.

6.4.1 | Aspect and tenses

The use of the perfective and imperfective aspect of verbs interacts with tenses in Polish.

The choice of either perfective or imperfective is only possible in past and future tenses in Polish. In other words only in the past and future can the

311

status of an action be described as ongoing or completed. All actions in the present tense typically denote ongoing, repeated, or habitual action (non-completed) and therefore can only be expressed through the imperfective form of verbs, e.g., **czytam** 'I'm reading/I read.'

When the main verb refers to something happening at the moment of speech, it must be in the imperfective.

> **Ojciec słucha** <IMPFV> **radia.** 'Father is listening to the radio.'
> **Matka śpi** <IMPFV>. 'Mother is sleeping.'
> **Pies szczeka** <IMPFV>. 'The dog is barking.'
> **Chcę** <MAIN VERB, IMPFV> **przeczytać** <PFV VERB> **ten artykuł.** 'I want to read this article.'
> **Mówię,** <MAIN VERB, IMPFV> **że zadzwonię** <PFV VERB> **wieczorem.**
> 'I am saying that I will call in the evening.'

In the sentences below, please note that the time reference is determined by the main verb. If the main verb refers to an action or state happening at the moment of speech, it can only be in the imperfective.

> **Chcę** <IMPFV> **coś powiedzieć** <PFV>. 'I want to say something.'
> **Chciałabym** <IMPFV> **przeczytać** <PFV> **tę książkę.** 'I would like to read this book.'
> **Proszę** <IMPFV> **wyjść** <PFV>. 'Please leave <PFV>.'
> **Mam** <IMPFV> **nadzieję, że zdałam** <PFV>. 'I hope that I passed.'

Imperfective forms of verbs are also used when referring to temporal structures that do not involve a change, e.g.,

> **Było zimno. Ojciec słuchał radia, a matka spała.**
> 'It *was* cold. Father *was listening* to the radio, and mother *was sleeping*.'

> *Mieszkaliśmy* **w Londynie.**
> 'We *were living/we lived* in London.'

Imperfective forms are used for verbs that inherently have no ending, which are continuous, e.g.,

> **Ciężko** *pracowaliśmy*. 'We *were working/worked* hard.'
> **Ewa** *studiowała* **prawo.** 'Ewa *was studying/studied* law.'

Perfective forms of verbs can only refer to temporal structures with an action that has ended or will have ended.

The perfective (resultative) treats the entire action as one uninterrupted moment with an ending that involves a change. That action is finished just before the moment of stating it, or will have finished just after the moment of stating it:

Entire, uninterrupted action just after the time of speech

poda chleb 'he/she will pass the bread'
kopnie piłkę 'he/she will hit the ball'
zbije szklankę 'he/she will break the glass'
napisze e-mail 'he/she will write an email'

Entire, uninterrupted action just before the time of speech:

podał chleb 'he passed the bread'
kopnął piłkę 'he hit the ball'
zbił szklankę 'he broke the glass'
napisał e-mail 'he wrote an email'

To create a perfective form from an imperfective verb, in Polish a prefix is often added to the imperfective verb, e.g.,

malować <IMPFV>/**na-malować** <PFV> 'to paint'
czytać <IMPFV>/**prze-czytać** <PFV> 'to read'

The future tense of most perfectives looks a lot like the present tense of the imperfective, e.g.,

Present	Future
czytam <IMPFV> 'I am reading'	prze-*czytam* <PFV> 'I will read'
czytasz <IMPFV> 'you are reading'	prze-*czytasz* <PFV> 'you will read'
maluję <IMPFV> 'I am painting'	na-*maluję* <PFV> 'I will paint'
malujesz <IMPFV> 'you are painting'	na-*malujesz* <PFV> 'you will paint'

therefore the term "non-past form" is often used when referring to the present and future in comparison to the past tense.

6.4.2 Aspect of the main verb

	Imperfective	Perfective
Present	√	*does not exist*
Past	√	√
Future	√	√

"Aspect" allows the action to be examined from different angles, emphasizing its result and implying a shift of action or describing the action as something that is not happening in the present. The final decision of whether to translate a verb into the imperfective or perfective form is based on the context in which the sentence is presented:

Napisałam referat i wyłączyłam komputer.
'I *finished writing* [my] paper and turned off the computer.'

Napisałam referat.
'I *wrote* [my] paper.'

Verbs that inherently refer to an action with an ending have either imperfective or perfective forms. The imperfective is used when the action is ongoing, continued or will continue to unfold, and the perfective is used to emphasize an event that has happened or will have happened and will involve a change.

Since the imperfective form is used for an action that is ongoing, continued or will continue, it is often used (1) to answer the question: what is/was/will be going on?, and hence to: (2) describe an action, (3) describe two or more actions happening simultaneously, in parallel, ongoing actions unfolding over a period of time, non-stop or repetitively occurring actions, closely linked actions, as in a temporal structure with the verbs **zaczynać** 'to start,' 'to begin,' **kończyć** 'to finish,' **przestać** 'to stop doing something,' e.g.:

zaczynać/zacząć padać 'to start raining'
kończyć/skończyć pisać 'to finish writing'
przestawać/przestać palić 'to stop smoking'

Perfective forms, on the other hand, are used to emphasize completion, and hence that aspect is used in sentences with a sequence of events, when one must finish in order for the other to begin, e.g.,

Skończyłam pracę i poszłam do domu 'I finished work and went home.'

Verbs with no ending have only imperfective forms, e.g.,

bać się 'to be afraid'
umieć 'to know how'
zajmować się 'to take care of'
rozmawiać 'to talk'

Some verbs are biaspectual: they serve both in imperfective and perfective contexts, such as **awansować** 'to promote,' **aresztować** 'to arrest.'

6.4.3 | Choosing the aspect

Czego szukałeś? <IMPFV> 'What were you looking for?' (only process, no results)
Co znalazłeś? <PFV> 'What have you found?' (results, completion)

Verbs that inherently refer to an action with an ending have either imperfective or perfective forms. The imperfective form is used when the action is ongoing, continued or will continue to unfold, and the perfective form is used to emphasize an event that has happened or will have happened and will involve a change.

Choosing between the imperfective and perfective form depends on the informant's intentions, e.g., *pisałam* referat emphasizes the action itself, that in the past 'I (a female) *was writing/wrote* [my] paper.' In the sentence *napisałam* referat the informant wants to point out the result: 'I *have written* [my] paper.' With perfective forms one can expect a change in action. Imperfective forms of verbs describe the action in a continuing mood, without bringing any change of affairs.

Napisałam **referat i wyłączyłam komputer.** '*I finished writing* [my] paper and turned off the computer.'
Pisałam **referat i słuchałam muzyki.** '*I was writing* [my] paper and listening to music.'

However, our conversations usually involve sentences with more than one verb and these sentences are presented in a context. Context and formal language restrictions (like in English using the present tense in the sentence 'if she comes,' not 'if she will come') usually dictate which aspect to choose in Polish or which tense to choose in English.

Zawiesił <PFV> *mi się komputer,* **kiedy** *pisałam* <IMPFV> **referat.**
'My computer crashed <PFV> when I *was writing* [my] <IMPFV> paper.'

Zawiesił <PFV> *mi się komputer,* **kiedy** *napisałam* <PFV> **referat.**
My computer crashed <PFV> when I *wrote* [my] <IMPFV> paper.'

Skończyłam <PFV> *pisać* <IMPFV> **referat, kiedy nagle zawiesił** <PFV> **mi się komputer.**
'I finished writing [my] paper, when all of a sudden the computer crashed.'

Kończyłam <IMPFV> *pisać* <IMPFV> **referat, kiedy nagle zawiesił** <PFV> **mi się komputer.**
'I was finishing writing [my] paper, when all of a sudden the computer crashed.'

The choice of either aspect of the main verb 'to finish,' **kończyć** (imperfective) or **skończyć** (perfective), is possible, but the verb that follows, according to formal restrictions, must be in the imperfective form in Polish.

A choice of aspect has to be made almost every time a verb is used, and the meaning of the sentence will be affected by the chosen aspect. Below is a list of instances where only one aspect is grammatically possible. As a rule of thumb use the imperfective form of the verb by default.

6.4.4 | *Imperfective*

(*process* in all three tenses)

1. Is used in *all three tenses*: present, past and compound future (**czytam**—'I am reading,' **czytałem**—'I was reading' <MSC>, **będę czytać**—'I will be reading'), and in participles that end with *-ąc*: *czytając* 'while reading' and *-ący*: *czytający* 'the one who is reading.'
2. Denotes an *incomplete*, *continued* or *repeated* action – one which was, is or will be *in progress* without regard to its beginning, end or result. Also an action unfolding over a period of time, or an action without reference to a definite termination or result.
3. Is used *by default* when no other restrictions occur to describe an action in the past or future.

   Rano jadłam śniadanie. 'In the morning I had breakfast.'

   This sentence uses an imperfective form of the verb because it emphasizes the action of the verb rather than a result: compare with **Rano zjadłam śniadanie i dlatego teraz nie jestem głodna.** 'In the morning I have had breakfast and so now I am not hungry.'

4. Denotes *repetition*: frequent and repeated action, often accompanied by adverbs of frequency and duration: **zawsze** 'always,' **często** 'often,' **zwykle** and **zazwyczaj** 'usually,' **co godzinę** 'every hour,' etc.

   Codziennie rano piję mocną kawę.
   'Every day in the morning I have strong coffee.'

   Zawsze jem drugie śniadanie.
   'I always eat elevenses [UK, (lit.) second breakfast].'

Note: In Polish some verbs have more than one imperfective form. Forms such as **pijać** 'to drink,' **jadać** 'to eat' as opposed to **pić** 'to drink' and **jeść** 'to eat,' suggest that action occurs frequently (see 6.4.13).

O tej porze zwykle pijam herbatę. 'At this time of the day I usually drink tea.'

Czasami jadam mięso wołowe. 'I occasionally eat beef.'

5. Is used with words suggesting *continuity*: ciągle, stale, non stop, bez przerwy, nadal 'constantly, permanently.'

Ciągle leczyła <IMPFV> **się za granicą.** 'She was constantly undergoing treatment abroad.'

Stale zadawał <IMPFV> **to samo pytanie.** 'He was constantly asking the same question.'

Mówił <IMPFV> **bez przerwy.** 'He was talking all the time.'

6. Is used in constructions referring to our *likes* and *dislikes*, and *hobbies* in general, e.g.:

a. Lubię . . . 'I like . . .' Nie lubię . . . 'I don't like . . .'
Lubię tańczyć. 'I like dancing.'
Co lubisz robić? 'What do you like doing?'
Nie lubię prasować. 'I don't like ironing.'

b. "I used to . . ."
Kiedyś częściej chodziliśmy do kina.
'We used to go to the movies more often in the past.'

c. "Have you (ever) . . .?"

These sentences use an imperfective form of the verb because there is no emphasis on completion. Instead the emphasis is on getting information about whether an attempt at action has taken place.

Both questions and answers use imperfective forms:

Czy czytałeś <IMPFV> **wiersze Norwida?** 'Have you (ever) read poems by Norwid?'

Tak, czytałem <IMPFV>. 'Yes, I have.'

Czy widziałeś <IMPFV> **nowy film Wajdy?** 'Have you seen Wajda's new film?'

Tak, widziałem <IMPFV>. **Jest bardzo poruszający.** 'Yes, I have. It is very moving.'

Czy jadłeś <IMPFV> **(kiedyś) pierogi?** 'Have you (ever) had pierogi?'

By using the perfective form of the verb, emphasis is put on *completion*. I asked you to read the poems and now I am asking whether or not you have done that.

Czy przeczytałeś <PFV> **wiersze Norwida?**
'Have you read [the] poems by Norwid?'

7. Is used *after "start" and "finish" verbs*.

The imperfective form is always used in the form of imperfective infinitive after verbs that denote beginning **zaczynać** (IMPFV)/**zacząć** (PFV) or finishing **kończyć** (IMPFV)/**skończyć** (PFV) or **przestawać** (IMPFV)/**przestać** (PFV) doing something, because if you start or finish an action, you are already within the spectrum of an ongoing action.

> **Zaczęłam** <PFV> **planować** <IMPFV> **wakacje.**
> 'I've started planning [the] vacation.'

> **Zwykle zaczynam** <IMPFV> **planować** <IMPFV> **wakacje w maju.**
> 'I usually start planning [the] vacation in May.'

> **Właśnie kończę** <IMPFV> **załatwiać** <IMPFV> **sprawy związane z przeprowadzką.**
> 'I'm about to finish everything related to the move.'

> **Właśnie skończyłam** <PFV> **załatwiać** <IMPFV> **sprawy związane z przeprowadzką.**
> 'I have just finished everything related to the move.'

> **Przestało** <PFV> **padać** <IMPFV>.
> 'It stopped raining.'

8. Is used in *general requests and commands*.

> **Proszę mówić** <IMPFV> **po polsku.**
> 'Please speak in Polish.'

(In comparison, asking for specificity would use the perfective form of the verb: **Proszę powiedzieć** <PFV> **to po polsku.** 'Please say *it* in Polish.')

> **Mów** <IMPFV> **wolno i wyraźnie.**
> 'Speak slowly and clearly.'

9. Is used in *negative requests and commands*.

> **Proszę tego nie robić** <IMPFV>. 'Please do not do it.'
> **Nie opierać** <IMPFV> **się o drzwi.** 'Do not lean on the door.'
> **Nie trać** <IMPFV> **czasu.** 'Don't waste time.'

Note: The perfective form of the verb is used to convey the sense of a warning:

> **Nie zgub** <PFV> **kluczy!**
> 'Don't lose the keys!'

> **Nie wypij** <PFV> **mojej kawy.**
> 'Do not drink my coffee.'

10. Is used after *impersonal modal verbs* **można, trzeba, warto, wolno** and personal **chcieć, móc, musieć, powinien, woleć** *to express general ideas and truths*:

> **Co można robić** <IMPFV> **na urlopie?** 'What can one do on vacation?' (process)
>
> **Co można zrobić** <PFV> **na urlopie?** 'What one can get done on vacation? (results)
>
> **Kwiaty warto kupować** <IMPFV> **na rynku.** 'Flowers are worth buying at the market.' (more than once, repetitive process)
>
> **Muszę się uczyć** <IMPFV>. 'I must study.' (ongoing process)

The perfective form would be used to emphasize an action completed at one time:

> **Warto kupić** <PFV> **jej kwiaty.**
> 'It is worth buying her flowers.'
>
> **Muszę się nauczyć** <PFV> **tego wiersza na pamięć.**
> 'I must learn the poem by heart.'

11. Is used to express *simultaneous actions*:

> **Jedli popcorn i oglądali film.**
> 'They were eating popcorn and watching a movie.'

12. Is often used as an imperative to convey the sense of *invitation*: **mów, mów** 'talk (more),' **bierz, bierz** 'take it,' **siadaj i opowiadaj** 'sit down and tell (us all),' **śpiewaj!** 'sing,' **tańcz!** 'dance.'

The imperative is usually repeated.

13. Is used in a question: **Co mam robić?** 'What shall I do?' is asking for action. **Co mam zrobić?** is asking 'what results do you expect from me?' (See 6.5.1.1)

6.4.5 | Perfective

(focusing on *completion*)

1. Is used for an *action that has been or will be completed*. The perfective form of the verb is used to emphasize the completion, result or achievement of an action: **mur runął** 'the wall collapsed,' **mur runie** 'the wall will collapse.'

2. Is used to describe a simple action *completed in a moment*: **usiadł** 'he sat down,' **zawył z bólu** 'he howled with pain.'

It is often used after the words **nagle** 'suddenly,' **za chwilę** 'in a moment,' **zaraz** 'immediately,' 'at once,' **w końcu** 'at last,' 'finally' when referring to an *immediate future*:

> **Za chwilę oszaleję.** 'I'll lose my mind in a moment.'
> **Zaraz zrobię śniadanie.** 'I'll make breakfast in a sec.'
> **Wreszcie się ustatkowałaś.** 'You have finally settled down.' <FEM>

Note: **Zaraz wracam** 'I'll be right back' on the store window instead of **Zaraz wrócę** 'I'll be right back' may suggest that I will probably not be back very soon.

3. Is used in *sequential actions*.

The perfective form of the verb is used in a sequence of events to emphasize *a change from one situation to another*:

> **Wróciłam do domu, przebrałam się, umyłam, a potem zjadłam lekką kolację.**
> 'I came home, changed, washed and then ate a light supper.'

> **Rano napisałam e-mail, a następnie wysłałam go do pracodawcy.**
> 'In the morning I wrote an email and then sent it to my employer.'

The e-mail could not have been sent if it had not been written (finalized).

4. Is used for *cumulative action*

> **Zjadłam cały tort i wypiłam całą butelkę wina.**
> 'I ate the whole cake and finished the whole bottle of wine.'

5. Is used *to emphasize that something has been done thoroughly*.

> **Przeczytałem instrukcję od A do Z i nadal nie wiem, jak to działa.** 'I read the manual from A to Z and I still don't know how it works.'
> **Gruntownie przeszukaliśmy akta.** 'We searched the files thoroughly.'
> **Dokładnie wysprzątaliśmy strych.** 'We cleaned the attic carefully.'
> **Lekarz dokładnie go zbadał.** 'The doctor examined him thoroughly.'

6. Is used *when we expect results*.

> **Czy zadzwoniłeś do rodziców?**
> Have you called your parents?

7. Is used in situations of trying and failing (versus imperfective which can denote a lack of any attempt). Perfective is used to express trying (regardless of the results) to do something, while imperfective is used to emphasize absence of any attempt to do something.:

Nic nie zrobiłam <PFV>. 'I did nothing.' [I tried but it did not work out.]
Nic nie robiłam <IMPFV>. 'I did nothing.' [I did not even try.]

—**Kto wziął** <PFV> **pilot?** 'Who took the remote control?'
—**Ja nie brałem** <IMPFV>. 'I didn't take it.'

Some verbs do not have perfective forms—verbs with no inherent ending, e.g., **być** 'to be,' **móc** 'can,' **podróżować** 'to travel,' **studiować** 'to study,' **pracować** 'to work,' **mieszkać** 'to reside.' For such verbs, a form with the suffix **po** serves as a potential perfective form with a meaning of "temporary," e.g.,

Czas trochę popodróżować po świecie.
'It's time to travel a bit around the world.'

Kiedy trochę popracujesz, zrozumiesz czym jest praca.
'When you work for some time, you will understand what work is.'

Pobyłem trochę sam, a teraz trochę z tobą pobędę.
'I stayed by myself for a bit, and now I will stay with you for a bit.'

Some verbs do not have imperfective forms, e.g., **runąć** 'to tumble.'

6.4.6 | Triggers

There are key words that trigger the imperfective or perfective aspect.

They are especially useful for beginners of Polish. However, many of adverbs of frequency and words that usually signalize a perfective form can also be used the with imperfective forms. As a rule of thumb, use the imperfective form when you describe an unfolding, ongoing action that does not involve a change.

Use the perfective form in temporal structures that involve a change and signalize an event completed at one time, e.g.:

Ewa od czasu do czasu powie <PFV> **coś po francusku.**
'From time to time Ewa will say something in French.'
Ewa od czasu do czasu mówi <IMPFV> **po francusku.**
'From time to time Ewa speaks French.'

Między ósmą a dziesiątą *nauczyłam* **się** <PFV> **20 nowych słów.**
'Between eight and ten o'clock *I memorized* 20 new words.'
Między ósmą a dziesiątą *uczyłam* **się** <IMPFV> **do egzaminu.**
'Between eight and ten o'clock *I was studying* for the exam.'

Właśnie kończyłam <IMPFV> **pić kawę, kiedy zadzwonił** <PFV> **telefon.**
'I was just finishing drinking [my] coffee, when the phone rang.'
Właśnie skończyłam <PFV> **pić kawę, kiedy zadzwonił** <PFV> **telefon.**
'I had just finished drinking my coffee, when the phone rang.'

Imperfective aspect	Perfective aspect
jak często? 'how often?'	**nagle** 'suddenly'
ile razy? 'how many times?'	**zaraz** 'immediately'
jak długo? 'how long?'	**za chwilę** 'momentarily'
zawsze 'always'	**raptem** 'all of a sudden'
zwykle/zazwyczaj 'usually'	**wkrótce** 'soon'
często 'often'	**nareszcie/wreszcie/w**
czasem/czasami 'sometimes'	**końcu** 'finally'
od czasu do czasu 'from time to time'	**natychmiast** 'at once'
rzadko 'rarely'	**właśnie** 'just'
okazjonalnie 'occasionally'	**już** 'already'
nigdy nie 'never'	**kiedy** 'when'
codziennie 'daily'	
co godzinę 'every hour'	
co tydzień/miesiąc/rok 'every week/ month/year'	
każdego dnia/tygodnia/miesiąca/roku 'each day/week/month/year'	
w/co każdy wtorek/weekend 'each/ every Tuesday/weekend'	
każdego roku w maju/latem 'every May/year'	
ciągle/wciąż/stale/non stop 'constantly'	
całymi dniami/tygodniami/latami 'all days/weeks/years'	
nieraz 'many times'	

6.4.7 | *Aspect and clauses*

Adverbial clauses: **kiedy** 'when,' **gdy** 'when,' **podczas gdy** 'while,' **w czasie gdy** 'when,' **jak** 'as' are used with imperfective or perfective based on the following criteria.

1. Use the *imperfective* aspect when describing simultaneous events. Events in both clauses occur in the same tense.

> **Podczas gdy on pracował, ja musiałam siedzieć w domu sama.**
> 'While he was working, I had to stay at home alone.'
> **W czasie gdy ty zdawałeś na studia, ja zdawałam do liceum.**
> 'When you were passing exams to go to college, I was passing exams to go to high school.'
> **Jem, kiedy/jak się denerwuję.** 'I eat when I'm nervous.'

2. Use the *perfective* aspect when one event will have caused or had caused another. Events in both clauses occur in the same tense, unlike in English.

> **Zadzwonię** <PFV>, **jak wrócę** <PFV>. 'I'll call when I get back.'
> **Cieszyłam się** <past IMPFV>, **kiedy go zobaczyłam** <past PFV>.
> 'I was happy when I saw him.'
> **Ucieszę się** <future PFV>, **kiedy go zobaczę** <future PFV>.
> 'I'll be happy when I see him.'

The adverbs **już** and **właśnie** can take imperfective or perfective forms of verbs.

> **Kiedy weszłam do pokoju, dzieci już jadły** <IMPFV> **obiad.** 'When I entered the room, the children were already eating lunch.'
> **Kiedy weszłam do pokoju, dzieci już zjadły** <PFV> **obiad.** 'When I entered the room, the children had already finished lunch.'

The perfective form of the verb after **już** suggests a sequence: the children ate lunch before I entered the room.

In general statements, **jeśli** is followed by the present tense when referring to a conditional:

> **Jeśli kocha, to poczeka.** 'If (s)he loves, (s)he will wait.'

| 6.4.7.1 | **Zanim** *'before'* with the perfective *aspect*

The word **zanim** connects two events, of which one will take or took place earlier than the other. **Zanim** is followed by the *perfective form* of the verb in the past or future tenses.

> **Zanim rozpoczął** <PFV> **pracę w radiu, zajmował się** <IMPFV> **tłumaczeniami.** 'Before he started working at the radio, he was doing translations.'

Zjedz <PFV> **zupę, zanim wystygnie** <PFV>. 'Finish your soup before it gets cold.'

Nauczyłam się <PFV> **grać na pianinie, zanim nauczyłam się** <PFV> **czytać.** 'I learned how to play piano before I learned how to read.'

Wrócę<PFV>, **zanim zrobi się** <PFV> **późno.** 'I'll be back before it gets late.'

Zastanów się <PFV>, **zanim coś powiesz** <PFV>. 'Think for a while, before you say something.'

6.4.7.2 | **Aż** and **dopóki nie** 'until' with the perfective aspect

The action in the main clause will continue or continued, using the imperfective form of the verb, *only until* the event with **dopóki nie** or **aż** occurs, using the perfective form of the verb. Note that **dopóki** takes a negated verb. Both **aż** and **dopóki nie** are followed by the perfective form of the verb.

Jadł <past IMPFV>, *aż* **najadł się do syta** <past PFV>.
Jadł <past IMPFV>, *dopóki nie* **najadł się do syta** <past PFV>.
'He ate until he got full.'

Siedzieliśmy <past IMPFV> **na balkonie, dopóki nie zrobiło się** <past PFV> **zimno.**
Siedzieliśmy <past IMPFV> **na balkonie, aż zrobiło się** <past PFV> **zimno.**
'We sat on the balcony until it got cold.'

Będziesz siedział przy stole, dopóki nie skończysz obiadu.
'You'll remain sitting at the table until you have finished [your] dinner.'

6.4.7.3 | **Dopóki** and **tak długo, jak** 'as long as' with the imperfective aspect (simultaneous events)

If the main clause is in the past or future tense, the subordinate clause is in the past or future tense as well. If the main clause is in the present tense, the subordinate clause can be in the present or future.

Miałem pieniądze, dopóki pracowałem.
Miałem pieniądze tak długo, jak pracowałem.
'I had money as long as I was working.'

Dopóki pracujesz, masz pieniądze.
'As long as you work, you have money.'

Będę was wspierała <future IMPFV> **tak długo, jak będzie**
  <future IMPFV> **to możliwe.** 'I will support you as long as possible.'
Dopóki żyję <present>, **będę o was dbał** <future IMPFV>. 'As long
  I live, I'll take care of you.'

Grałem w kasynie, dopóki nie wygrałem. 'I played in the casino
  until I won.'
Grałem w kasynie, dopóki wygrywałem. 'I played in the casino as
  long as I was winning.'
Będę grał, dopóki nie wygram. 'I'll play until I win.'
Będę grał, dopóki wygrywam. 'I'll play as long as I'm winning.'

6.4.8 | *Aspectual pairs of verbs*

The imperfective and perfective can be formed by:

1. adding a prefix to the imperfective infinitive, e.g., **pisać** <IMPFV>/**na-pisać**
   <PFV> 'to write.' In English the process is rendered by a preposition,
   e.g., **napisać** 'to write something down.'

The choice of prefixes can be fairly distinctive and is limited with
any specific verb but it is *not* possible to give clear rules for when a
particular prefix is added to an imperfective infinitive to create its
perfective counterpart in the primary aspectual pair. (A primary aspectual pair consists of the imperfective and perfective forms of a verb
with the same meaning.) Often language tradition dictates the usage of
a given prefix:

> **chować** <IMPFV>/**s-chować** <PFV> 'to hide,' **pakować** <IMPFV>/
> **za-pakować** <PFV> 'to wrap, to pack,' **myć** <IMPFV>/**u-myć** <PFV>
> 'to wash,' **kąpać** <IMPFV>/**wy-kąpać** <PFV> 'to bath.'

It is more obvious to see which prefix to add when it comes to verbs
of motion, as many prefixes describe spatial awareness (6.4.14.13).

> **w-ejść** 'to enter'   **z-ejść** 'to go down'
> **wy-jść** 'to exit'   **ob-ejść** 'to go (a)round'

Lists of commonly used imperfective verbs with their perfective counterpart in the primary aspectual pair are given under point 2 below.

2. contracting (shortening) or modifying the stem in the imperfective and perfective aspects:

> **oceniać** <IMPFV>—**ocenić** <PFV> 'to assess,' **zaczynać** <IMPFV>—
> **zacząć** <PFV> 'to begin,' **krzyczeć** <IMPFV>—**krzyknąć** <PFV>
> 'to shout,' **kupować** <IMPFV>—**kupić** <PFV> 'to buy,' **zdobywać**
> <IMPFV>—**zdobyć** <PFV> 'to achieve,' **odpoczywać** <IMPFV>—
> **odpocząć** <PFV> 'to rest.'

It is not possible to clearly distinguish between imperfective and perfective forms based on the length of the verb, but below are some tips that may help. In the aspectual pair:

a. The infinitive with a prefix is perfective, while its counterpart without a prefix is imperfective. It is the prefix that made the verb form perfective:

Imperfective	Perfective
czytać 'to read'	**prze-czytać**
dzwonić 'to call'	**za-dzwonić**
jechać 'to go'	**po-jechać**
kończyć 'to finish'	**s-kończyć**
pisać 'to write'	**na-pisać**
prosić 'to request'	**po-prosić**
pytać 'to inquire'	**za-pytać**
robić 'to do'	**z-robić**
uczyć się 'to learn'	**na-uczyć się**

b. When both forms have identical ends and beginnings, it is often the shorter form that is perfective:

Imperfective	Perfective
dawać 'to give'	**dać**
dostawać 'to get'	**dostać**
obiecywać 'to promise'	**obiecać**
otrzymywać 'to receive'	**otrzymać**
poznawać 'to get to know'	**poznać**
spotykać się 'to meet'	**spotkać się**
ubierać się 'to dress'	**ubrać się**
wstawać 'to get up'	**wstać**
wychowywać się 'to grow up'	**wychować się**
wyjeżdżać 'to go out'	**wyjechać**
zasypiać 'to oversleep'	**zaspać**

c. When both forms have identical beginnings but one form ends with -ać and the other one with -ić/yć, -eć, -ąć, the -ać form is often imperfective:

Imperfective	Perfective
dokuczać 'to bother'	**dokuczyć**
kupować 'to buy'	**kupić**
opowiadać 'to tell'	**opowiedzieć**
otwierać 'to open'	**otworzyć**
powtarzać 'to repeat'	**powtórzyć**
przeprowadzać się 'to move'	**przeprowadzić się**
wracać 'to return'	**wrócić**
zaczynać 'to begin'	**zacząć**
zajmować 'to occupy'	**zająć**
zamykać 'to close'	**zamknąć**
zapominać 'to forget'	**zapomnieć**
zapraszać 'to invite'	**zaprosić**
zasypiać 'to fall asleep'	**zasnąć**
zwiedzać 'to tour'	**zwiedzić**
odwiedzać 'to visit'	**odwiedzić**

Note: When two infinitives have the same length but one ends with -ąć, the one with -ąć is the perfective one. Most of the verbs ending with -ąć are perfective.

Imperfective	Perfective
krzyczeć 'to shout'	**krzyknąć**

3. Using two different verbs. *These forms should be memorized.* Do not rely on the length of the infinitive.

Imperfective	Perfective
brać 'to take'	**wziąć**
mówić 'to talk'	**powiedzieć**
oglądać 'to watch'	**obejrzeć**
spoglądać na 'to look at'	**spojrzeć**
widzieć 'to see'	**zobaczyć**
znajdować 'to locate'	**znaleźć**
kłaść 'to put'	**położyć**

6.4.9 Biaspectual verbs

A verb is biaspectual if it has one form serving for both aspects, imperfective and perfective. It means that the verb can be used both to describe unfolding events and in a temporal structure that involves a change. Such verbs are often borrowed from languages that do not distinguish between imperfective and perfective. Over time, such verbs can develop an imperfective/perfective pair, e.g., **parkować** <IMPFV>/**zaparkować** <PFV> 'to park.'

aresztować 'to arrest'
awansować 'to promote'
cudzołożyć 'to commit adultery'
desygnować 'to designate'
mianować 'to appoint'
potrafić 'to be able to do something'
rozbrykać się 'to go wild' (coll.)
rozmyślić się 'to change one's mind'

Nie potrafię spojrzeć prawdzie prosto w oczy.
'I am not able to face the truth.'

W 1967 roku papież mianował arcybiskupa Karola Wojtyłę kardynałem.
'In 1967 the Pope appointed archbishop Karol Wojtyła cardinal.'

Tuż przed meczem policja aresztowała awanturujących się kibiców.
'Just before the game, the police arrested fighting fans.'

6.4.10 Perfective only verbs

Some verbs can only be used in the perfective form (*perfectivum tantum*), when the action cannot be described as ongoing:

oniemieć 'to be (left) speechless'
owdowieć 'to become a widow/a widower'
runąć 'to tumble'

6.4.11 Imperfective only verbs

Some verbs that describe continuing actions and states are only used in the imperfective form (*imperfectivum tantum*):

asystować 'to accompany'	**potrzebować** 'to need'
deportować 'to deport'	**pracować** 'to work'
domagać się 'to demand'	**uczestniczyć** 'to participate'
guzdrać się 'to dawdle'	**umieć** 'to know how'
(**guzdra się/guzdrze się**)	**uprawiać (sport)** 'to go in for
kontynuować 'to continue'	sports'
leżeć 'to lie'	**woleć** 'to prefer'
marudzić na <+ACC> 'to gripe'	**towarzyszyć** 'to accompany'
mieć 'to have'	**zazdrościć** 'to envy'
należeć do <+GEN> 'to belong to'	**żyć** 'to be alive'

Anestezjolog asystuje przy operacji.
'An Anesthesiologist assists at the surgery.'

Minister spraw zagranicznych często towarzyszy premierowi w oficjalnych wizytach zagranicznych.
'The Minister of Foreign Affairs often accompanies the Prime Minister during official visits abroad.'

6.4.12	*Additional aspectual pairs*

An aspectual pair is often formed by adding a prefix to an imperfective verb to form a perfective verb (**prosić/<u>po</u>prosić**). When other prefixes are used with such a verb (**<u>za</u>prosić**), a new form is needed for the imperfective (**za<u>praszać</u>**).

Imperfective	Perfective
prosić 'to request'	**po-prosić** 'to request'
	za-prosić 'to invite'
	prze-prosić 'to apologize'
	wy-prosić 'to turn somebody out'

In some verbs the traces of the original infinitive are more visible, in some less. Creating the imperfective forms in the second aspectual pair usually requires the stem to be contracted or modified, here **i** is changed to **a**.

Imperfective	Perfective
zapraszać 'to invite'	**za-prosić**
przepraszać 'to apologize'	**prze-prosić**
wypraszać 'to turn somebody out'	**wy-prosić**
spraszać 'to invite' (coll.)	**s-prosić**
upraszać 'to get somebody to do something'	**u-prosić**
dopraszać się 'to entreat'	**do-prosić się**
napraszać się 'to plead, to beg'	**na-prosić się**

329

Ile się ich **naprosiłam, żeby naprawili klimatyzację.** 'How many times have I asked for the AC to be fixed?'
Matka z trudem doprosiła się syna o ciszę. 'The mother couldn't get her son to be quiet.'
Daj się uprosić—chodź na kawę. 'Come on, let me buy you coffee.'
Proszę go wyprosić z pokoju. 'Please make him leave.'
(-praszać by itself does not exist)

Prefixes are very diversified, with multi-meanings, of which some are more, some are less distinct. Prefixes, first of all, signalize spatial location and hence most distinctively prefixed modifications are seen with motion verbs, e.g., **wnieść** 'to carry into,' **podnieść** 'to pick up,' **wynieść** 'to take out,' **przynieść** 'to bring.' (See 6.4.14.13)

Below is a list of some prefixes and their common usage:

do- (reaching a destination, supplementary action, adjustment)

a. Often used with verbs that require some time to get to the point of destination, where **do-** suggests the final leg of the process, e.g., **dobiec do mety** 'to reach the finishing line.'

Do-... **się** suggests obstacles on the final leg just before reaching the finishing line: **doczekać się sprawiedliwości** 'to wait and achieve justice,' **doczekać się awansu** 'to finally get promoted.'

For verbs of motion in particular, the preposition that corresponds to the verbal prefix can often be used following the verb, e.g., **podwieźć kogoś pod dom** 'to give someone a lift home,' **dojść do drzwi** 'to reach the door,' **przejść przez ulicę** 'to cross the street,' **Złodzieje napadli na bank.** 'The thieves attacked the bank.' However, verbs are not limited to the prepositions that correspond to the verbal prefix, and a range of prepositions can be used.

> <u>do</u>trzeć <u>do</u> **centrum** 'to get to the center'
> **dotknąć sufitu** 'to touch the ceiling'
> **doręczyć list** 'to deliver a letter'
> **dokończyć remont** 'to finish a renovation'
> **dopłynąć do brzegu** 'to reach the shore'
> **dogonić złodzieja** 'to catch up with a thief'
> **doholować samochód do warsztatu** 'to tow a car to the workshop'
> **doszorować się** 'to scrub clean'
> **dopić piwo** 'to finish up beer'

dosmażyć 'to finish frying'
dopracować szczegóły 'to touch up details'
Kiedy ty dorośniesz? 'When will you (finally) grow up?'
Nie mogę się dodzwonić do rodziców. 'I can't get through to my parents.'
Nie mogę się doczekać wakacji. 'I can't wait to go on vacation.'
Wreszcie dostaliśmy się do wyjścia. 'We finally got to the exit.'

b. To be supplementary to something:

> **dodać** 'to add,' **dosypać** 'to sprinkle more,'
> **dosolić** 'to add more salt,' **dopieprzyć** 'to add more pepper,'
> **dosłodzić** 'to add more sugar,' **doprawić do smaku**
> 'to season to taste,' **dolać mleka do kawy** 'to pour more
> milk into coffee,' **dopisać** 'to write in,' **mogę się dosiąść?**
> 'may I join you?'

c. To adjust so the two objects are equal:

> **dofinansować** 'to subsidize,' **dowartościować** 'to feel
> appreciated,' **dorównać rywalowi** 'to be equal with a rival,'
> **dostosować się** 'to adjust,' **dopasować krawat do koszuli**
> 'to match a tie to a shirt,' **dorobić klucze** 'to make duplicate
> keys,' **dotlenić się** 'to get some fresh air'

od- (repetition to give precision, a return action, subtraction, separation)

a. It is added to verbs to signalize that an action is performed with precision to achieve optimal results, and the action is repeated until the optimal result is reached. Od- suggests a reconstructive, reproductive character of motions with a positive result:

> **odegrać rolę Hamleta** 'to play the role of Hamlet,'
> **odrysować** 'to copy a pattern,' **odtworzyć** 'to reconstruct,'
> **odrestaurować** 'to renovate,' **odzyskać dane** 'to retrieve a date,'
> **odnowić stosunki dyplomatyczne** 'to renew diplomatic
> relations,' **odczytać** 'to decipher'

Od- can also mean that the action was performed in an unsatisfactory manner. Usually such verbs are colloquial: **odbębnić godziny w pracy** 'to rattle off hours at work,' **odfajkować/odwalić robotę** 'to get the job over and done with.'

b. To signalize a return action:

> **odpisać** 'to write back,' **oddać** 'to give back,' **odnieść** 'to carry back,' **odmówić** 'to refuse,' **odpowiedzieć** 'to respond,' **odkupić** 'to buy back,' **odrobić zaległości w szkole** 'to catch up with material at school,' **odespać zarwaną noc** 'to sleep off the night before,' **odblokować ulicę** 'to make the street passable/unblock the street,' **odpolitycznić media** 'to depoliticize the media'

c. To substract:

> **odjąć, odlać** 'to pour out (liquid),' **odsypać** 'to pour out (powder),' **odłożyć** 'to put back,' **odzyskać** 'to regain,' **odliczyć** 'to count out,' **odchudzić się** 'to lose weight'

d. Movement away and separation:

> **odjechać** 'to go away,' **oddalić się** 'to move away,' **odciągnąć** 'to pull away,' **minister odbył podróż to Chin** 'the minister went on an official trip to China,' **odłamać** 'to break off,' **odciąć** 'to cut off,' **oderwać** 'to rip off,' **odpruć** 'to unstitch,' **odkurzyć** 'to dust off,' 'to vacuum'

prze- (from one (side, source) to the other (side, source), through, acting thoroughly)

It is often used with verbs to signalize that an action is performed from one end to the other (inside to outside, start to finish, top to bottom, diagonally or horizontally through with results that could be complete and last for a while when the action was long enough, or incomplete when the action was quick and only on the surface:

> **przekopać tunel** 'dig a tunnel,' **przeczytać książkę** 'to read (through) a book,' **przebadać pacjenta** 'to examine a patient,' **przesunąć meble/spotkanie** 'to move the furniture/to postpone a meeting,' **przemyśleć sytuację** 'to think through the situation,' **przepchać (się) do przodu** 'to push through forward (to elbow),' **przejść na drugą stronę ulicy** 'to cross the street,' **przeskoczyć przez** <+ACC> **płot** 'to jump through the fence,' **przetłumaczyć z polskiego na angielski** 'to translate from Polish to English,' **przegrać dane z dysku na dyskietkę** 'to copy data from a hard disk to a floppy disk,' **przepisać** 'to copy,' **przelać piwo z butelki do szklanki** 'to pour beer from a bottle into a glass,' **przesypać sól ze słoika do solniczki** 'to pour salt from a jar into a salt

shaker,' **przejrzeć kogoś na wylot** 'to see through somebody,' (to find out the truth) **przemoknąć do suchej nitki** 'to get soaked through,' **przedostać się** 'to force one's way through,' **przebaczyć** 'to forgive,' **przekupić** 'to bribe'

Sometimes the action brings unwanted results:

przegapić wyprzedaż 'to miss a sale,' **przeziębić się** 'to catch a cold,' **przegrać pieniądze** 'to lose money,' **przespać zajęcia** 'to oversleep and miss a class,' **przesolić zupę** 'to oversalt the soup,' **przejeść się** <+INS> **chipsami** 'to eat too many chips,' **przepłukać gardło** 'to rinse out [one's] throat,' **przerwać dyskusję** 'to interrupt a discussion'

Nie przerywaj mi!
'Don't interrupt me!'

W Londynie, musi się pan przesiąść.
'You have to transfer in London, sir.'

roz- (augmentation, movement into separate parts, signalizing the beginning of a sudden change in action, distribution)

a. It is often added to verbs to signalize enlargement (augmentation) of the object:

rozbudować dom 'to extend a house,' **rozszerzyć Unię Europejską** 'to enlarge the E.U.,' **rozlać kawę** 'to spill coffee,' **rozłożyć stół** 'to unfold table,' **rozpowszechnić film** 'to distribute a film,' **rozpisać się** 'to go on' (coll.), **rozgadać się** 'to go on and on (talking)' (coll.), **rozpić się** 'to take to drink'

b. It is often used to show movement from the center outwards into many directions or parts, which can result in disintegration:

rozpaść się 'to disintegrate':

Związek Radziecki (ZSRR) rozpadł się w 1991 roku.
'The Soviet Union (U.S.S.R.) fell apart in 1991.'

rozciągnąć sweter 'to stretch a sweater,' **rozerwać na strzępy** 'to rip something to shreds,' **rozbić gang** 'break up a gang,' **rozchorować się** 'to get sick,' **rozpuścić się** 'to dissolve,' **rozejść się** 'to go separate ways,' **rozwieść się** 'to divorce,' **roztrwonić majątek** 'to squander,' 'to waste wealth,' **rozkraść** 'to steal'

c. It is often added to verbs to signalize the beginning of a sudden change in action:

> **rozkrzyczeć się** 'to start yelling/bawling' (of a child), **rozpłakać się** 'to burst into tears,' **roześmiać się** 'to start laughing,' **rozzłościć się** 'to get angry,' **rozluźnij się!** 'relax,' 'loosen up!,' **rozbrykać się** 'to go wild' (coll.), **rozmyślić się** 'to change one's mind,' **rozpoznać** 'to recognize'

d. It is often used to signalize distribution from the same source:

> **rozdać prace** 'to hand out homework,' **rozstawić talerze** 'to set out plates,' **rozreklamować** 'to advertise,' **rozsławić się** 'to become famous,' **rozlosować nagrody** 'to distribute prizes by lottery'

u- (sudden action, finalizing prolonged action, making improvements, getting a piece of something, satiation)

a. It is added to verbs to signalize an action with sudden results:

> **ukłuć** 'to prick,' **ugryźć** 'to bite'
> **Ugryzł mnie komar.** 'A mosquito bit me'.
> **uśmiechnąć się** 'to smile,' **usłyszeć** 'to hear,' **ukryć** 'to hide,' **ubrudzić się** 'to get dirty,' **upuścić książkę** 'to drop a book,' **usunąć plamę** 'to remove a stain,' **nie szczyp mnie!** 'don't pinch me!' **uszczypnąć kogoś** 'to pinch somebody,' **uprzedzić** 'to warn,' **uszkodzić** 'to harm,' **uderzyć** 'to strike,' **uścisnąć rękę** 'to shake a hand,' **Uściśnij babcię!** 'give grandma a hug!,' **utonąć** 'to drown'

b. It is added to verbs whose action continues for a while and is then finalized:

> **uspać dziecko** 'to put the baby to sleep,' **uspokoić (się)** 'to calm (oneself) down,' **uciszyć** 'to silence,' **ubić pianę** 'to beat up,' **uczesać (się)** 'to comb (oneself),' **ubłagać rodziców, żeby zostać z dziadkami** 'to plead [with one's] parents to be able to stay with [one's] grandparents,' **uleczyć** 'to cure' (**choroba nieuleczalna** 'incurable disease'), **upiec** 'to bake,' **ugotować** 'to cook,' **usmażyć** 'to fry,' **udusić** 'to stew,' **udokumentować** 'to substantiate,' **udowodnić** 'to prove,' **ugruntować** 'to establish,' **upełnomocnić** 'to empower,' **usankcjonować** 'to sanction,' **uwierzytelnić** 'to authenticate'

Maybe soon we may see the verb **grillować** with its potential counterpart **ugrillować** (1,610 results on Google 7.26.2010)

The potential form **ugrillować** from **grillować** is used occasionally in Polish but has not yet become standardized.

c. To make something better:

> **ulepszyć** 'to improve,' **umilić czas** 'to spend the time in a nicer way,'
> **usprawnić komunikację miejską** 'to improve city transportation,'
> **umożliwić** 'to make possible,' **unowocześnić** 'to modernize,'
> **usamodzielnić (się)** 'to become independent,' **uszczęśliwić** 'to
> make happier,' **uregulować** 'to regulate,' **umeblować** 'to furnish,'
> **umundurować** 'to provide with uniforms'

d. To signalize a reduction of the object, or getting a piece of the object:

> **ukrócić** 'to curb,' **uszczuplić budżet** 'to deplete a budget,'
> **ugryźć kawałek** 'to bite a piece,' **upić trochę** 'to drink a little,'
> **ukroić kawałek** 'to cut a piece'

e. **u . . . się** is added to verbs to signalize satiation of the subject:

> **ubawić się** 'to have fun,' **uśmiać się** 'to laugh hard,' **umęczyć się**
> 'to get tired'
> **Ale się ubawiłam!** <FEM> 'I had so much fun.'

na- (lasting results, to apply to the surface/to act onto a surface, satiation)

a. It is often used with verbs to signalize methodical action whose results will last:

> **na-uczyć się** 'to learn,' **na-malować** 'to depict,' **na-ostrzyć**
> **ołówek** 'to sharpen a pencil,' **na-oliwić zawiasy u drzwi** 'to
> oil door hinges,' **na-pisać książkę** 'to write a book,' **na-robić**
> **zaległości w pracy** 'to fall behind at work,' **na-pracować się**
> 'to work hard,' **na-karmić dziecko** 'to feed up a child'

b. Action onto a surface (usually with the preposition **na** <+ACC>):

> **nałożyć słuchawki na** <+ACC> **uszy** 'to put headphones on
> [one's] ears'
> **nałożyć krem na twarz** 'to put cream on [one's] face'
> **nacisnąć na przycisk** 'to press the button'

c. **na- . . . się** to signalize satiation, saturation

> **Polski rynek nasycił się hipermarketami.** 'The Polish market
> became saturated with hypermarkets.'
> **najeść się do syta** 'to eat one's fill,' **naoglądać się filmów**
> 'to watch too many movies,' **nasłuchać się bzdur** 'to hear too
> much rubbish'

nad- (to act with extra and excessive power, to abuse)

nad-użyć władzy/zaufania 'to overuse authority/to betray someone's trust,' **nadrobić zaległości w pracy** 'to catch up at work'

to weaken: nadszarpnąć, nadwerężyć

pod- (acting below the object to lower the object or its quality)

a. It is used to signalize placing an object under another object, usually followed by the preposition pod <+ACC>:

podłożyć sweter pod <+ACC> **głowę** 'to put a sweater under [one's] head,' **podsunąć pod nos** 'to place very close'

b. To describe a shady action, an action below the level of legality:

podrobić podpis 'to forge a signature,' **podrobić pieniądze** 'to counterfeit,' **podsłuchać** 'to eavesdrop,' **Nie podsłuchuj!** 'Stop eavesdropping!,' **podpatrzeć** 'to observe,' **podkraść się** 'to steal,' **podburzyć** 'to incite,' **podjudzać** 'to instigate'

c. Motion upward:

podskoczyć 'to jump up,' **podnieść** 'to pick up,' **podciągnąć rękawy** 'to pull up [one's] sleeves,' **podkręcić włosy** 'to curl hair'

d. To approach:

podejść do stolika 'to approach the table,' **podjechać pod sam sklep** 'to drive close to the store,' **podbiec do matki** 'to run up to a mother,' **podlecieć do lampy** 'to fly up to the lamp'

e. To improve partially someone's condition over time:

podleczyć się w sanatorium 'to get better in a sanatorium'

przy- (arriving, connecting)

a. It is often used to signalize arrival by different forms of transportation:

przyjechać 'to arrive by car, bus and train,' **przybyć** 'to arrive (official),' **przyjść** 'to arrive on foot'

b. To unite:

przylepić 'to stick,' **przyjąć** 'to accept,' **przyłączyć** 'to join,' **przybić** 'to nail,' **przykleić** 'to glue,' **przysiąść się** 'to accompany,' **przylgnąć** 'to cling,' **przypiąć** 'to attach,' 'to pin,' **przytulić się** 'to embace,' **przynieść** 'to bring,' **przysłać** 'to send in'
Czy mogę się przysiąść? 'Can I join you?'

w(e)-

a. Movement inside an object:

> **wciasnąć** 'to squeeze in,' **wgnieść** 'to dent,' **wejść** 'to come in,' **wjechać** 'to drive in,' **wpłynąć** 'to flow in,' 'to enter,' **wlecieć** 'to fly in,' **wlać** 'to pour in,' **włożyć** 'to put in,' 'to invest,' **wsiąść** 'to get in,' **wbiec** 'to run in(to),' **wbić** 'to hammer something into,' **wetrzeć** 'to rub into'

b. To include something into an object, to integrate:

> **wcielić** 'to incarnate,' **włączyć** 'to incorporate,' **wpisać** 'to register,' 'to enter one's name,' **wkleić** 'to stick into'

wy- (out)

a. Movement out:

> **wyjść** 'to go out,' **wyjechać** 'to drive out,' **wysiąść** 'to get out,' **wyciągnąć** 'to draw out,' **wypłynąć** 'to sail out,' **wyrwać** 'to pull out,' **wybuchnąć** 'to break out,' **wyrzucić** 'to throw out,' **wybiec** 'to run out,' **wybrać** 'to choose,' **wyprowadzić się** 'to move out,' **wydać** 'to spend' (money, not time)

b. To act on the surface and perform entirely successfully:

> **wyszyścić zęby** 'to brush [one's] teeth,' **wysprzątać pokój** 'to clean a room,' **wymyć okna** 'to wash windows,' **wygrać** 'to win,' **wyjaśnić** 'to explain,' 'to clear up,' **wymyślić** 'to think up,' **wyciągnąć wnioski** 'to draw conclusions'
>
> **wywnioskować** 'to deduce'
> **wypatrzeć, wypatrzyć** 'to look out for somebody, something'

wy- (się) can signify satiation:

> **wypocząć** 'to rest up,' **wyspać się** 'to get enough sleep,' **wytańczyć się** 'to dance up a heart'

z-/s-

a. To put together:

> **złożyć** 'to put together,' **złączyć** 'to join,' **skleić** 'to glue together' (**s** is written before voiceless consonants) (See 6.4.14.13)

b. Action that brings instant results:

> **zrobić** 'to do,' **skończyć** 'to finish,' **schować** 'to hide,' **splamić** 'to stain,' 'to smudge,' **zblednąć** 'to turn pale'

c. Movement down:

> **zjechać** 'to go down,' **zsunąć** 'to slide down,' **zbiec** 'to run down,' 'to run away'

d. To wear out, destroy:

> **zniszczyć** 'to destroy,' **znosić** 'to wear out,' **zmarnować** 'to waste,' **zniekształcić** 'to distort'

e. To remove from the surface:

> **zmyć lakier do paznokci** 'to wash off nail polish,' **zetrzeć** 'to rub off,' **spłukać** 'to rinse off,' **zedrzeć** 'to wear out,' **ściągnąć ubranie** 'take off clothes'

f. To make something smaller:

> **zmniejszyć** 'to diminish,' **zredukować** 'to reduce,' **zwolnić** 'to slow down,' 'to dismiss,' **skrócić** 'to shorten'

za-

a. To cover totally a surface:

> **zalać** 'to pour over,' 'to flood,' **zadymić** 'to fill with smoke,' **zapisać** 'to record,' **zasypać** 'to cover,' 'to fill up,' **zanurzyć** 'to sink in,' **zastawić drogę** 'to block the road'

b. To reach a destination:

> **zajechać** 'to arrive to pick up somebody,' 'to drive up,' **zaparkować** 'to park,' **zanieść do pralni** 'to take to the laundry'

c. The beginning of a process, to initiate a process:

> **zacząć** 'to begin,' 'to commence,' **zainicjować dyskusję** 'to initiate a discussion,' **zapowiedzieć** 'to announce,' **zapamiętać** 'to note,' **zasłabnąć** 'to become ill'

d. Initial verbs:

> **zacząć** 'to begin'

e. Final action (no more):

> **zasnąć** 'to fall asleep,' **zamknąć** 'to lock up,' 'to lock in,'
> **zatrzasnąć** 'to slam,' **zabić** 'to kill,' **zastrzelić** 'to shoot dead,'
> **zakopać** 'to bury' [therefore **Zakopane** (city in the south of
> Poland), 'the buried city,' because it is in the valley], **zamrozić**
> 'to freeze,' **zakończyć wojnę** 'to finish the war'

o-/ob-

a. To act around:

> **okrążyć** 'to circle,' **otoczyć** 'to surround,' **ogrodzić** 'to fence in,'
> **okleić** 'to paste on,' **obsypać prezentami** 'to sprinkle,' 'to
> shower with gifts,' **objechać cały świat** 'to go around/tour
> around the world,' **obejść** 'to walk around,' **opłynąć** 'to sail
> around,' **obiec** 'to run around,' **oblizać** 'to lick'

b. 'To deceive,' 'act around the truth':

> **okłamać** 'to lie,' **oszukać** 'to cheat,' **osłabić** 'to weaken'

c. Indirect action:

> **opowiedzieć** 'to narrate,' **opisać** 'to describe,' **omówić** 'to review,'
> **opracować** 'to prepare'

6.4.13 | Frequentative/iterative verbs

Some verbs (including all motion verbs) have two forms of the imperfective
aspect. Frequentative forms of verbs emphasize repetition, and are used to
describe someone's habits. They constitute a subtype of the imperfective
aspect. In English frequentative verbs could be expressed with the verb
keep, e.g., 'he kept having headaches' **miewał bóle głowy**, instead of 'he
had headaches' **miał bóle głowy**.

> **Na obiad często jem pizzę.** 'I often eat pizza for lunch.'
> **Na obiad jadam pizzę.** 'I eat pizza for lunch.'

Frequentative verbs can be accompanied by adverbs of frequency, but don't
have to be.

As a rule, Polish verbs of motion have two forms of the imperfective aspect.

A list of non-motion verbs with two imperfective forms is given below.
Note that frequentative imperfective forms are created from verbs without

prefixes—e.g., czytać 'to read' **czytywać**—by extending the stem of the infinitive by the infixes -wa-, -y(wa)-, -a-. Note the changes to vowels and consonants: ó:o (mówić—mawiać), e:a (jeść—jadać). Frequentative infinitives, e.g., **mawiać** 'to talk' often become a stem for imperfective verbs with specific meanings, e.g., **zamawiać** 'to order.'

Frequentative/iterative verbs without prefixes are used in present, past and future tenses, but their usage is decreasing.

Verbs that denote imperfective habitual, repetitive action:

> **być—bywać** 'to be,' **pić—pijać** 'to drink,' **jeść—jadać** 'to eat,'
> **grać—grywać** 'to play,' **mieć—miewać** 'to have,'
> **chodzić—chadzać** 'to go,'
> **pisać—pisywać** 'to write,' **widzieć—widywać** 'to see,'
> **spać—sypiać** 'to sleep,' **mówić—mawiać** 'to speak'

Compare the present tense conjugation of **czytać** <IMPFV> 'to read'—**czytywać** <IMPFV iterative> 'to read (habitually)' and **mieć** <IMPFV> 'to have'—**miewać** <IMPFV iterative> 'to have (on an ongoing basis)':

czytać	czytywać	mieć	miewać
ja czyt-am	czyt-uję	m-am	miew-am
ty czyt-asz	czyt-ujesz	m-asz	miew-asz
on/a/o czyt-a	czyt-uje	m-a	miew-a
my czyt-amy	czyt-ujemy	m-amy	miew-amy
wy czyt-acie	czyt-ujecie	m-acie	miew-acie
oni/e czyt-ają	czyt-ują	m-ają	miew-ają

6.4.14 Verbs of motion

6.4.14.1 Overview

Verbs of motion have two imperfective forms:

multidirectional, such as **chodzić** 'to walk,' **jeździć** 'to ride,' **biegać** 'to run/jog,' **pływać** 'to swim,' **latać** 'to fly,' to indicate repeated trips,

and *unidirectional*, such as **iść** 'to walk,' **jechać** 'to ride,' **biec** 'to run,' **płynąć** 'to swim,' **lecieć** 'to fly' to indicate a single trip.

1. Multidirectional (IMPFV): **Chodzić, jeździć, biegać, pływać, latać** are used for traveling around, repeated and habitual trips.

2. Unidirectional (PFV): **Pójść, pojechać, pobiec, popłynąć, polecieć** indicate a single uninterrupted round- or completed trip.
3. Unidirectional (IMPFV): **Iść, jechać, biec, płynąć, lecieć** focus on the process of the trip, the trip itself, or uncompleted travel.

Note for students of Russian: The distinctions in Polish are different from Russian and less rigid.

> **Codziennie chodzę do pracy.** *'Everyday I go* to work.' (habitual trip)
> **Jak często chodziłaś do kina, kiedy byłaś na studiach?**
> *'How often did you go* to the movies when you were a student?'
> (repeated trips)
> **Latem każdego dnia będę chodzić na basen.** *'In the summer
> I will be going* to the pool every day.' (habitual trip)
> **W piątek wieczorem** *poszliśmy* **z kolegą do kina.** 'Friday night
> *we went* to the movies with a friend.' (single round trip)
> **W weekend** *pójdę* **na jogę.** *'I am going* to yoga this weekend.'
> (single round trip)
> **Dwie godziny jechaliśmy na lotnisko.** 'It *took two hours to get* to the
> airport.' (focus on time during the trip)
> **Zadzwoń do mnie, kiedy** *będziecie szli* **do kina.** 'Call me when
> you are on the way to the movies.' (focus on time during the trip)
> **Idę do pracy.** *'I am going* to work.' (focus on process of uncompleted trip)

Motion verbs can be unprefixed, e.g., **chodzić, jeździć** and prefixed, e.g., **wychodzić, wyjeżdżać**.

Prefixed verbs can be divided into verbs with the prefix **po-** and verbs with other prefixes, e.g., **wy-, przy-, prze-, w(e)-,** etc.

| 6.4.14.2 | *Single round-trip*

To indicate a single (uninterrupted) round-trip in the past or future use **pójść, pojechać** in the past or future, respectively.

> **Wczoraj rano** *poszłam* **do pracy.** 'Yesterday morning *I went* to work.'
> **Wczoraj po zajęciach** *poszłam* **do biblioteki.** 'Yesterday after
> classes *I went* to the library.'
> **Jutro rano, jak zwykle,** *pójdę* **do pracy.** 'Tomorrow morning, as
> usual, *I will go* to work.'
> **Jutro po zajęciach** *pójdę* **do biblioteki.** 'Tomorrow after classes
> *I will go* to the library.'

It is common to use the verb **być** 'to be' to indicate a place of destination as a result of a single round-trip in the past.

> **Wczoraj po zajęciach *byłam* w bibliotece.** 'Yesterday after classes I *was* at the library.'
> **Czy *byłeś* kiedyś w Australii?** 'Have you ever *been to* Australia?'

6.4.14.3 | *Repetitive round-trips*

To indicate a repetitive round-trip use **chodzić** and **jeździć**.

> **Codziennie chodzę do pracy.** '*Everyday I go* to work.'
> **Jak często chodziłaś do kina, kiedy byłaś na studiach?** '*How often did you go* to the movies when you were a student?'
> **Latem każdego dnia będę chodzić na basen.** 'In the summer I *will be going* to the pool every day.'
> **Codziennie jeżdżę do pracy autobusem.** '*Every day I go* to work by bus.'
> **Wczoraj *trzy razy jeździłam* na lotnisko.** '*I went* to the airport *three times* yesterday.'

Verbs of motion can be without spatial prefixes—**chodzić** and **iść**, both meaning 'to walk,' and **jeździć** and **jechać**, both meaning 'to ride'—and with spatial prefixes, e.g., **wychodzić** 'to go out' <IMPFV> and **wyjść** 'to walk out,' 'to go out' <PFV>, and **wyjeżdżać** 'to drive out' <IMPFV> and **wyjechać** 'to depart' <PFV>, respectively.

6.4.14.4 | *Choosing the verb of motion: on foot or by vehicle*

In Polish, it is common to choose verbs that indicate going on foot when the place is within walking distance, to an event or when there is no emphasis on the mode of transportation:

> **W każdą niedzielę chodzimy do kościoła.** 'Every Sunday we go to church.'
> **Po co idziesz do sklepu?** 'What are you going to the store for?'
> **W piątek idziemy z klasą do teatru.** 'On Friday we are going to the theater with our class.'
> **Słyszałam, że wkrótce idziesz na urlop.** 'I've heard that you are going on vacation soon.'

Each trip could be done by vehicle; however the mode of transportation is not important. The place of destination or the movement is important.

W niedzielę pojedziemy do kościoła moim samochodem. 'We will drive in my car to the church on Sunday.'
W piątek jedziemy na wycieczkę. 'On Friday we are going on a trip.'
Jedziesz z nami na lotnisko? 'Are you going with us to the airport?'

The emphasis is that the trip cannot be within walking distance.

It is common to use **jeździć** to mean 'flying' when the emphasis is not on the mode of transportation:

Ile razy w roku jeździ pan na konferencje?
'How often do you go to conferences, sir?'

Często jeździmy w góry.
'We often travel to the mountains.'

Some of these trips can by made by plane, but no emphasis is placed on the type of transportation.

| 6.4.14.5 | *Multidirectional (indeterminate) unprefixed verbs of motion* |

biegać 'to run,' **chodzić** 'to walk,' **jeździć** 'to ride,' **latać** 'to fly,' **pływać** 'to swim'

All of these verbs are *imperfective* and can be used in the present, past and future. Biegać, latać and **pływać** belong to conjugation I: -am, -a, -ają, and chodzić and jeździć belong to conjugation IV: -ę, -i, -ą. Note the stem change in the first person singular and third person plural for jeździć and chodzić. From the second person singular, the stem goes back to the one used in the infinitive.

Infinitive	Meaning	Conjugation
biegać	'to run'	**(ja) biegam, (on) biega, (oni) biegają**
latać	'to fly'	**(ja) latam, (on) lata, (oni) latają**
pływać	'to swim'	**(ja) pływam, (on) pływa, (oni) pływają**
chodzić	'to walk'	**(ja) chodzę, (on) chodzi, (oni) chodzą**
jeździć	'to ride'	**(ja) jeżdżę, (on) jeździ, (oni) jeżdżą**

In the present and past multidirectional, unprefixed, imperfective verbs of motion:

a. refer to trips in several directions;

b. refer to repeated trips in one direction;

c. state the ability to move or the skills for motion.

In the future multidirectional unprefixed imperfective verbs of motion:

d. refer to repeated trips;

e. refer to the ability to move.

Present:

a. **Lubię chodzić po lesie.** 'I like walking in the woods.'

Lubię biegać i pływać. 'I like to jog and swim.'

Latem pływam w jeziorze, a zimą w basenie. 'In the summer I swim in a lake, and in the winter in the pool.'

Zakupoholiczki codziennie biegają po sklepach. 'Shopaholics go shopping every day.'

Często biegam na bieżni. 'I often run on the race course.'

Nigdy nie pływam bez czepka. 'I never swim without a cap.'

Rzadko latam klasą biznes. 'I rarely fly business class.'

Mąż Ewy jest pilotem i nigdy nie ma go w domu—wiecznie dokądś lata. 'Ewa's husband is a pilot and he is never at home—he is always flying somewhere.'

b. **Po zajęciach chodzę do biblioteki.** 'I go to library after classes.'

Co rok jeździmy na wakacje do Włoch. 'Every year we go to Italy on vacation.'

Od czasu do czasu chodzimy z mężem do kina. 'From time to time [my] husband and I go to the movies.'

Po co tam chodzisz? 'Why do you [regularly] go there?'

Po co tam idziesz? 'Why do you [at the moment] go there?'

c. **Dlaczego nie lubisz chodzić ze mną na jogę?** 'Why don't you like going to yoga with me?'

Boję się latać. 'I am afraid of flying.'

Nie umiem jeździć samochodem. 'I can't drive a car.'

Nasz sześciomiesięczny synek już chodzi! 'Our six-month-old little son is already walking.'

Past:

a. **Wczoraj chodziłam po sklepach.** 'Yesterday I went shopping.'

Kiedyś codziennie rano biegałam. 'In the past I used to run every morning.'

b. **Rok temu często jeździłam z córką do lekarza.** 'Last year I often went to the doctor's with [my] daughter.'

c. **Po dwóch miesiącach rehabilitacji, syn znowu chodził.** 'After two months of rehabilitation, [our] son was walking again.'
   Wczoraj chodziłam po lesie. 'Yesterday I was walking in the woods.'
   W weekend jeździłam rowerem. 'I was biking over the weekend.'

Future:

d. **Od września co tydzień będę chodzić na basen.** 'As of September, every week I will be going to the pool.'
   Rodzice kupili dom nad morzem i teraz często będziemy tam jeździć. '[My] parents bought a house by the sea, and now we will be going there often.'
   Od jutra będę biegać codziennie. 'As of tomorrow I will be jogging every day.'

e. **Jutro całe przedpołudnie będziemy jeździć na nartach.** 'Tomorrow will be skiing the whole morning.'
   Za miesiąc będziesz chodził, zobaczysz. 'In a month you will be walking, you will see.'

Note: To express 'let's go (home),' Poles often use chodźmy (do domu), jedźmy już 'let's go (by vehicle)'.

Idiomatic expressions using multidirectional imperfective verbs of motion without prefixes (biegać 'to run,' chodzić 'to walk,' jeździć 'to ride,' latać 'to fly,' pływać 'to swim')

chodzić pieszo or **chodzić piechotą** or **chodzić na piechotę**
   'to walk on foot'—to emphasize motion on foot
Nie lubię chodzić pieszo do pracy, wolę jeździć rowerem.
   'I do not like going to work on foot, I prefer biking.'
Nie lubię chodzić do pracy. 'I don't like going to work.'
O co chodzi? 'What's the problem?'
nieszczęścia chodzą parami 'when it rains it pours'
chodzić na rzęsach 'to go crazy' (coll.)
Ciarki <+DAT> **mi chodzą po plecach.** 'I'm afraid.'
chodzić z <+INS> **kimś** 'to date somebody'
chodzić z głową w chmurach 'to walk with one's head in the clouds'
chodzić spać (razem) z kurami 'to go to bed very early'
   [lit. 'to go to bed (along) with hens']
słuchy chodzą, że odchodzisz 'rumour has it that you are leaving'

Ten autobus nie chodzi w niedziele i święta. 'The bus does not run on Sundays and public holidays.'

Twój zegarek źle chodzi. 'Your watch shows the wrong time.'

Co ci chodzi po głowie? 'What's on your mind?'

biegać po <+LOC> **sklepach, urzędach** 'to run around the shops, offices'

Od tygodnia biegam za <+INS> **prezentem dla żony.** 'for a week now I've been running around to get my wife a present.'

Chodzić is also used to express wearing something frequently or constantly:

Często chodzę w dżinsach. 'I often wear jeans.'

Use dokąd? 'where to?', when asking about the point of destination and gdzie? 'where?' when asking about whereabouts:

Dokąd pani idzie? 'Where are you going to, madam?'

6.4.14.6 *Unidirectional (determinate) unprefixed verbs of motion*

iść 'to go on foot,' **jechać** 'to ride,' **biec** 'to run,' **płynąć** 'to swim,' **lecieć** 'to fly'

All of these verbs are *imperfective* and refer to ongoing action.

The conjugation in the present tense:

Note that **biec**, like many verbs having an infinitive ending with -c, has a -g sound in all the conjugation in the present and past tenses.

Iść, like jechać, has an irregular conjugation.

Infinitive	Meaning	Conjugation
biec	'to run'	**(ja) biegnę, (on) biegnie, (oni) biegną**
lecieć	'to fly'	**(ja) lecę, (on) leci, (oni) lecą**
płynąć	'to swim'	**(ja) płynę, (on) płynie, (oni) płyną**
iść	'to walk'	**(ja) idę, (on) idzie, (oni) idą**
jechać	'to ride'	**(ja) jadę, (on) jedzie, (oni) jadą**

These verbs are strictly used to describe one trip in one direction in progress at the moment of talking about the trip or to refer to a trip in one direction that is to happen in the immediate future or a trip in one direction that is planned to happen in the near future:

Idę do sklepu. 'I am going to the store.'

Dokąd idziemy? 'Where are we going [now]?'

Jedziemy do centrum. Jedziesz z nami? 'We are going to the center. Are you going with us?'

Dzisiaj lecę do Gdańska. 'I am flying to Gdańsk today.'

Płyniemy do brzegu? 'Are we swimming/sailing to the shore?'

Jutro idziemy do lekarza. 'Tomorrow we are going to the doctor's.'

Za tydzień lecę do Bostonu. 'In a week I'm flying to Boston.'

Słyszałam, że wkrótce idziesz na urlop. 'I've heard that you are going on vacation soon.'

Kiedy idziesz na urlop? 'When are you going on vacation?'

They are used in the past tense to describe one trip in one direction in progress at the moment of talking about the trip:

Spotkałam Ewę, kiedy szłam do pracy.
'I met Ewa when I was walking to work.'

Kiedy ostatnio jechałeś metrem do pracy?
'When was the last time you went to work by metro?'

or to describe one stage of a trip that was in the past:

Z Ełku do Zakopanego jechaliśmy moim samochodem, a z Zakopanego do Pragi jechaliśmy samochodem Piotra.
'From Ełk to Zakopane we drove my car, and from Zakopane to Prague we drove Piotr's car.'

Z Talina do Helsinek płynęliśmy promem.
'From Tallin to Helsinki we went by ferry.'

Z Waszyngtonu do Nowego Jorku lecieliśmy tylko 45 minut.
'From Washington DC to New York we flew only 45 minutes.'

They are used in the future tense to describe one stage of a trip that will happen in the future:

Za rok o tej porze będziemy lecieli samolotem do Anglii.
'Next year at this time we will be flying on a plane to England.'

or planned action in the near future:

Po pracy idę do fryzjera. 'After work I'm going to the hairdresser's.'

Zadzwoń, kiedy będziesz szła do fryzjera. 'Call me, when you are on the way to the hairdresser's.'

Nie zapomnij książeczki zdrowia, kiedy będziesz szedł do przychodni. 'Don't forget the health insurance card [booklet] when you are going to the clinic.'

6.4.14.7 *Imperfective verbs of motion without spatial prefixes*

Multidirectional	Unidirectional
(repeated trips in one direction or one trip in many directions)	(single trip in one direction in progress)
Gdzie jesteś?	**Dokąd idziesz?**
'Where are you?'	'Where are you going?'
Chodzę po sklepach.	**Idę do sklepu.**
'I'm shopping.'	'I'm going to the store.'
[going from store to store]	

Some phrases typically signal use of a multidirectional or unidirectional verb:

Multidirectional verbs	Unidirectional verbs
(e.g., **chodzić** 'to walk,' **jeździć** 'to travel,' **biegać** 'to run,' **latać** 'to fly,' **pływać** 'to swim, sail')	(e.g., **iść** 'to walk,' **jechać** 'to travel,' **biec** 'to run,' **lecieć** 'to fly,' **płynąć** 'to swim, sail')
często 'often'	**teraz** 'now'
nigdy nie 'never'	**jutro** 'tomorrow'
co tydzień 'every week'	**pojutrze** 'the day after tomorrow'
w soboty 'on Saturdays'	**właśnie** 'right now'
codziennie 'every day'	**w sobotę** 'on Saturday'
raz na miesiąc 'once a month'	**za chwilę** 'in a moment'

Co tydzień chodzę na basen. Teraz idę do kina.
'Every week I go to the pool. I'm going to the movies now.'

Dwa razy w roku jeżdżę na konferencję. W piątek jadę do Krakowa.
'Twice a year I go on a conference. On Friday I'm going to Krakow.'

Idiomatic expressions with unidirectional imperfective verbs of motion without prefixes (biec 'to run,' iść 'to walk,' jechać 'to ride,' lecieć 'to fly,' płynąć 'to swim')

czas leci 'time flies'
Jak leci? 'How is it going? (coll.)
Wszystko leci <+DAT> **mi z rąk.** 'I'm so nervous, I can't do anything.'
Zofia czyta/kupuje wszystko jak leci. 'Zofia reads/buys everything that she can hold on to.'
lecieć na łeb na szyję or **biec na złamanie karku** 'to run like hell' (coll.)

płynąć żabką/kraulem 'to do the breast stroke/the crawl'
biec co sił w nogach 'to run as fast as one can'
biec na pomoc 'to rush to help'

6.4.14.8 Perfective verbs of motion with the prefix po-

Perfective verbs of motion with the prefix po- are created by adding the prefix po- to the unidirectional imperfective verbs of motion iść 'to walk,' jechać 'to ride,' biec 'to run,' lecieć 'to fly,' płynąć 'to swim.'

Perfective verbs of motion with the prefix po- indicate one trip in one direction.

Infinitive	Meaning	Conjugation in the future tense
pobiec	'to run'	(ja) pobiegnę, (on) pobiegnie, (oni) pobiegną
polecieć	'to fly'	(ja) polecę, (on) poleci, (oni) polecą
popłynąć	'to swim'	(ja) popłynę, (on) popłynie, (oni) popłyną
pójść	'to walk'	(ja) pójdę, (on) pójdzie, (oni) pójdą
pojechać	'to ride'	(ja) pojadę, (on) pojedzie, (oni) pojadą

There are *no* present tense forms. Note the conjugation of pójść with ó in all persons.

They are used in the past to indicate one trip in one direction. Emphasis is on the point of destination. The usage is usually triggered by the absence of the actors.

Gdzie są rodzice? 'Where are the parents?'
Pojechali z babcią do szpitala. '[They] went [by vehicle] with grandma to the hospital.'

Mamy nie ma—poszła do pracy. 'Mom isn't here—she went to work.'
Ewy nie ma—poleciała na angielski. (coll.) 'Ewa isn't here—she rushed to an English class.'
Ceny paliwa znowu poleciały w górę. 'Gas prices went up (sharply) again.'

They are used in a sequence:

Po zajęciach poszłam do biblioteki. 'After classes I went to the library.'
Zjadł i poszedł spać. 'He ate and went to bed.'
Po pracy ojciec poszedł popływać. 'Father went swimming after work.'

They are used in the future to indicate one trip in one direction. Emphasis is on the point of destination.

Po zajęciach pójdę do biblioteki.
'After classes I'll go to the library.'

Zanim pojedziemy do Polski, chcemy nauczyć się mówić po polsku.
'Before going to Poland, we want to learn to speak Polish.'

Dokąd zamierzasz pojechać latem?
'Where are you going in the summer?'

Idiomatic expressions with perfective verbs of motion with the prefix po-:

Jak <+DAT> **ci poszło?** 'How did it go?'
Wszystko poszło dobrze. 'Everything went well.'
ceny poszły w górę/w dół 'prices went up/down'
pójść na kompromis w sprawie <+GEN> 'to compromise on something'
pójść na współpracę 'to agree to cooperate'
pójść do wojska 'to join the army'
pojechać za granicę 'to go abroad'
pobiec po lekarza 'to rush for a doctor'

6.4.14.9 *Imperfective verbs of motion with temporal* **po-**

While unidirectional verbs of motion with the prefix po- create perfective verbs of motion, when po- is added to multidirectional imperfective verbs of motion without spatial prefixes, like **chodzić, jeździć, biegać, latać, pływać,** they gain the meaning of walking around for a while, riding around for a while, running around for a while, flying around for a while and swimming around for a while, respectively. These verbs can be used in the present, past and future tenses:

Lubię pochodzić po ogrodzie, kiedy jestem zmęczona.
'I like to walk around the garden for a while when I am tired.'

Rano pobiegałam po parku, a potem wzięłam prysznic.
'In the morning I ran around the park for a while, and then I took a shower.'

Popływamy w basenie przed obiadem?
'How about going swimming in the pool for a while before lunch?'

Note: **Pochodzić** has one more meaning: 'to originate from':

Skąd pani pochodzi? Where are you from, madam?'
Pochodzę z Francji. 'I come from France.'

| 6.4.14.10 | *Imperfective and perfective verbs of motion with spatial prefixes* |

Spatial prefixes refer to a location in space (**z/od** 'from,' **do/przy** 'to,' **w** 'in,' **wy** 'out') and can be attached to multidirectional verbs of motion (**chodzić, jeździć, biegać, pływać**) to form *imperfective prefixed verbs with specific meanings of motion* in one direction or repeated trips in one direction to denote specific motion (coming in, going out, arriving) in the present, past and future tenses:

wy + chodzić = wychodzić 'to leave, to go out'

Note: **Jeździć** changes to *prefix* + **jeżdżać**, e.g., **odjeżdżać** 'to leave from' (*jeżdżać* by itself does not exist!).

Prefix + **jeżdżać** verbs are conjugated like **czytać**: -am, -a, -ają (ja) **odjeżdżam**, (on) **odjeżdża**, (oni) **odjeżdżają**.

Latać changes to *prefix* + **latywać**, e.g., **odlatywać** 'to depart' (*latywać* by itself does not exist!).

Prefix + **latywać** verbs are conjugated like **pracować**: -uję, -uje, -ują (ja) **odlatuję**, (on) **odlatuje**, (oni) **odlatują**.

They are used in the present for trips with specific motion in one direction:

Wychodzę. 'I'm going out.'

or repeated trips with specific motion:

Codziennie, około ósmej rano, wychodzę do pracy.
'Every day around eight I'm leaving for work.'

Często przychodzisz tu na kawę?
'Do you often come here for coffee?'

O której godzinie wyjeżdża pociąg/wylatuje samolot z Krakowa do Warszawy? 'What time does the train leave/the plane depart from Cracow to Warsaw?'
O której godzinie przyjeżdża autobus/przylatuje samolot z Warszawy? 'What time does the bus/plane arrive from Warsaw?'

They are used for set plans in the immediate future

Wyjeżdżamy wcześnie rano. 'We are leaving very early in the morning.'
W maju wychodzę za mąż. 'I'm getting married in May.'

They are used in the past for trips with specific motion in one direction or repeated trips with specific motion:

Elizabeth Taylor osiem razy wychodziła za mąż.
'Elizabeth Taylor got married [to a man] eight times. [(lit.) left for a husband]'

Kiedyś przychodziliście do nas częściej.
'You used to visit us more often.'

They are used in the future for trips with specific motion in one direction or repeated trips with specific motion (promises):

Od dzisiaj będę wychodził z biura przed osiemnastą.
'As of today I will be leaving the office before 6 p.m.'

Od jutra będę przychodził na zajęcia punktualnie.
'As of tomorrow I will be coming to classes on time.'

Hiszpanie będą przechodzili na pełną emeryturę w wieku 67 lat.
'The Spanish will be retiring at the age of 67.'

Idiomatic expressions with imperfective verbs of motion with spatial prefixes:

wychodzić za mąż 'to get married' (only about a woman)
przechodzić na emeryturę 'to retire'
to przechodzi ludzkie pojęcie 'it is beyond human understanding'
to przechodzi wszelkie oczekiwania 'it is beyond all expectations'

| 6.4.14.11 | Perfective verbs of motion with spatial prefixes

When the same spatial prefixes (**z/od, do/przy, w(e), wy**) are attached to the unidirectional verbs of motion **iść, jechać, biec, lecieć, płynąć**, perfective prefixed verbs are created. These verbs express a single movement in one direction. They are used in the past and future.

Past:

wyjść 'to go out'
    <MSC SG> **wyszedłem** 'I left/went out,' **wyszedłeś** 'you left,'
       wyszedł 'he left'
    <FEM SG> **wyszłam** 'I left,' **wyszłaś** 'you left,' **wyszła** 'she left'

<NT SG> **dziecko wyszło** 'the child left'

<MHPL> **wyszliśmy** 'we left,' **wyszliście** 'you left,' **wyszli** 'they left'

<NO-MHPL> **wyszłyśmy** 'we left,' **wyszłyście** 'you left,' **wyszły** 'they left'

wybiec 'to run out'

<MSC SG> **wybiegłem** 'I ran out,' **wybiegłeś** 'you ran out'
  wybiegł 'he ran out'

<FEM SG> **wybiegłam** 'I ran out,' **wybiegłaś** 'you ran out'
  wybiegła 'she ran out'

<NT SG> **dziecko wybiegło** 'the child ran out'

<MHPL> **wybiegliśmy** 'we ran out,' **wybiegliście** 'you ran out'
  wybiegli 'they ran out'

<NO-MHPL> **wybiegłyśmy** 'we ran out,' **wybiegłyście** 'you ran out,'
  wybiegły 'they ran out'

wylecieć 'to fly out,' 'to take off'

<MSC SG> **wyleciałem** 'I flew out,' **wyleciałeś** 'you flew out,'
  wyleciał 'he flew out'

<FEM SG> **wyleciałam** 'I flew out,' **wyleciałaś** 'you flew out,'
  wyleciała 'she flew out'

<NT SG> **dziecko wyleciało** 'the child flew out'

<MHPL> **wylecieliśmy** 'we flew out,' **wylecieliście** 'you flew out,'
  wylecieli 'they flew out'

<NO-MHPL> **wyleciałyśmy** 'we flew out,' **wyleciałyście** 'you flew out,'
  wyleciały 'they flew out'

wypłynąć 'to sail out'

<MSC SG> **wypłynąłem** 'I sailed out,' **wypłynąłeś** 'you sailed out,'
  wypłynął 'he sailed out'

<FEM SG> **wypłynęłam** 'I sailed out,' **wypłynęłaś** 'you sailed out,'
  wypłynęła 'she sailed out'

<NT SG> **dziecko wypłynęło** 'the child sailed out'

<MHPL> **wypłynęliśmy** 'we sailed out,' **wypłynęliście** 'you sailed out,'
  wypłynęli 'they sailed out'

<NO-MHPL> **wypłynęłyśmy** 'we sailed out,' **wypłynęłyście** 'you sailed
  out,' **wypłynęły** 'they sailed out'

Future:

wyjść

<I PR SG> **wyjdę** 'I will go out,' <2 PR SG> **wyjdziesz** 'you will go out,'
  <3 PR SG> **wyjdzie** 's/he, it will go out,' <I PR PL> **wyjdziemy** 'we will
  go out,' <2 PR PL> **wyjdziecie** 'you will go out,' <3 PR PL> **wyjdą** 'they
  will go out'

wybiec

<1 PR SG> **wybiegnę** 'I will run out,' <2 PR SG> **wybiegniesz** 'you will run out,' <3 PR SG> **wybiegnie** 's/he, it will run out,' <1 PR PL> **wybiegniemy** 'we will run out,' <2 PR PL> **wybiegniecie** 'you will run out,' <3 PR PL> **wybiegną** 'they will run out'

wylecieć

<1 PR SG> **wylecę** 'I will fly out,' <2 PR SG> **wylecisz** 'you will fly out,' <3 PR SG> **wyleci** 's/he, it will fly out,' <1 PR PL> **wylecimy** 'we will fly out,' <2 PR PL> **wylecicie** 'you will fly out,' <3 PR PL> **wylecą** 'they will fly out'

wypłynąć

<1 PR SG> **wypłynę** 'I will sail out,' <2 PR SG> **wypłyniesz** 'you will sail out,' <3 PR SG> **wypłynie** 's/he, it will sail out,' <1 PR PL> **wypłyniemy** 'we will sail out,' <2 PR PL> **wypłyniecie** 'you will sail out,' <3 PR PL> **wypłyną** 'they will sail out'

They are used in the past for a single specific movement in one direction. Emphasis is on the specific movement:

Wyjechaliśmy z Polski w 1989 roku. 'We left Poland in 1989.'
Premier Tusk przyjechał do Gdańska. 'Prime Minister Tusk came to Gdańsk.'

Or a single specific movement in one direction in a sequence:

Po zajęciach studenci wyszli z sali. 'After classes [the] students left the room.'
Piotr wyszedł z pokoju, zanim zdążyłam coś powiedzieć. 'Piotr left the room before I had time to say something.'
Zanim rodzice przyszli z pracy, dzieci posprzątały cały dom. 'Before [their] parents came home from work, the children had cleaned the whole house.'

They are used in the future for a single specific movement in one direction. Emphasis is on the specific movement:

Przyjedziesz na Święta? 'Will you <informal> come for Christmas?'

A single specific movement in one direction in a sequence:

Przyjdę do was, jak tylko skończę rozmawiać. 'I will come [and join you] as soon as I finish talking.'
Wyjedziemy zanim się ściemni. 'We will leave before it gets dark.'

Idiomatic expressions:

Kto późno przychodzi sam sobie szkodzi. 'first come, first served' (saying)

Zaszła pomyłka/zaszło nieporozumienie. 'There was a mistake/ there was a misunderstanding.'

zajść w ciążę 'to get pregnant'

| 6.4.14.12 | **Pójść** *versus* **wyjść**

Poszłam na zakupy. 'I went shopping.' (the focus is on the place of destination: I have gone shopping and I will not come back soon.)

Wyszłam na pocztę. 'I went to the post office.' (the focus is on leaving the place: I have gone to the post office but I will come back soon.)

Codziennie o ósmej rano wychodzę do pracy.
'Every morning I leave for work at eight.'

Ania wyszła z domu wczoraj rano i nie wiem, dokąd poszła.
'Ania left home yesterday morning and I don't know where she went.'

| 6.4.14.13 | *Spatial prefixes*

Below are spatial prefixes along with their meaning, examples and common prepositions.

Table 6.1 Spatial prefixes

Prefix	Meaning	Verb with prefix	prepositions
wy-	'going out,' 'exit'	**wychodzić** **wyjść**	**do** <+GEN> 'to' **na** <+ACC> 'to'
przy-	'arrive,' 'coming to'	**przychodzić** **przyjść**	**z/od** <+GEN> 'from'
w(e)-	'enter into,' 'coming in'	**wchodzić** **wejść**	
z(e)-	'descend/run down,'	**zjechać**	
s-	'coming from different places,' 'dismount from'	**schodzić**	

355

The prefix z- changes to s- before voiceless consonants (**f, k, p**):

spaść
schodzić
spłynąć

Write the prefix z- when combined with vowels and voiced consonants:

z-jechać <PFV> 'to drive down' and **s-chodzić** <IMPFV> 'to walk down'
j-voiced, **ch**-voiceless consonants

z-badać 'to examine' and   **b**-voiced, **p**-voiceless consonants
s-padać 'to fall'

z-dobyć 'to achieve' and   **d**-voiced, **t**-voiceless consonants
s-toczyć 'to fight'

Write ze- when combined with a consonant cluster or when the verb stem begins with s-:

zejść <PFV> 'to walk down'
zeskoczyć <PFV> 'to jump down'

The prefix z is often pronounced ź [ʑ] before a verb stem beginning with dź/dzi:

zdziałać 'to accomplish'
zdziwić się 'to be astonished'
zdziecinnieć 'to dote'

Write the prefix ś- when the verb stem begins with ci/ć: ściemniać się 'to get dark,' ścisnąć 'to press.'

Sportowcy zjechali do Pekinu. 'Sportsmen arrived in Beijing.'
Samolot schodzi do lądowania. 'A plane is descending to land.'
Proszę zejść z roweru. 'Please dismount from the bicycle.'
O której godzinie wychodzisz do pracy? 'What time do you leave for work?'
Wyszłam na pocztę. Zaraz wrócę. 'I have gone to the post office. I'll be back in a moment.'
Kto zwykle pierwszy przychodzi do biura? Who usually comes to the office first?
Kto zwykle ostatni wychodzi z biura? Who usually leaves the office last?
Wchodzisz czy wychodzisz? Are you coming in or going out?
wjechać na rondo 'to enter a roundabout'

zjechać z ronda 'to exit a roundabout'

zjechać windą do garażu 'to go down on the elevator to the garage'

zbiegać 'to run down'

zjeździć <+ACC> **całą Amerykę** 'to travel across the U.S.'

Prefix	Meaning	Verb with prefix	Prepositions
od(e)-	'going away from'	**odjechać** **odejść** **odlecieć**	**do** <+GEN> 'to' **na** <+ACC> 'to' **z/od** <+GEN> 'from'
do-	'up to' (but no contact)	**dojechać** **dojść** **dolecieć**	**pod** <+ACC> 'close to'
pod(e)-	'toward,' 'approach'	**podejść** **podbiec** **podpłynąć** **podwieźć**	

podwieźć <PFV> **kogoś pod dom** 'to give someone a lift home'

podejść <PFV>/**podpłynąć** <PFV> **bliżej** 'to come/swim closer'

prze-	'through,' 'across'	**przejść** **przejechać**	**przez** <+ACC> 'across' **obok** <+GEN> 'nearby'

przejechać obok pomnika
'to drive near to a monument'

przejść przez ulicę
'to cross the street'

przejechać przez most/przez tunel
'to drive over the bridge/through the tunnel'

ob-	'go round'	**objechać**	<+ACC>

Pare lat temu objechaliśmy Polskę południową.
'A few years ago we traveled around southern Poland.'

za-	'to detour to stop/fetch someone or something'		**do** <+GEN> 'to' **na** <+ACC> 'for' **po** <+ACC> 'for'

Po drodze do domu zajadę do rodziców.
'On the way home I will stop by my parents.'

Zajdź jutro jak będziesz miał czas.
'Drop by if you have time tomorrow.'

Zajadę po ciebie wieczorem.
'I'll come pick you up in the evening.'

Po drodze na lotnisko zajechaliśmy na obiad.
'On the way to the airport we stopped for lunch.'

Prefix	Meaning	Verb with prefix	Prepositions
roz-	'going to different destinations'	**rozjechać się rozejśc się**	**do** <+GEN> 'to'/**na** <+ACC> 'to' **z** <+GEN> 'from'

Write the prefix **roz-** even though you hear [ros], as in **rozstać się** 'to part,' **rozpocząć** 'to begin,' **rozsławić** 'to make famous.' Write **roze-** with a consonant cluster: **rozejść się** 'to go separate ways,' **rozesłać** 'to send out.'

wz-/ws-	'to go up'	**wznieść się/wzejść wbiec**	**na co?** <+ACC>

Idioms with prefixed verbs of motion:

wychodzić/wyjść za mąż 'to get married [to a man]'
przechodzić/przejść na emeryturę/na rentę 'to retire'
zachodzić/zajść w ciążę 'to get pregnant'

Verbs of shipment, like verbs of motion as a rule, have two imperfective forms: multidirectional and unidirectional.

Multidirectional	Unidirectional
nosić <IMPFV> 'to carry'	**nieść** <IMPFV>
wozić <IMPFV> 'to transport'	**wieźć** <IMPFV>

Nosić is also used to express wearing something frequently or constantly.

Used in the present, past and future tenses:

nosić <IMPFV multidirectional>:
(**ja**) **noszę** 'I carry,' (**on**) **nosi**, (**oni**) **noszą**; (**on**) **nosił** 'he was carrying'; (**on**) **bedzie nosił** 'he will be carrying'

nieść <IMPFV unidirectional>:

    (ja) niosę, (on) niesie, (oni) niosą; (on) niósł 'he was carrying,'
    (ona) niosła; (on) bedzie niósł 'he will be carrying'

Ponosić <IMPFV> 'to carry for a while' is used in present, past and future tenses.

Ponieść <PFV> 'to carry', to carry in one direction in one trip, is used in past and future tenses.

    ponosić dziecko na rękach 'to carry a baby in arms for a while'
    ponieść klęskę 'to suffer a defeat'
    ponieść konsekwencje <+GEN> to suffer the consequences of
       something
    Nerwy mnie poniosły. 'I lost my nerve.'

Spatial prefixes added to multidirectional forms create imperfective verbs with the specific movement of carrying into, bringing and carrying out *in progress*:

    nosić 'to carry,' 'to wear (clothes)'
    wozić 'to carry in a vehicle'

wynosić 'to carry out'	**wywozić** 'to transport out'
wnosić 'to carry in'	**wwozić** 'to transport in'
przynosić 'to bring'	**przywozić** 'to bring (by vehicle)'
podnosić 'to lift'	**podwozić** 'to give a lift'
przenosić 'to carry forward'	**przewozić** 'to transport'
zanosić 'to carry'	**zawozić** 'to carry (in a vehicle)'

Added to unidirectional forms, they create perfective verbs with the specific movement of carrying into, bringing, and carrying out:

nieść:	**wynieść**	**wieźć:**	**wywieźć**
	wnieść		**wwieźć**
	przynieść		**przywieźć**
	podnieść		**podwieźć**
	przenieść		**przewieźć**
	zanieść		**zawieźć**

Koleżanka codziennie przynosi coś słodkiego do pracy, ale dzisiaj nie przyniosła.
'[My] colleague brings something sweet to work every day, but today she did not bring anything.'

Według tradycji, po ślubie mężczyzna przenosi kobietę przez próg.
'According to tradition, after the wedding the husband carries [his] wife through the door.'

Insekty przenoszą choroby.
'Insects transfer diseases.'

Wczoraj wyniosłem śmieci i zaniosłem ubrania do pralni.
'Yesterday I took out the trash and took the clothes to the laundry.'

Codziennie wynoszę śmieci i zanoszę ubrania do pralni.
'Every day I take out the trash and take the clothes to the laundry.'

Co wolno wnieść, a czego nie wolno wnosić do samolotu.
'What one can carry in, and must not carry in on the plane.'

Co wolno wwieźć i czego nie wolno wywozić z kraju? 'What can one bring in and what is one not allowed to deport from the country?'

Codziennie wynoszę śmieci, ale jutro nie wyniosę.
'Every day I carry out the trash, but tomorrow I will not carry [it] out.'

Nasi sąsiedzi cały dzień wnosili swoje meble.
'Our neighbors were carrying in their furniture the whole day.'

Muzyka przestała grać, bo na salę wnieśli ogromny tort.
'The music stopped playing because they carried a giant cake into the room.'

| 6.4.15 | *Verbs of placement and positioning* |

Some verbs describe the horizontal and vertical placement of different objects and their position after being placed: **położyć** 'to place something horizontally.' Some verbs describe how people position themselves: **położyć** *się* **na brzuchu** 'to lie down on one's stomach.'

Table 6.2 Verbs of placement

Imperfective repetitive (in progress)	Perfective	Position of the object: (cannot take a direct object)
kłaść 'to place horizontally'	położyć	leżeć 'to be lying'
		poleżeć 'to be lying for a while'
		leż! <IMPER>
stawiać 'to place vertically'	postawić	stać 'to be standing'
		postać 'to be standing for a while'
		stój! <IMPER>
wieszać 'to hang something'	powiesić	wisieć 'to be hanging'
		powisieć 'to be hanging for a while'
		wiś! <IMPER>
sadzać 'to seat someone'	posadzić	siedzieć 'to be sitting'
		posiedzieć 'to be sitting for a while'
		siedź! <IMPER>

6.4.15.1 | *Conjugation:*

kłaść: (ja) **kładę**, (on) **kładzie**, (oni) **kładą**
położyć: (ja) **położę**, (on) **położy**, (oni) **położą**
leżeć: (ja) **leżę**, (on) **leży**, (oni) **leżą**

Codziennie kładę syna spać o 19.00, ale dzisiaj położyłam go o 21.00. 'I put my son to bed at 7 p.m. every day, but today I put him [to bed] at 9 p.m.'

Zwykle wieszasz kurtkę w przedpokoju. Dlaczego dzisiaj nie powiesiłeś? 'Usually you hang your jacket in the closet. Why didn't you hang it [there] today?'

Nie lubię stać w kolejkach. 'I don't like standing in lines.'
Kto siedzi obok Marka? 'Who's sitting next to Marek?'

stawiać: (ja) **stawiam**, (on) **stawia**, (oni) **stawiają**
postawić: (ja) **postawię**, (on) **postawi**, (oni) **postawią**
(po)stać: (ja) **(po)stoję**, (on) **(po)stoi**, (oni) **(po)stoją**

wieszać: (ja) **wieszam**, (on) **wiesza**, (oni) **wieszają**
powiesić: (ja) **powieszę**, (on) **powiesi**, (oni) **powieszą**
(po)wisieć: (ja) **(po)wiszę**, (on) **(po)wisi**, (oni) **(po)wiszą**

sadzać: (ja) **sadzam**, (on) **sadza**, (oni) **sadzają**
posadzić: (ja) **posadzę**, (on) **posadzi**, (oni) **posadzą**
(po)siedzieć: (ja) **(po)siedzę**, (on) **(po)siedzi**, (oni) **(po)siedzą**

Posadzić also means to imprison someone or to plant something.

6.4.15.2 *How do we position ourselves?*

Table 6.3 Verbs of positioning

Imperfective repetitive (in progress)	Perfective	Position of the object: (cannot take a direct object)
kłaść się 'to lie down'	**położyć się**	**leżeć** 'to be lying' **poleżeć** 'to be lying for a while'
wstawać 'to get up'	**wstać**	**stać** 'to be standing' **postać** 'to be standing for a while'
siadać 'to take a seat'	**usiąść**	**siedzieć** 'to be sitting' **posiedzieć** 'to be sitting for a while'

Conjugation:

> *wstawać* <IMPFV>: **wstaję, wstaje, wstają**   **wstawaj!** 'get up'
> *wstać* <PFV>: **wstanę, wstanie, wstaną**   **wstań!**
>
> *siadać* <IMPFV>: **siadam, siada, siadają**   **siadaj!** 'sit down'
> *usiąść* <PFV>: **usiądę, usiądzie, usiądą**   **usiądź!** 'take a seat'

Proszę usiąść. 'Please take a seat.'
Chcę posiedzieć w domu. 'I want to stay at home for a while.'
Proszę nie siadać. 'Please don't take a seat.'

When used with spatial prefixes, imperfective verbs of horizontal and vertical placement, e.g., **kłaść, stawiać** and verbs indicating how people position themselves can denote different ways of "putting something in," e.g., **przełożyć** 'to rearrange' (from **włożyć**), **wsiadać** 'to get in,' **wysiadać** 'to get off,' etc. Some common examples:

Imperfective   Perfective

wkładać 'to put (on)'   **włożyć** <+ACC>

Proszę włożyć płaszcz i buty. 'Please put on a coat and shoes.'
Nie lubię wkładać butów. 'I don't like putting on shoes.'

wstawiać 'to put'   **wstawić** <+ACC>   **do** <+GEN> 'to'

Wstaw mleko do lodówki.
'Put the milk into the refrigerator.'

Nie cierpię wstawiać naczyń do zmywarki.
'I really do not like putting dishes into the washer.'

Imperfective	Meaning	Verb with prefix	Perfective
wsiadać	'to get in'	**wsiąść**	**do** <+GEN> 'to'
wysiadać	'to get off'	**wysiąść**	**z** <+GEN> 'from'
przesiadać się	'to transfer'	**przesiąść się**	**z** <+GEN> 'from'

6.4.15.3 *Idiomatic expressions*

wisieć na telefonie 'to spend hours on the phone'
wisieć na włosku 'hanging by a thread'

6.4.16 **Prefix po-**

6.4.16.1 *Temporal meaning of* **po-**

When the prefix **po-** is combined with:

1. imperfective verbs without spatial prefixes: **tańczyć** 'to dance,' **śpiewać** 'to sing,' **ruszać** 'to move,' **czekać** 'to wait'
2. imperfective multidirectional motion verbs without spatial prefixes: **chodzić** 'to walk,' **jeździć** 'to ride,' **pływać** 'to sail,' 'to swim,' **latać** 'to fly'

it expresses the temporal meaning 'for a while'

potańczyć 'to dance for a while'
pośpiewać 'to sing for a while'
poczekać 'to wait for a while'
pochodzić 'to walk around for a while'
pojeździć na nartach 'to go skiing for a while'
popływać 'to sail, swim around for a while'

In colloquial use, these verbs are often accompanied by **sobie** 'oneself.'

Najpierw chcę poćwiczyć, a potem wezmę prysznic.
'First I want to exercise for a while, and then I'll take a shower.'

Wczoraj potańczyłam, pośpiewałam, a potem zasnęłam w fotelu.
'Yesterday I danced for a while, sang for a while and then fell asleep in the armchair.'

Porozmawiali chwilę i zaczęli grać.
'They talked for a moment and started playing.'

Jutro muszę z tobą chwilę porozmawiać.
'Tomorrow I need to talk to you for a moment.'

Może popływamy przed obiadem?
'How about swimming for a while before lunch?'

6.4.16.2 *Perfective meaning of* **po-**

When the prefix **po-** is combined with unidirectional verbs of motion: iść 'to walk,' jechać 'to ride,' płynąć 'to swim,' 'to sail,' lecieć 'to fly,' it expresses movement on a single trip with the emphasis on *departure* in the past or the future:

pójść <PFV> 'to walk'
pojechać <PFV> 'to ride'
polecieć <PFV> 'to fly'
popłynąć <PFV> 'to swim, to sail'

Rodzice pojechali po brata na lotnisko.
'[My] parents went to the airport to pick up [my] brother.'

Pojadę za tobą na koniec świata.
'I'll follow you to the end of the world.'

Pojedźmy pod namiot.
'Let's go camping.'

Premier poleciał do Moskwy.
'The PM flew to Moscow.'

Poszłam do domu.
'I went home.'

6.4.16.3 *Distributive perfective* **po-**

The prefix **po-** can be combined with prefixed imperfective verbs, in other words, it can be attached to imperfective verbs with prefixes, e.g., zjadać 'to eat up' <IMPFV>, zamawiać 'to order' <IMPFV> in order to signalize distributive cumulative action performed by many subjects and/or on many objects:

zjadać 'to eat up' <IMPFV>—**pozjadać** 'to eat up' <PFV>
zamawiać 'to order' <IMPFV>—**pozamawiać** 'to order' <PFV>

poprawiać <IMPFV>—**poprawić** <PFV> 'to correct'
popoprawiać <PFV> **błędy** 'to correct mistakes'

Prefixed imperfective verbs +po are perfective and do not have imperfective counterparts.

Other verbs include: **poprzewracać krzesła** 'to overturn chairs,' **poprzestawiać krzesła** 'to move chairs,' *poprzenosić książki* z jednego pokoju do drugiego 'to carry books from one room to another,' **pozmywać naczynia** 'to wash the dishes,' **poprzyklejać znaczki** 'to glue stamps,' *poprzyszywać guziki* do marynarki 'to sew buttons on a jacket,' **pozapinać guziki** 'to button up.'

Zanim wrócili rodzice, pozmywaliśmy naczynia i poprzenosiliśmy sprzęty z jednego pokoju do drugiego.
'Before [our] parents returned, we had washed the dishes and moved the equipment from one room to the other.'

w głowach im się poprzewracało 'they lost their mind'
huragan poprzewracał drzewa 'a windstorm overturned the trees'

6.4.16.4 *Starting and turning point* **po-**

When combined with the prefixes **po-** and **z-**, non-prefixed verbs that express a process often signalize a beginning phase of a process and a radical change that will last: **polubić** 'to get to like,' **pokochać** 'to fall in love,' **poznać** 'to get to know,' **pogodzić się** 'to come to an agreement,' **połączyć się** 'to connect,' **posmutnieć** 'to get sad,' **poczuć** 'to get to feel,' **postarzeć się** 'to get older,' **pogorszyć się** 'to deteriorate,' **posiwieć** 'to turn gray,' **zrozumieć** 'to understand,' **zważyć się** 'to become sour,' **mleko zważyło się** 'the milk became sour.'

Dzięki tobie poczułam się lepiej. 'You made me feel better.'
Dlaczego pani posmutniała? 'Why did you get sad, madam?'

6.4.16.5 *Intensifying* **po-**

Po- often signalizes enlargement. It is often a perfective counterpart of a verb with the prefix **po-** and ending -ać: *pogłębiać* <IMPFV> **pogłębić** <PFV> 'to become deeper,' *poszerzać* <IMPFV> **poszerzyć** <PFV> 'to become wider,' *pogrubiać* <IMPFV> **pogrubić** <PFV> 'to make something bolder,' *powiększać* <IMPFV> **powiększyć** <PFV> 'to make something bigger,' *podwajać* <IMPFV> **podwoić** <PFV> 'to double,' *potrajać* <IMPFV> **potroić** <PFV> 'to triple.'

6.5 Conjugation

Just as Polish nouns are declined, Polish verbs are conjugated. This means that the verb form changes in order to agree with its subject in all forms which the verb can assume. There are four conjugations (the patterns according to which Polish verbs are conjugated).

The personal pronouns 'I,' 'you' singular and plural, 'we' are usually omitted in the sentence (because each person has a distinct ending by which the subject can be recognized), if there is no emphasis on the actor:

Często pracuję wieczorami. 'I often work in the evenings.'
Tylko ja pracuję wieczorami. 'Only I work in the evenings.'

For the third person singular and plural, personal pronouns are required unless the subject is obvious:

Ewa nie przyjdzie. Wczoraj wieczorem wyjechała do Wiednia.
'Ewa won't come. She left for Vienna last night.' (See 6.1)

6.5.1 Infinitive

The infinitive is the dictionary form of the verb, to give its lexical meaning. The infinitive does not provide information about time, mood, person, class or number.

Most Polish infinitives end with: -ć: **czytać** 'to read,' **brać** 'to take,' **wziąć** 'to take.'

Some infinitives, usually with irregular conjugations, end with:

-ść: **iść** 'to walk,' **kłaść** 'to place horizontally,'

-źć: **wieźć** 'to transport,' **ugrząźć** 'to become bogged down' or 'to get stuck' (coll.)

A group of verbs end with -c: **móc** 'can,' 'be able,' **tłuc** 'to break.' There are stem-consonant mutations in all forms of these verbs, both in past and non-past forms: (c:g:ż) **móc** (ja) **mogę,** (on) **może;** (c:k:cz) **tłuc** (ja) **tłukę,** (on) **tłucze.**

The infinitive is used in the following situations:

1. After modal verbs and impersonal modal expressions in which the speakers express their position towards the information provided, from

obligation to possibility and permission. It is important, however, to remember that in the future tense with być 'to be,' modal verbs cannot be used in the infinitive: e.g., **będę musiał** (not: będę musieć)

> **musieć** 'to have to,' 'need to,' 'must,' **chcieć** 'to want,' **móc** 'to be able to,' 'can,' 'may,' **powinien** 'should'
>
> **można** 'it is possible,' **trzeba** 'it is necessary,' **wolno** 'it is allowed'
>
> **warto** 'it is worthwhile'
>
> **wypada** 'it is polite'
>
> **należy** 'one should, it should'
>
> **Zawsze należy o tym pamiętać.** 'One should always remember this.'

> **Nie warto mówić prawdy, wystarczy mówić byle co.** 'It is not worth telling the truth, it is enough to tell anything.'
>
> **Chciałbym cię o coś zapytać.** 'I'd like to ask you something.'
>
> **Muszę zadzwonić do rodziców.** 'I have to call [my] parents.'
>
> **Nie wypada dzwonić tak późno.** 'It is not polite to call that late.'
>
> **Wypadałoby podziękować za prezent.** 'It'd be polite to thank them for the gift.'
>
> **Co powinienem zrobić?** 'What should I do?'
>
> **Możesz zaczekać do jutra.** 'You can wait till tomorrow.'
>
> **Nie chcę czekać do jutra.** 'I don't want to wait till tomorrow.'
>
> **Możesz podać telefon?** 'Can you pass the phone?'

2. After verbs of preference, will and expectation:

> być w stanie 'to be able to do something,' kochać 'to love,' lubić 'to like,' mieć 'to be supposed to,' 'to have to,' mieć nadzieję 'to hope,' nienawidzić 'to detest,' obiecywać 'to promise,' planować 'to plan,' potrafić 'to be capable of doing something,' pragnąć 'to desire,' prosić 'to request,' umieć 'to know how,' uwielbiać 'to love,' 'to adore,' woleć 'to prefer,' zamierzać or mieć zamiar 'to plan,' 'to intend,' zdołać 'to manage to do something'

> **Masz jeść, nie marudzić.** 'You have to eat, not to whine.'
>
> **Proszę powtórzyć.** 'Please repeat.'
>
> **Lubię przebywać w ich towarzystwie.** 'I like being in their company.'
>
> **Uwielbiam pływać.** 'I love swimming.'
>
> **Wolę chodzić po górach. Nie umiem pływać.** 'I prefer hiking. I can't swim.'

Kiedy zamierza pan wrócić? 'When are you planning to return?'
Mam nadzieję skończyć tę książkę w sierpniu. 'I hope to
  finish the book in August.'

3. When modifying a noun: **czas/pora** 'it is time to,' **wstyd** 'it's a shame
   to,' **żal** 'it is a pity to,' **szkoda** 'it is a waste to,' **grzech** 'it is a sin to.'

   Pora umierać *'Time to die'* [film title]
   Czas wracać do hotelu. 'It is time to go back to the hotel.'
   Wstyd mi znowu prosić cię o pieniądze. 'I am ashamed to
     ask you for money again.'
   szkoda gadać 'it is a waste of breath' (coll.)
   grzech wyrzucać 'it is a sin to throw [something] away'

4. When modifying adverbs: **trudno** 'it is difficult,' **łatwo** 'it is easy,'
   miło/przyjemnie 'it is a pleasure,' **przykro** 'it is painful to.' (See 2.4.7)

   Przyjemnie było go posłuchać, ale trudno zrozumieć.
     'It was a pleasure to listen to him, but difficult to understand.'
   Aż przykro patrzeć jak oni traktują swoje dzieci. 'It is
     painful to see how they treat their own children.'
   Myć się w zimnej wodzie jest zdrowo. 'It is healthy to wash
     in cold water.'

5. After verbs that mean 'to start' and 'to finish':

   Zaczynać—zacząć 'to begin,' **s-kończyć/przestawać—
   przestać** 'to finish.'

   Zaczyna/przestało padać.
   'It has started to rain/stopped raining.'

6. With motion verbs to express going somewhere in order to fetch
   something. The subject is the same in both clauses:

   Idę do sklepu kupić chleb. 'I'm going to the store to get
     [some] bread.'
   Jadę do Anglii uczyć się języka. 'I go to England to study the
     language.'
   Przyszłam z tobą porozmawiać. 'I came to talk to you.'

7. To express the idea of making someone do something:

   Nasz szef kazał nam przyjść w weekend. 'Our boss told us
     to come [to work] on the weekend.'
   Profesor zabronił używać telefonów w klasie. '[The]
     professor forbade the use of cell phones in class.'

Pułkownik rozkazał wycofać wojska. 'The colonel ordered the withdrawal of the army.'

8. To express the idea of letting someone do something:

pozwolić **komuś coś zrobić** 'to let somebody do something'
Dlaczego pozwoliłeś im to zrobić? 'Why did you allow them to do it?'

9. In the process of making decisions: **zdecydować się/postanowić** 'to make up one's mind,' **wahać się** 'to hesitate,' **próbować** 'to try,' 'to make an attempt,' **zapomnieć** 'to forget.'

Zdecydowaliśmy się wyjechać. 'We have decided to leave.'
Spróbuj nas zrozumieć. 'Try to understand us.'
Zapomniałam wyłączyć żelazko. 'I forgot to turn off the iron.'

10. The infinitive is often used without a subject in a rhetorical question:

Co robić? 'What [shall we] do?' **Kupować czy sprzedawać?** 'Buy or sell?'

11. In an exclamation: **Żyć nie umierać!** 'This is the life!'

12. As an equivalent to an imperative: **podawać schłodzone** 'serve chilled,' **zażywać co cztery godziny** 'take every four hours.'

13. After constructions with a subject in the dative case:

Chce mi się płakać/jeść/pić. 'I want to cry/eat/drink.'
Co ci kupić? 'What do you want [us to] buy you?'
Jak wam pomóc? 'How [can I] help you?'

14. In subjectless constructions with verbs of perception:

nic nie widać 'nothing can be seen'
słychać hałas 'the noise can be heard'
czuć spalenizną 'there is a smell of burning'

| 6.5.1.1 | *Infinitive contexts: perfective and imperfective* |

The aspect of the infinitive depends to a large extent on the context:

Co można robić <IMPFV> **na wakacjach?** 'What can one do on vacation?'
Co można zrobić <PFV> **na wakacjach?** 'What can one get done on vacation?'

Ona lubiła wypić. 'She used to like to get drunk.'
Ona lubi pić. 'She likes drinking.'

When an infinitive follows a verb with the meaning to start or to finish, it must be in the imperfective form:

Przestań do mnie dzwonić <IMPFV>. 'Stop calling me.'
Zaczynam rozumieć <IMPFV>, **dlaczego odeszłaś.** 'I am starting to understand why you left.'

6.5.2 | Agreement

Subjects and verbs agree in person, number, category, and class. The subject dictates the person marker of the verb.

6.5.2.1 | Subject–verb number agreement

Syn wyszedł. <3 PR MSC SG past> '[The] son left.'
Synowie wyszli. <3 PR PL past> '[The] sons left.'
Spodnie są mokre. '[The] pants are wet.'

With personal pronouns: the same number and person

Ty jesteś wysoki. 'You are tall.'
My jesteśmy wysocy. 'We are tall.'

When the subject is compound, and with the conjunctions **i** 'and,' **oraz** 'and,' the verb is plural:

Ewa i Kasia uczą się do egzaminu. 'Ewa and Kasia are studying for the exam.'
Będą potrzebne sok, kawa i herbata. 'We will need juice, coffee and tea.'
Emanowały z niej dobroć i spokój. 'Goodness and calmness emanated from her.'
Podrożały euro i ropa. 'The prices of the euro and gas increased.'

With the conjunctions: **ani . . . , ani** 'neither . . . , nor' and **lub** 'or,' it is preferable to make the verb plural:

Ani dziadek, ani ojciec nie żyją. 'Neither grandfather, nor father is alive.'
"Stagnacja lub regres wstrzymywały bieg w kierunku rozwoju wielu krajów."[1] 'Stagnation or decline postponed a move toward development in many countries.'

The verb is singular in the following instances:

1. because of (diplomatic) hierarchy, or to emphasize the first of a number of subjects:

> **Królowa Elżbieta z mężem *przyjechała* do Polski.**
> 'Queen Elizabeth with her husband came to Poland.'

> **Na pokładzie samolotu *był* prezydent z żoną.**
> 'On the plane there was the president and his wife.'

In such sentences, the verb usually precedes the subject.

> **Do Polski przyleciała Królowa Elżbieta z mężem.**
> lit. 'To Poland came Queen Elizabeth with her husband.'

> **Na pokładzie samolotu był prezydent z żoną.**
> lit. 'On the plane was the president with his wife.'

> **Do sklepu weszła kobieta z dzieckiem.**
> lit. 'To the store came in a woman with a baby.'

2. when referring to a group subject:

> **Większość jego prac *powstała* w poprzednim dziesięcioleciu.**
> 'The majority of his work was created in the last decade.'

> **Wiele kobiet *jest* zadowolonych z dłuższego urlopu macierzyńskiego.**
> 'Many women are happy because of the longer maternity leave.'

> **W grupie *było* ośmioro dzieci.**
> 'There were eight children in the group.'

3. with the disjunctive conjunction **albo** 'or':

> **Za obiad *zapłacił* Adam, albo Piotr.** 'Either Adam or Piotr paid for dinner.'
> ***Grała* matka albo syn.** 'A mother or a son played.'

The first noun that follows the verb decides the class of the verb.

4. with appositions:

> **Nasz dziadek, tak jak i jego matka, *mieszkał* przed wojną w Łodzi.**
> 'Our grandfather, like his mother, lived in Łódź before the war.'

Sometimes a verb can be singular or plural when the subjects are in front of the verb and they agree in class:

> **Ani matka** <FEM>, **ani córka** <FEM> **nie lubią** <PL>/**nie lubi** <SG> **gotować.**
> 'Neither mother nor daughter likes to cook.'

In a construction with **nie ma** <3 PR SG present> 'there isn't, it is not, there aren't, there are not' to express nonexistence of the subject(s) or object(s), the verb is always in the third person singular, regardless of the subject(s):

> **syn jest** <3 PR SG present> **w domu** '[the] son is at home'
> **syna nie ma** <3 PR SG present> **w domu** '[the] son is not at home'
> **synowie są** <3 PR PL present> **w domu** '[the] sons are at home'
> **synów nie ma** <3 PR SG present> **w domu** '[the] sons are not at home'

In the past **nie ma** changes to **nie było** <3 PR SG past> but it is still in the *singular* form.

> **synów nie było w domu** '[the] sons were not at home.' (See 2.6.4)

6.5.2.2	Subject–verb class agreement

There is class agreement in verbal endings in the past tense (e.g., <u>czytaliśmy</u> 'we were reading'), in conditional mood (<u>czytałabyś</u> 'you <FEM> would be reading'), and in future with the past tense form (e.g. **będą** <u>czytali</u> 'they will be reading'). The basic form is the past tense ending, as conditional mood and future tense can be formed from the past tense form. In the singular, the past tense ending formations agree with the subject, with masculine (-łem, -łeś, -ł), feminine (-łam, -łaś, -ła), and neuter (-ło) forms. In the plural, the past tense ending formations agree with the subjects, with male human plural (-liśmy, -liście, -li) and no-male human plural forms (-łyśmy, -łyście, -ły). (See also 6.3.1 and 6.3.2, as well as 3.4 and 3.2.16 for information on classes of noun phrases.)

The male human plural forms are used for groups of at least one male human being. This includes groups of all men/boys and mixed groups with at least one male human being.

The no-male human plural forms are used for groups with no male human beings in them.

Exceptionally, when a female and a male animal are the subject of the sentence, the verb in the plural takes the ending -li, completely ignoring the female element.

Matka i pies *poszli* **na spacer.** 'Mother and the dog went for a walk.'
Dziewczynki i pies *poszli* **na spacer.** '[The] girls and a dog went for a walk.'

Note:
Dzieci poszły na spacer.
'[The] children went for a walk.'

Osoby poszły na spacer.
'[Some] persons went for a walk.'

Ludzie *poszli* **na spacer.**
'[The] people went for a walk.'

Rodzice *poszli*.
'[My] parents went for a walk.'

Appositions do not change the class of the main clause:

Niebezpieczne związki <PL>, **powieść** <FEM SG> **francuskiego pisarza Choderlosa de Laclosa,** *są* <PL> **utworem opiewającym wielką siłę miłości w świecie ludzkiego zakłamania.** '*Dangerous Liaisons*, a novel by the French writer Choderlosa de Laclosa, [are] is a work glorifying the power of love in the world of human hypocrisy.'

However, in sentences with female titles, the verb has the ending -ła, not -ł:

Sekretarz <MSC> **stanu Madeleine Albright** <FEM> **konsultowa***ła* **się w sprawie sytuacji na Bliskim Wschodzie z szefami dyplomacji Francji, Niemiec i Wielkiej Brytanii.**
'Secretary of State Madeleine Albright discussed the situation in the Middle East with the ministers of foreign affairs from France, Germany and Great Britain.' (see Chapter 12)

6.6 Indicative

Speakers can express their attitude as real, probable, speculative, or unreal using different moods, just like using modal verbs.

There are four moods in Polish:

- indicative (**tryb oznajmujący**)
- imperative (**tryb rozkazujący**)
- conditional (**tryb przypuszczający**)
- subjunctive (**tryb łączący**)

All six persons can be used with the indicative mood. It can be expressed in the present, past and future.

373

| 6.6.1 | **Present** |

The Polish phrase (**ja**) **czytam** can be expressed by the English present tense 'I read' and present continuous 'I am reading.' In Polish the present tense is called **czas teraźniejszy**, which literally means 'time now.'

The present tense expresses action which is ongoing, the non-accomplished aspect. (See 6.4.1 and 6.6.3)

The present tense can also express the immediate future.

The present tense has four main conjugation groups (I–IV) plus irregular verbs. In present tense conjugations, there is a correlation between the endings in the first person singular **ja** 'I' and the third person plural **oni/one** 'they,' e.g., **proszę** and **proszą**, **idę** and **idą**.

The ending of the third person singular in most regular verbs equals the verb stem, e.g., **czyta(ć)**, **mówi(ć)**, **uczy(ć)**, **musi(eć)**, **chodzi(ć)**.

This chapter examines each verb class with its conjugation patterns.

The imperfective present and perfective future conjugation groups are:

Singular	I	II	III	IV
1st person	**-am**	**-em**	**-ę**	**-ę**
2nd person	**-asz**	**-esz**	**-esz**	**-ysz/-isz**
3rd person	**-a**	**-e**	**-e**	**-y/-i**

Plural	I	II	III	IV
1st person	**-amy**	**-emy**	**-emy**	**-ymy/-imi**
2nd person	**-acie**	**-ecie**	**-ecie**	**-ycie/-icie**
3rd person	**-ają**	**-eją** or **-edzą**	**-ą**	**-ą**

The second person singular and plural are used when referring to someone in an informal setting. In formal settings, the forms of **pan, pani, państwo** are used with the third person singular and plural, e.g.:

> **Gdzie mieszkasz?** 'Where do you live?' (asking one person informally)
> **Gdzie mieszkacie?** 'Where do you live?' (asking more than one person informally)
> **Gdzie pan mieszka?** 'Where do you live?' (asking a man in a formal setting)

Gdzie pani mieszka? 'Where do you live?' (asking a woman in a formal setting)

Gdzie państwo mieszkają? 'Where do you live?' (asking a group or a couple in a formal setting)

(See 5.2.10 for a discussion of the multiple forms of rendering 'you' in Polish.)

| 6.6.1.1 | *Conjugation I:* **-am, -a, -ają**

Conjugation I includes infinitives that end in **-ać** (but not in **-ować, -ywać, -iwać, -awać** and a group of **-ać** verbs conjugated according to conjugation III, see 6.6.1.3). Both imperfective and perfective verbs with the same stems conjugate with the same set of endings. When conjugated with these endings, imperfective verbs form the present tense and perfective verbs form the future tense (see 6.6.3.2).

The root is the infinitive minus the final **-ać**. The endings are:

Singular	Plural
-am	**-amy**
-asz	**-acie**
-a	**-ają**

czytać <IMPFV> 'to read' is a regular verb:

Singular	Plural
(ja) czyt-am	**(my) czyt-amy**
'I read/I'm reading'	'we read/we're reading'
(ty) czyt-asz	**(wy) czyt-acie**
'you read/you're reading'	'you read/you're reading'
on/ona/ono/pan/	**oni/one/panie/panowie/**
pani czyt-a	**państwo czyt-ają**
'he/she/it/sir/madam reads/is reading'	'they/ladies/gentlemen/ladies and gentlemen read/are reading'

Note there are two forms of informal "you" (singular and plural) as well as formal forms (see 5.2.10).

All first person plural **my** 'we' forms have the ending **-my** in all conjugations, the second person singular has **-sz** at the end in all present tense conjugations, and all second person plural **wy** 'you pl.' forms have the ending **-cie** in all conjugations.

mieć <IMPFV> 'to have' is irregular:

Singular	Plural
(**ja**) **mam** 'I have'	(**my**) **mamy** 'we have'
(**ty**) **masz** 'you have'	(**wy**) **macie** 'you have'
on/**ona**/**ono ma** 'he/she/it has'	**oni**/**one mają** 'they have'

dać <PFV> 'to give' is irregular:

Singular	Plural
(**ja**) **dam** 'I'll give'	(**my**) **damy** 'we'll give'
(**ty**) **dasz** 'you'll give'	(**wy**) **dacie** 'you'll give'
on/**ona**/**ono da** 'he/she/it'll give'	**oni**/**one dadzą** 'they'll give'

Note the irregular ending in the third person plural where the regular **j** changes to **dz**.

Dać is a perfective form of the imperfective **dawać** (see 6.6.1.3).

Other commonly used verbs that conjugate like **czytać** include:

> **biegać** 'to run'
> **czekać na** <+ACC> 'to wait for'
> **grać w** <+ACC> 'to play sports'
> **kochać** <+ACC> 'to love'
> **mieszkać** 'to reside'
> **opowiadać** <+ACC> **o** <+LOC> 'tell something *about* something'
> **otwierać** <+ACC> 'to open'
> **pomagać** <+DAT> 'to help'
> **przepraszać za** <+ACC> 'to apologize for'
> **pytać o** <+ACC> 'to inquire about'
> **siadać** 'to take a seat'
> **umierać** 'to die'
> **używać** <+GEN> 'to use'
> **zamykać** <+ACC> 'to close'

The following list of "pseudo" -**ać** verbs do not belong to Conjugation I.

The first and second person singular conjugations for these verbs are provided in brackets. For the full conjugation pattern, see the conjugation group listed in parentheses. (It is useful to note that based on the first and second person singular, the whole pattern can be constructed. Also note that if the verb ends in -**ę** in the first person singular, it has the ending -**ą** in the third person plural.)

Note: Verbs with prefixes are conjugated the same as the root verb, e.g., **napisać** [napiszę, napiszesz] 'to write' is conjugated like **pisać** [piszę, piszesz].

1. **pisać** [piszę, piszesz] 'to write' <IMPFV> and verbs with the root -**pisać**, e.g., **napisać** [napiszę, napiszesz] 'to write' <PFV>, **zapisać się** 'to enroll' <PFV> (Conjugation III)

2. verbs with ending -**ować**, e.g., **pracować** [pracuję, pracujesz] 'to work' <IMPFV> (Conjugation III)

3. verbs with ending -**iwać**, e.g., **przesłuchiwać** [przesłuchuję, przesłuchujesz] 'to interrogate' <IMPFV> (Conjugation III)

4. verbs with ending -**ywać**, e.g., **wychowywać** (**się**) [wychowuję (się), wychowujesz (się)] 'to raise, (to grow up)' <IMPFV> **zapisywać się** 'to enroll <IMPFV>, **pokazywać** 'to show' <IMPFV> (Conjugation III)

5. **dawać** [daję, dajesz] 'to give' <IMPFV> and verbs with the root -**dawać**, e.g., **sprzedawać** 'to sell' <IMPFV>, **wydawać** 'to spend money <IMPFV>, **zdawać** 'to pass an exam' <IMPFV> (Conjugation III)

6. **stawać** [staję, stajesz] 'to stand' <IMPFV> and verbs with the root -**stawać**, e.g., **wstawać** 'to get up' <IMPFV>, **dostawać** 'to receive' <IMPFV> (Conjugation III)

7. verbs with the ending -**znawać**, e.g., **poznawać** [poznaję, poznajesz] 'to meet' <IMPFV>, **zeznawać** 'to confess' <IMPFV> (Conjugation III)

8. **stać się** [stanę się, staniesz się] 'to become' <PFV>, **stawać się** [staję się, stajesz się] 'to become' <IMPFV>, **zostać** [zostanę, zostaniesz] 'to become, to stay' <PFV>, **zostawać** [zostaję, zostajesz] 'to stay' <IMPFV> (Conjugation III)

9. **brać** [biorę, bierzesz] 'to take' <IMPFV> and verbs with the root -**brać**, e.g., **wybrać** 'to choose' <PFV> (Conjugation III)

10. **prać** [piorę, pierzesz] 'to do laundry' <IMPFV> and verbs with the root -**prać**, e.g., **wyprać** 'to do laundry' <PFV> (Conjugation III)

11. **rwać** [rwę, rwiesz] 'to tear' <IMPFV> (Conjugation III)

12. verbs with the stem -**zać**, e.g., **pokazać** [pokażę, pokażesz] 'to show' <PFV>, **kazać** 'to order' <IMPFV> (Conjugation III)

13. verbs with the stem -**sać**, e.g., **czesać** (**się**) [czeszę (się), czeszesz (się)] 'to brush (oneself)' <IMPFV>, **uczesać się** 'to brush (oneself)' <PFV> (Conjugation III)

14. **płakać** [płaczę, płaczesz] 'to cry' <IMPFV>, **płukać** [płuczę, płuczesz] 'to rinse' <IMPFV> and verbs with the same stems, e.g., **przepłukać** 'to rinse out' <PFV> (Conjugation III)

15. **skakać** [skaczę, skaczesz] 'to jump' <IMPFV> (Conjugation III)

16. **kąpać** (**się**) [kąpię (się), kąpiesz (się)] <IMPFV>, **wykąpać** (**się**) 'to bathe (oneself)' <PFV> (Conjugation III)

17. the motion verb **jechać** [jadę, jedziesz] 'to travel' <IMPFV> (Conjugation III)
18. **śmiać się** [śmieję się, śmiejesz się] 'to laugh' <IMPFV> (Conjugation III)
19. **stać** [stanę, staniesz] 'to stand' <PFV> and verbs with the ending -stać, e.g., **wstać** 'to get up' <PFV>, **dostać** 'to receive' <PFV> (Conjugation III)
20. **stać** [stoję, stoisz] 'to be standing' <IMPFV> (Conjugation IV)
21. **spać** [śpię, śpisz] 'to sleep' <IMPFV> and verbs with the root -spać, e.g., **wyspać się** 'to get enough sleep' (Conjugation IV)
22. **bać się** [boję się, boisz się] 'to be afraid' <IMPFV> (Conjugation IV)

6.6.1.2   *Conjugation II: -em, -e, -eją/-edzą*

The root is the infinitive minus the final -eć. The endings are:

Singular	Plural
-em	**-emy**
-esz	**-ecie**
-e	**-eją**

rozumieć 'to understand' is a regular verb:

Singular	Plural
(ja) rozumi-em 'I understand'	**(my) rozumi-emy** 'we understand'
(ty) rozumi-esz 'you understand'	**(wy) rozumi-ecie** 'you understand'
on/ona/ono/pan/ pani rozumi-e 'he/she/it/sir/madam understands'	**oni/one/panie/panowie/ państwo rozumi-eją** 'they/ladies/gentlemen/ladies and gentlemen understand'

A derivative of the root verb **rozumieć** is conjugated similiarly:

zrozumieć <PFV>. However, as a perfective verb, it produces the future tense.

(ja) zrozumi-em 'I'll understand'	**(my) zrozumi-emy** 'we'll understand'
(ty) zrozumi-esz 'you'll understand'	**(wy) zrozumi-ecie** 'you'll understand'
on/ona/ono/pan/ pani zrozumi-e 'he/she/it/sir/madam'll understand'	**oni/one/panie/panowie/ państwo zrozumi-eją** 'they/ladies/gentlemen/ladies and gentlemen'll understand'

A small group of verbs conjugate similiarly. Note the third person plural form **umieją**, **rozumieją** (not: umią, rozumią).

> **umieć** <INF> 'to have a skill,' 'to know how to'
> **śmieć** 'to dare'

wiedzieć 'to know' has an irregular conjugation. Note that **wiedzieć** has the meaning of 'to know information' and is followed by interrogatives or other clauses (not a direct object) (e.g., **Wiem, gdzie on mieszka.** 'I know where he lives.'). **Znać** has the meaning of 'to know someone or something' and is followed by a direct object (e.g., **Znam jego adres.** 'I know his address.'; **Znam ją.** 'I know her.'; **Znam język polski.** 'I know Polish.')

Singular	Plural
(**ja**) **wiem** 'I know'	(**my**) **wiemy** 'we know'
(**ty**) **wiesz** 'you know'	(**wy**) **wiecie** 'you know'
on/ona/ono wie 'he/she/it knows'	**oni/one wiedzą** 'they know'

jeść 'to eat' is irregular:

Singular	Plural
(**ja**) **jem** 'I eat'	(**my**) **jemy** 'we eat'
(**ty**) **jesz** 'you eat'	(**wy**) **jecie** 'you eat'
on/ona/ono je 'he/she/it eats'	**oni/one jedzą** 'they eat'

Note the third person plural ending -**edzą**.

A derivative of the root verb **jeść** with the prefix z-: **zjeść** <PFV> is conjugated similiarly. However, as a perfective verb, it produces the future tense.

(**ja**) **zj-em** 'I'll eat'	(**my**) **zj-emy** 'we'll eat'
(**ty**) **zj-esz** 'you'll eat'	(**wy**) **zj-ecie** 'you'll eat'
on/ona/ono/pan/pani zj-e 'he/she/it/sir/madam'll eat'	**oni/one/panie/panowie/państwo zj-edzą** 'they/ladies/gentlemen/ ladies and gentlemen'll eat'

6.6.1.3	*Conjugation III:* -ę, -e, -ą

This class of verbs is very diverse, because many pseudo -ać verbs belong to this group: **pracować** 'to work,' **dawać** 'to give' <IMPFV>, **kazać** 'to order,' pisać 'to write,' and żyć 'to live,' and the motion verbs iść 'to walk' and jechać 'to ride' (see list of pseudo -ać verbs at end of section 6.6.1.1). Additionally, there are many stem–consonant mutations, e.g., c: g: ż, e.g., móc: mogę: możesz 'can.' Note the correlation between the first person singular and the third person plural. The first person singular has the ending of one nasal -ę, while the third person plural has -ą, and when stem-consonant mutations occur, the two forms have an identical stem: mogę <1 PR SG>—może <3 PR SG>—mogą <3 PR PL>.

The root is the infinitive minus the final consonant -ć or -c, or double consonants -ść, -źć. The endings are:

Singular	Plural
-ę	-emy
-esz	-ecie
-e	-ą

The group of verbs that belong to this class can be further divided into subgroups:

1. Verbs with systematic stem changes:

- with the productive suffix -ować, e.g., pracować 'to work'
- with the suffix -awać, e.g., dawać 'to give.'

Verbs in this subgroup are well represented in Polish. Many -ować verbs are loan translations, e.g., parkować 'to park,' rezerwować 'to reserve,' decydować 'to decide,' anulować 'to cancel,' importować 'to import,' eksportować 'to export,' krytykować 'to criticize,' logować się 'to log in.'

A defective verb belongs to this subgroup: brakować 'to be lacking.'

The -ować part is changed to -uj-, and then regular endings are attached.

pracować 'to work' <IMPFV>

Singular	Plural
(ja) prac-uj-ę 'I work'	(my) prac-uj-emy 'we work'
(ty) prac-uj-esz 'you work'	(wy) prac-uj-ecie 'you work'
on/ona/ono prac-uj-e 'he/she/it works'	oni/one prac-uj-ą 'they work'

To conjugate verbs with the suffix -dawać 'to give' <IMPFV>, replace -wać- with -j-, and then add regular endings.

dawać 'to give' <IMPFV>

Singular	Plural
(ja) **d-aj-ę** 'I give'	(my) **d-aj-emy** 'we give'
(ty) **d-aj-esz** 'you give'	(wy) **d-aj-ecie** 'you give'
on/ona/ono **d-aj-e** 'he/she/it gives'	oni/one **d-aj-ą** 'they give'

The following are conjugated similarly:

dodawać 'to add'	**sprzedawać** 'to sell'
dostawać 'to receive'	**wstawać** 'to get up'
oddawać 'to give back,' 'to return'	**wydawać** 'to spend money'
podawać 'to pass'	**zadawać** 'to ask a question,' 'to give a task to do'
poznawać 'to meet'	**zeznawać** 'to testify'
przyznawać 'to admit'	**zostawać** 'to stay'

Most of the verbs with -awać are imperfective.

The perfective forms are created by removing -aw- to leave dodać (from dostawać), poznać (from pozn<u>aw</u>ać), wstać (wst<u>aw</u>ać), etc.

2. Pseudo -ać verbs with systematic stem-consonant mutations in all forms when non-past endings are added, e.g., s:sz pisać 'to write,' r:rz karać 'to punish,' k:cz skakać 'to jump.'

This is not a numerous subgroup, but a few commonly used verbs belong here, e.g., czesać 'to comb,' kołysać 'to swing' are conjugated similarly to pisać with s:sz; ciosać 'to hew' has two forms: cioszę/ ciosam; żebrać 'to beg' and bazgrać 'to scribble' are conjugated similiarly to karać; and płakać 'to cry,' and płukać 'to rinse' are conjugated similiarly to skakać.

pisać 'to write' s:sz <IMPFV>

Singular	Plural
(ja) **piszę** 'I write'	(my) **piszemy** 'we write'
(ty) **piszesz** 'you write'	(wy) **piszecie** 'you write'
on/ona/ono **pisze** 'he/she/it writes'	oni/one **piszą** 'they write'

karać 'to punish' r:rz <IMPFV>

Singular	Plural
(**ja**) **karzę** 'I punish'	(**my**) **karzemy** 'we punish'
(**ty**) **karzesz** 'you punish'	(**wy**) **karzecie** 'you punish'
on/ona/ono karze 'he/she/it punishes'	**oni/one karzą** 'they punish'

skakać 'to jump' k:cz <IMPFV>

Singular	Plural
(**ja**) **skaczę** 'I jump'	(**my**) **skaczemy** 'we jump'
(**ty**) **skaczesz** 'you jump'	(**wy**) **skaczecie** 'you jump'
on/ona/ono skacze 'he/she/it jumps'	**oni/one skaczą** 'they jump'

The perfective counterpart of **skakać** is **skoczyć**, with the consonant **cz**.

3. Monosyllabic verbs with -**yć** and -**uć** plus a few -**ić** verbs.

In all forms of non-past the short stem is compensated by a -**j**- infix, and regular endings are added.

żyć 'to be alive'

Singular	Plural
(**ja**) **ży-j-ę** 'I am alive'	(**my**) **ży-j-emy** 'we are alive'
(**ty**) **ży-j-esz** 'you are alive'	(**wy**) **ży-j-ecie** 'you are alive'
on/ona/ono ży-j-e 'he/she/it is alive'	**oni/one ży-j-ą** 'they are alive'

Other verbs that conjugate similarly include: **bić** (**się**) 'to beat (oneself),' **myć** (**się**) 'to wash (oneself),' **pić** 'to drink,' **czuć** (**się**) 'to feel,' **współczuć komuś** <DAT> 'to sympathize,' **szyć** 'to sew,' **tyć** 'to gain weight.'

Note that **być** 'to be,' **śnić** 'to dream,' **goić się** 'to heal,' **kpić** 'to mock' do not belong here. (See 6.6.1.4)

4. Verbs with the productive ending -**ąć**.

These are mostly built on -**jąć** or -**nąć** roots. While some -**nąć** verbs are either perfective or imperfective, -**jąć** verbs are all perfective future.

To conjugate these verbs, delete -**ąć**, add -**m**-/-**n**- in the first person singular and third person plural, and -**mi**-/-**ni**- in all other persons, and then add the regular non-past endings. Note that the extra -**m**-/-**n**- element is also present in the imperfective forms, e.g., **wynajmować, zaczynać**.

wynająć 'to hire,' 'to rent' <PFV> wynajmować <IMPFV>

Singular   Plural

(**ja**) **wyna-jm-ę** 'I'll rent'   (**my**) **wyna-jmi-emy** 'we'll rent'
(**ty**) **wyna-jmi-esz** 'you'll rent'   (**wy**) **wyna-jmi-ecie** 'you'll rent'
on/ona/ono wyna-jmi-e   **oni/one wyna-jm-ą**
  'he/she/it'll rent'   'they'll rent'

Verbs that conjugate similarly are derivatives of **jąć** 'to commence' (bookish): **wy-jąć** 'to take something out' <PFV>, **przy-jąć** 'to accept' <PFV>, **prze-jąć** 'to take over' <PFV>, **za-jąć** 'to occupy' <PFV>, **na-jąć** 'to hire' <PFV>, **ob-jąć** 'to hug' <PFV>, **od-jąć** 'to take something away' <PFV>, **po-jąć** 'to comprehend' <PFV>, **zd-jąć** 'to take something off' <PFV>.

It may be easier to remember the extra -**m**- if we realize that **sejm**, the name for the Polish parliament, comes from the -**jąć** root, namely, **s-jąć** 'to get together.'[2]

zacząć 'to begin,' 'to commence' <PFV> zaczynać <IMPFV>

Replace the **ąć** ending with **n** (first person singular and third person plural) or **ni** (all other persons) and then add the regular endings. Note that the extra -**n**- element is present in the imperfective form **zaczynać**.

Singular   Plural

(**ja**) **zacz-n-ę** 'I'll begin'   (**my**) **zacz-ni-emy** 'we'll begin'
(**ty**) **zacz-ni-esz** 'you'll begin'   (**wy**) **zacz-ni-ecie** 'you'll begin'
on/ona/ono zacz-ni-e   **oni/one zacz-n-ą** 'they'll begin'
  'he/she/it'll begin'

Verbs that conjugate similarly: **pragnąć** 'to desire' <IMPFV>, **minąć** 'to pass' <PFV>, **biegnąć** 'to run' <IMPFV>, **runąć** 'to tumble' <PFV>, **tonąć** 'to go under' <IMPFV>, **usnąć** 'to fall asleep' <PFV>, **ginąć** 'to die' <IMPFV>, **chudnąć** 'to lose weight' <IMPFV>.

Irregular -**ąć**: **wziąć** 'to take' <PFV>, **brać** <IMPFV>

This commonly used verb is conjugated as follows:

Singular   Plural

(**ja**) **wez-m-ę** 'I'll take'   (**my**) **weź-mi-emy** 'we'll take'
(**ty**) **weź-mi-esz** 'you'll take'   (**wy**) **weź-mi-ecie** 'you'll take'
on/ona/ono weź-mi-e   **oni/one wez-m-ą** 'they'll take'
  'he/she/it'll take'

Note the soft ź in all forms except the first person singular and the third person plural which differ by the nasal sounds ę:ą, and the imperfective form **brać**.

Powziąć 'to come to a decision' (bookish), **zawziąć się** 'to be determined,' conjugate like **wziąć**.

5. Verbs built on **brać** 'to take' <IMPFV>, **prać** 'to do laundry' <IMPFV>.

These have systematic consonant and vowel shifts in all persons before non-past endings. The vowels -io- appear in the first person singular and third person plural; -ie- and the consonant change r:rz appears in all other persons before non-past endings are added.

brać 'to take' <IMPFV>

Singular	Plural
(ja) biorę 'I take'	**(my) bierzemy** 'we take'
(ty) bierzesz 'you take'	**(wy) bierzecie** 'you take'
on/ona/ono bierze 'he/she/it takes'	**oni/one biorą** 'they take'

These verbs conjugate similarly: **wybrać** 'to select,' **zabrać** 'to take,' **ubrać (się)** 'to put on (oneself),' **przebrać się** 'to change' (clothes), **zebrać** 'to collect'—all verbs built on **-brać** and **-prać** are perfective. Imperfective prefixed verbs have their stem extended by -ie-, e.g., **wybierać** 'to select' <IMPFV> and are conjugated like **czytać** 'to read' (see 6.6.1.1).

6. Pseudo -ać monosyllabic verbs built on the stem **lać** 'to pour'

These verbs have a systematic vowel shift in all persons. To conjugate these verbs, replace the final -ać with the infix -ej-, and then add regular non-past endings.

Singular	Plural
(ja) leję 'I pour'	**(my) lejemy** 'we pour'
(ty) lejesz 'you pour'	**(wy) lejecie** 'you pour'
on/ona/ono leje 'he/she/it pours'	**oni/one leją** 'they pour'

Perfective future derivatives of -lać conjugate similarly: **wylać** 'to pour something out,' 'to spill,' **zalać** 'to flood,' **dolać** 'to fill up,' and **śmiać się** *z kogo, czego* <GEN> 'to laugh at somebody, something'; **dziać się** 'to happen,' which is usually used in the third person singular and plural: **Co się dzieje?** 'What is going on?' Two weather-related verbs belong here. They are mostly used in the third person singular and plural: **wiatr** wieje 'the wind blows,' **słońce grzeje** 'the sun is warm.' The irregular verbs **mdleć** 'to faint' and **siwieć** 'to turn gray' belong here.

7. Infinitives with the double consonant ending -ść: **kłaść** 'to place horizontally' <IMPFV>, **iść** 'to walk' <IMPFV>, **usiąść** 'to take a seat' <PFV>.

To conjugate these verbs delete -ść, add -d (for **iść, kłaść, usiąść**) and then add regular endings: -ę for the first person singular, and -ą for the third person plural, e.g., **iść** i-d-ę 'I am going,' i-d-ą 'they are going.' For the second person singular and plural delete -ść, add -dzi, and then add regular endings -esz, -emy, e.g., **iść** i-dzi-esz 'you are going,' i-dzi-emy 'we are going'. For the third person singular, delete -ść, add -dzi, and then add the regular ending -e, e.g., idzi-e 's/he is going.'

Note that the first person singular and third person plural differ by the nasal sound only **idę:idą**.

iść 'to walk'

Singular	Plural
(ja) idę 'I'm walking'	**(my) idziemy** 'we're walking'
(ty) idziesz 'you're walking'	**(wy) idziecie** 'you're walking'
on/ona/ono idzie 'he/she/it's walking'	**oni/one idą** 'they're walking'

The irregular verbs **nieść** 'to carry in hands' and **wieźć** 'to transport' and their future perfective derivatives with spatial prefixes: **wynieść** 'to carry out,' **przywieźć** 'to bring in' are conjugated as follows:

nieść 'to carry in hands'

Singular	Plural
(ja) niosę 'I carry'	**(my) niesiemy** 'we carry'
(ty) niesiesz 'you carry'	**(wy) niesiecie** 'you carry'
on/ona/ono niesie 'he/she/it carries'	**oni/one niosą** 'they carry'

wieźć 'to transport'

Singular	Plural
(ja) wiozę 'I transport'	**(my) wieziemy** 'we transport'
(ty) wieziesz 'you transport'	**(wy) wieziecie** 'you transport'
on/ona/ono wiezie 'he/she/it transports'	**oni/one wiozą** 'they transport'

385

The irregular verb **kraść** 'to steal':

Singular	Plural
(ja) kradnę 'I steal'	**(my) kradniemy** 'we steal'
(ty) kradniesz 'you steal'	**(wy) kradniecie** 'you steal'
on/ona/ono kradnie 'he/she/it steals'	**oni/one kradną** 'they steal'

Note the additional **-n-** in the first person singular and third person plural and **-ni-** in all other persons.

8. Infinitives ending with **-c**.

These have a unique but predictable type of stem–consonant change in all persons of non-past tenses. Their pattern is either **g:ż** or **k:cz**. In the first person singular and third person plural use the velar consonants **g** or **k**, and use **ż** or **cz** in all other persons. Words with the same root—nouns, verbs, adjectives—have either **g** or **k**: **można** 'it is possible,' 'can do,' **piekarnia** 'bakery.'

móc 'may,' 'can,' 'be able,' 'have permission to do something'

Singular	Plural
(ja) mogę 'I can'	**(my) możemy** 'we can'
(ty) możesz 'you can'	**(wy) możecie** 'you can'
on/ona/ono może 'he/she/it can'	**oni/one mogą** 'they can'

Pomóc 'to help' is conjugated similarly.

piec 'to bake' <IMPFV>

Singular	Plural
(ja) piekę 'I bake'	**(my) pieczemy** 'we bake'
(ty) pieczesz 'you bake'	**(wy) pieczecie** 'you bake'
on/ona/ono piecze 'he/she/it bakes'	**oni/one pieką** 'they bake'

9. This subgroup of verbs with the infinitive ending **-eć** has the systematic final-stem—consonant change **rz:r**. To conjugate these verbs, delete **-eć**, add **-r** in the first person singular and third person plural and **-rz-** in all other persons then attach regular non-past endings.

umrzeć 'to die' <PFV>

Singular	Plural
(ja) umrę 'I'll die'	(my) umrzemy 'we'll die'
(ty) umrzesz 'you'll die'	(wy) umrzecie 'you'll die'
on/ona/ono umrze 'he/she/it'll die'	oni/one umrą 'they'll die'

Oprzeć (się) o/na coś <ACC> 'to lean against/on something,' drzeć 'to tear' conjugate similarly.

The modal verb chcieć 'to want'

Singular	Plural
(ja) chcę 'I want'	(my) chcemy 'we want'
(ty) chcesz 'you want'	(wy) chcecie 'you want'
on/ona/ono chce 'he/she/it wants'	oni/one chcą 'they want'

The verb brakować <IMPFV>, zabraknąć <PFV> 'to lack something, not be in sufficient amount' is mostly used in the third person singular. The item that is lacking is expressed in the genitive case.

w mieście brakuje <present> lekarzy 'there are not enough doctors in the city'

w mieście brakowało <past imperfective> lekarzy 'there were not enough doctors [for some time] in the city'

w mieście zabrakło <past imperfective> lekarzy 'there were not enough doctors in the city [suddenly]'

w mieście będzie brakowało <future imperfective> lekarzy 'there will not be enough doctors in the city'

w mieście zabraknie <future imperfective> lekarzy 'there will be not enough doctors in the city' [for sure]

If there is a person who is lacking/missing something, that person is expressed in the dative case.

brakuje mi <DAT> wolnego czasu 'I am lacking free time'

Zawsze brakowało mi czasu. Teraz mam czas, ale brakuje mi zdrowia. 'I was always lacking [free] time. Now, I have time, but am lacking [good] health.'

Kiedyś zabraknie mi cierpliwości, żeby go zrozumieć. 'One day I will not have enough patience to understand him.'

niczego nam nie brakuje 'we are not lacking anything'
czego pani brakuje? 'what are you missing?' (asking a woman in a formal setting)

The verb **brakować** can be used interchangeably with the noun **brak** 'lack of' → See 2.6.9.

6.6.1.4 | *Conjugation IV:* **-ę, -i/-y, -ą**

The root is the infinitive minus the final -yć/-ić/-eć. The endings are:

Singular	Plural
-ę	**-imy/-ymy**
-isz/-ysz	**-icie/-ycie**
-i/-y	**-ą**

Verbs with final "historically" soft consonants in the infinitive: **rz, ż, cz, sz** always have -y in all persons except for **ja** and **oni**, e.g., **tańczyć** 'to dance': **tańczę** 'I'm dancing,' **tańczysz** 'you're dancing,' **tańczą** 'they're dancing'; **krzyczeć** 'to shout, scream': **krzyczę** 'I'm screaming,' **krzyczysz** 'you're screaming,' **krzyczą** 'they're screaming.'

Verbs with the soft consonants **-l, -ni** in the infinitive have -i in all persons except for **ja** and **oni**, e.g., **palić** 'to smoke': **palę**, 'I'm smoking,' **palisz** 'you're smoking,' **palą** 'they're smoking'; **myśleć** 'to think': **myślę** 'I'm thinking,' **myślisz** 'you're thinking,' **myślą** 'they're thinking.'

Infinitives with soft stem-final consonants have the following systematic shifts in: si→sz, ci→c, zi→ż, dzi→dz, ści→szcz, ździ→żdż in **ja** and **oni** forms, e.g., **musieć** 'must': **muszę, musisz**; **prosić** 'to request': **proszę, prosisz**. In all other forms the stem goes back to its original form.

tańczyć 'to dance'

Singular	Plural
(**ja**) **tańczę** 'I dance'	(**my**) **tańczymy** 'we dance'
(**ty**) **tańczysz** 'you dance'	(**wy**) **tańczycie** 'you dance'
on/ona/ono tańczy 'he/she/it dances'	**oni/one tańczą** 'they dance'

słyszeć 'to hear'

Singular	Plural
(ja) słyszę 'I hear'	**(my) słyszymy** 'we hear'
(ty) słyszysz 'you hear'	**(wy) słyszycie** 'you hear'
on/ona/ono słyszy 'he/she/it hears'	**oni/one słyszą** 'they hear'

The following verbs are conjugated similarly:

cieszyć (się) 'to please' ('to be glad')
krzyczeć 'to shout'

Verbs ending in a vowel + -ić have a predictable shift from i to j in the first person singular and third person plural.

kroić 'to cut'

Singular	Plural
(ja) kroję 'I cut'	**(my) kroimy** 'we cut'
(ty) kroisz 'you cut'	**(wy) kroicie** 'you cut'
on/ona/ono kroi 'he/she/it cuts'	**oni/one kroją** 'they cut'

leczyć 'to treat,' **kończyć** 'to end'
leżeć 'to be lying'
liczyć 'to count,' **łączyć** 'to connect,' **patrzyć/patrzeć na** <+ACC> 'to look at'
położyć 'to place horizontally' <PFV>, **suszyć** 'to dry,' **tłumaczyć** 'to translate'
uczyć (się) 'to teach' ('to learn'), **wierzyć** 'to believe,' **zobaczyć** 'to see' <PFV>
życzyć komuś <DAT> **czegoś** <GEN> 'to wish somebody something'

When an infinitive has the soft consonant l, ci, dzi, mi, bi, pi, si, ni, zi before -eć/-ić, always add -i, never -y in all persons except the first person singular and third person plural.

myśleć 'to think'

Singular	Plural
(ja) myślę 'I think'	**(my) myślimy** 'we think'
(ty) myślisz 'you think'	**(wy) myślicie** 'you think'
on/ona/ono myśli 'he/she/it thinks'	**oni/one myślą** 'they think'

szkolić (się) 'to train' ('to undergo training')

Singular	Plural
(ja) szkolę 'I train'	(my) szkolimy 'we train'
(ty) szkolisz 'you train'	(wy) szkolicie 'you train'
on/ona/ono szkoli 'he/she/it trains'	oni/one szkolą 'they train'

The following verbs are conjugated similarly: woleć 'to prefer,' palić 'to smoke,' śnić 'to dream,' kpić/drwić 'to mock,' zwolnić 'to dismiss (oneself),' 'to slow down,' oznajmić 'to announce,' dzielić (się) 'to divide' ('to share').

| 6.6.1.5 | *Systematic shifts in stem-final consonants* |

The changes occur only in **ja** and **oni/one** forms. In all other persons the stem goes back to its root (without -ić/-(i)eć), and then the regular non-past endings are added:

ci→c	płacić 'to pay'	płacę, płacisz
	lecieć 'to fly'	lecę, lecisz
dzi→dz	chodzić 'to walk'	chodzę, chodzisz
	siedzieć 'to be sitting'	siedzę, siedzisz
si→sz	prosić 'to request'	proszę, prosisz
	musieć 'to have to'	muszę, musisz
ści→szcz	czyścić 'to clean'	czyszczę, czyścić
	pościć 'to fast'	poszczę, pościsz
zi→ż	wozić 'to transport'	wożę, wozisz
	grozić 'to threaten'	grożę, grozisz
ździ→żdż	jeździć 'to ride'	jeżdżę, jeździsz

Chrzcić 'to baptize' conjugates (ja) chrzczę, (ty) chrzcisz, oni chrzczą.

prosić 'to request'

Singular	Plural
(ja) proszę 'I request'	(my) prosimy 'we request'
(ty) prosisz 'you request'	(wy) prosicie 'you request'
on/ona/ono prosi 'he/she/it requests'	oni/one proszą 'they request'

Verbs with the final labial consonants **b, p, w, f**, e.g., -**bić: lubić** 'to like,' **robić** 'to do'; -**wić: mówić** 'to speak,' **martwić się o kogoś/o coś** <ACC> 'to worry about somebody/something'; -**pić: kupić** 'to purchase' <PFV>, **wątpić** 'to doubt,' **trafić** 'to hit,' **potrafić** 'to be able to,' carry the -i- sound in all persons.

lubić kogoś/coś 'to like somebody/something'

Singular	Plural
(**ja**) **lubię** 'I like'	(**my**) **lubimy** 'we like'
(**ty**) **lubisz** 'you like'	(**wy**) **lubicie** 'you like'
on/ona/ono lubi 'he/she/it likes'	**oni/one lubią** 'they like'

Irregular verbs: **spać** 'to sleep,' **bać się kogoś/czegoś** <GEN> 'to be afraid of somebody/something,' 'to worry'

Singular	Plural
(**ja**) **śpię** 'I sleep'	(**my**) **śpimy** 'we sleep'
(**ty**) **śpisz** 'you sleep'	(**wy**) **śpicie** 'you sleep'
on/ona/ono śpi 'he/she/it sleeps'	**oni/one śpią** 'they sleep'
(**ja**) **boję się** 'I am afraid'	(**my**) **boimy się** 'we are afraid'
(**ty**) **boisz się** 'you are afraid'	(**wy**) **boicie się** 'you are afraid'
on/ona/ono boi się 'he/she/it is afraid'	**oni/one boją się** 'they are afraid'

6.6.2 Past

The past tense in Polish is used to express a process, action or event in the past.

The imperfective, non-accomplished aspect of the verb is used to express a process: **wczoraj robiłam naleśniki** 'I was making pancakes yesterday.'

The perfective, accomplished aspect is used to express actions or events in the past, with emphasis on the results of the action: **wczoraj zrobiłam naleśniki** 'I made pancakes yesterday.'

A phrase taken out of its wider context can be interpreted as either imperfective or perfective, e.g., **czytałem tę książkę** can be 'I read <past> this book' or 'I was reading this book.' What English expresses through different past tenses, Polish expresses through aspects in the past tense. (See 6.4)

<table>
<tr><td>6.6.2.1</td><td>Formation</td></tr>
</table>

To form the past tense of the majority of verbs, drop the infinitive ending -ć, and add the past tense endings agreeing with the person, number and class of the subject.

Table 6.4 Past tense endings

| Singular | | | |
Person	MSC	FEM	NT
1st 'I'	**-łem**	**-łam**	(potential form **-ł-om**)
2nd 'you'	**-łeś**	**-łaś**	(potential form **-ł-oś**)
3rd 'he,' 'she,' 'it'	**-ł**	**-ła**	**-ło**

| Plural | | |
Person	MHPL form	NO-MHPL form
1st 'we'	**-liśmy**	**-łyśmy**
2nd 'you'	**-liście**	**-łyście**
3rd 'they'	**-li**	**-ły**

In the singular past tense verbs can have three classes: masculine, feminine and neuter. In the plural there are only two forms:

1. with -li, when referring to male human beings or a group with at least one male human being, e.g.:

   chłopcy *byli* **w domu** '[the] boys *were* at home'
   kobiety i mężczyźni *byli* **w domu** '[the] women and men *were* at home'

2. with -ły, when referring to a group with no male human beings:

   kobiety i dzieci *były* **w domu** '[the] women and children *were* at home'

Note: In the same way, when a female and a male animal constitute the group it is referred to with -li, e.g., **córka z psem byli w domu** 'my daughter and a dog were at home,' **dwie dziewczynki i cztery psy byli w domu** 'two girls and four dogs were at home.'

Below is the conjugation of the verb **być** 'to be' in the past tense. Note that the past tense indicators -ł-/-l- are added to the root of the verb (after deleting the infinitive ending -ć) and are present in all persons of the past tense. Then the indicators are followed by the gender indicator -e for masculine forms and -a for feminine forms, -o for neuter forms in the singular, -i for groups of/with a human male, -y for groups without a male human, then person indicators are added: -m for the first person, ś for the second person, and finally the number indicator is added: -my, -cie for the plural.

by-	**-ł-**	**-a-**	**-ś**
root	past tense indicator	feminine form	second person singular

Table 6.5 Past tense of **być**

Singular			
Person	MSC	FEM	NT
1st 'I was'	by-ł-em	by-ł-am	(potential form **by-ł-om**)
2nd 'you were'	by-ł-eś	by-ł-aś	(potential form **by-ł-oś**)
3rd 'he, she, it was'	by-ł	by-ła	by-ło

Plural	MHPL form	NO-MHPL form
1st 'we were'	by-li-ś-my	by-ły-ś-my
2nd 'you were'	by-li-ś-cie	by-ły-ś-cie
3rd 'they were'	by-li	by-ły

In order to emphasize the actor(s), the past tense endings -ś, -śmy, -ście can be detached from the verb and added to question words. When moving -ś, the remaining e or a at the end of the verb disappears. This construction has a more informal register.

Gdzie byłeś? 'Where were you?'
Gdzieś był? 'Where were you?'
Co zrobiliście? 'What have you done?'
Coście zrobili? 'What have you done?'

| 6.6.2.2 | *Potential forms* **-łom, -łoś** |

Ja 'I' and **ty** 'you' neuter past tense forms do not exist, although potentially they can be formed. It is assumed that each subject of neuter grammatical class has a biological gender which dictates the form of the verb, e.g., **dziecko** 'a child' would say **byłam** or **byłem**, depending on its sex. Objects of neuter class, such as **słońce** 'the sun,' **piwo** 'beer' do not have the ability to express themselves (except in situations such as fairy tales with anthropomorphized inanimate objects, e.g., **Dzień dobry słońce! Gdzie byłoś w nocy?** 'Hello, sun! Where were you at night?').

Without past tense and gender indicators, the endings would be the following. You can consider this as scaffolding for the past tense, the conditional mood, and the future with the past tense form that could be used with neuter nouns.

	Singular	Plural
1st person	**-m**	**-śmy**
2nd person	**-ś**	**-ście**
3rd person	-∅	-∅

| 6.6.2.3 | *Stress in the past tense plural* **my** *'we' and* **wy** *'you' forms* |

In the past tense **my** 'we' and **wy** 'you' forms, stress falls on the third syllable from the last (on the last vowel directly before -li/-ły). In other words, the stress never falls on the past tense endings -li/-ły, -śmy/-ście, e.g., **pracowaliśmy, poszliście** (1.4).

| 6.6.2.4 | *Past tense conjugation* |

Verbs with the infinitive endings -ać, -ić, -yć such as **czytać, pracować, pić, mówić, myć, tańczyć** have a very regular past tense conjugation. Simply delete the final -ć and add regular past tense endings.

Note that -ować verbs do not change to -uj-, as was the case in the present (non-past) forms.

pracować 'to work'

Table 6.6 Past tense of **pracować**

Singular			
Person	MSC	FEM	NT
1st 'I worked'	**pracowałem**	**pracowałam**	
2nd 'you worked'	**pracowałeś**	**pracowałaś**	
3rd 'he/she/it worked'	**pracował**	**pracowała**	**pracowało**

Plural		
Person	MHPL	NO-MHPL
1st 'we worked'	**pracowaliśmy**	**pracowałyśmy**
2nd 'you worked'	**pracowaliście**	**pracowałyście**
3rd 'they worked'	**pracowali**	**pracowały**

Verbs with the infinitive ending -eć, e.g., **mieć** 'to have': e→a in all forms except male human forms.

Table 6.7 Past tense of **mieć** 'to have'

Singular			
Person	MSC	FEM	NT
1st 'I had'	**miałem**	**miałam**	
2nd 'you had'	**miałeś**	**miałaś**	
3rd 'he/she/it had'	**miał**	**miała**	**miało**

Plural		
Person	MHPL	NO-MHPL
1st 'we had'	**mieliśmy**	**miałyśmy**
2nd 'you had'	**mieliście**	**miałyście**
3rd 'they had'	**mieli**	**miały**

Similarly: **chcieć** 'to want,' **musieć** 'must,' **myśleć** 'to think,' **widzieć** 'to see,' **wiedzieć** 'to know'

Verbs with the infinitive ending -ąć, e.g., **wziąć** 'to take' <PFV>: the final nasal vowel -ą becomes the other nasal -ę in all persons except the male singular. Note that -ął is pronounced -oł [wziołem], and -ął is pronounced -eł [wziełam], [wzieli], [wzięły].

Table 6.8 Past tense of **wziąć** 'to take'

Singular Person	MSC	FEM	NT
1st 'I took'	**wziąłem**	**wzięłam**	
2nd 'you took'	**wziąłeś**	**wzięłaś**	
3rd 'he/she/it took'	**wziął**	**wzięła**	**wzięło**

Plural Person	MHPL	NO-MHPL
1st 'we took'	**wzięliśmy**	**wzięłyśmy**
2nd 'you took'	**wzięliście**	**wzięłyście**
3rd 'they took'	**wzięli**	**wzięły**

Similarly: **zacząć** 'to begin' <PFV>, **wynająć** 'to hire,' 'to rent' <PFV>, **objąć** 'to hug' <PFV>, **zginąć** 'to die (from unnatural causes)' <PFV>.

Verbs with the infinitive ending -ść, e.g., **jeść** 'to eat,' **kłaść** 'to put something horizontally' and **usiąść** 'to take a seat': delete -ść, add -d-, and then attach regular past tense endings. Note that **jeść** also changes final e→a in all forms except the male human form.

Table 6.9 Past tense of **jeść** 'to eat'

Singular Person	MSC	FEM	NT
1st 'I ate'	**jadłem**	**jadłam**	
2nd 'you ate'	**jadłeś**	**jadłaś**	
3rd 'he/she/it ate'	**jadł**	**jadła**	**jadło**

Plural Person	MHPL	NO-MHPL
1st 'we ate'	**jedliśmy**	**jadłyśmy**
2nd 'you ate'	**jedliście**	**jadłyście**
3rd 'they ate'	**jedli**	**jadły**

Usiąść 'to take a seat' <PFV> conjugates like **jeść**, with -siad- in all forms except male human plural forms (-sied-).

Table 6.10 Past tense of **iść/(pójść)** 'to go, walk'

Singular Person	MSC	FEM	NT
1st 'I was going (went)'	(po)szedłem	(po)szłam	
2nd 'you were going'	(po)szedłeś	(po)szłaś	
3rd 'he/she/it was going'	(po)szedł	(po)szła	(po)szło

Plural Person	MHPL	NO-MHPL
1st 'we were going'	(po)szliśmy	(po)szłyśmy
2nd 'you were going'	(po)szliście	(po)szłyście
3rd 'they were going'	(po)szli	(po)szły

Nieść 'to carry in hands' and wieźć 'to carry in a vehicle, to transport' and their prefixed forms have the following conjugation in the past tense: delete -ść, change the stem to **nios/wioz** (like in the first person singular present tense form **niosę/wiozę** 'I'm carrying') and then add regular past tense endings. The **on** 'he' form is **niósł/wiózł**, and male human forms have their stem changed to **nieś-/wieź** (identical to imperative forms).

Table 6.11 Past tense of **nieść** and **wieźć**

Singular Person	MSC	FEM	NT
1st 'I carried'/'I carried by vehicle'	nios-łem/ wioz-łem	nios-łam/ wioz-łam	
2nd 'you carried'	nios-łeś/ wioz-łeś	nios-łaś/ wioz-łaś	
3rd 'he/she/it carried'	niósł/wiózł	nios-ła/wioz-ła	nios-ło/ wioz-ło

Plural Person	MHPL	NO-MHPL
1st 'we carried'	nieśliśmy/wieźliśmy	nios-łyśmy/wiozłyśmy
2nd 'you carried'	nieśliście/wieźliście	nios-łyście/wiozłyście
3rd 'they carried'	nieśli/wieźli	nios-ły/wiozły

To conjugate **znaleźć** 'to find,' delete **źć**, add all singular and plural no male human past tense endings to the modified stem **znalazł**, e.g., **znalazłem** 'I found it' <MSC SG>.

Add all male human forms to the modified stem **znaleźli**.

Verbs with the infinitive ending -c: **móc/pomóc** (ó:o alternation), **biec, piec**, add past tense endings to -*mog*-, -*bieg*-, -*piek*-. The 'he' form is **mógł, biegł, piekł**.

Table 6.12 Past tense of verbs ending **-c**

Singular Person	MSC	FEM	NT
1st 'I could'	**mogłem**	**mogłam**	
2nd 'you could'	**mogłeś**	**mogłaś**	
3rd 'he/she/it could'	**mógł**	**mogła**	**mogło**

Plural Person	MHPL	NO-MHPL
1st 'we could'	**mogliśmy**	**mogłyśmy**
2nd 'you could'	**mogliście**	**mogłyście**
3rd 'they could'	**mogli**	**mogły**

6.6.2.5 *Past perfect*

Past perfect forms are used mostly in literary works to express past actions.

The past tense forms of the particular verb we want to use in the past perfect are added to the forms of the third person singular or plural of the verb **być** 'to be': **był, była, było, byli, były**: **Czytałem** <1 PR SG MSC> **był** <3 PR SG MSC> **onegdaj tę księgę** 'I had read the book once.'

6.6.3 **Future**

The future tense expresses actions that will continue or will happen in the future after the moment of speaking. As opposed to past actions, which are known, the future can involve probability, possibility and uncertainty.

The future has two tenses: simple and compound.

The immediate future places a process in continuation and is often expressed through present tense constructions: **idę zrobić pedicure** 'I'm going to get a pedicure.' (See 6.6.3.2.1)

Table 6.13 Future tense of **być**

Person	Singular	Plural
1st	**będę** 'I will be'	**będziemy** 'we will be'
2nd	**będziesz** 'you will be'	**będziecie** 'you will be'
3rd	**będzie** 'he/she/it will be'	**będą** 'they will be'

The verb **być** in the future translates "will be"; **jutro będzie gorąco** 'tomorrow will be hot' (not: będzie być).

6.6.3.1 | Imperfective: compound future

The compound future is used to express a process that is going to continue in the future. The compound future referring to an unfolding process does not emphasize the outcome, since the future is in a sense uncertain, so it uses imperfective forms of verbs.

> **Kiedyś _będziemy robić_ to, na co mamy ochotę.** 'One day _we will be doing_ what we want.'

The compound future referring to an outcome which is expected to be reached emphasizes the outcome and so uses perfective forms of the passive participle.

> **Projekt _będzie zrobiony_ na jutro.** 'The project _will be done_ for tomorrow.'
> **Za tydzień dom będzie sprzedany.** 'In a week the house will be sold.'

6.6.3.1.1 | Formation

The future tense of imperfective verbs, also known as the compound future, can be made up in two ways.

1. The future tense forms of the verb 'to be' plus the imperfective infinitive. This gives us no information about the speaker's gender, unless the subject specifies it.

> **Będę głosować na ekologów.** 'I will vote for ecologists.'

2. The future tense forms of the verb 'to be' plus the third person singular or plural of the past tense (-ł, -ła, -ło, -li, -ły forms). This gives us information about the speaker's gender.

Będę głosowała <FEM> **na ekologów.**
'I will vote for ecologists.'

Będę głosował <MSC> **na ekologów.**
'I will vote for ecologists.'

Constructions with the past tense must be used to form the future with modal verbs.

Będę musiał coś z tym zrobić.
'I will have to do something with it.'

Za rok będziesz mógł robić to, co będziesz chciał.
'In a year you will be able to do what you [will] want to do.'

Do not use perfective verbs with the future forms of the verb 'to be.'

będę kupować or **będę kupował** <MSC>
'I will buy,' not: będę kupić.

Table 6.14 Future tense of **grać**

Singular Person	MSC	FEM	NT	
1st	**będę grał**	**będę grała**	—	'I will play'
2nd	**będziesz grał**	**będziesz grała**	—	'you will play'
3rd	**będzie grał**	**będzie grała**	**będzie grało**	'he/she/it will play'

Plural Person	MHPL	NO-MHPL	
1st	**będziemy grali**	**będziemy grały**	'we will play'
2nd	**będziecie grali**	**będziecie grały**	'you will play'
3rd	**będą grali**	**będę grały**	'they will play'

The future tense in Polish, unlike in English, is used after conjunctions of time (od) **kiedy** '(since) when,' **jeśli** 'if,' **jak tylko** 'as soon as'

Kiedy/Jeśli będziesz w Krakowie, zadzwoń. 'When/If you are [will be] in Cracow, call [me].'

| 6.6.3.1.2 | Compound future word order |

To negate the compound future, place **nie** in front of the future tense form of the verb 'to be,' e.g.:

Nie będę głosować na ekologów. 'I will not vote for ecologists.'

Changing the word order and placing the future tense form of the verb 'to be' after the imperfective infinitive will result in an emotionally charged sentence.

Na ekologów głosować nie będę. 'For ecologists I will *not* vote.'
Więcej na ten temat rozmawiać nie będę. 'I won't talk about it any more.'

| 6.6.3.2 | *Perfective: simple future* |

The future tense of perfective verbs, also known as the simple future, is simple because it is made up of the conjugated perfective verb, with endings identical to the present tense.

In Polish, to create a perfective form from an imperfective verb, a prefix is often added to the imperfective verb (see 6.4.8), e.g.,

malować <IMPFV>/**na-malować** <PFV> 'to paint'
czytać <IMPFV>/**prze-czytać** <PFV> 'to read'

The future tense of most perfective verbs looks a lot like the present tense of the imperfective, e.g.,

Present	Future
czytam <IMPFV> 'I am reading'	**prze-***czytam* <PFV> 'I will read'
czytasz <IMPFV> 'you are reading'	**prze-***czytasz* <PFV> 'you will read'
maluję <IMPFV> 'I am painting'	**na-***maluję* <PFV> 'I will paint'
malujesz <IMPFV> 'you are painting'	**na-***malujesz* <PFV> 'you will paint'

Therefore the term "non-past form" is often used when referring to the present and future in comparison to the past tense.

The simple future in independent clauses is used to express (see 6.4.4, 6.4.5):

• an order

   Pójdziesz do babci i ją przeprosisz. 'You will go to grandma and will apologize to her.'

- a request

  Na jutro proszę przeczytać ten artykuł. 'For tomorrow, please read the article.'

- an offer

  Zatańczymy? 'Shall we dance?'
  Pomogę pani. 'I'll help you, madam.'
  Zrobię kawę. 'I'll make some coffee.'

- a prediction

  Jestem pewna, że czegoś zapomnę. 'I'm sure that I'll forget something.'
  Ona nigdy go nie pokocha. 'She will never fall in love with him.'
  Niedługo się zobaczymy. 'We'll see each other soon.'
  Zaraz się rozpada. 'It'll start to rain steadily any minute.'

- determination

  Do maja nauczę się gotować. 'I'll learn to cook by May.'
  W przyszłym roku kupię dom. 'Next year I'll buy a house.'
  Prawda zwycięży. 'The truth will prevail.'

- reassurance

  Czy przeczytasz artykuł?
  'Will you finish the article?' (as I asked you to)
  Spróbujesz z nim porozmawiać?

  'Will you try to talk to him?'

- completion of events in the future

  Zadzwonię wieczorem. 'I'll call in the evening.'
  Skończysz do jutra?. 'Will you finish by tomorrow?'

- a sequence of events

  Kupię kwiaty i pójdę do niej.
  'I'll buy flowers and will go to see her.'

  Pójdziemy, kiedy skończę.
  'We'll go when I [will] finish.'

  Zadzwonię, jak tylko dojedziemy na miejsce.
  'I'll call as soon as we get to the place.'

6.6.3.2.1 Future expressed in present tense: Future event is planned

Set plans are often expressed through the present tense (imperfective aspect).

Wyjeżdżam za godzinę. 'I'm leaving in an hour.'
Jutro rano idę do dentysty. 'I'm going to the dentist's tomorrow morning.'

The immediate future is often expressed through the present tense accompanied by time specifiers such as **właśnie, zaraz** 'just':

Zaraz wracam. 'I'll be right back.'
Właśnie wychodzimy. 'We are (about) to leave.'

6.6.3.2.2 Future expressed in present tense: Future event is certain to occur

Jutro jest piątek. 'Tomorrow is Friday.'
Jutro mam urodziny. 'Tomorrow is my birthday.'

6.6.3.2.3 Expressing intentions in the future

Zamierzać/planować 'to be going to do something'

The future tense is often expressed by the verbs **zamierzać** 'to be going to do something' or **planować** 'to plan to do something.' Both verbs are followed by perfective or imperfective infinitives.

Zamierzam często was odwiedzać <IMPFV>. 'I plan to visit you often.'
Zamierzam was jutro odwiedzić <PFV>. 'I plan to visit you tomorrow.'

6.6.3.2.4 Future of the past

A future event is seen as being in progress from a viewpoint in the past.

Wiedziałem, że będziesz czekała.
'I knew that you would be waiting.'

Miałam nadzieję, że będziesz szczęśliwy w Paryżu.
'I hoped that you would be happy in Paris.'

A future event is seen as completed from a viewpoint in the past.

Wiedzieliśmy, że nas nie zawiedziesz.
'We knew that you would not let us down.'

Czułem, że do mnie napiszesz.
'I had a feeling that you would write to me.'

403

6.7 Conditional

The marker of the conditional mood is the suffix **-by**. The conditional mood expresses actions and events that are not guaranteed to happen; they can or could happen *if* certain conditions are met. It corresponds to English constructions with "would," "could," "might."

Conditional forms of the verb **kupić** <PFV> 'to buy':

> **Gdybym miał pieniądze, kupiłbym ten dom.**
> 'If I had money, I would buy this house.'

> **Kupiłbyś mi coś słodkiego?**
> 'Would you buy me something sweet?'

The conditional mood is made up of the third person form of the past tense (forms with **-ł, -ła, -ło, -li, -ły**) of both imperfective and perfective verbs, and combined with the appropriate form of the suffix **-by**.

Table 6.15 Conditional suffixes

Person	Singular	Plural
1st	**-bym**	**-byśmy**
2nd	**-byś**	**-byście**
3rd	**-by**	**-by**

Table 6.16 Conditional of **kupić** <PFV>

Singular Person	Masculine	Feminine	Neuter	
1st	**kupiłbym**	**kupiłabym**	—	'I would buy'
2nd	**kupiłbyś**	**kupiłabyś**	—	'you would buy'
3rd	**kupiłby**	**kupiłaby**	**kupiło by**	'he/she/it would buy'

Plural Person	MHPL	NO-MHPL	
1st	**kupilibyśmy**	**kupiłybyśmy**	'we would buy'
2nd	**kupilibyście**	**kupiłybyście**	'you would buy'
3rd	**kupiliby**	**kupiłyby**	'they would buy'

For stress in the conditional mood, see 1.4.

6.7.1 | Movable -by

In order to emphasize the actor, the particle -by can be detached from the verb and placed directly after the personal pronoun.

Ja bym nie odmówił. 'I would not refuse.'
Oni by nie zapomnieli. 'They would not forget.'
Ja bym mu <DAT> **dał.** 'I would teach him.' (coll.)
A co ty byś zrobił na moim miejscu? 'And you, what would you do in my situation?'

The suffix -by can also be attached to the auxiliary verb **być** before adverbs to emphasize the continuation of an action.

Zawsze byłbym cię kochał. 'I would always have loved you.'
Zawsze bym cię kochał. 'I would always love you.'

6.7.2 | Use

It is important to emphasize that in Polish the time of the sentence is determined by the main verb.

Poradzisz sobie. 'You will succeed.'
Wiem, że sobie poradzisz. 'I know that you will succeed.'
Wiedziałem, że sobie poradzisz. 'I knew that you would [will] succeed.'

In the last sentence the future event seen from a viewpoint in the past uses the future simple tense in Polish, while in English it requires the *would* form.

The conditional mood can express:

* requests/demands:

> **Czy mógłby pan zamknąć okno?**
> 'Could you please close the window?'
>
> **Przestałbyś palić w domu.**
> 'Could you stop smoking at home.'

* wishes:

> **Chciałbym dokądś wyjechać.** 'I'd like to go somewhere.'
> **Zjadłabym coś słodkiego.** 'I would/might eat something sweet.'

405

- supposition:

> **Mogłabyś to zrobić?** 'Could you do it?'
> **Wolałbym** <MSC IMPFV> **nie myśleć, co mogłoby się stać.**
> 'I would rather not think what might have happened.'

To express a hypothetical condition, a subordinate clause is required. The marker of the subordinate clause is the conjunction **gdy-** '*if*'.

In hypothetical sentences, the markers of a hypothetical condition (**gdy-** 'if') and the conditional mood (-**by** 'would') are attached to each other to form **gdyby**, and then the endings of the suffix **by-** are added. There are no markers attached to the verb in the subordinate clause (the one without "if")

Hypothetical condition in the present:

> **Gdybyś kupił ser, zrobiłabym pizzę.**
> 'If you bought cheese I would make pizza.'

In Polish, the verbs in both clauses are used in the conditional mood. In English, the verb in the main clause is used in the conditional mood, but the clause with "if" is in the past tense.

Hypothetical condition in the past:

> **Gdybyś kupił ser, zrobiłabym pizzę.**
> 'If you had bought cheese, I would have made pizza.' (but you did not)

> **Gdybym wiedział, zadzwoniłbym.**
> 'Had I known, I would have called.' (but I didn't know)

In Polish, the verbs in both clauses are used in the conditional mood. In English, the verb in the main clause is used in the conditional mood, but the clause with "if" is in the past perfect.

Note: There is a past conditional in Polish which is used less often:

> **Gdybyś był kupił ser, zrobiłabym pizzę.**
> 'If you had bought cheese, I would have made pizza.' (but you did not)

> **Gdybym był wiedział, zadzwoniłbym.**
> 'Had I known, I would have called.' (but I didn't know)

Both imperfective and perfective verbs are used in the conditional mood:

> **Gdybym tylko miała czas, cześciej chodziłabym** <IMPFV> **do kina.**
> 'If only I had had time, I would have gone to the movies more often.'

Gdybym tylko miała czas, poszłabym <PFV> **do kina.**
'If only I had had time, I would have gone to the movies.'

The conditional endings **-bym/-byś/-by/-byśmy/-byście/-by** are written together or separately.

They are written together with the past tense form of verbs: **czytałbym** 'I would write' <MSC> (not: czytałemby), and with the conjunction "if" **gdyby/jeśliby**.

Conditional endings are written separately after all other parts of speech:

Co by było, gdyby ...? 'What would happen if ...?'
Pożyczyć byś mogła coś do czytania. 'You could lend something to read.'

6.7.2.1 | *Hypothesis without* **gdyby**

Na twoim miejscu, zacząłbym szukać pracy. 'In your place (= If I were you), I would start looking for a job.'
Co byś zrobił na moim miejscu? 'What would you do if you were in my situation?'

Chcę, żebyś skończył studia. 'I want you to graduate.' (see 6.20)

6.7.3 | *Impersonal*

The impersonal conditional is created by combining modal verbs and impersonal verbs (with the endings **-no, -to**) with the suffix **-by** (*written separately*).

Można by pójść na spacer. 'One might go for a walk.'
Można by było pójść na spacer. 'One could go for a walk.'
Trzeba by zadzwonić do rodziców. 'We/you/etc. should call [our/your/etc.] parents.'
Szkoda by było to wyrzucić. 'It would be a waste to throw it out.'
Warto by było pójść na tę wystawę. 'It would be worth going for the exhibition.'
Powinni byście zadzwonić. 'You should have called.'
Mówiono by o nas wszędzie. 'They would talk about us everywhere.'
Nagrodę przyznano by wcześniej. 'The award would be given earlier.'

6.8 Imperative

Za króla Sasa jedz, pij i popuszczaj pasa! (saying)
[lit. 'During the Saxon times, eat, drink and loosen your belt.']

The imperative is used to give orders, and express commands and prohibitions. It is also used to make suggestions and requests: **Nie pal!** 'Don't smoke!'

It is mostly used in spoken Polish, in the second persons singular and plural **ty** and **wy** and the first person plural **my**. It can also be used in a form of infinitive, e.g., **Nie deptać trawników!** 'Do not step on the grass!' or in a form of indicative mood with a strong intimation, e.g., **Weźmiesz go ze sobą!** 'You *will* take him with you!' For suggestions and polite requests, but still imposing an action on somebody, a conditional mood can be used, e.g., **Może zrobiłbyś kolację.** 'Maybe you could make dinner.' Additionally, a construction with **proszę** 'please' followed by an infinitive can be used (e.g., **Proszę wejść.** 'Please come in.') or **proszę** followed by an imperative (e.g., **Proszę wejdź!** 'Please come in!' <informal>).

The imperative mood can be used with imperfective and perfective verbs. With perfective verbs, it relates to the completion of the command: **Napij się!** 'Have a drink!' **Usiądź!** 'Have a seat!' With imperfective verbs, it relates to the process of fulfilling the command: **Pij!** 'Drink!' **Siedź spokojnie!** 'Sit still!' (See 6.8.3)

Płacz, płacz, poczujesz się lepiej! 'Cry, cry, you will feel better.'
Nie śpij! 'Don't sleep!'
Jesteś w ciąży? Nie pij! 'Are you pregnant? Don't drink!'

6.8.1 Formation

The forms of the imperative are based on the present indicative.

Verbs with -am, -a, -ają

Drop the final -ą in the third person plural and this will create the imperative form for **ty**, then add -**cie** to form the imperative for **wy**, add -**my** to form the imperative for **my** in the meaning of "let's."

czytać: **czytaj!** 'read!' (you, SG)   (present indicative: *oni czytają*)
czytaj-cie! 'read!' (you all)
czytaj-my! 'let's read!'

The difference between the present indicative and imperative mood in the first and second persons plural is in the -j- sound:

(my) **czytamy** 'we're reading,' **czytajmy!** 'let's read!'

(wy) **czytacie** 'you're reading,' **czytajcie!** read! (you all)

For all other verbs drop the final letter in the third person singular.

kupić:	**Kup** *coś ładnego!* 'Buy *something nice!*'
	Kupcie *chleb!* 'Buy *some bread!*'
	Kupmy *nowy komputer!* 'Let's buy *a new computer!*'
(za)tańczyć:	**(za)tańcz!** 'dance!'
	(za)tańczcie! 'dance!'
	(za)tańczmy! 'let's dance!'
(na)pisać:	**(na)pisz!** 'write!'
	(na)piszcie! 'write!'
	(na)piszmy! 'let's write!'
(po)myśleć:	**(po)myśl!** 'think!'
	(po)myślcie! 'think!'
	(po)myślmy! 'let's think!'
(z)robić:	**(Z)rób** *coś!* 'Do *something!*'
	(Z)róbcie *zakupy!* 'Do *shopping!*'
	(Z)róbmy *jej niespodziankę!* 'Let's *surprise her!*'

Verbs that end in the third person singular with -ie drop the vowel -e and add -j.

zacząć:	**Zacznij** *mówić!* 'Start *talking!*'
(on zacznie)	**Zacznijcie** *beze mnie!* 'Start *without me!*'
	Zacznijmy *nowe życie!* 'Let's start *a new life!*'

All imperatives based on the motion verbs **iść, chodzić** and **jechać** end with **dź** (pronounced [ć], if at the end of the word).

Idź do domu! 'Go home!'
Chodźmy spać! 'Let's go to bed!'
Wyjdź <PFV> **z mojego pokoju!** 'Get out of my room!'
Nie wychodź sama! 'Do not go out alone!'
Chodź tu! 'Come here!'
Chodźmy już! 'Let's go!'
Jedźcie sami! 'Go (ride) by yourself!'

Verbs that end in the third person singular with -oi, change to -ój:

(Po)krój cebulę! 'Chop the onion!'
Stój! 'Stand!' 'Halt!'
Nie bój się mnie! 'Don't be afraid of me!'

Verbs that end in the third person singular with -i (Conjugation IV) take -j.

Śpij! 'Sleep!' (derived from <u>spać</u>/<u>on śpi</u>)

A few irregular frequently used imperative forms:

Weź to! 'Take it!'
Weź się w garść! 'Pull yourself together!'
Nie bierz tego! 'Don't take it!'
(Z)jedz coś! 'Eat something!'
Znajdź dla mnie czas! 'Find time for me!'
(O)powiedz nam jak było! 'Tell us how it was!'
Bądź ostrożny! 'Be careful!'
Bądźmy w kontakcie! 'Let's stay in touch.'

To make an imperative referring to a man or a woman, or a group of people, simply add the particle **niech** in front of the conjugated third person singular/plural verb.

Niech pani odda moje pieniądze! 'Give me my money!' (talking to a woman)
Niech pan odda moje pieniądze! 'Give me my money!' (talking to a man)
Niech państwo oddadzą moje pieniądze! 'Give me my money!' (talking to a couple or a group of people)

6.8.2 | Using infinitive

The infinitive can be used to give written orders or instructions in an impersonal way.

Podawać schłodzone. 'Serve chilled.'
Zażywać co cztery godziny. 'Take every four hours.'
Jeść, nie marudzić! 'You have to eat, not to whine!'
Żyć nie umierać! 'This is the life.'

(See also 2.4.7)

6.8.3 | Negative commands

Generally, negative commands are expressed with imperfective verbs.

Wróć <PFV> **przed północą!** 'Come back before midnight.'
Nie wracaj <IMPFV> **późno!** 'Do not come back late!'
Nie mów <IMPFV> **nikomu!** 'Do not tell anyone!'
Wypijmy <PFV> **za zdrowie gospodyni!** 'Let's drink to our host's health.'
Nie pijmy <IMPFV> **już!** 'Let's not drink any more!'

Sometimes negative commands are used with perfective verbs to express a warning. Negative commands are mostly used with the verbs (z)gubić 'to lose,' and zapomnieć 'to forget,' powiedzieć 'to tell,' pozwolić 'to allow.'

Tylko nie powiedz <PFV> **mamie.** 'Don't you dare tell mother!'
Tylko powiedz <PFV> **ojcu, a zobaczysz!** 'Tell father, and you will see [what I'm going to do to you].'
Nie zgub <PFV> **kluczy.** 'Don't lose the keys!'
Nie zapomnij <PFV> **wziąć paszport!** 'Don't forget to take [your] passport!'
Nie pozwól mu odejść <PFV>**!** 'Do not let him go!'

6.9 Participles

Participles have the dual nature of a verb and an adjective. They are formed from verbs, and based on the verbal stem the lexical meaning of the participle can be determined, but are declined like adjectives. They correspond in English to the "-ing" form, and replace **który** 'who/which' (adjectival participles) or **kiedy** 'while' (adverbial participles) clauses in a sentence.

dziecko, które śpi 'a child who sleeps'
śpiące dziecko 'a sleeping child'

Dziecko, kiedy śpi, rośnie. 'A child, when it is sleeping, grows.'
Dziecko śpiąc rośnie. 'A child, while sleeping, grows.'

Śpiąca królewna '*Sleeping Beauty*,' **znany artysta** 'known artist,'
mówiąc między nami 'just between you and me'

There are three adjectival participles (present active -ący, present passive and past passive, both -any, -ony, -ty) and two adverbial participles (-ąc, -wszy/-łszy).

Adjectival participles are formed from imperfective and perfective verbs, and are declined like adjectives.

Adverbial participles are also formed from imperfective and perfective verbs, but unlike adjectival participles, are indeclinable.

6.9.1 | Negated

All adjectival participles are written as one word when negated:

niepalący, niepijący człowiek 'non-smoking, non-drinking person'
Od tygodnia pada nieustający deszcz. 'It's been raining non-stop for a week.'

The exception to the rule is in phrases with conjunctions: **ani . . . ani** 'neither . . . nor'; **ale/lecz** 'but':

nie pijący, ale/lecz palący mężczyzna 'not a drinking but a smoking man'

Nie is written separately with adverbial participles:

nie wiedząc 'not knowing'
nie dowiedziawszy się 'not having known'

6.9.2 | Present active adjectival

Dla chcącego, nie ma nic trudnego.
'If there is a will, there is a way.' (saying)

Present active participles carry the meaning of the present tense and are formed from present tense (imperfective) verbs, that is, from the third person plural of the verb, to which the marker -ąc "-ing" is attached, followed by adjectival endings—nominative singular: -y <MSC>, -a <FEM>, -e <NT> and nominative plural: -y <MHPL>, -e <NO-MHPL>). These participles are used to replace a relative clause with **który** 'who/which.' In English the present active adjectival participle is often translated as "-ing," or "the one which is . . . -ing": "burning, the one which is burning," e.g., **płonący** <NOM MSC SG> **budynek** 'burning building.'

Present active participles are declined like adjectives and must agree in class, number and case with their subject. The subject or object, which the present active participle is modifying, is *active* in the construction in which it appears, e.g.:

To jest budynek <NOM MSC SG>**, który płonie.**
'This is the building which is burning.'

To jest płonący <NOM MSC SG> **budynek.**
'This is the burning building.'

W budynku <LOC MSC SG>**, który płonie, strażacy szukają dziecka.** 'In the building, which is burning, firefighters are looking for a child.'

W płonącym <LOC MSC SG> **budynku strażacy szukają dziecka.** 'In the burning building firefighters are looking for a child.'

obcokrajowiec <NOM SG>**, który mówi po polsku** 'a foreigner who speaks Polish'

obcokrajowiec <NOM SG>**, mówiący** <NOM SG> **po polsku** 'a Polish-speaking foreigner'

Mieszkam z obcokrajowcem <INS SG>**, który mówi po polsku.** 'I live with a foreigner that speaks Polish.'

Mieszkam z obcokrajowcem <INS SG>**, mówiącym** <INS SG> **po polsku.** 'I live with the Polish-speaking foreigner.'

<table><tr><td>6.9.2.1</td><td>Formation</td></tr></table>

Adjectival verbal participles decline like adjectives. Attach the present active adjectival participle marker -ąc to the third person plural of a present tense (imperfective) verb, and then add the appropriate adjectival ending—nominative singular: -y <MSC>, -a <FEM>, -e <NT> and nominative plural: -y <MHPL>, -e <NO-MHPL> (or other appropriate adjectival case endings)—so that the ending agrees in case, class and number with the noun it modifies.

The adjectival ending -y is characteristic for all male singular and all plural forms with male humans: **tańczący chłopiec** 'dancing boy,' **tańczący chłopcy** 'dancing boys,' **tańczący ludzie** 'dancing people.'

Infinitive	3rd person PL	Participle
spać	**śpią**	**śpią-cy/śpią-ca/śpią-ce** 'sleeping'
kochać	**kochają**	**kochają-cy/kochają-ca/kochją-ce** 'loving'
chodzić	**chodzą**	**chodzą-cy/chodzą-ca/chodzą-ce** 'walking'

The declinable active participle of the verb **być** 'to be' is **będący** <MSC NOM SG/ NOM MHPL>, **będąca** <FEM NOM SG>, **będące** <NT NOM SG/NOM NO-MHPL>.

śpiące <NT> **dziecko** 'sleeping child'
kochający <MSC> **mąż** 'loving husband'
chodząca <FEM> **encyklopedia** 'walking encyclopedia'

Tekst, będący istotną częścią kompozycji muzycznej, powinien być zrozumiały. The text, being an essential part of a musical composition, should be understandable.

A present active participle used in a sentence replaces a **który** 'who/which' clause or serves as an adjective or noun.

Pasażerowie, *którzy odlatują* do krajów strefy Schengen, przechodzą przez kontrolę bezpieczeństwa i kierują się do poczekalni odlotowych.
'Passengers *who fly* to Schengen zone, pass through safety control and then go through to the departure gates.'

Pasażerowie *odlatujący* do krajów strefy Schengen przechodzą przez kontrolę bezpieczeństwa i kierują się do poczekalni odlotowych.
'Passengers *flying* to Schengen zone, pass through safety control and then go through to the departure gates.'

The present active participle can serve as a noun but is declined like an adjective:

kupujący, kupująca 'shopper,' **sprzedający, sprzedająca** 'vendor,' **służący, służąca** 'servant,' **cierpiący, cierpiąca** 'sufferer,' **niepalący, niepaląca** 'non-smoker,' **niepijący, niepijąca** 'non-drinker,' **umierający, umierająca** 'dying person,' **przewodniczący** 'chairperson.'

Wagon dla niepalących 'Non-smoking compartment.'

Present active participle as adjective:

przekonywający 'convincing'

Nagle rozległ się ogłuszający huk.
'Suddenly a deafening roar blasted out.'

Idiomatic expressions with present active participles:

zrobić coś niechcący 'to do something accidentally'
Niechcący rozlałam kawę. 'I accidentally spilt the coffee.'
latający dywan 'magic carpet' [lit. 'flying carpet']

Uciekać jak szczury z tonącego okrętu. 'To run away like rats from a sinking ship.'
Tonący brzytwy się chwyta. 'A drowning man grasps for a straw' [lit. 'for a straight razor']

Do not form present active participles from perfective verbs.

Szukamy ludzi umiejących (not: potrafiący) **wykorzystywać najnowsze osiągnięcia techniki.**
'We are looking for people who are able to use the latest achievements in technology.'

Potrafić is a perfective verb and does not form a present active participle.

Passive participles correspond to English participles: **mówiony** 'spoken,' **importowany** 'imported,' **używany** 'used,' **zrobiony** 'done.' They are formed from imperfective and perfective infinitives of transitive verbs (verbs that must be followed by a direct object); they are not formed from reflexive verbs (verbs with **się**). They are declined like adjectives.

Their markers are **-any, -ony, -ty**, such as in **znany** 'known,' **zamknięty** 'closed,' **pieczony** 'baked.'

Passive participles formed from imperfective verbs inform us about an ongoing process.

język mówiony 'spoken language/the language that is being spoken'
używany samochód 'used car/the car that is being used'

Passive participles formed from perfective verbs (used more often) inform us that an event has been accomplished. The people and things the past passive participles modify are *passive* in the construction in which they appear, as things can be closed, opened, built, finished, forgotten, made, purchased.

To są zużyte baterie.
'These are worn out batteries.'

Co zrobić ze zużytymi bateriami?
'What do we do with worn out batteries?'

The passive participle is used to form the passive voice (see 6.12).

6.9.3.1 *Formation*

Passive participles are formed from imperfective or perfective transitive verbs (verbs that are followed by a noun in the accusative case and non-reflexive verbs) by dropping -(ś)ć, -c from the infinitive, and adding the suffix -n-, -on-, -t- followed by the adjectival ending (-y, -a, -e, -i). They decline like adjectives.

1. Passive participles formed from verbs ending in -ać and -eć (not derived from -rzeć, such as **drzeć** 'to tear') in the infinitive are formed by dropping -ć and adding the suffix -n- followed by the adjectival endings (-y, -a, -e, -i).

Passive participles formed from verbs ending in -ać

INF	drop the INF ending -ć	add suffix -n-	add adjectival endings
znać 'to know'	**zna-**	**znan-**	**znan-y aktor** 'known actor' <MSC SG> **znan-a aktorka** 'known actress <FEM SG> **znan-e imię** 'known name' <NT SG> **znan-e dzieci** 'known kids' <NO-MHPL> **znan-i aktorzy** 'known actors' <MHPL>

Passive participles formed from verbs ending in -eć:

INF	drop the INF ending -ć	add suffix -n-	attach adjectival endings
widzieć 'to see'	**widzie-**	shift **e** to **a** **widzia-**	**napiwek mile widzian-y** 'a tip is welcome' <MSC SG> **opinia mile widzian-a** 'opinion is welcome <FEM SG> **zdjęcie mile widziane** 'photo is welcome' <NT SG> **dzieci mile widzian-e** 'kids are welcome' <NO-MHPL> **studenci mile widzian-i** 'students are welcome' <MHPL>

Neuter forms and plural forms with no male human both have the ending -e, e.g., **kochane dziecko** 'beloved child' and **kochane dzieci** 'beloved children.' -i is used for plural forms with a male human, e.g., **kochani chłopcy** 'beloved boys.'

Infinitive	Passive participles
kocha-ć 'to love'	**kocha-ny** <MSC SG> 'beloved'
	kocha-na <FEM SG> 'beloved'
	kocha-ne <NT SG> 'beloved'
	kocha-ne <NO MALE HUMAN FORM> 'beloved'
	kocha-ni <MALE HUMAN FORM> 'beloved'

Kochani rodzice i przyjaciele! 'Beloved parents and friends!'

zamykać 'to close'	**zamykan-y (-a, -e, -i)** 'closed'
torturować 'to torture'	**torturowan-y (-a, -e, -i)** 'tortured'
brać 'to take'	**bran-y (-a, -e, -i)** 'taken'
sprzedać <PFV> 'to sell'	**sprzedan-y (-a, -e, -i)** 'sold'
sprzedawać <IMPFV> 'to sell'	**sprzedawany (-a, -e, -i)** 'sold'

Vowel shift in -eć verbs, final e:a:

Infinitive	Passive participles
widzieć 'to see'	**widziany, widziana, widziane, widziani** 'seen'

Politechnika Warszawska: cudzoziemcy mile widziani.
'Warsaw University of Technology: foreign students are welcome.'

2. Passive participles formed from verbs ending in -ić/-yć, -ść/-źć and -c in the infinitive are formed by dropping -ić/-yć, -ść/-źć and -c and adding the suffix -on- followed by the adjectival endings (-y for masculine nouns, -a for feminine nouns, -e for neuter nouns in the singular, and -e for no male human plural nouns, -i for male human plural nouns).

Infinitive	drop **-yć**	add suffix **-on**	attach adjectival endings
zmęczyć	**zmęcz-**	**zmęczon-**	**zmęczon-y syn** 'tired son' <MSC SG>
			zmęczon-a córka 'tired daughter' <FEM SG>
			zmęczon-e dziecko 'tired child' <NT SG>
			zmęczon-e dzieci 'tired children' <NO-MHPL>
			zmęczen-i ludzie 'tired people' <MHPL>

In the male human plural form the ending is, exceptionally, *-eni*.

Predictable consonant shifts in the formation of passive participles occur within the infinitives that end in -sić, -cić, -zić, -ścić, -dzić, -oić, -źć e.g., si:sz, ci:c, zi:ż, ści:szcz, dzi:dz, oi:oj, ź:zi, respectively.

Infinitive	drop **-ć**	shift	add suffix **-on**	attach adjectival endings
zaprosić 'to invite'	**zaprosi**	**si:sz**	**zaproszon-**	**zaproszon-y gość** 'invited guest' <MSC SG>
				zaproszon-a rodzina 'invited family' <FEM SG>
				zaproszon-e dziecko 'invited child' <NT SG>
				zaproszon-e rodziny 'invited families' <NO-MHPL>
				zaprosz*eni* goście 'invited guests' <MHPL>

Infinitive	shift	Passive participles
prosić 'to request'	**si:sz**	**proszony, proszona, proszone, proszeni** 'requested'
zaprosić 'to invite'	**si:sz**	**zaproszon-y (-a, -e, zaproszeni)** 'invited'
(za)płacić 'to pay'	**ci:c**	**(za)płacon-y (-a, -e, (za) płaceni)** 'paid'
(o)słodzić 'to sweeten'	**dzi:dz**	**(o)słodzon-y (-a, -e, (o) słodzeni)** 'sweetened'
(wy)czyścić 'to clean'	**ści:szcz**	**(wy)czyszczon-y (-a, -e, wyczyszczeni)** 'cleaned'
kroić 'to cut'	**i:j**	**krojon-y (-a, -e, krojeni)** 'cut'
obrazić 'to insult'	**zi:ż**	**obrażon-y (-a, -e, obrażeni)** 'insulted'
wozić <IMPFV> 'to transport'	**zi:ż**	**wożon-y (-a, -e, wożeni)** 'transported'
wieźć <PFV> 'to transport'	**ź:zi**	**wiezion-y (-a, -e, wiezieni)** 'transported'
nosić <IMPFV> 'to carry'	**ź:zi**	**noszon-y (-a, -e, noszeni)** 'carried'
nieść <PFV> 'to carry'	**ś:si**	**niesion-y (-a, -e, niesieni)** 'carried'

Consonantal shifts c:cz, ci:cz, ść:dzi, c:ż:

(o)chrzcić 'to baptize'	**(o)chrzczon-y (-a, -e,** **(o)chrzczeni)** 'baptized'
okraść 'to rob'	**okradzion-y (-a, -e, okradzieni)** 'robbed'
ukraść 'to steal'	**ukradzion-y (-a, -e, ukradzieni)** 'stolen'
ostrzec 'to warn'	**ostrzeżon-y (-a, -e, ostrzeżeni)** 'warned'
strzec 'to guard'	**ostrzeżon-y (-a, -e, ostrzeżeni)** 'guarded'
(u)piec 'to bake'	**(u)pieczon-y (-a, -e, (u)pieczeni)** 'baked'

Irregular:

(z)jeść 'to eat'	**(z)jedzon-y (-a, -e, (z)jedzeni)** 'eaten'

Stany *Zjednoczone* Ameryki '*United* States of America (USA)'
ONZ Organizacja Narodów Zjednoczonych 'United Nations
 Organization'
kurczak *pieczony* '*roasted* chicken'

3. Passive participles formed from verbs ending in -ąć in the infinitive are formed by dropping -ąć and adding the suffix -ęt- followed by the adjectival endings (-y, -a, -e, -i).

Neuter forms and plural forms with no male human both have the ending -e, e.g., **zmoknięte dziecko** 'wet child' and **zmoknięte dzieci** 'wet children.'

-i is used for plural forms with a male human and -ęty changes to -ęci: **zmoknięci chłopcy** 'wet boys.'

The vowel shift ą:ę occurs in all forms.

Infinitive	Passive participles
zacząć 'to begin'	**zaczęty, zaczęta, zaczęte, zaczęci** 'begun, started'
zamknąć \<PFV\> 'to close'	**zamknięt-y (-a, -e, zamknięci)** 'closed'
wynająć 'to hire'	**wynajęt-y (-a, -e, wynajęci)** 'hired, rented'
zmarznąć 'to freeze'	**zmarznięt-y (-a, -e, zmarznięci)** 'frozen, cold'
wziąć 'to take'	**wzięt-y (-a, -e, wzięci)** 'taken'

419

4. Passive participles formed from monosyllabic verbs ending in -ić/-yć and -uć (and their derivatives) in the infinitive, plus participles derived from -drzeć, such as **podrzeć** 'to tear something up' are formed by dropping -ć and adding the suffix -t- followed by the adjectival endings (-y, -a, -e, -i).

Neuter forms and plural forms with no male human both have the ending -e, e.g., **bite dziecko** 'beaten child' and **bite dzieci** 'beaten children.'

-i is used for plural forms with a male human and -ty changes to -ci: **bici chłopcy** 'beaten boys.'

Infinitive	Passive participles
zabić 'to kill'	**zabity, zabita, zabite, zabici** 'killed'
(u)myć 'to wash'	**(u)myt-y (-a, -e, (u)myci)** 'washed'
(u)kłuć 'to prick'	**(u)kłut-y (-a, -e, (u)kłuci)** 'pricked'
(ze)psuć 'to break'	**(ze)psut-y (-a, -e, (ze)psuci)** 'broken'

Infinitives with the endings -rzeć, -rzyć drop the whole ending, add the suffix -art-, and then attach adjectival endings.

INF	drop -rzeć/ -(o)rzyć	add -art-	attach adjectival endings
otworzyć 'to open' <PFV>	**otw-**	**otwart-**	**otwart-y mężczyzna** 'open man' <MSC SG> **otwarc-i ludzie** 'open people' <MHPL>
podrzeć 'to tear up' <PFV>	**pod-**	**podart-**	**podart-y** 'torn up' <MSC SG>

The male human plural has the ending -ci (predictable consonant shift t:ci), e.g., **otwarci ludzie** 'open people.'

Idiomatic expressions with passive participles:

Kradzione nie tuczy. 'Ill-gotten gains seldom prosper' (saying)
Strzeżonego Pan Bóg strzeże. 'Better safe than sorry.' (saying)
[Lit. 'The one who is guarded, God guards.']

Darowanemu koniowi nie zagląda się w zęby. 'Don't look a gift horse in the mouth.' (saying)
Tu jest pies pogrzebany. 'Here is the problem.' (coll.)
coś jest szyte grubymi nićmi 'something is manipulated' [lit. 'sewed with thick threads']

Doniesienia medialne były grubymi nićmi szyte.

'The news was manipulated.'

parking strzeżony 'attended parking'

zamknięte 'closed' **otwarte** 'open'

urząd nieczynny 'office closed'

zepsuty do szpiku kości 'rotten to the core'

zmarznięty na kość 'frozen to the marrow' [lit. 'bone']

czuć się jak zbity pies 'to feel miserable'

mieć obrażoną minę 'to look offended'

śmiertelnie ranny 'fatally wounded'

6.9.3.2	Use

Passive participles may function as adjectives, are used in phrases and sentences to replace **który** 'which/who,' and with the adverbial ending **-o** are used in subjectless constructions (often translated by "they").

To jest książka, którą bardzo lubię. 'This is the book I like a lot.'

To jest moja ulubiona książka. 'This is my favorite book.'

Nie jestem z tego zadowolony. 'I am not happy (satisfied) with that.'

Nic w tej sprawie nie zrobiono. 'They did nothing about it.'

Passive participles are used when the active voice is changed into the passive voice. In sentences where past participles are often used with the logical subject in the accusative case, preceded by the preposition **przez** 'done by,' the subject is the actor responsible for the action (see also 6.12):

Chirurg operuje pacjenta. (active, present tense)

'The surgeon is operating on a patient.'

Pacjent jest operowany przez chirurga (passive, present tense)

'The patient is operated on by a surgeon.'

Chirurg zoperował pacjenta (active, past tense, PFV)

'The surgeon operated on a patient.'

Pacjent został zoperowany (passive, past tense PFV)

'The patient has been operated on by a surgeon.'

6.9.4	Indeclinable adverbial

Adverbial participles are formed from present tense (imperfective) verbs with the marker **-ąc**; and from past tense (perfective) verbs, with the markers

-wszy/-łszy. Adverbial participles modify the verb in the main clause (hence adverbial), answering the question **kiedy?** 'when?', and are indeclinable.

> **Uśmiecham się, kiedy cię widzę.** 'I smile, when I see you.'
> **Widząc cię, uśmiecham się.** 'Seeing you, I am smiling.'

> **Uśmiechnąłem się, kiedy cię zobaczyłem.** 'I smiled when I saw you.'
> **Zobaczywszy cię, uśmiechnąłem się.** 'Having seen you, I smiled.'

| 6.9.4.1 | Formation of indeclinable imperfective adverbial participles |

Imperfective adverbial participles are formed from present tense (imperfective) verbs, that is, from the third person plural form of the verb, to which the marker -c '-ing' is attached. The people and things the imperfective adverbial participles modify are *active* in the constructions in which they appear.

Infinitive	3rd person PL	Indeclinable imperfective participle
czytać	**czytają**	**czytając** 'while reading'
słuchać	**słuchają**	**słuchając** 'while listening'
chodzić	**chodzą**	**chodząc** 'while walking'
kończyć	**kończą**	**kończąc** 'while finishing'

| 6.9.4.2 | Use |

The indeclinable imperfective adverbial participle with the marker -ąc is used in a sentence where action is happening simultaneously in both clauses, to replace a clause with **kiedy** 'while.' Both clauses must have the same subject expressed in the nominative case, must be in the same tense (present or past) and the duration of the action in both clauses is not too distant in the past.

> **Piotr czyta książkę i słucha muzyki.** (present tense) 'Piotr is reading a book and listening to music.'
> **Piotr czyta książkę, słuchając muzyki.** 'Piotr is reading a book *while* listening to music.'

> **Wczoraj wieczorem Piotr czytał książkę i słuchał muzyki.** (past tense) 'Last night Piotr was reading a book and listening to music.'
> **Wczoraj wieczorem Piotr czytał książkę, słuchając muzyki.** 'Last night Piotr was reading a book *while* listening to music.'
> **Piotr przeczytał książkę, słuchając muzyki.** (perfective) 'Piotr finished the book *while* listening to music.'

Spotkałam koleżankę, kiedy wracałam do domu. 'I met my friend, when I was coming back home.'

Wracając do domu, spotkałam koleżankę. 'While coming back home, I met my friend.'

But:

Kiedy byłam mała, dużo czytałam. 'When I was a little girl I used to read a lot.' (Not: Będąc dziewczynką dużo czytałam. 'Being a little girl, I used to read a lot.'—the time is too distant.) This participle informs us that the action is happening almost simultaneously.

6.9.4.3 | *Formation of indeclinable perfective adverbial participles*

Indeclinable perfective adverbial participles are formed from a perfective verb, that is from the third person singular, masculine form, of the past tense. Simply drop the -ł in the third person past tense masculine form, and then add -wszy 'having done something,' when the stem ends with a vowel; add -łszy 'having done something,' when the stem ends with a consonant or cluster.

3rd person past tense, PFV MSC form	Participle
zrobi-ł (vowel+ł)	**zrobiwszy** 'having done'
wszed-ł (consonant+ł)	**wszedłszy** 'having entered'

Wszedłem do pokoju i przywitałem się ze wszystkimi.
'I entered the room and [then] I greeted everyone.'

Wszedłszy do pokoju, przywitałem się ze wszystkimi.
'Having entered the room, I greeted everyone.'

6.9.4.4 | *Use*

The people and things that perfective adverbial participles modify are *active* in the construction in which they appear. Unlike imperfective adverbial participles, which inform us about action that is happening simultaneously, indeclinable perfective adverbial participles inform us about an event that happened prior to the event in the main clause.

These forms with -wszy/-łszy carry the meaning of the past tense and their actors are active. In English this construction is rendered by "having done. . . ."

Indeclinable adverbial participles with the marker -wszy/-łszy are used in a sentence with action in both clauses happening in sequence, to replace a clause with **kiedy** 'while, when.' Both clauses must have the same subject expressed in the nominative case.

6.9.5 | Summary

Participles divide into adjectival participles (which decline like adjectives), and adverbial participles (which are indeclinable).

Adjectival participles divide into:

a) active, formed from imperfective verbs, e.g., **śpiące dziecko** 'sleep*ing* child' which equals 'the child who is sleeping' (marker '-ing' in English)

b) passive, formed from both imperfective and perfective verbs, e.g., **wyspane dziecko** 'well-rest*ed* child' which equals 'the child who slept well' (marker '-ed' in English)

Adverbial participles are all indeclinable and active.

a) adverbial participles can be formed from imperfective verbs, e.g., **Śpiąc, chrapię.** 'I snore while I sleep.' [both actions at the same time] (marker 'while')

b) adverbial participles can be formed from perfective verbs, e.g., **Skończywszy studia, zaczął pracować jako nauczyciel.** 'Having finished his studies, he started working as a teacher.' [sequence of actions] (marker 'having done something')

Use adjectival participles when you replace clauses with 'which?'

śpiące dziecko 'sleeping child'

Które **dziecko?** '*Which* child?'
Dziecko, które śpi. 'The child who is sleeping.'

Use indeclinable adverbial participles when you replace clauses with 'while' or 'when?'

Skończywszy studia, zaczął pracować jako nauczyciel. 'Having finished [his] studies, he started working as a teacher.'

Kiedy **zaczął pracować jako nauczyciel?** '*When* did he start working as a teacher?'
Skończywszy studia. 'Having finished [his] studies.'

Compare the sentences below to see the differences between the use of adjectival and adverbial participles.

Adjectival participles modify the things or people who are active in the sentence, answering the question **jaki?** 'what kind?'

Kobieta, która jest w ciąży, powinna dużo spać.
'A woman who is pregnant should sleep a lot.'

Kobieta, będąca w ciąży, powinna dużo spać.
'A woman, while being pregnant, should sleep a lot.'

Będąca w ciąży kobieta powinna dużo spać.
'A pregnant woman should sleep a lot.'

Do not separate the subject from the verb with a comma. You can insert additional information and then use commas on both sides of the inserted text.

Adverbial participles modify the verb, and answer the question **kiedy?** 'when?'

Kobieta powinna dużo spać, kiedy jest w ciąży.
'A woman should sleep a lot, when she is pregnant.'

Kobieta powinna dużo spać będąc w ciąży.
'A woman should sleep a lot while pregnant.'

| 6.9.5.1 | *Past passive adjectival participles* |

Past passive participles can be formed from both imperfective and perfective verbs.

odzież używana 'second hand, used clothes' versus **odzież zużyta**
'worn out clothes'
Co zrobić ze zużytymi bateriami? 'What do we do [to do] with worn out batteries?'
Baterie używane w telefonach komórkowych są ładowane określonym prądem. 'The cell phone batteries are being charged with the proper electrical current.'

6.10   Impersonal voice of personal verbs

Co się stało, to się nie odstanie. 'What's done cannot be undone.'
(saying)

The impersonal voice of personal verbs (verbs that provide forms for all persons, "I," "you," etc.) is used when the identity of the subject, the agent, which performs the action (expressed by the verb), is unknown (impersonal). It is quite popular in Polish, especially in the media.

It can be used instead of an active or passive voice in past and non-past tenses.

Kiedyś ludzie rzadko wyjeżdżali na wakacje za granicę.
'In the past people rarely went abroad on vacation.' (active voice, past)

Kiedyś rzadko *wyjeżdżało się/wyjeżdżano* na wakacje za granicę.
'In the past going abroad on vacation was rare.' (impersonal voice, past)

Teraz ludzie często wyjeżdżają na wakacje za granicę.
'Now people often go abroad on vacation.' (active voice, present)

Teraz często *wyjeżdża się* na wakacje za granicę.
'Now going abroad is frequent.' (impersonal voice, present)

Za kila lat ludzie będą wyłącznie jeździć na wakacje za granicę.
'In a couple of years people will only be going abroad on vacation.' (active voice, future)

Za kilka lat *będzie jeździło się* wyłącznie na wakacje za granicę.
'In a couple of years going abroad on vacation will be the only option.' (impersonal voice, future)

The impersonal voice of personal verbs is not to be confused with impersonal verbs such as **widać**, **słychać**, which do not have personal forms, "I," "you," "he," etc.).

The impersonal voice is used:

1. When the passive form is required and the verb in Polish does not have a passive form (reflexive verbs and intransitive verbs do not have passive forms, see 6.13).

   ***Domagano się* ponownego przeliczenia głosów.**
   'A recount of votes was demanded.'

   ***Zaleca się* picie półtora litra wody dziennie.**
   'It is recommended to drink one and a half liters of water daily.'

   ***Zabrania się* palenia tytoniu**
   'Smoking is forbidden'

Tu *się* **nie** *pali*
'Do not smoke here'

Przebacz*ono* **mu.**
'He was forgiven.'

D*ano* **nam wreszcie spokój.**
'We were finally left alone.'

Powiedziano jej o wypadku.
'She was informed about the accident.'

Only transitive verbs (with a noun in the accusative case) can be passive. Intransitive verbs (with an object in the dative case) cannot be passive.

2. In the media, instead of a transitive verb that has a passive meaning.

Muzeum Powstania Warszawskiego *zostało otwarte* **w Warszawie.** (passive perfective)
'The Warsaw Uprising Museum was opened in Warsaw.'

W Warszawie *otwarto* **Muzeum Powstania Warszawskiego.**
'In Warsaw they opened the Warsaw Uprising Museum.'

Coraz więcej samochodów *jest sprowadzanych* **z zagranicy.** (passive imperfective)

Coraz więcej samochodów *sprowadza się* **z zagranicy.**
'More and more cars are being imported from abroad.'

6.10.1 Formation

The impersonal voice of personal verbs can be formed in two ways:

1. With passive participles ending -o, e.g., **pisano** 'it was written' to express past-tense action and events. For passive participle formation, see 6.9.3.

   Replace infinitive endings -ać/-eć with -ano:

   czytać-czytano 'read,' **myśleć-myślano** 'thought' (note the shift e:a).

   Replace infinitive endings -ić/-yć with -ono:

   mówić-mówiono 'said,' **tańczyć-tańczono** 'danced,' **chodzić-chodzono** 'walked,' **jeździć-jeżdżono** 'driven' (note the shifts ci:c, zi:z, si:sz, ści:szcz, dzi:dz, ździ:żdż).

427

Replace infinitive endings -ąć and monosyllabic infinitive endings -ić/-yć or -uć with -to:

zacząć-zaczęto 'started' (shift ą:ę), **bić-bito** 'beaten,' **ukłuć-ukłuto** 'pricked.'

2. With the reflexive pronoun **się** added to past tense third person neuter singular (marker -ło) **pisało się** 'it was written' to express past tense action and events; by adding the reflexive pronoun **się** to present tense third person singular **pisze się** to express present-tense action and events; and by adding **się** to future compound third person with neuter past tense form **będzie się pisało** to express future tense action and events.

Kiedyś wyłącznie *pisano* list. 'In the past only letters were written.'
Teraz *pisze się* listy i e-maile. 'Now letters and emails are [being] written.'
W przyszłości *będzie się pisało* tylko e-maile lub SMS-y. 'In the future only emails and SMSs will be written.'

The impersonal voice of personal verbs is formed from imperfective or perfective verbs, depending on the context.

Use imperfective verbs to express the ongoing action and events in the past or in the future. Use perfective verbs to refer to action and an event that was or will be accomplished in the past or in the future.

Powiedziano jej o wypadku. 'She was told [informed] about the accident.'
Powie się jej o wypadku, kiedy wrócimy. 'She will be told [informed] about the accident when we return.'

Jeśli (jak) *się powiedziało* a, (to) trzeba powiedzieć b.
'When A is said <PFV>, then B has to follow.' (saying)

Nie od razu Kraków *zbudowano*. 'Rome wasn't built in a day.'
[Lit. 'Cracow wasn't built right away.'] (saying)

6.11 Verbal nouns

Apetyt rośnie w miarę *jedzenia*. (saying)
'Appetite comes with eating.'

Verbal nouns have the dual nature of a verb and a noun. They are formed from verbs, and based on the verbal stem the lexical meaning of the verbal noun can be determined, but they are declined like neuter nouns. They are formed by adding the endings -nie/-ienie/-ęcie/-cie to the stems of verbs. Verbal nouns are in the neuter class (have the ending -e). (For verbal nouns as subjects, see 2.4.7.)

Verb	Verbal noun
czytać 'to read'	**czytanie** 'the reading'
jeść 'to eat'	**jedzenie** 'the food'
leżeć 'to be lying'	**leżenie** 'to be in a horizontal position'
mieszkać 'to reside'	**mieszkanie** 'the apartment'
przejść 'to cross'	**przejście** 'the crosswalk'

Verbal nouns are used

1. To express linkage after the English "*something to* eat/drink/read," etc. The preposition **do** imposes the genitive case on a verbal noun.

   W samolocie zawsze mam coś do czytania. 'On the plane I always have something to read.'
   mieć chęć do życia 'to have the will to live'
   Czy podać coś zimnego do picia? 'Should I bring something cold to drink?'
   W domu nie ma nic do jedzenia. 'There is nothing to eat at home.'

2. To inform about something that is **niemożliwy** (cannot possibly be accomplished). **Nie do** is followed by a verbal noun formed from the perfective verb, in the genitive case.

   Ta sprawa jest nie do wykrycia. 'This case is impossible to detect.'
   To jest nie do opisania. 'It cannot be described.'
   bariera nie do pokonania 'insurmountable obstacle'
   propozycja nie do przyjęcia 'an unacceptable proposal'

   Sometimes this can have a positive meaning.

   Wizerunek miasta zmienił się nie do poznania.
   The city image changed beyond recognition.

3. To emphasize the purpose of one product in regard to the other

   pokój/mieszkanie do wynajęcia 'room/apartment to rent'
   płyn do mycia naczyń/do płukania 'dishwashing liquid/fabric softener'
   proszek do pieczenia/do prania 'baking powder/washing powder'

4. To express **przed** 'before' <+INS> and **po** 'after' <+LOC>, mostly with verbal nouns formed from motion verbs.

> **przyjazd** 'arrival' **odjazd** 'departure'
> **wyjazd/wyjście** 'take off/exit'
> **wjazd/wejście** 'entrance'

> **Po przyjeździe, poszliśmy na plażę.**
> 'After [our] arrival, we went to the beach.'

> **Przed wyjazdem z Polski mieliśmy dużo pracy.**
> 'Before leaving Poland, we had to do a lot.'

> **Przed wyjściem z biura, nie zapomnij wyłączyć komputer.**
> 'Before you leave the office, don't forget to turn off the computer.'

> **Sytuacja Polski się zmieniła po wstąpieniu/po wejściu do NATO i Unii Europejskiej.**
> 'The situation of Poland changed after entering NATO and the EU.'

"Before" can be expressed by **zanim** + perfective verb (see 6.4.7.1).

> **Zanim wyjdziesz, wyłącz komputer.**
> 'Before you leave, turn off the computer.'

"After" can be expressed by **od kiedy** 'since' + verb.

> **Od kiedy Polska weszła do NATO, wiele się zmieniło.**
> 'Since Poland entered NATO, a lot has changed.'

Verbal nouns formed from verbs that require the accusative case, follow the *genitive case*. It is as if the two nouns become linked.

> **rozumieć** <ACC> **tekst** 'to understand a text'
> **rozumienie** <GEN> **tekstu** 'understanding of the text'
> (reading comprehension)

Verbal nouns formed from verbs that require case governance other than the accusative case, require the same case governance, and the same preposition to follow, as the original verb.

> **mówić** <INS> **szeptem** 'to speak in a whisper'
> **mówienie** <INS> **szeptem** 'whispering'
> **leżeć na** <LOC> **słońcu** 'to bask in the sun'
> **leżenie na** <LOC> **słońcu** 'basking in the sun'

Even though, formally, verbal nouns can be made up from almost all Polish verbs (**chcieć** 'to want,' **chęć** 'a desire,' not: chcenie, **apelować** 'to appeal,' apelowanie (potential form), **apel** 'the appeal'), the "unadorned" noun is often used instead of verbal nouns.

> **pracować** 'to work,' **pracowanie** (potential), **praca** 'the job'
> **jeździć** 'to ride,' **jeżdżenie** (potential), **jazda** 'the driver'
> **pamiętać** 'to remember,' **pamiętanie** (potential), **pamięć** 'the memory'
> **biegać** 'to run,' **bieganie** (potential), **bieg** 'the run'
> **potrzebować** <GEN> 'to need,' **potrzeba** <GEN> 'the need'

but

> **losować** 'to draw,' **losowanie** 'the draw'

6.11.1 Formation

With verbs that end in -(a)ć and -e(ć) as well as -i(ć) and -y(ć), take off the ć and add -nie. In verbs that end with -i(ć), -i changes to -e.

przesłuchać 'to interrogate'	**przesłuchanie** 'the interrogation'
pytać 'to ask'	**pytanie** 'the question'
(z)rozumieć 'to understand'	**(z)rozumienie** 'the comprehension'
spotkać 'to meet'	**spotkanie** 'the meeting'
zwolnić (się) 'to be excused'	**zwolnienie** 'the sick note'
spóźnić się 'to be late'	**spóźnienie** 'the tardiness'
upomnieć 'to reprimand'	**upomnienie** 'the admonition'

Consonantal shifts occur with -i(ć) verbs: si:sz, zi:ż, ździ:żdż.

Add -enie to verbs that end in -ść/-źć. Ś and ź become si, zi before the vowel -e.

nieść 'to carry'	**niesienie** 'carrying'
wieźć 'to transport'	**wiezienie** 'transporting'
jeść 'to eat'	**jedzenie** 'the food'

Add -cie to verbs that end in -ąć, -nąć.

zdjąć 'to take off'	**zdjęcie** 'the picture' (shift ą:ę)
wynająć 'to rent'	**wynajęcie** 'the rent'

Sometimes verbs with the ending nąć form verbal nouns with the ending -ienie, e.g.:

pragnąć 'to desire'	**pragnienie** 'the desire'
cisnąć 'to press'	**cieśnienie** 'the pressure'
skinąć 'to nod'	**skinienie** 'the nod'

Add -**cie** to monosyllabic verbs that end in -**ić**/-**yć** and their derivatives:

myć 'to wash'	**mycie** 'the wash'
żyć 'to live'	**życie** 'the life'
pić 'to drink'	**picie** 'the drink'

Być gotowym na czyjeś każde skinienie. (saying)
'To be at everybody's beck and call.'

6.12 Passive voice

Dobrymi chęciami piekło jest wybrukowane.
'(The road to) hell is paved with good intentions.'

Saint Bernard of Clairvaux

In the active voice, the performer of the action (the agent) is the subject of the verb and performs the action on the object, the recipient of the action.

In the passive voice, the recipient (transformed into the subject) does not act, but is acted upon, and comes before the agent which performs the action upon it. The preposition **przez** 'done by' <+ACC> comes before the performer of the action. Sometimes the presence of the agent is not necessary.

Policja	**aresztowała** <+ACC>	**młodego mężczyznę.** (active)
performer	action/transitive verb	recipient of the action
'The police	arrested	a young man.'

Młody mężczyzna	**został**	**aresztowany**	**przez** <ACC>	**policję.** (passive)
subject	auxiliary verb	past participle	preposition	agent in the accusative case
'A young man	was	arrested	by	the police.'

Matka	**myje**	**dziecko.** (active)
subject	action	recipient of the action
'Mother	washes	the child.'

Dziecko	**jest**	**myte.** (passive)
subject	auxiliary verb	past participle
A child	is being	washed.

Listonosz	**dostarczył**	**przesyłkę.** (active)
Subject	action	direct object
'The mailman	delivered	the package.'

Przesyłka	**została**	**dostarczona.** (passive)
Subject	auxiliary verb	past participle
'A package	has been	delivered.'

Only *transitive verbs followed by a direct object* can be used in the passive voice. Verbs with the reflexive pronoun **się** cannot be used in the passive voice: *bać się* 'to be afraid.' (See 6.13)

6.12.1 Construction

The passive voice is constructed with the help of the verb **być** 'to be' (with imperfective verbs), or **zostać** 'to become' (with perfective verbs), followed by the past participle of the transitive verb of the active sentence (with the marker -any, -ony, or -ty) (see 6.9.3.1). The past participle agrees with the object of the transformation in class, number and case, not with the performer of the action. The tense in the passive voice is identical to the tense in the active, original voice.

Chirurg operuje pacjenta. (active, present)
The surgeon operates on the patient.

Pacjent jest operowany przez chirurga. (passive, present)
The patient is being operated on by the surgeon.

In certain passive voice constructions, when the transitive verb governs cases other than the accusative, the preposition **przez** 'done by' <+ACC> is not used. In English, such constructions are rendered by the preposition "with."

List został napisany <+INS> **zielonym atramentem.**
'The letter was written with green ink.'

Ulice są pokryte <+INS> **śniegiem.**
'The streets are covered with snow.'

placki polane <+INS> **śmietaną**
'pancakes with sour cream on top'

Kraj rządzony jest <+INS> **żelazną ręką (przez** <+ACC> **agresywny reżim).**
'The country is being ruled with an iron fist (by an aggressive regime).'

433

Passive voice constructions in past and non-past tenses, as well as in the conditional mood, are given below:

| 6.12.1.1 | *Present*

Piotr pisze list. 'Piotr writes/is writing a letter.' (active)
List jest pisany przez Piotra. 'The letter is being written by Piotr.'
(passive)

| 6.12.1.2 | *Past imperfective*

Piotr pisał list.
'Piotr wrote/was writing a letter.' (active)

List był pisany przez Piotra.
'The letter was being written by Piotr.' (passive)

| 6.12.1.3 | *Past accomplished (with perfective verbs)*

Piotr napisał list.
'Piotr wrote the letter.' (active)

List został napisany przez Piotra.
'The letter was written/has been written by Piotr.' (passive)

| 6.12.1.4 | *Future compound*

Piotr będzie pisać/będzie pisał list. 'Piotr will be writing a letter.'
(active)
List będzie pisany przez Piotra. 'The letter is going to be written
by Piotr.' (passive)

| 6.12.1.5 | *Future perfective*

Piotr napisze list. 'Piotr will finish writing the letter.'
List zostanie napisany przez Piotra. 'The letter will be written
by Piotr.'

| 6.12.1.6 | *Conditional mood (not conditional construction with "if")* |

Piotr pisałby list. 'Piotr might write a letter.'
List byłby pisany. 'The letter might be written.'
Piotr napisałby list. 'Piotr would write the letter.'
List zostałby napisany przez Piotra. 'The letter would have been written by Piotr.'

Note: When the recipient of the action is in the plural, use the plural form of the verb "to be" or "to become," so that the verb agrees with the recipient(s).

Piotr pisze listy. 'Piotr writes/is writing letters.' (active)
Listy są pisane. 'Letters are being written.' (passive)
Policja nas aresztowała. 'The police arrested us.' (active)
My zostaliśmy aresztowani. 'We were arrested.' (passive)

When the recipient of the action is in an unidentified number or in a number larger than five, use the past or non-past tense of the verb "to be" or "to become" in the third person singular (in the past, use the neuter form with -ło), and put the transformed subject in the genitive case.

Piotr pisze dużo listów. 'Piotr writes/is writing many letters.' (active)
Dużo listów jest <3 PR SG VERB> **pisanych** <GEN>. 'Many letters are being written.' (passive)
Piotr napisał osiem listów. 'Piotr wrote eight letters.' (active)
Osiem listów zostało <3 PR SG NT VERB> **napisanych** <GEN>. 'Eight letters were written.' (passive)

Verbs that take an indirect object cannot be used in the passive voice. To express them in the passive, use the impersonal voice (see 6.10).

Rodzice mu przebaczyli. 'His parents forgave him.'
Przebaczono <+DAT> **mu.** 'He was forgiven.'
Matka powidziała nam o wszystkim. 'Mother told us about everything.'
Powiedziano nam o wszystkim. 'We were informed about everything.'

6.13 Transitive and intransitive verbs

Transitive verbs are those used with a direct object (noun or adjectival noun) in the accusative, genitive or instrumental cases, and whose object can be transformed into the subject. In other words, transitive verbs have the ability to act upon the object *directly* (direct causation without any prepositions). Reflexive verbs cannot be transitive, e.g., **myć się** 'to wash oneself.'

Chłopiec myje <+ACC> **samochód.** 'The boy is washing a car.'
Dziecko zbiera <+ACC> **znaczki.** 'The child is collecting stamps.'
Policjant kieruje <+INS> **ruchem.** 'The policeman is directing traffic.'
Firma zarządza <+INS> **kapitałem.** 'The company is administering capital.'
Student używa <+GEN> **komputera.** 'The student is using the computer.'
Broker dokonuje <+GEN> **transakcji na giełdzie.** 'The broker is trading on the stock exchange.'

Transitive verbs can be transformed from the active voice to the passive voice, that is, the object can be transformed into the subject of the passive voice sentence.

Samochód jest myty przez chłopca. 'The car is washed by the boy.'
Znaczki są zbierane przez dziecko. 'Stamps are being collected by the child.'
Ruch jest kierowany przez policjanta. 'The traffic is being directed by the policeman.'
Komputer jest używany przez studenta. 'The computer is being used by the student.'
Transakcje są dokonywane przez brokera. 'Transactions are being made by the broker.'

Transitive verbs, e.g., **dawać co?** 'to give what?' **mówić co?** 'to say what?' **tłumaczyć co?/kogo?** 'to translate what?' are not to be confused with intransitive verbs such as **dawać komu** 'to give somebody,' **mówić komu** 'to tell somebody,' and pseudointransitive verbs such as **zaręczyć się** 'to get somebody engaged,' **całować się** 'to kiss each other or one another,' where the verb can function without the pronominal object.

Many Polish verbs can be followed by more than one case, depending on their role in the sentence (without being preceded by a preposition).

zaręczyć kogoś z kimś 'to engage somebody to somebody'
<transitive verb>
zaręczyć się 'to become engaged to each other'
<pseudotransitive verb>
Ewa i Jan zaręczyli się. 'Ewa and Jan got engaged.' <active voice>
Ewa jest zaręczona. 'Ewa is engaged.' <passive voice>

The verb **iść** is intransitive as it does not take a direct object. **Jechać** might be seen as transitive—we can say **jechać samochodem** 'to ride by car'—but we actually drive a car rather than ride. If we ride, then this is *in* the car (as a passenger), and therefore the verb **jechać** is not a transitive verb (because of the preposition "*in*": **jechać w samochodzie**). **Prowadzić samochód** means 'to drive a car,' and it is a transitive verb. It can be transformed into **samochód prowadzony przez kobietę** 'the car driven by a woman.' Additionally, the verb *ujeżdżać* 'to compact,' or 'to break in a horse' can be used as a transitive verb: *ujeżdżona droga* 'compacted road,' *ujeżdżony koń* 'broken-in horse.'

> **Matka daje dzieciom pieniądze.** 'Mother gives money to the children.'
>
> **Pieniądze są dawane dzieciom przez matkę.** 'The money is given to the children by the mother.'
>
> **Ewa tłumaczy koledze pracę domową.** 'Ewa explains the homework to her friend.'
>
> **Praca domowa jest tłumaczona koledze.** 'The homework is being explained to the friend.'
>
> **Ewa tłumaczy tekst.** 'Ewa is translating the text.'
>
> **Test jest tłumaczony.** 'The text is being translated.'

Transitive verbs used without an object become intransitive.

> **Piotr czyta książkę.** 'Piotr is reading a book.' <transitive verb **czytać** 'TO READ'>
>
> **Piotr czyta.** 'Piotr is reading.' <INTRANSITIVE VERB>

6.14 Reflexive verbs

Reflexive verbs are those where the suffix **się** is present in all forms of the verb, including verbal nouns, e.g., **mycie się zimną wodą** 'washing oneself with cold water.' Many transitive verbs change into intransitive by adding **się**, e.g., **myć dziecko** 'to wash a child' and **myć się** 'to wash oneself.'

Verbs with **się** can be reflexive, reciprocal, and used in set phrases (idiomatic).

'Reflexive' means the subject performs an action on himself or herself.

> **myję się** 'I wash myself'
>
> **Oni codziennie budzą się przed siódmą.** 'They wake up before 7 a.m. every day.'

Note: Some sentences are not reflexive in a sense, because the subject does not perform an action on him- or herself:

Pani Ewa często czesze się u fryzjerki. 'Miss Ewa often has her hair done at the hairdresser's.'

'Reciprocal' means the action is performed by two or more participants and they are the objects (recipients) of the action (see 5.3.1.2).

> **Dziewczyna i chłopak się całują.** 'A girl and a boy are kissing each other.'
> **Oni znają się od zawsze.** 'They have known each other for ever.'
> **Politycy często kłócą się o pieniądze.** 'Politicians often argue about money.'

Note: Sometimes it could be unclear whether the verb is reflexive or reciprocal. There is no ambiguity once the sentence is used in context.

> **Psy się liżą.** 'Dogs lick themselves' *or* 'Dogs lick each other.'
> **Dziewczynki się czeszą.** 'Girls comb themselves' *or* 'Girls comb each other.' (See 5.3.14)

To avoid ambiguity the word **wzajemnie** 'each other' could be added.

6.14.1 Się in set phrases

When *się* is used with a verb it often gains a new meaning, but can be related in some way to the original verb:

uczyć 'to teach'	**uczyć się** 'to learn'
urodzić 'to give birth'	**urodzić się** 'to be born'
zatrzymać 'to stop' <+noun>	**zatrzymać się** 'to stay at somebody's place'
czuć 'to detect by smell'	**czuć się** 'to feel'
oglądać 'to watch'	**oglądać się na coś/na kogoś** 'to rely on something/somebody'

Jan uczy czy uczy się francuskiego? 'Does Jan teach or learn French?'
Zatrzymajmy się w hotelu. 'Let's stay at the hotel.'
Zatrzymaj się! 'Stop (halt)!'
Zatrzymaj samochód. 'Stop the car.'

najeść się do syta 'to eat one's fill'
nasiedziałam się 'I have been sitting for a long time'

Verbs such as **najeść się** 'to eat up,' **wytańczyć się** 'to dance up,' that is verbs with the prefixes **na** or **wy** attached to them, and followed by the reflexive pronoun **się**, denote satiation.

There are verbs in Polish that occur only as reflexive verbs.

bać się 'to be afraid'   **uśmiechać się** 'to smile'
napić się 'to have a drink'   **pojawić się** 'to appear'
śmiać się 'to laugh'

See 5.3.1.6 for the positioning of the reflexive particle **się** in a phrase.

6.15   Być

The verb **być** "to be" is mostly used as a linking verb.

Imię Róży jest **powieścią Umberta Eco.**
'*The Name of the Rose* is a novel by Umberto Eco.'

Jan *był* **oddanym profesorem.**
'Jan was a dedicated professor.'

Będziecie **świetnym rodzicami.**
'You will be great parents.'

When used as a linking verb, it is followed by the noun and its modifiers in the instrumental case (2.9).

It is also used as an auxiliary verb:

• in the compound future tense

   Jutro *będę spać* **do południa.** 'I will be sleeping till noon tomorrow.'

• in passive voice constructions

   Jestem zaproszony **na kolację do przyjaciół.**
   'I am invited for dinner to [my] friends'.'

   Kiedy to *będzie skończone?*
   'When will it be finished?'

• with modal verbs

   Nie wolno będzie. 'It will not be allowed.'

• with impersonal expressions

   Będzie widać. 'It will be seen.'

Być can also be used as an independent verb.

Jest mi niedobrze.
'I'm not feeling well.'

Będzie dobrze.
'It will [all] be fine.'

Byliśmy, jesteśmy, będziemy.
'We were, we are, we will be.'

For the omission of forms of 'to be' in present tense after 'this,' see 2.4.4.

6.15.1 Negated być

To express a lack of somebody or something in the present tense, the negated verb "to have" in the third person singular, **nie ma**, is used for all forms, instead of "to be." In the past tense the verb "to be" in the third person singular in the neuter form **nie było** is used for all persons, and in the future **nie będzie** is used for all persons. The noun or adjective whose lacks are to be expressed is in the genitive case (for constructions of absence, see 2.4.9 and 2.6.4).

'He is not here,' 'we are not here,' etc. **nie ma go, nie ma nas.**

Mamy nie ma, brata nie ma, dziadków nie ma—nikogo nie ma. Jestem w domu sam. 'Mom is not [here], [my] brother is not [here], [my] grandparents are not [here]—nobody is [here]. I am by myself.'

Nikogo nie było w domu. 'Nobody was at home.'
Nie będzie mnie przez tydzień. 'I will not be [here] for a week.'

Table 6.17 Conjugation of **być**

The verb **być** 'to be' has an irregular present tense conjugation.

Present

Person	Singular	Plural
1st	**jestem**	**jesteśmy**
2nd	**jesteś**	**jesteście**
3rd	**jest**	**są**

Past

Person	Singular	Plural
	MSC/FEM/NT	Male human form/No male human form
1st	byłem/byłam/—	byliśmy/byłyśmy
2nd	byłeś/byłaś/—	byliście/byłyście
3rd	był/była/było	byli/były

Future

Person	Singular	Plural
1st	będę	będziemy
2nd	będziesz	będziecie
3rd	będzie	będą

Conditional Mood

Person	Singular	Plural
	MSC/FEM/NT	Male human form/No male human form
1st	byłbym/byłabym/—	bylibyśmy/byłybyśmy
2nd	byłbyś/byłabyś/—	bylibyście/byłybyście
3rd	byłby/byłaby/byłoby	byliby/byłyby

Imperative Mood

Person	Singular	Plural
1st	—	bądźmy
2nd	bądź	bądźcie
3rd	niech będzie	niech będą

Participles

	Adjectival Active	Adjectival Passive	Adverbial
MSC	będący	—	
FEM	będąca	—	będąc
NT	będące	—	

Verbal noun: **bycie**

6.15.2 *"To be" or "to have"?*

Some common constructions with the verb **być** 'to be,' are rendered in English by the verb **mieć** 'to have,' and some with the verb "to have" in Polish, are rendered in English by "to be."

Polish	English
"to have"	"to be"
Age:	
Mam 20 lat.	'I am 20 years old.'
Measurements:	
Mam prawie dwa metry.	'I am almost two meters.'
Metr ma sto centymetrów.	'One meter is a hundred centimeters.'
Idiomatic expressions:	
mieć rację	'to be right'
nie mieć racji	'to be wrong'

6.16 Mieć

Mieć 'to have' has the following conjugation:

Table 6.18 Conjugation of **mieć**

Present

Person	Singular	Plural
1st	**mam**	**mamy**
2nd	**masz**	**macie**
3rd	**ma**	**mają**

Past

Person	Singular MSC/FEM/NT	Plural Male human form/No male human form
1st	**miałem/miałam/—**	**mieliśmy/miałyśmy**
2nd	**miałeś/miałaś/—**	**mieliście/miałyście**
3rd	**miał/miała/miało**	**mieli/miały**

Future

Person	Compound Singular	Plural
1st	będę mieć	będziemy mieć
2nd	będziesz mieć	będziecie mieć
3rd	będzie mieć	będą mieć

The future can also be formed as: będę miał/miała, będziesz miał/miała, będzie miał/miała/miało, będziemy mieli/miały, będziecie mieli/miały, będą mieli/miały.

Conditional Mood

Person	Singular MSC/FEM/NT	Plural Male human form/No male human form
1st	miałbym/miałabym/—	mielibyśmy/miałybyśmy
2nd	miałbyś/miałabyś/—	mielibyście/miałybyście
3rd	miałby/miałaby/miałoby	mieliby/miałyby

Imperative Mood

Person	Singular	Plural
1st	—	miejmy
2nd	miej	miejcie
3rd	niech ma	niech mają

Participles

	Adjectival active	Adjectival passive	Adverbial
MSC SG	mający	—	
FEM SG	mająca	—	mając
NT SG	mające	—	

Impersonal form: miano; impersonal conditional: miano by

Common and idiomatic expressions with the verb mieć 'to have':

mieć nadzieję 'to have hope'
mieć ochotę 'to feel like doing something'
którego dzisiaj mamy? 'what's the date today?'

co mam robić? 'what am I *supposed to* do?'

Jutro ma być cieplej. 'Tomorrow is supposed to be warmer.'

Masz to zrobić. 'You *have to/are to* do it.'

Jak się mają pańscy rodzice? 'How are your parents doing, sir?'

się ma! 'hi!' (coll.)

6.17 Modal verbs

Modal verbs are verbs that are used with the main verb to convey a speaker's position regarding a given action or state (a situation, person and a thing). Modal verbs can express, among other things, possibility, necessity, permission, obligation, lack of ability, and prohibition. When using **móc**, **chcieć** and **musieć** in the future, use the past -ł/-ła/-ło/-li/-ły forms. Do not combine the future tense of the verb "to be" with the infinitive:

będę mógł/chciał/musiał 'I will be able/may want/will have to'
   (not: będę móc/chcieć/musieć)

Muszę już iść. 'I have to go.' (practical necessity)

Mogę już iść? 'Can I go now?'

Powinieneś już iść. 'You should go now.'

To translate the English 'can' to express skill, use the Polish verb **umieć** 'to know how,' followed by the infinitive.

Umiem pływać i nurkować. 'I can swim and dive.'

Umiem mówić po polsku. 'I can speak Polish.'

To express requests in English: "Can I have it?," use the Polish verb **prosić** followed by the object in the accusative case.

Proszę rachunek. 'Check, please.'
   ['Can I have the check, please?']

Modal verbs are followed by infinitives and have the same subject as the main verb. They are:

1. Mieć 'to have to'/'to be supposed to'/'I am to . . .'
2. Musieć 'must'
3. Móc 'can,' 'may,' 'be able,' 'have permission'
4. Powinien (defective verb) 'should,' 'ought to'
5. Chcieć 'to want'
6. Potrzebować 'need to'

There are defective modals that do not have personal endings. They are used when the actor is not specified:

1. **Można** 'it is possible'
2. **Powinno się** 'one should'
3. **Trzeba** 'it is necessary'
4. **Warto** 'it is worthwhile'
5. **Wolno** 'it is allowed'

6.17.1 Mieć 'I am/you are/he is to, to be supposed to'

- to express necessity or obligation
- to express intention or expectation.

   Masz jeść, nie marudzić. 'You are to eat, not whinge.'
   Masz to zrobić i już. 'You are to do it and that's that.' (period)
   Gdzie miałem mieszkać? 'Where was I supposed to live?'

6.17.2 Musieć "to have to/must"

- To express necessity and obligation

   Musiałem nosić \<IMPFV\> **mundurek, kiedy chodziłem do szkoły.**
   'I had to wear a uniform when I was a student.' (habitual action)

   Musimy wracać \<IMPFV\>.
   'We have to get going back.' (intended action)

   Będę musiał wziąć \<PFV\> **kredyt na studia.**
   'I will have to take a student loan.'

   Muszę być w domu przed dziesiątą.
   'I have to be at home before 10 p.m.'

Musieć is used in all tenses, with imperfective and perfective verbs. The imperfective verbs indicate habitual or intended actions.

- To express a lack of compulsion: "not to have to," "not to be obliged to"

   Nie musimy się spieszyć. 'We do not have to hurry.'
   Kiedyś nie musieliśmy płacić za studia. 'We did not have to pay for [our] studies in the past.'
   Tak nie musi być. 'It does not have to be this way.'

• To express logical implication and assumption: "must be," "has to be," "ought to"

> **Złodziej musiał wejść tylnymi drzwiami.**
> 'It is logical that the thief must have entered through the rear door.'
> **Gdzieś musi być błąd.** 'There has to be/ought to be a mistake somewhere.'
> **Musiało ci smakować, skoro tyle zjadłeś.** 'You must have liked it, since you ate so much.'

• To express prohibition: nie wolno '*must not*'

> **Nie wolno dotykać obrazów.** 'You must not touch the paintings.'
> **Tutaj nie wolno palić.** 'You must not smoke here.'

Negated **móc** 'not to have permission' is weaker than **nie wolno** 'must not.' With the construction **nie wolno** 'not permitted,' the subject who is not being permitted to do something is placed in the dative case.

> **Nie możesz wychodzić z domu po 22.00.**
> 'You cannot leave the house after 10 p.m.'

> **Nie wolno ci** <DAT> **wychodzić z domu po 22.00.**
> 'You must not leave the house after 10 p.m.'

| 6.17.3 | Móc *'can/be able/may/have permission'* |

• To express physical ability by virtue of law

> **Pracodawca może wypowiedzieć pracę pracownikowi.**
> An 'employer can dismiss an employee.'

• To express physical ability

> **Po roku intensywnych ćwiczeń pacjent mógł ponownie chodzić.** 'After a year of intensive exercises the patient could walk again.'
> **Z przejedzenia nie mogę zasnąć.** 'I cannot sleep because of overeating.'

• To express a lack of ability (disability)

> **Ojciec tracił wzrok i nie mógł czytać.** 'Father was losing his sight and could not read.'
> **Długo nie mogłam zajść w ciążę.** 'I was not able to get pregnant for a while.'

Often permanent disability is expressed without modal verbs.

Ona cię nie widzi—jest niewidoma.
'She does not [cannot] see you—she is blind.'

- To express possibility/opportunity

  W rok możesz skończyć studia magisterskie. 'You can
  complete [your] graduate studies in a year.'
  Ceny mogą ulec <PFV> **zmianie.** 'Prices can be subject to change.'
  W centrum mogą być korki. 'There could be a traffic jam in
  the center.'

- To give or seek permission

  Mogę wejść? 'Can/may/could I come in?'

- To make requests

  Możesz powtórzyć? 'Can/could you repeat [that]?'
  Mogę wyjść wcześniej? 'Can/could I leave earlier?'

- To express reproach

  Mogłeś zadzwonić! 'You could/might have called!'
  Nie mogłeś mnie uprzedzić? 'Couldn't you have warned me?'

- To indicate unrealized possibility (past perfective)

  Mogłam zginąć! 'I could have died!'

6.17.4 Powinien *'should/ought to'*

- To express suggestion/obligation

  Powinieneś zadzwonić. 'You should call.'

Note: The English use of "shall" and "will" to express intention does not
have an equivalent in Polish using modals.

'Shall we go?' **Pójdziemy?**   'We will see.' **Zobaczymy.**

6.17.5 Usage

Modal verbs with personal endings can be conjugated in past and non-past
tenses (except for **mieć** 'to be supposed to,' and **powinien** 'should'), and
they do not have aspectual forms.

Present	Past <MSC>	Future <MSC>
mam 'I am supposed to'	**miałem** 'I was supposed to'	—
mogę 'I can'	**mogłem** 'I could'	**będę mógł** 'I will be able'
muszę 'I must'	**musiałem** 'I had to'	**będę musiał** 'I will have to'
powinienem <MSC> 'I should'	**powinienem był** 'I should have'	—
potrzebuję 'I am in need of'	**potrzebowałem** 'I was in need of'	**będę potrzebował** 'I will be in need of'

Modal verbs without personal endings can be used in past and non-past tenses, with the help of the auxiliary verb **być** 'to be'

Present	Past	Future
można 'it is possible'	**można było** 'it was possible'	**można będzie** 'it will be possible'
trzeba 'it is necessary'	**trzeba było** 'it was necessary'	**trzeba będzie** 'it will be necessary'
warto 'it is worthwhile'	**warto było** 'it was worthwhile'	**warto będzie** 'it will be worthwhile'
wolno 'it is allowed'	**wolno było** 'it was allowed'	**wolno będzie** 'it will be allowed'

In conditional impersonal forms -by is written separately.

można by 'one could'   **można by było** 'one could have'

Jak można by im pomóc? 'How could one help them?'
Można by było z nimi negocjować. 'One could have negotiated with them.'

Modal verbs can be combined, but caution should be taken not to combine contradictory verbs (not: he must may):

Być może będę musiał pójść do pracy w sobotę. 'I may have to go to work on Saturday.'
Powinieneś umieć to zrobić. 'You should be able to do it.'

There are many ways, not only using modal verbs, to convey a speaker's position towards a given situation, person or thing, for instance adverbs and adjectives:

być może 'maybe,' na pewno 'definitely,' oczywiście 'of course,' prawdopodobnie 'probably': być może wrócę o piątej 'I may be back at five o'clock' versus na pewno wrócę o piątej 'I'll definitely be back at five o'clock.'

6.18 Impersonal verbs

An impersonal verb (czasownik nieosobowy) does not have the personal forms "I," "you," "he," "she," etc. It is often used in a form of infinitive or in the third person singular in all tenses (in the past tense and the future tense with past participles, the neuter gender with the marker -ło is used).

Impersonal verbs are used in subjectless sentences—the subject is not expressed overtly in the nominative case.

Leje (jak z cebra). 'It's raining (cats and dogs).'
Trzeba czekać. 'It is necessary to wait.'
Ściemnia się. 'It is getting dark.'
Będzie padało. 'It is going to rain.'
Warto by go zobaczyć. 'It would be worthwhile to see him.'

Past	Present	Future
padało 'it was raining'	pada 'it rains'	będzie padało 'it will rain' or będzie padać 'it will rain'

Impersonal verbs are not to be confused with the impersonal voice of personal verbs, e.g., Zabrania się palenia tytoniu. 'It is forbidden to smoke' (see 6.10).

Impersonal verbs are often used with weather verbs:

Padało całą noc. 'It has been raining all night.' or 'It has been snowing all night.' (depending on the context)
dżdży 'it's drizzling,' kropi 'it's dripping'
ociepla się 'it's getting warm,' ociepli się 'it will get warm'
oziębiać się 'it's getting cold,' oziębiło się 'it got cold'
wieje 'it is windy'
ściemnia się 'it's getting dark,' ściemniło się 'it got dark'
widnieje 'it's getting light outside'
wypogadzać się 'it's getting clear,' wypogodziło się 'it cleared up'
chmurzy się 'it's getting cloudy'
dnieje 'it's growing dusk'
grzmi 'it's thundering' grzmiało 'it thundered'
zachmurzyło się 'it became overcast'

Some modal verbs are impersonal:

można 'it is possible'   **warto** 'it is worthwhile'
powinno się 'one should'   **wolno** 'it is allowed'
trzeba 'it is necessary'   **należy** 'should' (synonym of **powinno się**)

(6.17)

Dlaczego należy dbać o zdrowie? 'Why should one take care of
one's health?'
nie należy 'should not' (less formal than **nie wolno** 'must not' and
not as strong as '**nie wolno**')
Dlaczego nie należy jeść późno kolacji? 'Why should one not eat
dinner late?'
Dlaczego nie wolno jeść późno kolacji? 'Why must one not eat late?'
Dziecka nie należy karmić za często. 'A child should not be fed
too often.'
Dziecka nie wolno karmić surowym mięsem. 'A child must not
be fed raw meat.'

Some modal verbs are impersonal. Impersonal modal verbs take the
infinitive, e.g.,

Trzeba <+INF> **mieć wizę, żeby wjechać do Uzbekistanu.** 'It is
necessary to have a visa to enter Uzbekistan.'
Warto <+INF> **obejrzeć nowy film Różyczka.** 'The movie *Little Rose*
is worth watching.'

Verbs that are used in the infinitive form only are mostly used to denote
perception:

widać 'see'   **słychać** 'hear'   **czuć** 'feel/smell'

These are often used in idiomatic expressions:

Nic nie widać. 'Can't see anything.' (lit. 'Nothing is visible.')
Co słychać? 'What's up?' (lit. 'What is heard?')
Czuć go na kilometr. 'You can smell him a mile/kilometer away.'

Many impersonal verbs are used in the third person singular or plural
and often take the equivalent of the English object in the nominative case
(see 2.4.12).

boleć 'to hurt'
Boli mnie głowa <NOM>. 'My head hurts.'
Bolą mnie nogi. 'My legs hurt.'

dłużyć się 'to drag (on)'
spotkanie dłużyło się 'the meeting dragged on'
dogasać/dogasnąć 'to burn out'
pożar dogasał 'the fire was burning out'
mdlić/zemdlić 'to feel sick/nauseate'
słodki tort mnie zemdlił 'the sweet cake made me sick'
nurtować 'to niggle'
wątpliwości mnie nurtowały 'I was nagged by doubt'
odbywać się/odbyć się 'to happen'

6.19 "There is/there are"

The English construction "there is/there are" is rendered in Polish by **jest** and **są**.

> **W budynku jest winda.** 'There is an elevator in the building.'
> **W budynku są dzieci.** 'There are children in the building.'

In comparision, **tam** 'over there' is used to emphasize the location.

Tam jest winda. 'There is an elevator over there.'

Present	Past	Future
jest 'there is'	**był/była/było** 'there was'	**będzie** 'there will be'
	byli/były 'there were'	**będą** 'there will be'

In the past tense the form of the verb has to agree with its subject in number, class and case.

> **W budynku była jedna mała winda.** 'There was one small elevator in the building.'
> **W budynku było jedno wyjście awaryjne.** 'There was one emergency exit in the building.'

Plural nouns without numerals and nouns used in the quantity of two, three or four as separate digits, such as two, twenty-two, one hundred and two (not twelve, thirteen, fourteen) are used with the plural forms of the verb "to be": **są/byli/były/będą**.

Byli is used to denote a group with one or more male humans. **Były** is used to denote a group without (fully developed) male humans.

> **W budynku są/były/będą dwie/trzy/cztery windy.**
> 'There are/were/will be two/three/four elevators in the building.'

451

Plural forms with an unidentified quantity, e.g., **dużo** 'many/much/a lot/ lots,' **mało** 'few/a little,' **kilka** 'several,' **parę** 'a couple,' or with a quantity higher than five (except those with the separate digits two, three, or four) are used with the singular form of the verb "to be": **jest/było/będzie**. In the past tense use the neuter form (-**ło**).

> **W budynku jest/było/będzie kilka/pięć wind.**
> 'There are/were/will be several/five elevators in the building.'

6.19.1 | Negated forms

"There is/are not," "there was/were not", "will be/will not be" are rendered in Polish by **nie ma, nie było, nie będzie** for all persons, classes, and numbers. The object which is lacking is expressed in the genitive case. In the past, the neuter form of the verb "to be," **było**, is used for singular and plural nouns (2.4.9).

> **W budynku nie ma** <SG present> <+GEN SG> **windy.** 'There is not an elevator in the building.'
> **W budynku nie ma** <SG present> <+GEN PL> **dzieci.** 'There are not children in the building.'
> **W budynku nie było** <SG past NT> <+GEN SG> **windy.** 'There was not an elevator in the building.'
> **W budynku nie było** <SG past NT> <+GEN PL> **dzieci.** 'There were not children in the building.'
> **W budynku nie będzie** <SG FUT> <+GEN SG> **windy.** 'There will not be an elevator in the building.'
> **W budynku nie będzie** <SG FUT> <+GEN PL> **dzieci.** 'There will not be children in the building.'

Present	Past	Future
nie ma	**nie było**	**nie będzie**
'there is not'	'there was/were not'	'there will not be'

(See also 2.4.9 and 2.6.4)

6.20 Subjunctive

To express a wish, desire, request or action that has not yet occurred, the subjunctive mood is very often used in everyday Polish. Time in subjunctive constructions is determined by the main verb. Depending on who the addressee of the wish, desire or request is, either the infinitive or a past tense with the conjunction **żeby** 'that' is used.

Chcę skończyć studia. 'I want to graduate.' [lit. 'I want to finish studies.']

Chcę, żeby oni skończyli \<male human form>/**one skończyły** \<no male human form> **studia.** 'I want them to graduate.' [lit. 'I want that they graduate.']

Chciałabym być wyższa. 'I wish I were taller.' (referring to a woman)

Chciałbym być wyższy. (referring to a man)

Chciałabym, żebyś była wyższa. 'I wish you \<FEM> were taller.'

Chciałabym, żebyś był wyższy. 'I wish you \<MSC> were taller.'

6.20.1 With infinitive

The infinitive is used when the addressee of the wish or desire is the subject of the sentence.

Chcę stąd wyjechać. 'I want to leave here.'

Chciałbym \<MSC> **stąd wyjechać.** 'I would like to leave here.'

Chciałem \<MSC> **stąd wyjechać.** 'I wanted to leave here.'

The infinitive is also used with impersonal constructions

Proszono, żeby nie rozmawiać. 'We were asked not to talk.'

Mówiło się, żeby głosować na ekologów. 'They were saying to vote for ecologists.'

6.20.2 Żeby clauses

In clauses beginning with **żeby** 'that,' the past tense is used with either the perfective or imperfective verb, depending on context.

Ewa chce, żeby Piotr stąd wyjechał \<MSC>.
'Ewa wants Piotr to leave here.'

Ewa chciałaby \<FEM>, **żeby Piotr stąd wyjechał** \<MSC>.
'Ewa would like Piotr to leave here.'

Ewa chciała \<FEM>, **żeby Piotr stąd wyjechał** \<MSC>.
'Ewa wanted Piotr to leave here.'

The form of the past tense (singular or plural, masculine, feminine, neuter, male human or no male human forms) in the subordinate clause (introduced by żeby) depends on the subject in the subordinate clause.

Ewa chce, żeby Piotr stąd wyjechał <MSC>.
'Ewa wants Piotr to leave here.'

Ewa chce, żeby Anna stąd wyjechała <FEM>.
'Ewa wants Anna to leave here.'

Ewa chce, żeby rodzice stąd wyjechali <male human form>.
'Ewa wants [her] parents to leave here.'

Ewa chce, żeby dzieci stąd wyjechały <no male human form>.
'Ewa wants the children to leave here.'

The form of the conjunction żeby depends on the subject in the subordinate clause (introduced by the conjunction żeby), not on the subject in the main clause. Żeby agrees in person and number with the subject in the subordinate clause.

Rodzice chcą, żebym skończył studia. 'My parents want me <MSC> to graduate.'

Rodzice chcą, żebym skończyła studia. 'My parents want me <FEM> to graduate.'

Rodzice chcą, żebyś skończył studia. 'My parents want you <MSC SG> to graduate.'

Rodzice chcą, żebyś skończyła studia. 'My parents want you <FEM SG> to graduate.'

Rodzice chcą, żeby ona skończyła studia. 'My parents want her to graduate.'

Rodzice chcą, żeby on skończył studia. 'My parents want him to graduate.'

Rodzice chcą, żebyśmy skończyli studia. 'My parents want us <MHPL> to graduate.'

Rodzice chcą, żebyśmy skończyły studia. 'My parents want us <NO-MHPL> to graduate.'

Rodzice chcą, żebyście skończyli studia. 'My parents want you <PL MHPL> to graduate.'

Rodzice chcą, żebyście skończyły studia. 'My parents want you <PL NO-MHPL> to graduate.'

Rodzice chcą, żeby oni skończyli studia. 'My parents want them <MHPL> to graduate.'

Rodzice chcą, żeby one skończyły studia. 'My parents want them <NO-MHPL> to graduate.'

Rodzice chcą, żebym skończył <MSC>/**skończyła** <FEM> **studia.**

'My parents want me to graduate.' [lit. 'My parents want that I finish
[my] studies.']

Ojciec chce, żebym skończył <MSC>/**skończyła** <FEM> **studia.**

'My father wants me to graduate.' [lit. 'My father wants that I finish
[my] studies.']

Dlaczego chcesz, żebym skończył <MSC>/**skończyła** <FEM> **studia?**

'Why do you <SG> want me to graduate?' [lit. 'Why do you <SG> want
that I finish my studies?']

Dlaczego chcecie, żebym skończył <MSC>/**skończyła** <FEM>
studia?

'Why do you <PL> want me to graduate?' [lit 'Why do you <PL> want
that I finish my studies?']

| 6.20.2.1 | *Translation of żeby in subjunctive constructions*

żebym 'that I'
żebyś 'that you' (both masculine and feminine)
żeby 'that he, that she, that it, that they'
żebyśmy 'that we' (accent falls on **że**)
żebyście 'that you' male human and no male human forms
   (accent falls on **że**)

| 6.20.2.2 | *Respectful forms of address*

żeby pani 'that you,' referring to a woman
żeby pan 'that you,' referring to a man
żeby państwo 'that you,' referring to a couple or a group of people
żeby panie 'that you,' referring to women
żeby panowie 'that you,' referring to men

6.21   Expressing English tenses in Polish

Time in subjunctive constructions is determined by the main verb
(see 6.20).

Time in reported speech stays in the same tense as in the original phrase
(see 6.22).

6.21.1 Present

1. Events happening at the precise moment of speaking.

> Polish: present simple
> English: present continuous or present simple

> **Ewa słucha muzyki pop.** 'Ewa is listening to pop music.'
> **Widzę cię.** 'I see you.'

2. Action taking place at or around the time of speaking.

> Polish: present simple
> English: present continuous

> **Słońce zachodzi i robi się zimno.**
> 'The sun is setting and it is getting dark.'

3. Habitual or repeated action in the present.

> Polish: present or present frequentative
> English: present simple

> **Ewa słucha muzyki pop.** 'Ewa listens to pop music.'
> **Ewa je/jada obiady w stołówce akademickiej.** 'Ewa eats
> lunches in the school cafeteria.'

4. Scientific truths, definitions, legal documents, sayings.

> **Ziemia krąży wokół słońca.**
> 'The earth revolves around the sun.'
> **Zło dobrem zwyciężaj.** 'Evil fights with good.'

6.21.2 Past

1. To express an action at a specific moment in the past. The action is
viewed as non-accomplished, still in progress.

> Polish: past imperfective
> English: past simple or past continuous

> **W 1981 mieszkałam w Polsce.**
> 'In 1981 I was living in Poland.' or 'In 1981 I lived in Poland.'

> **W 2001 budowaliśmy dom.**
> 'In 2001 we were building a house.'

2. To express an action at a specific moment in the past. The action is viewed as accomplished.

Polish: past perfective
English: past simple

W 1981 zamieszkałam W Polsce.
'In 1981 I settled down in Poland.'

W 2001 zbudowaliśmy nasz dom.
'In 2001 we built our house.'

3. The results of the action completed in the past are tangible in the present.

Polish: past perfective
British English: present perfect
American English: past simple

Wyszłam za mąż.
'I <FEM> got married [to a man]. [(lit.) left for a husband]'

Spociłam się.
'I got sweaty.'

Spłaciłam długi.
'I paid off my debts.'

4. The action has not been completed in the past but is tangible in the present.

Polish: past imperfective
English: present perfect continuous

Robiłam ciasto.
'I have been making a cake.' (and I have flour all over my face)

5. Past events or actions continue for a specific time period. Duration is emphasized.

Polish: past imperfective
English: past continuous or simple past

Mieszkaliśmy w Krakowie przez dwa lata.
'We were living in Cracow for two years.'

Ewa kochała Piotra przez całe życie.
'Ewa loved Piotr all [her] life.'

6. Events or actions occurred in the past and are continuing. Duration is emphasized.

> Polish: present
> English: present perfect continuous

Od 1981 roku mieszkam w Polsce.
Since 1981 I have been living in Poland.'

Od 2001 roku budujemy dom.
'Since 2001 we have been building a house.'

7. To express habitual or repeated action in the past.

> Polish: past imperfective or past frequentative
> English: "used to" or "would" with infinitive

Piotr dzwonił do rodziców w każdą sobotę.
'Piotr used to call his parents every Saturday.'

Na studiach Ewa jadła/jadała obiady w stołówce akademickiej.
'In college Ewa would eat lunches in the school cafeteria.'

8. Two events occurred simultaneously: adverbs **podczas gdy** 'while,' **kiedy** 'when/while.'

> Polish: past imperfective
> English: past continuous

Czytałam gazetę, kiedy Piotr oglądał film.
'I was reading a paper while Piotr was watching a movie.'

9. One event occurred during another event: adverbs **podczas gdy** 'while,' **kiedy** 'when/while.'

> Polish: past imperfective/past perfective
> English: past simple/past perfect

Czytałam gazetę, kiedy zadzwonił telefon.
'I was reading a paper when the phone rang.'

10. Events occurred in sequence.

> Polish: past perfective
> English: past simple, past perfect or past perfect continuous

Przeczytałam artykuł i/zanim zadzwoniłam do Ewy.
'I had read the paper and/before I called Ewa.'

Kiedy przeczytałam artykuł, zadzwoniłam do Ewy.
'When I finished reading the paper, I called Ewa.'

Mieszkałem w Nowym Jorku, zanim przyjechałem do Waszyngtonu.
'I lived in New York before I came to Washington, DC.'
'I had been living in New York before I came to Washington, DC.'

| 6.21.3 | *Future*

1. An event will be accomplished.

Polish: future perfective
English: "will/shall" with infinitive

Jutro zadzwonię do rodziców. 'I will call my parents tomorrow.'

2. An event will be taking place in the future.

Polish: future imperfective
English: future continuous

Jutro o tej porze będę dzwonił do rodziców.
'This time tomorrow I will be calling my parents.'

3. An event will be accomplished before a time in the future.

Polish: future perfective
English: future perfect

Jutro przed obiadem zadzwonię do rodziców.
'Tomorrow I will have called my parents before lunch.'

4. To express intentions.

Polish: **mieć zamiar/zamierzać** with perfective infinitive
English: "to be going to" with infinitive.

Jutro mam zamiar zadzwonić do rodziców.
'I am going to call my parents tomorrow.'

5. A future event is planned in the present or is a fact.

Polish: present
English: present continuous/present simple

459

Jutro dzwonię do rodziców.
'Tomorrow I am calling my parents.'

Samolot ląduje o 6.30.
'The plane lands at 6:30.'

6. To express near future.

Polish: present imperfective
English: "to be about to" with infinitive

Właśnie kupuję bilet.
'I am about to buy the ticket.'

7. Two events will occur in sequence in the future.

Polish: future perfective
English: "will/shall" with infinitive and present simple

Zadzwonię, jak tylko dojedziemy.
'I'll call as soon as we get there.'

(See 6.6.3.2.4)

6.22   Reported (indirect) speech

The tense of reported speech in Polish stays the same as in the original sentence, unlike in English, where the reported speech involves tense changes. Use **że** 'that' with the statements.

Present

Adam: Ewa jest <PRESENT> **chora.** 'Adam: Ewa is sick' (direct speech, original sentence)

Adam mówi <PRESENT>, **że Ewa jest** <PRESENT> **chora.**
'Adam says that Ewa is sick.' (reported speech)

Adam powiedział <PERFECTIVE PAST>, **że Ewa jest** <PRESENT> **chora.**
'Adam said that Ewa was sick.' (reported speech)

Past

Adam: Wczoraj Ewa była <IMPERFECTIVE PAST> **chora.**
'Adam: Ewa was sick yesterday.' (direct speech, original sentence)

Adam mówi <PRESENT>, **że wczoraj Ewa była** <IMPERFECTIVE PAST>
chora. 'Adam says that yesterday Ewa was sick.'

Adam powiedział <PERFECTIVE PAST>, **że wczoraj Ewa była**
<IMPERFECTIVE PAST> **chora.** 'Adam said that yesterday Ewa had been
sick yesterday.'

Adam: Wczoraj Ewa kupiła <PERFECTIVE PAST> **psa.** 'Adam: Ewa bought a dog yesterday.' (direct speech, original sentence)

Adam mówi <PRESENT>, **że Ewa wczoraj kupiła** <PERFECTIVE PAST> **psa.** 'Adam says that Ewa bought a dog yesterday.'

Adam powiedział <PERFECTIVE PAST>, **że Ewa wczoraj kupiła** <PERFECTIVE PAST> **psa.** 'Adam said that Ewa had bought a dog yesterday.'

Future:

Adam: Jutro Ewa będzie <IMPERFECTIVE FUTURE> **zajęta.** 'Adam: Ewa will be busy tomorrow.' (direct speech, original sentence)

Adam mówi <PRESENT>, **że jutro Ewa będzie** <IMPERFECTIVE FUTURE> **zajęta.** 'Adam says that tomorrow Ewa will be busy.'

Adam powiedział <PERFECTIVE PAST>, **że jutro Ewa będzie** <IMPERFECTIVE FUTURE> **zajęta.** 'Adam said that tomorrow Ewa would be busy.'

Adam: Jutro Ewa kupi <PERFECTIVE FUTURE> **psa.** 'Adam: Ewa will buy a dog tomorrow.' (direct speech, original sentence)

Adam mówi <PRESENT>, **że jutro Ewa kupi** <PERFECTIVE FUTURE> **psa.** 'Adam says that Ewa will buy a dog tomorrow.'

Adam powiedział <PERFECTIVE PAST>, **że jutro Ewa kupi** <PERFECTIVE FUTURE> **psa.** 'Adam said that Ewa would buy a dog tomorrow.'

6.22.1 With questions

The tense of the reported speech in Polish stays the same as in the original sentence, unlike in English, where the reported speech involves tense changes. Use **czy** 'whether' with general yes/no questions. Reported speech with specific questions, e.g., **gdzie?** 'where?', **kiedy?** 'when?' etc. also use the specific questions in Polish.

Adam: Chcesz pójść do kina?
'Adam: Do you want to go to the movies?' (direct speech, original sentence)

Adam pyta <PRESENT>, **czy chcesz pójść do kina.**
Adam is asking whether you want to go to the movies.

Adam zapytał <PAST>, **czy chcesz pójść do kina.**
Adam asked whether you would like to go to the movies.

Adam: Będziesz <FUTURE> **jutro w biurze?** 'Adam: Will you be in the office tomorrow?' (direct speech, original sentence)
Adam pyta <PRESENT>, **czy będziesz** <FUTURE> **jutro w biurze.**
Adam is asking whether you will be in the office tomorrow.
Adam zapytał <PAST PERFECTIVE>, **czy będziesz** <FUTURE> **jutro w biurze.** Adam asked whether you would be in the office tomorrow.

Adam: Gdzie byłaś <PAST> **wczoraj?** 'Adam: Where were you yesterday?' (direct speech, original sentence)
Adam pyta <PRESENT>, **gdzie byłaś** <PAST> **wczoraj.** 'Adam is asking where you were yesterday.'
Adam zapytał <PAST PERFECTIVE>, **gdzie byłaś** <PAST> **wczoraj.** 'Adam asked where you were yesterday.'

6.22.2 With commands, wishes, requests, desires

When one subject wants, asks, or tells other subject(s) to do something, the tense in the subordinate clause is always past, regardless of the tense in the original sentence.

(See also → Subjunctive 6.20)

Adam mówi do Ewy: Bądź ostrożna! 'Adam is telling Ewa: Be careful!' (direct speech, original sentence)
Adam mówi <PRESENT>, **żeby Ewa była** <PAST> **ostrożna.** 'Adam tells Ewa to be careful.'

Adam powiedział <PAST> **do Ewy: Bądź ostrożna!** 'Adam told Ewa: Be careful!'
Adam powiedział <PAST>, **żeby Ewa była** <PAST> **ostrożna!** 'Adam told Ewa to be careful!'

Chapter 7

Adverbs and adverbial phrases

7.1   Overview

Adverbs are often formed from descriptive adjectives. In Polish, adverbs are generally used to provide information about the action (as opposed to adjectives, which provide information about the subject and objects), and answer the questions: **kiedy** 'when'? **gdzie** 'where'? and **jak** 'how'? They describe the manner in which someone is doing, has done or will do something or how something is, has been or will be done.

> **Jedź ostrożnie.** 'Drive *safely*.'
> **Profesor mówił *głośno* i *wyraźnie*.** 'The professor spoke *loudly* and *clearly*.'
> **Źle się czuję.** 'I am *not* feeling *well*.'

Many constructions that use an adverb in Polish use an adjective in English (7.14).

> ***Ciepło*** <ADV> **tu.** 'It is *warm* <ADJ> in here.'
> ***Ładnie*** <ADV> **dziś wyglądasz.** 'You look *nice* <ADJ> today.'
> **W Paryżu jest *drogo*** <ADV>. 'It is *expensive* <ADJ> in Paris.'
> ***Zimno*** <ADV> **mi.** 'I am cold <ADJ>.'

Adverbs do not have cases, class and number—they are, unlike adjectives—invariable.

Most adverbs, similarly to adjectives, have comparative and superlative forms. (See 7.13.2)

> **Studenci mówili *głośniej* niż profesor.** 'The students spoke *louder* than the professor.'
> **W mieście jest *głośniej* niż na prowincji.** 'It is *louder* in the city than [it is] in the suburbs.'
> **Wczoraj czułam się dużo *gorzej*.** 'I felt *much worse* yesterday.'

Some adverbs do not have the comparative and superlative forms.

wczoraj 'yesterday'   **dość** 'quite'
tutaj 'here'   **prawie** 'almost'
nigdy 'never'   **wkrótce** 'soon'

Adverbs can modify:

- a verb: **mów wyraźnie** 'speak clearly'
- an adjective: **zupełnie zimna herbata** 'completely cold tea,' **wyjątkowo spostrzegawczy** 'very observant'
- another adverb: **bardzo dobrze** 'very well,' **dość spokojnie** 'quite calm'
- whole sentences: **oczywiście przyzna się do wszystkiego** 'surely he will confess to everything'
- sometimes, adverbs can modify nouns: **karp po żydowsku** 'Jewish-style carp.'

Adverbs can indicate: time, manner, place, degree of intensity, frequency.

Wkrótce zadzwonię. 'I'll call *soon*.'
Ewa *ostrożnie* jeździ samochodem. 'Ewa drives *safely*.'
Ewa *intensywnie* trenuje przed zawodami. 'Ewa trains *intensively* before the tournament.'
***Często* biegam.** 'I run *frequently*.'

7.2 Formation

Many adverbs are normally formed by adding the suffix -o or -e to a descriptive adjective. The choice between -e or -o is mostly based on the softness of the adjectival stem.

7.2.1 Suffix -e

-e is used with adverbs which are mostly formed from adjectives that end in -(consonant+)ny, -ły, -wy (not -owy).

Regular and predictable changes occur: ł:l, n:ni, st:ści, w:wi, sny:śnie, sty:ście.

Adjective	Adverb	Meaning	Shift
biegły	**biegle**	'fluently'	**ł:l**
ciekawy	**ciekawie**	'interestingly'	**w:wi**

doskonały	doskonale	'perfectly'	ł:l
dyskretny	dyskretnie	'discreetly'	n:ni
groźny	groźnie	'dangerously'	n:ni
hałaśliwy	hałaśliwie	'noisily'	w:wi
ładny	ładnie	'prettily'	n:ni
niezręczny	niezręcznie	'awkwardly'	n:ni
osobisty	osobiście	'personally'	sty:ście
poufały	poufale	'familiarly'	ł:l
radosny	radośnie	'joyfully'	sn:śni
spokojny	spokojnie	'calmly'	n:ni
wspaniały	wspaniale	'wonderfully'	ł:l
wyraźny	wyraźnie	'clearly'	n:ni
zgryźliwy	zgryźliwie	'abrasively'	w:wi
zły	źle	'wrongly'	ł:l

but:

mroźny	mroźno	'freezing'
późny	późno	'late'
wolny	wolno	'slowly'
dyszny	duszno	'stuffy'

7.2.2 | Suffix -o

-o is used with adverbs mostly formed from descriptive adjectives that end in a soft (-ni, -pi, -wi, -si), velar (-ki, -gi) or "historically" soft (-cy, -czy, -ży, -chy, -szy) consonant or in -owy.

Adjective	Adverb	Meaning
bliski	blisko	'closely'
cichy	cicho	'quietly'
cierpki	cierpko	'tartly'
daleki	daleko	'far'
drogi	drogo	'expensively'
duży	dużo	'a lot'
gęsi	(chodzić) gęsiego	'(to walk) in a single line'
głęboki	głęboko	'deeply'
głupi	głupio	'foolishly'
gorący	goraco	'hot'
kojący	kojąco	'soothingly'

lek**ki**	lek**ko**	'lightly,' 'gently'
nis**ki**	nis**ko**	'low'
ostat**ni**	ostat**nio**	'lately'
pies**zy**	(**chodzić**) pie**szo**	'(to walk) on foot'
su**chy**	su**cho**	'dry'
szero**ki**	szero**ko**	'widely'
śpią**cy**	śpią**co**	'sleepy'
śred**ni**	śred**nio**	'on average'
świe**ży**	świe**żo**	'freshly'
ta**ni**	ta**nio**	'cheaply'
uro**czy**	uro**czo**	'charmingly'
wą**ski**	wą**sko**	'narrowly'
wyso**ki**	wyso**ko**	'high'

-owy	**-owo**	
wyjątk**owy**	wyjątk**owo**	'exceptionally'
zdrowy	zdrowo	'healthy'
szacunkowy	szacunkowo	'approximately'
typowy	typowo	'typically'

świeżo malowane '*freshly*-painted wet paint'
Dzisiaj jest bardzo *gorąco*. 'It is *very* hot today.'

-ry (without irregular **dobry** 'good': **dobrze** 'well')

sta**ry**	sta**ro**	'[looking] old'
ponu**ry**	ponu**ro**	'grimly'

7.2.2.1 | *Colors*

Colors have the ending -o in adverbs.

biały 'white'	**(na) biało** '(in) white'
czarny 'black'	**na czarno** 'in black'
czerwony 'red'	**na czerwono** 'in red'
niebieski 'blue'	**na niebiesko** 'in blue'
szary 'gray'	**na szaro** 'in gray'
zielony 'green'	**na zielono** 'in green'
żółty 'yellow'	**na żółto** 'in yellow'
jasny 'light'	**na jasno** in bright colors
ciemny 'dark'	**na ciemno** in dark colors

Pomalowaliśmy kuchnię _na zielono_. 'We painted [our] kitchen _[in]_ green.'

Dlaczego ubrałeś się _na czarno_? 'Why did you dress [all] _in black?_'

7.2.3 | Two forms

Some adverbs can have two distinct forms, used in certain phrases:

miło and **mile** 'nicely'
ledwo and **ledwie** 'barely,' 'hardly'
wysoko 'high' (about height) and **wysoce** 'high' (about hierarchy)
pochmurno and **pochmurnie** 'cloudy'
mglisto 'foggy' (about weather) and **mgliście** 'vaguely' (about concepts)

Bardzo mi _miło_ (not: mile) '_Pleased_ to meet you.'
   [**miło** is used with the logical subject in the dative case]
Byłam _mile_ zaskoczona telefonem od Ewy. (not: miło)
   'I was _pleasantly_ surprised by Ewa's phone call.'
   [**mile** is used with the subject in the nominative case]

Ledwie żyję. 'I am barely alive, I am exhausted.'
Pochmurno dziś. 'It is _cloudy_ today.'

7.3 Placement

The placement of adverbs depends on the part of speech that the adverb modifies (See also 7.14.3). An adverb can be placed:

1. Immediately before or after the verb.
2. In front of the adjective.
3. In front of another adverb it modifies.
4. After the noun it modifies (for manner).

1. _Szybko_ chodzisz. 'You walk _fast._'
   Mieszkam _blisko_. 'I live _close by._'
   Mówię _po polsku_. 'I speak _Polish_ [lit. in Polish way]'
2. _Bardzo_ ładny dom. '_Very_ pretty house.'
   Wyjątkowo otwarta osoba. '_Exceptionally_ open [minded] person.'
   On jest _dostatecznie_ dorosły, żeby sobie poradzić. 'He is adult _enough_ to manage.'

467

3. Jest *dość* zimno. 'It is *quite* cold.'
   Mieszkam *bardzo* blisko. 'I live very *close*.'
4. Dania <PL> *na gorąco*. '*Hot* entrées.'

7.4 Adverbs of time

Adverbs of time are used to express time in the present, past and future and to answer the question **kiedy** 'when'?

dzisiaj 'today' [pronounced dzisi<u>a</u>j not <u>e</u>j]
dziś 'today'
jutro 'tomorrow'
kiedyś 'one day'
teraz 'now'
wczoraj 'yesterday' [pronounced fczor<u>a</u>j not fczor<u>e</u>j]

Dawno **pani nie widziałam.** 'I have not seen you (madam) *for a long time*.'
Do zobaczenia *wkrótce*. 'See you *soon*.'

7.4.1 Translating English word "time"

'Time' can be translated in different ways, depending on what the term "time" refers to, e.g., hour, season, or time period.

wówczas 'at that time'
jednocześnie 'at the same time'
wtedy 'at the time'
od czasu do czasu, chwilami
  'at times'
za każdym razem
  'each (every) time'
godzina 'hour of the day'
w czasach or **za czasów** 'in times'
[praca] w niepełnym wymiarze
  'part-time [job]'

za pierwszym razem
  'the first time around'
po raz ostatni or **poprzednim razem** 'the last time'
pora dnia 'time of the day'
pora roku 'time of the year'
wyprzedzać swoją epokę to
  be ahead of the times [lit. 'to be
  ahead of one's own epoch']

Za każdym razem **kiedy cię widzę, wyglądasz pięknie.**
'*Every time* I see you, you look beautiful.'
Po raz ostatni **proszę cię, żebyś przestał.** 'This is *the last time* I am asking you to stop.'

***Poprzednim razem* byłem na czas.** '*The last time* I came on time.'
Zdałem egzamin na prawo jazdy *za pierwszym razem*. 'I passed
the driver's license exam *the first time around*.'

7.4.2 | Stages of life, periods

To był bardzo trudny *okres* w moim życiu. 'It was a very difficult
time in my life.'
***okres* pokoju** '*time* of peace'

7.4.3 | Time now

aktualnie 'at present' (false friend, does not mean "actually")
dzisiaj 'today'
obecnie 'currently'
teraz 'now'
Właśnie wychodzę <+IMPFV>. 'I am about to go out.'
współcześnie 'in our times' (bookish)

7.4.4 | First, then, next and finally

najpierw 'first'   **następnie** 'next'
potem 'then'   **w końcu** 'finally'

***Najpierw* pobiegam, *potem* wezmę prysznic, *następnie* zrobię
kawę, i *w końcu* coś zjem.**
'*First*, I will go for a jog, *then* I will take a shower, *next* I'll make coffee
and *finally* I'll eat something.'

7.4.5 | Early/late; earlier/later

wcześnie 'early' ≠ **późno** 'late'
wcześniej 'earlier' ≠ **później** 'later'
Jest *już późno*. Przepraszam, ale muszę już iść. 'It is *already late*.
I am sorry, but I have to go now.'
Jest *jeszcze wcześnie*. Naprawdę musisz już iść? 'It is *still early*.
Do you really have to go already?'

469

| 7.4.6 | **Time passed** |

dawniej 'in the past'
dawno temu 'long ago'
kiedyś 'in the past'
niedawno 'not so long ago'
od kiedy? 'since when?'

ostatnio 'lately'
przedwczoraj 'the day before yesterday'
tydzień temu 'a week ago'
wczoraj 'yesterday'
właśnie wtedy 'just then'

Ostatnio **dużo podróżowałam.** '*Lately* I have traveled a lot.'
To było w 1955 roku. *Właśnie wtedy* **poznałam Ewę.** 'It was in
 1955. *Just then* I met Ewa.'

| 7.4.7 | **Time to come** |

do kiedy? 'until when?'
dopóki nie <+PFV> 'until'
jutro 'tomorrow'
zawczasu 'in advance' **[z góry]**

właśnie kiedy <+PFV> 'just when'
pojutrze 'the day after tomorrow'
wkrótce 'soon'

Nie odezwę się, *dopóki* **mnie** *nie przeprosisz.* 'I won't say a word
 until you *apologize* to me.'
Zrób to *zawczasu,* **a nie w ostatniej chwili.** 'Do it *in advance* and
 not at the last minute.'

| 7.4.8 | **Duration** |

ciągle 'never stops'
długo 'for a long time'

nadal 'still'
niedługo 'briefly'

| 7.4.8.1 | *During time to come* |

dopiero jutro 'not until tomorrow'
dopiero za tydzień
 'not until after a week'

wkrótce 'soon'
niedługo
 'soon, before long'

| 7.4.9 | **Translation difficulties** |

jeszcze nie 'not yet' ≠ **już nie** 'no more'
Jeszcze 'still' is a synonym of **nadal** 'still.'

Rodzice *już nie pracują*—są emerytami. '[My] parents *do not work any more*—they are retired.'

Jestem studentką—*jeszcze nie pracuję*. 'I am a student—*I do not work yet*.'

nadal versus **ciągle**

Ewa *ciągle rozmawia* przez telefon. 'Ewa *never stops talking* on the phone' (negative connotation)

Ewa *nadal rozmawia* przez telefon. 'Ewa *is still on the phone*' (neutral connotation)

Syn *ciągle* śpi. '[My] son *always* sleeps.'

Syn *nadal* śpi, ale kiedy się obudzi, proszę go nakarmić. '[My] son is *still* sleeping, but when he wakes up, please feed him.'

For days of the week, months of the year and seasons, see 9.2.6. For clock time, see 8.2.

7.5   Age

Asking about age in Polish actually means asking about the number of summers **lato—lat** <GEN PL> one has acquired.

Ile on ma lat? 'How old is he?' [lit. 'How many years does he have?']

Ile lat ma pan Piotr? 'How old is mister Piotr?'

Ile masz lat? 'How old are you?' <familiar form>

Ile lat ma nasz dom? 'How old is our house?'

7.5.1   Rok—lat—lata

Rok [lit. 'a year'] is only reserved for a period of 365 or 366 days. Unlike in Russian, any compound numbers with **jeden** take **lat** (not **rok**).

Komputer ma rok. 'The computer is one year old.'

Mam 21 lat. 'I am 21 years old.'

Mam 11 lat. 'I am 11 years old.'

Numerals that end in the words **dwa, trzy, cztery** take **lata**.

Komputer ma dwa lata. 'The computer is two years old.'

Mam 34 lata. 'I am 32 years old.'

Mam 82 lata. 'I am 82 years old.'

All numerals that do not end in the words **dwa**, **trzy**, **cztery** or in the word **rok** take **lat**.

> **Komputer ma pięć lata.** 'The computer is five years old.'
> **Mam 12 lat.** 'I am 12 years old.'

7.5.2 | *Approximate age*

There are many ways to express approximate age and number in general. The most popular are: **około** 'about' <+GEN>, **ponad** 'more than' <+ACC>, **mniej więcej** 'more or less' <+ACC>.

> **Komputer ma *ponad* dwa** <ACC=NOM> **lata** <ACC=NOM>.
> 'The computer is *more than* two years old.'

> **Komputer ma *około* dwóch** <GEN> **lat** <GEN PL>.
> 'The computer is about two years old.'

Notice that both the number and the year are in the genitive case.

> **Nasza drukarka ma *mniej więcej* dwa** <ACC=NOM> **lata** <ACC=NOM>.
> 'Our printer is *more or less* ten years old.'

Because of the complexity of expressing approximate numbers with the preposition **około**, the construction **mniej więcej** is recommended.

For more on how to express approximate age and different stages of life see 9.2.6.

7.6 Weather

There are many ways to ask about the weather in Polish. Like in English, generally one type of question asks about the weather itself, i.e., 'what's the weather like [today],' and the other type is about the conditions outside 'how is it; is it cold?' Such duality is also observed in Polish.

> *Jaka* <ADJ> **(jest) dzisiaj *pogoda*?** '*What* is *the weather like* today?'
> **Dzisiaj jest *piękna*** <ADJ> ***pogoda*!** 'Today [it] is *beautiful weather*!'

> *Jak* <ADV> ***jest na zewnątrz?* Zimno** <ADV> **czy *ciepło*** <ADV>?
> '*How is it* outside? *Cold* <ADJ> or *warm* <ADJ>?'

> **Jaka pogoda była wczoraj?**
> 'What was the weather like yesterday?'

Jaka pogoda będzie jutro?
'What will the weather be like tomorrow?'

Jaka jest prognoza pogody na jutro?
'What is the weather forecast for tomorrow?'

Weather conditions in Polish are described with adverbs and verbs in the third person singular, in the past tense the neuter form with the marker -ło is used.

When the answer includes the actual word **pogoda** 'weather,' an adjective is used. Otherwise an adverb is used to describe the weather.

Dzisiaj jest *piękna pogoda*. 'Today [it] is *beautiful weather*.'
Dzisiaj jest *pięknie*. 'Today is *beautiful*.'

Bez względu na pogodę, jutro idziemy w góry.
'Come rain or shine, we will go hiking tomorrow.'

Weather conditions are expressed with the verb "to be" in the third person singular; in the past tense using the singular neuter form—with marker -ło + adverb.

[Dzisiaj] *jest ciepło*. 'It *is warm* [today].'
Wczoraj *było ciepło*. 'Yesterday *was warm*.'
Jutro też *będzie ciepło*. 'Tomorrow *will be warm*, too.'

Other adverbs commonly used with the weather:

jest chłodno 'it's cool'	**jest mroźno** 'it's freezing'
jest duszno 'it's muggy'	**jest pochmurno** 'it's overcast'
jest gorąco 'it's hot'	**jest przyjemnie** 'it's pleasant'
jest słonecznie 'it's sunny'	**jest zimno** 'it's cold'
jest wilgotno 'it's humid'	

7.7 Adverbs of place

Adverbs of place are generally used after verbs that indicate location and positioning:

być 'to be'
znajdować się 'to be located, to be situated' <IMPFV>
znaleźć się 'to be located, to be situated, to be placed' <PFV>
leżeć 'to be situated, to be placed'

Gdzie leży Turcja? 'Where is Turkey located?'
Jestem już blisko. 'I am very close.'

blisko 'close'	**tam** 'over there
daleko 'far'	**tutaj/tu** 'here''
gdzie? 'in where?' (interrogative)	**wszędzie** 'everywhere'
gdziekolwiek 'anywhere'	**z przodu** 'ahead'
gdzieś 'somewhere'	**z tyłu** 'behind'
na dole 'down(stairs)'	**niezbyt daleko**
na górze 'above, up(stairs)'	'not very far'
na lewo 'on the left'	**niedaleko stąd**
na prawo 'on the right'	'not far from here'

Przepraszam, *gdzie* **jest wyjście?** 'Excuse me, *where* is the exit?'
Wyjście jest *na dole.* '[The exit is] *downstairs.'*
Gdzie **chcesz się spotkać?** '*Where* do you want to meet?'
Gdziekolwiek. '*Anywhere*' (everywhere that works well for you)
Siedź *tu!* 'Keep sitting!'
Siedź *z tyłu,* *z przodu* **nie ma miejsca.** 'Stay sitting *in the back,*
   there is no room *in the front.'*
Usiądź *z tyłu!* 'Take a seat *in the back!'*
Śpisz *na górze,* **czy** *na dole?* 'Are you sleeping *on the top* bunk or
   on the bottom bunk?' (**łóżka piętrowego** 'of the bunk bed')

| 7.7.1 | *Directional adverbs* |

Adverbs of direction are generally used after verbs expressing motion.
(6.4.14)

skręcać/skręcić 'to turn'
jechać 'to go', etc.

do przodu 'forward'	**pod górę** 'uphill'
do tyłu 'backward'	**tam** 'over there'
dokąd? '[to] where?'	**tutaj/tu** 'here'
(interrogative)	**w dół** 'downward'
dokądkolwiek '[to] anywhere'	**stąd** '[from] here'
dokądś '[to] somewhere'	**w lewo** 'on the left'
iść prosto 'to go straight'	**w prawo** 'on the right'
na górę 'above, up(stairs)'	**skąd?** 'where [from]?'
	niedaleko stąd 'not far from here'

Dokąd to? 'Where [are you] *off to?*' (coll.)

Idź do przodu, tam jest więcej miejsca. 'Go *forward [to the front]*, there is more room over there.'

Dlaczego jedziemy do tyłu? 'Why are we *going backward?*'

W górę, w górę, śmiało! '*Up, up*, go ahead!'

Dokąd chcesz pójść? 'Where do you want to go?'

Dokądkolwiek. Byle daleko stąd? '*Anywhere.* As long as it is far *from here.*'

Zejdź! 'Get down!' (e.g., from a ladder)

Skąd jesteś? '*Where* are you *from?*' **Z Ameryki.** 'From America.'

7.8   Adverbs of manner

Adverbs of manner are used to indicate the method or style in which something is, has been or will be done.

Many adverbs of manner are in a form of adverbial expression (more than one word). Commonly used adverbial expressions are: **na . . . -o /-e, po . . . -u.**

Kto z państwa mówi *po polsku?* 'Who of you speaks *Polish?*'

U nas wszystko *po staremu.* 'We are doing *the same as always.*'

Zrobiłeś to *naumyślnie.* 'You did it *intentionally.*'

Gdzie pan mieszka *na stałe?* 'Where do you live *permanently?*'

Lubię skrzydełka *na ostro.* 'I like *spice* wings.'

Jestem tu tylko *przejazdem.* 'I am just *passing through.*'

Commonly used adverbs of manner:

robić coś 'to do something' (**jak?** 'how?', **w jaki sposób?** 'in what way?')

dobrze 'well'	**odręcznie** 'immediately'
inaczej 'differently'	**odruchowo** 'impulsively'
jakoś 'somehow'	**po kryjomu** 'in secret'
mimowolnie 'unintentionally'	**po swojemu** 'in one's own way'
na miejscu 'on the spot'	**podobnie** 'similarly'
na trzeźwo 'soberly'	**potajemnie** 'in secret'
natychmiast(owo) 'immediately'	**stopniowo** 'gradually'
naumyślnie 'intentionally'	**szybko** 'fast'
niechcący 'accidentally'	**wolno** 'slowly'
nieostrożnie 'carelessly'	**złośliwie** 'maliciously'
niespodziewanie 'unexpectedly'	**źle** 'wrong', 'not well'

poznać kogoś *osobiście, przypadkowo* 'to meet somebody *in person, accidentally*'

poinformować kogoś *pisemnie, ustnie, listownie* 'to inform somebody *in writing, orally, by mail*'

sterować czymś *elektronicznie, manualnie, ręcznie* 'to navigate something *electronically, manually, by hand*'

mówić na okrągło *po cichu, szeptem, po angielsku* 'to speak *all the time, quietly, in English*'

chodzić *boso, po omacku, bezszelestnie* 'to walk *barefoot, to feel your way through the dark, noiselessly*'

mieszkać *na stałe* 'to live *permanently*,' ***na zawsze*** 'forever'

być gdzieś *przejazdem* 'to be somewhere for a short period of time—passing through'

coś do jedzenia *na zimno, na gorąco, na ostro, na słodko, na wynos* 'something to eat *cold, hot* (temperature), *spicy, sweet, take out*'

jajko *na twardo, na miękko* '*hard-boiled* egg, *soft-boiled* egg'

czuć się 'too feel,' **świetnie** 'great,' **dobrze** 'well,' **fantastycznie** 'fantastic,' **tak sobie** 'so so,' **względnie dobrze** 'fairly well'

7.8.1 | Using a language

To speak, read or write in a language is expressed with the combination po + adjective that pertains to the language + u.

Mówić *po arabsku*. 'To speak *Arabic*.'
Pisać *po chińsku*. 'To write *in Chinese*.'
Rozumieć *po rosyjsku*. 'To understand *Russian*.'
Znam pięć słów *po japońsku*. 'I know five words *in Japanese*.'

But **tekst napisany po łacinie** 'a text written in Latin.'

7.8.2 | po . . . .-u

The pair po . . .-u is popular to express the manner in which something is, has been or will be done.

po mału 'little by little'	**po prostu** 'simply'
po ciemku 'in the dark'	**po przyjacielsku** 'amicably'
po mistrzowsku 'skillfully'	**po kryjomu** 'in secret'

7.9 Adverbs of degree

Adverbs of degree are used to intensify action (i.e., the verb that conveys the action), or a feature (i.e., the adjective that describes it).

bardziej 'more' (not więcej)
bardzo 'very'
całkiem 'entirely'
co najmniej 'at least'
dosyć 'quite'
dość 'quite'
kompletnie 'completely'
ledwo 'hardly'
mniej 'less'
najbardziej 'most'
najmniej 'least'
nieprzytomnie 'madly'
trochę 'a little'
wystarczająco 'enough'
dostatecznie 'enough'

tak 'so, that'
o mało nie 'close call'
okropnie 'horribly'
prawie (nikt)
　(+negatives) 'hardly (anybody)'
prawie 'almost'
strasznie 'terribly'
w ogóle 'in general'
wcale '(not) at all'
więcej (nie) '(not) any more'
za 'too'
zbyt 'too'
zupełnie 'fully'

mało kto 'almost nobody' is a synonym of **prawie nikt** 'hardly anybody'
mało gdzie 'almost nowhere' is a synonym of **prawie nigdzie**
　'hardly anywhere'

Ewa jest *dostatecznie* silna, żeby sobie poradzić. 'Ewa is strong *enough* to manage.'
Ewa jest *nieprzytomnie* zakochana. 'Ewa is *madly* in love.'
***Całkiem* o tym zapomniałam.** 'I *completely* forgot about it.'
***Wcale* jej *nie* rozumiem.** 'I *don't* understand her *at all*.'
***Więcej* do niej *nie* napiszę.** 'I won't write to her *any more*.'
***Prawie nigdy nie* dzwonisz.** 'You *hardly ever* call.'
Dlaczego jest *tak* zimno? 'Why is it *so* cold?'

7.9.1 "More"

bardziej + adjective, another adverb or a verb
więcej + noun or a noun phrase to specify quantity
Jestem *bardziej zaangażowany* niż ty. 'I am *more involved* than you are.'
Dzisiaj mam *więcej czasu*. 'I have *more time* today.'

(See 4.17.6.2)

7.10 Adverbs of frequency

Generic question: **Jak często?** 'How often?'

czasami 'sometimes'
czasem 'now and then'
często 'often, frequently'
nieczęsto 'not often,
  infrequently'
nigdy nie 'never'

od czasu do czasu
  'from time to time'
rzadko 'rarely'
zawsze 'always'
zazwyczaj 'in general'
zwykle 'usually'

7.10.1 *Adverbial phrases of frequency*

Adverbial phrases of frequency express frequency within a described period of time. The prepositions **na** <+ACC> and **w** <+LOC> are generally used with weeks, months, and years to indicate frequency. The preposition **co** 'every' is followed by the accusative case or the nominative case. **Co rok** 'every year' has a synonymous phrase **co roku**, which is more popular than co rok, e.g., **jak co roku** 'like every year.'

co <+ACC> **sobotę** 'every Saturday' or **co** <+NOM> **sobota** 'every Saturday'
co <+ACC> **chwilę** or **co** <+NOM> **chwila** 'every moment'
co <+ACC> **rok** 'every year' or as a set phrase **co** <+GEN> **roku** 'every year'

raz na <+ACC> **tydzień**
  'once a week'
raz w <+LOC> **tygodniu**
  'once a week'
raz dziennie 'once a day'
[cardinal number] + **razy**
  'more than once'

dwa razy na tydzień
  'twice a week'
dwa razy w tygodniu
  'twice a week'
dwa razy dziennie 'twice a day'
kilka razy 'several times'
parę razy 'a couple of times'

When using different numbers of days, weeks, months, years, etc. remember that the numbers 2, 3, and 4 and compound numbers with 2, 3, and 4 follow the nominative plural form. Number five and its multiples follow the genitive plural form as do 12, 13, and 14. As part of a compound number, such as 21, 51 "one" follows the genitive plural.

co <+ACC or NOM> **tydzień** 'every week'
co <+NOM> **dwa, trzy, cztery** <+NOM PL> **tygodnie** 'every two, three, four weeks'
co pięć <+GEN PL> **tygodni** 'every five weeks'

co <+NOM> **miesiąc** 'every month'

co <+NOM> **dwa, trzy, cztery** <+NOM PL> **miesiące** 'every two, three, four months'

co <+NOM> **pięć** <+GEN PL> **miesięcy** 'every five months'

co <+NOM> **dwa, trzy, cztery** <+NOM PL> **lata** 'every two, three, four years'

co <+NOM> **pięć** <+GEN PL> **lat** 'every five years'

co <+NOM> **dzień** 'every day' = **codziennie** 'daily'

co <+NOM> **dwa, pięć**, etc. **dni** <NOM PL=GEN PL> 'every two, five, etc. days'

co noc <ACC=NOM> 'every night'

co godzinę 'every hour'

co <+NOM> **dwie, trzy, cztery** <+NOM PL> **godziny** 'every two, three, four hours'

co <+NOM> **pięć** <+GEN PL> **godzin** 'every five hours'

7.11   Interrogative adverbs

Interrogative adverbs are used to inquire about time, place, manner, and purpose:

dlaczego? 'why?'	**dokąd?** '[to] where?'
do kiedy? 'until when?'	**na jak długo?** 'for how long?'
gdzie? 'where?'	**od kiedy?** 'since when?'
ile? 'how much/many?'	**skąd?** '[from] where?'
jak długo? 'how long?'	**jak?** 'how?'
kiedy? 'when?'	

Skąd **pan jest?** '*Where* are you *from*, sir?'
Od kiedy **pan tutaj mieszka?** '*Since when* have you been living here, sir?'
Na jak długo **pan wyjeżdża?** '*How long* are you going *for*, sir?'
Jak długo **pani będzie w Polsce?** '*How long* will you be in Poland, madam?'

7.12   Negative adverbs

Nie is written as one word with adverbs that are formed from adjectives.

Jest mi *niedobrze.* 'I am *not [feeling] well.*'
Tutaj jest *niedrogo* **i bardzo smacznie.** 'It is *inexpensive* and very tasty here.'

479

Wyglądasz *nieatrakcyjnie* **w tej bluzie.** 'You look *unattractive* in this sweatshirt.'

***Nieładnie* się zachowałeś.** 'You behaved *unpleasantly*.'

Ewa *niesmacznie* **gotuje, za to piecze pyszne ciasta.** 'Ewa *does not cook well* but bakes delicious cakes.'

and

niezbyt 'not too much'   **nieraz** 'many times'

However, when a clear contrast or contradiction is being made (usually with the conjuctions **lecz, ale** 'but'), the **nie** in negated adverbs is written separately.

Wyglądasz nie ładnie, lecz cudownie. '[lit.] You look not pretty, but gorgeous.'

Nie is written separately from adverbs that are not formed from adjectives.

nie bardzo 'not too much'   **nie raz, a dwa razy**
nie dzisiaj 'not today'   'not once but twice'
nie dość 'not enough'   **nie za bardzo** 'not too much'

Nie is written seperately from the comparative and superlative forms.

nie lepiej 'not better'   **nie najlepiej** 'not best'

7.13 Comparative and superlative

Adverbs and adjectives have comparative forms (**stopień wyższy**) and super-lative forms (**stopień najwyższy**). Adverbs form comparatives by adding the suffix **-ej** to the positive degree (basic form) and superlatives by adding the prefix **naj-** to the comparative degree.

To form comparatives from adverbs that end in **-e**, simply add **-j** to the adverb.

To form comparatives from adverbs that end in **-o**, simply drop the **-o** and add the suffix **-ej**. Predictable consonant changes to soften the stem will occur: r:rz, d:dzi, ł:l, n:ni, st:ści. (See 1.3.4)

zimno 'cold'	**n:ni**	**zimniej** 'colder'	**najzimniej** 'coldest'
pięknie 'beautifully'		**piękniej** 'more beautifully'	**najpiękniej** 'most beautifully'
tanio 'cheaply'		**taniej** 'more cheaply'	**najtaniej** 'most cheaply'

wyraźnie		**wyraźniej**	**najwyraźniej**
'clearly'		'more clearly'	'most clearly'
staro	r:rz	**starzej**	**najstarzej**
'old'		'older'	'oldest'
młodo	d:dzi	**młodziej**	**najmłodziej**
'young'		'younger'	'youngest'
ciepło	ł:l	**cieplej**	**najcieplej**
'warmly'		'more warmly'	'most warmly'
często	st:ści	**częściej**	**najczęściej**
'frequently'		'more frequently'	'most frequently'

To form comparatives from adverbs that end in -(o)ko and -(o)go, simply drop the -ko and -go and add the suffix -ej to the stem. Predictable consonant changes occur s:ż, g:ż, t:c, d:dzi. (See 1.3.4)

nisko 'low'	**niżej** 'lower'	**najniżej** 'lowest'
wysoko 'high'	**wyżej** 'higher'	**najwyżej** 'highest'
drogo	**drożej**	**najdrożej**
'expensive'	'more expensive'	'most expensive'
krótko 'shortly'	**krócej** 'more shortly'	**najkrócej** 'most shortly'
długo 'long'	**dłużej** 'longer'	**najdłużej** 'longest'
lekko 'light'	**lżej** 'lighter'	**najlżej** 'the lightest'
blisko 'closely'	**bliżej** 'more closely'	**najbliżej** 'most closely'
rzadko 'rarely'	**rzadziej** 'more rarely'	**najrzadziej** 'most rarely'

Some adverbs, like in English, have irregular comparative and superlative forms.

dobrze 'well'	**lepiej** 'better'	**najlepiej** 'best'
źle 'badly'	**gorzej** 'worse'	**najgorzej** 'worst'
dużo 'many'	**więcej** 'more'	**najwięcej** 'most'
mało 'little, a few'	**mniej** 'less'	**najmniej** 'least'

7.13.1 (naj)bardziej/(naj)mniej + adverb

Adverbs can also form comparatives by adding the intensifiers **bardziej** 'more' and **najbardziej** 'most' or diminishers **mniej** 'less' and **najmniej** 'least' to the positive degree (basic form) of the adverb.

najbardziej obiecująco 'the most promisingly'

najmniej obiecująco 'the least promisingly'

Relational adverbs have no semantic content other than that of the noun they were formed from. Relational adverbs do not have comparative or superlative forms.

> **po polsku** 'of or referring to Poland and its inhabitants'
> **na pewno** 'for sure'
> **za darmo** 'free of charge' (cannot be more or less free of charge)

7.13.3 *Comparative constructions*

To compare two qualities or quantities using the positive degree (basic form) of an adverb, constructions such as **tak . . . , jak** 'as . . . as;' **nie tyle . . . , co** 'so much . . . as,' or just **jak** 'as,' are used.

> **Powiedziała to *tak spokojnie jak* umiała.**
> 'She said it *as calmly as* she could.'

> **W Nowym Jorku *jest tak drogo jak* w Paryżu.**
> 'In New York *it is as expensive as* in Paris.'

> **Wyglądasz *tak młodo jak* dwadzieścia lat temu.**
> 'You look *as young as* 20 years ago.'

7.13.3.1 *Comparative of superiority*

To compare two qualities or quantities certain constructions are used, rendered in English by 'more . . . than'

1. Comparative form of the adverb + **niż** 'than' <+NOM>
2. Comparative form of the adverb + **niż** 'than' <+noun phrase>
3. Comparative form of the adverb + **od** 'than' <+GEN>
4. **Coraz** + a comparative form of the adverb. Continuous increase/decrease.
5. **Im . . . tym** 'the more . . . the. . . .'
6. **jest tym bardziej . . . ponieważ** 'all the more/less . . . than/as'

> **Ewa *lepiej* prowadzi samochód *niż* Piotr.** 'Ewa drives *better than* Piotr.'
> **Ewa *lepiej* prowadzi samochód *od* Piotra.** 'Ewa drives *better than* Piotr.'

> **W Waszyngtonie jest *cieplej niż* w Warszawie.** 'In Washington, DC it is *warmer than* in Warsaw.'

Studia zaoczne są teraz *bardziej popularne niż* dawniej.
'External studies are now *more popular than* in the past.'
Mam *coraz mniej* wolnego czasu. 'I have *less and less* time.'
Zużywamy *coraz więcej* energii. 'We use *more and more* energy.'
Im częściej **biegam *tym lepiej* się czuję.** '*The more frequently* I jog,
the better I feel.'

7.13.4 Superlative constructions

To compare superlative qualities or quantities certain constructions are used.

Superlative form of the adverb + **w** 'in,' **na** 'at, in' <+LOC>
Comparative form of the adjective + **z(e)** 'than' <+GEN PL>

(An extra e is used before many consonant clusters. See 1.3.8.1.)

Mieszkamy *najdalej ze wszystkich*.
'*Out of everyone* we live *the farthest*.'

Kto *w klasie najszybciej* biega?
'*Who in the class* runs *the fastest*?'

Kto biega najszybciej na świecie?
'Who runs the fastest in the world?'

7.14 Differences between English and Polish adverbs

7.14.1 Use of senses

In English, constructions with the senses mostly take adjectives. In Polish
they take adverbs.

Ładnie <ADV> **wyglądasz.** 'You look *nice* <ADJ>.'
Ładnie <ADV> **[to wygląda].** '[It looks] *nice* <ADJ>.'
Ładnie <ADV> **pachniesz.** 'You smell *nice* <ADJ>.'
Ładnie <ADV> **pachnie.** 'It smells *nice* <ADJ>.'
or: **To ma miły** <ADJ> **zapach.** [lit. 'It has a nice smell.']
Świetnie **smakuje.** <ADV> 'It tastes *great* <ADJ>.'
or: **To jest smaczne.** <ADJ> 'It is tasty <ADJ>.'
Ładnie <ADV> **śpiewa.** 'She sounds nice <ADJ>.'
or: **Ona ma ładny** <ADJ> **głos.** 'She has a pretty <ADJ> voice.'
Ładnie <ADV> **brzmi.** 'It sounds *nice* <ADJ>.'

483

Idiom:

> **W porządku.** [lit. 'in order'] 'Sounds good <ADJ>.'

> **Jest** *przyjemny* <ADJ> **w dotyku.** 'He feels *nice* <ADJ>.' (e.g., a dog)
> **To jest** *przyjemne* <ADJ> **w dotyku.** 'It feels *nice* <ADJ>.' [lit. 'It is nice
>   in touch.']
> *Przyjemnie* <ADV> **być w domu.** 'It feels *nice* <ADJ> being at home.'
> **Jak mi** *dobrze!* 'This feels so *nice*.' (e.g., I am so comfortable right now)

(Infinitives are also modified by adverbs; see 2.4.7.)

7.14.1.1 English–Polish Agreement with senses

English and Polish constructions with the senses are expressed using adverbs
when it is the action performed in a certain manner that is modified.

> **Ewa słucha** *uważnie* <ADV>. 'Ewa is listening *attentively* <ADV>.'
> **Dotknij psa** *delikatnie* <ADV>. 'Touch the dog *nicely* <ADV>.'

English and Polish use adjectives to describe the object or subject of a
sentence or clause.

> **Ona wygląda na** *skupioną* **osobę** <ADJ, ACC>. 'She looks *attentive* <ADJ>.'
> [lit. 'She looks as the attentive person.']

7.14.2 Empty "it"

generally takes adjective in English, and adverb in Polish.

Most constructions in English that begin with "it"—where "it" cannot be
classified—are omitted in Polish and the whole construction is modified
by an adverb.

> **W pokoju było** *ciemno* <ADV>. 'It was *dark* <ADJ> inside the room.'

(There is no answer to the question: what is dark? It means that the "it"
is empty. As a consequence an adverb is used in Polish, and an adjective
in English.)

> *Ciemno* <ADV> **tu.** 'It is *dark* <ADJ> in here.' (no answer for what is
>   dark—empty "it")
> **Dzisiaj jest** *słonecznie* <ADV>. 'It's *sunny* today <ADJ>.'

(There is no answer for what is sunny in the sentence, we know when but
not what, **dzisiaj** is an adverb of time.)

W Nowym Jorku jest *drogo* <ADV>. 'It is *expensive* <ADJ> in
New York.'

(No answer for what is expensive in New York, we only know where it
is expensive, "where" is an adverb of place.)

Slightly modified sentences can classify "it," but then instead of the adverb,
the adjective will be used in Polish and English.

Dzisiaj jest *słoneczny dzień*. 'Today it is *a sunny day*.'
Nowy Jork jest *drogim* <ADJ, INS NT> ***miastem*** <NOUN INS NT>.
  'New York is *an expensive* <ADJ> city <NOUN>.'

(**miasto** is modified; the instrumental case is used after the verb "to be")

Nowy Jork to drogie <ADJ NOM> **miasto.** 'New York is an expensive
  <ADJ> city.'

(**miasto** is modified; the nominative case is used after the demonstrative
pronoun "to")

Constructions that pertain to physical or mental health are generally used
with an adverb in Polish.

***Zimno* mi.** 'I am *cold*.'
***Smutno* nam.** 'We are *sad*.'

7.14.3 Placement

Adverbs of place such as **tu** 'here,' **tutaj** 'here,' and **tam** 'over there' are
generally used immediately in front or after the verb in longer sentences
in Polish, and at the end of the sentence in English.

Mieszkał w Bostonie i *tam* szukał pracy. 'He lived in Boston and
  was looking for a job *over there*.'
Dlaczego *tam* zaparkowałeś? 'Why did you park *over there*?'
Co się *tutaj* dzieje? 'What is going on in *here*?'
***Tu* mnie boli.** 'It hurts *here*.'
Co pani *tam* robi? 'What are you doing *over there*?'

In short phrases, the placement of **tu, tutaj** in Polish and English can be
similar.

Chodź *tu*. 'Come *here*.'
Nie chodź *tam*. 'Don't go *there*.'

485

7.14.4 **Dostatecznie, też, również, także**

The adverb **dostatecznie** "enough" (= sufficiently) is used after the adjective in English but, before the adjective in Polish.

Piotr jest *dostatecznie* dorosły, żeby sobie poradzić.
'Piotr is adult *enough* to manage.'

Także 'as well' is used to add additional information to a sentence and is often used in phrases that start from **a także** 'and also/and additionally.'

Też is used in regular speech, in both written and spoken Polish. In Polish, unlike in English, **też, również,** and **także** are used immediately before or after the verb. In Polish **też, również** hardly ever begin the sentence. Także is often used in the phrase **a także.**

Ja *też* jestem głodna.
'I am hungry, *too.*'

Ewa lubi kino. Operę *też* lubi.
'Ewa likes movies. She likes opera, *too.*'

Ewa lubi kino. Lubi *też* operę.
'Ewa likes movies. She *also* likes opera.'

Ewa mówi po polsku i rosyjsku, a także po arabsku.
'Ewa speaks Polish and Russian, and also Arabic.'

Chapter 8

Numerals and clock time

8.1 Numerals

8.1.1 Cardinal numbers

Cardinal numbers are used to specify a certain number of things. They are:

0	zero	30	trzydzieści
1	jeden	40	czterdzieści
2	dwa	50	pięćdziesiąt
3	trzy	60	sześćdziesiąt
4	cztery	70	siedemdziesiąt
5	pięć	80	osiemdziesiąt
6	sześć	90	dziewięćdziesiąt
7	siedem	100	sto
8	osiem	125	sto dwadzieścia pięć
9	dziewięć	200	dwieście
10	dziesięć	300	trzysta
11	jedenaście	400	czterysta
12	dwanaście	500	pięćset
13	trzynaście	600	sześćset
14	czternaście	700	siedemset
15	piętnaście	800	osiemset
16	szesnaście	900	dziewięćset
17	siedemnaście	1000	tysiąc
18	osiemnaście	1235	tysiąc dwieście trzydzieści pięć
19	dziewiętnaście		
20	dwadzieścia	2000	dwa tysiące
21	dwadzieścia jeden	3000	trzy tysiące

4000	**cztery tysiące**	10 000	**dziesięć tysięcy**
5000	**pięć tysięcy**	100 000	**sto tysięcy**
6000	**sześć tysięcy**	1 000 000	**milion**
7000	**siedem tysięcy**	1 000 000 000	**miliard**
8000	**osiem tysięcy**	2 000 000 000	**dwa miliardy**
9000	**dziewięć tysięcy**	5 000 000 000	**pięć miliardów**

Note: In Polish, unlike in English, neither a comma nor a dot are used in thousands and higher numbers. A space after every three zeros is used.

Raz is used instead of **jeden** for counting. **Raz, dwa, trzy, raz, dwa, trzy . . .**

8.1.1.1	Numeral governance with **dwa**, **trzy**, **cztery**

- **dwa** refers to masculine nouns (except for male humans) and neuter inanimate nouns (see 8.1.1.6 for neuter animate)
- **dwie** refers to feminine nouns
- **trzy** and **cztery** refer to masculine and feminine nouns (except for male humans) and neuter inanimate nouns (see 8.1.1.6)
- numerals that end in the words **dwa**, **trzy**, **cztery** take no male human forms in the nominative plural and the no male human plural form of verbs (marker -**ły**)

Dwa/trzy/cztery małe koty śpią <PL>.
'Two/three/four small cats are sleeping.'

Dwie/trzy/cztery małe dziewczynki śpią <PL>.
'Two/three/four small girls are sleeping.'

Dwa/trzy/cztery małe okna są brudne <PL>.
'Two/three/four small windows are dirty.'

8.1.1.2	Numeral governance with **dwaj**, **trzej**, **czterej**

Dwaj, trzej, czterej are the numerals used in the subject position when referring to male human beings. They take the male human plural form of verbs (marker -**li**), and male human forms in the nominative plural.

Dwaj/trzej/czterej wysocy mężczyźni śpią.
'Two/three/four tall men are sleeping.'

Number—noun agreement:

NOM	**Dwa małe koty śpią.**	'Two small cats are sleeping.'
ACC	**Widzę dwa małe koty.**	'I see two small cats.'
GEN	**Nie widzę dwóch małych kotów.**	'I don't see two small cats.'
DAT	**Daję mleko dwu/dwóm małym kotom.**	'I give milk to two small cats.'
LOC	**o dwu/dwóch małych kotach**	'about two small cats'
INS	**z dwoma małymi kotami**	'with two small cats'

Idiom: **chodzić na czworakach** 'to walk on all fours' (to crawl)

8.1.1.3	Number—noun—verb discrepancy with five and up

From the cardinal number **pięć** 'five' upwards (except for the cardinal numbers that end in **dwa/dwie, trzy, cztery**), the verb that modifies the cardinal number **pięć** 'five' upwards is in the singular, in the past tense the neuter form with the marker **ło** is used, in the passive the form **-o** is used, and with nouns and noun phrases the genitive plural is used.

Pięć osób <GEN PL> **mieszka** <PRESENT SG> /**mieszkało** <PAST SG> **w naszym domu.**
'Five people live/lived in our house.'

Pięć osób <GEN PL> **zakwaterowano** <PASSIVE> **w jednym pokoju.**
'Five people were lodged in one room.'

Please note that compound numerals with the final number 2, 3, 4 do not follow this rule.

Dzisiaj *jest* 5 stopni. 'Today [it] *is* 5 degrees.'
Dzisiaj *są* 24 stopnie. 'Today [it] *is* 24 degrees.'
Dzisiaj rano *było* 10 stopni, teraz *są* 22 stopnie. 'This morning [it] *was* 10 degrees, now [it] *is* 22.'

Pięć/dziesięć/sto <+GEN PL> **małych kotów śpi** <SG verb>.
'Five/ten/a hundred small cats are sleeping.'
Pięć/dziesięć/sto <+GEN PL> **małych dziewczynek śpi** <SG verb>.
'Five/ten/a hundred small girls are sleeping.'
Pięć/dziesięć/sto <+GEN PL> **małych okien jest** <SG verb> **brudnych.**
'Five/ten/a hundred small windows are dirty.'

Collective and indefinite numbers in the subject position

Collective numbers **dwoje** 'two' and upwards and indefinite numbers in the subject position take a verb in the singular. In the past tense formation, the verb takes the neuter marker -ło. Nouns and noun phrases following the numbers are in genitive plural. (See also 8.1.2 and 8.1.5)

> **Pięcioro posłów mieszka poza Warszawą.**
> 'Five members of parliament live outside of Warsaw.'

> **Na spotkanie przyszło dwoje ludzi.**
> 'Two [man and woman] people came for the meeting.'

> **Dużo ludzi mówi po angielsku.**
> 'Many people speak English.'

| 8.1.1.4 | **zero** |

Zero declines like a neuter noun, e.g., **metro.**

> **Wczoraj było dziesięć stopni poniżej** <GEN> **zera.**
> 'Yesterday was ten degrees *below zero*.'
> **zaczynać od zera** 'to start *from scratch*' (idiom)

Zero is used with singular (uncountable) or plural nouns or noun phrases in the genitive case.

> **Zero poczucia humoru.** 'Zero sense of humor.'
> **Zero tolerancji dla pijanych kierowców.** 'Zero tolerance for drunk drivers.'
> **On ma zero kwalifikacji na to stanowisko.** 'He has zero qualifications for this job.'
> **Zero wydatków i zero przychodów.** 'Zero expenses and zero income.'

Table 8.1 Declension of **zero**

Case	Singular	Plural
NOM	zero	zera
ACC	zero	zera
GEN	zera	zer
DAT	zeru	zerom
LOC	zerze	zerach
INS	zerem	zerami

| 8.1.1.5 | **Jeden** |

Jeden declines similarly to the pronoun **tamten, tamta, tamto**. It has masculine **jeden**, feminine **jedna**, and neuter **jedno** forms that agree with the noun or noun phrase in class, number and case. **Jeden, jedna, jedno** combine with singular nouns when they denote *one* item.

> **Mamy *jedno*** (not: jedne) ***dziecko.*** 'We have *one child*.'
> ***Jeden chleb nie wystarczy.*** '*One* [loaf of] *bread* will not be enough.'
> **Zamówiłam *jedną książkę*, a otrzymałam dwie.** 'I ordered *one book*, but I received two.'
> ***Jedli z jednego talerza.*** 'They were eating *from one plate*.'

| 8.1.1.5.1 | **Jeden** as a separate digit |

For compound numbers ending in jeden 'one' (e.g., 21, 101, etc.) the number jeden is not declined.

> **W sali jest dwadzieścia** <NOM> ***jeden*** <NOM> **osób.**
> 'There are twenty-one people in the room.'

> **Dyrektor rozmawiał z dwudziestoma** <INS> ***jeden*** <UNDECLINED> **osobami** <INS PL>.
> 'The manager was talking with twenty-one people.'

> **Dyrektor rozmawiał o dwudziestu** <LOC> ***jeden*** <UNDECLINED> **osobach** <LOC PL>.
> 'The manager was talking about twenty-one people.'

> **Na stu** <LOC> ***jeden*** <UNDECLINED> **stronach** <LOC PL> **tego dokumentu znalazłam tylko jeden błąd.**
> 'On the one hundred and one pages of this document I found only one mistake.'

When jeden is used by itself (not a part of a compound number), the number jeden <MSC>, jedna <FEM>, jedno <NT> declines like an adjective, and agrees with the noun it modifies in class, case, and number.

> **W pokoju jest tylko *jedna*** <FEM NOM SG> ***osoba, jeden*** <MSC NOM SG> ***pracownik, jedno*** <NT NOM SG> ***dziecko.***
> 'There is only one person, one employee, one child in the room.'

> **Dyrektor rozmawiał z *jedną*** <FEM INS SG> ***osobą/z jednym*** <MSC INS SG> ***pracownikiem/z jednym*** <NT INS SG> ***dzieckiem.***
> 'The manager was talking with one person/one employee/one child.'

Dyrektor rozmawiał o jednej <FEM LOC SG> **osobie/o jednym**
<MSC LOC SG> **pracowniku/o jednym** <NT LOC SG> **dziecku.**
'The manager was talking about one person/one employee/one child.'

| 8.1.1.5.2 | **Jedne** and **jedni** with plural nouns |

The plural forms of "number one": **jedne** for no male human nouns, and **jedni** for male human nouns, are used in the meaning of *some* in opposing sentences, and also in the meaning of *both* (accompanied by the connector **i** 'and').

> **Jedne kobiety płakały, inne krzyczały.** 'Some women were crying, others were screaming.'
> **Jedni spali, kiedy drudzy pracowali.** 'Some were sleeping, while others were working.'
> **Jedne i drugie warunki były nie do przyjęcia.** 'Both conditions were unacceptable.'
> **Jedni i drudzy byli przemili.** 'Both [mixed groups of men and women, or just men] were very nice.'

With plural tantum nouns (a noun that is invariably plural in form but singular in sense, e.g., **spodnie** 'pants'), "number one" is sometimes used in its plural no male human form **jedne**.

> **W domu mamy tylko jedne nożyczki.**
> 'We have only one [pair of] scissors at home.'
> (better: **W domu mamy tylko jedną parę nożyczek.**)

| 8.1.1.5.3 | *jeden/jedna/jedno z . . .* |

Jeden is often used in the construction "*one of . . .*" followed by the noun in the genitive plural.

> **Piotr jest jednym z moich najlepszych przyjaciół.** 'Piotr is one of my best friends.'
> **Zabić drozda to jedna z moich ulubionych książek.** 'To Kill a Mockingbird is one of my favorite books.'

| 8.1.1.5.4 | **Jedyny** |

Jedyny is used with the meaning 'the *only one*'—there are no other options or people.

> **Piotr jest jedynym okulistą w mieście.**
> 'Piotr is the only optician in town.'

Jedyne metro w Polsce jest w Warszawie.
'The only metro in Poland is in Warsaw.'

To *jedyne rozwiązanie*, które przychodzi mi do głowy.
'It is the only solution that comes to my mind.'

Note: "An only child" in Polish is **jedynak** (boy) or **jedynaczka** (girl).

Table 8.2 Declension of **jeden**

Case	Singular			Plural	
	MSC	FEM	NT	NO-MHPL	MHPL
NOM	jeden	jedna	jedno	jedne	jedni
ACC	= NOM/GEN	jedną	jedno	jedne	jednych
GEN	jednego	jednej	jednego	jednych	jednych
DAT	jednemu	jednej	jednemu	jednym	jednym
LOC	jednym	jednej	jednym	jednych	jednych
INS	jednym	jedną	jednym	jednymi	jednymi

8.1.1.6 | Dwa

There are many forms of the number two in the nominative case: **dwa** and **dwie**; **dwaj** and **dwoje** (8.1.2). The use of these forms depends on the class of the nouns they describe.

1. **Dwa** is used with masculine nouns (except male humans) and neuter inanimate nouns; the verb is in the plural; nouns are in the nominative plural.

   W pokoju są/były *dwa stoły i dwa krzesła*.
   'There are/were *two tables* and *two chairs* in the room.'

2. **Dwie** is used with feminine nouns (objects, people and animals); the verb is in the plural, nouns are in the nominative plural.

   W pokoju są/były *dwie szafy i dwie kobiety*.
   'There are/were *two dressers* and *two women* in the room.'

3. **Dwaj** is used with male human nouns; the verb is in the plural, nouns are in the nominative plural.

   W pokoju są/byli *dwaj mężczyźni*.
   'There are/were *two men* in the room.'

4. **Dwoje** is used with animate neuter nouns in genitive plural (people and animals).

W pokoju jest/było *dwoje dzieci* i *dwoje szczeniąt*.
'There are/were *two children* and *two puppies* in the room.'

5. **Dwoje** is also used for groups of mixed male and female humans, *the verb is in the singular*, the past tense form is the neuter form with the marker -ło, and *nouns are in the genitive plural* case. (See 8.1.2)

W pokoju jest/było *dwoje ludzi*.
'There are/were *two people* in the room (one male and one female).'

| 8.1.1.6.1 | **Dwaj** and **dwóch/dwu** with male human nouns |

Dwaj can be used interchangeably with **dwóch/dwu** in the nominative case. However, **dwóch/dwu** impose on the noun the form of the genitive plural and the verb is in the singular; the past tense is the neuter form with the marker -ło.

W pokoju są/byli *dwaj mężczyźni*. 'There are/were *two men* in the room.'

W pokoju jest/było *dwóch mężczyzn*. 'There are/were *two men* in the room.'

Table 8.3 Declension of **dwa**

Case	NO MALE HUMAN PL			MALE HUMAN PL
	MSC no human	NT inanimate	FEM	
NOM	dwa	dwa	dwie	dwaj/dwu (dwóch)
ACC	= NOM	= NOM	= NOM	dwu (dwóch)
GEN	dwu (dwóch)	dwu (dwóch)	dwu (dwóch)	dwu (dwóch)
DAT	dwu (dwóm)	dwu (dwóm)	dwu (dwóm)	dwu (dwóm)
LOC	dwu (dwóch)	dwu (dwóch)	dwu (dwóch)	dwu (dwóch)
INS	dwoma	dwoma	dwiema/dwoma	dwoma

| 8.1.1.7 | **Oba** *'both'* |

| 8.1.1.7.1 | As subject |

1. Referring to humans

Obaj/obydwaj: male human, verb in plural, noun in the nominative case
Obie/obydwie: female human, verb in plural, noun in the nominative case

Oboje/obydwoje: with married couples; verb in plural, noun in the nominative case

but

Oboje/obydwoje: mixed groups, including children; verb in singular, noun in the genitive plural (**rodzeństwo** in genitive singular)

Obaj/obydwaj synowie pracują w centrum.
'Both sons work in the center.'

Obie/obydwie siostry studiują historię.
'Both sisters study history.'

Oboje rodzice są/byli na spotkaniu.
'Both parents are/were at the meeting.'

Oboje państwo Kwaśniewscy byli na balu.
'Both Mr. and Mrs. Kwaśniewski were at the ball.'

but

Oboje dzieci jest/było na spotkaniu.
'Both children are/were at the meeting.'

Oboje studentów jest/było na spotkaniu.
'Both students are/were at the meeting.'

Oboje rodzeństwa mieszka/mieszkało w Polsce.
'Both sister and brother live/lived in Poland.'

or: **I siostra, i brat mieszkają w Polsce.**
or: **Zarówno siostra, jak i brat mieszkają w Polsce.**

2. Referring to inanimate (objects) and non humans (animals) *of the same kind*

Oba/obydwa: masculine animals and objects, and neuter objects, verb in plural, noun in the nominative case
Obie/obydwie: feminine animals and objects, verb in plural, noun in the nominative case
Oboje/obydwoje: neuter animals (offspring), and with collective nouns, such as **oczy** 'eyes,' **uszy** 'ears'; verb in singular, noun in the genitive plural

Oba/obydwa domy są/były na sprzedaż. *'Both houses are/were* for sale.'
Obie/obydwie lampy są/były nasze. *'Both lamps are/were ours.'*
Oboje uszu jest/było czyste. *'Both ears are clean.'*
Oboje szczeniąt jest/było słodkie. *'Both puppies are/were cute.'*

495

Note: *Both* refers to objects of the same kind:

> **Oba łóżka są wygodne.** '*Both beds* are comfortable.'
> **Łóżko i sofa są bardzo wygodne.** (not: łóżko i sofa są oba bardzo wygodne) '*The bed and the sofa are both* very comfortable.'

| 8.1.1.7.2 | As object or complement |

> **Dom przekazany *przez oboje małżonków*.** 'A house handed over
> *by both spouses*.'
> **Na *obojgu oczach/uszach* były plamy.** '*On both eyes/ears* were spots.'
> **Czytam artykuł *o obojgu studentach*.** 'I am reading an article *about
> both students*.'

> **Rozmawiałeś z matką czy z ojcem?** 'Did you talk with mom,
> or with dad?'
> **Z obojgiem.** 'With both.'

> **Myślisz o Kasi czy o Basi?** 'Are you thinking about Kasia or Basia?'
> **O obu/o obydwu./O jednej i o drugiej.** 'About both.'

Oba/obydwa, obie/obydwie cannot refer to two different objects.

> **Chcesz ciastko czy kawę?** 'Do you want a pastry or coffee?'
> **I ciastko, i kawę. *Jedno i drugie*.** '*Both*.' or: **I to, i to.**

> **Jeździsz metrem czy autobusem?**
> **I metrem, i autobusem. *Jednym i drugim*.** '*Both*.' or: **I tym, i tym.**

Oba/obydwa, obie/obydwie can be used when referring to two objects of
the same kind.

> **Chcesz ciastko czekoladowe, czy waniliowe?** 'Do you want a
> chocolate or vanilla pastry?'
> **Poproszę oba/obydwa.** 'Both, please.'

Idiom:

> **bilet w obie strony** 'a return ticket,' 'a round-trip ticket'

| 8.1.1.7.3 | Zarówno . . . , jak i . . . 'both . . . and . . .' |

> **On jest *zarówno mądry, jak i zabawny*.**
> 'He is *both smart and funny*.'

> **Jest *zarówno słonecznie, jak i mroźno*.**
> 'It is *both sunny and freezing*.'

Zarówno *on, jak i ona* kupili bilety.
'Both *he and she* bought tickets.'

Zaczęli zarówno *tańczyć, jak i śpiewać*.
'They started *to both dance and sing*.'

8.1.1.7.4 | Translation difficulties

"Both came" can be translated into Polish as:

Obaj/obydwaj przyszli (if two of them are male human)
Obie/obydwie przyszły (if two of them are female human)
Oboje przyszli (if one of them is male and the other is female human)

8.1.1.7.5 | *Dziadkowie* 'grandparents/grandfathers'

o **obojgu/obydwojgu dziadkach** 'about both grandparents'
o **obu/o obydwu/o obydwóch dziadkach** 'about both grandfathers'
z **obojgiem/z obydwojgiem dziadków** 'with both grandparents'
z **obu/z oboma/z obydwu dziadkami** 'with both grandfathers'

Table 8.4 Declension of **oba**

Case	MHPL	FEM	NO-MHPL
NOM	obaj/obydwaj	obie/obydwie	oba/obydwa
ACC	obu/obydwu/obydwóch	obie/obydwie	oba/obydwa
GEN	obu/obydwu/obydwóch	obu/obydwu/obydwóch	obu/obydwu/obydwóch
DAT	obu/obydwu/obydwóm	obu/obydwu/obydwóm	obu/obydwu/obydwóm
LOC	obu/obydwu/obydwóch	obu/obydwu/obydwóch	obu/obydwu/obydwóch
INS	obu/obydwu/obydwoma	obiema/obydwiema	obu/oboma/obydwoma

Note: The above forms of 'both' refer to two people of the same sex, two things or ideas, or two animals. These forms of 'both' are not used with neuter nouns that end in ę in the nominative singular (e.g., **szczenię** 'puppy'), to refer to couples of mixed sex, or to refer to children.

Obaj mężczyźni są lekarzami. 'Both men are doctors.'
Obie kobiety są lekarkami. 'Both women are doctors.'
Ludzie stali po obu stronych ulicy. 'People were standing on both sides of the street.'
Babcia nazywała mnie obydwoma imionami: Anna Maria.
'[My] grandmother used to call me both names: Anna Maria.'

8.1.1.7.6 | Couples

NOM **oboje państwo Kwaśniewscy** both Mr. and Mrs. Kwaśniewski
      oboje rodzice both parents

ACC **oboje państwa Kwaśniewskich**
      oboje rodziców

GEN **obojga państwa Kwaśniewskich**
      obojga rodziców

DAT **obojgu państwu Kwaśniewskich**
      obojgu rodzicom

LOC **obojgu państwu Kwaśniewskich**
      obojgu rodzicach

INS **obojgiem państwa Kwaśniewskich**
      obojgiem rodziców

8.1.1.8 | **Trzy** *and* **cztery**

8.1.1.8.1 | **Trzy, trzech, trzej** and **troje**, and **cztery, czterech, czterej**
and **czworo** as a subject

Both forms of the cardinal number **trzy** 'three' <NOM> and **trzech** 'three'
<GEN>, **cztery** 'four' <NOM> and **czterech** 'four' <GEN> can be used as a
subject, but take different forms of nouns and verbs.

Trzy <NOM> and **cztery** <NOM> take no male human plural nouns and
noun phrases in the nominative plural forms, the verb is in the plural.

Trzech <GEN>, **czterech** <GEN> take male human plural nouns and noun
phrases in the genitive plural forms, in the past tense the neuter form with
the marker **-ło** is used, in the passive the form **-o** is used, and with nouns
and noun phrases the genitive plural is used.

Trzej, czterej are used with male human nouns; the verb is in the plural,
nouns are in the nominative plural.

Troje, czworo are used with animate neuter nouns (people and animals)
and with groups of mixed male and female humans.

> **Mam** *trzech/czterech braci.* 'I have *three/four brothers.*'
> **W pokoju są/były** *trzy/cztery stoły i trzy/cztery krzesła.* 'There
> are/were *three/four tables* and *three/four chairs* in the room.'
> **W pokoju są/były** *trzy/cztery szafy i trzy/cztery kobiety.* 'There
> are/were *three/four dressers* and *three/four women* in the room.'

W pokoju są/byli *trzej/czterej mężczyźni.* 'There are/were *three/four men* in the room.'

W pokoju jest/było *troje/czworo dzieci* **i** *troje/czworo szczeniąt.* 'There are/were *three/four children* and *three/four puppies* in the room.'

W pokoju jest/było *troje/czworo ludzi.* 'There are/were *three/four people* in the room.' (mixed group of male and female)

<hr>

8.1.1.8.2 | **trzej** and **trzech; czterej** and **czterech** with male human nouns, as subjects

Trzej and czterej can be used interchangeably with trzech and czterech, respectively, in the subject position. However, trzech and czterech impose on the noun the form of the genitive plural and the verb is in the singular; the past tense form is the neuter form with the marker -ło.

W pokoju są/byli *trzej/czterej mężczyźni.*
'There are/were *three/four men* in the room.'

W pokoju jest/było *trzech/czterech mężczyzn.*
'There are/were *three/four men* in the room.'

Table 8.5 Declension of **trzy** and **cztery**

Case	NO-MHPL	NT inanimate	FEM	MHPL
NOM	**trzy/cztery**	**trzy/cztery**	**trzy/cztery**	**trzej/czterej;**
				trzech/czterech
ACC	= NOM	= NOM	= NOM	**trzech/czterech**
GEN		**trzech/czterech**		
DAT		**trzem/czterem**		
LOC		**trzech/czterech**		
INS		**trzema/czterema**		

8.1.1.9 | **Pięć** *and up*

These numerals have one ending for the no male human form: pięć, sześć, siedem, etc. and one for the male human form: pięciu, sześciu, siedmiu, etc.

pięć **kobiet** 'five women'
pięciu **mężczyzn** 'five men'
dziewięćdziesiąt **matek** '90 mothers'
dziewięćdziesięciu **ojców** '90 fathers'

Numbers five and up (except for compound cardinal numbers with the separate digits 2, 3, 4): in the subject position the verb is in the singular (in the past tense with the neuter marker **-ło**, in the passive with **-no, -ło**) and nouns or noun phrases are in the genitive plural.

> **Pięć kobiet jest/było w pokoju.** *'Five women are/were in the room.'*
> **Sześć sklepów zostało zniszczonych.** *'Six stores were destroyed.'*
> **Dwanaście psów jest/było głodnych.** *'Twelve dogs are/were hungry.'*

| 8.1.1.9.1 | 5, 15, 50 |

Male human numbers end in **-u** in the nominative case. These numerals have only three forms: a nominative—accusative form, a genitive—locative—dative form, and an instrumental form. The instrumental form can be the same as the dative, locative and genitive form.

Table 8.6 Declension of 5, 15, 50

Case	NO-MHPL	MHPL
NOM	**pięć/piętnaście/pięćdziesiąt**	**pięciu/piętnastu/pięćdziesięciu**
ACC	= NOM	= NOM
GEN	**pięciu/piętnastu/pięćdziesięciu**	= NO-MHPL
DAT	= GEN	= NO-MHPL
LOC	= GEN	= NO-MHPL
INS	= GEN	= NO-MHPL
	or **pięcioma/piętnastoma/**	= NO-MHPL
	pięćdziesięcioma	

Widzę *pięć* <ACC NO-MHPL> **kobiet.**
'I see five women.'

Widzę *pięciu* <ACC MHPL> **mężczyzn.**
'I see five men.'

Pracuję z *pięciu* <INS NO-MHPL> **kobietami.**
'I work with five women.'

Pracuję z *pięciu* <INS MHPL> **mężczyznami.**
'I work with five men.'

Pracuję z *pięcioma* <INS NO-MHPL> **kobietami.**
'I work with five women.'

Pracuję z *pięcioma* <INS MHPL> **mężczyznami.**
'I work with five men.'

Table 8.7 Declension of **sto/stu** and **dwieście/dwustu**

Case	NO-MHPL	MHPL
NOM	**sto, dwieście**	**stu, dwustu**
ACC	= NOM	= NOM
GEN	**stu, dwustu**	**stu, dwustu**
DAT	**stu, dwustu**	**stu, dwustu**
LOC	**stu, dwustu**	**stu, dwustu**
INS	**stu/stoma, dwustu/dwustoma**	**stu/stoma, dwustu/dwustoma**

Trzysta and czterysta decline similarly to dwieście, dwustu.

8.1.1.10 *500–900*

Five hundred–nine hundred have two forms, one for male human; the other for everything else.

Table 8.8 Declension of 500, 600, 700, 800, 900

Case	NO-MHPL	MHPL
NOM	**pięćset, sześćset, siedemset, osiemset, dziewięćset**	One form for all MHPL cases: **pięciuset, sześciuset, siedmiuset, ośmiuset, dziewięciuset**
ACC	= NOM	
GEN	**pięciuset, sześciuset, siedmiuset, ośmiuset, dziewięciuset**	
DAT	= GEN	
LOC	= GEN	
INS	= GEN	

Male human plural form

One form for all cases: NOM = ACC = GEN = DAT = LOC = INS

pięciuset, sześciuset, siedmiuset, ośmiuset, dziewięciuset

Ośmiuset pasażerów **zostało uratowanych**.
'*Eight hundred passengers* were saved.'

Rozmawiamy o *ośmiuset pasażerach*.
'We are talking *about the eight hundred passengers*.'

| 8.1.1.11 | **Tysiąc** *and* **milion** |

Zero, **tysiąc** 'thousand,' and **milion** 'million' decline like nouns, similarly to **pióro**, **miesiąc**, and **banan**, respectively.

> **od tysiąca do miliona złotych** 'from one thousand to
>   one million zloty'
> **w tysiącu są trzy zera** 'there are three zeros in one thousand'
> **w pięć miesięcy zarobił pięć tysięcy** 'in five months he made
>   five thousand'

| 8.1.1.11.1 | **Tysiąc** and **milion** with nouns and verbs |

Tysiąc and **milion** as subjects combine with nouns in the genitive plural and with verbs in the singular (in the past tense with the neuter marker -ło, in the passive with -no, -ło), or plural when they denote 2–4 thousand or million).

> *Tysiąc osób jest/było* **na wiecu.** 'A thousand people are/were at
>   the rally.'
> *Pożar zagraża tysiącowi domów.* 'Fire is a threat *to thousands of*
>   *homes.*'
> *Milion złotych został* **przeznaczony na szkoły.** '*One million zloty*
>   *were* allocated for schools.'

Note: the plural form of verbs is often used with numbers 2–4 and with **tysiące**, **miliony** in the meaning of "thousands of ...," "millions of. . . ."

> **Na wiecu** *były dwadzieścia dwa tysiące ludzi.* '*Twenty-two thousand*
>   *people were* at the rally.'
> *Tysiące osób były* **na wiecu.** 'Thousands of people are/were at the rally.'

Table 8.9 Declension of **tysiąc** and **milion**

Case	Singular	Plural
NOM	**tysiąc, milion**	**tysiące, miliony**
ACC	**tysiąc, milion**	**tysiące, miliony**
GEN	**tysiąca, miliona**	**tysięcy, milionów**
DAT	**tysiącowi, milionowi**	**tysiącom, milionom**
LOC	**tysiącu, milionie**	**tysiącach, milionach**
INS	**tysiącem, milionem**	**tysiącami, milionami**

8.1.2 | Collective numbers

Collective numbers are used to specify a certain number of animate neuter nouns, such as **dzieci** 'children,' or the offspring of animals that end in -ę such as **szczenię** 'puppy,' or when collective numbers refer to a group of mixed male and female humans. When collective numbers are used as a subject, the *verb is in the singular*, the past tense is the neuter form with the marker **-ło**, and *nouns are in the genitive plural* case.

Dwoje/troje/kilkoro dzieci było głodnych.
'Two/three/several children were hungry.'

When the verb is in front of the noun it could be:

Głodnych było dwoje/troje/kilkoro dzieci.
'Two/three/several children were hungry.'

or:

Głodne było dwoje/troje/kilkoro dzieci.
'Two/three/several children were hungry.'

The collective numbers are:

2 **dwoje**	8 **ośmioro**
3 **troje**	9 **dziewięcioro**
4 **czworo**	10 **dziesięcioro**
5 **pięcioro**	50 **pięćdziesięcioro**
6 **sześcioro**	90 **dziewięćdziesięcioro**
7 **siedmioro**	

8.1.2.1 | *"Several" with collective numbers*

kilkoro dzieci, szczeniąt 'several (up to 10) children, puppies'
kilkanaścioro studentów było w pokoju 'several (11–19) students, people were in the room'

8.1.2.2 | *Talking about siblings and children*

Mam *dwoje/troje/czworo rodzeństwa*. 'I have *two/three/four siblings*.'
Mam *dwóch/trzech/czterech braci*. 'I have *two/three/four brothers*.'
Mam *dwie/trzy/cztery siostry*. 'I have *two/three/four sisters*.'

503

Mam *dwoje/troje/czworo dzieci.* 'I have *two/three/four children.*'
Mam *dwóch/trzech/czterech synów.* 'I have *two/three/four sons.*'
Mam *dwie/trzy/cztery córki.* 'I have *two/three/four daughters.*'

8.1.2.3 | Use

Collective numbers are used with:

- *pluralia tantum*: **dwoje drzwi** 'two doors,' **troje spodni** (usually replaced by **trzy pary spodni** 'three pairs of pants'), **dwoje sań** 'two sleighs';
- neuter animate nouns that end with -ę, such as **szczenię; dwoje szczeniąt** 'two puppies'
- the plural form of **dziecko—dzieci; dwoje dzieci** 'two children'
- some objects that naturally occur in pairs: **dwoje oczu, uszu, rąk** 'two eyes, ears, hands' (of the same person)
- a mixed group of people or a group of people where we are not sure of their sex: **dwoje studentów** 'two students,' **troje pasażerów** 'three passengers,' **czworo uczniów** 'four pupils' (if there were only men in the group it would be **dwóch studentów, trzech pasażerów, czterech uczniów;** if there were only women in the group it would be **dwie studentki, trzy pasażerki, cztery ucznnice)**
- the preposition **w(e)** <+ACC> to indicate "togetherness" of a mixed group: **byliśmy tam *we troje* '*all three of us* were there,' mieszkamy *w pięcioro* '*all five of us* live together'**

Table 8.10 Declension of **dwoje, troje, czworo, pięcioro**

Case	
NOM	**dwoje, troje, czworo, pięcioro rodzeństwa/dzieci**
	'two, three, four, five siblings/children'
ACC	**dwoje, troje, czworo, pięcioro rodzeństwa/dzieci**
GEN	**dwojga, trojga, czworga, pięciorga rodzeństwa/dzieci**
DAT	**dwojgu, trojgu, czworgu, pięciorgu rodzeństwu/dzieciom**
LOC	**dwojgu, trojgu, czworgu, pięciorgu rodzeństwie/dzieciach**
INS	**dwojgiem, trojgiem, czworgiem, pięciorgiem rodzeństwa/dzieci**

8.1.3 | **Substantive numerals**

Substantive numerals are the names used for cardinal numbers. Substantive numerals do not have a lexical equivalent in English.

1	**jedynka**	'a one'	(F grade)
2	**dwójka**	'a two'	(D grade)
3	**trójka**	'a three'	(C grade)
4	**czwórka**	'a four'	(B grade)
5	**piątka**	'a five'	(A– grade)
6	**szóstka**	'a six'	(A grade)
7	**siódemka**	'a seven'	
8	**ósemka**	'an eight'	
9	**dziewiątka**	'a nine'	
10	**dziesiątka**	'a ten'	

8.1.3.1 | *Formation*

In order to make a substantive numeral, drop the final vowel in the ordinal numeral (**-ny** in "a hundredth"), and add -**ka**.

jedenasty → **jedenastka**	'an eleven'
pięćdziesiąty → **pięćdziesiątka**	'a fifty'
setny → **setka**	'a hundred'

8.1.3.2 | *Use*

Substantive numerals are generally used for school grades, bus numbers, apartment numbers, approximate age, and to indicate a number of people doing something together.

As subjects, **dzisiątki** and **setki** (the plural forms of **dzisiątka** and **setka**) indicate an estimated number in tens and hundreds.

Masz ósemkę? 'Do you have *an eight?*' (a card number)
Piotr dostał jedynkę z historii. 'Piotr *got F* in history.'
Ewa dostaje *same szóstki*. 'Ewa gets *only As.*'
Mieszkamy *pod ósemką*. 'We live *in apartment number eight.*'
Zwykle gramy *we czwórkę*, ale dzisiaj zagramy *we trójkę*.
  'We usually play *in a group of four,* but today we will play *in a group of three.*'
Piotr ma *pięćdziesiątkę na karku*. 'Piotr is *in his fifties.*' (coll.)
Ewa jest *przed trzydziestką*. 'Ewa is *in her late twenties.*' (coll.)
Piotr jest *dobrze po czterdziestce*. 'Piotr is *in his late forties.*'

| 8.1.4 | *Ordinal numbers* |

Ordinal numbers are used to indicate the order and position of objects or people. They correspond to the English numbers with the marker "-th," e.g., "fourth" (**czwarty**).

Ordinal numbers are declined like adjectives; they have masculine, feminine, and neuter forms in the singular, and no male human forms in the plural. Ordinal numbers agree in number, class and case with the noun or noun phrase they qualify.

The ordinal numbers "first" to "fourth" have male human plural forms: **pierwsi** 'first,' **drudzy** 'second,' **trzeci** 'third,' **czwarci** 'fourth.'

> 'The men finished *first*.' **Mężczyźni skończyli *pierwsi*.**

Note that the ordinal number *third* in the masculine singular form **trzeci** is the same as that for the male human plural, e.g.,

> **Mężczyzna był *trzeci*** <MSC SG> **w kolejce.**
> 'The man was third in line.'

> **Mężczyźni byli *trzeci*** <MHPL> **w kolejce.**
> 'The men were third in line.'

The ordinal numbers "fifth" and above are not usually used in male human plural forms. Instead the sentence is typically reworded so that the male human plural form is not needed. For example:

> **Mężczyźni byli *na szóstym miejscu*.** 'The men finished sixth.'
> (lit. 'The men were in sixth place.')

Potential forms exist for the male human plural, such as 'fifth' **piąci**, 'sixth' **szóści**, 'seventh' **siódmi**. However, they are not usually used.

Neuter singular forms are identical to the no male human plural forms.

> ***pierwsze* dziecko** <NT SG>
> 'first child'

> ***pierwsze* objawy grypy** <NO-MHPL>
> 'first symptoms of flu'

> ***trzydzieste* dziecko** <NT SG>
> 'thirtieth child'

> **lata *trzydzieste*** <NO-MHPL>
> 'the thirtieths'

Table 8.11 Ordinal numbers

	MSC	FEM	NT	NO-MHPL	MHPL
0	zerowy	zerowa	zerowe	zerowe	zerowi
1st	pierwszy	pierwsza	pierwsze	pierwsze	pierwsi
2nd	drugi	druga	drugie	drugie	drudzy
3rd	trzeci	trzecia	trzecie	trzecie	trzeci
4th	czwarty	czwarta	czwarte	czwarte	czwarci
5th	piąty	piąta	piąte	piąte	—
6th	szósty	szósta	szóste	szóste	—
7th	siódmy	siódma	siódme	siódme	—
8th	ósmy	ósma	ósme	ósme	—
9th	dziewiąty	dziewiąta	dziewiąte	dziewiąte	—
10th	dziesiąty	dziesiąta	dziesiąte	dziesiąte	—
11th	jedenasty	jedenasta	jedenaste	jedenaste	—
12th	dwunasty	dwunasta	dwunaste	dwunaste	—
13th	trzynasty	trzynasta	trzynaste	trzynaste	—
14th	czternasty	czternasta	czternaste	czternaste	—
15th	piętnasty	piętnasta	piętnaste	piętnaste	—
16th	szesnasty	szesnasta	szesnaste	szesnaste	—
17th	siedemnasty	siedemnasta	siedemnaste	siedemnaste	—
18th	osiemnasty	osiemnasta	osiemnaste	osiemnaste	—
19th	dziewiętnasty	dziewiętnasta	dziewiętnaste	dziewiętnaste	—
20th	dwudziesty	dwudziesta	dwudzieste	dwudzieste	—
21st	dwudziesty pierwszy	dwudziesta pierwsza	dwudzieste pierwsze	= NT	—
22nd	dwudziesty drugi	dwudziesta druga	dwudzieste drugie	= NT	—
23rd	dwudziesty trzeci	dwudziesta trzecia	dwudzieste trzecie	= NT	—
24th	dwudziesty czwarty	dwudziesta czwarta	dwudzieste czwarte	= NT	—
30th	trzydziesty	trzydziesta	trzydzieste	trzydzieste	—
40th	czterdziesty	czterdziesta	czterdzieste	czterdzieste	—
50th	pięćdziesiąty	pięćdziesiąta	pięćdziesiąte	pięćdziesiąte	—
100th	setny	setna	setne	setne	—
101st	sto pierwszy	sto pierwsza	sto pierwsze	sto pierwsze	sto pierwsi
200th	dwusetny	dwusetna	dwusetne	dwusetne	—
1000th	tysięczny	tysięczna	tysięczne	tysięczne	—
1010th	tysiąc dziesiąty/ -a, -e				
2000th	dwutysięczny	dwutysięczna	dwutysięczne	dwutysięczne	—
2010th	dwa tysiące dziesiąty	dwa tysiące dziesiąta	dwa tysiące dziesiąte	= NT	—
last	ostatni	ostatnia	ostatnie	ostanie	ostatni

8.1.4.1 | *Compound ordinal numbers*

In compound ordinal numbers with two digits, both parts are declined.

przed *dwudziestą drugą* 'before 10 p.m.'
po *dwudziestej trzeciej* 'after 11 p.m.'

In compound numbers with three and more digits, only the last two digits
are declined.

W 1989 (tysiąc dziewięćset *osiemdziesiątym dziewiątym*) roku.
'In 1989.'
W 2011 (w dwa tysiące *jedenastym*) roku. (not: w dwutysięcznym
jedenastym) 'In 2011.'

8.1.4.2 | *Use*

The ordinal numbers answer the questions **który?, która?, które?** 'Which
one in order, in turn?'

Na którym piętrze mieszkasz? 'Which floor do you live on?'
Na ósmym (na 8.) piętrze. 'On the 8th floor.'

Ordinal numbers are often used in time constructions:

- to indicate the hour (minutes are expressed in cardinal numbers)

Która jest godzina? 'What time is it?'
Jest pierwsza (godzina), dziesięć (minut). 'Ten past five.'
O której godzinie wrócisz? 'At what time will you be back?'
Wrócę o *dwudziestej trzeciej*. 'I'll be back at 11 p.m.'

(See 8.2)

- to ask about the date

Który dzisiaj jest? 'What date is it today?'
**Dzisiaj jest dwudziesty drugi maja, dwa tysiące dziesiąty
rok** (05.22.2010). 'Today is May 22nd, 2010.'

- to indicate that something occurred on a specific day (in genitive)

Jedenastego listopada Polska odzyskała niepodległość.
'On the *eleventh* of November Poland regained its independence.'
**Urodziłem się *dwudziestego drugiego* lutego dwa tysiące
pierwszego roku.** 'I was born on January *twenty second* two
thousand and *one*.'

- to indicate a place or position (in a contest)

    Kto przybiegł *pierwszy* do mety? 'Who finished *first?*'
    Kto zdobył *drugie miejsce*? 'Who got *second place?*'
    Kto był ostatni? 'Who was last?'

- to indicate a year in school

    Jestem *na pierwszym/drugim/trzecim/czwartym* roku.
    'I am a freshman/sophomore/junior/senior.'

- to indicate an anniversary

    Jutro jest nasza *dwudziesta trzecia* rocznica ślubu.
    'Tomorrow is our *23rd* wedding anniversary.'

8.1.4.2.1 | With titles and historical events

Papież Jan Paweł II reads: **Papież Jan Paweł Drugi**
'Pope John Paul the second'

Królowa Elżbieta II reads: **Królowa Elżbieta Druga**
'Queen Elizabeth the second'

II wojna światowa reads: **druga wojna światowa**
'The Second World War'

8.1.4.2.2 | Ordinal and cardinal numbers

***Pierwsze dwie minuty* spotkania były niepewne.**
'*The first two minutes* of the meeting were unsure.'

***Pierwsze dwa lata* na studiach były trudne.**
'*The first two years* in college were difficult.'

8.1.5 | *Indefinite numerals*

Indefinite numerals answer the question **ile?** 'How much?' 'How many?'
Indefinite numerals (**parę/paru, kilka/kilku, wiele/wielu, ile/ilu**) decline similarly to the cardinal numbers **pięć/pięciu**. (See Table 8.6)

Indefinite numerals are:

Ile? 'How much?' 'How many?'
dużo 'a lot' (indeclinable)
niedużo/mało 'not a lot' (indeclinable)
nieco 'a little bit' (indeclinable)

509

liczny, liczna, liczne, liczni (decline like an adjective) 'numerous,'
   'many'
kilka 'a few'
parę 'a couple'
niewiele 'little/few'
wiele 'many/much'
kilkanaście 'several' (11–19) (declines like **piętnaście**, see Table 8.6)
kilkadziesiąt 'several tens'
kilkaset 'several hundred'
niejeden <MSC>, **niejedna** <FEM>, **niejedno** <NT> (decline like **jeden,
   jedna, jedno**, see Table 8.2) 'more than one'

Male human forms of certain indefinite numerals have the ending **-u**:

Ilu? 'How many?'	**wielu** 'many/much'
kilku 'a few'	**kilkunastu** 'several' (11–19)
paru 'a couple'	**kilkudziesięciu** 'several tens'
niewielu 'little/few'	**kilkuset** 'several hundred'

Kilku mężczyzn przyszło na spotkanie. 'A few men came to the
   meeting.'
Ilu mężczyzn przyszło na spotkanie? 'How many men came to
   the meeting?'
but
Ile osób przyszło na spotkanie? 'How many people came to the
   meeting?'
Kilka kobiet przyszło na spotkanie. 'A few women came to
   the meeting.'

| 8.1.5.1 | *Indefinite numerals and verbs* |

Most indefinite numerals take a *singular* verb in Polish.

Kilka osób spało.
'A few people were sleeping.'

Kilkaset komputerów było zepsutych.
'A few hundred computers were broken.'

Some indefinite numerals, namely **większość** 'the majority,' **część** 'a part,'
may take the past-tense singular neuter form (characteristic for indefinite
numerals) or past tense singular feminine form (because as nouns, **większość**
and **część** are feminine).

Większość głosowało ... 'The majority voted ...'
Większość głosowała ... 'The majority voted ...'

Dużo and **mało** as complements

Do not use **dużo** or **niedużo/mało** in cases other than the nominative, accusative or genitive, instead use **wiele, liczny** or **kilka**.

W parku było dużo ludzi. 'There were *many people* in the park.'
Rozmawiałem z wieloma (not: z dużo) **ludźmi.** 'I talked *to many people*.'
W Waszyngtonie jest dużo bezpłatnych muzeów. 'There are many free museums in Washington, DC.'
Byliśmy w wielu bezpłatnych muzeach w Waszyngtonie. 'We were in many free museums in Washington, DC.'

"Many times"

Wiele **razy** is used to denote "many times."

raz 'once,' 'one time'
dwa razy 'two and more times' (use **razy** to indicate multiple times)
dwa—pięć razy 'two—five times'

Raz w roku **chodzę do dentysty.**
'Once a year I go to the dentist's.'

Dwa razy w roku **chodzę do dentysty.**
'Twice a year I go to the dentist's.'

Mam próchnicę i dlatego chodzę do dentysty
kilka razu w roku.
'I have decay so I go to the dentist's many times a year.'

Trzy razy w tygodniu **chodzę do siłowni.**
'Three times a week I go to the gym.'

Wielokrotnie and wielokroć (bookish) also mean 'many times'

Pisaliśmy do prezesa *wielokrotnie.*
'We wrote *many times* to the president of the company.'

511

Note: To denote an approximate number in tens, hundreds, thousands, dzisiątki, setki, tysiące are used respectively. The verb form is the plural.

Setki/tysiące ludzi były na wiecu.
'Hundreds/thousands of people were at the rally.'

8.1.6 | Fractions

Common fractions are:

¼ **jedna czwarta**
½ **jedna druga**
¾ **trzy czwarte**

pół 'half' (indeclinable), **połowa** 'half' (declinable)
ćwierć 'quarter'
półtora 'one and a half' with masculine and neuter nouns
półtorej 'one and a half' with feminine nouns

The numerator is a cardinal number; the denominator is an ordinal number. Both the numerator and denominator take the *feminine form* of the number (if applicable), as they qualify część <FEM> 'a part.'

⅔ **dwie trzecie**
⅛ **jedna ósma**
⅜ **trzy ósme**
⅝ **pięć ósmych**
1⅞ **jeden i siedem ósmych** (See 8.1.9)

8.1.6.1 | Fractions and verbs

In Polish, fractions take verbs in the *singular*.

Dwie trzecie rządu głosowało za ustawą.
'Two thirds of the government voted for the bill.'

Dwie trzecie ludności żyje w biedzie.
'Two thirds of the population live in poverty.'

Jedna trzecia zabawek została wycofana ze sklepów.
'One third of the toys were taken off the shelves.'

Nouns can be in both singular and plural forms.

Jednej czwartej <+GEN PL> **udziałów nie udało się sprzedać.**
'*One quarter of the shares* were not sold.'

Kup ćwierć <+GEN SG> **kilo orzechów.**
'Buy *a quarter kilo* of nuts.'

Za półtora <+GEN SG> **roku skończę studia.**
'I will graduate *in a year and a half*.'

Spotkanie trwało półtorej <+GEN SG> **godziny.**
'The meeting lasted *an hour and a half*.'

Chcesz pół <+GEN SG> **jabłka?**
'Do you want *half of an apple*?'

Chcesz połowę <+GEN SG> **jabłka?**
'Do you want *half of an apple*?'

Przed półtora <+INS> **rokiem nie pracowałem.**
'*A year and a half ago* I was not working.'

Przed półtorej <+GEN> **godziny zadzwonił Piotr.**
'Piotr called *an hour and a half ago*.'

Po pół <+LOC> **godzinie wszyscy spali.**
'*After half an hour* everyone was sleeping.'

8.1.6.2	Pół

While **pół** 'half' is indeclinable, **połowa** (not used with **godzina** 'hour') is declinable. **Połowa** declines like the noun **głowa**.

Ktoś zjadł pół/połowę tortu. 'Somebody ate *half of the tart*.'

In Polish, **pół** combines with nouns in the *genitive singular*.

Cztery i pół roku (not: lata) **mieszkałem w Anglii.**
'I have lived in England for *four and a half years*.'

Dwa i pół miesiąca (not: miesiące) **mieszkał sam.**
'He lived by himself for *two and a half months*.'

Dwa i pół punktu (not: punkta) **zabrakło mi do piątki.**
'I was $2^1/_2$ points short of an "A".'

But: **dwa i pół** *razy* (not: raza) 'two and a half times.'

8.1.7 | Double, triple

To refer to items that come in a single unit, pair, triplet, or quadruplet use
the words **pojedynczy**, **podwójny**, **potrójny**, **poczwórny**, respectively.

> **Gra pojedyncza** (e.g., **w tenisie**) 'singles' (in tennis)
> **Gra podwójna** (e.g., **w tenisie**) 'doubles' (in tennis)

A group of more than four uses the word **-krotny** combined with cardinal
numbers, e.g., **pięciokrotny** 'quintuple,' **sześciokrotny** 'sextuple,' **siedmi-
okrotny** 'septuple.'

> **twaróg *podwójnie mielony***
> 'doubly ground cottage cheese'

> ***podwójna porcja***
> 'double portion'

> ***Podwójne życie Weroniki***
> '*The double life of Veronique*' (a film by K. Kieślowski)

> ***podwójny agent***
> 'double agent'

8.1.8 | Preposition po

8.1.8.1 | With distribution

The preposition **po** is often used with numbers to indicate an equal number
of items for each individual or object.

> **Dostaliśmy *po pięć złotych.***
> 'We each got 5 zloty.'

> **Mamy *po 22 lata.***
> 'We each are 22 years old.'

8.1.8.2 | Numeral adverbs

> **po pierwsze** 'first(ly)'
> **po drugie** 'second(ly)'
> **po trzecie** 'third(ly)'

8.1.9 | Decimals

In Polish, a comma is used to indicate decimals.

0,025 zero przecinek zero dwadzieścia pięć or: **dwadzieścia pięć tysięcznych**

0,25 zero przecinek dwadzieścia pięć or: **dwadzieścia pięć setnych**

0,2 zero przecinek dwa or: **dwie dziesiąte**

NOM **dwie dziesiąte**	DAT **dwóm dziesiątym**
ACC = NOM	LOC = GEN
GEN **dwóch dziesiątych**	INS **dwoma dziesiątymi**

Zabrakło mi *dwóch dziesiątych punktu*, żeby wygrać. 'I was 0.2 points short of winning.'

8.1.10 | Measurements

Measurements can be expressed in many ways. Height, length, depth and width use the genitive case, preceded by the optional preposition o.

wysoki 'high'; **wysokość** 'height' <FEM>
długi 'long'; **długość** 'length' <FEM>
głęboki 'deep'; **głębokość** 'depth' <FEM>
szeroki 'wide'; **szerokość** 'width' <FEM>
gruby 'thick'; **grubość** 'thickness' <FEM>

wieżowiec (o) wysokości <+GEN> **dwustu trzydziestu jeden metrów** 'a skyscraper is 231 meters high'
wieżowiec wysokości <+GEN> **dwustu trzydziestu jeden metrów**

or

wieżowiec ma wysokość <+GEN> **dwustu trzydziestu jeden metrów** 'a skyscraper has the height of 231 meters'
wieżowiec ma <+NOM> **dwieście trzydzieści jeden metrów wysokości**

dziesięciometrowy basen 'a pool ten meters long,' 'a ten-meter long pool'
basen (o) długości <+GEN> **dziesięciu metrów** 'a pool has ten meters length'

515

basen ma <+NOM> **dziesięć metrów długości**
basen ma długość <+GEN> **dziesięciu metrów**

basen (o) głębokości pięciu metrów 'a pool five meters deep'
basen ma głębokość pięciu metrów
basen ma pięć metrów głębokości

basen o szerokości pięciu metrów 'a pool five meters wide'
basen ma szerokość pięciu metrów
basen ma pięć metrów szerokości

deska ma sześć centymetrów grubości 'a plank 6 cm thick'
deska o grubości sześciu centymetrów
deska ma grubość sześciu centymetrów

Ona ma metr sześćdziesiąt wzrostu. 'She is 160 cm tall.'
pięćdziesiąt metrów kwadratowych '50 square meters'
50 na 20 metrów '50 meters by 20 (meters)'

8.1.11 **Liczba, numer** *and* **cyfra**

Liczba indicates the numerical status of something, an equivalent that is used to designate an amount (sum) of things or people when you count. It is also used in a mathematical sense.

liczba osób zatrudnionych 'the number of employed people'
liczba pokojów w hotelu 'the number of rooms at the hotel'
liczba autobusów w godzinach szczytu 'the number of buses
   during the rush hour'
parzysta liczba 'even number'
liczba dwucyfrowa 'two-digit number'

Numer indicates the number of something, e.g., a hotel room, phone number, registration number, area code

mieszkanie numer 10 'apartment number 10'
numer telefonu 'a phone number'
numer pokoju w hotelu 'a room number at a hotel'
numer autobusu 'a bus number'
numer rejestracyjny samochodu 'a car's registration number'
numer kierunkowy do Warszawy jest 0–22 'the phone code for
   Warsaw is 0–22'

cyfra means 'digit,' a graphic sign of a number

napisać cyfry 'to write out the digits'

Table 8.12 Number summary

Number **Liczba**	Cardinal **Główna**	Ordinal **Porządkowa**	Collective **Zbiorowa**	Substantive **Rzeczownik**
0	zero	zerowy	zero	zerówka
1	jeden, jedno, jedna, jedni	pierwszy	jeden, jedno, jedna, jedni	jedynka
2	dwa, dwie	drugi	dwoje	dwójka
3	trzy	trzeci	troje	trójka
4	cztery	czwarty	czworo	czwórka
5	pięć	piąty	pięcioro	piątka
6	sześć	szósty	sześcioro	szóstka
7	siedem	siódmy	siedmioro	siódemka
8	osiem	ósmy	ośmioro	ósemka
9	dziewięć	dziewiąty	dziewięcioro	dziewiątka
10	dziesięć	dziesiąty	dziesięcioro	dziesiątka
11	jedenaście	jedenasty	jedenaścioro	jedenastka
12	dwanaście	dwunasty	dwanaścioro	dwunastka
13	trzynaście	trzynasty	trzynaścioro	trzynastka
14	czternaście	czternasty	czternaścioro	czternastka
15	piętnaście	piętnasty	piętnaścioro	piętnastka
16	szesnaście	szesnasty	szesnaścioro	szesnastka
17	siedemnaście	siedemnasty	siedemnaścioro	siedemnastka
18	osiemnaście	osiemnasty	osiemnaścioro	osiemnastka
19	dziewiętnaście	dziewiętnasty	dziewiętnaścioro	dziewiętnastka
20	dwadzieścia	dwudziesty	dwadzieścioro	dwudziestka
30	trzydzieści	trzydziesty	trzydzieścioro	trzydziestka
40	czterdzieści	czterdziesty	czterdzieścioro	czterdziestka
50	pięćdziesiąt	pięćdziesiąty	pięćdziesięcioro	pięćdziesiątka
60	sześćdziesiąt	sześćdziesiąty	sześćdziesięcioro	sześćdziesiątka
70	siedemdziesiąt	siedemdziesiąty	siedemdziesięcioro	siedemdziesiątka
80	osiemdziesiąt	osiemdziesiąty	osiemdziesięcioro	osiemdziesiątka
90	dziewięćdziesiąt	dziewięćdziesiąty	dziewięćdziesięcioro	dziewięćdziesiątka
100	sto	setny	setka	setka
200	dwieście	dwusetny		
300	trzysta	trzechsetny		
400	czterysta	czterechsetny		
500	pięćset	pięćsetny		
600	sześćset	sześćsetny		
700	siedemset	siedemsetny		
800	osiemset	osiemsetny		
900	dziewięćset	dziewięćsetny		
1000	tysiąc	tysięczny		
million	milion	milionowy		
billion	miliard	miliardowy		
trillion	bilion	bilionowy		

8.2 Clock time

8.2.1 *Generic questions*

Która (jest) godzina? 'What time is it?'
A construction without **jest** is less formal.

O której (godzinie) **jest pociąg?**
'*At what (time)* is the train?'

Na którą (godzinę) **mam zarezerwować stolik?**
'*For what time* should I make a reservation?'

8.2.1.1 *Other ways of asking and telling time*

Którą masz godzinę?
[lit. 'What time do you have?'] (familiar form)

Wiesz, która jest godzina?
'Do you know what time it is?' (familiar form)

Masz zegarek? Która jest godzina?
'Do you have a watch? What time is it?' (familiar form)

8.2.2 *Generic answers*

8.2.2.1 *Full hours*

Teraz jest pierwsza godzina. 'Right now it is one o'clock.'
Jest pierwsza godzina. 'It is one o'clock.'
Jest pierwsza. 'It is one [o'clock].'
Pierwsza. '[It is] one [o'clock].'

Incomplete constructions are considered less formal.

8.2.2.1.1 Precise and approximate time

Jest *równo* pierwsza. 'It is one o'clock *on the dot*.'
Jest pierwsza *zero zero*. 'It is one o'clock *zero zero* [minutes].'
***Wybiła* pierwsza.** 'The clock *struck* one.'
Jest *prawie* pierwsza. 'It's *almost* one.'
***Za parę* minut będzie pierwsza.** '*In a few* minutes it will be one.'

Other than full hours

8.2.2.2.1 | Simplified, spoken forms

A simplified answer includes the hour in the ordinal number in the feminine form because it modifies the feminine noun **godzina;** minutes are in cardinal numbers.

Jest druga pięć. 'It is two-oh-five.'
Jest druga piętnaście. 'It's two fifteen.'
Jest druga trzydzieści. 'It's two-thirty.'
Jest druga czterdzieści pięć. 'It's two forty-five.'

8.2.2.2.2 | First half of the hour

The preposition **po** followed by the ordinal number in the locative case is used to express the first half of the hour.

Jest minuta *po* <+LOC> **piątej.** 'It is a minute *after* five.'
Jest dwie *po* <+LOC> **piątej.** 'It is two [minutes] *past* five.'
Jest pięć po <+LOC> **drugiej.** 'It is five past two.'
Jest 25 po <+LOC> **trzeciej.** 'It is 25 past three.'

8.2.2.2.3 | Second half of the hour

The preposition **za** followed by the ordinal number in the accusative case is used to express the second half of the hour. The number indicating the hour is the feminine ordinal in the nominative case.

Jest za <+ACC> **pięć** <+NOM> **druga [godzina].** It is five to two.
 [lit. 'five minutes to the second hour']
Jest za <+ACC> **dwie** <+NOM> **druga [godzina].** It is two [minutes] to two. [lit. 'two minutes to the second hour']

8.2.2.2.4 | Half to the next hour

To express half of the hour, the preposition **do** 'to' is used, followed by the ordinal number in the genitive case. "Half" is expressed by **wpół,** or rarely as **pół.**

Jest wpół *do* <+GEN> **drugiej.** 'It is half past one.' [lit. 'half to the second hour']

8.2.2.2.5 | Shared endings

Notice that to express some time after the hour and half of the hour the ordinals have identical endings. This is because the genitive and the locative adjectival endings overlap.

> **Jest pięć po** <+LOC> **piątej.** 'It is five past five.'
> **Jest wpół do** <+GEN> **piątej.** 'It is half past four.'

8.2.3 | At what time?

When answering the question "at what time?", the preposition **o** is dropped before the preposition **za** 'in' and it is optional before **wpół** 'half.'

> **Wrócę o drugiej pięć.** 'I'll be back at two-oh-five.'
> **Wrócę pięć po drugiej.** 'I'll be back at five past two.'
>
> **Wrócę za pięć druga.** 'I'll be back at five to two.'
> **Wrócę (o) wpół do drugiej.** 'I'll be back at half past one.'

8.2.4 | 24-hour clock

The 24-hour clock is generally used for official purposes: in the military, in official correspondence, timetables, etc.

> **Pociąg odjeżdża o 15.30.** 'The train leaves at 3:30 p.m.'
> **Samolot wylądował o 22.30.** 'The plane landed at 10:30 p.m.'
> **Wiadomości o 19.30.** 'The 7:30 news.'

8.2.5 | 12-hour clock

To specify the time of day, the following specific words can be added:

> **rano** 'in the morning'
> **po południu** 'in the afternoon'
> **wieczorem** 'in the evening'
> **w nocy** 'at night'
> **nad ranem** 'at dawn'

> **Wróciliśmy o siódmej wieczorem.** 'We came back at 7 p.m.'
> **Wróciliśmy o siódmej rano.** 'We came back at 7 a.m.'
> **Wróciliśmy o czwartej nad ranem.** 'We came back at 4 a.m.'

8.2.6 | *Translation difficulties*

'Last night' is **wczoraj wieczorem** when it means the time before sleeping time.

'Last night' is **wczoraj w nocy** when it means the time considered as sleeping time.

> ***Wczoraj wieczorem* poszliśmy do kina.** '*Last night* we went to the movies.'
>
> **Okradziono ją *wczoraj w nocy*.** 'She was robbed *last night*.'

For days of the week, months of the year, and seasons, see 9.2.6. For adverbs of time, see 7.4.

Chapter 9

Prepositions

9.1   Overview

A preposition, **przyimek** in Polish, is an indeclinable part of speech that expresses the relationship of one word to another. **Przyimek** in Polish literally means **przy**—'at' **imię**—'name.'

> **Rozmawiam o polityce.** 'I am talking *about* politics.'
> **Jestem w domu.** 'I am *at* home.'
>
> **Dziewczynki lubią bawić się w** <+ACC> ***dom***. 'Girls like to play *house*.'
>
> **Dziewczynki lubią bawić się w** <+LOC> ***domu***. 'Girls like to play *at home*.'

Prepositions specify, pin down, or target a location, place, time, person, state, purpose, etc. They are multifunctional and can express various meanings by themselves and through the use of various cases. It is therefore important to learn prepositions together with the specific contexts within which they are used and the cases the can govern.

> **Mieszkam w Krakowie.** 'I live in Crakow.' (place)
> **Wrócę o ósmej.** 'I will be back at eight.' (time)
> **kwiaty dla mamy** 'flowers for mom' (person)
> **Jestem w świetnym humorze.** 'I am in a great mood.' (state)
> **Odkładam na komputer.** 'I'm saving for a computer.' (purpose)

In English, many nuances in meaning are expressed with the help of prepositions, e.g., 'a house for a son' **dom dla syna**, 'a letter to the prime minister' **list do premiera**.

Prepositions signalize relations between words.

In many languages, including Polish, prepositional phrases are increasing in order to be more specific and more precisely describe the relationships between words.

łyżeczka cukru 'a spoon of sugar'
łyżeczka do cukru 'a teaspoon' (lit. 'a spoon to sugar')
prawo własności 'ownership'
prawo do własności 'right to property'

In many cases, prepositions and prefixes—this is particularly obvious with motion verbs—combine to reflect a specific relation in time and space.

Zjechał z drogi. 'He pulled off the road.'
Najechał na chodnik. 'He ran onto a sidewalk.'
Przejechał przez most. 'He drove across the bridge.'
Wjechał w kałużę. 'He drove into a puddle.'
Dojechał do centrum. 'He got to the center.'

All prepositions govern a certain case or cases. The correct case must be used to impart the correct meaning. For prepositions that govern multiple cases, using a different case with the same preposition will generate a different meaning. Each preposition has a set case or a set group of cases that it can govern; the preposition cannot be used with any other cases.

sałatka z <+INS> **krewetkami**
'a salad with shrimp'

sałatka z <+GEN> **krewetek**
'a shrimp salad, [lit.] salad made from shrimp'

Prepositions could be paired with a noun, e.g., **na stole** 'on a table,' an adjective, e.g., **wygląda na śpiącą** 'she looks sleepy,' **uznany za niewinnego** 'to find somebody innocent,' a numeral, e.g., **do dwunastej godziny** 'until twelve (o'clock),' **z dwiema kobietami** 'with two women,' **do wszystkich** 'to everyone,' or a pronoun, e.g., **nad nami** 'above us,' **dla ciebie** 'for you' (informal).

When prepositions are used with personal pronouns, the pronoun takes an extra n- prefix: **niego, niemu, nim, nią, niej, nich, nimi.** (See 5.2.8)

Dużo o nich słyszałem. 'I have heard a lot *about them*.'
Czekasz na niego? 'Are you waiting *for him*?'

Prepositions with the masculine personal pronoun **on** 'he' can be written as one word. Those forms cannot be applied to the personal pronoun 'she.'

Such forms, even though still used by many, are less common than using the pronoun and preposition separately.

na niego = nań (See 5.2.8.1)
Patrzą nań z zazdrością. 'They look at him with envy.'

dla niego = dlań

Dlań była gotowa na wszystko. 'For him she was ready to do anything.'

z niego = zeń

Nie spuszczała zeń oczu. 'She kept a close eye on him.'

Prepositions can also come into a relationship with adverbs, and then effectively do not govern any case, since adverbs do not decline.

jajko na miękko 'soft-boiled egg'

porozmawiajmy na poważnie 'let's talk seriously'

There is also a relationship between prepositions and verbs in Polish. The meaning of the verbs that are used with prepositional phrases changes, depending on the preposition the verbs come into relation with.

kłócić się z żoną przyjaciela 'to argue *with [one's] friend's* wife'

kłócić się o żonę przyjaciela 'to argue *about [one's] friend's* wife'

Some verbs, if followed by prepositional phrases, may completely change their meaning.

Matka pożyczyła pieniądze córce. 'The mother lent the money to the daughter.'

Matka pożyczyła pieniądze od córki. 'The mother borrowed the money from the daughter.'

The sentence **Matka pożyczyła pieniądze** is ambiguous since in Polish the verb **pożyczyć** means 'to lend' and 'to borrow,' and only the connection of the verb with either the prepositional phrase **pożyczyć od kogoś** 'to borrow from someone,' or the non-prepositional construction with the dative **pożyczyć komuś** 'to lend to someone' can determine the meaning of the verb.

Because of the multi-meaning of prepositions, they should *not* be learnt separately, but along with the prepositional phrase and case governance.

9.1.1 *General characteristics*

In general, prepositional phrases are written as two words:

na przykład 'for example,' **na razie** 'so far,' 'for the time being,' **na pewno** 'for sure,' 'certainly,' **w ogóle** 'in general'

In some situations prepositions have become compound words, and in modern Polish are written as one word, e.g., **naprawdę** 'really,' 'truly,' dlaczego 'why,' 'what for,' **przedtem** 'before (that),' 'earlier,' **popojutrze** 'in three days' time, ['lit. after after tomorrow'], **przedwczoraj** 'the day before yesterday,' **naprzeciwko** 'across from.'

Be careful. Sometimes the meaning of the phrase depends on whether it is written as one or two words:

> **współpraca z zagranicą** 'cooperation with foreign countries'
> **w kraju i za granicą** 'in the country and abroad' [lit. 'beyond the borders']
> **wrócić z zagranicy** 'to come back from abroad'
> **sąsiedzi zza (wschodniej) granicy** 'neighbors from beyond the (eastern) border'
> **W tę i we w tę stronę uciekali ludzie.** 'People were running to this and to that side.'
> **wte i wewte** 'there and back' (coll., set phrase)
> **chodzić wte i wewte** 'to walk there and back'

9.1.1.1 | **w** *with numeral* **pół**

The preposition **w** in a phrase with the numeral **pół** 'half' can be written as two words to mean 'in the middle' or with the phrase 'in half an hour':

> **przerwać w pół słowa** 'to stop in mid-word'
> **zrobiła obiad w pół godziny** 'she made lunch in 30 minutes'

With time, and when it means 'semi' or 'in half,' **wpół** is written as one word:

> **Jest wpół do piątej.** 'It is half past four.'
> **Był wpół przytomny.** 'He was half conscious.'
> **Jestem na wpół żywy.** 'I am half-dead.'

9.1.2 | **Position in a sentence**

Polish prepositions mainly precede the phrase they govern.

> **prezent** *dla* <+GEN> **syna** 'a gift *for* a son'

A few prepositions follow the phrase they govern.

> **dwa dni** *temu* 'two days *ago*'
> **chodź, wyjdziemy mamie naprzeciw** 'let's go to meet mom'

Polish adverbial prepositions, such as **dookoła** 'around,' **blisko** 'close,' **wokół** 'around,' etc. precede the word they govern.

> **Mieszkam blisko pracy.** 'I live close to [my] work.'

When an adverb in used in front of a noun or a noun phrase to which it is referring it is an adverbial preposition and as such imposes a case on the noun or the noun phrase. When occupying other positions or when referring to a verb it is an adverb.

> **Dzieci biegały dookoła** <+GEN> **drzewa.** 'Children were running around the tree.'
> **Dzieci biegały dookoła.** <ADV> 'Children were running around.'
> **Mieszkam blisko** <+GEN> **apteki.** 'I live next to the pharmacy.'
> **Mieszkam blisko.** <ADV> 'I live nearby.'
> **Spacer wokół** <+GEN> **domu.** 'A walk round the house.'
> **Wokół sami lunatycy.** <ADV> 'Around are only sleepwalkers.'
> [Lyrics by **Dżem**]
> **Zamiast** <ADV> **samochodem pojechałam na uczelnię autobusem.** 'Instead of going by car I went to school by bus.'
> **Zamiast** <+GEN> **samochodu, wypożyczyliśmy autobus.** 'Instead of a car we rented a bus.'

9.2 Types

Prepositions can be divided into:

1. Primary prepositions, or in other words simple single, independent words, e.g., **z** 'from,' **z** 'together with,' **za** 'behind,' **pod** 'under,' **przed** 'before.'

2. Compound prepositions, also called secondary prepositions, which combine primary prepositions, e.g., **zza** (**z**+**za**) 'from behind,' **spod** (**z**+**pod**) 'from under,' **sprzed** (**z**+**przed**) 'from before,' **ponad** (**po**+**nad**) 'above,' **sponad** (**z**+**po**+**nad**) 'from over,' etc. They are written as one word: **zza ściany** 'from behind the wall,' **sprzed domu** 'from the front of the house,' **znad morza** 'from the seaside,' but **z ponad** in the meaning of 'from more than,' e.g., **Z ponad trzystu prac wybrano tylko pięć.** 'From over three hundred works they chose only five.'

   Z before **p** becomes **s**, like in **spod** 'from under.'

3. Adverbial prepositions, e.g., **blisko** 'near' <+GEN>, **wokół** 'around' <+GEN>, etc.

Adverbial prepositions normally precede the phrase they govern e.g., **Mieszkam** *blisko* **dworca.** 'I live close to the train station,' **Ziemia obraca się** *wokół* **Słońca.** 'The earth revolves around the sun.' When adverbial prepositions are used at the end of the sentence or clause they are treated as adverbs, e.g., mieszkam *blisko* 'I live nearby,' rozglądać się *wokół* 'to look around.'

4. Prepositions derived from nouns and verbs belong to secondary prepositions, e.g., **celem** 'in order to do something, [lit.] with the goal of' <+GEN> derived from **cel** 'aim,' 'goal,' **względem** 'regarding' <+GEN> derived from **wzgląd** 'account,' 'consideration,' **dzięki** 'thanks to' <+DAT> derived from the verb **dziękować** 'to thank.'

> **Spotkali się celem omówienia szczegółów wizyty.** 'They met in order to discuss the details of the visit.'
>
> **Spotkali się w celu omówienia szczegółów wizyty.** 'They met with the purpose of discussing the details of the visit.'
>
> **Rodzice mają pewne plany względem ciebie.** '[Your] parents have some plans regarding you.'
>
> **Dzięki twojej pomocy udało mi się.** 'Thanks to you I succeeded.'

In modern Polish the increasing popularity of prepositional phrases over already existing constructions that do not require a preposition is noticeable, for example: **daj to dla mamy** 'lit. give it for mother' instead of **daj to mamie** 'give it to mother,' which is considered the standard Polish; **kupić prezent dla mamy** and **kupić mamie prezent.** The construction *daj to dla mamy* used to be more of a regional one, and it is not considered standard. The increasing popularity of prepositional phrases is also observed in constructions such as **specjalista** *od* **komputerów, specjalista** *w zakresie* **komputerów** ('computer specialist'). The increasing number of prepositional phrases is often explained as the result of an increasing need to look for more precise phrasing.

9.2.1 | *Primary*

Primary prepositions are mostly monosyllabic: **o** 'about,' **na** 'on,' **do** 'to,' **przy** 'at,' or non-syllabic **w** 'in,' **z** 'from.' Variants with an extra e, like **we** 'in,' **ze** 'from,' **pode** 'underneath' are used to avoid consonant clusters (two or more consonants in a row), and facilitate the pronunciation of primary prepositional phrases, for example **we wtorek** 'on Tuesday' (see 1.3.8.1).

It is worth mentioning that in the south and west parts of Poland variants with an extra e sometimes occur in words that start with a consonant in general, even though this is not a consonant cluster, **we wodzie** 'in water,' *ze* **sokiem** 'with juice.'

Table 9.1 presents the most common primary prepositions that govern different cases along with their main meanings. Note that some prepositions are hard to define as they denote both a literal and figurative relationship between the words.

Table 9.1 Primary prepositions

Case	Prepositions
Nominative	**jako** 'as,' 'in the capacity of,' **jak** 'like,' 'than,' **niż** 'than'
Genitive	**do** 'to,' **dla** 'for,' **od(e)** 'from,' **podczas** 'during,' **u** 'at somebody's place,' **z(e)** 'from,' **bez(e)** 'without,' **naprzeciw(ko)** 'opposite,' 'across from'
Accusative	**między** 'between' [destination], **na** 'on to,' 'for,' **nad(e)** 'above' [destination], **o** 'against' [destination], 'for,' 'about,' **przez(e)** 'through,' **po** 'for,' **pod(e)** 'under' [destination] **w(e)** 'in' [destination], **za** 'behind' [destination], 'for,' **przed(e)** 'before,' 'in front of' [destination]
Instrumental	**między** 'between,' **nad(e)** 'above,' **pod** 'below,' **przed(e)** 'before,' 'in front of,' **z(e)** 'together with,' **za** 'behind'
Locative	**na** 'on,' **o** 'about,' **przy** 'at,' **po** 'after,' **w(e)** 'in'
Dative	**ku** 'towards,' **przeciw(ko)** 'against,' **wbrew** 'against,' **dzięki** 'thanks to'

Notes

1. **Jako, między, podczas, przeciw(ko), naprzeciw(ko), dzięki** are not primary prepositions but are included in the list for reference.

2. **Niż** expresses comparison and does not have an effect on the case of the other words of the prepositional phrase. It follows the verb governance. It can be treated as a preposition and/or a conjunction.

> **Jan jest wyższy** *niż* **Adam.** 'John is taller than Adam.' (niż+NOM)
> **Jan woli kawę** *niż* **herbatę.** 'John prefers coffee to tea.' (niż+ACC)
> **Bardziej boję się kotów** *niż* **psów.** 'I am more afraid of cats than dogs.' (niż+GEN)
> **Jan bardziej ufa ojcu** *niż* **matce.** 'John trusts his father more than his mother.' (niż+DAT)
> **Jan bardziej interesuje się filmem** *niż* **muzyką.** 'John is more interested in film than music.' (niż+INS)

3. The forms of the preposition **przeciw** and **przeciwko**, both in the meaning of 'against,' are interchangeable.

4. The preposition **naprzeciw** can also be written as **naprzeciwko** 'opposite from,' 'across.' This preposition governs two different cases depending on its place being before or after the phrase it governs. If used before the phrase it governs, in the meaning of 'opposite,' 'across from,' **naprzeciw(ko)** governs the genitive case:

   Mieszkam naprzeciwko rodziców. 'I live across from my parents.'
   Zaparkowałem naprzeciwko apteki. 'I parked across from the pharmacy.'

When **naprzeciw(ko)** is used in the meaning of 'coming towards,' 'meeting half way,' it can precede the phrase it governs and then follows either the genitive or the dative case:

   Wyjść naprzeciw <+GEN> **dziecka.**
   Wyjść naprzeciw <+DAT> **dziecku.** 'To go meet a child.'

However, when the preposition **naprzeciw** is used after the phrase it governs, it takes the dative case:

   wyjść dziecku <+DAT> **naprzeciw** 'to go to meet a child'
   wyjść rodzicom <+DAT> **naprzeciw** 'to go to meet parents'

| 9.2.1.1 | *Stress* |

Primary prepositions, e.g., **z** 'from,' **do** 'to,' **dla** 'for,' are normally unstressed, however when they precede a monosyllabic pronoun, e.g., **mną** 'me,' **was** 'you, PL,' **nas** 'us,' the stress shifts to the preposition: pisz <u>*do* mnie</u> często 'write to me often,' co masz <u>*dla* mnie</u>? 'what do you have for me?', trzymamy <u>*za* was</u> kciuki 'we keep our fingers crossed for you.'

When a monosyllabic preposition e.g., **na** 'on,' **do** 'to,' **za** 'behind' is added to a monosyllabic noun (e.g., **most** 'bridge,' **dom** 'house,' **krzyż** 'cross,' **wieś** 'countryside,' 'village'), or to a possessive pronoun (**mój** 'my,' **swój** 'my own,' 'your own,' etc. **nasz** 'our') or numeral (e.g., **trzy** 'three,' **dwóch** 'two'), the stress falls on the noun, possessive pronoun or numeral: pracować <u>za *dwóch*</u> 'to do the work of two (men),' czekać <u>na *cud*</u> 'to wait for a miracle,' przejść <u>przez *most*</u> 'to cross the bridge,' zbierać <u>na *krzyż*</u> 'to collect (money) for a cross,' <u>na *mój koszt*</u> 'at my expenses,' liczyliśmy <u>na *głos*</u> senatorów w tej sprawie 'we counted on [the] senators' vote on this issue,' spał <u>na *wznak*</u> 'he slept on his back.'

Set phrases are an exception to that rule. Then the stress falls on the prepositions: wyszła <u>*za* mąż</u> 'she got married,' miał kilka włosów <u>*na* krzyż</u> 'he was practically bald,' liczyć <u>*na* głos</u> 'to count out loud,' zejdź <u>*na* dół</u> 'come downstairs,' wyprowadzić się <u>*na* wieś</u> 'to move to the country,' pochodzę <u>*ze* wsi</u> 'I come from a village.'

Sometimes the meaning of the phrase differs depending on the stress:

> **z dnia *na* dzień** or **dzień po dniu** 'day by day'
> **żyć z dnia *na* dzień** 'to live day by day'
>
> **z dnia na *dzień*** or **nagle, w ciągu doby** 'suddenly, within 24 hours'
> **Z dnia na *dzień* straciliśmy wszystko.** 'We lost everything within 24 hours.'

For more on stress, see 1.4.

9.2.2 | Compound

Compound prepositions occur when more than one preposition combines to express in a more detailed way a location or destination, mostly by adding the preposition **z** 'from' to the instrumental case prepositions (**nad** 'above,' **pod** 'under,' **przed** 'in front of,' **za** 'behind'). Note that the case changes when two prepositions combine.

> **z** <+GEN> 'from' + **nad** <+INS> 'above, over' = **znad** <+GEN> 'from above,' 'from over'
> **Wracamy znad morza.** 'We are returning from over the sea.'
>
> **z** <+GEN> 'from' + **pod** <+INS> 'under' = **spod** <+GEN> 'from under'
> **Wyszedł spod łóżka.** 'He came from under the bed.'

Note: **z** becomes **s** in front of the unvoiced consonant **p**, e.g., **sprzed** (z + przed), **spod** (z + pod):

z <+GEN> 'from' + przed <+INS> 'in front of' = **sprzed** <+GEN> 'from in front of'

> **Panna młoda uciekła sprzed ołtarza.** 'The bride ran away from in front of the altar.'

z <+GEN> 'from' + za <+INS> 'behind' = **zza** <+GEN> 'from behind'

> **Samochód wyjechał zza rogu.** 'A car came from round the corner.'

Compound prepositions also represent a combination of the preposition **po** with the instrumental case prepositions (e.g., **nad** 'above,' **pod** 'under,' **przed** 'in front of,' **za** 'behind'). The preposition **po** suggests a lack of closeness/proximity in the relationship between the words, e.g., **ponad** <+ACC> '(over and) beyond' (po + nad 'above'), **pomiędzy** <+INS [location]/ACC [destination]> 'between, among' (po + między 'between'), **poza** <+INS [location]/

ACC [destination]> 'outside, besides' (**po** + **za** 'behind') and **poprzez** <+ACC> 'throughout.' Those compound prepositions also pair with the preposition **z** <+GEN> 'from' + **ponad** <+INS> 'beyond' = **sponad** <+GEN> 'from beyond': **sponad gór** 'from beyond the mountains.'

z <+GEN> 'from' + **pomiędzy** <+INS> 'between, among' = **spomiędzy** <+GEN> 'from between, from among': **Wyszedł spomiędzy drzew.** 'He stepped out from between the trees.'

z <+GEN> 'from' + **poza** <+INS> 'outside' = **spoza** <+GEN> 'from outside': **osoby spoza partii** 'persons outside of the party'

Table 9.2 shows the most common meanings of compound prepositions. Note that some prepositions can have a range of meanings as they can denote both a literal and figurative relationship between the words.

Table 9.2 Compound prepositions

Preposition	Case	Meaning	Example
ponad 'over,' 'above,' 'beyond'	ACC	in comparison, beyond the level	**Kochał ją ponad życie.** 'He loved her more than anything else.'
			To ponad nasze siły. 'This is beyond our level of strength.'
ponad 'over,' 'above'	INS	higher than	**Samolot leciał wysoko ponad miastem.** 'A plane was high above the city.'
ponad [destination] 'above,' 'over'	ACC	go beyond	**wznieść się ponad podziały społeczne** 'to rise above social differences'
			wznieść się ponad przeciętność 'to rise above mediocrity'
poprzez 'through,' 'throughout' (suggests an obstacle)	ACC	spatial temporal via, as a medium by (means of)	**dostrzec coś poprzez mgłę** 'to see something through the mist'
			poprzez dzieje 'throughout history'
			komunikować się poprzez Internet 'to communicate via the Internet'
			zwiększyć podaż poprzez obniżenie cen 'to increase the supply through the reduction of prices'

Table 9.2 (*cont'd*)

Preposition	Case	Meaning	Example
pomiędzy	INS	among, between	**pomiędzy ludźmi** 'among people'
	ACC	(destination) among, between	**wejść pomiędzy skały** 'to go between the rocks' **Rozdał swój majątek pomiędzy najbiedniejszych.** 'He distributed his wealth among the poorest.'
pomimo **(mimo)**	GEN	in spite of, despite	**Pomimo złego nastroju poszłam na spotkanie.** 'Despite the bad mood I went to the meeting.'
	ACC	in spite of, despite	only in phrases: **pomimo to, pomimo wszystko** 'despite it,' 'despite everything'
poza	INS	besides, beyond	**poza tym** 'besides it' **być poza zasięgiem** 'to be beyond reach'
	ACC	(destination) beyond	**wyjść poza temat** 'to go beyond the subject' **W sobotę jedziemy poza miasto.** 'On Saturday we are going beyond the city [outside the city].'
spomiędzy	GEN	from between	**Słońce wyłoniło się spomiędzy chmur.** 'The sun emerged from between the clouds.'
spod	GEN	from under, to come from around a place, near	**Wyszedł spod prysznica.** 'He came from under the shower.' **Jestem spod Gdańska.** 'I come from around Gdańsk.' **Wyskoczył spod łóżka.** 'He jumped [out] from under the bed.'
sponad	GEN	from over	**Dźwięk dolatywał sponad wierzchołków drzew.** 'The sound was coming from over the tops of the trees.'
spoza	GEN	from outside	**Jesteś spoza Krakowa?** 'Are you from outside of Cracow?' **spoza kręgu znajomych** 'from outside the group of colleagues'

Table 9.2 (*cont'd*)

Preposition	Case	Meaning	Example
sprzed	GEN	from in front of before (temporal)	**Samochód odjechał sprzed bramy.** 'A car left from in front of the gate.'
			koszt utrzymania sprzed roku 'the cost of living before a year [last year]'
			stare fotografie sprzed wojny 'old pictures from before the war'
znad	GEN	from above	**suche powietrze znad Ukrainy** 'dry air from above Ukraine'
zza	GEN	from behind, through	**Słońce wyszło zza chmur.** 'The sun came from behind the clouds.'

but: **z ponad** (= 'from more than'): **Z ponad tysiąca wierszy wybraliśmy sto naj-lepszych.** 'From more than a thousand poems we have chosen the best one hundred.'

9.2.3 | Derived from nouns and verbs

Prepositions can be derived from nouns, e.g., **celem** 'in order to do something,' from the noun **cel** 'aim,' 'purpose,' **względem** 'regarding,' from **wzgląd** 'account,' 'consideration', or verbs, e.g., **dzięki**, from the verb **dziękować** 'to thank' or can be prepositional phrases, e.g., **w celu** 'in order to do something,' derived from the noun **cel** 'aim,' 'purpose,' **ze względu na kogoś, na coś** 'regarding, on account of somebody, something.'

In Polish single prepositions are often being replaced by prepositional phrases e.g., **dla** 'for' with **na rzecz** 'for the purpose of,' **od** 'from' with **do spraw** 'lit. to the matter.' This could be explained by the need for precision in expressing relations between words, e.g., **Fundusze dla dzieci głuchoniemych** 'Funds for children orally and aurally challenged,' **Fundusze na rzecz dzieci głuchoniemych** '[lit.] Funds for the purpose of children orally and aurally challenged.' **Specjalista od oprogramowań komputerowych** 'a computer program specialist,' **specjalista w zakresie oprogramowania komputerowego** 'a specialist in computer programming.'

In formal registers of Polish, these prepositional phrases are often replaced, when possible, with a single-word preposition, e.g., in the sentence below, do spraw 'to the matter' can be very successfully replaced with the preposition **celem** and can still target the goal: **Powołać komisję <u>do spraw</u> ustalenia przyczyn katastrofy** '[lit.] To appoint a committee to the matter of determination of the causes of the disaster' can become **Powołać komisję <u>celem</u> ustalenia przyczyn katastrofy** 'To appoint a committee in order to determine the causes of the disaster.'

Functions of prepositions

Spatial

Spatial prepositions describe a place where something is located, or a direction or goal to and/or from a place:

1. **Klucze są** *na* **stole.** 'The keys are on the table.'
2. **Mieszkam** *w* **centrum.** 'I live in the center.'
3. **Tłum stał za** <+INS> **drzwiami.** 'A crowd was standing behind the door.'
4. **Idę** *do* **muzeum.** 'I'm going to the museum.'
5. **Zaczekam** *przed* **budynkiem.** 'I'll wait in front of the building.'

Temporal

Temporal prepositions describe events in time:

6. **Wrócę** *przed* **północą.** 'I'll be back before midnight.'
7. **Spotkajmy się** *za* **godzinę.** 'Let's meet in an hour.'
8. *podczas* **przerwy** 'during the break'
9. **W lecie jeździmy do Włoch.** 'In the summer we go to Italy.'
10. **Mam wolne** *do* **środy.** 'I am off until Wednesday.'
11. *w* **piątek** 'on Friday' (See 9.2.6)
12. *w* **maju** 'in May' (See 9.2.6.9)

Causal relations

Prepositions of causal relations are used to point out the reason and/or cause of a situation:

13. *Przez* **przypadek dowiedziałem się o wszystkim.** 'By accident I found out about everything.'
14. *dzięki* **rodzicom** 'thanks to [my] parents'

15. *wskutek* or *na skutek* trzęsienia ziemi 'as a result of the earthquake'
16. *wbrew* zdrowemu rozsądkowi 'in spite of common sense'
17. *Mimo* zakazu zaparkował przed urzędem. 'Despite a ban he parked in front of the office.'
18. zaniemówić *ze* zdumienia (z/ze <+GEN>) 'to be struck dumb with astonishment'
19. *Od* palenia papierosów masz żółte zęby. 'You have yellow teeth as a result of smoking.'

| 9.2.4.4 | To denote purpose |

Prepositions of purpose occur in phrases describing the aim or the recipient of an action:

20. *na rzecz* dzieci 'for children'
21. *na* znak solidarności 'as a sign of solidarity'
22. *na* cześć gospodyni 'in honor of the host'
23. *za* zdrowie młodej pary 'to the health of the newlyweds'
24. *na* wszelki wypadek 'just in case'
25. *na* czarną godzinę 'for a rainy day'
26. *na* pomoc powodzianom 'to help flood victims'

| 9.2.4.5 | To express a way in which something is done |

27. *pod* <+INS> narkozą 'under an anesthetic'
28. wczasy *pod* <+INS> gruszą 'vacation in the country'
29. wczasy *w* <+LOC> siodle 'horse riding vacation'
30. spódnica *w* <+ACC> kratkę 'checked skirt'

| 9.2.4.6 | Conditional |

31. *w razie* <+GEN> awarii powiadomić policję 'in case of damage, notify the police'

| 9.2.4.7 | To express comparisons |

32. Jestem starsza *od* <+GEN> niej. 'I am older than her.'
33. najwyższy *w* <+LOC> klasie 'the tallest in class'

34. *Przy* <+LOC> **mężu choleryku była uosobieniem spokoju.** 'Next to her hothead husband she was the personification of calmness.'
35. **W** *porównaniu* **z** <+INS> **zeszłym rokiem, podaż gwatownie zmalała.** 'In comparison with the previous year, the supply drastically decreased.'

Note that the same preposition could be used to denote different functions. **Przed** <+INS> in spatial relations (5) means 'in front of' something, but in temporal relations (6) it means 'before' something, **za** <+INS> in spatial relations (3) describes location behind, and **za** <+ACC> in temporal relations (7) denotes a time after which something will happen. The preposition **w** in temporal relations may denote 'on a given day' (11), as in **w** <+ACC>, or 'in a particular month' (12), as in **w** <+LOC>.

9.2.5 | *Location versus destination*

Spatial prepositions show the location of a person or an object, indicate motion to/towards a point of destination, or show motion in space:

Jedziemy w <+ACC> **góry.** 'We are going to the mountains.' [destination]
Jesteśmy w <+LOC> **górach.** 'We are in the mountains.' [location]
Chodzimy po <+LOC> **górach.** 'We are hiking in the mountains.'
   [motion at the location, not to a destination]
latać w <+LOC> **powietrzu** 'fly in the air' [motion within a location, not to a destination]
wzbić się w <+ACC> **powietrze** 'to rise up into the air' [destination]

Prepositions may take different cases. The most important difference in the usage of prepositions is whether the preposition shows location or indicates motion to or towards a destination. (See 9.3.5.1)

The idea of describing location ("she is *at* the concert") and movement towards a goal ("she is going *to* the concert") is often expressed by using the same preposition in Polish, unlike in English. To distinguish both functions, the preposition governs different cases. In other words, the same preposition can take one case if it shows a location, and a different case when it denotes movement toward a destination.

To denote motion to/towards a destination, the genitive or accusative cases are used. To show the location of a person or an object, the instrumental or locative cases are used.

Note that in rare situations the dative case is also used to denote motion towards a destination, mostly in a figurative meaning, e.g., **zbliżamy się** ku końcowi 'we move closer to the end' or idziemy ku Europie 'we are moving towards Europe.'

Constructions with the preposition ku <+DAT> are often replaced with the preposition do <+GEN>.

Zbliżamy się do finału. 'We are getting closer to the finals.'

The usage of either genitive or accusative cases to denote motion to a place of destination is not optional, but is strongly observed and tied to the place one is going to.

Table 9.3 below shows general rules about when to use the genitive or the accusative case to indicate motion to/towards a place of destination. Prepositions that show a location and motion toward a destination have been included to show that some prepositions (**nad, na, w**) can be used for more than one function. **Na** is used in the accusative case to denote motion *onto the surface of*. It is also used to show location *on the surface of*, but in the locative case. The same occurs with **w** and **nad**. **W** denotes motion *to the inside of*, but it is also used to show location *inside of something*. **Nad** is used to denote *motion above* or *by* (mostly with expanse of water, **ocean** 'ocean,' **morze** 'sea,' etc.), but it is also used to show *location above* or *by*.

Similar correlations occur with the prepositions **między, pod, przed, za**.

Motion from always takes the genitive case.

Table 9.3 Spatial prepositions **to, at, from**

	Motion to dokąd? 'where to?'	Being at/in gdzie? 'where?'	Motion from skąd? 'from where?'
Places			
physical buildings cities	do <+GEN>	w <+LOC>	z <+GEN>
mountains	w <+ACC>	w <+LOC>	z <+GEN>
expanses of water	nad <+ACC>	nad <+INS>	znad <+GEN>
Events/functions	na <+ACC>	na <+LOC>	z <+GEN>
People	do <+GEN>	u <+GEN>	od <+GEN>

Idę do <+GEN> **sklepu.** 'I'm going *to* the store.'
Jestem w <+LOC> **sklepie.** 'I'm *in* the store.'
Idę nad <+ACC> **rzekę.** 'I'm going *to* the river.'
Jestem nad <+INS> **rzeką.** 'I'm *at* the river.'

Idę w <+ACC> **góry.** 'I'm going to the mountains.'

Jestem w <+LOC> **górach.** 'I'm in the mountains.'

Idę _na_ <+ACC> **koncert.** 'I'm going _to_ the concert.'

Jestem _na_ <+LOC> **koncercie.** 'I'm _at_ the concert.'

Idę _do_ <+GEN> **babci.** 'I'm going _to_ [my] grandma's.'

Jestem _u_ <+GEN> **babci.** 'I am at [my] grandma's.'

Wracam _od_ <+GEN> **babci.** 'I am coming back _from_ [my] grandma's.'

Expressing motion to/towards a place of destination, showing a location, and describing returning from it, should be learned and practised lexically, within a meaningful context.

Below are commonly used "sets of prepositions" which indicate motion to and from, and show location.

do 'going towards,' 'to,' 'into' <+GEN>

w 'being in,' 'inside' <+LOC>

z 'coming from' <+GEN>

9.2.5.1 | Do

Do 'toward,' 'to' is the most popular preposition for expressing movement to a goal. It always takes the genitive case. It is often used with physical destinations (buildings, cities, movies, restaurants, etc.).

Jedziemy _do Warszawy_. 'We are going _to Warsaw_.'

Chodźmy _do teatru_. 'Let's go _to the theater_.'

Idę _do restauracji_. 'I'm going _to a restaurant_.'

włożyć ubrania _do walizki_ 'to put clothes _into a suitcase_'

9.2.5.2 | W

W 'being in, inside' is the most popular preposition for showing location inside physical objects (boxes, suitcases, buildings, cities, movies, restaurants, etc.) The locative case shows location.

Jesteśmy _w Warszawie, w teatrze, w restauracji_.

'We are _in Warsaw, in a theater, in a restaurant_.'

Ubrania są _w walizce_.

'The clothes are _inside the suitcase_.'

9.2.5.3 | Z

Z 'from' followed by the genitive case denotes returning or withdrawal from these places (buildings, cities, movies, restaurants, etc.)

Wracamy z *Warszawy, z kina, z restauracji.*
'We are returning from Warsaw, from the theater, from the restaurant.'

Wyjęłam ubrania z *walizki.*
'I took the clothes *out of the suitcase*.'

9.2.5.4 | *Na* and *w*

na 'going to, going onto, on top of' <+ACC>
na 'being at, being on, on top of' <+LOC>
z 'from' <+GEN>

Na 'going to,' 'going onto,' 'going on top of,' is the second most popular preposition for expressing motion toward a destination. **Na** is mostly used with functions and events, but also with large, spacious and open areas such as a stadium, cemetery, or roof. A few enclosed places, such as **poczta** 'post office,' **uniwersytet** 'university,' **lotnisko** 'airport' belong to the group as well. (See also 9.2.5.7)

Jedziemy na <+ACC> **koncert/na cmentarz/na lotnisko.**
'We're going to the concert/to the cemetary/to the airport.'

Jesteśmy na <+LOC> **koncercie/na cmentarzu/na lotnisku.**
'We're at the concert/at the cemetary/at the airport.'

Wracamy z <+GEN> **koncertu/z cmentarza/z lotniska.**
'We're coming back from the concert/from the cemetary/from the airport.'

Idę na <+ACC> **dach.** 'I'm going on the roof.'
Jestem na <+LOC> **dachu.** 'I'm on the roof.'
Schodzę z <+GEN> **dachu.** 'I'm walking down from the roof.'

w 'going in, inside' <+ACC>
w 'being in, inside' <+LOC>
z 'from' <+GEN>

Mężczyzna stał w <+LOC> **tłumie.** 'A man was standing *inside the crowd.*'

Mężczyzna wszedł w <+ACC> **tłum.** 'A man went into the crowd.'

Mężczyzna wyszedł z <+GEN> **tłumu.** 'A man stepped out of the crowd.'

9.2.5.5 | *"Sets" to express visiting people and coming back*

do 'to visit' <+GEN>

u 'at somebody's place,' also at people's businesses <+GEN>

od 'away from,' 'back from' <+GEN>

Idziemy *do fryzjera.* 'We are going *to the hairdresser's.*'

Byliśmy *u fryzjera.* 'We were *at the hairdresser's.*'

Wróciliśmy *od fryzjera.* 'We came *back from the hairdresser's.*'

U 'at' can also refer to a group of people who share the same values, address, interests, etc.

U nas [in Poland] **służba wojskowa jest obowiązkowa.**

Czy u was (w Stanach Zjednoczonych) również?

'In Poland military service is compulsory. Is it the same in the United States?'

spotkajmy się u mnie

'let's meet at my place'

u nas 'at our place, in our country'

u was 'at your place, in your country'

9.2.5.6 | **Do, na, w** *with geographical names*

9.2.5.6.1 | Countries

Do <+GEN> is used to express "going to" to most countries.

Jedziemy do Polski, do Wielkiej Brytanii, do Stanów Zjednoczonych, do Rosji, do Niemiec.

'We are going to Poland, to Great Britain, to the United States, to Russia, to Germany.'

Exceptionally, **Słowacja** 'Slovakia,' **Węgry** 'Hungary,' **Białoruś** 'Belarus' and **Ukraina** 'Ukraine' take the preposition **na** 'to' when talking about going to the country.

The preposition **na** with these countries takes nouns and noun phrases in the accusative case.

> **Jadę na** <+ACC> **Słowację, na Węgry, na Białoruś, na Ukrainę.**
> 'I'm going to Slovakia, Hungary, Belarus, Ukraine.'

Lithuania and Latvia may take either the preposition **do** or **na** to express "going there," but **na** is much more popular.

> **Jadę na Litwę** (or **do Litwy**), **na Łotwę** (or **do Łotwy**).
> 'I am going to Lithuania, Latvia.'

W <+LOC> is used to show "being" in most countries.

> **Mieszkam w Polsce, w Wielkiej Brytanii, w Stanach Zjednoczonych, w Rosji, w Niemczech, w Czechach.**
> 'I live in Poland, in Great Britain, in the United States, in Russia, in Germany, in the Czech Republic.'

Exceptionally, **na** <+LOC> is used to show "being" in certain countries.

> **Pracuję na Węgrzech, na Słowacji, na Ukrainie.**
> 'I work in Hungary, in Slovakia, in Ukraine.'

It is possible but less common to use the preposition **do** when talking about going to Slovakia, Ukraine, Latvia and Lithuania.

> (less common) **Jadę do Słowacji, do Ukrainy, do Łotwy, do Litwy.**
> 'I'm going to Slovakia, to Ukraine, to Latvia, to Lithuania.'

To express being *in* Slovakia, Hungary, Lithuania, Latvia, Belarus, and Ukraine, exceptionally, the preposition **na** is used.

> **Mieszkam na** <+LOC> **Słowacji, na Węgrzech, na Litwie, na Łotwie, na Białorusi, na Ukrainie.**
> 'I live in Slovakia, Hungary, Lithuania, Latvia, Belarus, Ukraine.'

The preposition **na** with these countries takes nouns and noun phrases in the locative case.

When the country is modified by an adjective, being in the country is often expressed with the preposition **w**.

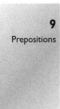
Mieszkaliśmy w <+LOC> **zachodniej Słowacji, w komunistycznych Węgrzech.**
'We lived in western Slovakia, communist Hungary.'

Na <+LOC> is used to show location on peninsulas, islands, archipelagoes and places apart from the mainland.

pobyt na Florydzie, na Karaibach, na Kubie, na Helu, na Mauritiusie, na Alasce, na Syberii
'staying in Florida, in the Caribbean, in Cuba, in Hel, on Mauritius, in Alaska, in Siberia.'

Na <+ACC> is used to express going to those places.

Jedziemy na Florydę, na Karaiby, na Kubę, na Hel, na Mauritius, na Alaskę, na Syberię.
'We are going to Florida, to the Caribbean, to Cuba, to Hel, to Mauritius, to Alaska, to Siberia.'

Do <+GEN> is used to express "going to" many regions in the world but only two regions in Poland – **Wielkopolska** 'Greater Poland' and **Małopolska** 'Lesser Poland' – both being regions of Poland that have the name **Polska** 'Poland' within the regional name.

Jedziemy do Toskanii, do Alzacji, do Burgundii, do Wielkopolski, do Małopolski.
'We are going to Tuscany, to Alsace, to Burgundy, to Greater Poland, to Lesser Poland.'

W <+LOC> is used to show "being" in almost all regions, but only two regions in Poland – **Wielkopolska** 'Greater Poland' and **Małopolska** 'Lesser Poland' – two regions of Poland that have the name **Polska** 'Poland' within the regional name. (See 9.3.7)

Mieszamy w Toskanii, w Alzacji, w Burgundii, w Wielkopolsce, w Małopolsce, w Galicji.
'We live in Tuscany, in Alsace, in Burgundy, in Greater Poland, in Lesser Poland, in Galicia.'

Na <+ACC> is used to express "going to" Polish regions (except do <+GEN> for **Wielkopolska** 'Greater Poland' and **Małopolska** 'Lesser Poland').

Jedziemy na Śląsk, na Mazowsze, na Kujawy, na Pomorze, na Mazury.
'We are going to Silesia, to Mazovia, to Kuyavia, to Pomerania, to Masuria.'

Na <+LOC> is used to show "being" in Polish regions (except w <+LOC> for **Wielkopolska** 'Greater Poland' and **Małopolska** 'Lesser Poland')

Mieszamy na Śląsku, na Mazowszu, na Kujawach, na Pomorzu, na Mazurach.
'We live in Silesia, in Mazovia, in Kuyavia, in Pomerania, in Masuria.'

| 9.2.5.6.4 | Mountain ranges |

W <+ACC> is used to express going to or near a mountain range.

Jedziemy w góry. 'We are going to the mountains.'
Jedziemy w Tatry. 'We are going to the Tatra mountains.'
Pojedźmy w Himalaje. 'Let's go to the Himalayas.'
Jedziemy w góry Kaukazu. 'We are going to the Caucasus mountains.'
but **jedziemy na Kaukaz, na Ural** (mountains or region)

| 9.2.5.6.5 | Open spaces |

Na <+ACC> is used to express "going" to open spaces e.g., meadow, desert, flatlands, lowland, forest clearing.

Idziemy na łąkę, na pustynię, na równinę, na nizinę, na polanę.
'We are going to a meadow, to a desert, to a flatland, to a lowland, to a forest clearing.'

Na <+LOC> is used to show "being" in an open space.

Odpoczywamy na łące, na pustyni, na równinie, na nizinie, na polanie, na plaży.
'We rest at a meadow, at a desert, at flatlands, at a lowland, at a forest clearing, at the beach.'

but *W pustyni i w puszczy* '*In Desert and Wilderness*,' a novel by Nobel Prize winning author Henryk Sienkiewicz.

| *Usage of* **na**

The preposition **na** has a very rich repertoire. The most common usages of *na* are as follows.

Table 9.4 Cardinal directions

Na <+LOC> is used with points of the compass:	[**Na Zachodzie** written with the capital letter 'Z' means in the West, referring to the countries in the "Western world."]
na południu 'in the south'	**na południowym wschodzie** 'in the southeast'
na północy 'in the north'	**na południowym zachodzie** 'in the southwest'
na wschodzie 'in the east'	**na północnym wschodzie** 'in the northeast'
na zachodzie 'in the west'	**na północnym zachodzie** 'in the northwest'

Also: **na Bliskim Wschodzie** 'in the Middle East', **na Dalekim Wschodzie** 'in the Far East.'

Na <+ACC> together with **od** <+GEN> are used when giving directions and describing the location of one city with reference to another city or place.

Kraków jest *na* <+ACC> **południe od** <+GEN> **Zakopanego.**
'Cracow is *to* the south of [lit. *from*] Zakopane.'

Warszawa jest *na* **południowy zachód od Gdańska.**
'Warsaw is *to* the south-west of [lit. *from*] Gdańsk.'

Jedziemy *na* **północ.**
'We are going to the north.'

Jedziemy *na* **Kraków.**
'We are going in the direction of Cracow.'

Na <+LOC> is used to show location at the following:

droga 'road'	**róg** 'corner'
dworzec 'railway station'	**schody** 'stairs'
plac 'square'	**skwer** 'green square'
postój 'taxi stand'	**stacja** 'station'
przedmieścia 'suburbs'	**teren** 'terrain'
przejście dla pieszych, graniczne 'cross for pedestrians,' 'check point'	**ulica** 'street'
	wybrzeże 'seaside,' 'coast'
przystanek 'bus stop'	**zakręt** 'turning'

Jesteśmy w kawiarni *na placu* **Wolności,** *na ulicy* **Chopina,** *na przedmieściach* **Londynu,** *na skwerze* **Kościuszki.**
'We are in a café *on* Freedom *Square, on* Chopin *Street, in* the suburbs of London, *on* Kościuszko *Square.*'

Na <+ACC> is used to express "going" to those places where we use the preposition na to describe the location.

Wychodzę *na* **ulicę,** *na* **przedmieścia,** *na* **skwer.**
'I'm going *to* the street, *to* the suburbs, *onto* a square.'

Na <+ACC> expresses "going" to spacious areas where the surface essentially constitutes the place.

Jadę na cmentarz. 'I go to the cemetery.'
Jadę na lotnisko. 'I go to the airport.'
Jadę na stadion. 'I'm going to a stadium.'
Jadę na poligon. 'I'm going to a training ground.'
Jadę na dworzec. 'I'm going to a station.'
wypłynąć na powierzchnię 'to swim to the surface'
pójść na dno 'to go down'
jechać na ulicę Długą 'to go to Długa Street'

Na <+LOC> is used to show the location of the places for which we used the preposition na to express "going to":

być na cmentarzu, lotnisku, stadionie, poligonie, rynku, dworcu, froncie, powierzchni, dnie, ulicy
'to be at the cemetery, airport, stadium, training ground, market square, station, front, surface, bottom, street'

Na <+ACC> is used to express "going to" such places as **poczta** 'the post office' and **uniwersytet** 'the university.'

Idę *na pocztę.* 'I'm going *to the post office.*'
Idę *na uniwersytet.* 'I am going *to the university.*'

The preposition na <+LOC> is used to denote location at those places:

Jestem *na poczcie.* 'I'm *at the post office.*'
Jestem *na uniwersytecie.* 'I'm *at the university.*'

Na <+ACC> is used to express "going to" meetings, events and functions.

Na 'on,' 'at' <+LOC> is used to show attendance at various meetings, events and functions.

545

Idziemy *na* <+ACC> ***spotkanie.*** 'We are going *to the meeting.*'
Jesteśmy *na* <+LOC> ***spotkaniu.*** 'We are *at the meeting.*'
Idę *na* <+ACC> ***zajęcia.*** 'I'm going *to class.*'
Jestem *na* <+LOC> ***zajęciach.*** 'I'm *in class.*'

Below find an extensive list of nouns that take the preposition *na* <+ACC> to express "going to" an event or function and *na* <+LOC> to express attendance or being at an event or function.

badanie 'medical exam'
balet 'ballet'
ceremonia 'ceremony'
chrzciny 'baptism'
dyskusja 'discussion'
film 'film'
imieniny 'name day'
kamping 'camping'
koncert 'concert'
lekcja 'lesson'
lektorat 'foreign
   language course'
msza 'mass'
nabożeństwo
   '[church] service'
obóz harcerski
   'scout camp'
odczyt 'lecture'
operacja 'surgery'
pogrzeb 'funeral'
pokaz 'show'
posiedzenie 'session'

prelekcja 'talk'
promocja (książki)
   'promotion (book launch)'
przerwa 'break,' 'recess'
prześwietlenie 'X-ray'
przyjęcie 'reception'
randka 'date'
rozmowa kwalifikacyjna 'job interview'
ślub 'wedding ceremony'
spotkanie 'meeting'
sztuka 'play'
urodziny 'birthday'
wernisaż 'vernissage'
wesele 'wedding'
wieczór (poezji, kawalerski, panieński)
   'evening (poetic, bachelor, bachelorette)'
wykład 'lecture'
wystawa 'exhibition'
zabawa 'dance'
zakupy 'shopping'
zaręczyny 'engagement party'
zebranie 'gathering'

Na 'at' is used with meals:

drugie śniadanie 'elevenses'
kawa 'coffee'
kolacja 'supper'
lunch 'lunch'

obiad 'midday meal'
podwieczorek 'afternoon tea'
posiłek 'meal'
śniadanie 'breakfast'

Idę *na obad.* 'I'm going *for lunch.*'

Na is also used to mean 'at': **training** 'practice,' **zawody** 'competition,' **olimpiada** 'olympics,' **mistrzostwa** 'championships,' **safari** 'safari' (indeclinable).

(See 9.3.7)

9.2.6 | *Temporal relations*

Prepositions are used in various constructions to express time, a period of time, a specific time, etc.

Note that while **w** <+ACC> is mostly used with days of the week (**w poniedziałek** 'on Monday'), **w** <+LOC> is used with months (**w maju** 'in May') and years (**w 2011 roku** 'in 2011'). (See 8.1.4.1)

o 'at' <+LOC>

o drugiej (godzinie) 'at two (o'clock)'

o której godzinie? 'at what time?'
o pierwszej 'at one o'clock'
o północy 'at midnight'

za 'to,' 'in' ('in the future') <+ACC>

za kwadrans pierwsza '(it's) a quarter to one'
Za tydzień wyjeżdżamy. 'We are leaving in a week.'
Za godzinę mam ważne spotkanie. 'In an hour I have an important meeting.'
za dwie (minuty) dwunasta '(it's) two (minutes) to twelve'
za pół godziny 'in half an hour'

po 'after' <+LOC>

kwadrans po pierwszej 'a quarter after one'
po północy 'after midnight'
po tygodniu wreszcie zadzwonił 'he finally called after a week'

ponad 'more than' <+ACC>

Film trwał ponad godzinę. 'The movie lasted more than an hour.'
Pracował w Paryżu ponad rok. 'He worked in Paris for more than a year.'

około 'around,' 'about' <+GEN>

około południa 'around noon'
około północy 'around midnight'
około pierwszej 'around one o'clock'
Około miesiąca czekał na odpowiedź. 'He waited for about a month for a response.'

w 'within' <+ACC>

w minutę 'within a minute'
W rok zbudowali dom. 'They built a house within a year.'
w godzinę 'within an hour'
zrobić coś w mig 'to do something in no time'

w 'in' <+LOC>

w ostatniej chwili 'at the last minute'
w godzinach szczytu 'during rush hour'
w nocy 'at night'
przed 'before,' 'earlier,' 'ago' <+INS>

Wrócę przed piątą (godziną). 'I'll be back before five (o'clock).'
przed północą 'before midnight'
przed południem 'before noon'
przed obiadem 'before lunch'
przed rokiem 'a year ago'
Przed chwilą wyszedł. 'He left a moment ago.'

na 'for (how long),' 'by' <+ACC>

Jedziemy na rok do Francji. 'We're going to France for a year.'
Wychodzę na pół godziny. 'I'm leaving for half an hour.' (I'll be back
   in 30 minutes.)
Chcę to skończyć na poniedziałek. 'I want to finish it by
   Monday.'
raz na miesiąc 'once a month'
raz na tysiąc lat 'once every thousand years'
na starość/na stare lata 'in the old days'
na przestrzeni wieków 'over the course of a few centuries'

do 'to, till' <+GEN>
do jutra 'till tomorrow'
do siedmiu dni 'up to seven days'

od 'from,' 'since' <+GEN>
od dzieciństwa 'since childhood'

Pracuję od ósmej do piątej. 'I work from eight to five (o'clock).'
Lekarz przyjmuje od poniedziałku do piątku oprócz środy.
   'The doctor sees patients from Monday to Friday except Wednesday.'
Od stycznia do marca byłam na zwolnieniu. 'From January till
   March I was on sick leave.'
od świtu do nocy 'from dawn till dusk'

od rana do wieczora 'from the morning till the evening'
pada od tygodnia 'it's been raining for a week'
od miesiąca 'for the past month'
od wielu lat 'for (the past) many years'
od (niepamiętnych) wieków 'since time (immemorial)' but
nie widzieliśmy się kupę lat (coll.) 'we haven't seen each other for
   a really long time ([lit.] a heap of years)'

Note that **kupa** 'a heap, a lot' used above in **kupa lat** 'many years' is an colloquial word not typically used in formal settings.

Table 9.5 Days of the week

w(e) 'on' <+ACC> with days of the week 'on a day'		
poniedziałek	w poniedziałek	'on Monday'
wtorek	we wtorek	'on Tuesday'
środa	w środę	'on Wednesday'
czwartek	w(e) czwartek	'on Thursday'
piątek	w piątek	'on Friday'
sobota	w sobotę	'on Saturday'
niedziela	w niedzielę	'on Sunday'

Note that variants with an extra e, like **we wtorek**, **we czwartek** are used to avoid consonant clusters (two or more consonants in a row), and to ease pronunciation.

w <+ACC> when denoting days

w tę sobotę 'this Saturday'
w ten piątek 'this Friday'
w przyszły piątek 'next Friday'
w przyszłą sobotę 'next Saturday'
w piątek tydzień temu 'last Friday'
w zeszły piątek 'last Friday'
w zeszłą sobotę 'last Saturday'
w ostatni piątek miesiąca 'on the last Friday of a month'
w pierwszą sobotę maja 'on the first Saturday of the month of May'

but: **w ciągu doby** 'in one day' (**w dwadzieścia cztery godziny** 'in 24 hours')

Note that days of the week do not begin with a capital letter, and the week starts on Monday. (See 1.7)

9.2.6.1 | *Essential parts of the day*

rano 'in the morning'
po południu 'in the afternoon'
wieczorem 'in the evening'
w nocy 'at night'
w <+ACC> **sobotę rano** 'on Saturday morning'
w <+ACC=NOM> **piątek wieczorem** 'on Friday evening'

9.2.6.2 | *Parts of day throughout the day*

dzisiaj rano 'this morning'
dzisiaj po południu 'this afternoon'
dzisiaj wieczorem 'this evening'
dzisiaj w nocy 'tonight'

do nocy 'until night'
do północy 'until midnight'
do południa 'until the afternoon'
do rana 'until the morning'
do wieczora 'until the evening'
o północy 'at midnight'
o świcie 'at dawn' but: **wyjechać skoro świt/bladym świtem**
  'to leave/left as soon as dawn breaks/broke'
o wschodzie słońca 'at sunrise'
o zachodzie słońca 'at sunset'
o zmierzchu 'at dusk,' 'at twilight'
od (samego) rana 'since the (very) morning'
po północy 'after midnight'
po południu 'in the afternoon'
po zmierzchu 'after dark'
pod wieczór 'towards the evening'
przed północą 'before midnight'
przed południem 'before afternoon'
w nocy 'at night'
późnym rankiem 'in the mid-morning'
w nocy z <+GEN> **dwunastego na** <+GEN> **trzynastego maja** 'on the
  night of May 12'
w południe 'at noon'
z (samego) rana '(first thing) in the morning'

9.2.6.3 *To express time going by: minute by minute, hour by hour/day by day/week by week, year by year*

Z <+GEN> **minuty na** <+ACC> **minutę robiło się coraz zimniej.** 'It was getting colder minute by minute.'

Z godziny na godzinę sytuacja stawała się nie do zniesienia. 'Hour by hour the situation was becoming unbearable.'

żyć z dnia na dzień 'to live day by day'

z tygodnia na tydzień 'week by week'

z roku na rok 'year by year'

9.2.6.4 *To express phases of something being in process*

Idiom: **Mieć coś na końcu języka.** 'To have something on the tip of the tongue.'

początek 'beginning,' **koniec** 'end,' **być w toku** 'pending, to be under way'

na początku czegoś 'at the beginning of something'

na samym początku/zaraz na początku 'at the very beginning'

na początek 'to begin with'

od początku roku 'since the beginning of the year'

z początku myśleliśmy, że to żart 'initially we thought it was a joke'

od początku do końca 'from beginning to end'

na końcu 'at the end, last of all'

na samym końcu 'at the very end'

pod koniec lekcji 'toward the end of class'

w końcu wyszedł 'in the end/finally he left'

z końcem semestru 'with the end of the semester'

z początkiem lata 'with the beginning of the summer'

z nadejściem zimy 'with the approch of winter'

piąty od końca 'the fifth from the end'

policzyć do dziesięciu od końca 'to count to ten backwards'

od końca do końca 'from end to end'

pojechać na koniec świata 'to go to the end of the world'

9.2.6.5 *Stages of life* **w** 'in' <+LOC>/**od** 'since' <+GEN>

Często chorowałam w niemowlęctwie. 'I was often sick in babyhood.'

Od niemowlęctwa był radosnym dzieckiem. 'Since babyhood he was a cheerful child.'

Mieszkał u babci w dzieciństwie. 'He lived at grandma's in his childhood.'

Od dzieciństwa mieszkam u babci. 'I have been living at grandma's since my childhood.'

w latach młodzieńczych 'during the youthful years'

od lat młodzieńczych 'since the youthful years'

W młodości dużo podróżował. 'In [his] youth/when young he traveled a lot.'

we wczesnej młodości 'in early youth'

Czym skorupka za młodu nasiąknie, tym na starość trąci
(saying) 'Just as the twig is bent the tree is inclined.'

9.2.6.6 | *To express approximation* **około** 'around' <+GEN>, **z** 'about' <+ACC>

Mam około dwóch metrów. 'I am about two meters tall.'

Ona ma około trzydziestu lat. 'She is around 30 years old.'

Ona ma około trzydziestki. (coll.) 'She is around 30 years old.'

Kosztował około stu złotych. 'It cost around/approximately one hundred zloty.'

Bilet do Polski kosztuje z tysiąc dolarów. 'A ticket to Poland costs almost two thousand dollars.'

Miał ze dwa metry. 'He was almost two meters tall.'

Note that the prepositional phrases **w przybliżeniu/w zaokrągleniu** mean 'in round numbers, about':

podać sumę w przybliżeniu 'to give the sum in round figures'

(To express approximate age, see 7.5.2 and 8.1.3.2.)

9.2.6.7 | **W** <+LOC> *with seasons*

w lecie 'in summer'
w jesieni 'in fall'
w zimie 'in winter'
but: **na** <+ACC> **wiosnę** 'in spring'

w sezonie letnim/zimowym/grzewczym 'in the summer/winter/ heating season'

Note that all seasons can also be expressed in the instrumental case:

wiosną 'in spring'   **jesienią** 'in fall'
latem 'in summer'   **zimą** 'in winter'

9.2.6.8 | *Holidays*

Idziemy na Boże Narodzenie. 'We're going for Christmas.'
Na/w Wielkanoc zawsze robimy biały barszcz.
  'For/during Easter we always make white borsch soup.'
iść na sylwestra 'to go to a New Year's Eve party'
Co dostałeś na gwiazdkę? 'What did you get for Christmas?'
W Święto Dziękczynienia jemy indyka.
  'For Thanksgiving we eat turkey.'

W Święto Zmarłych odwiedzamy groby bliskich. 'On All Souls'
  day we visit our relatives' graves.'
We Wszystkich Świętych pójdziemy na cmentarz. 'For All
  Saints' day we will go to the cemetery.'

9.2.6.9 | **W** <+LOC> *with weeks, months, years, centuries, ages, periods, eras*

To express 'in' + a month, use the preposition **w** <+LOC>.

Table 9.6 Months

1	styczeń	w styczniu	'(in) January'
2	luty	w lutym	'(in) February
3	marzec	w marcu	'(in) March
4	kwiecień	w kwietniu	'(in) April'
5	maju	w maju	'(in) May'
6	czerwiec	w czerwcu	'(in) June'
7	lipiec	w lipcu	'(in) July'
8	sierpień	w sierpniu	'(in) August'
9	wrzesień	we wrześniu	'(in) September'
10	październik	w październiku	'(in) October'
11	listopad	w listopadzie	'(in) November'
12	grudzień	w grudniu	'(in) December'

Note that all months except February (**w lutym**) and November (**w listo-padzie**) have the ending **u** in locative singular.

w tym/w przyszłym/w zeszłym/w następnym tygodniu/ miesiącu/roku '(in) this/next/last/following week/month/year'

w pierwszym tygodniu maja 'in the first week of May' but:

w bieżącym roku 'in this (current) year'

w maju tego roku 'this May'

w maju zeszłego roku 'in May last year' or **rok temu w maju** 'in May, a year ago'

w maju przyszłego roku 'in May next year' or **za rok w maju** 'in a year in May'

Ewa jest w piątym miesiącu ciąży. 'Eva is in her fifth month of pregnancy.'

w dwa tysiące jedenastym roku 'in the year 2011'

w tym/w zeszłym/w przyszłym/następnym wieku 'this/last/next/ following century'

w tym/w poprzednim stuleciu 'this/previous century'

w tym/w minionym tysiącleciu 'in this/last millennium'

w minionym roku 'last year'

w epoce baroku 'during the baroque period'

w epoce Szekspira 'during the Shakespearean era'

w średniowieczu 'during the medieval period'

Note that to express 'during the time of . . .' the preposition **za** <+GEN> is used:

za Kościuszki 'during the Kościuszko time'

za komuny 'during the communist time'

Za króla Sasa jedz, pij i popuszczaj pasa (saying) 'During the Saxon reign, eat, drink and loosen your belt.'

9.2.6.10 **U schyłku** 'at the close of' <+GEN>

u schyłku XVIII wieku 'at the close of the eighteenth century'

u schyłku drugiego tysiąclecia 'at the close of the second millennium'

u schyłku dnia 'at the close of day'

u schyłku życia 'at the end of life'

9.2.6.11 *Temporal* **z** 'from, of' <+GEN>

gazeta z zeszłego wtorku 'a newspaper from last Tuesday'
pismo z dnia 7 marca 'a letter dated March 7th'
ratusz z szesnastego wieku 'a town hall from the sixteenth century'
e-mail z ósmego maja 'email of the eighth of May'
resztki z wczorajszej kolacji 'leftovers from last night's dinner'

9.3 Governing cases

In Polish, prepositions *govern* their noun or noun phrase. As a consequence, each preposition requires the noun or noun phrase to be used in the nominative, accusative, genitive, dative, instrumental, or locative case. A preposition can govern one, two, or even three different cases depending on its function in the sentence.

9.3.1 One case

Examples of prepositions governing one case (for extensive list see Table 9.9):

do 'to' <+GEN>: **idę do pracy** 'I go to work'
bez 'without' <+GEN>: **herbata bez cukru** 'tea without sugar'
dla 'for' <+GEN>: **prezent dla mamy** 'a present for mom'
od 'from' <+GEN>: **list od niej** 'a letter from her'
u 'at (someone's)' <+GEN>: **u mnie** 'at my place'
przez 'through, across, done by' <+ACC>: **przejść przez ulicę** 'to cross the street'
dzięki 'thanks to' <+DAT>: **dzięki tobie czuję się lepiej** 'thanks to you I feel better'

9.3.2 Two cases

Most prepositions that govern two different cases are used (1) to show location and (2) to express motion toward a destination—this is a very important difference in preposition usage. (See 9.2.5)

Table 9.7 presents the prepositions that govern two cases.

Note that some prepositions are hard to define as they denote both a literal and figurative relationship with the words.

Table 9.7 Prepositions governing two cases

Preposition	Case	Translation	Example
między	INS	between, among	**Stół stoi między fotelami.** 'The table stands between armchairs.' **między dobrem a złem** 'between good and evil'
	ACC	between, among [destination]	**wcisnąć walizkę między torby** 'to squeeze a suitcase between bags'
na	LOC	on, at, in [open area, island, events]	**urlop na Krecie** 'vacation on Crete' **Zupa jest na stole.** 'The soup is on the table.' **tańczyć na koncercie** 'to dance at the concert'
	ACC	to [destination], onto, for	**jechać na Kretę** 'to go to Crete' **iść na koncert** 'to go to a concert' **zaproszenie na kolację** 'an invitation for dinner'
nad (nade)	INS	over, above, by, at	**Obraz wisi nad łóżkiem.** 'A painting is hanging above the bed.' **wakacje nad morzem** 'vacation by the sea'
	ACC	over, above, by (when describing an expanse of water) [destination]	**jechać nad morze** 'to go by/to the sea'
o	LOC	(talk, think) about, concerning, at [time]	**Rozmawiam o artykule.** 'I talk about an article.' **Będę o drugiej.** 'I will be [there] at two.'
	ACC	(up) against, [destination], (ask) about, for	**opierać się o ścianę** 'to lean against the wall' **proszę o ciszę** 'silence, please'
po	LOC	along, around, after [time] [noun]	**chodzić po sklepach** 'to go along the stores' **podróżować po Europie** 'to travel around Europe' **po wojnie** 'after the war' **spotkanie po latach** 'a meeting after years' (a reunion)
	ACC	for (in order to get) [destination] up to, as far as	**Poszła po lekarstwa.** 'She went for medicine.' **Wody było po pas.** 'The water was waist-deep.'

Table 9.7 (*cont'd*)

Preposition	Case	Translation	Example
pod (**pode**)	INS	under, beneath, below, beyond	**Książka jest pod stołem.** 'A book is under the table.'
	ACC	up to [destination, incl. figurative] up-(wind, etc.) to beyond, under(neath) approaching the end of a time period	**wejdź pod stół** 'go underneath the table' **Pod koniec roku dostanę podwyżkę.** 'By the end of the year I will get a raise.' **Dziadkowie często spacerowali pod rękę.** 'Grandparents often walk hand in hand.' [lit. 'to walk hand under hand']
poza	INS	beyond, besides, outside	**poza godzinami pracy** 'beyond working hours' **Poza tobą świata nie widzę.** 'I don't see the world besides you.' **poza tym** (participle), 'besides'
	ACC	beyond, outside [destination]	**Nie wolno wychodzić poza bramę.** 'Going outside/beyond the gate is not allowed.'
przed (**przede**)	INS	before, in front of	**Zaparkował przed wejściem.** 'He parked in front of the entrance.' **przed wojną** 'before the war' **Wrócę przed północą.** 'I will be back before midnight.'
	ACC	in front of [destination]	**wyjść przed dom** 'to go in front of the house'
w (**we**)	LOC	in, at, inside [enclosed area]	**być w domu** 'to be at home'
	ACC	into, in [destination]	**wjechać w ulicę** 'to enter the street' **wjechać w bramę** 'to go into a gate' **wścibiać nos w cudze sprawy** 'to put one's nose into someone else's business'

Idioms and sayings:

> **być między młotem a kowadłem** 'to be caught between a rock and a hard place' [lit. 'to be between hammer and anvil']

wpaść po same uszy 'to fall head over heels' [lit. 'to fall up to the ears' level']

wpaść pod samochód 'to be hit by the car' [lit. 'to fall under the car']

iść pod prąd 'to go upstream/against the current'

lubię mieć wszystko pod ręką 'I like to have everything under (the reach of) my hand'

zapaść się pod ziemię (ze wstydu) 'vanish into the earth (because of shame)'

Na *and* **w** *with nouns to describe different meanings*

Sometimes both prepositions **na** and **w** can be used to describe a different meaning:

basen as a whole spacious facility

Idę na basen. 'I'm going to the swimming pool.'
Jestem na basenie. 'I'm at the swimming pool.'

basen as a basin filled with water:

pływam w basenie. 'I'm swimming in the pool.'

na terenie Warszawy 'in the Warsaw area'
w terenie 'away from being in the office'
Geolodzy często pracują w terenie. 'Geologists often work outside their offices.'

pływać w rzece 'to swim in the river'
pływać na rzece 'to swim on the river'

znajomość języka w mowie i w piśmie 'spoken and written command of the language'
Proszę to na piśmie. 'Can I have it in writing, please?'
w powietrzu 'up in the air'
na świeżym powietrzu 'in the fresh open air'

wygrzewać się na słońcu 'to bask in the sun'
w słońcu (w cieniu) 'in the sun' (in the shade)

na wysokości dwóch metrów 'at the height of two meters'
w wysokości tysiąca złotych
'in the amount of one thousand zloty'

miała łzy w oczach 'she had tears in her eyes'
rosnąć w oczach 'to grow rapidly' (idiom)
na naszych oczach 'in front of our very eyes'

w górze/w dole 'up in the air, in the sky'
trzymać rękę w górze 'to keep your hand up'
winda jeździ w górę/w dół 'the elevator goes up/down'
leżeć w dole 'to lie in a hole'
na górze/na dole 'at the top/bottom' *also* 'upstairs/downstairs' in
    a building

w szczycie 'in peak hours,' 'in the gable wall'
na szczycie 'at the summit,' 'on the top of the mountain'

we dworze 'in the manor house'
napijemy się kawy na dworze 'we will drink coffee outside'
sługa na dworze 'a servant at the court'

w ustronnym miejscu 'in a secluded spot'
zginął na miejscu 'died on the spot'
miał wszystko na swoim miejscu 'he had everything in its proper place'

Na <+ACC> is also used when the destination is towards the upper point
of something or a surface:

Idziemy *na zamek*. 'We are going to the castle.' (the area around
    the castle)
Idziemy *do zamku*. 'We are going to the castle.' (a particular building)

Oko *na Polsce* (a CNN program reporting about Poland). Oko *na Polsce* means
that literally the eye is located on Poland. Oko **na Polskę** would imply that
the program covers Poland and all the major issues about the country.

Całe lato dzieci spędziły *na obozie* żeglarskim. 'The children
    spent the whole summer at the sailing camp.'
ludzie umierali *w obozie* 'people were dying in the camp'

(See 9.2.5.6)

9.3.3 | Three cases

Table 9.8 presents the prepositions that govern three cases.

Note that some prepositions are hard to define as they denote both a literal
and figurative relationship between the words.

559

Table 9.8 Prepositions governing three cases

Preposition	Case	Translation	Example
z (ze)	GEN	from, off, out of, (made) of/from	**Jestem z Ameryki.** 'I am from America.'
			Sernik jest zrobiony z sera i jajek. 'Cheesecake is made from cheese and eggs.'
	INS	(together) with	**Z kim idziesz do kina?** 'With whom are you going to the movies?'
			Idę razem z rodziną. 'I'm going together with my family.'
	ACC	about [approx. age, value, time, distance]	**Ten obraz ma ze sto lat.** 'the painting is about a hundred years [old].' [lit. 'has about a hundred years']
			Bilet do Polski kosztuje z tysiąc dolarów. 'A ticket to Poland costs about a thousand dollars.'
za	ACC	for, by, in [time]	**Do zobaczenia za godzinę.** 'See you in an hour.'
			Za zdrowie gospodyni! (toast) 'To [our] host's health!'
			za naszą i waszą wolność 'for our and your freedom'
	ACC	beyond, behind [destination]	**jechać za granicę** 'to go abroad'
			Kot wszedł za kredens. 'A cat went in behind the dresser.'
	GEN	during (the time of), as far as back	**Za króla Sasa jedz, pij i popuszczaj pasa.** 'During the Saxon times, eat, drink and loosen your belt.'
			za komuny 'during the communist time'
			za mojej młodości 'at the time of my youth'
			za dnia 'during the daytime, by day'
	INS	behind, beyond	**za domem** 'behind the house'
			za granicą 'abroad'

The preposition **za** 'for' can also govern the nominative in idiomatic phrases, e.g., **wyjść za mąż** 'to get married,' **być z kimś za pan brat** 'to have a good relationship with somebody, to know the subject well,' **z gramatyką za pan brat** 'to know grammar well.'

9.3.4 | Nominative

Jako 'as,' 'in the capacity of,' underlines the specific character of the deter-miner, its function and role in connection to something:

Pracował jako nauczyciel. 'He worked as a teacher.'

Jak 'as,' 'like,' 'than' with negation introduces a comparison: the first part of the sentence is negated and the adjective is in the comparative form.

Nie ma nic gorszego jak gorące mleko. 'There is nothing worse than hot milk.'
biały jak ściana 'white as a wall'

Note that **jak** could be treated as a particle **wracaj jak najszybciej** 'come back as soon as possible,' **jak nie trzaśnie drzwiami** 'suddenly (s)he slams the door,' **mieszkanie jak się patrzy** 'top quality apartment.'

For lists of prepositions and each case that they govern, (see 2.5.7 and 9.2.5).

9.3.5 | Accusative

The accusative case is used after particular prepositions. These include **przez** and **poprzez**, after which the accusative case is always used, **na, po, w, o,** which can take either the accusative or the locative, **między, nad, pod, pomiędzy, ponad, poza, przed, za,** which can take either the accusative or the instru-mental, and **z,** which can take either the accusative or the genitive (see Tables 9.1 and 9.9).

These prepositions take an object in the accusative case when motion is specified into or onto something. In the example 'a car drove *into* the tunnel' **samochód wjechał w tunel**, the preposition **w** takes an object in the accusative case because of the specific motion into the tunnel.

The list below includes only two prepositions that *always* take the accusa-tive: **przez** and **poprzez**. Other examples of when a preposition takes an object in the accusative case are listed under 9.3.5.1.

między 'in between, in among'
na 'onto,' 'for,' 'toward'
nad 'to' (with expanse of water), 'to above'
po 'up to,' 'as far as,' 'in order to get'
pod 'to under,' 'beneath'
pomiędzy 'to under,' 'beneath'
ponad 'to beyond,' 'above'

poprzez 'through'
poza 'to beyond'
przed 'to in front of'
przez 'through,' 'via,' 'go across'
o 'lean against something'
w 'into,' 'on,' 'to' (with mountains)
z 'about,' (approx. measurement)
za 'to behind,' 'for,' 'in'

Since these prepositions can be translated into English in many ways, the list below provides only some examples.

przez 'through,' 'via,' 'go across'

pociąg z Warszawy do Gdańska przez Malbork 'train from Warsaw to Gdańsk via Malbork'
wejść przez okno 'to come through the window'
Przeszedł przez ulicę, park, most. 'He went across the street, park, bridge.'
rozmawiam przez telefon 'to talk on the phone'
zakupy przez Internet 'shopping through the Internet'
mówić przez nos 'to speak through your nose'
Przeszła przez piekło. 'She went through hell.'

It is worth noting that in modern Polish **przez** is often used to express talking via new technology, such as through Skype and other means via the Internet.

Często rozmawiamy przez Skype'a, bo jest taniej niż przez telefon.
'We often talk on Skype, because it is cheaper than on the phone.'

przez 'across,' 'over'

przebiec przez ulicę 'to run across the street'
przeskoczyć przez kałużę 'to jump over the puddle'
przejść przez granicę 'to cross the border'

przez 'for,' 'during' (temporal)

Przez cały wieczór słuchałam muzyki. 'During the whole evening I was listening to music.'
Nie widziałam go przez miesiąc. 'I haven't seen him for a month.'

przez 'by' arithmetical operation

osiem podzielić przez dwa 'eight divided by two'
dwa pomnożyć przez cztery 'two multiplied by four'

przez 'by' in passive voice sentences

Polon został odkryty przez Marię Skłodowską-Curie i Piotra Curie. 'Polonium was discovered by Maria Skłodowska-Curie and Pierre Curie.'
Papier został wynaleziony w Chinach. 'Paper was invented in China.'

Poprzez is similar to **przez** 'through,' 'via' but is more intense, and often suggests obstacles.

szliśmy poprzez bagna, lasy, krzaki
'we were going through bogs, woods, bushes'

uczyć się poprzez zabawy i gry 'to learn through fun and games'

Poprzez emphasizes a long time and/or process.

od średniowiecza do współczesności poprzez romantyzm
'from the Middle Ages to the present time through Romanticism'

9.3.5.1 | With motion/toward a destination

Most of the accusative case prepositions govern more than one case. For example, **o** can govern the accusative in the meaning of 'for,' while predominantly it is rendered in English by 'about' and governs the locative case. The distinction between one case and another relates to motion toward a destination. The general rule is that if motion to or towards the goal is involved, the accusative case will follow, if no motion toward a destination is involved, the prepositions take either the instrumental or locative case. This distinction can also be shown by the questions words **dokąd?** 'where to?' [destination] versus **gdzie?** 'where?' [location].

Note that some verbs have less obvious or more figurative motion toward a destination: **ubiegać się o <+ACC>** 'to run/apply for,' **opierać się o <+ACC>** 'to lean on,' **włożyć na <+ACC>** 'to put on.'

The preposition **na <+LOC>** denotes a location, and the same preposition **na <+ACC>** denotes destination; **w <+LOC>** denotes location, **w <+ACC>** denotes destination; **nad <+INS>** denotes location, **nad <+ACC>** denotes destination. (See Table 9.3)

Accusative (destination)	**Instrumental/Locative** (location)
między 'between, among' <+ACC>	**między** 'between,' 'among' <+INS>
na 'onto,' 'for,' 'toward'	**na** 'on,' 'at' <+LOC>
nad 'to over,' 'above'	**nad** 'over,' 'above' <+INS>
po 'up to,' 'as far as,' 'in order to get'	**po** 'after,' 'along' <+LOC>
pod 'to under,' 'beneath'	**pod** 'under,' 'beneath' <+INS>
pomiędzy 'between, among'	**pomiędzy** 'between,' 'among' <+INS>
ponad 'to beyond,' 'above'	**ponad** 'beyond,' 'above' <+INS>
poza 'to beyond'	**poza** 'beyond,' 'outside' <+INS>
przed 'before,' 'to in front of'	**przed** 'before,' 'in front of' <+INS>
w 'into,' 'on'	**w** 'in' <+LOC>
z 'about,' 'approximate measurement'	**z** 'together with' <+INS>
za 'to behind,' 'for,' 'in'	**za** 'behind' <+INS>
o 'lean against something'	**o** 'about' <+LOC>

Note that the predominant meaning of the preposition **z** is 'from' <+GEN>.

> **Dziecko wdrapało się *na* stół.** 'A child climbed on the table.'
> **Samochód wjechał *w* tunel.** 'A car drove into the tunnel.'
> **Samochód wjechał *na* tory kolejowe.** 'A car drove on the railway tracks.'
> **Kot wszedł *pod* łóżko.** 'A cat went under the bed.'
> **Jedziemy *nad* morze.** 'We are going to the sea.'
> **Jedziemy *w* góry.** 'We are going to the mountains.'
> **Nie opieraj się *o* ścianę.** 'Do not lean on the wall.'
> **Bilet do Polski kosztuje *z* tysiąc euro.** 'A ticket to Poland costs approximately one thousand euro.'

The examples below illustrate the differences in the use of **na**, **w**, **po**, and **o**, which can take either the accusative or the locative.

Object in the accusative case (towards a destination)	Object in the locative case (location)
Dziecko wdrapało się *na* stół. 'A child climbed on the table.'	**Dziecko siedzi *na* stole.** 'A child is sitting on the table.'
Samochód wjechał *w* tunel. 'A car drove into the tunnel.'	**Samochód zepsuł się *w* tunelu.** 'A car broke down in the tunnel.'

Kto pójdzie *po* lód?
'Who will go to get ice?'

Nie opieraj się *o* ścianę.
'Do not lean on the wall.'

**Niebezpiecznie
jest chodzić *po* lodzie.**
'It is dangerous to walk on ice.'

The examples below illustrate the differences in the use of prepositions which can take either the accusative or the instrumental.

Object in the accusative case (towards a destination)	Object in the instrumental case (location)
Kot wszedł *pod* łóżko. 'A cat went under the bed.'	**Kot śpi *pod* łóżkiem.** 'A cat is sleeping under the bed.'
Nie wychylaj się *za* okno. 'Do not lean out of the window.'	**Co widzisz *za* oknem?** 'What do you see though the window?'
Jedziemy *nad* morze. 'We are going to the sea.'	**Jesteśmy *nad* morzem.** 'We are at the sea.'

9.3.6 | Genitive

The group of prepositions requiring the genitive (**dopełniacz**) is very rich. Many of these prepositions refer to spatial relation, often to describe that something is far, close, near, or around the goal (see Tables 9.1 and 9.9).

bez 'without'
blisko 'close to'
dla 'for'
do 'to'
dokoła/dookoła 'around,' 'round'
koło 'by,' 'next to'
mimo 'in spite of,' 'despite'
na skutek 'as a result of'
naokoło 'round'
naprzeciw(ko) 'opposite'
nieopodal 'near'
o 'with' (concerning measurement)
obok 'next to'
od 'from' (people and time)
około 'about,' 'near' (used with time)

opodal 'near by'
oprócz 'except'
podczas 'during'
pomimo 'in spite of'
poniżej 'below,' 'beneath'
pośrodku 'in the middle'
spod 'from under'
spomiędzy 'from among'
sponad 'from above'
spoza 'from behind'
sprzed 'from before'
u 'at somebody's place,' *chez* 'in French'
według 'according to'
z 'from'
znad 'from above,' 'from' (expanse of water)

bez 'without'

Po polsku mówił bez akcentu. 'He spoke Polish without an accent.'
bez wątpienia 'without doubts'
bez chwili wahania 'without a moment of hesitation'

sayings:

bez pracy nie ma kołaczy 'without work there is no reward'
nie ma róży bez kolców 'there is no rose without a thorn'
nie ma reguły bez wyjątku 'there is no rule without an exception'

blisko 'close'

Mieszkam blisko szkoły. 'I live close to school.'

dla 'for a purpose,' 'for the benefit of' (see 9.7.2)

Zrobiłem to dla nas. 'I did it for us.'

do 'to,' 'till'

do poniedziałku 'till Monday'
Idę do pracy. 'I go to work.'

dokoła 'around,' 'round'

Dzieci biegały dokoła choinek. 'Children were running around the Christmas trees.'

dookoła 'around,' 'round'

Ziemia obraca się dookoła Słońca. 'The earth revolves around the sun.'

koło 'by,' 'next to'

Zaparkowałem koło sklepu. 'I parked by the store.'

mimo 'in spite of,' 'despite'

Mimo wczesnej pory byłam w dobrym nastroju. 'Despite the early time I was in a good mood.'

Note: **Mimo** in the set phrase **mimo wszystko** 'after all' is with the accusative case.

The old meaning of **mimo** is 'by,' 'next to' and it governs the genitive case.

Przeszedł mimo domu.   **Przeszedł obok domu.**
'He walked by the house.'   'He walked by the house.'

Przeszedł mimo.
'He walked by.'

Przeszedł obok.
'He walked by.'

Mimo że is a conjunction meaning 'although.'

Mimo że padało cały tydzień, wszyscy świetnie się bawili.
'Although it rained for the whole week, everyone had a great time.'

A comma comes after the whole phrase.

na skutek 'as a result of'

Na skutek dewaluacji złotego wartość nagrody zmalała do zera. 'As a result of zloty devaluation the value of the prize decreased to zero.'

naokoło 'around,' 'round'

Biegał naokoło ogrodu. 'He was running around the garden.'
naprzeciw 'opposite,' 'in the opposite direction'
Helena usiadła naprzeciw nas. 'Helen sat opposite us.'

naprzeciwko 'opposite'

Po chwili siedzieliśmy naprzeciwko siebie.
'After a moment we were sitting opposite each other.'

nieopodal 'near'

Jan dostał mieszkanie nieopodal parku.
'John got a flat near the park.'

o 'with'

koło o średnicy 20 cm 'a wheel with a 20 cm diameter'

obok 'next to'

Przechodząc obok recepcji, słyszałem dyskusję z udziałem ministra transportu. 'Passing by the reception desk I overheard a discussion with the minister of transport.'

od 'from'

poznać kogoś od kuchni
'to get to know somebody from the inside'
wracamy od lekarza 'we are coming back from the doctor'

około 'about,' 'near'

Wrócę około piątej. 'I will be back about five.'

oprócz 'except'

Wszyscy świetnie się bawili oprócz mnie.
'[They] all had a great time except me.'

oprócz 'apart from that,' 'besides'

Oprócz <+GEN> **historii Polski pasjonował się** <+INS>
językoznawstwem.
'Besides Polish history he was passionately fond of linguistics.'

Please note that the preposition **oprócz** is often replaced by the preposition
poza <+INS>. However, it is more precise to use **oprócz** to denote a supplement, an addition.

Poza mną, przyszły tylko dwie osoby. 'Besides me, only two
people came.'
Oprócz mnie, przyszły tylko dwie osoby. 'Except for me, only
two people came.'

podczas 'during'

podczas Powstania Warszawskiego
'during the Warsaw Uprising'
podczas przeprowadzki 'during the move'

podług = według 'according to'

Była ubrana podług panującej mody.
'she was dressed according to the dominant fashion.'

Czy według ciebie to dobry pomysł?
'Is it a good idea in your opinion [lit. according to you]?'

poniżej 'below'

Zarabiam poniżej średniej krajowej.
'I make below the country's average.'

pośrodku 'in the middle of'

Stół zwykle stoi pośrodku pokoju, a telewizor pod ścianą.
'A table usually stands in the middle of the room, and a TV by the wall.'

sprzed 'from before'

plakat sprzed wojny 'a poster from before the war'

u 'at,' 'at somebody's place' (like *chez* in French)

Jestem u lekarza. 'I am at the doctor's.'
Jestem u rodziny. 'I am at my family's place.'
u mnie 'at my place'

u Ewy 'Chez Eva' (as a name for a café, restaurant, business, etc.)
pokoje u Szymka 'rooms at Simon's'
u fryzjera 'at the hairdresser's'

u 'as a part of' (in idiomatic expressions)

palce u rąk 'fingers'
palce u nóg 'toes'

u 'at one's home/country'

U nas w domu na Wigilię zawsze jemy śledzie.
'In my home on Christmas Eve we always eat herring.'
Czy u was też jest tak zimno?
'Is it this cold in your country too?'

z 'from'

Jestem z Warszawy. 'I am from Warsaw.'
zrobić coś z rozpaczy/gniewu/miłości
'to act out of despair, anger, love'
konstytucja z 1791 roku 'the constitution of 1791'

z 'made of'

kolczyki ze srebra 'earrings made of silver'
sok ze świeżych owoców 'juice made of fresh fruit'
Z czego to jest zrobione? 'What is this made of?'
zastawa z porcelany 'porcelain tableware'

znad 'from above'

Podniósł wzrok znad krzyżówki. 'He raised his eyes from the
crossword.'
Wróciliśmy znad morza. 'We are coming back from the sea.'
niż znad Bałkanów 'low from above the Balkans'

9.3.7	*Locative*

The locative case is used for positioning objects (see Tables 9.1 and 9.9).

na 'on' (position on top or on the surface of another object), 'at'
o 'about,' 'at' (temporal)
po 'after,' 'along'
przy 'at'
w 'in' (inside of another object)

na 'on' (see 9.2.5.6)

> **na stole** 'on the table'
> **na ulicy** 'on the street'
> **na podłodze** 'on the floor'
> **na ścianie** 'on the wall'
> **na powierzchni** 'on the surface'
> **na** 'on' open spaces

> **na stadionie** 'at the stadium'
> **na cmentarzu** 'at the cemetery'
> **na świeżym powietrzu** 'in the fresh air'

Na is exceptionally used with **poczta** 'post office,' **lotnisko** 'airport,' **dworzec** 'railway station,' **uniwersytet** 'university' to express location.

> **na poczcie** 'at the post office' (in the past, like Fedex does today, mail was exchanged on the streets, and the preposition **na** still reflects that)
> **na lotnisku** 'at the airport' (even though airports are located in walled spaces, **na** refers to the main purpose of the airport, the area outside the airport building)
> **na dworcu** 'at the railway station' (even though the station is a building, **na** reflects the essential purpose of the station, the rails that are located in the open area)
> **na uniwersytecie**

na 'at' participating in events and functions

> **Wczoraj byliśmy na śniadaniu/obiedzie/kolacji w restauracji.**
> 'We were at the restaurant for breakfast/lunch/dinner yesterday.'
> **Jedzenie na przyjęciu było pyszne.** 'The food at the reception was delicious.'
> **Czy będzie pani na spotkaniu dziś wieczorem?**
> 'Will you [formal] be at the meeting this evening?'

na 'in' (with directions or points of the compass)

> **na południu** 'in the south'
> **na północy** 'in the north'
> **na wschodzie** 'in the east'
> **na zachodzie** 'in the west'
> **na południowym/północnym wschodzie**
> 'in the south/north east'
> **na południowym/północnym zachodzie**
> 'in the south/north west'

w 'in,' 'inside,' also often rendered by 'at' in English

w pokoju 'in the room'
w pudełku 'in the box'
w tłumie 'in the crowd'
w szkole 'in school'
w domu 'inside the house,' 'at home'
w pracy 'at work'

W <+LOC> is used to show 'being' in almost all regions, but only two Polish regions: **Małopolska** 'Lesser Poland' and **Wielkopolska** 'Greater Poland' (see 9.2.5.6.3).

9.3.8 | Dative

dzięki 'thanks to'
ku 'to,' 'towards'
na przekór 'in spite of,' 'despite'
przeciw 'against'
przeciwko (= **przeciw**)
wbrew 'against,' 'contrary to'

zbrodnia przeciwko ludzkości 'a crime against the people'
Jestem przeciwko wojnom. 'I am against wars.'
Dzięki twojej pomocy znaleźliśmy to mieszkanie. 'Thanks to your help we found this apartment.'
Nigdy nie działaj wbrew własnej woli. 'Never act against your own will.'
Nasza córka robi wiele rzeczy na przekór naszym radom. 'Our daughter does many things against our advice.'

(See Tables 9.1 and 9.9)

9.3.9 | Instrumental

między 'between,' 'among'
nad 'above,' 'over,' 'at with expanse of water'
pod 'below,' 'under(neath)'
pomiędzy 'among,' 'amid'
ponad 'over,' 'above,' 'near'
poza 'outside,' 'besides'
przed 'in front of,' 'before'
w porównaniu z 'in comparison with'
z 'together with'
za 'behind,' 'to be in favor of,' 'long for'
zgodnie z 'in accordance with'

palić za sobą mosty (saying) 'to burn one's bridges'

Polska leży *między* **Rosją a Niemcami.** 'Poland is between Russia and Germany.'

Lampa wisi *nad* **stołem.** 'A lamp is hanging above the table.'

Krzesło stoi *przed* **biurkiem.** 'A chair is standing in front of the desk.'

Ceny żywności *w porównaniu* **z zeszłym rokiem są dwa razy wyższe.** 'Food prices in comparison to last year are twice as high.'

Często rozmawiam z rodzicami. 'I often talk with [my] parents.'

Z kim wychodzisz? 'Who are you going out with?'

Nad is often rendered in English by 'at' with water.

Mieszkamy nad rzeką. 'We live by the river.'

Urlop spędzimy nad morzem. 'We will spend [our] vacation at the sea.'

(See also section 9.3.5.1 and Tables 9.1 and 9.9.)

Idiomatic usage

psu na budę 'to be a dead loss'
z deszczu pod rynnę 'from bad to worse'
groch z kapustą 'disorder, chaos'
bułka z masłem 'piece of cake'
żyć jak pies z kotem lit. 'to live like dog with cat'
z duszą na ramieniu 'to have your heart in your mouth'
być w siódmym niebie 'to be in seventh heaven'
wpaść jak śliwka w kompot 'to get into hot water'
iść komuś na rękę 'to meet somebody half-way'
zapaść się pod ziemię 'to vanish'
jak kamień w wodę 'to disappear, to vanish'
przyjąć za dobrą monetę 'as a good sign'
człowiek z krwi i kości 'a flesh and blood person'
musztarda po obiedzie 'miss the boat'
porywać się z motyką na słońce 'to bite off more than one can chew'
zrobić coś od ręki 'to do something on the spot'
mieć muchy w nosie 'be moody'

9.5 Repetition

Prepositions are not usually repeated if they govern the same case and are used in the same clause.

Rozmawiałem z matką i (z) ojcem.
'I talked with mother and (with) father.'

za naszą i (za) waszą wolność
'to your and (to) our freedom'

Byłem w szpitalu w środę i (w) sobotę.
'I was at the hospital on Wednesday and (on) Saturday.'

Opowiadał o domu, (o) pogodzie i (o) rodzinie.
'He was talking about home, (about) the weather and (about)
   [his] family.'

człowiek z krwi i (z) kości
'a flesh and blood person'

Sometimes, however, to underline and emphasize a word in a phrase you can encounter:

Jestem *za* wolnością i *za* demokracją.
'I am *for* freedom and *for* democracy.'

Prepositions that govern the *same case* are repeated when they are used in different clauses:

Rano poszłam do biblioteki, a wieczorem do kina.
'In the morning I went to the library and in the evening to the movies.'

or they are used with clitic or stressed forms:

Rozmawiam z tobą, nie z nią.
'I am talking to you, not to her.'

Prepositions which govern *two different cases* require repetition of the nouns they refer to.

In English it is possible to omit the noun in sentence such as: "Newspapers were on (the table) and under the table." In Polish, the prepositions *on* and *under* govern different cases, so it is necessary to repeat the noun.

Gazety leżały na <+LOC> stole i pod <+INS> stołem.
'Newspapers were lying on the table and under the table.'

In such situations, when a determiner is described by two different prepositions that govern two different cases, it is much better to replace the second noun with a personal pronoun.

Gazety leżały na stole i pod nim.
'Newspapers were lying on the table and under it.'

In general, try to avoid listing two prepositions in a row. Insead of: (!) **za około pięć minut** 'in about five minutes,' involving the preposition **za** <+ACC>, and **około** <+GEN>, use the construction **za mniej więcej pięć minut** 'in more or less five minutes.' In a sentence like **daliśmy dzieciom w prezencie po około sto złotych** 'we gave the children a present of about one hundred zloty each,' involving **po** <+LOC>, **około** <+GEN>, it might be unclear which preposition takes precedence, so it is better to modify the sentence to **daliśmy dzieciom w prezencie mniej więcej po sto złotych** 'we gave the children a present of more or less one hundred zloty each.' Sometimes we cannot avoid two prepositions next to each other: **odwlec na po wyborach** 'to postpone until after the election.'

If prepositions govern the *same case* it is possible to omit one of the nouns:

pozdrowienia dla (znajomych) i od znajomych
'greetings for (friends) and from friends'

9.6 Paired prepositions

Polish prepositions often occur in pairs. The most common combinations are:

od <+GEN> **. . . do** <+GEN> **. . .** 'from . . . to . . .'

For pairs of prepositions denoting going to, being at, and returning from a place, see Table 9.3.

A very popular pair of prepositions used to express temporal relation and personal relation:

od wtorku do piątku 'from Tuesday to Friday'
od rana do wieczora 'from morning till evening'
od świtu do zmierzchu 'from dusk till dawn'
Chodzę od lekarza do lekarza i nadal nie wiem, co mi dolega.
'I go from doctor to doctor and I still don't know what's wrong.'

Chodzić od Annasza do Kajfasza (going from one office to another and not being successful) 'to go from pillar to post' (saying)

To set the limits, or a specific certain distance:

Chodziliśmy od domu do domu. 'We were going from home to home.'
od morza do Tatr 'from the sea to the Tatra mountains'
czytać od deski do deski 'to read from cover to cover'
od stóp do głów 'from head to toe'
od czubka głowy do pięt 'from head to heels'

Note that the prepositional pair **od ... do** is used on train tickets to suggest that among all the routes the Polish railway system offers, you plan to put limits on your trip. Normally a distance from one place to another is expressed by the prepositions **z ... do**.

Note that to underline a fragment of the route, Poles use the set of prepositions **od ... do**:

Autokar z Warszawy do Gdańska. Spałam od Elbląga do Malborka.
'A bus from Warsaw to Gdańsk. I was sleeping from Elbląg to Malbork.'

Elbląg and Malbork are cities on the way from Warsaw to Gdańsk.

od <+GEN> **... po** <+ACC> **...** 'from ... up to/till ...,'

Zwolniono dużo osób: od prezesa po pracowników fizycznych.
'Many people were laid off: from the president down to the manual workers.'
Był sparaliżowany od pasa po szyję. 'He was paralyzed from his waist up to his neck.'

z <+GEN> **... do** <+GEN> **...** 'from ... to ...'

A very popular pair of prepositions used to express spatial relation:

Wracamy z Warszawy do Krakowa.
'We are coming from Warsaw to Cracow.'

Jedziemy z Paryża do Berlina.
'We are going from Paris to Berlin.'

z <+GEN> **... na** <+ACC> **...** 'from ... to ...'

A pair of prepositions to express temporal, consecutive events:

z roku na rok 'year after year'
z miesiąca na miesiąc 'month after month'
z dnia na dzień 'day after day'
z minuty na minutę 'minute by minute'

This pair also expresses translating from one language to another, converting from one scale to another, going up and down, changing lanes:

tłumaczenie z polskiego na angielski
'translation from Polish to English'

Przeprowadziliśmy się z trzeciego piętra na parter.
'We moved from the third floor to the ground floor.'

Wymieniłam euro na dolary.
'I have changed the euros into dollars.'

biegać z góry na dół
'to run up and down'

zjechać z lewego (pasa) na prawy pas
'change lanes from the left to the right'

zjechać z drogi na pobocze
'pull over'

Zamienił stryjek siekierkę na kijek
(saying) 'a bad bargain' [lit. 'uncle exchanged a hatchet for a stick']

It is also very popular for expressing spatial relation. Note that the preposition **na** in spatial relation is mostly used with events, functions, open, spacious areas, and islands (see 9.2.5.7).

Lecimy z Polski na Hawaje.
'We are flying from Poland to Hawaii.'

Uczę się z lekcji na lekcję.
'I study from lesson to lesson.' (systematically)

Constructions of the type neck and neck, one-on-one, tit for tat:

łeb w łeb 'neck and neck'
oko w oko 'to be eyeball to eyeball'
sam na sam 'one-on-one'
wet za wet 'tit for tat'
od deski do deski 'from beginning to end' 'read from cover to cover'
wte i wewte 'there and back'

9.7 Translation difficulties

9.7.1 "With"

The preposition z 'together with' seems to be problematic for those learning Polish. It is used in the literal meaning of 'together with,' e.g., żona z mężem 'wife together with husband.' When "with" is used as a medium, like in the title *Ogniem i mieczem* '*With fire and sword*' by Henryk Sienkiewicz, Polish does not use the preposition z.

Walczyli z ogniem kilka dni.
'They fought with the fire for a few days.' (lit. 'with flames')

In English constructions like 'a house with a garden' **dom z ogródkiem,** 'wife with husband' **żona z mężem,** 'dance with me' **zatańcz ze mną** the preposition z is used. However, when in English the meaning is more that a tool is being used to fulfill a task, like 'write with a pen,' then in Polish the preposition z is omitted.

Tańcowała igła z nitką '*Needle dancing with thread*'—a popular children's poem by Brzechwa (two objects dancing together)

Szyła białymi nićmi. 'She was sewing with white threads.' (medium)
skakać nożycami (a way of jumping, a scissor jump)
skakać z nożycami do kogoś 'to jump at somebody with scissors in hands'
leżeć bykiem (coll.) 'to loaf around'
leżeć z bykiem 'to lie down together with a bull'
usprawiedliwić nieobecność bólem głowy 'to excuse one's absence with a headache'
poszła do pracy z bólem głowy 'she went to work with a headache'
najechać kursorem 'move the cursor'
najechać z piskiem opon 'to run with squeal of tires'

(See 2.9)

9.7.2 "For"

1. dla <+GEN> 'for (the benefit of)'

perfumy dla żony 'perfume for [my] wife'
Dla świętego spokoju. 'for the sake of peace and quiet' (idiom)

Codziennie biegam dla zdrowia. 'I jog every day for [my] health.'
korzyści dla firmy 'profits for a firm'

2. za <+ACC> 'for (in exchange/compensation for; to be thankful /apologetic for)'

Dziękuję za pomoc. 'Thank you for your help.'
Dam ci zegarek za telefon. 'I will give you a watch for your phone.'
za nic na świecie 'for nothing in the world' (idiom)
przeprosić za szkody 'to apologize for the damage'
dostać sto złotych za dzień pracy 'to get a hundred zloty for a day of work'
Za jakie grzechy? 'What did I do to deserve this? [lit.] For what sins?' (idiom)

3. na <+ACC> 'for' with specified events, means of transportation, purposes, times

pojemnik na szkło 'a container for glass'
pieniądze na studia 'money for studies'
dom na sprzedaż 'house for sale'
Zapraszam panią na kawę/na lody/na obiad. 'I invite you [formal] for coffee/ice cream/lunch.'
Umówiłam się na piątą. 'We have made arrangements for five o'clock.'
Spieszę się na pociąg. 'I hurry for the train.'
To są pieniądze na urlop. 'This is the money for [our] vacation.'
Odkładam na czarną godzinę. 'I am saving for a rainy day.' (idiom)

4. po <+ACC> 'in order to get,' 'to fetch'

Poszłam po bilety. 'I went to get tickets.'
Idź po chleb. 'Go to get bread.'
Po co wróciłeś? 'What did you come back for?'
Wróciłam po swoje rzeczy 'I came back to get my stuff.'

5. do <+GEN> 'for (sets, for the use of, for things that go together)'

szampon do włosów 'hair shampoo' (lit. 'shampoo for hair')
nóż do sera 'cheese knife' (lit. 'a knife for cheese')
proszek do prania 'washing detergent' (lit. 'detergent for washing')
miejsce do spania/do jedzenia 'a space for sleeping/eating'
pokój do nauki 'a room for studying'
lampa do czytania 'reading lamp' (lit. 'lamp for reading')

6. za <+INS> (in set phrases)

wyjechać za chlebem, za pracą 'to go for bread, money'

9.8 Buffer vowel -e

The buffer **e** (1.3.8.1) eases pronunciation. As a phonological result, e is added in prepositional phrases when a preposition that ends with a consonant precedes a word that starts with another consonant. An extra e is always added when a monosyllabic preposition ends with a consonant before derivatives of the pronoun **ja** 'I': **mną, mnie**.

beze mnie 'without me'	**nade mną** 'above me'
ode mnie 'from me'	**spode mnie** 'from under me'
we mnie 'in me'	**ze mną** 'with me'
pode mną 'under me'	**ze mnie** 'from me'
przede mną 'in front of me'	

Table 9.9 List of prepositions

Preposition (Przyimek)	Case (Przypadek)	Translation (Tłumaczenie)
bez (beze)	GEN	'without'
blisko	GEN	'near'
daleko	GEN	'far'
dla	GEN	'for (the benefit of)'
do	GEN	'to,' 'towards,' 'up to,' 'till,' 'for,' 'at,' 'in'
dokoła	GEN	'(all) around,' 'all about'
dookoła	GEN	'(all) around,' 'all about'
dzięki	DAT	'due to,' 'thanks to,' 'as a result of'
koło	GEN	'around,' 'near,' 'by,' 'approximately'
ku	DAT	'towards'
między	INS	'between,' 'among'
	ACC	'between,' 'among [destination]'
mimo	GEN	'despite,' 'in spite of,' 'past,' 'by'
	ACC	'despite' [only **mimo to** and **mimo wszystko**]
na	LOC	'on,' 'at,' 'in' [open area]
	ACC	'to' [destination], 'for'
na kształt	GEN	'in the shape of'
nad (nade)	INS	'above,' 'over,' 'on top of'
	INS	'at' [e.g., **nad morzem, jeziorem**]
	ACC	'to' [destination], 'for'
naokoło	GEN	'around,' 'all about'
naprzeciw(ko)	GEN	'opposite (from),' 'across (from)'
niedaleko	GEN	'near'
o	LOC	'about,' 'concerning,' 'at' [time]
	ACC	'(up) against,' 'for,' 'about'
obok	GEN	'near(by),' 'beside,' 'alongside'
od (ode)	GEN	'from,' 'since,' 'than'

Table 9.9 (cont'd)

Preposition (Przyimek)	Case (Przypadek)	Translation (Tłumaczenie)
około	GEN	'around,' 'about'
oprócz	GEN	'besides,' 'apart from,' 'except'
po	LOC	'along,' 'according to,' 'after' [time]
	ACC	'(to go) for,'[1] 'after' [destination]
pod (pode)	INS	'under,' 'beneath,' 'below'
	ACC	'up to' [destination], 'up-' (wind, etc.)
podczas	GEN	'during'
podług	GEN	'according to'
pomiędzy	INS	'between,' 'among'
	ACC	'between,' 'among' [destination]
pomimo	GEN	'despite,' 'in spite of,' 'past,' 'by'
	ACC	'despite' [only **pomimo to** and **pomimo wszystko**]
ponad	ACC	'(over and) beyond'
poniżej	GEN	'below,' 'downstream from'
poprzez	ACC	'through,' 'throughout'
pośrodku	GEN	'in the middle of'
pośród	GEN	'among'
powyżej	GEN	'above,' 'upstream from'
poza	INS	'beyond,' 'besides'
	ACC	'beyond' [destination]
prócz	GEN	'besides,' 'apart from,' 'except'
przeciw(ko)	DAT	'against,' 'in opposition to'
przed (przede)	INS	'before,' 'in front of'
	ACC	'in front of' [destination]
przez (przeze)	ACC	'through,' 'across,' 'during,' 'because of'
przy	LOC	'at,' 'near,' 'next to'
spod	GEN	'from near' [town]
spomiędzy	GEN	'from among'
sponad	GEN	'from (over and) beyond'
spośród	GEN	'from among,' 'out of'
spoza	GEN	'from beyond'
sprzed	GEN	'from in front of'
u	GEN	'at,' 'near'
w (we)	LOC	'in,' 'at,' 'inside' [enclosed area]
	ACC	'into,' 'in' [destination]
w ciągu	GEN	'in the course of'
w pobliżu	GEN	'near'
w przeciągu	GEN	'in the course of'
wbrew	DAT	'in spite of,' 'contrary to'
według	GEN	'according to'
wewnątrz	GEN	'inside,' 'within'
wobec	GEN	'in regard to,' 'in view of'
wokoło	GEN	'around'
wokół	GEN	'around'

Table 9.9 (cont'd)

Preposition (Przyimek)	Case (Przypadek)	Translation (Tłumaczenie)
wskutek	GEN	'as the result of,' 'on account of'
wszerz	GEN	'along the width of'
wśród	GEN	'among'
wzdłuż	GEN	'along the length of'
z (ze)	GEN	'from,' 'off,' 'out of' '(made) of'
	INS	'(together) with'
	ACC	'about' [age, value, time, distance]
z powodu	GEN	'because of,' 'due to'
za	INS	'behind,' 'beyond'
	ACC	'for,' 'by,' 'in'
	ACC	'beyond' [destination]
	GEN	'during (the time of),' 'as far back as'
	(ADV.)	'too' [e.g., za dużo, za mała]
za pomocą	GEN	'with the help of'
zamiast	GEN	'instead of'
na zewnątrz	GEN	'outside'
znad	GEN	'from near' [water], 'from above'
zza	GEN	'from behind'

¹ **Po** can mean 'for,' as in **Idę do sklepu po mleko.** 'I am going to the store for milk.'

Chapter 10

Conjunctions

10.1 Overview

A conjunction (**spójnik**) is a part of speech that links together words, phrases, clauses, and sentences.

woda *i* ogień 'water *and* fire'
ani duży, *ani* mały '*neither* big, *nor* small'
Martwię się, *że* sobie nie poradzisz. 'I worry (*that*) you won't be able to handle it.'

Conjunctions are indeclinable.

Conjunctions do not govern the case of the words they combine.

matka *i* ojciec 'mother <NOM> *and* father <NOM>'
dla matki *i* ojca 'for mother <GEN> *and* father <GEN>'

There are two main categories of conjunctions: coordinating (10.2) and subordinating (10.3). Coordinating conjunctions link words and clauses of equal relevance. Subordinating conjunctions introduce a clause that is dependent on a main clause, e.g., "**Muszę do niego lecieć, *bo* zaraz się obudzi.**"[1] 'I have to hurry to him *because* he's about to wake up.'

10.2 Coordinating

Coordinating conjunctions (**spójniki współrzędne** or **koniunktory**) join words, phrases and clauses of equal relevance, e.g., **duży i mały** 'big and small,' **Ja czytam, a on pisze** 'I am reading and he is writing,' **Dziecko jest zdolne, ale leniwe** 'The child is talented but lazy.'

Coordinating conjunctions can be subdivided by function.

1. Connective (łączne) (10.2.1)
2. Contrastive or adversative (przeciwstawne) (10.2.2)
3. Disjunctive (rozłączne) (10.2.3)
4. Consecutive or resultative (wynikowe) (10.2.4)
5. Inclusive or explanatory (włączne, synonimiczne, wyjaśniające) (10.2.5)

Punctuation with conjunctions:

A comma is required before contrastive and resultative conjunctions.

A comma is not required before connective and disjunctive conjunctions, unless the conjunction repeats (i to, i tamto), or is used after interjections or subordinate clauses.

Powiedział, że wychodzi, i wyszedł.
'He said that he was leaving and left.'

10.2.1 Connective

Connective conjunctions (spójniki łączne) are used to link similarities between words, phrases and sentences *that are located at the same time and/or in the same space.*

i 'and'	**ni** 'nor' (bookish)
oraz 'and'	**ni . . . , ni . . .** 'neither . . . nor . . .'
a także 'as well as'	**i . . . , i . . .** 'both . . . and . . .'
jak również 'as well as'	**ani . . . , ani . . .** 'neither . . . nor . . .'
tudzież 'as well (as),' 'also'	(verb is negated)
(bookish)	**a** 'and' (can also mean 'but';
ani '(n)or'	see 10.2.1.10)

10.2.1.1 i 'and'

i links words

brat i siostra 'brother and sister'

Kobieta i życie '*Woman and life*' (a popular magazine for women).

Kupiłam dobry i tani słownik. 'I bought a good and cheap dictionary.'
Dziewczyny i chłopcy idą do kina. 'Girls and boys go to the movies.'

Lubię mówić po polsku i po angielsku. 'I like to speak Polish and English.'

Proszę bilet i legitymację szkolną. 'Ticket and student ID please.'

Położył się i zasnął. 'He lay down and fell asleep.'

Trzasnęła drzwiami i wyszła. 'She slammed the door and left.'

Oglądali telewizję i rozmawiali. 'They were watching TV and talking.'

| 10.2.1.2 | **oraz** 'and,' 'as well as'

Oraz usually links words in the meaning of **i** 'and' and **a także** 'as well as.' It usually replaces **i** 'and' to avoid repetitiveness in a consecutive position. *Oraz* is also used to add a complementary meaning.

Matki i ojcowie oraz dzieci, a także dziadkowie uważnie słuchali wykładu.
'Mothers *and* fathers, *and* children, *as well as* grandparents were listening attentively to the lecture.'

Na spotkanie zaproszono osoby prywatne oraz przedstawicieli firm.
'Individuals were invited to the meeting, *as well as* firms' representatives.'

Wesołych Świąt Bożego Narodzenia oraz Szczęśliwego Nowego Roku
'Merry Christmas and a Happy New Year.'

Zwolennicy oraz przeciwnicy projektu przyszli na spotkanie.
'Supporters *and* opponents came for a meeting.'

Na lekcji rozmawialiśmy o rzeczownikach i przymiotnikach oraz ich odmianie przez przypadki.
'In class we were talking about nouns and adjectives, and their declination.'

Note: Jadacka adds a hierarchy aspect, when using the connective conjunctions: **i, oraz, a także**, and illustrates it in the sentence: "**W sali sejmowej byli już premier i marszałek oraz posłowie opozycji, a także nieliczni postronni obserwatorzy.**" 'In the parliamentary room were already present the Prime Minister and the Speaker of the House, and opposition members of parliament, as well as a few observers from outside.' Jadacka says that replacing either of the conjunctions with a different one will lead to "negative stylistic consequences."[2]

The example below also illustrates the dynamics of connective conjunctions.

(!)Hillary a także Bill Clinton. (!)'Hillary as well as Bill Clinton.'
Hillary i Bill Clinton. 'Hillary and Bill Clinton.'

| 10.2.1.3 | **a także** (or **jak również**) 'as well as,' 'and'

This usually suggests the last component listed and added.[3]

**Rozmawialiśmy o dzieciach, pracy, wakacjach, a także planach
na przyszły rok.** 'We were talking about children, work, vacation,
as well as plans for the next year.'
Kupiłam chleb i masło oraz mleko, a także wędliny. 'I bought
bread and butter and milk, as well as cold cuts.'

| 10.2.1.4 | **ani** 'or'

Nie myślał o nim ani o jego siostrze. 'He did not think about him
or about his sister.'
Nie chcę jeść ani pić. 'I don't want to eat, or drink.'

Ani is often used as a particle.

Nie miał ani grosza. 'He did not have a penny.'

| 10.2.1.5 | **ni** 'nor' (bookish, archaic)

Ni is often used in set phrases, or sayings:

ni diabła nie można zrozumieć '[lit.] even the devil can't
understand; it doesn't make any sense' (coll.)

**Gdy z oczu znikniesz, nie mogę ni razu
W myśli twojego odnowić obrazu** '[lit.] When you
disappear from my eyes, I can't even a single time,
In my thoughts recreate your image'
[**Niepewność** 'Uncertainty', Adam Mickiewicz]

| 10.2.1.6 | **ni . . . , ni . . .** 'neither . . . nor . . .'

This is often used in set phrases, or sayings. A comma is required before
the second **ni**.

ni pies, ni wydra 'neither fish nor fowl'
ni z tego, ni z owego 'suddenly'
ni to, ni owo 'neither this, nor that'

| 10.2.1.7 | **i . . . , i . . .** 'and . . . and . . .', 'both . . . and . . .'

A comma is required before the second i.

Brakuje nam i żywności, i pieniędzy. 'We lack both food and money.'

Pożyczyliśmy i rower, i namiot od znajomych. 'We borrowed both [the] bicycle and [the] tent from friends.'

I chcę rozmawiać tylko serca biciem, 'And I want to talk only with beating hearts'
I westchnieniami, i ucałowaniami 'And with sighs and with kisses'
I tak rozmawiać godziny, dni, lata, 'And to talk for hours, days, years'
Do końca świata i po końcu świata. 'Until the end of the world, and after that.'
[**Rozmowa** '*Conversation*,' Adam Mickiewicz]

| 10.2.1.8 | **ani . . . , ani . . .** 'neither . . . nor . . . ,' 'either . . . or . . .'

The verb is negated, and a comma is required before the second **ani**

Nie byłem ani w Paryżu, ani w Berlinie. 'I haven't been to either Paris or Berlin.'
Ani w bibliotece, ani w księgarni nie mogłam znaleźć tej książki. 'Neither in a library, nor in a bookstore could I find the book.'
W łazience nie było ani ręcznika, ani mydła. 'There was neither a towel nor soap in the bathroom.'

| 10.2.1.9 | **a** 'and'

'**A**' links words, except when it is used in the prepositional phrase **między . . . a . . .** 'between . . . and . . . ,' when no comma is required.

A 'and' is used as a contrastive conjunction: **Ja pracuję, a on studiuje.** 'I work, *and* he studies.'

Autobus kursuje między Warszawą a Krakowem.
'The bus runs between Warsaw *and* Cracow.'

Na koncercie wystąpił młody a rezolutny pianista Adam Wnęka.
'Adam Wnęka, a young *and* clever pianist, performed at the concert.'

A 'and' is also used to introduce follow-up statements or questions, e.g., **Mam na imię Alicja. A ty?** 'My name is Alice. And you?'

| 10.2.1.10 | *When do I use* **i** *and when* **a***?*

Both can be translated in English as 'and.'

i 'and' indicates similar things, ideas, types, shapes, etc.

Brzoza i kasztan to drzewa liściaste.
'The birch and the chestnut are broadleaved trees.'

Adam i Ewa mieszkają piętro wyżej.
'Adam and Eva live one floor above.'

a 'and, but' indicates a contrast, shows differences between things, ideas, types, shapes, etc. It rarely links words, e.g., **Autobus kursuje między Warszawą a Krakowem.** 'The bus runs between Warsaw *and* Cracow.'

a is used to contrast or introduce new information, e.g.,

Kasztan to drzewo liściaste, a świerk to drzewo iglaste.
'The chestnut is a broadleaved tree, and the spruce is a coniferous tree.'

Matka jest Polką i córka też jest Polką.
'The mother is a Pole *and* [her] daughter is a Pole too.'

Matka jest Polką, a córka jest Amerykanką.
'The mother is a Pole, *and* [her] daughter is an American.'

Matka jest Polką, (a) nie Amerykanką.
'The mother is a Pole, *(and) not* an American.'

Rodzice i dzieci chcą odpocząć tydzień nad morzem, a potem chcą pojechać w góry.
'The parents *and* children want to rest for a week by the sea, *and* then they want to go to the mountains.'

587

Żona chciałaby pojechać na Florydę, a mąż wolałby spędzić urlop na Alasce.
'The wife would like to go to Florida, *and* [her] husband would prefer to spend the vacation in Alaska.

In English "and" is used to join words and phrases, like in the phrase 'Parents *and* children . . . ,' but it is also used to contrast, for example different plans: '(they) . . . want to rest for a week by the sea, *and* then they want to go to the mountains.' In Polish, to show differences, as well as to emphasize a contrast between two words, phrases or sentences, the conjunction **a** is used. In such cases **a** could also be translated as 'but.'

W tym roku jedziemy na Wielkanoc do rodziców męża, a za rok do moich rodziców.
'This year we are going to my husband's parents for Easter, and next year to my parents.'

10.2.1.11 *More examples of connective conjunctions*

Lubię tańczyć i głośno śpiewać na koncertach. 'I like to dance and sing loud at concerts.'
Nie chcę jeść ani pić. 'I don't want to eat, or drink.'

Firma oferuje dzieciom zniżki na nocleg oraz śniadanie gratis.
'The company offers a lodging discount for children and a free breakfast.'

10.2.1.12 *Commas in sentences with connective conjunctions*

1. When more than one of the same conjunction occurs in a row, a comma is put before each additional conjunction, e.g.:

Kupiłam masło i ser, i chleb, i wędliny.
'I bought butter and cheese and bread and cold cuts.'

In order to avoid repetition of the conjunction **i** 'and,' it is preferred to replace the second **i** with the connective conjunction **oraz** 'and,' and replace the third **i** with the conjunction **a także** or **jak również** 'as well as.' A comma appears in front of **a także** or **jak również**, but not in front of **oraz**. Stylistically, it is better not to change the order of the conjunctions.

Kupiłam masło i ser oraz chleb, a także wędliny.
Wesołych Świąt Bożego Narodzenia i szczęśliwego Nowego Roku oraz wszelkiej pomyślności życzy Alicja.
'Merry Christmas and a Happy New Year, as well as best of luck from Alice.'

2. A comma is put before the conjunction **a** 'and' when it occurs as a connector, and combines clauses (not parts) which can function without each other, e.g.:

Przed sklepem stał samochód, a w nim płakało dziecko.
'A car was standing in front of the store, and a baby was crying inside' (clauses)
między ziemią a niebem 'between the earth and the sky' (parts)

The word **niebem** cannot function by itself, it needs more information from the first clause. No comma is required.

3. A comma is required when the conjunction **i** occurs as a consecutive conjunction (= **więc, toteż**) meaning 'so,' and not as a connective one:

Pracowałaś <FEM> **cały dzień, i dlatego jesteś bardzo zmęczona.**
'You have been working the whole day, and therefore you are very tired.'

but note:

Poszedł do sklepu i kupił masło i chleb.
'He went to the store and bought butter and bread.'

Even though the conjunction **i** is repeated, a comma is not required, because in the first part of the sentence **i** connects two verbs (**poszedł i kupił**), and in the second part two nouns (**masło i chleb**).

10.2.2	*Contrastive or adversative*

Contrastive conjunctions (**spójniki przeciwstawne**) are used to point to differences between words, phrases and ideas, and to mark a contrast between them. A comma is required before each contrastive conjunction.

a 'and,' 'but'
aczkolwiek (= **chociaż, jednak**) 'although'
ale 'but'
aliści 'yet,' 'but' (archaic, bookish)
atoli 'howbeit' (archaic, bookish)
choć (= **chociaż**) 'although'

589

chociaż 'although'

inaczej 'otherwise,' 'or (else)'

jednak 'but,' 'yet,' 'although,' 'though,' 'however'

jednakże (= **jednak**)

lecz 'but'

mimo iż 'even though,' 'in spite of,' 'despite'

mimo że 'even though,' 'in spite of,' 'despite'

natomiast (= **podczas gdy**) 'while,' 'whereas,' (= **zaś**)

owszem 'on the contrary'

raczej 'but,' 'yet,' 'though,' 'however'

tylko 'but,' 'only'

tylko że 'but,' 'however'

tymczasem 'meanwhile' (= **jednak, natomiast**)

wszakże (bookish) 'however'

wszelako (bookish) 'however'

za to 'but,' 'yet'

zaś 'while,' 'whereas' (= **natomiast**) [never occurs in the initial
position]

a 'and,' 'but' [contrasting]

Matka jest lekarką, a ojciec jest prawnikiem. 'Mother is
a doctor, and father is a lawyer.'

**Robert studiuje stosunki międzynarodowe, a Agnieszka
medycynę.**

'Robert studies international relations, and Agnieszka medicine.'

**Po południu pójdę na basen, a wieczorem zadzwonię do
rodziców.**

'In the afternoon I will go to the swimming pool, and in the evening
I will call my parents.'

Jestem lekarzem, a nie weterynarzem. or **Nie jestem
lekarzem, lecz (ale) weterynarzem.**

'I am a doctor, and not a veterinarian.' or 'I am not a doctor,
but a veterinarian.'

(Nie jestem lekarzem, a weterynarzem. In the sentence where the first part
has a negated verb, it is stylistically better to replace the conjunction a
with ale or lecz, both meaning 'but.')

Matka jest niska, a ojciec wysoki. 'Mother is short, and father
is tall.'

Najważniejsza jest zabawa, a nie praca. 'The most important
thing is fun, and not work.'

Nie oddał pracy na czas, a zaliczył semestr. 'He did not hand in
the paper on time, but he passed the semester.'

Nie miał dużych szans, a wygrał. 'He did not have a big chance,
but he won.'

aczkolwiek 'although' (= **chociaż, jednak**)

Ta sztuka była dziwna aczkolwiek ciekawa, prawda?
'The play was strange but interesting, don't you think?'

ale 'but' (= **lecz**)

Teściowa czuje się dobrze, ale teść narzeka na zdrowie.
'Mother-in-law is well, but father-in-law complains about his health.'

Nie chcę, ale dla ciebie to zrobię. 'I don't want to,
but for you I'll do it.'

Rozumiem cię, ale się z tobą nie zgadzam. 'I understand you,
but I do not agree with you.'

Słuchałam wykładu, ale nic nie rozumiałam. 'I was listening to
the lecture, but I understood nothing.'

**Dziadek dużo wiedział o wojnie, ale nigdy o niej nie
opowiadał.** 'Grandfather knew a lot about the war,
but he never talked about it.'

choć = **chociaż** 'although'

choćby choćbym/choćbyś/choćby etc. 'although': choć plus conditional
endings of the verb

Nie zrobię tego, choćbyś mnie prosił na kolanach. 'I will not do
it, although [even if] you ask me on your knees.'

inaczej 'otherwise,' 'or (else)'

Wyślij ten list, inaczej będziesz miał problem. 'Send the letter
otherwise you will have a problem.'

jednak 'but,' 'yet,' 'although,' 'though,' 'however'

Lubię kino, jednak wolę teatr. 'I like movies, but I prefer the
theater.'

Kupił pierścionek zaręczynowy, jednak się nie oświadczył.
He bought an engagement ring, but he did not propose.

Muszę lecieć, ty jednak zostań. 'I must be going (lit. flying),
but you stay.'

Musimy jednak z nimi porozmawiać. 'We need, however,
to talk to them.'

mimo iż 'even though,' 'in spite of,' 'despite'

Jutro, mimo iż mam wolne, pójdę do pracy. 'Tomorrow, even though I have a day off, I will go to work.'

mimo że 'even though,' 'in spite of,' 'despite'

Mimo że miał samochód, jeździł do pracy rowerem.
'Even though he had a car, he was riding a bike to work.'

natomiast 'while,' 'whereas'

Studenci wolą zajęcia po południu, natomiast profesorowie wolą zajęcia wcześnie rano. 'Students prefer classes in the afternoon, whereas professors prefer classes early in the morning.'

owszem 'on the contrary'

Owszem is mostly used as a particle meaning 'certainly,' 'indeed': Ładna pogoda, prawda? Owszem. 'Pretty weather, isn't it?' 'Indeed.'

Nie jesteś idealny, owszem zrobiłeś wiele złego w swoim życiu.
'You are not perfect; on the contrary, you did a lot of evil in your life.'

raczej 'but,' 'yet,' 'though,' 'however'

Ja pojadę, ty raczej zostań. 'I will go, you stay though.'

tylko 'but,' 'only'

This is also used as a particle to emphasize only one object, subject, idea, etc., Proszę tylko wodę. 'Only water, please.'

Dziewczynka nic nie powiedziała, tylko zaczęła płakać.
'The little girl did not say anything, but started to cry.'

Nie jestem zła, tylko głodna. 'I am not angry, but hungry.'

Nie śpię, tylko mam zamknięte oczy. 'I am not sleeping, only my eyes are closed.'

Mogę przyjść każdego dnia, tylko nie w piątek. 'I can come every day but Friday.'

Nie jestem twoją przyjaciółką, tylko matką. 'I am not your friend, but (your) mother.'

tylko że 'but,' 'however'

Przeczytałeś artykuł? 'Have you read the article?'

Tak, tylko że nic nie zrozumiałem. 'Yes, however I understood nothing.'

tymczasem 'meanwhile,' often translates as 'but/however'

Miało być zabawnie, tymczasem było strasznie nudno. 'It was supposed to be funny but it was terribly boring.'

Mieliśmy być w Warszawie wcześnie rano, tymczasem wylądowaliśmy na Okęciu dopiero w południe. 'We were to be in Warsaw early in the morning, but we landed only at noon.'

za to 'but,' 'yet'

Mój samochód jest mały, za to bardzo wydajny i oszczędny. 'My car is small, but (yet) efficient and very economical.'

zaś 'while,' 'whereas'

Syn wybrał francuski, zaś córka rosyjski. '[My] son chose French, whereas [my] daughter [chose] Russian.'

| 10.2.2.1 | *What's the difference between* **i, a, ale** *and* **lecz**?

i 'and'	**ale** 'but'
a 'and/but'	**lecz** 'but'

All of these conjunctions except for **i** are translated into English as 'but.'

A and **ale** are mostly used in the spoken language, whereas **lecz** is used in written Polish. **Lecz** used in spoken expressions can be seen as pretentious.

Sometimes both conjunctions (**a** and **ale**) work:

Babcia była Czeszką, a (ale) dziadek Niemcem.
'Grandmother was Czech, and (but) grandfather was German.'

In general **ale** is stronger, and better emphasizes contrast:

Słuchałam wykładu, ale nic nie rozumiałam.
'I was listening to the lecture, but I understood nothing.'

"**Nie chcę, ale muszę**" "I don't want to, but I have to"—a popular saying of Lech Wałęsa, the former president of Poland.

When the first clause is negated, it is better to use **ale** or **lecz** than **a**.

Nie dzieci powinny rządzić światem, ale (lecz) dorośli.
'Children should not rule the world but adults.'

Nie proszę o sprawiedliwość, ale jej żądam.
'I do not ask for justice, but I demand it.'

Jestem lekarzem, a nie weterynarzem.
'I am a doctor, and not a veterinarian.'

Nie jestem lekarzem, ale weterynarzem.
'I am not a doctor, but a veterinarian.'

Nie jestem lekarzem, tylko weterynarzem.

A 'but' can be used as an exception, when the negated first part of the sentence permits the second, even though logically it should not.

Nie oddał pracy na czas, a zaliczył semestr.
'He did not hand in the paper on time, but he passed the semester.'

Nie miał dużych szans, a wygrał.
'He did not have a big chance, but he won.'

| 10.2.2.2 | When do I use **bo, ponieważ, dlatego, dlatego że,** or **gdyż?**

Bo, ponieważ, gdyż, and **dlatego że** are possible equivalents of 'as,' 'because,' 'since,' 'for,' and are subordinating conjunctions. **Dlatego** is a coordinating conjunction translated into English as 'therefore,' 'so,' 'that is why.' Its synonym is **więc** 'therefore,' 'so.'

Bo is mostly used in spoken expressions and SMS, whereas **ponieważ** is mostly used in written standard Polish, and is rarely used in dialects.

Wyszłam, bo byłam głodna. 'I left cos I was hungry.'

Ponieważ is a Czech borrowing,[4] very popular in Polish. It is used much more often than **dlatego że.**[5] Even though short enough to be used in spoken language, **gdyż** is more bookish, and replacing **bo** with **gdyż** in oral expressions might sound pretentious.

Ponieważ, dlatego że, bo answer the question **dlaczego?** 'why?', however **bo** should not begin the sentence, unless it is colloquial.

Dlaczego zjadłaś moją kanapkę? 'Why did you eat my sandwich?'
Bo byłam głodna. 'Because I was hungry.' (coll.)
Ponieważ byłam głodna. 'Because I was hungry.'
Zjadłam, bo byłam głodna. 'I ate, because I was hungry.'
Zjadłam, dlatego że byłam głodna. 'I ate, because I was hungry.'

All of these conjunctions are subordinating conjunctions, whereas **dlatego** 'therefore,' 'so' is a coordinating conjunction that links two equally important sentences, where one can exist without the other.

Byłam głodna, dlatego zjadłam kanapkę.
'I was hungry, therefore I ate a sandwich.'

Ponieważ, dlatego że, bo, gdyż are used when the result is first: **Zjadłam kanapkę** 'I ate a sandwich,' then there is the cause: **byłam głodna** 'I was hungry.' When we use **dlatego**, the order is the opposite: first the cause: **Byłam głodna**, and then the result: **zjadłam kanapkę**. To combine the two clauses we use a consecutive coordinating conjunction: **dlatego**, or its synonym **więc**.

> **Byłam głodna** [cause], **dlatego zjadłam kanapkę** [result].
> 'I was hungry, therefore I ate the sandwich.'

> **Byłam głodna** [result], **ponieważ/dlatego że nie zjadłam śniadania** [cause].
> 'I was hungry, because I had not had breakfast.'

> **Byłam głodna, więc zjadłam kanapkę.**
> 'I was hungry, so I ate the sandwich.'

> **Zjadłam kanapkę** [result], **ponieważ byłam głodna** [cause].
> 'I ate the sandwich because I was hungry.'

A comma should be used in front of all of the conjunctions: ponieważ, dlatego że, bo, gdyż, dlatego and więc.

The conjunction **zaś** 'while,' 'whereas' is used in oral expressions, and **natomiast** 'while,' 'whereas' is preferred in written Polish.

> **Córka jest blondynką, zaś syn ma ciemne włosy i oczy.**
> '[My] daughter is blonder, whereas [my] son has dark hair and [dark] eyes.'

> **Kasztan jest drzewem liściastym, natomiast świerk iglastym.**
> 'The chestnut is a leafy tree, whereas the spruce is a coniferous tree.'

10.2.3 Disjunctive

Disjunctive conjunctions (**spójniki rozłączne**) suggest either exchangeability or exclusiveness. All of the disjunctive conjunctions can be repeated: albo . . . albo . . . , czy . . . , czy . . . , bądź . . . bądź . . . except for **lub**. A comma is required when the conjunction is repeated more than once. Pairs of conjunctions should not be mixed, e.g. (!) Czy chcesz iść do kina, albo do teatru?

> **Czy chcesz iść do kina, czy do teatru?** 'Do you want to go to the movies or to the theater?'
> **albo** 'or'
> **albo . . . albo . . .** 'either . . . or . . .'
> **bądź** 'or'

bądź . . . bądź . . . 'either . . . or . . .'
czy 'or'
czy . . . czy . . . 'either . . . or . . .'
lub 'or' (bookish) does not start a sentence

Spotkamy się jutro albo pojutrze. 'We will meet tomorrow or
the day after tomorrow.'
W niedziele jem obiad u rodziców albo u siostry. 'On Sundays
I eat lunch at [my] parents' or at [my] sister's.'
Mam zostać czy wyjść? 'Should I stay or leave?'
Wieczorem poczytam albo upiekę ciasto. 'In the evening I will
read a little or I will bake a cake.'
Zadzwoń jutro albo pojutrze. 'Call tomorrow or the day after
tomorrow.'
Zadzwoń jutro czy pojutrze. 'Call tomorrow or the day after
tomorrow.'
Zadzwonisz jutro, czy pojutrze? 'Will you call tomorrow or the
day after tomorrow?' (coll.)
Czy zadzwonisz jutro, czy pojutrze? 'Will you (lit. whether you will)
call tomorrow or the day after tomorrow?'
Zadzwonię albo jutro, albo pojutrze. 'I'll call tomorrow or the
day after tomorrow.'
Czujesz się lepiej czy gorzej? 'Are you feeling better or worse?' (coll.)
Czy czujesz się lepiej czy gorzej? 'Are you (lit. whether you are)
feeling better or worse?'
Wcześniej czy później rodzice dowiedzą się o wszystkim.
'Sooner or later [my] parents will find out about everything.'
Żartujesz, czy mówisz prawdę? 'Are you joking or are you telling
the truth?'
Jesteś chora, czy udajesz? 'Are you sick, or are you pretending?'

10.2.4 Consecutive or resultative

Consecutive or resultative coordinating conjunctions (**spójniki wynikowe**)
link the clauses in the way that one results from the other. They emphasize
the cause-result connection.

dlatego 'thus'
i (= więc, toteż) 'so'
przeto 'hence' (bookish)
skutkiem tego 'thereby'

tedy 'so,' 'wherefore' (archaic)
to 'then'
toteż (bookish) 'that is why,' 'hence'
więc 'therefore,' 'so' [occurs in the middle of sentences, not at the beginning]
zatem 'therefore,' 'so'

Note: With i (= więc, toteż), we can put a comma before i when it means więc, toteż 'therefore, so':

Zapomniałam skasować bilet, i musiałam zapłacić karę.
'I forgot to validate the ticket, and I had to pay a fine.'
Zapomniałam skasować bilet, więc musiałam zapłacić karę.
'I forgot to validate the ticket, so I had to pay a fine.'
Zapomniałam skasować bilet, toteż musiałam zapłacić karę.
'I forgot to validate the ticket, that is why I had to pay a fine.'

Zapomniał parasol, dlatego zmókł. 'I forgot my umbrella so I got wet.'

Nie ubezpieczyliśmy mieszkania, skutkiem tego nie otrzymamy odszkodowania. 'We have not insured the house, therefore we will not receive compensation.'

Nie chcesz, to nie mów. 'If you don't want it, then don't say it.'
Nie chciałeś zabrać głosu wcześniej, to teraz nie przeszkadzaj. 'You did not want to take the floor earlier, so do not interrupt now.'

Byłam głodna, więc poszłam do stołówki na obiad. 'I was hungry, so I went to the cafeteria for lunch.'
Jego zachowanie było obcesowe, dlatego wyszliśmy z sali.
'His behavior was unceremonious, so we left.'

Kupiłeś bilety, zatem chodźmy do filharmonii. 'You have bought the tickets, therefore let's go to the philharmonic.'

| 10.2.5 | *Inclusive or explanatory*

Explanatory conjunctions, (spójniki włączne, synonimiczne, wyjaśniające) link two words with the same meaning in an explanatory way.

czyli 'that is'
to jest 'that is'
to znaczy 'that is'

inaczej (= innymi słowy) 'or,' 'also known as'
innymi słowy 'in other words'

Jego dziadek był stomatologiem, inaczej dentystą. 'His grandfather was a stomatologist, also known as a dentist.'

Spotkajmy się jutro, to jest we wtorek. 'Let's meet tomorrow, that is on Tuesday.'

Zniknąłeś na tydzień, nikogo nie powiadomiłeś o swoich planach—innymi słowy, jesteś nieodpowiedzialny. 'You disappeared for a week, and did not let anyone know about your plans—in other words, you are not responsible.'

Zgasło światło, to znaczy wszyscy poszli spać. 'The light went off so everybody went to sleep.'

Nie oddałeś pracy na czas, czyli nie zaliczyłeś przedmiotu. [so, więc] 'You did not turn the paper in on time, which means that you failed the subject.'

10.3 Subordinating

Subordinating conjunctions (**spójniki podrzędne**) link a subordinate clause (dependent clause, that cannot stand alone as a sentence because it does not give a complete thought) with the main clause, e.g.:

Kiedy **byłam mała** [subordinate clause], **nie lubiłam jeść szpinaku** [main clause].
'*When* I was little [subordinate clause], I did not like to eat spinach [main clause].'

Jeżeli **nie oddasz książek w terminie** [subordinate clause], **zapłacisz karę** [main clause].
'*If* you do not return the books on time [subordinate clause], you will pay a fine [main clause].'

Gdybyś **oddał książki w terminie** [subordinate clause], **nie zapłaciłbyś kary** [main clause].
'*If* you had returned the books on time [subordinate clause], you would not have paid a fine [main clause].'

Chociaż **byłam chora** [subordinate clause], **poszłam na zajęcia** [main clause].
'*Although* I was sick [subordinate clause], I went to classes [main clause].'

Ponieważ **przeprosiłeś** [subordinate clause], **postanowiłem dać ci jeszcze jedną szansę** [main clause].
Because you have apologized [subordinate clause], I have decided to give you one more chance [main clause].'

Tak się spieszyłam, że zapomniałam torebki.
'I was so much in a hurry *that* I forgot [my] purse.'
Wiem [main clause], **że nie powinienem palić** [subordinate clause].
'I know *that* I should not smoke.'

The most common Polish subordinating conjunctions:

albowiem 'because' (bookish)
aby 'in order to'
aż 'until'
bo 'because'
bowiem 'because' (bookish)
choć 'although,' 'even though,' 'though'
choćby on/ona/to/oni/ one 'even if he/she/it/ they'
choćbym 'even if I'
choćbyś 'even if you' <SG, Informal>
choćbyście 'even if you' <PL>
choćbyśmy 'even if we'
chociaż 'although,' 'even though,' 'though'
czy 'whether'
dlatego że 'because'
dopóki nie 'until' <+PFV verb>
gdy 'when'
gdy . . . to . . . 'when . . . then . . .' (coll.)
gdyby 'if'
gdyż 'because'
im . . . tym . . . 'the [more] the [better]'
iż 'that' (bookish)
iżby 'that' (bookish)
jak 'as,' 'like'
jak 'if'
jak 'when,' 'since,' 'while'
jak gdyby 'as though'
jak tylko 'as soon as'
jakby 'as though'
jednak 'however'
jeśli 'if'
jeśli tylko 'if only'

jeśli ... to ... 'if ... then ...'
jeśliby 'if'
jeżeli 'if'
jeżeliby 'if'
kiedy 'when'
kiedy ... to ... 'when ... then ...'
mimo że 'although,' 'even though,' 'though'
nim 'before'
niż 'than'
o ile? 'as far as'
pod warunkiem, że 'provided'
pomimo że 'although,' 'even though,' 'though'
ponieważ 'because'
tak długo jak 'as long as'
zanim 'before'
że 'that'
żeby 'in order to,' 'in order that'

10.3.1 | Resultative conjunctions

These conjunctions answer the question 'why?' They highlight causes and results:

dlatego 'that's why'	**ponieważ** 'because'
bo 'because' (coll.)	**bowiem** 'because' (bookish)
dlatego że 'because'	**albowiem** 'because' (bookish)
gdyż 'because'	

Podróżuję, *ponieważ/bo/dlatego że/gdyż* **chcę zwiedzić każde państwo na świecie.** 'I travel, *because* I want to visit every country in the world.'

Chcę zwiedzić każde państwo na świecie, *dlatego* **podróżuję.** 'I want to visit every country in the world, *that's why* I travel.'

10.3.2 | Conditional conjunctions

These answer the question 'in what circumstances?' 'Under what condition?'

jeżeli 'if'
jeśli 'if'

jak 'if'
gdyby 'if'
jeśliby 'if'
jeżeliby 'if'
o ile? 'as far as'
tak długo jak 'as long as'
pod warunkiem, że 'provided'
jeśli tylko 'if only'
jeśli . . . to . . . 'if . . . then . . .'
kiedy . . . to . . . 'when . . . then . . .'
gdy . . . to . . . 'when . . . then . . .' (coll.)

Jeżeli dostanę podwyżkę, pojedziemy na Jamajkę. 'If I get a rise, we will go to Jamaica.'
Gdybym dostał podwyżkę, pojechalibyśmy na Jamajkę. 'If I had got a rise, we would have gone to Jamaica.' (about the past)
Gdybym dostał podwyżkę, pojechalibyśmy na Jamajkę. 'If I get a rise, we might go to Jamaica.' (hypothetical)

10.3.3 Concessional conjunctions

These give consent to do something despite the disadvantage of the action:

choć 'although/even though/though'
chociaż 'although/even though/though'
mimo że 'although/even though/though'
pomimo że 'although/even though/though'
jednak 'however'
choćbym 'even if I'
choćbyś 'even if you' <SG, informal>
choćby on/ona/to/oni/ one 'even if he/she/it/ they'
choćbyśmy 'even if we'
choćbyście 'even if you' <PL>

Chociaż było zimno, poszliśmy na spacer do parku. '*Although* it was cold, we went for a walk to the park.'
Choćbyś błagał, nie kupię ci tej gry. '*Even if you* were begging me, I would not buy you the game.'
Spóźnił się na spotkanie, jednak wcześniej zdążył zadzwonić i uprzedzić o spóźnieniu. 'He was late for the meeting, however he called earlier and informed about [his] delay.'

10.3.4 Temporal conjunctions

These answer the question 'when?' They sequence or specify events in time:

kiedy 'when'
gdy 'when' <informal>
jak 'when' <informal> 'since,' 'while'
od kiedy 'since when'
zanim 'before' <+PFV verb>
nim 'before' <informal>
jak tylko 'as soon as'
aż 'until'
dopóki nie 'until'

Dwa lata minęły, jak/od kiedy przestałem palić. 'It has been two years since I stopped smoking.'
Kiedy/Gdy/Jak miałem dwadzieścia lat, służyłem w wojsku. 'When I was twenty years old, I served in the army.'
Zanim wyjdziesz, wyłącz komputer. 'Before you leave, turn off the computer.'
Nim wrócisz, będę gotowa. 'Before you are back, I will be ready.'
Będę pisał, aż skończę. 'I will be writing until I have finished.'
Będę pisał, dopóki nie skończę. 'I will be writing until I have finished.'
Jak tylko przestałem palić, zacząłem tyć. 'As soon as I stopped smoking, I started to gain weight.'

10.3.5 Comparative conjunctions

im ... tym ... 'the [more] ... the [better]'
niż 'than'
jak 'as,' 'like'
jak gdyby 'as if'
jakby 'as though'

Jej mąż wygląda jakby był bardzo chory. 'Her husband looks as though he was very sick.'
Im więcej czytam, tym więcej mam wątpliwości. 'The more I read, the more doubts I have.'
Wolałem z nią tańczyć, niż z nimi rozmawiać. 'I preferred to dance with her, than to talk to them.'
Malujesz jak prawdziwy artysta. 'You paint like a real artist.'

Chapter 11

Interjections

Interjections are remarks or comments interjected by the speaker to show his or her emotions or to influence the listener. They can also create statements.

cóż 'oh well' (indifference)
hm (hesitation)
szkoda 'pity' (regret)
Fuj, **niedobre!** *Ugh,* not good! (disgust)
oj, **boli** *'ouch,* it hurts!' (pain)
brr, **jak zimno!** *brr*! 'it's cold!'
Ach! **Daj spokój! Nie przejmuj się!** 'Oh, chill out! Don't worry.'
Aha! **Teraz rozumiem.** *'Oh*! Now I get it.' (a clarification)

Interjections are used to replace a description of the full action.

Szliśmy ulicą i nagle *bum*! **Eksplodował samochód.** 'We were walking on the street and suddenly *boom*! 'The car exploded.'
Byliśmy w lesie i nagle *trach*! **Drzewo się złamało.** 'We were in the forest and suddenly *crack*! The tree fell down.'
Idę ulicą i nagle *łup*! **Ktoś mnie uderzył i straciłem przytomność.** 'I'm walking on the street and suddenly *wham*! I got hit and lost consciousness.'
no to *siup* 'bottoms up'
I nagle sterta talerzy *łubu-du* **na podłogę!** 'And suddenly a pile of plates *bang* on the floor!'
Aha, **miałam zadzwonić.** 'Oh [and] I was supposed to call.' (a reminder)
hopla! jump!
ha ha **bardzo śmieszne** *'ha ha* very funny'
no 'yes' (coll.)

no no no, **nie tak szybko** 'hello, not so fast' [omit commas in order
   not to slow the speed of pronouncing such phrases]

no, **rusz się!** *'come on,* move!'

Och! **Jak tu pięknie!** 'Wow! How beautiful it is in here!'

Ojejku, **co z tobą!** Oh, what's with you?

puk, puk 'knock, knock'

Uwaga! 'Attention!'

wara 'hands off'

wara **ode mnie** *'hands off* of me'

y (filler) **Kiedy tam byłem? yyyy nie pamiętam.**
   'When was I there? *aaaa* I don't remember.'

Chapter 12

Gender issues of address

12.1 Overview

In recent years, as women are increasingly achieving equal status in the political, economic and social arenas in Poland, the need is being recognized for female equivalents of male-gendered professions.

From a linguistic point of view, the Polish language itself is prepared to create feminine forms from almost all masculine nouns denoting titles and professions.

Patterns that already exist include the suffixes which follow.

12.2 Suffixes

-ka

	Masculine	Feminine
'actor'	aktor	aktor*ka*
'partner'	partner	partner*ka*
'teacher'	nauczyciel	nauczyciel*ka*
'friend'	przyjaciel	przyjació*łka*
'journalist'	dziennikarz	dziennikar*ka*
'cook'	kucharz	kuchar*ka*
'artist'	malarz	malar*ka*
'writer'	pisarz	pisar*ka*
'soccer player'	piłkarz	piłkar*ka*
'activist'	działacz	działacz*ka*
'auditor'	słuchacz	słuchacz*ka*
'researcher'	badacz	badacz*ka*

'smoker'	palacz	palacz*ka*
'debtor'	dłużnik	dłużnicz*ka*
'spokesperson'	rzecznik	rzecznicz*ka*
'manager'	kierownik	kierownicz*ka*
'guard'	strażnik	strażnicz*ka*
'Norwegian'	Norweg	Norweż*ka*

-ca

	Masculine	Feminine
'worker'	pracownik	pracowni*ca*
'physical worker'	robotnik	robotni*ca*
'martyr'	męczennik	męczenni*ca*

-ini/-yni

	Masculine	Feminine
'member'	członek	członk*ini*
'host'	gospodarz	gospody*ni*
'teacher'	wychowawca	wychowawczy*ni*
'winner'	zwycięzca	zwyciężczy*ni*
'adviser'	doradca	doradczy*ni*

-owa

	Masculine	Feminine
'tailor'	krawiec	krawc*owa*
'king/queen'	król	król*owa*

This means that the Polish language can accommodate the names of professions in which women have only recently become recognized.

	Masculine	Feminine
'taxi driver'	szofer	szoferka
'movie director'	reżyser	reżyserka
'soldier'	żołnierz	żołnierka
'mountain climber'	wspinacz	wspinaczka
'psychologist'	psycholog	psycholożka

12.3 Creating feminine forms

There are two limitations that arise with the creation of new feminine forms from traditional male forms:

1. There are limitations within the suffixes -ka, -ini, -yni, -owa, -ca when forming a female title or profession.
2. There are limitations within social preference.

On the one hand, there are more and more women who speak up about their need to be able to create a term that describes their profession without assigning them a male gender, and therefore, we can observe a strong tendency in the Polish language to modify masculine forms to provide feminine ones for professions. On the other hand, the means available within the language to create feminine titles and professions sometimes have limiting parameters, as discussed below.

-ka

1. The suffix -ka happens to be largely used to create feminine diminutive forms, which are construed as smaller and emotionally charged, such as: **kobietka** 'little woman,' **dziewczynka** 'little girl,' **zupka** diminutive of 'soup.' The forms with the suffix -ka can also be construed as belittling with a negative tinge, e.g., **kobietka** 'little woman,' and therefore female professions formed by adding the -ka suffix to existing male professions may not be perceived to be on an equal footing with the masculine form, e.g., **profesor/profesorka** 'professor,' **prezes/prezeska** 'president.'
2. Sometimes limitations can occur due to resulting difficulties of pronunciation, e.g., **adiunkt/adiunktka(!)** 'lecturer.'
3. Some feminine forms which could be created with the -ka suffix from masculine terms for professions already have a different established meaning.

szofer 'taxi driver'	**szoferka** 'driver's cab'
reżyser 'director'	**reżyserka** 'control room'
żołnierz 'soldier'	**żołnierka** 'soldiering'
wspinacz 'mountain climber'	**wspinaczka** 'climbing'
cukiernik 'pastry cook'	**cukierniczka** 'small sugar bowl'
sekretarz 'secretary'	**sekretarka** 'personal assistant' and 'answering machine'
dziekan 'dean'	**dziekanka** 'student's leave'

-owa

Currently military ranks and occupations are used only with male forms: **sierżant** 'sergeant,' **pułkownik** 'colonel,' **kapitan** 'captain,' **generał** 'general.' Forms such as **kapitan*owa***, **pułkownik*owa***, **generał*owa***, although feminine, only refer to the wife of the **kapitan**, **pułkownik**, **generał**, and not to a woman who bears such a rank.

The forms with **-owa** may also refer to a wife of other professions, such as a doctor, director, or president, **doktorowa, dyrektorowa,** or **prezesowa,** respectively.

Additionally, the **-owa** suffix resembles the Russian form for creating patronymic names (a second name based on the father's name).

Since the form **-owa** would bring some confusion as it also denotes "a wife of," that suffix is not used to denote a female title or profession.

Today, it is more common to refer to the wife in a descriptive form: **Pani Iksińska, żona prezesa Iksińskiego.** 'Mrs. X, the wife of President X.'

-ca

The **-ca** suffix is often used to create emotive nouns referring to a female, such as:

> **awanturnica** 'argumentative woman'
> **złośnica** 'a complaining, disagreeable woman'
> **diablica** 'she-devil'

When adding the **-ca** suffix to some male professions, the new word already has an existing meaning in Polish.

cukiernik 'pastry cook'	**cukiernica** 'sugar bowl'
kierowca 'driver'	**kierownica** 'steering wheel'

The suffixes **-ini** and **-yni** are less productive in creating new female titles and professions.

12.4 Social preference

'Secretary of State' **Sekretarz Stanu** vs. **Sekretarka Stanu**(!)

A female form of **sekretarz stanu** 'secretary of state' such as **sekretarka stanu** is not used. The male forms are used in **Sekretarz Stanu Hillary Clinton, Sekretarz Stanu Madeleine Albright.** While the feminine form **sekretarka** exists, it is not used, as **sekretarka** is conceived of as limited to an administrative position of 'secretary.' Also, **sekretarka** in Polish means 'an answering machine,' as in the common phrase: **nagrałam się na twoją sekretarkę** 'I left a message on your answering machine.'

As another example of social preference, on occasion a woman in Poland will prefer to use the male form of her husband's family name, such as with names that are descriptive adjectives, **Zielony** 'Green,' **Śmiały** 'Bold,' **Mocny** 'Strong,' in preference to changing the name into the feminine form, e.g., **Zielona** (or adopting other options). To some Poles, the female forms can sound less serious than the male forms (**Ewa Zielona** vs. **Ewa Zielony/Jan Zielony**).

The awareness of *gender issues* in Polish is increasing. Language publications openly and frequently try to use and propose female forms of professions that have a chance of being accepted by society, e.g., **psycholożka** 'psychologist,' **biolożka** 'biologist,' **polityczka** 'politician,' **mecenaska** 'lawyer,' **adwokatka** 'lawyer,' with the idea that the more often they are heard, the higher the likelihood that they will be assimilated into the language. Another example is **koordynatorka** 'coordinator.' Women have begun to use this form and it is increasingly recognized in Polish language references and other sources. In Polish media, some other forms are appearing, such as **żołnierka** referring to a female soldier, instead of **żołnierz**, and **działowa** instead of **działowy**, 'a tank operator.'

Conversely, many professions represented by feminine words do not provide masculine forms, such as: **sprzątaczk***a* 'cleaning woman,' **nian***ia* 'nanny,' **bon***a* 'nursemaid,' **kosmetyczk***a* 'beautician,' **przedszkolank***a* 'pre-school teacher.' This raises the question of creating masculine forms, potentially: sprzątacz(?), niań(?), nianiek(?), przedszkolanek(?).

12.5   Addressing a woman

Pani Nowak 'Miss Nowak'
Prezes Kowalska 'President Kowalska'

To address or refer to a woman with a masculine title or a profession before the name, the masculine title or profession is used in the nominative case, regardless of the position in the sentence, e.g.,

Rozmawiałem z Sekretarz Stanu Hillary Clinton. 'I spoke with Secretary of State Hillary Clinton.'
spotkanie u Ambasador Jareckiej 'a meeting at Ambassador Jarecka's'

Compare:

Spotkanie z Ambasador Nowak. 'A meeting with Ambassador Nowak. (a woman)'
Spotkanie z Ambasadorem Nowakiem. 'A meeting with Ambassador Nowak. (a man)'

Only first and last names with the ending -a are declined, when referring to women, e.g.,

Rozmawiamy o Hillary Clinton.
'We are talking about Hillary Clinton.'

compare with a masculine name:

Rozmawiamy o Edmundzie Hillarym.
'We are talking about Edmund Hillary.'

Last names with the ending -y, -i, -e are declined according to the adjectival pattern.

Only last names in -a referring to a female human being are declined, e.g., Kościuszko:

Znam Tadeusza Kościuszkę! 'I know Tadeusz Kościuszko!'
Znam Ewę Kościuszko. 'I know Ewa Kościuszko.'

12.6 Female titles

Titles and professions with a final consonant, e.g., **komisarz** 'commissar,' **redaktor** 'editor,' **psycholog** 'psychologist,' are modified by masculine adjectives when referring to a woman. Both the noun and adjective are declined according to the masculine pattern. Past tense verbs have feminine forms, e.g.:

spotkanie ze znanym psychologiem, Ewą Kowalską
'a meeting with the famous psychologist Ewa Kowalska'

Psycholog Ewa Kowalska była <PAST TENSE FEM> **na spotkaniu.**
'Ewa Kowalska, the psychologist, was at the meeting.'

Titles and professions ending in a consonant can be modified by feminine adjectives when referring to a woman, but the profession must remain in the nominative, and be followed by the name.

spotkanie ze znaną psycholog, Ewą Kowalską
'a meeting with the famous psychologist Ewa Kowalska'

Titles and professions with the final endings -ca (not -ica) and -ta cannot be modified by feminine adjectives.

spotkanie ze znanym doradcą, Ewą Kowalską
'a meeting with the famous adviser Ewa Kowalska'

(incorrect!) spotkanie ze znaną doradcą, Ewą Kowalską
'a meeting with the famous adviser Ewa Kowalska'

Ewa była świetnym kierowcą.
'Ewa was a great driver.'

Piotr był świetnym kierowcą.
'Piotr was a great driver.'

Od Ewy, świetnego kierowcy, nauczyłam się jeździć.
'From Ewa, a great driver, I have learnt how to drive.'

Od Piotra, świetnego kierowcy, nauczyłam się jeździć.
'From Piotr, a great driver, I have learnt how to drive.'

wybitny iranista
'outstanding Iranian expert (female)'

Dzięki Ewie, wybitnemu iraniście, rozumiem islam.
'Thanks to Ewa, an outstanding Iranian expert, I understand Islam.'

To dzięki Piotrowi, wybitnemu iraniście, rozumiem islam.'
'Thanks to Piotr, an outstanding Iranian expert, I understand Islam.'

Kierowca autobusu jechała bardzo wolno.
'The (female) bus driver was going very slowly.'

Unijna komisarz przyjechała do Gdańska.
'The EU Commissioner (female) came to Gdansk.'

Była minister finansów zrezygnowała z mandatu radnej.
'A former (female) minister of finance resigned from the council seat.'

Danuta Hübner <FEM> **jest znanym** <MSC> **polskim** <MSC>
dyplomatą <FEM>.
'Danuta Hübner is a well-known Polish diplomat.'

For other gender issues, see also sections 3.2.1, 3.2.9.3, and 4.7.3.

Notes

I Pronunciation and spelling

[1] Karaś and Madejowa (1977), p. 212.
[2] Timberlake (2004), p. 179.
[3] Ibid.

2 Case usage

[1] Mędak (2005).
[2] Nagórko (2005), p. 286.
[3] Mędak (2005).
[4] Mizerski p. 489.
[5] Mędak (2005).
[6] Mędak (2005).
[7] Mędak (2005).

3 Nouns

[1] Nagórko (2005), p. 144.
[2] Westfal (1956), p. 337.
[3] Ibid.
[4] Długosz-Kurbaczowa and Dubisz (2006), p. 202.
[5] Dąbrowska (1998), p. 111.

4   Adjectives

[1] Jadacka (2005), p. 80.
[2] *Kuchnia*, no. 8, Warsaw (1998); PWN Corpus.

6   Verbs

[1] *Rzeczpospolita*, no. 04.14, Warsaw (2001); PWN Corpus.
[2] Brückner (1998), p. 484.

10   Conjunctions

[1] *Przekrój*, no. 2922, Kraków (2001); PWN Corpus.
[2] Jadacka (2005), pp. 221–2.
[3] Ibid.
[4] Bańkowski (2000), p. 696.
[5] 62,320 vs. 13,763 instances; IPI PAN Corpus.

Bibliography

Bańko, Mirosław, ed. (2006) *Polszczyzna na co dzień*. Warsaw: Wydawnictwo Naukowe PWN.

——(2007) *Wykłady z polskiej fleksji*. Warsaw: Wydawnictwo Naukowe PWN.

Bańkowski, Andrzej (2000) *Etymologiczny słownik języka polskiego*. 2 vols. Warsaw: Wydawnictwo Naukowe PWN.

Bartnicka, Barbara, and Halina Satkiewicz (1990) *Gramatyka języka polskiego: Podręcznik dla cudzoziemców*. Warsaw: Wydawnictwo Wiedza Powszechna.

Bąk, Piotr (2007) *Gramatyka języka polskiego*. Warsaw: Wydawnictwo Wiedza Powszechna.

Bielec, Dana (2002) *Basic Polish: A Grammar and Workbook*. London and New York: Routledge.

——(2004) *Intermediate Polish: A Grammar and Workbook*. London and New York: Routledge.

——(2004) *Polish: An Essential Grammar*. London and New York: Routledge.

Bolanowski, J. E. (1962) *A New Polish Grammar*. Milwaukee: Polonia Publishing Company.

Boruc, Irena, Helena Sprengel, and Elżbieta Werkowska (2006) *Język polski: Tablice polonistyczne*. Gdańsk: Wydawnictwo Podkowa.

Brooks, Maria Zagórska (1975) *Polish Reference Grammar*. The Hague: Mouton & Co.

Brückner, Aleksander (1998) *Słownik etymologiczny języka polskiego*. Warsaw: Wydawnictwo Wiedza Powszechna.

Cieślikowa, Aleksandra, ed. (2008) *Mały słownik odmiany nazw własnych*. Warsaw: Oficyna Wydawnicza RYTM.

Comrie, Bernard, and Greville G. Corbett, eds (2002) *The Slavonic Languages*. London and New York: Routledge.

Crystal, David (1999) *A Dictionary of Language*. Chicago: The University of Chicago Press.

Cząstka-Szymon, Bożena, Helena Synowiec, and Krystyna Urban (2005) *Mały słownik terminów gramatycznych*. Warsaw: Oficyna Wydawnicza RYTM.

Dąbrowska, Anna (1998) *Język polski*. Wrocław: Wydawnictwo Dolnośląskie.

Defense Language Institute, Foreign Language Center (1966) *Polish Basic Course: Compiled Grammar Notes, Lessons 1-108*. Monterey: Defense Language Institute.

Derwojedowa, Magdalena, Halina Karaś, and Dorota Kopcińska, eds (2005) *Język polski*. Warsaw: Świat Książki.

Długosz-Kurczabowa, Krystyna (2005) *Słownik etymologiczny języka polskiego*. Warsaw: Wydawnictwo Naukowe PWN.

Długosz-Kurczabowa, Krystyna, and Stanisław Dubisz (2006) *Gramatyka historyczna języka polskiego*. Warsaw: Wydawnictwa Uniwersytetu Warszawskiego.

Dubisz, Stanisław, ed. (2002) *Nauka o języku dla polonistów*. Warsaw: Wydawnictwo Książka i Wiedza.

Dutka, Wojciech, Beata Gajewska, and Anna Willman (2008) *Słownik ortograficzny z zasadami gramatyki*. Warsaw: Wydawnictwo Szkolne PWN.

Dyszak, Andrzej S. (2007) *Mały słownik czasowników osobliwych (o niepełnej odmianie)*. Warsaw: Oficyna Wydawnicza RYTM.

——(2007) *Mały słownik rzeczowników osobliwych (o nietypowej odmianie)*. Warsaw: Oficyna Wydawnicza RYTM.

Dzigański, Artur (2005) *Słownik interpunkcyjny*. Kraków: Wydawnictwo Zielona Sowa.

Feldstein, Ronald F. (2001) *A Concise Polish Grammar*. Durham: Slavic and East European Language Research Center.

Fisiak, Jacek, Maria Lipińska-Grzegorek, and Tadeusz Zabrocki (1978) *An Introductory English-Polish Contrastive Grammar*. Warsaw: Wydawnictwo Naukowe PWN.

Gladney, Frank Y. (1983) *Handbook of Polish*. Urbana: G & G Press.

Grala, Maria, and Wanda Przywarska (1978) *Z polskim na co dzień*. Warsaw: Państwowe Wydawnictwo Naukowe.

Gruszczyński, Włodzimierz, and Jerzy Bralczyk (2002) *Słownik gramatyki języka polskiego*. Warsaw: Wydawnictwa Szkolne i Pedagogiczne.

Grzegorczykowa, Renata, Roman Laskowski, and Henryk Wróbel (1984) *Gramatyka współczesnego języka polskiego: Morfologia*. Warsaw: Państwowe Wydawnictwo Naukowe.

Grzenia, Jan (2002) *Słownik nazw własnych*. Warsaw: Wydawnictwo Naukowe PWN.

Gussmann, Edmund (2007) *The Phonology of Polish*. Oxford: Oxford University Press.

IPI PAN Corpus (Korpus, Instytut Podstaw Informatyki, Polska Akademia Nauk). (2006) Warsaw. <http://korpus.pl>.

Jadacka, Hanna (2005) *Kultura języka polskiego: Fleksja, słowotwórstwo, składnia*. Warsaw: Wydawnictwo Naukowe PWN.

Janecki, Klara (2000) *301 Polish Verbs*. New York: Barron's.

Jodłowski, Stanisław, and Witold Taszycki (1987) *Zasady pisowni polskiej i interpunkcji ze słownikiem ortograficznym*. Wrocław: Ossolineum.

Kaleta, Zofia (1995) *Gramatyka języka polskiego dla cudzoziemców*. Kraków: Uniwersytet Jagielloński.

Karaś, Mieczysław, and Maria Madejowa (1977) *Słownik wymowy polskiej PWN* (Dictionary of Polish pronunciation). Warsaw: Wydawnictwo Naukowe PWN.

Klemensiewicz, Zenon (1953) *Zarys składni polskiej*. Warsaw: Wydawnictwo Naukowe PWN.

Kłosińska, Anna, Elżbieta Sobol, and Anna Stankiewicz (2007) *Wielki słownik frazeologiczny PWN z przysłowiami*. Warsaw: Wydawnictwo Naukowe PWN.

Kłosińska, Katarzyna (2005) *Skąd się biorą słowa*. Warsaw: Świat Książki.

Kłosińska, Katarzyna, ed. (2004) *Formy i normy, czyli poprawna polszczyzna w praktyce*. Warsaw: Wydawnictwo FELBERG SJA.

Kryżan-Stanojević, Barbara, and Irena Sawicka (2007) *Ćwiczenia z fleksji języka polskiego dla cudzoziemców*. Toruń: Wydawnictwo Uniwersytetu Mikołaja Kopernika.

Kubiak-Sokół, Aleksandra, ed. (2007) *Poprawnie po polsku: Poradnik językowy PWN*. Warsaw: Wydawnictwo Naukowe PWN.

——(2008) *Piszemy poprawnie: Poradnik językowy PWN*. Warsaw: Wydawnictwo Naukowe PWN.

——(2008) *Słownik ortograficzny PWN z wymową*. Warsaw: Wydawnictwo Naukowe PWN.

Linde-Usiekniewicz, Jadwiga, ed. (2004) *Wielki słownik angielsko-polski PWN-Oxford*. Warsaw: Wydawnictwo Naukowe PWN and Oxford University Press.

——(2004) *Wielki słownik polsko-angielski PWN-Oxford*. Warsaw: Wydawnictwo Naukowe PWN and Oxford University Press.

Lipińska, Ewa (1999) *Nie ma róży bez kolców: Ćwiczenia ortograficzne dla cudzoziemców*. Kraków: Universitas.

——(2004) *Z polskim na ty*. Kraków: Universitas.

Lipińska, Ewa, and Elżbieta Grażyna Dąmbska (2005) *Kiedyś wrócisz tu . . . Część II: By szukać swoich dróg i gwiazd.* Kraków: Universitas.

Lipińska-Grzegorek, Maria (1977) *Some Problems of Contrastive Analysis: Sentences with Nouns and Verbs of Sensual Perception in English and Polish.* Edmonton: Linguistic Research, Inc.

Litwinski, Victor (2008) *Polish Learner's Grammar.* Washington, DC: Foreign Service Institute.

Łaziński, Marek (2006) *O panach i paniach: Polskie rzeczowniki tytularne i ich asymetria rodzajowo-płciowa.* Warsaw: Wydawnictwo Naukowe PWN.

Madelska, Liliana, and Małgorzata Warchoł-Schlottmann (2008) *Odkrywamy język polski.* Kraków: Prolog.

Madelska, Liliana, and Małgorzata Witaszek-Samborska (2003) *Zapis fonetyczny: Zbiór ćwiczeń.* Poznań: Wydawnictwo Naukowe Uniwersytetu im. Adama Mickiewicza.

Markowski, Andrzej (2007) *Język polski: Poradnik prof. Markowskiego.* Warsaw: Langenscheidt.

——(2007) *Kultura języka polskiego.* Warsaw: Wydawnictwo Naukowe PWN.

Markowski, Andrzej, ed. (2002) *Nowy słownik poprawnej polszczyzny PWN.* Warsaw: Wydawnictwo Naukowe PWN.

Matthews, P. H. (2007) *Concise Dictionary of Linguistics.* Oxford: Oxford University Press.

Mazur, Bolesław W. (2007) *Colloquial Polish.* New York and London: Routledge.

Mędak, Stanisław (2002) *Co z czym?* Kraków: Universitas.

——(2003) *Słownik odmiany rzeczowników polskich.* Kraków: Universitas.

——(2004) *Liczebnik też się liczy!* Kraków: Universitas.

——(2004) *Słownik form koniugacyjnych czasowników polskich.* Kraków: Universitas.

——(2005) *Praktyczny słownik łączliwości składniowej czasowników polskich.* (A practical dictionary of Polish verbal collocations) Kraków: Universitas.

Miodek, Jan (1996) *Nie taki język straszny: O polszczyźnie do uczniów.* Gdańsk: Gdańskie Wydawnictwo Oświatowe.

Miodunka, Władysław, and Janusz Wróbel (1986) *Polska po polsku.* Vol. II. Warsaw: Wydawnictwo Interpress.

Mizerski, Edmund, ed. (2005) *Język polski: Encyklopedia w tabelach.* Łódź: Wydawnictwo Adamantan.

Moszyński, Leszek (2006) *Wstęp do filologii słowiańskiej.* Warsaw: Wydawnictwo Naukowe PWN.

Nagórko, Alicja (2005) *Zarys gramatyki polskiej*. Warsaw: Wydawnictwo Naukowe PWN.

Ostaszewska, Danuta, and Jolanta Tambor (2006) *Fonetyka i fonologia współczesnego języka polskiego*. Warsaw: Wydawnictwo Naukowe PWN.

Paryski, Marie (1938) *A Practical Polish Grammar*. USA: Paryski Publishing Company.

Patkaniowska, Maria (1944) *Essentials of Polish Grammar for English-Speaking Students*. Glasgow: Książnica Polska.

Pawelec, Radosław, and Dorota Zdunkiewicz-Jedynak (2007) *Język polski: Poradnik korespondencji użytkowej*. Warsaw: Langenscheidt.

Polański, Edward (2008) *Zasady pisowni i interpunkcji*. Warsaw: Wydawnictwo Naukowe PWN.

Przybylska, Renata (2006) *Schematy wyobrażeniowe a semantyka polskich prefiksów czasownikowych do-, od-, prze-, roz-, u-*. Kraków: Universitas.

PWN Corpus (Korpus Języka Polskiego Wydawnictwa Naukowego PWN). <http://korpus.pwn.pl>.

Pyzik, Józef (2000) *Przygoda z gramatyką: Fleksja i słowotwórstwo imion*. Kraków: Universitas.

——(2003) *Iść czy jechać?* Kraków: Universitas.

Rospond, Stanisław (2005) *Gramatyka historyczna języka polskiego*. Warsaw: Wydawnictwo Naukowe PWN.

Saloni, Zygmunt (2001) *Czasownik polski*. Warsaw: Wydawnictwo Wiedza Powszechna.

Saloni, Zygmunt, and Marek Świdziński (2007) *Składnia współczesnego języka polskiego*. Warsaw: Wydawnictwo Naukowe PWN.

Strutyński, Janusz (2005) *Gramatyka polska*. Kraków: Wydawnictwo Tomasz Strutyński.

Swan, Oscar E. (1983) *A Concise Grammar of Polish*. Washington, DC: University Press of America.

——(2002) *A Grammar of Contemporary Polish*. Bloomington: Slavica.

——(2009) *Polish Verbs and Essentials of Grammar*. New York: McGraw Hill.

Szober, Stanisław (1962) *Gramatyka języka polskiego*. Warsaw: Państwowe Wydawnictwo Naukowe.

Szpyra-Kozłowska, Jolanta (2002) *Wprowadzenie do współczesnej fonologii*. Lublin: Wydawnictwo Uniwersytetu Marii Curie-Skłodowskiej.

Szymczak, Mieczysław, et al., eds (1999) *Słownik języka polskiego PWN*. 3 vols. Warsaw: Wydawnictwo Naukowe PWN.

Teslar, J. A. (1941) *A New Polish Grammar*. Edinburgh: Oliver and Boyd.

Timberlake, Alan (2004) *A Reference Grammar of Russian*. Cambridge: Cambridge University Press.

Trask, R. L. (1993) *A Dictionary of Grammatical Terms in Linguistics*. London and New York: Routledge.

Tytuła, Magdalena, and Marta Łosiak (2008) *Polski bez błędów: Poradnik językowy dla każdego*. Warsaw: Wydawnictwo Szkolne PWN.

Urbańczyk, Stanisław, ed. (1994) *Encyklopedia języka polskiego*. Wrocław: Ossolineum.

Wade, Terence (2000) *A Comprehensive Russian Grammar*. Oxford: Blackwell Publishing.

Westfal, Stanisław (1956) *A Study in Polish Morphology: The Genitive Singular Masculine*. The Hague: Mouton & Co.

Wiśniewski, Marek (2001) *Zarys fonetyki i fonologii współczesnego języka polskiego*. Toruń: Wydawnictwo Uniwersytetu Mikołaja Kopernika.

Wyrwas, Katarzyna (2007) *www.poradniajęzykowa.pl*. Katowice: Wydawnictwo Uniwersytetu Śląskiego.

Index

The page numbers for key listings are in bold. Polish letters with diacritical marks are alphabetized separately (e.g., **prosić** precedes **prócz**).